North America

North America

BY

ANTHONY TROLLOPE

EDITED

WITH AN INTRODUCTION, NOTES

AND NEW MATERIALS BY

DONALD SMALLEY AND BRADFORD ALLEN BOOTH

A DA CAPO PAPERBACK

Library of Congress Cataloging in Publication Data

Trollope, Anthony, 1815–1882.
  North America.

  (A Da Capo paperback)
  Reprint. Originally published: New York: Knopf,
1951.
  Bibliography: p.
  Includes index.
  1. United States—Description and travel—1848-1865.
2. Canada—Description and travel—1763-1865. 3. United
States—Politics and government—Civil War, 1861-1865.
4. Trollope, Anthony, 1815-1882—Journeys—North America.
I. Smalley, Donald Arthur, 1907-   . II. Booth,
Bradford Allen, 1909-   . III. Title.
E167.T84   1986   917.3′047   86-11481
ISBN 0-306-80278-3 (pbk.)

This Da Capo Press paperback edition of *North America* is an unabridged
republication of the edition published in New York in 1951. It is
reprinted by arrangement with Alfred A. Knopf, Inc.

Published by Da Capo Press, Inc.
A Subsidiary of Plenum Publishing Corporation
233 Spring Street
New York, N.Y. 10013

Manufactured in the United States of America

INTRODUCTION

ANTHONY TROLLOPE IN AMERICA

IT is somewhat difficult for us Americans not to accept our national heritage unemotionally as part of the inevitability of history. We do not always remember that the great social and political experiment which the Revolutionary War made possible was under skeptical surveillance in all quarters of the world, and that its challenge became increasingly insistent for "our British cousins," in particular, in the middle of the nineteenth century. There is now no doubt that the Civil War was a crucial moment in our history. The author of the Gettysburg Address saw clearly the tremendous implications of the struggle. In point of fact the conflict did prove that a nation dedicated to the proposition that all men are created equal could endure. In 1861–2 many of the best-informed and best-disposed English observers were certain that it could not. Even Anthony Trollope, convinced that the North must win, did not think that the Union could be reconstituted on the old basis. The issue profoundly concerned the British people, and they followed the daily news from the battlefronts with the closest attention. Trollope's report in *North America* created a great stir, for it offered an eyewitness account of democracy's struggle for survival, plus a shrewd, objective commentary on the characteristic features of American life, from the pen of a high-ranking British civil servant who was also a distinguished man of letters.

It would be unwise to assert for Trollope any great originality as a spectator and transcriber of the American scene. What he did in *North America* had largely been done before. The warm-heartedness, the goodwill, the tolerance he brought to his task had by no means been absent from the work of other commentators. It might be said, however, that one of Trollope's distinctions as a travel writer is that he never confused what was good for Englishmen with what was good for people of other countries. He knew that a social climate tolerable in one community may be quite intolerable in another of different traditions; his internationalism has not always been sufficiently recognized. But it is not on such qualities of insight, welcome as they may be, that Trollope's appeal rests. Rather, it is on his sharp perception of the significance of details, on the fine balance of his eager curiosity and steady rationalism, on the dry whimsicality of his low-pitched *obiter dicta,* and on the spontaneity of his style.

I

The Cunard steamer *Arabia* reached Boston on September 5, 1861. Among the hundred passengers disembarking from her early that morning were Anthony Trollope and his wife, Rose. Trollope, at forty-six, was an established novelist in the prime of his career. *The Warden, Barchester Towers,* and *Framley Parsonage* already lay behind him, as did also an excellent travel book, *The West Indies and the Spanish Main.* To use a measure of success that he was fond of applying to himself, his returns from his books had been steadily increasing: for *Framley Parsonage* he had been paid one thousand pounds, a sum that few writers could then command for a single work. The work that he had come to America to prepare was to bring him still more, but his motives in coming were by no means purely mercenary. It had been the ambition of his literary life to write a book about the United States. Two years earlier, stopping at New York between steamers on his return from the West Indies, he had paid a brief visit to Niagara Falls, Saratoga Springs, and a portion of Canada. He had declined at that time to go into his opinions of the country at any length, for it was not his purpose, he said, to deal with the United States or even New York at the fag end of a volume about the West Indies. In *The West Indies and the Spanish Main* he had written:

On the United States I should like to write a volume, seeing that the government and social life of the people there—of that people who are our children—afford the most interesting phenomena which we find as to the new world;—the best means of prophesying, if I may say so, what the world will next be, and what men will next do. There, at any rate, a new republic has become politically great and commercially active. . . .

Trollope had now come to make an extended tour of the country and to produce his book. By doing so he felt that he could wipe out a family debt of thirty years' standing, a debt owed to the citizens of the United States. It had been incurred by his remarkable but politically irresponsible mother.

Anthony had indeed some reason to feel that his mother had treated Americans with less than justice. In her *Domestic Manners of the Americans* (1832) Frances Trollope had not willfully distorted her picture of American life, but her point of sight had been highly personal. Her own experiences in the country had been unfortunate and almost disastrous; she had found a great deal in the modes and manners of the raw New World that was distasteful to her, and she had not hesitated to say as much, in what she chose to call her "gossipy pages," with a wealth of graphic detail and lively anecdote. The injustice lay not so much in what she said as in the fact that she said it so effectively. She portrayed one side of the picture—a side of American life that undoubtedly existed—with such wit and vividness that many Englishmen took it for the whole truth. Many Americans realized that their English cousins were so taking it. Her book became a best-seller in both England and America, but in America it was reviled almost as often as it was read. Newspapers throughout the country upbraided her in the strongest terms, though they gave liberal extracts from her pages. Even the more refined quarterlies decried her "coarse exaggeration" and "bitter caricature"; a Western editor indexed his review under "Lies of an English lady." American journalists soberly repeated, and probably believed, that "libeling the United States" had netted her "the immense profit of between one hundred and thirty and one hundred and forty thousand dollars." She was lampooned in prose and poetry and on the stage; she was travestied in cartoons. She became a folk character presented in crude effigy as a "trollop" in museums and carnivals. There was fear among responsible Americans that the heat of this anger among their fellow citizens might be sufficient to touch off an international "incident." Although the intensity of the anger gradually died down, even by the time of Anthony's arrival the name Trollope was a byword in the United States for British superciliousness. "My mother," Anthony wrote in *An Autobiography*,

had thirty years previously written a very popular, but, as I had thought, a somewhat unjust book about our cousins over the water. She had seen what was distasteful in the manners of a young people, but had hardly recognised their energy. I had entertained for many years an ambition to follow her footsteps there, and to write another book.

Quite aside from his labors as a novelist, Trollope was a hardworking and responsible official in the Post Office, a service he had followed for twenty-seven years. It was not easy for him to get a nine-month leave of absence from his duties. He had persisted, however, until he obtained it; the time had come, he felt, to write his book about the United States if he was ever to write it. The outbreak of the war between the North and the South might make the sort of inquiry he intended to carry out more difficult than it would be in time of peace, but on the other hand the war would guarantee an audience for a new book on America.

II

Soon after landing, Trollope must have realized with new force the obstacles that lay in his road. To do justice to the Americans and their way of life—even to perceive their characteristic way of life with any degree of clarity—must have seemed in the fall of 1861 a task of no mean proportions. The passage from Liverpool had taken twelve days. It was the time separating a world at peace from a world engaged in internecine warfare. Trollope had been abruptly "set down among a people whose whole minds were filled with affairs of the war." The surrender of Fort Sumter had taken place less than five months earlier; the Battle of Bull Run was only six weeks past. The Confederate forces were on the Potomac and almost within cannon-shot of Washington.

If Trollope gathered the newspapers of recent days, the view they offered must have appalled him. The details of war and the rumors of war, the significant and the trivial, shared headings and columns; but they were all about the war, and they were all sensational. If a routine exercise of a few heavy guns in the Northern fortifications was replied to by Southern rifles, that was enough to start bulletins that a full-scale attack on Washington had begun. The Potter Committee had uncovered two hundred employees of government departments who were of doubtful loyalty to the Union. Recent arrests on suspicion of treason included those of the Mayor of Washington, the Baltimore Commissioner of Police, and three wives and two daughters of former members of Congress. A Mrs. Hennington, in spite of a close search of her effects, had reached Richmond from New York with over thirty pounds of quinine, five revolvers, and a galvanic battery. In Missouri a Confederate army of "about ten thousand men" was pushing northward and had reached Lebanon on the road to Rolla. Two Union warships threw shells for half an hour into Galveston, Texas. A Union fleet had captured Fort Hatteras on the North Carolina coast. Jefferson Davis was dead. At least, reports to this effect had reached the stage of "apparently strong confirmation." And always there were the calls for volunteers. Ohio, Governor Dennison proclaimed, had already sent into the field thirty thousand men armed and equipped. Twenty-nine new regiments of infantry, with a proportionate force of artillery and cavalry, were being organized in the state. It was up to the people of Ohio to perfect these organizations as rapidly as possible.

War was the subject and the mood of the time; it dominated the press, the costume, the gatherings, the talk of the people. Trollope soon found reassurance, however, that beneath the turbulent surface the life of the country went on substantially as it did in time of peace.

I worked very hard at the task I had assigned to myself [Trollope says in An Autobiography], *and did, I think, see much of the manners and institutions of the people. Nothing struck me more than their persistence in the ordinary pursuits of life in spite of the war which was around them. Neither industry nor amusement seemed to meet with any check. Schools, hospitals, and institutes were by no means neglected because new regiments were required.*

This is a leading theme in *North America,* and it is the one that governs what is probably the greatest value of the book for the modern reader. More than anything else, *North America* is a record of the other side of the early 1860's, an account of those parts of American life which kept along on or fairly close to their accustomed courses despite the Civil War.

Trollope was well qualified to handle such a subject. He had chosen for his peculiar field as a novelist the quiet, almost commonplace, life of an English cathedral town and its environs. He had developed a special knack for setting down the characteristic life of people without heightening or distortion—"just as real," Nathaniel Hawthorne described the world of Trollope's novels, "as if some giant had hewn a great lump out of the earth and put it under a glass case, with all its inhabitants going about their daily business, and not suspecting that they were being made a show of." *North America,* like the novels, is set in a casual key; it contains far more of faithful detail and trenchant observation than it does of any of the more poetic qualities evoked from many writers by the stirring time. Trollope did see something of life near the front, but he was not greatly moved by the pageantry of war. "In the days of Hector and Ajax," he remarks, "the thing was done in a more picturesque manner, and the songs of battle should, I think, be confined to those ages." His own purpose was "to see what I could of the people, rather than to scrutinize the ways of the army."

It was as well that Trollope defined his subject in this way, for he had but a limited period at his disposal. He was an experienced traveler, however, with a quick eye trained to catch the significant in passing. In the first months, Trollope and his wife Rose visited Boston and New York, took a rapid trip to Canada, and made a hurried tour of the Western states, as far north as St. Paul and as far west as Dubuque. On November 27 Rose sailed from Boston to return to England, and Trollope began a more leisurely survey of the United States, revisiting many places he had already seen hurriedly, spending some weeks at Washington, and devoting an additional month to the West. He wrote as he traveled, putting down his impressions while they were still fresh upon him, for he had a theory, expressed at length in *An Autobiography*, that while such a system did not make for absolute accuracy of the sort achieved by a writer who relied upon research and based every word upon a "rock of facts," the total impression created by his method was the truer; it was the best way, he felt, "of producing to the eye of the reader, and to his ear, that which the eye of the writer has seen and his ear has heard."

Few writing travelers have seemed so independent of the works that preceded them. Aside from his mother's book, of which he is indeed often conscious, it would be hard to name a single work that markedly influenced Trollope out of all the multitude that had been written on the United States. He must have had an acquaintance with some of the classics of American travel, such as Basil Hall's *Travels in North America* (1829), Harriet Martineau's *A Retrospect of Western Travel* (1838) and her *Society in America* (1839), Dickens's *American Notes* (1842), and Alexander Mackay's *The Western World* (1850); he does refer on one occasion to Alexis de Tocqueville's *Democracy in America* (1835–40) and in another instance to the American Frederick Law Olmsted's accounts of his travels in the South (1856–61).[1] But, for good or for ill (and for something of both), Trollope gives no indication of having done any special reading as a background for *North America*. As Allan Nevins has said, Trollope "stood squarely on his own feet," dealing elaborately and freshly with many of the same subjects that had already been dealt with often and at length by previous travelers, but treating these subjects as though he were the first tourist to set eyes on American life.[2] By the time that he took ship at New York on March 12, 1862, a large part of his manuscript was already in the hands of the printer, and most of the rest had been written.

[1] See the note on page 429 for further particulars regarding Olmsted and his books of travel.

[2] *American Social History as Recorded by British Travellers*, compiled and edited by Allan Nevins (New York, 1923), p. 302. See also Henry T. Tuckerman: *America and Her Commentators* (New York, 1864), p. 233. Tuckerman considers Trollope's failure to study his predecessors a positive fault.

III

The America that Anthony Trollope toured and examined in 1861–2, even aside from the fact of the war, was in many respects a different country from the one that his mother had seen three decades earlier. The nation had grown tremendously; it had more than doubled in population and had now reached a total of nearly thirty-two million. Cincinnati, his mother's chief place of residence in the United States and her major specimen for dissection in *Domestic Manners of the Americans,* had been transformed in the space of thirty years from a youthful, roaring town of slightly over twenty thousand to an opulent city over eight times that size, mature, settled, and remote from the frontier. This community, which Mrs. Trollope had flayed for its crudities, was now an important center for the arts, noted for its contributions to music and to literature. Mrs. Trollope's Bazaar, the fantastic structure she had reared as a beacon for culture in the raw town, was a shabby derelict obscured by newer and taller neighbors. It is true that in some ways the city had not altered. Anthony discovered that its great business was "hog killing now, as it used to be in the old days of which I have so often heard." The captains of this industry had increased the efficiency of their plants to a point where they could put through "a hog a minute." Anthony took a walk above Cincinnati much like one his mother had described, to visit the picturesque hills overlooking the city and the Ohio River. Like her, he found that the chief occupation of the city made itself felt even here. There was "a rising flavour in the air. . . . It was the odour of hogs going up to the Ohio heavens;—of hogs in a state of transit from hoggish nature to clothesbrushes, saddles, sausages, and lard." Nevertheless, Anthony found Cincinnati a well-built American city of breadth and grandeur, with an attitude of substantial civic dignity. The banner for noise, bustle, crudity, and headlong growth had long since passed on to St. Louis, then to Chicago. During the preceding ten years Chicago had grown from about thirty thousand inhabitants to nearly one hundred and ten thousand.

In the West that Mrs. Trollope had seen, farming had meant clearing land and raising crops and cattle for little beyond subsistence. With the cultivation of the Great Plains and the development of the reaper and binder, American farming had come to mean the production for profit of vast seas of grain, channeled eastward by water and railroad in enormous quantities. The sight so impressed Anthony that he gave a chapter to the subject. But greater than the growth and change in farming in the thirty years had been the development of industry. Iron-mills, factories, and machine shops had sprung up throughout the seaboard states, the Pittsburgh area, and the cities of the West. A succession of new inventions had done much to give a novel character to American living—the sewing machine, the typesetting machine, the Otis elevator, central heating, sleeping cars, ocean steamboats, improved plows, Colt revolvers, tinned milk and vegetables, rubber goods, power looms, the Bessemer steel process, the hydraulic turbine. Americans surpassed the English in contriving new conveniences, but sometimes, as Anthony discovered, they had effected new inconveniences as well:

The great glory of the Americans is in their wondrous contrivances,— in their patent remedies for the usually troublous operations of life. In their huge hotels all the bell-ropes of each house ring on one bell only, but a patent indicator discloses a number, and the whereabouts of the ringer is shown. One fire heats every room, passage, hall, and cupboard,—and does it so effectually that the inhabitants are all but stifled. Soda-water bottles open themselves without any trouble of wire or strings. Men and women go up and down stairs without motive power of their own. Hot and cold water are laid on to all the chambers;—though it sometimes happens that the water from both taps is boiling, and that when once turned on it cannot be turned off again by any human energy.

But the difference between the United States that Trollope visited and the land of thirty years earlier was above all a question of change in communications. The West that Mrs. Trollope saw had been a formidable distance from the Eastern seaboard. The trip from Cincinnati to Baltimore had taken three days by Ohio steamboat, then another three or more, depending upon the hazards of the road, by stagecoach through the Alleghenies. Now news came by telegraph, and the sections of the country were connected by thirty thousand miles of railroad. The frontier had been brought close in point of time to the centers of civilization. The men of Dubuque or Prairie du Chien read Eastern newspapers, and their wives kept abreast of New York fashions. A new type of pioneer settlement, the railroad town, had come into being. Such communities fascinated Trollope. He found them ugly to the eye, with their sidings and branches, and hard on the ear, with the continual panting and groaning and whistling of slow freights, fast freights, and passenger trains. The houses clung in rows close to the iron rails. Yet these places had an air of meaning about them. They had taken the locomotive to their bosoms as their domestic animal; no one feared it, and little children ran about almost among its wheels. In this young world the cities had come first. Railroad towns rose up in the forests and on the prairies, where the only connecting road was the thin iron track, where the face of the country between one settlement and another was still in many places unknown. Large hotels were reared in such communities before a clientele was visible for them. In "the States of America," Trollope says with some abandon in his sparkling chapter on hotels, "the first sign of an incipient settlement is an hotel five stories high, with an office, a bar, a cloak-room, three gentlemen's parlours, two ladies' parlours, a ladies' entrance, and two hundred bedrooms."

The railroad figures prominently in Trollope's account; locomotion seemed to him a vital aspect of American life. "The railways and the hotels have between them so churned up the people that an untravelled man or woman is a rare animal." A young man would step into a car, sit down with the air of a person passing between stations, and remark in the course of conversation that he was going seven or eight hundred miles. He would buy papers as the train passed through the larger cities, eat a large assortment of gumdrops and apples, and make himself, on the whole, very much at ease and at home. "He knows nothing of the ennui of travelling, and never seems to long for the end of his journey, as travellers do with us." Whole families boarded train or boat for distant points with scarcely greater show of concern. Although the uncontrolled energies of their many offspring round his legs sometimes made Trollope less than comfortable, he did not, from a longer perspective, disapprove. American railways offered points for an Englishman's admiration. The sleeping car, in which the seats could be converted to beds in a few minutes, was among the most remarkable of America's multitude of remarkable contrivances, and Trollope confessed to a delight in seeing the beds made up.

IV

The people, however, had not changed so much as some of the exterior conditions of their lives. Trollope makes a distinction between the men of the Atlantic states and the men of the West, but the Westerners he sometimes treats with as little flattery as his mother had done before him. He found the men gloomy and silent. They answered him in monosyllables, or even with a nod or shake of the head, showing neither pleasure nor displeasure in being addressed.

They care nothing for the graces,—or shall I say, for the decencies of life? They are essentially a dirty people. Dirt, untidiness, and noise, seem in nowise to afflict them. Things are constantly done before your eyes, which should be done and might be done behind your back. . . . I have eaten in Bedouin tents, and have been ministered to by Turks and Arabs. I have sojourned in the hotels of old Spain and of Spanish America. I have lived in Connaught, and have taken up my quarters with monks of different nations. I have, as it were, been educated to dirt, and taken out my degree in outward abominations. But my education had not reached a point which would enable me to live at my ease in the western States. A man or woman who can do that may be said to have graduated in the highest honours, and to have become absolutely invulnerable, either through the sense of touch, or by the eye, or by the nose. Indifference to appearances is there a matter of pride. A foul shirt is a flag of triumph. A craving for soap and water is as the wail of the weak and the confession of cowardice.

Toward Western women he was scarcely more polite. They were hard, dry, and melancholy; all the softness seemed to have been trodden out of them even before they had reached their mid-twenties. Trollope granted that, like their more gracious Eastern sisters, they possessed a high degree of intelligence: "They are sharp as nails, but then they are also as hard." They were tyrants to their parents and later to their husbands. Anthony could forgive Eve for tempting Adam to eat the apple: "Had she come from the West country she would have ordered him to make his meal, and then I could not have forgiven her."

Nothing in his mother's book is much sharper than this or better designed to offend the American sensibilities; but Anthony, even when writing in bleak hotel rooms with the irritations of travel in the West still upon him, often shows more tolerance and understanding. He could conceive "rather an affection" for a group of extremely dirty teamsters who came his way at a Kentucky hostelry. They were orderly and well-behaved; they showed less clumsiness and more intelligence than a group of Englishmen of comparable rank would have shown. The silence of Western Americans, despite his best efforts to draw them into conversation, was a trait that strongly impressed this genial Englishman and one to which he returns more than once in his narrative; but he came to accept and almost to admire it:

An American has the power of seating himself in the close vicinity of a hot stove and feeding in silence on his own thoughts by the hour to-

*gether. It may be that he will smoke; but after a while his cigar will
come to an end. He sits on, however, certainly patient, and apparently
contented. It may be that he chews, but if so, he does it with motionless jaws, and so slow a mastication of the pabulum on which he feeds,
that his employment in this respect only disturbs the absolute quiet of
the circle when, at certain long, distant intervals, he deposits the secretion of his tobacco in an ornamental utensil which may probably be
placed in the furthest corner of the hall. But during all this time he
is happy. It does not fret him to sit there and think and do nothing.
He is by no means an idle man,—probably one much given to commercial enterprise. Idle men out there in the West we may say there are
none. How should any idle man live in such a country? . . . An Englishman, if he be kept waiting by a train in some forlorn station in
which he can find no employment, curses his fate and all that has led to
his present misfortune with an energy which tells the story of his deep
and thorough misery. Such, I confess, is my state of existence under
such circumstances. But a western American gives himself up to "loafing," and is quite happy.*

The men who sat thus in the hall of the Crosslines, Ohio, hotel
were farmers, mechanics, and storekeepers, with two lawyers and one
clergyman in the complement—so much Trollope got out of them before, balanced on the back legs of their armchairs, their feet on the
stove railing, they lapsed into the Western American brand of nirvana.
Patience was of all virtues the one Trollope had least expected to find
in the people of the West, but the quality was manifest in the social,
the business, and the political aspects of their lives. Even more admirable was the air of self-respect and manly dignity which showed itself
among them. Anthony's extreme case in point is the restless land-
clearing farmer still to be met with on the outskirts of the rich corn
and wheat land. Mrs. Trollope had made much of this type of American for his squalor and wretchedness, comparing him most unfavor-
ably with the lowest of English farm laborers. Anthony found the man
destitute of love for his land or his home, willing to sell out at a moment's notice if there was a chance to turn a sizable amount of dollars.

*But yet this man has his romance, his high poetic feeling, and
above all his manly dignity. Visit him, and you will find him without
coat or waistcoat, unshorn, in ragged blue trousers and old flannel
shirt, too often bearing on his lantern jaws the signs of ague and sickness; but he will stand upright before you and speak to you with all
the ease of a lettered gentleman in his own library. . . . He is his own*

master, standing on his own threshold, and finds no need to assert his equality by rudeness. He is delighted to see you, and bids you sit down on his battered bench without dreaming of any such apology as an English cottier offers to a Lady Bountiful when she calls. He has worked out his independence, and shows it in every easy movement of his body. He tells you of it unconsciously in every tone of his voice. You will always find in his cabin some newspaper, some book, some token of advance in education. When he questions you about the old country he astonishes you by the extent of his knowledge. I defy you not to feel that he is superior to the race from whence he has sprung in England or in Ireland. To me I confess that the manliness of such a man is very charming. He is dirty and perhaps squalid. His children are sick and he is without comforts. His wife is pale, and you think you see shortness of life written in the faces of all the family. But over and above it all there is an independence which sits gracefully on their shoulders, and teaches you at the first glance that the man has a right to assume himself to be your equal.

V

Trollope made sturdy efforts to warm to the Western Americans. He scrubbed away the dirt (for he carried his own tub and scrubbing implements about with him), slept through much of the noise, and persisted in asking questions of hostile women and their taciturn mates; he even joined the men in lighting their cigars, tilting their chairs, and putting their feet on the counter, thereby assuming the American male posture of which his mother had so highly disapproved. But though he learned to respect and sometimes to admire the people of the West, he could not, except on rare occasions, like them. He had thought before starting his tour that he would actually enjoy the "roughness of the West" and find a repelling arrogance among Easterners. He found instead that Westerners, though they were not intentionally uncivil, managed to make themselves unpleasant to him, whereas the East abounded with "clever genial men" and "clever pretty women." "As the general result of my sojourn in the country," he says toward the end of his book, "I must declare that I was always happy and comfortable in the eastern cities, and generally uncomfortable in the West." His pages often fail to bear out this generality in anything but the shakiest sort of way; but the fact seems to be that in the last few years, the years of his establishment as a successful novelist, Anthony had taken to preferring the polished to the rough side of society more than he liked to realize.

Boston was by all odds his favorite city. He admired its recreations, its public library, Beacon Street, the Common, Harvard College, and the literary men he met in the city and its environs. He came in time to like the great yellow-painted dome of the State House. Although Boston still cultivated the reputation of being a Puritan city, he found that people knew how to have a good time withindoors even of a Sunday. Champagne and canvasback ducks were frequently met with. Men savored their cigars and sometimes lighted up when ladies were in the room, often dispensing altogether with the withdrawal of the ladies after dinner. This relaxing of the social code was thoroughly congenial to him (as it would have been to his mother). "I fear," Trollope confesses, "that there is within me an aptitude to the milder debaucheries which makes such deviations pleasant. I like to drink and I like to smoke, but I do not like to turn women out of the room."

Not long after Trollope had landed at Boston, James Russell Lowell met him at a dinner. Lowell set down in a letter his impressions of the English novelist and recorded also the exchange of volleys that took place between Trollope and Oliver Wendell Holmes. In *James Russell Lowell: a Biography* (1901), Horace Elisha Scudder quoted this letter as follows:

I dined the other day with Anthony Trollope, a big, red-faced, rather underbred Englishman of the bald-with-spectacles type. A good roaring positive fellow who deafened me (sitting on his right) till I thought of Dante's Cerberus. He says he goes to work on a novel "just like a shoemaker on a shoe, only taking care to make honest stitches." Gets up at 5 every day, does all his writing before breakfast, and always writes just so many pages a day. He and Dr. Holmes were very entertaining. The Autocrat started one or two hobbies, and charged, paradox in rest—but it was pelting a rhinoceros with seed-pearl.

Dr. *You don't know what madeira is in England?*

T. *I'm not so sure it's worth knowing.*

Dr. *Connoisseurship in it with us is a fine art. There are men who will tell you a dozen kinds, as Dr. Wagen would know a Carlo Dolci from a Guido.*

T. *They might be better employed!*

Dr. *Whatever is worth doing is worth doing well.*

T. *Ay, but that's begging the whole question. I don't admit it's worse doing at all. If they earn their bread by it, it may be worse doing (roaring).*

Dr. *But you may be assured—*

wagons. Mounted sentries with drawn sabers, "shivering in the cold and besmeared with mud," were posted at corners, and "muddy, clattering dragoons" sat about the streets with dirty woolen comforters round their ears.

Trollope did not admire the celebrated physical plan of Washington; the city was "a ragged, unfinished collection of unbuilt broad streets" as deep in mud as a plowed field, the most ungainly place that he had seen, and the most presumptuous. He believed that there was little hope it would ever grow enough to occupy the space set off for it. "Unfinished" was the proper word for the city. Parts of Pennsylvania Avenue would be heavy going for most hunting men. Massachusetts Avenue was, on the maps, a full-blown street about four miles in length, but long before reaching the end of it the explorer found himself in an uncultivated, undrained wilderness, wading through bogs with his trousers tucked to his knees. In the distance loomed the unfinished dome of the Capitol. Trollope considered the Washington Monument a fair type of the city. "It is unfinished,—not a third of it having as yet been erected,—and in all human probability ever will remain so." He had seen a plate-glass box kept for contributions toward completing the monument. There were two half dollars in the box, both of them counterfeit.

VI

Even when he was dealing with the cities of the East, then, Trollope let many comments make their way into his account which are as unflattering as those his mother had made in *Domestic Manners*. He was aware that this was so. When he had composed his first, hopeful chapter, he had aspired to write things that would help "to mitigate the soreness" that had long divided the two countries. As in a novel he was to write a few years later, however, his first plans did not prosper. His ugly spinster heroine Miss Mackenzie, in the novel of that name, was to make a match for herself in spite of him. In *North America* also, the plot and characters got out of hand. "I went among them wishing to write of them good words," Anthony says in his last chapter, "—words which might be pleasant for them to read, while they might assist perhaps in producing a true impression of them here at home. But among my good words there are so many which are bitter, that I fear I shall have failed in my object as regards them." He was sure that even his favorite American city, once it had read his book, would deny him. "I know that I shall never again be at Boston, and that I have said that about Americans which would make me unwelcome as a guest if I were there. . . . They who will expect blessings from me, will say among themselves that I have cursed them."

When he finally saw the American notices of his book, Trollope must have found them an agreeable surprise. There were a few carpers, including the *Ladies' Repository*, published at Cincinnati—the ladies of Cincinnati had not yet forgotten or forgiven his mother's strictures on them. But the reaction of the American press was predominantly favorable, even enthusiastic. Newspapers quoted long sections from his pages with approval. The powerful *North American Review* pronounced his account "one of the most readable books of travel we have ever met with." Trollope, it stated, had achieved "an appreciation of the fundamental idea of American society." If there was to be a series of Trollope commentaries on the United States, the *North American's* wish was that the next might be "as great an improvement on our friend as he is on his mother." The influential *American Theological Review* trusted that Americans, even the most thin-skinned among them, would not resent his "good-natured satire at our faults and follies . . . for the critic has a generous and manly soul." Trollope's handling of American scenes and attitudes it found "frank, interesting, and cordial." The house of Harper published vast quantities of *North America* in a cheap edition; the enthusiasm of the reviewer in *Harper's New Monthly Magazine* may therefore need to be taken at some discount. But he would never have dared to say anything so laudatory of Mrs. Trollope's *Domestic Manners. North America,* excepting only de Tocqueville's classic, was the best book "which has been produced by any foreigner upon us."

One reason for Trollope's receiving such kind treatment was that in the summer and fall of 1862 the North was grateful for friends, and especially English friends. Trollope had a good deal to say in favor of the Northern cause in the Civil War. He held that the South possessed no constitutional or ethical right to secede, that slavery was an abominable practice, and that the Northern armies would ultimately win the war. But Trollope was not by any means a glowing propagandist for the North. He viewed the South's necessities, as opposed to its abstract rights, with much sympathy. He scored the corruptness of a number of Northern officials and military men, and he argued that the Union as it had been would never be restored. The South would remain a separate country; eventually the West would, he thought, become a third and separate nation.

There was a stronger reason for the cordial reception of *North America*. Trollope's comments upon his own adventures in the United

States and the details of his day-to-day experiences were often as acid
as his mother's had been; but his generalizations upon the American
way of life were with rare exceptions highly favorable. Frances Trollope had seldom drawn a line in *Domestic Manners* between what was
displeasing to her personally and what was in itself bad. She had been
very hard upon the lower classes, who did most to make her stay in the
United States uncomfortable. She held that the country could never
achieve anything like a satisfactory state of civilization until the citizens of the lower orders gave up a good deal of their crude familiarity
and their vaunted independence for a proper attitude of humility and
respect toward their betters. An argument over the placement of luggage in a stagecoach had sent her into a query whether the Indians had
not been better civilized than the crude republicans who had replaced
them. Anthony saw his traveling desk tossed seven yards by a careless
railway porter; he heard its "poor weak intestines rattle in their death-
struggle," and then heard the porter and a crowd of fellow porters jeer
at his remonstrances. He was quite unhappy as he picked up the
broken desk and made his way into a coach. "This was very sad, and
for the moment I deplored the ill-luck which had brought me to so
savage a country." But on a little reflection he could take a less personal view of the matter: ". . . though I was badly off on that railway
platform,—worse off than I should have been in England,—all that
crowd of porters round me were better off than our English porters.
They had a 'good time' of it." This is a recurrent theme in *North
America*. The United States was often an uncomfortable place for a
traveling Englishman, but it was an excellent place for Americans.

*For myself, I do not like the Americans of the lower orders. I am not
comfortable among them. They tread on my corns and offend me.
They make my daily life unpleasant. But I do respect them. I acknowledge their intelligence and personal dignity. I know that they are men
and women worthy to be so called; I see that they are living as human
beings in possession of reasoning faculties; and I perceive that they
owe this to the progress that education has made among them. . . .
Civilization does not consist in the eschewing of garlic or the keeping
clean of a man's finger-nails. It may lead to such delicacies, and probably will do so. But the man who thinks that civilization cannot exist
without them imagines that the church cannot stand without the spire.*

Trollope, it is clear from such passages, was very conscious that he
was retracing his mother's footsteps. She had looked upon the demand
for equality among citizens of the United States as a sort of disease eat-

ing away the grace and beauty from American life and leaving it raw and hideous. Anthony viewed this demand as a symptom of the country's health and a proof that its government was, on the whole, a good government:

It is always the same story. With us there is no level of society. Men stand on a long staircase, but the crowd congregates near the bottom, and the lower steps are very broad. In America men stand upon a common platform, but the platform is raised above the ground, though it does not approach in height the top of our staircase. If we take the average altitude in the two countries, we shall find that the American heads are the more elevated of the two.

VII

Although Trollope's *North America,* unlike his mother's book, was cordially received in the United States, in England it met with a good deal of unfavorable criticism. Much of the hostility was political rather than literary. By favoring the cause of the North in the Civil War, Anthony was taking the unpopular side on one of the livest issues of the day. The upper classes of England felt a kinship with the landowning gentry of the South as opposed to the merchants, industrialists, and small farmers of the North. They did not approve of slavery, but they minimized the importance of that question and held that the main cause of the war was the effort of the North to make the South stay in the Union against her own will. Although the middle and lower classes of the industrial section of England were largely sympathetic with the North despite the dependence of the English mills upon Southern cotton, the political leaders of the Liberals as well as of the Conservatives were decidedly pro-South. In the last months of 1861 the *Trent* affair had brought England close to actual war with the Union, and in 1862 the feeling against the North was still intense and bitter.

Writing some years later in *An Autobiography,* Trollope expressed no very high opinion of *North America.* It "was not a good book. I can recommend no one to read it now in order that he may be either instructed or amused,—as I can do that on the West Indies. It served its purpose at the time and was well received by the public and by the critics." Trollope's memory was playing him false, for *North America* was rather roughly handled by the English critics, who, indeed, found the book's principal justification in its lively and amusing manner. Some of them made no attempt to write a balanced, impartial review.

The critic for *Blackwood's Magazine*, for example, frankly declared that the prime target for his attack was the North Americans rather than Trollope and proclaimed that "politically we dislike them extremely." The people of the North were "content to follow with senseless shouting the pigmy impostors who are conducting them into such frightful quagmires."

None of the other reviews was quite so vehement in its language or so sweeping in its rejection of *North America*, but a large number of writers attacked Trollope for his opinions and found his book prolix and poorly organized. Others accused him of inaccuracy and superficiality. In fact, of all the British reviews we have examined, only one granted the book unqualified approval—and that one was published in Ireland! [4] A respectable majority, however, granted that *North America*, for all its faults, political and literary, was fresh, graphic, and highly readable. A minority held the book to be "sensible," and the *Westminster Review* went so far as to describe it as "intelligent." The *Spectator*, while finding Trollope sometimes tedious and superficial, granted his book "the charm that attaches to style."

It is the talk of a cultivated, tolerant gentleman, who has good eyes and uses them, who can make apologies for the things most offensive to his own prejudices, and who never forgets that conversation should not degenerate into a lecture. A club man sauntering through the States, and talking to himself of his own honest opinions, would say pretty much what Mr. Trollope has said . . . in a pleasant, chatty, though somewhat verbose style, which carries the listener with him to the end, and when he stops leaves the impression that the speaker, if not the most far-sighted of men, is one of the most agreeable.

Reading *North America* a half century later, another English critic, James Bryce—the author of *The American Commonwealth*—was willing to call the book "excellent."

VIII

Trollope could forget the sharp things English reviewers said about *North America*, but another unpleasant aspect of his experiences with the book made a more lasting impression upon him. Before sailing for the United States he had completed arrangements with Edward and Frederick Chapman for the publication of his manuscript within two

---

[4] *The Dublin University Magazine.* For a listing of reviews examined, see Bibliography.

months after his return. The English edition duly appeared in May
1862. A few days before leaving the United States he had made arrangements with J. B. Lippincott, of Philadelphia, for an American
edition. Harper & Brothers anticipated this edition with a low-priced
pirated volume, and the resulting imbroglio has some interest in literary history.

In accordance with the provisions of the American contract Trollope sent proof sheets of *North America* to Lippincott before publication in England. But by some stratagem Harper's managed to rush
through the presses an edition to sell for sixty cents, outmaneuvering
Lippincott's both in time and in price. Mr. Lippincott wrote Trollope
in high dudgeon that Harper's had dropped all its other work to
concentrate on this piracy.[5] Harper's seems to have printed its edition in seventy-two hours and got it on the streets four days before Lippincott's book appeared. Trollope was furious and asked Mr. Lippincott's permission to make the matter public. To this Lippincott agreed.
Trollope then sat down and wrote a 2,500-word open letter to James
Russell Lowell, with whom he had discussed copyright problems in
Boston, and who, Trollope knew, would be sympathetic. The letter,
which was published in the *Athenæum* for September 6, 1862, tells the
whole story in detail. In a personal interview Fletcher Harper had assured Trollope that he would not publish a competing text if Trollope
chose to take his manuscript elsewhere. Trollope's forthright statement
of the facts must have made Harper most uncomfortable; at any rate,
he replied at some length, but rather lamely and irrelevantly. Trollope
immediately availed himself again of the *Athenæum's* columns (for
October 25, 1862), answering Harper paragraph by paragraph in a
letter of a thousand words. However just Trollope's moral claim
against Harper may have been, he had no legal rights whatever in his
own property. Acknowledging himself beaten, he vented his anger in
print and scrawled in red ink across the face of his schedule of earnings
from *North America* the single word "Cheated." Trollope had known
that by exposing the episode he had nothing personal to gain, for by
September virtually all the major reviews had spoken and sales of the
book must have passed their peak. He hoped only to bring to public
attention the need for an international copyright.

[5] Letters from J. B. Lippincott to Anthony Trollope dated June 26, 1862, and
July 24, 1862. These are preserved among Trollope's business papers at the Bod-
leian Library. Trollope's letters to Lippincott's were destroyed in a fire many years
ago.

IX

Whatever faults Trollope may have found with America, he cherished for Americans a deep and sincere affection. Essentially gregarious, he enjoyed people; his open, responsive nature encouraged sociability and cut through false dignity and reserve. He made friends wherever he went. One would not gather this from *North America,* because, though it is a very human book, it is not a personal diary. As a travel writer Trollope concerned himself with "political, social, and material conditions." Hence he does not give us a running account of social contacts established and friendships made. Indeed, it may be with some surprise that we learn, in the last chapter, of the strength of his ties with Boston friends, of the sentimental regret with which he contemplates his departure. Characteristically, he mentions no names, but from his account book and from personal letters one can compile a list of those whom he saw most frequently.

In Boston these were James T. Fields, the publisher, and his wife, Annie; Dr. Samuel Kirkland Lothrop, the prominent Unitarian minister; Mr. and Mrs. Charles D. Homans; and the Peabodys. In Cambridge it was Longfellow and Agassiz; in Quincy the Adams family; in New York the Bancrofts; in Philadelphia the Biddles and the Reeds. But, above all, it was Kate Field. Mary Katherine Keemle Field (1838–96), a vivacious St. Louis girl of varied though minor talents, had met the Tom Trollopes in Florence. Anthony Trollope, seeing her at his brother's, was charmed by her beauty, her easy grace and spontaneity, and her pert manners. That he quite lost his heart to her is an inescapable conclusion from the veiled but unmistakable reference to her in *An Autobiography* as his closest friend outside the family. Trollope's attitude toward Kate was avuncular in the main, but there is a touch of gallantry in his letters, which are the most personal he ever wrote. No doubt there is much of Kate Field in Caroline Spaulding and Isabel Boncassen, self-reliant American heroines of *He Knew He Was Right* and *The Duke's Children,* respectively. But for her part, to judge from letters and from laconic entries in her diary, Kate seems to have valued Trollope chiefly as a means toward the furtherance of her career as writer, lecturer, and actress. Nevertheless, Trollope welcomed her companionship, and the fact that she was in America added interest, and perhaps spice of adventure, to his trips here. Although remarkably self-sufficient, Trollope knew the inevitable loneliness of the stranger in a foreign land. Kate Field bridged the gap between England and America, and she helped him to recognize and to understand some of the more obscure facets of the national character.

Trollope came to know the national character rather well, for the 1861–2 visit was not, as he then thought, his last. In fact, he was to make three more trips. Early in 1868 he was asked by the Post Office, from which he had just retired, to negotiate a treaty in Washington. This he did. At the same time he received a commission from the Foreign Office to press for an international copyright agreement. His unhappy experience over the publication of the American edition of *North America* had taught him what Dickens and other popular novelists had long since learned: that writers on both sides of the Atlantic were the victims of unscrupulous pirate publishers and that they had no recourse whatever. Trollope was unsuccessful both on this occasion and later in 1876 when he sat as a member of the Royal Copyright Commission. Not until after his death was agreement reached on this point of fundamental justice for the creative artist.

Trollope's fourth visit came at the end of his 1871–2 trip to Australia, from which he chose to return to London via Honolulu, San Francisco, and New York. About this trip he is strangely silent. One would have expected an experienced English traveler to turn to account such promising material as a view of California in 1872. But of his stop-over and the long journey across the plains we are given in his *An Autobiography* only a tantalizing anecdote about a courtesy call paid on Brigham Young.

I did not achieve any great intimacy with the great polygamist of the Salt Lake City. I called upon him, sending to him my card; apologising for doing so without an introduction, and excusing myself by saying that I did not like to pass through the territory without seeing a man of whom I had heard so much. He received me in his doorway, not asking me to enter, and inquired whether I were not a miner. When I told him that I was not a miner, he asked me whether I earned my bread. I told him I did. "I guess you're a miner," said he. I again assured him that I was not. "Then how do you earn your bread?" I told him that I did so by writing books. "I'm sure you're a miner," said he. Then he turned upon his heel, went back into the house, and closed the door. I was properly punished, as I was vain enough to conceive that he would have heard my name.

Of the fifth trip, which repeated the itinerary of the fourth, we know much more. In 1875 Trollope again visited Australia and returned through the United States. A series of recently recovered travel letters, written for the *Liverpool Mercury* and perhaps other newspapers, includes a rather whimsical account of the perils of life in San

Francisco and of the railway journey to New York. This letter will be found in an appendix to the present volume.[6] It will suffice here to say that Trollope's somewhat grudging praise of the attractions of California comes with imperfect grace from one who had just experienced the hardships of frontier Australia. Although he tried always to free himself from bias in his criticism of American customs, the English squire in him protested against inconveniences, major and minor, and against the American philosophy of opportunism. Having already pointed out instances of economic madness in the gold fields of Australia, he should have been prepared to understand the speculative fever of San Francisco and to turn his attention to the city's virtually unrivaled natural advantages. But what did he see? San Francisco is the least interesting city he had ever visited in all his travels; there is almost nothing worth seeing; strangers will desire to get out of the city as quickly as they can! One wonders if the experienced traveler did not observe one of the world's most magnificent harbors. What were his thoughts as the *City of Melbourne* steamed into the Golden Gate? According to his own account, he was digesting the news of the failure of the Bank of California! This amazing circumstance is not without significance, for it points up what was important to Trollope. Like Browning, Trollope was less interested in nature than in human nature. He wanted to know how people live. He could not understand why, when his Mississippi River steamer was delayed with a broken paddlewheel, he was the only passenger who went ashore to knock at settlers' doors and ask questions. As a traveler Trollope was neither a philosopher nor a poet, but a student of human nature with both patience and imagination.

Trollope's interest in people and in the economics of living emphasizes the fact that he was first of all a novelist, a novelist concerned with man in his social relationships. Because America was of all countries the one in which the role of man in society was of keenest importance, it is natural that the novelist's eye should have turned toward situations that might be artistically useful. Trollope observed a good deal in the American character and American scene which stimulated his imagination, and later he introduced into both novels and short stories familiar character types and plot situations from his American experiences. He was particularly struck, as was Henry James, by the fictional possibilities of the American abroad. Because his treatment of this material illustrates his considered attitude toward Americans and

6 Pages 541–7.

develops his concept of the need for mutual tolerance and understanding, it might be well to examine briefly the novels in which Americans are given a prominent place.

Winifred Gregory Gerould and James Thayer Gerould in their valuable compilation *A Guide to Trollope* note that thirty-four Americans play more than incidental roles in Trollope's works. These characters appear in a total of eight novels and six short stories, covering the years 1860–82; that is, from "The Courtship of Susan Bell," set in Saratoga Springs and written immediately after the first visit, to *The Landleaguers,* on which Trollope was at work at the time of his death. America and Americans would therefore seem to have been a pervasive influence on his life and on his art. The three novels in which this influence may be traced most importantly are *He Knew He Was Right, The American Senator,* and *The Duke's Children.*

He Knew He Was Right was begun in England late in 1867, but a large part of it was written in the United States in the following spring. The story is set in Italy, and one of the sub-plots introduces Jonas Spaulding, the American Minister. Spaulding has with him two nieces, one of whom, Caroline, becomes engaged to Lord Peterborough. The predicament of innocents abroad is exploited fully in a comedy-of-manners treatment, but the social implications of the marriage are debated earnestly and at length. Trollope had a personal interest, one may guess, in his American heroine, for this segment of his story was probably written for Kate Field, whom he was seeing frequently and with whom he was corresponding regularly at the time. It is more than possible that Caroline Spaulding represents Kate Field as she had charmed Trollope in 1860 at Florence, and that the stiff and opinionated American poetess Wallachia Petrie, whom Caroline laughingly calls "the American Browning," represents what Trollope in 1868 feared that Kate might become. Indeed, he must have intimated so much to Kate, for she protested, and he replied in a letter dated April 15, 1870: "I never said you were like W. Petrie. I said that that young woman did not entertain a single opinion on public matters which you could repudiate." Miss Petrie is an insufferably loud feminist, a man-hating lecturer with a violent and irrational antipathy toward all things English. Trollope never lost his aversion for the type. Caroline, on the other hand, while not without spirit, is quiet and self-deprecating; she comes to believe, quite mistakenly, that she is not fit to be the wife of an English lord. Trollope was charmed by the cleverness of American girls and by their beauty, but he perhaps agreed with his charac-

ter Louis Trevelyan, who says that "they want the weakness which a
woman ought to have." Caroline is attractive because she combines
American independence of character with English femininity.

But most of what Trollope has to say about American life is developed through the mildly satiric portrait of Jonas Spaulding, a proto-
type of Elias Gotobed, the American Senator. Spaulding is pompous
and rhetorical, full of windy hyperbole about the national "institootions." He is on the defensive, suffering from that social malaise which
is at the root of much protective blustering. He is a bore, to be sure,
but a likable bore, and in his orotund but by no means unintelligent
way he scores many home thrusts against foreign contradictions and
absurdities. Trollope understands the Minister's point of view and ac-
knowledges that there is something to be said in his defense.

In *An Autobiography* Trollope admitted that the novel he wrote
in Australia in 1875 might well have been entitled "The Chronicle of
a Winter at Dillsborough," but over his publisher's protests he called
it *The American Senator*. Elias Gotobed, Senator from the state of
Mickewa, is merely a fringe character in a complicated story, but
around him Trollope frames most precisely his concept of rational
Anglo-American relations. By virtue of his travel experience Trollope
was gaining the perspective to judge of men and manners internation-
ally, and, as a result, to see more clearly the chinks in British armor.
While he was in Australia there appeared the closing numbers of his
novel *The Way We Live Now,* a powerful and a bitter indictment of
"the commercial profligacy of the age." Now, a stranger in an English-
speaking country, Trollope saw an opportunity to comment further,
and objectively, on the mores of his epoch. Professor David Stryker has
recently pointed out [7] the parallels between Elias Gotobed in England
and Anthony Trollope in America. On this occasion the American has
the better case. It is English habits and customs that are under attack.
The Senator is no paragon of diplomacy; he is usually tactless and often obtuse. But the strength of his position and the weakness of English counterattacks are perfectly clear. Trollope not only shows his
countrymen how others see them, but indicates precisely how vulner-
able they are to serious criticism. *The American Senator* should be
read as a companion piece to *North America*.

The last of this group of Americans used as major characters is
Isabel Boncassen, charming heroine of *The Duke's Children*. The sit-

[7] See "The Significance of Trollope's *The American Senator*," *Nineteenth-
Century Fiction*, V (September 1950). *The Way We Live Now* had presented two
Americans of some interest in the handsome and headlong Western woman, Wini-
fred Hurtle, and the affable but less than scrupulous spectator, Hamilton K. Fisker.

I   Portrait of Anthony Trollope

Appleton's Journal, III (*May* 14, 1870), 552

II The Bathe at Newport: "For here ladies and gentlemen bathe in
decorous dresses. . . ."

Harper's Weekly, II *(September* 4, 1858), 568

uation explored here is that of *He Knew He Was Right:* a beautiful American girl captivates and ultimately marries the most eligible bachelor in England. The interest is somewhat dulled, however, by the familiarity of the action.[8] Isabel is the daughter of a wealthy American scholar studying at the British Museum. Lord Silverbridge is the eldest son of the Duke of Omnium. The Duke is not happy to see his son go outside his class for a bride, but he does nothing to prevent the marriage. Trollope has not yet subdued all his prejudices, and Americans are made uncomfortable by talk of Isabel's "unworthiness." Although the author makes it clear that Silverbridge's sacrifices are justified, the fact of the sacrifice has seemed to some American readers to be emphasized too persistently. Trollope is quite willing to accept talented Americans into ducal society, but he holds firmly to the idea of rank. He never surrendered the social ideals that he brought to America on his trip to the West Indies in 1859. For the American achievement of leveling up to a higher standard of material and cultural prosperity than Europe had ever known, he had the highest admiration. But he died convinced that the English social order produced a finer, more highly cultivated group at the top.

Trollope's task, however, was not to point out instances of British superiority or make invidious comparisons, but to foster international understanding, to encourage a meeting of minds among two peoples whom he loved. This could be achieved, he knew, only by dispassionate appraisal and objective analysis. Of hasty and biased generalizations the literature of American travel had been too full. His own approach he described in the introductory chapter to *Australia and New Zealand* (1873):

> *An Englishman visiting the United States, if he have any purpose of criticism in his mind,—any intention of judging how far the manner of life there is a good manner, and of making comparison between British and American habits, should be ever guarding himself against the natural habit of looking at things only from his own point of view. . . . Should he find Americans to be educated, plenteously provided, honest, moral, and Godfearing, he might perhaps, in such case, safely conclude that they were prosperous and happy, even if they talked through their noses and called him Sir at every turn in their speech. . . . Such things may influence the happiness of an individual, may make the United States an uncomfortable home for a middle-aged Englishman, or London a dreary domicile for an American well estab-*

---

[8] For another use of the same situation see "Miss Ophelia Gledd" in *Lotta Schmidt and Other Stories* (1867).

lished in his own customs. They have no bearing at all on the well being of a people, and yet they have often been taken as indicating a national deformity, and sometimes national calamity. Our writers have fallen into this mistake in writing of America.

Trollope avoided this mistake. That is his distinction among nineteenth-century travelers.

DONALD SMALLEY
BRADFORD ALLEN BOOTH

CONTENTS

xxxiv CONTENTS

ILLUSTRATIONS

A KEY

to the notes of this edition

Notes by ANTHONY TROLLOPE (there are but a few
of them) are marked by asterisks.

Notes by the EDITORS OF THIS EDITION are marked
by superior numbers.

CHAPTER I

INTRODUCTION

I T has been the ambition of my literary life to write a book about the United States, and I had made up my mind to visit the country with this object before the intestine troubles of the United States Government had commenced. I have not allowed the division among the States and the breaking out of civil war to interfere with my intention; but I should not purposely have chosen this period either for my book or for my visit. I say so much, in order that it may not be supposed that it is my special purpose to write an account of the struggle as far as it has yet been carried. My wish is to describe as well as I can the present social and political state of the country. This I should have attempted, with more personal satisfaction in the work, had there been no disruption between the North and South; but I have not allowed that disruption to deter me from an object which, if it were delayed, might probably never be carried out. I am therefore forced to take the subject in its present condition, and being so forced I must write of the war, of the causes which have led to it, and of its probable termination. But I wish it to be understood that it was not my selected task to do so, and is not now my primary object.

Thirty years ago my mother wrote a book about the Americans, to which I believe I may allude as a well known and successful work without being guilty of any undue family conceit. That was essentially a woman's book. She saw with a woman's keen eye, and described with a woman's light but graphic pen, the social defects and absurdities which our near relatives had adopted into their domestic life. All that she told was worth the telling, and the telling, if done successfully, was sure to produce a good result. I am satisfied that it did so. But she did not regard it as a part of her work to dilate on the nature and operation of those political arrangements which had produced the social absurdities which she saw, or to explain that though such absurdities were the natural result of those arrangements in their newness, the defects would certainly pass away, while the political arrangements, if good, would remain. Such a work is fitter for a man than for a woman. I am very far from thinking that it is a task which I can perform with satisfaction either to myself or to others. It is a work which some man will

and that whether or no all their institutions be at present excellent, and their social life all graceful, my wishes are that they should be so, and my convictions are that that improvement will come for which there may perhaps even yet be some little room.

And now touching this war which had broken out between the North and South before I left England. I would wish to explain what my feelings were; or rather what I believe the general feelings of England to have been, before I found myself among the people by whom it was being waged. It is very difficult for the people of any one nation to realize the political relations of another, and to chew the cud and digest the bearings of those external politics. But it is unjust in the one to decide upon the political aspirations and doings of that other without such understanding. Constantly as the name of France is in our mouth, comparatively few Englishmen understand the way in which France is governed;—that is, how far absolute despotism prevails, and how far the power of the one ruler is tempered, or, as it may be, hampered by the voices and influence of others. And as regards England, how seldom is it that in common society a foreigner is met who comprehends the nature of her political arrangements! To a Frenchman,—I do not of course include great men who have made the subject a study,—but to the ordinary intelligent Frenchman the thing is altogether incomprehensible. Language, it may be said, has much to do with that. But an American speaks English; and how often is an American met, who has combined in his mind the idea of a monarch, so called, with that of a republic, properly so named;—a combination of ideas which I take to be necessary to the understanding of English politics? The gentleman who scorned my wife for hugging her chains had certainly not done so, and yet he conceived that he had studied the subject. The matter is one most difficult of comprehension. How many Englishmen have failed to understand accurately their own constitution, or the true bearing of their own politics! But when this knowledge has been attained, it has generally been filtered into the mind slowly, and has come from the unconscious study of many years. An Englishman handles a newspaper for a quarter of an hour daily, and daily exchanges some few words in politics with those around him, till drop by drop the pleasant springs of his liberty creep into his mind and water his heart; and thus, earlier or later in life according to the nature of his intelligence, he understands why it is that he is at all points a free man. But if this be so of our own politics; if it be so rare a thing to find a foreigner who understands them in all their niceties, why is it that we are so confident in our remarks on all the niceties of those of other nations?

I hope that I may not be misunderstood as saying that we should not discuss foreign politics in our press, our parliament, our public meetings, or our private houses. No man could be mad enough to preach such a doctrine. As regards our Parliament, that is probably the best British school of foreign politics, seeing that the subject is not there often taken up by men who are absolutely ignorant, and that mistakes when made are subject to a correction which is both rough and ready. The press, though very liable to error, labours hard at its vocation in teaching foreign politics, and spares no expense in letting in daylight. If the light let in be sometimes moonshine, excuse may easily be made. Where so much is attempted, there must necessarily be some failure. But even the moonshine does good, if it be not offensive moonshine. What I would deprecate is, that aptness at reproach which we assume;—the readiness with scorn, the quiet words of insult, the instant judgment and condemnation with which we are so inclined to visit, not the great outward acts, but the smaller inward politics of our neighbours.

And do others spare us, will be the instant reply of all who may read this. In my counter reply I make bold to place myself and my country on very high ground, and to say that we, the older and therefore more experienced people as regards the United States, and the better governed as regards France, and the stronger as regards all the world beyond, should not throw mud again even though mud be thrown at us. I yield the path to a small chimney-sweeper as readily as to a lady; and forbear from an interchange of courtesies with a Billingsgate heroine, even though at heart I may have a proud consciousness that I should not altogether go to the wall in such an encounter.

I left England in August last—August 1861. At that time, and for some months previous, I think that the general English feeling on the American question was as follows. "This wide-spread nationality of the United States, with its enormous territorial possessions and increasing population, has fallen asunder, torn to pieces by the weight of its own discordant parts,—as a congregation when its size has become unwieldy will separate, and reform itself into two wholesome wholes. It is well that this should be so, for the people are not homogeneous, as a people should be who are called to live together as one nation. They have attempted to combine free-soil sentiments with the practice of slavery, and to make these two antagonists live together in peace and unity under the same roof; but, as we have long expected, they have failed. Now has come the period for separation; and if the people would only see this, and act in accordance with the circumstances which Providence and the inevitable hand of the world's ruler has prepared for them, all would be well. But they will not do this. They will go to war with each other. The South will make her demands for secession with an arrogance and instant pressure which exasperates the North; and the North, forgetting that an equable temper in such matters is the most powerful of all weapons, will not recognize the strength of its own position. It allows itself to be exasperated, and goes to war for that which if regained would only be injurious to it. Thus millions on millions sterling will be spent. A heavy debt will be incurred; and the North, which divided from the South might take its place among the greatest of nations, will throw itself back for half a century, and perhaps injure the splendour of its ultimate prospects. If only they would be wise, throw down their arms, and agree to part! But they will not."

This was, I think, the general opinion when I left England. It would not, however, be necessary to go back many months to reach the time when Englishmen were saying how impossible it was that so great a national power should ignore its own greatness, and destroy its own power by an internecine separation. But in August last all that had gone by, and we in England had realized the probability of actual secession.

To these feelings on the subject may be added another, which was natural enough though perhaps not noble. "These western cocks have crowed loudly," we said, "too loudly for the comfort of those who live after all at no such great distance from them. It is well that their combs should be clipped. Cocks who crow so very loudly are a nuisance. It might have gone so far that the clipping would become a work necessarily to be done from without. But it is ten times better for all parties that it should be done from within; and as the cocks are now clipping their own combs, in God's name let them do it and the whole world will be the quieter." That, I say, was not a very noble idea; but it was natural enough, and certainly has done somewhat in mitigating that grief which the horrors of civil war and the want of cotton have caused to us in England.

Such certainly had been my belief as to the country. I speak here of my opinion as to the ultimate success of secession and the folly of the war,—repudiating any concurrence of my own in the ignoble but natural sentiment alluded to in the last paragraph. I certainly did think that the Northern States, if wise, would have let the Southern States go. I had blamed Buchanan as a traitor for allowing the germ of secession to make any growth;—and as I thought him a traitor then, so do I him a traitor now.[1] But I had also blamed Lincoln, or rather the government of which Mr. Lincoln in this matter is no more than the exponent, for his efforts to avoid that which is inevitable. In this I think that I—or as I believe I may say we, we Englishmen—were wrong. I do not see how the North, treated as it was and had been, could have submitted to secession without resistance. We all remember what Shakespere says of the great armies which were led out to fight for a piece of ground not large enough to cover the bodies of those who would be slain in the battle; but I do not remember that Shakespere says that the battle was on this account necessarily unreasonable. It is the old point of honour, which, till it had been made absurd by certain changes of circumstances, was always grand and usually beneficent. These changes of circumstances have altered the manner in which appeal may be made, but have not altered the point of honour. Had the Southern States sought to obtain secession by constitutional means, they might or might not have been successful; but if successful there would have been no war. I do not mean to brand all the Southern States with treason, nor do I intend to say that having secession at heart they could have obtained it by constitutional means. But I do intend to say that acting as they did, demanding secession not constitutionally but in opposition to the constitution, taking upon themselves the right of breaking up a nationality of which they formed only a part, and doing that without consent of the other part, opposition from the North and war was an inevitable consequence.

It is, I think, only necessary to look back to the revolution by which the United States separated themselves from England to see this. There is hardly to be met, here and there, an Englishman who now regrets the loss of the revolted American colonies;—who now thinks that civilization was retarded and the world injured by that revolt; who now conceives that England should have expended more treasure and more lives in the hope of retaining those colonies. It is agreed that the revolt was a good thing; that those who were then rebels became patriots by suc-

[1] Trollope was not alone in thinking that Buchanan had been a traitor to the Union. Edward Dicey recorded, in *Six Months in the Federal States* (1863), that a portrait of Buchanan had once hung in the circular hall of the Capitol: ". . . but when the troops were quartered here, at the outbreak of the war . . . a Western regiment destroyed the portrait by squirting tobacco juice over it, leaving the other pictures untouched. 'And a vile indignity, too, sir,' said an Abolitionist, who told me the story, 'that was for the—tobacco juice.' "

Historians are now agreed that Buchanan was not a traitor. His administration was lamentably weak; he was timorously deferential toward the South; but his aim seems to have been to avoid civil war through compromise or, failing that, to delay the date of armed conflict until another president came into office.

cess, and that they deserved well of all coming ages of mankind. But not the less absolutely necessary was it that England should endeavour to hold her own. She was as the mother bird when the young bird will fly alone. She suffered those pangs which Nature calls upon mothers to endure.

As was the necessity of British opposition to American independence, so was the necessity of Northern opposition to Southern secession. I do not say that in other respects the two cases were parallel. The States separated from us because they would not endure taxation without representation—in other words because they were old enough and big enough to go alone. The South is seceding from the North because the two are not homogeneous. They have different instincts, different appetites, different morals, and a different culture. It is well for one man to say that slavery has caused the separation; and for another to say that slavery has not caused it. Each in so saying speaks the truth. Slavery has caused it, seeing that slavery is the great point on which the two have agreed to differ. But slavery has not caused it, seeing that other points of difference are to be found in every circumstance and feature of the two people. The North and the South must ever be dissimilar. In the North labour will always be honourable, and because honourable successful. In the South labour has ever been servile,—at least in some sense, and therefore dishonourable; and because dishonourable has not, to itself, been successful. In the South, I say, labour ever has been dishonourable; and I am driven to confess that I have not hitherto seen a sign of any change in the Creator's fiat on this matter. That labour will be honourable all the world over, as years advance and the millennium draws nigh, I for one never doubt.

So much for English opinion about America in August last. And now I will venture to say a word or two as to American feeling respecting this English opinion at that period. It will of course be remembered by all my readers that at the beginning of the war Lord Russell, who was then in the lower house, declared as Foreign Secretary of State that England would regard the North and South as belligerents, and would remain neutral as to both of them. This declaration gave violent offence to the North, and has been taken as indicating British sympathy with the cause of the seceders. I am not going to explain—indeed it would be necessary that I should first understand—the laws of nations with regard to blockaded ports, privateering, ships and men and goods contraband of war, and all those semi-nautical semi-military rules and axioms which it is necessary that all Attorneys-General and such like should at the present moment have at their fingers' end. But it must be evident to the most ignorant in those matters, among which large crowd I certainly include myself, that it was essentially necessary that Lord John Russell should at that time declare openly what England intended to do. It was essential that our seamen should know where they would be protected and where not, and that the course to be taken by England should be defined. Reticence in the matter was not within the power of the British Government. It behoved the Foreign Secretary of State to declare openly that England intended to side either with one party or with the other, or else to remain neutral between them.

I had heard this matter discussed by Americans before I left England, and I have of course heard it discussed very frequently in America. There can be no doubt that the front of the offence given by England to the Northern States was this declaration of Lord John Russell's. But it has been always made evident to me that the sin did not consist in the fact of England's neutrality,—in the fact of her regarding the two parties as belligerents,—but in the open declaration made to the world by a Secretary of State that she did intend so to regard them. If another proof were wanting, this would afford another proof of the immense weight attached in America to all the proceedings and to all the feelings of England on this matter. The very anger of the North is a compliment paid by the North to England. But not the less is that anger unreasonable. To those in America who understand our constitution, it must be evident that our Government cannot take official measures without a public avowal of such measures. France can do so. Russia can do so. The Government of the United States can do so, and could do so even before this rupture. But the Government of England cannot do so. All men connected with the Government in England have felt themselves from time to time more or less hampered by the necessity of publicity. Our statesmen have been forced to fight their battles with the plan of their tactics open before their adversaries. But we, in England, are inclined to believe, that the general result is good, and that battles so fought and so won will be fought with the honestest blows, and won with the surest results. Reticence in this matter was not possible, and Lord John Russell in making the open avowal which gave such offence to the Northern States only did that which, as a servant of England, England required him to do.

"What would you in England have thought," a gentleman of much weight in Boston said to me, "if when you were in trouble in India, we had openly declared that we regarded your opponents there as belligerents on equal terms with yourselves?" I was forced to say that, as far as I could see, there was no analogy between the two cases. In India

an army had mutinied, and that an army composed of a subdued, if
not a servile race.[2] The analogy would have been fairer had it referred
to any sympathy shown by us to insurgent negroes. But, nevertheless,
had the army which mutinied in India been in possession of ports
and sea-board; had they held in their hands vast commercial cities and
great agricultural districts; had they owned ships and been masters of
a wide-spread trade, America could have done nothing better towards
us than have remained neutral in such a conflict, and have regarded
the parties as belligerents. The only question is whether she would have
done so well by us. "But," said my friend in answer to all this, "we
should not have proclaimed to the world that we regarded you and
them as standing on an equal footing." There again appeared the true
gist of the offence. A word from England such as that spoken by Lord
John Russell was of such weight to the South, that the North could not
endure to have it spoken. I did not say to that gentleman,—but here I
may say, that had such circumstances arisen as those conjectured, and
had America spoken such a word, England would not have felt herself
called upon to resent it.

But the fairer analogy lies between Ireland and the Southern States.
The monster meetings and O'Connell's triumphs are not so long gone
by but that many of us can remember the first demand for secession
made by Ireland, and the line which was then taken by American sympathies.[3] It is not too much to say that America then believed that Ireland would secure secession, and that the great trust of the Irish re-
pealers was in the moral aid which she did and would receive from
America. "But our Government proclaimed no sympathy with Ireland," said my friend. No. The American Government is not called on
to make such proclamations; nor had Ireland ever taken upon herself
the nature and labours of a belligerent.

That this anger on the part of the North is unreasonable I cannot
doubt. That it is unfortunate, grievous, and very bitter I am quite sure.

[2] The Indian Mutiny of 1857 had started when a body of Sepoys, or Indian soldiers, refused to use greased cartridges, believing that the grease was made of
cow's fat and pig's lard and consequently offensive to both Hindus and Moham-
medans. Large areas of India were ripe for rebellion, and the mutiny quickly developed into a widespread and bloody war that was not completely suppressed until the
last months of 1858.

[3] The American press had been sympathetic toward Ireland, but surely, as Trollope himself implies, the analogy to events in 1861 is a very shaky one. During 1843
Daniel O'Connell had raised "monster meetings" throughout Ireland demanding repeal of the union with England. The agitation ended tamely when the government
forbade a scheduled assembly and O'Connell called off the meeting rather than resort to force.

But I do not think that it is in any degree surprising. I am inclined to think that did I belong to Boston as I do belong to London, I should share in the feeling, and rave as loudly as all men there have raved against the coldness of England. When men have on hand such a job of work as the North has now undertaken they are always guided by their feelings rather than their reason. What two men ever had a quarrel in which each did not think that all the world, if just, would espouse his own side of the dispute? The North feels that it has been more than loyal to the South, and that the South has taken advantage of that over-loyalty to betray the North. "We have worked for them, and fought for them, and paid for them," says the North. "By our labour we have raised their indolence to a par with our energy. While we have worked like men, we have allowed them to talk and bluster. We have warmed them in our bosom, and now they turn against us and sting us. The world sees that this is so. England, above all, must see it, and seeing it should speak out her true opinion." The North is hot with such thoughts as these, and one cannot wonder that she should be angry with her friend, when her friend, with an expression of certain easy good wishes, bids her fight out her own battles. The North has been unreasonable with England;—but I believe that every reader of this page would have been as unreasonable had that reader been born in Massachusetts.

Mr. and Mrs. Jones are the dearly beloved friends of my family. My wife and I have lived with Mrs. Jones on terms of intimacy which have been quite endearing. Jones has had the run of my house with perfect freedom, and in Mrs. Jones' drawing-room I have always had my own arm-chair, and have been regaled with large breakfast-cups of tea, quite as though I were at home. But of a sudden Jones and his wife have fallen out, and there is for a while in Jones' Hall a cat and dog life that may end—in one hardly dare to surmise what calamity. Mrs. Jones begs that I will interfere with her husband, and Jones entreats the good offices of my wife in moderating the hot temper of his own. But we know better than that. If we interfere, the chances are that my dear friends will make it up and turn upon us. I grieve beyond measure in a general way at the temporary break up of the Jones' Hall happiness. I express general wishes that it may be temporary. But as for saying which is right or which is wrong,—as to expressing special sympathy on either side in such a quarrel,—it is out of the question. "My dear Jones, you must excuse me. Any news in the City to-day? Sugars have fell; how are teas?" Of course Jones thinks that I'm a brute; but what can I do?

I have been somewhat surprised to find the trouble that has been taken by American orators, statesmen, and logicians to prove that this secession on the part of the South has been revolutionary;—that is to say, that it has been undertaken and carried on not in compliance with the constitution of the United States, but in defiance of it. This has been done over and over again by some of the greatest men of the North, and has been done most successfully. But what then? Of course the movement has been revolutionary and anti-constitutional. Nobody, no single Southerner, can really believe that the Constitution of the United States as framed in 1787, or altered since, intended to give to the separate States the power of seceding as they pleased. It is surely useless going through long arguments to prove this, seeing that it is absolutely proved by the absence of any clause giving such licence to the separate States. Such licence would have been destructive to the very idea of a great nationality. Where would New England have been as a part of the United States, if New York, which stretches from the Atlantic to the borders of Canada, had been endowed with the power of cutting off the six Northern States from the rest of the Union? No one will for a moment doubt that the movement was revolutionary, and yet infinite pains are taken to prove a fact that is patent to every one.

It is revolutionary, but what then? Have the Northern States of the American Union taken upon themselves in 1861 to proclaim their opinion that revolution is a sin? Are they going back to the divine right of any sovereignty? Are they going to tell the world that a nation or a people is bound to remain in any political status, because that status is the recognized form of government under which such a people have lived? Is this to be the doctrine of United States' citizens,—of all people? And is this the doctrine preached now, of all times, when the King of Naples and the Italian dukes have just been dismissed from their thrones with such enchanting nonchalance, because their people have not chosen to keep them? [4] Of course the movement is revolutionary; and why not? It is agreed now among all men and all nations that any people may change its form of government to any other, if it wills to do so,—and if it can do so.

There are two other points on which these Northern statesmen and logicians also insist, and these two other points are at any rate better worth an argument than that which touches the question of revolution. It being settled that secession on the part of the Southerners is revolution, it is argued, firstly, that no occasion for revolution had been given

[4] In September 1859 Garibaldi had entered Naples with his troops and proclaimed himself dictator of the kingdom.

by the North to the South! and, secondly, that the South has been dishonest in its revolutionary tactics. Men certainly should not raise a
revolution for nothing; and it may certainly be declared that whatever
men do, they should do honestly.

But in that matter of the cause and ground for revolution, it is so
very easy for either party to put in a plea that shall be satisfactory to
itself! Mr. and Mrs. Jones each had a separate story. Mr. Jones was
sure that the right lay with him: but Mrs. Jones was no less sure. No
doubt the North had done much for the South;—had earned money
for it; had fed it;—and had moreover in a great measure fostered all its
bad habits. It had not only been generous to the South, but over-indul-
gent. But also it had continually irritated the South by meddling with
that which the Southerners believed to be a question absolutely private
to themselves. The matter was illustrated to me by a New Hampshire
man who was conversant with black bears. At the hotels in the New
Hampshire mountains it is customary to find black bears chained to
poles. These bears are caught among the hills, and are thus imprisoned
for the amusement of the hotel guests. "Them Southerners," said my
friend, "are jist as one as that 'ere bear. We feeds him and gives him a
house and his belly is ollers full. But then, jist becase he's a black bear,
we're ollers a poking him with sticks, and a' course the beast is kinder
riled. He wants to be back to the mountains. He wouldn't have his
belly filled, but he'd have his own way. It's jist so with them Southerners."

It is of no use proving to any man or to any nation that they have
got all they should want, if they have not got all that they do want. If
a servant desires to go, it is of no avail to show him that he has all he
can desire in his present place. The Northerners say that they have
given no offence to the Southerners, and that therefore the South is
wrong to raise a revolution. The very fact that the North is the North,
is an offence to the South. As long as Mr. and Mrs. Jones were one in
heart and one in feeling, having the same hopes and the same joys, it
was well that they should remain together. But when it is proved that
they cannot so live without tearing out each other's eyes, Sir Cresswell
Cresswell,[5] the revolutionary institution of domestic life, interferes and
separates them. This is the age of such separations. I do not wonder
that the North should use its logic to show that it has received cause of

---

[5] The English probate and divorce court had been created as recently as January 1858. Sir Cresswell Cresswell (1794–1863) was the first judge to preside over the
new court. Himself a bachelor, Sir Cresswell Cresswell labored at his novel charge so
tirelessly and well that he is generally given credit for the success of the experiment.

CHAPTER II

NEWPORT—RHODE ISLAND

W E—the we consisting of my wife and myself—left Liverpool for Boston on the 24th August, 1861, in the "Arabia," one of Cunard's North American mail packets. We had determined that my wife should return alone at the beginning of winter, when I intended to go to a part of the country in which, under the existing circumstances of the war, a lady might not feel herself altogether comfortable. I proposed staying in America over the winter, and returning in the spring; and this programme I have carried out with sufficient exactness.

The "Arabia" touched at Halifax; and as the touch extended from 11 A.M. to 6 P.M. we had an opportunity of seeing a good deal of that colony;—not quite sufficient to justify me at this critical age in writing a chapter of travels in Nova Scotia, but enough perhaps to warrant a paragraph. It chanced that a cousin of mine was then in command of the troops there, so that we saw the fort with all the honours. A dinner on shore was, I think, a greater treat to us even than this. We also inspected sundry specimens of the gold which is now being found for the first time in Nova Scotia,[1]—as to the glory and probable profits of which the Nova Scotians seemed to be fully alive. But still, I think, the dinner on shore took rank with us as the most memorable and meritorious of all that we did and saw at Halifax. At seven o'clock on the morning but one after that, we were landed at Boston.

At Boston I found friends ready to receive us with open arms, though they were friends we had never known before. I own that I felt myself burdened with much nervous anxiety at my first introduction to men and women in Boston. I knew what the feeling there was with reference to England, and I knew also how impossible it is for an Englishman to hold his tongue and submit to dispraise of England. As for going among a people whose whole minds were filled with affairs of

[1] Gold was first discovered in Nova Scotia during the summer of 1860. There was considerable excitement, and a few adventurers rushed to the fields. The gold was not easily extractable from the quartz-veined granite, however, and it soon became clear that individual miners could get "no crumb of it." By 1883, when machinery for proper exploitation had been installed, the yield was still only 15,446 ounces for the year, an average return of $2.84 per man per day.

the war, and saying nothing about the war,—I knew that no resolution to such an effect could be carried out. If one could not trust oneself to speak, one should have stayed at home in England. I will here state that I always did speak out openly what I thought and felt, and that though I encountered very strong—sometimes almost fierce—opposition, I never was subjected to anything that was personally disagreeable to me.

In September we did not stay above a week in Boston, having been fairly driven out of it by the mosquitoes. I had been told that I should find nobody in Boston whom I cared to see, as everybody was habitually out of town during the heat of the later summer and early autumn; but this was not so. The war and attendant turmoils of war had made the season of vacation shorter than usual, and most of those for whom I asked were back at their posts. I know no place at which an Englishman may drop down suddenly among a pleasanter circle of acquaintance, or find himself with a more clever set of men, than he can do at Boston. I confess that in this respect I think that but few towns are at present more fortunately circumstanced than the capital of the Bay State, as Massachusetts is called, and that very few towns make a better use of their advantages. Boston has a right to be proud of what it has done for the world of letters. It is proud; but I have not found that its pride was carried too far.

Boston is not in itself a fine city, but it is a very pleasant city. They say that the harbour is very grand and very beautiful. It certainly is not so fine as that of Portland in a nautical point of view, and as certainly it is not as beautiful. It is the entrance from the sea into Boston of which people say so much; but I did not think it quite worthy of all I had heard. In such matters, however, much depends on the peculiar light in which scenery is seen. An evening light is generally the best for all landscapes; and I did not see the entrance to Boston harbour by an evening light. It was not the beauty of the harbour of which I thought the most; but of the tea that had been sunk there, and of all that came of that successful speculation. Few towns now standing have a right to be more proud of their antecedents than Boston.

But as I have said, it is not specially interesting to the eye—what new town, or even what simply adult town, can be so? There is an Athenæum, and a State Hall, and a fashionable street,—Beacon Street, very like Piccadilly as it runs along the Green Park,—and there is the Green Park opposite to this Piccadilly, called Boston Common. Beacon Street and Boston Common are very pleasant. Excellent houses there are, and large churches, and enormous hotels; but of such things as

these a man can write nothing that is worth the reading. The traveller
who desires to tell his experience of North America must write of people rather than of things.

As I have said, I found myself instantly involved in discussions on
American politics, and the bearing of England upon those politics.
"What do you think, you in England—what do you all believe will be
the upshot of this war?" That was the question always asked in those
or other words. "Secession, certainly," I always said, but not speaking
quite with that abruptness. "And you believe, then, that the South will
beat the North?" I explained that I, personally, had never so thought,
and that I did not believe that to be the general idea. Men's opinions
in England, however, were too divided to enable me to say that there
was any prevailing conviction on the matter. My own impression was,
and is, that the North will, in a military point of view, have the best of
the contest,—will beat the South; but that the Northerners will not prevent secession, let their success be what it may. Should the North prevail after a two years' conflict, the North will not admit the South to
an equal participation of good things with themselves, even though
each separate rebellious State should return suppliant, like a prodigal
son, kneeling on the floor of Congress, each with a separate rope of
humiliation round its neck. Such was my idea as expressed then, and I
do not know that I have since had much cause to change it.

"We will never give it up," one gentleman said to me—and, indeed,
many have said the same, "till the whole territory is again united from
the Bay to the Gulf! It is impossible that we should allow of two nationalities within those limits." "And do you think it possible," I asked,
"that you should receive back into your bosom this people which you
now hate with so deep a hatred, and receive them again into your arms
as brothers on equal terms? Is it in accordance with experience that a
conquered people should be so treated—and that, too, a people whose
every habit of life is at variance with the habits of their presumed con-
querors? When you have flogged them into a return of fraternal affection, are they to keep their slaves or are they to abolish them?" "No,"
said my friend; "it may not be practical to put those rebellious States
at once on an equality with ourselves. For a time they will probably be
treated as the Territories are now treated." (The Territories are vast
outlying districts belonging to the Union, but not as yet endowed with
State governments, or a participation in the United States Congress.)
"For a time they must, perhaps, lose their full privileges; but the Union
will be anxious to readmit them at the earliest possible period." "And
as to the slaves?" I asked again. "Let them emigrate to Liberia: back

to their own country." [2] I could not say that I thought much of the solution of the difficulty. It would, I suggested, overtask even the energy of America to send out an emigration of four million souls, to provide for their wants in a new and uncultivated country, and to provide after that for the terrible gap made in the labour market of the Southern States. "The Israelites went back from bondage," said my friend. But a way was opened for them by a miracle across the sea, and food was sent to them from heaven, and they had among them a Moses for a leader and a Joshua to fight their battles. I could not but express my fear that the days of such immigrations were over. This plan of sending back the negroes to Africa did not reach me only from one or from two mouths; and it was suggested by men whose opinions respecting their country have weight at home and are entitled to weight abroad. I mention this merely to show how insurmountable would be the difficulty of preventing secession, let which side win that may.

"We will never abandon the right to the mouth of the Mississippi." That in all such arguments is a strong point with men of the Northern States;—perhaps the point to which they all return with the greatest firmness. It is that on which Mr. Everett insists in the last paragraph of the oration which he made in New York on 4th of July, 1861. [3] "The Missouri and the Mississippi rivers," he says, "with their hundred tributaries give to the great central basin of our continent its character and destiny. The outlet of this system lies between the States of Tennessee and Missouri, of Mississippi and Arkansas, and through the State of Louisiana. The ancient province so called, the proudest monu-

2 Ever since 1820 Liberia, on the west coat of Africa, had been thought of as a place for sending freed slaves. In that year the American Colonization Society, which had acquired the territory, shipped out the first group. By 1845 the society and allied organizations had transported 4,500 colonists. In 1847 Liberia became an independent Negro republic.

3 Edward Everett (1794–1865), the noted American statesman, teacher, Unitarian clergyman, and orator, had been a personal friend of Anthony's mother ever since she had obtained an introduction to him in 1841. This fact does not deter Anthony from dealing rather roughly with him in Chapter xvi of North America, where there appears a full and unflattering description of Everett's manner and method on the lecture platform.

Trollope quotes above from the published text of Everett's oration entitled The Great Issues before Our Country: an Oration . . . Delivered at the New York Academy of Music, July 4, 1861. If the audience heard the whole of the forty-eight pages of fine print, one cannot but admire those who were in at the last paragraph. The right of the United States to fulfill her destiny by expanding her territories was a theme especially dear to Everett. As Secretary of State under Fillmore (for four months, 1852–3), he had declined a proposal from France and England to ensure Spain's continued possession of Cuba. Everett intimated in his reply that in time the United States might find it necessary to obtain this land.

ment of the mighty monarch whose name it bears, passed from the jurisdiction of France to that of Spain in 1763. Spain coveted it; not that she might fill it with prosperous colonies and rising States, but that it might stretch as a broad waste barrier, infested with warlike tribes, between the Anglo-American power and the silver mines of Mexico. With the independence of the United States, the fear of a still more dangerous neighbour grew upon Spain; and in the insane expectation of checking the progress of the Union westward, she threatened, and at times attempted, to close the mouth of the Mississippi on the rapidly increasing trade of the West. The bare suggestion of such a policy roused the population upon the banks of the Ohio, then inconsiderable, as one man. Their confidence in Washington scarcely restrained them from rushing to the seizure of New Orleans, when the treaty of San Lorenzo El Real, in 1795, stipulated for them a precarious right of navigating the noble river to the sea, with a right of deposit at New Orleans. This subject was for years the turning-point of the politics of the West; and it was perfectly well understood that, sooner or later, she would be content with nothing less than the sovereign control of the mighty stream from its head-spring to its outlet in the Gulf. *And that is as true now as it was then.*"

This is well put. It describes with force the desires, ambition, and necessities of a great nation, and it tells with historical truth the story of the success of that nation. It was a great thing done when the purchase of the whole of Louisiana was completed by the United States,— that cession by France, however, having been made at the instance of Napoleon, and not in consequence of any demand made by the States. The district then called Louisiana included the present State of that name, and the States of Missouri and Arkansas;—included also the right to possess, if not the absolute possession of, all that enormous expanse of country running from thence back to the Pacific; a huge amount of territory of which the most fertile portion is watered by the Mississippi and its vast tributaries. That river and those tributaries are navigable through the whole centre of the American continent up to Wisconsin and Minnesota. To the United States the navigation of the Mississippi was, we may say, indispensable; and to the States when no longer united the navigation will be equally indispensable. But the days are gone when any country, such as Spain was, can interfere to stop the highways of the world with the all but avowed intention of arresting the progress of civilization. It may be that the North and the South can never again be friends as the component parts of one nation. Such I take it is the belief of all politicians in Europe, and of many of those who live across the water. But as separate nations they may yet live together in amity, and share between them the great water-ways which God has given them for their enrichment. The Rhine is free to Prussia and to Holland. The Danube is not closed against Austria. It will be said that the Danube has in fact been closed against Austria, in spite of treaties to the contrary. But the faults of bad and weak governments are made known as cautions to the world, and not as facts to copy. The free use of the waters of a common river between two nations is an affair for treaty; and it has not yet come to that [,] that treaties must necessarily be null and void through the falseness of politicians.

"And what will England do for cotton? Is it not the fact that Lord John Russell with his professed neutrality intends to express sympathy with the South, intends to pave the way for the advent of Southern cotton?" "You ought to love us," so say men in Boston, "because we have been with you in heart and spirit for long, long years. But your trade has eaten into your souls, and you love American cotton better than American loyalty and American fellowship." This I found to be unfair, and in what politest language I could use I said so. I had not any special knowledge of the minds of English statesmen on this matter; but I knew as well as Americans could do what our statesmen had said and done respecting it. That cotton, if it came from the South, would be made very welcome in Liverpool, of course, I knew. If private enterprise could bring it, it might be brought. But the very declaration made by Lord John Russell was the surest pledge that England as a nation would not interfere, even to supply her own wants. It may easily be imagined what eager words all this would bring about; but I never found that eager words led to feelings which were personally hostile.

All the world has heard of Newport in Rhode Island as being the Brighton, and Tenby, and Scarborough of New England. And the glory of Newport is by no means confined to New England, but is shared by New York and Washington, and in ordinary years by the extreme South. It is the habit of Americans to go to some watering place every summer,—that is, to some place either of sea water or of inland waters. This is done much in England; more in Ireland than in England; but, I think, more in the States than even in Ireland. But of all such summer haunts, Newport is supposed to be in many ways the most captivating. In the first place it is certainly the most fashionable, and in the next place it is said to be the most beautiful. We decided on going to Newport,—led thither by the latter reputation rather than the former. As we were still in the early part of September we expected to find the place full, but in this we were disappointed;—disappointed, I say, rather than gratified, although a crowded house at such a place is certainly a nuisance. But a house which is prepared to make up six hundred beds, and which is called on to make up only twenty-five becomes, after a while, somewhat melancholy. The natural depression of the landlord communicates itself to his servants, and from the servants it descends to the twenty-five guests, who wander about the long passages and deserted balconies like the ghosts of those of the summer visitors, who cannot rest quietly in their graves at home.

In England we know nothing of hotels prepared for six hundred visitors, all of whom are expected to live in common. Domestic architects would be frightened at the dimensions which are needed, and at the number of apartments which are required to be clustered under one roof. We went to the Ocean Hotel at Newport, and fancied, as we first entered the hall under a verandah as high as the house, and made our way into the passage, that we had been taken to a well-arranged barrack. "Have you rooms?" I asked as a man always does ask on first reaching his inn. "Rooms enough," the clerk said. "We have only fifty here." But that fifty dwindled down to twenty-five during the next day or two.

We were a melancholy set, the ladies appearing to be afflicted in this way worse than the gentlemen, on account of their enforced abstinence from tobacco. What can twelve ladies do scattered about a drawing-room, so-called, intended for the accommodation of two hundred? The drawing-room at the Ocean Hotel, Newport, is not as big as Westminster Hall, but would, I should think, make a very good House of Commons for the British nation. Fancy the feelings of a lady when she walks into such a room intending to spend her evening there, and finds six or seven other ladies located on various sofas at terrible distances,— all strangers to her. She has come to Newport probably to enjoy herself; and as, in accordance with the customs of the place, she has dined at two, she has nothing before her for the evening but the society of that huge furnished cavern. Her husband, if she have one, or her father, or her lover, has probably entered the room with her. But a man has never the courage to endure such a position long. He sidles out with some muttered excuse, and seeks solace with a cigar. The lady, after half an hour of contemplation, creeps silently near some companion in the desert, and suggests in a whisper that Newport does not seem to be very full at present.

We stayed there for a week, and were very melancholy; but in our melancholy we still talked of the war. Americans are said to be given to bragging, and it is a sin of which I cannot altogether acquit them.

III Interior of an American Railway Car: "It will be said that the American cars are good enough for all purposes. The seats are not very hard, and the room for sitting is sufficient. Nevertheless, I deny that they are good enough for all purposes . . . to enter them and find a place often requires a struggle and almost a fight."

Illustrated London News, XXXVIII (*April* 6, 1861), 307

IV   The White Mountains—the Ride

Harper's Weekly, III (*August* 13, 1859), 521

But I have constantly been surprised at hearing the Northern speak of their own military achievements with anything but self-praise. "We've been whipped, sir; and we shall be whipped again before we've done; uncommon well whipped we shall be." "We began cowardly, and were afraid to send our own regiments through one of our own cities." This alluded to a demand that had been made on the Government, that troops going to Washington should not be sent through Baltimore, because of the strong feeling for rebellion which was known to exist in that city. President Lincoln complied with this request, thinking it well to avoid a collision between the mob and the soldiers.[4] "We began cowardly, and now we're going on cowardly, and darn't attack them. Well; when we've been whipped often enough, then we shall learn the trade." Now all this,—and I heard much of such a nature,—could not be called boasting. But yet with it all there was a substratum of confidence. I have heard northern gentlemen complaining of the President, complaining of all his ministers one after another, complaining of the contractors who were robbing the army, of the commanders who did not know how to command the army, and of the army itself which did not know how to obey; but I do not remember that I have discussed the matter with any Northerner who would admit a doubt as to ultimate success.

We were certainly rather melancholy at Newport, and the empty house may perhaps have given its tone to the discussions on the war. I confess that I could not stand the drawing-room—the ladies' drawing-room as such-like rooms are always called at the hotels, and that I basely deserted my wife. I could not stand it either here or elsewhere, and it seemed to me that other husbands,—ay, and even lovers,—were as hard pressed as myself. I protest that there is no spot on the earth's surface so dear to me as my own drawing-room, or rather my wife's drawing-room at home; that I am not a man given hugely to clubs, but one rather rejoicing in the rustle of petticoats. I like to have women in the same room with me. But at these hotels I found myself driven away, —propelled as it were by some unknown force,—to absent myself from

4 By the time that Lincoln gave this order, a collision had already occurred. The Baltimore Riot took place on April 19, 1861. The Sixth Massachusetts, passing through the city streets, had been stoned by a mob, and some of the soldiers had opened fire without orders. Rioters seized muskets from the ranks and turned the guns against their owners. Four soldiers and nine or more civilians were killed; many others were wounded. Fearing further riots if more soldiers appeared, Baltimore civil authorities requested that the railroad reroute troops and ordered the municipal bridges taken up. Pro-South bands tore out the railroad bridges. On April 21, Lincoln ordered that troops already under way be sent back to Harrisburg and routed outside the state in so far as possible.

the feminine haunts. Anything was more palatable than them; even
"liquoring up" at a nasty bar, or smoking in a comfortless reading-
room among a deluge of American newspapers. And I protest also,—
hoping as I do so that I may say much in these volumes to prove the
truth of such protestation,—that this comes from no fault of the American women. They are as lovely as our own women. Taken generally,
they are better instructed—though perhaps not better educated. They
are seldom troubled with *mauvaise honte*,—I do not say it in irony, but
begging that the words may be taken at their proper meaning. They
can always talk, and very often can talk well. But when assembled
together in these vast, cavernous, would-be luxurious, but in truth hor-
ribly comfortless hotel drawing-rooms,—they are unapproachable. I
have seen lovers, whom I have known to be lovers, unable to remain
five minutes in the same cavern with their beloved ones.

And then the music! There is always a piano in an hotel drawing-
room, on which, of course, some one of the forlorn ladies is generally
employed. I do not suppose that these pianos are in fact, as a rule,
louder and harsher, more violent and less musical, than other instru-
ments of the kind. They seem to be so, but that, I take it, arises from
the exceptional mental depression of those who have to listen to them.
Then the ladies, or probably some one lady, will sing, and as she
hears her own voice ring and echo through the lofty corners and round
the empty walls, she is surprised at her own force, and with increased
efforts sings louder and still louder. She is tempted to fancy that she is
suddenly gifted with some power of vocal melody unknown to her before, and filled with the glory of her own performance shouts till the
whole house rings. At such moments she at least is happy, if no one else
is so. Looking at the general sadness of her position, who can grudge
her such happiness?

And then the children,—babies, I should say if I were speaking of
English bairns of their age; but seeing that they are Americans, I
hardly dare to call them children. The actual age of these perfectly
civilized and highly educated beings may be from three to four. One
will often see five or six such seated at the long dinner-table of the
hotel, breakfasting and dining with their elders, and going through the
ceremony with all the gravity, and more than all the decorum of their
grandfathers. When I was three years old I had not yet, as I imagine,
been promoted beyond a silver spoon of my own wherewith to eat my
bread and milk in the nursery, and I feel assured that I was under the
immediate care of a nursemaid, as I gobbled up my minced mutton
mixed with potatoes and gravy. But at hotel life in the States the adult

infant lisps to the waiter for everything at table, handles his fish with epicurean delicacy, is choice in his selection of pickles, very particular that his beefsteak at breakfast shall be hot, and is instant in his demand for fresh ice in his water. But perhaps his, or in this case her, retreat from the room when the meal is over, is the *chef d'œuvre* of the whole performance. The little precocious, full-blown beauty of four signifies that she has completed her meal,—or is "through" her dinner, as she would express it,—by carefully extricating herself from the napkin which has been tucked around her. Then the waiter, ever attentive to her movements, draws back the chair on which she is seated, and the young lady glides to the floor. A little girl in Old England would scramble down, but little girls in New England never scramble. Her father and mother, who are no more than her chief ministers, walk before her out of the saloon, and then she,—swims after them. But swimming is not the proper word. Fishes in making their way through the water assist, or rather impede, their motion with no dorsal wriggle. No animal taught to move directly by its Creator adopts a gait so useless, and at the same time so graceless. Many women, having received their lessons in walking from a less eligible instructor, do move in this way, and such women this unfortunate little lady has been instructed to copy. The peculiar step to which I allude is to be seen often on the Boulevards in Paris. It is to be seen more often in second rate French towns, and among fourth rate French women. Of all signs in women betokening vulgarity, bad taste, and aptitude to bad morals, it is the surest. And this is the gait of going which American mothers,—some American mothers I should say,—love to teach their daughters! As a comedy at an hotel, it is very delightful, but in private life I should object to it.

To me Newport could never be a place charming by reason of its own charms. That it is a very pleasant place when it is full of people and the people are in spirits and happy, I do not doubt. But then the visitors would bring, as far as I am concerned, the pleasantness with them. The coast is not fine. To those who know the best portions of the coast of Wales or Cornwall,—or better still, the western coast of Ireland, of Clare and Kerry for instance,—it would not be in any way remarkable. It is by no means equal to Dieppe or Biarritz, and not to be talked of in the same breath with Spezzia.[5] The hotels, too, are all

---

[5] "In his somewhat disparaging estimate of Newport, R. I., Mr. Trollope strangely omits the chief attraction, and that is the peculiar climate, wherein it so much differs from the rest of the New England coast."—Henry T. Tuckerman: *America and Her Commentators* (1864).

built away from the sea; so that one cannot sit and watch the play of
the waves from one's window. Nor are there pleasant rambling paths
down among the rocks, and from one short strand to another. There
is excellent bathing for those who like bathing on shelving sand. I
don't. The spot is about half a mile from the hotels, and to this the
bathers are carried in omnibuses. Till one o'clock ladies bathe;—which
operation, however, does not at all militate against the bathing of men,
but rather necessitates it as regards those men who have ladies with
them. For here ladies and gentlemen bathe in decorous dresses, and are
very polite to each other. I must say, that I think the ladies have the
best of it. My idea of sea-bathing for my own gratification is not compatible with a full suit of clothing. I own that my tastes are vulgar and
perhaps indecent; but I love to jump into the deep clear sea from off a
rock, and I love to be hampered by no outward impediment as I do so.
For ordinary bathers, for all ladies, and for men less savage in their
instincts than I am, the bathing at Newport is very good.

The private houses—villa residences as they would be termed by
an auctioneer in England—are excellent. Many of them are, in fact,
mansions, and are surrounded with grounds, which, as the shrubs grow
up, will be very beautiful. Some have large, well-kept lawns, stretching
down to the rocks, and these to my taste give the charm to Newport.
They extend about two miles along the coast. Should my lot have made
me a citizen of the United States, I should have had no objection to
become the possessor of one of these "villa residences," but I do not
think that I should have "gone in" for hotel life at Newport.

We hired saddle-horses, and rode out nearly the length of the island.
It was all very well, but there was little in it remarkable either as regards cultivation or scenery. We found nothing that it would be possible either to describe or remember. The Americans of the United
States have had time to build and populate vast cities, but they have
not yet had time to surround themselves with pretty scenery. Outlying
grand scenery is given by nature; but the prettiness of home scenery is
a work of art. It comes from the thorough draining of land, from the
planting and subsequent thinning of trees, from the controlling of
waters, and constant use of minute patches of broken land. In another
hundred years or so Rhode Island may be, perhaps, as pretty as the Isle
of Wight. The horses which we got were not good. They were unhandy
and badly mouthed, and that which my wife rode was altogether ignorant of the art of walking. We hired them from an Englishman, who
had established himself at New York as a riding-master for ladies, and
who had come to Newport for the season on the same business. He com-

plained to me with much bitterness of the saddle-horses which came in his way,—of course thinking that it was the special business of a country to produce saddle-horses,—as I think it the special business of a country to produce pens, ink, and paper of good quality. According to him, riding has not yet become an American art, and hence the awkwardness of American horses. "Lord bless you, sir! they don't give an animal a chance of a mouth." In this he alluded only, I presume, to saddle-horses. I know nothing of the trotting-horses, but I should imagine that a fine mouth must be an essential requisite for a trotting-match in harness. As regards riding at Newport, we were not tempted to repeat the experiment. The number of carriages which we saw there,—remembering as I did that the place was comparatively empty,—and their general smartness, surprised me very much. It seemed that every lady with a house of her own had also her own carriage. These carriages were always open, and the law of the land imperatively demands that the occupants shall cover their knees with a worked worsted apron of brilliant colours. These aprons at first, I confess, seemed tawdry; but the eye soon becomes used to bright colours, in carriage aprons as well as in architecture, and I soon learned to like them.

Rhode Island, as the State is usually called, is the smallest State in the Union. I may perhaps best show its disparity to other States by saying that New York extends about 250 miles from north to south and the same distance from east to west; whereas the State called Rhode Island is about forty miles long by twenty broad, independently of certain small islands. It would, in fact, not form a considerable addition, if added on to many of the other States. Nevertheless, it has all the same powers of self-government as are possessed by such nationalities as the States of New York and Pennsylvania; and sends two senators to the Senate at Washington, as do those enormous States. Small as the State is, Rhode Island itself forms but a small portion of it. The authorized and proper name of the State is Providence Plantation and Rhode Island. Roger Williams was the first founder of the colony, and he established himself on the mainland at a spot which he called Providence. Here now stands the city of Providence, the chief town of the State; and a thriving, comfortable town it seems to be, full of banks, fed by railways and steamers, and going ahead quite as quickly as Roger Williams could in his fondest hopes have desired.

Rhode Island, as I have said, has all the attributes of government in common with her stouter and more famous sisters. She has a governor, and an upper house, and a lower house of legislature; and she is somewhat fantastic in the use of these constitutional powers, for she

calls on them to sit now in one town and now in another. Providence
is the capital of the State; but the Rhode Island parliament sits sometimes at Providence and sometimes at Newport. At stated times also it
has to collect itself at Bristol, and at other stated times at Kingston, and
at others at East Greenwich. Of all legislative assemblies it is the most
peripatetic. Universal suffrage does not absolutely prevail in this State,
a certain property qualification being necessary to confer a right to vote
even for the State Representatives. I should think it would be well for
all parties if the whole State could be swallowed up by Massachusetts or
by Connecticut, either of which lie conveniently for the feat; but I presume that any suggestion of such a nature would be regarded as treason
by the men of Providence Plantation.

We returned back to Boston by Attleborough, a town at which in
ordinary times the whole population is supported by the jewellers'
trade. It is a place with a speciality, upon which speciality it has thriven
well and become a town. But the speciality is one ill-adapted for times
of war; and we were assured that the trade was for the present at an
end. What man could now-a-days buy jewels, or even what woman, seeing that everything would be required for the war? I do not say that
such abstinence from luxury has been begotten altogether by a feeling
of patriotism. The direct taxes which all Americans will now be called
on to pay, have had, and will have much to do with such abstinence. In
the mean time the poor jewellers of Attleborough have gone altogether
to the wall.

CHAPTER III

MAINE, NEW HAMPSHIRE, AND VERMONT

PERHAPS I ought to assume that all the world in England knows that that portion of the United States called New England consists of the six States of Maine, New Hampshire, Vermont, Massachusetts, Connecticut, and Rhode Island. This is especially the land of Yankees, and none can properly be called Yankees but those who belong to New England. I have named the States as nearly as may be in order from the North downwards. Of Rhode Island, the smallest State in the Union, I have already said what little I have to say. Of these six States Boston may be called the capital. Not that it is so in any civil or political sense; —it is simply the capital of Massachusetts. But as it is the Athens of the Western world; as it was the cradle of American freedom; as everybody of course knows that into Boston harbour was thrown the tea which George III. would tax, and that at Boston, on account of that and similar taxes, sprang up the new revolution; and as it has grown in wealth, and fame, and size beyond other towns in New England, it may be allowed to us to regard it as the capital of these six Northern States, without guilt of *lèse majesté* towards the other five. To me, I confess, this Northern division of our once unruly colonies is, and always has been, the dearest. I am no Puritan myself, and fancy that had I lived in the days of the Puritans, I should have been anti-Puritan to the full extent of my capabilities. But I should have been so through ignorance and prejudice, and actuated by that love of existing rights and wrongs which men call loyalty. If the Canadas were to rebel now, I should be for putting down the Canadians with a strong hand; but not the less have I an idea that it will become the Canadas to rebel and assert their independence at some future period;—unless it be conceded to them without such rebellion. Who, on looking back, can now refuse to admire the political aspirations of the English Puritans, or decline to acknowledge the beauty and fitness of what they did? It was by them that these States of New England were colonized. They came hither stating themselves to be pilgrims, and as such they first placed their feet on that hallowed rock at Plymouth, on the shore of Massachusetts. They came here driven by no thirst of conquest, by no greed for gold, dreaming of no Western empire such as Cortez had achieved and Raleigh had meditated. They desired to earn their bread in the sweat of their brow, worshipping God according to their own lights, living in harmony under their own laws, and feeling that no master could claim a right to put a heel upon their necks. And be it remembered that here in England, in those days, earthly masters were still apt to put their heels on the necks of men. The Star Chamber was gone, but Jeffreys had not yet reigned. What earthly aspirations were ever higher than these, or more manly? And what earthly efforts ever led to grander results?

We determined to go to Portland, in Maine, from thence to the White Mountains in New Hampshire—the American Alps, as they love to call themselves,—and then on to Quebec and up through the two Canadas to Niagara; and this route we followed. From Boston to Portland we travelled by railroad,—the carriages on which are in America always called cars. And here I beg, once for all, to enter my protest loudly against the manner in which these conveyances are conducted. The one grand fault—there are other smaller faults—but the one grand fault is that they admit but one class. Two reasons for this are given. The first is that the finances of the companies will not admit of a divided accommodation; and the second is that the republican nature of the people will not brook a superior or aristocratic classification of travelling. As regards the first, I do not in the least believe in it. If a more expensive manner of railway travelling will pay in England, it would surely do so here. Were a better class of carriages organized, as large a portion of the population would use them in the United States as in any country in Europe. And it seems to be evident that in arranging that there shall be only one rate of travelling, the price is enhanced on poor travellers exactly in proportion as it is made cheap to those who are not poor. For the poorer classes, travelling in America is by no means cheap,—the average rate being, as far as I can judge, fully three-halfpence a mile. It is manifest that dearer rates for one class would allow of cheaper rates for the other; and that in this manner general travelling would be encouraged and increased.

But I do not believe that the question of expenditure has had anything to do with it. I conceive it to be true that the railways are afraid to put themselves at variance with the general feeling of the people. If so the railways may be right. But then, on the other hand, the general feeling of the people must in such case be wrong. Such a feeling argues a total mistake as to the nature of that liberty and equality for the security of which the people is so anxious, and that mistake the very one which has made shipwreck so many attempts at freedom in other countries. It argues that confusion between social and political equality which has led astray multitudes who have longed for liberty fervently, but who have not thought of it carefully. If a first-class railway carriage should be held as offensive, so should a first-class house, or a first-class horse, or a first-class dinner. But first-class houses, first-class horses, and first-class dinners are very rife in America. Of course it may be said that the expenditure shown in these last-named objects is private expenditure, and cannot be controlled; and that railway travelling is of a public nature, and can be made subject to public opinion. But the fault is in that public opinion which desires to control matters of this nature. Such an arrangement partakes of all the vice of a sumptuary law, and sumptuary laws are in their very essence mistakes. It is well that a man should always have all for which he is willing to pay. If he desires and obtains more than is good for him, the punishment, and thus also the preventive, will come from other sources.

It will be said that the American cars are good enough for all purposes. The seats are not very hard, and the room for sitting is sufficient. Nevertheless I deny that they are good enough for all purposes. They are very long, and to enter them and find a place often requires a struggle and almost a fight. There is rarely any person to tell a stranger which car he should enter. One never meets an uncivil or unruly man, but the women of the lower ranks are not courteous. American ladies love to lie at ease in their carriages, as thoroughly as do our women in Hyde Park, and to those who are used to such luxury, travelling by railroad in their own country must be grievous. I would not wish to be thought a Sybarite myself, or to be held as complaining because I have been compelled to give up my seat to women with babies and bandboxes who have accepted the courtesy with very scanty grace. I have borne worse things than these, and have roughed it much in my days from want of means and other reasons. Nor am I yet so old but what I can rough it still. Nevertheless I like to see things as well done as is practicable, and railway travelling in the States is not well done. I feel bound to say as much as this, and now I have said it, once for all.

Few cities, or localities for cities, have fairer natural advantages than Portland—and I am bound to say that the people of Portland have done much in turning them to account. This town is not the capital of the State in a political point of view. Augusta, which is further to the North, on the Kenebee river, is the seat of the State Government for Maine. It is very generally the case that the States do not hold their legislatures and carry on their Government at their chief towns. Augusta and not Portland is the capital of Maine. Of the State of New

York, Albany is the capital, and not the city which bears the State's name. And of Pennsylvania, Harrisburg and not Philadelphia is the capital. I think the idea has been that old-fashioned notions were bad in that they were old-fashioned; and that a new people, bound by no prejudices, might certainly make improvement by choosing for themselves new ways. If so the American politicians have not been the first in the world who have thought that any change must be a change for the better. The assigned reason is the centrical position of the selected political capitals: but I have generally found the real commercial capital to be easier of access than the smaller town in which the two legislative houses are obliged to collect themselves.

What must be the natural excellence of the harbour of Portland will be understood when it is borne in mind that the Great Eastern can enter it at all times, and that it can lie along the wharves at any hour of the tide.[1] The wharves which have been prepared for her—and of

[1] The *Great Eastern*, nearly six times the size of the largest ship before her, was one of the marvels of the age. Her iron hull, when she was ready for sea, displaced 27,384 long tons; the rail around her deck measured nearly a quarter mile; her six masts held 6,500 square yards of canvas; she was equipped as well with both side paddles and a screw, which derived their power from enormous steam engines.

Investors who sank an initial $6,000,000 into building the *Great Eastern* hoped to realize huge dividends, but from the start nearly everything went wrong with her. On November 3, 1857, when the ceremony of launching the hull took place, the iron mass made one lunge of forty inches and then refused to budge farther. Three months and an additional $600,000 later, she was finally got into the water. A further $1,600,000 would have to be raised before she could be properly fitted out for sea. The disheartened directors finally sold the ship itself for half that amount to a new body of promoters and thus finished the first link in the chain of disasters connected with her.

In September 1859 the *Great Eastern* at last weighed anchor. She had gone but a short distance down the Thames when a water preheater exploded, tearing a funnel to bits, wrecking the proudly furnished chief saloon, and scalding to death six stokers. I. K. Brunel, the designer of the ship, who had already taken to his bed from the strain of witnessing the engine trials, heard of the accident, sank into a coma, and died. A few months later the captain was drowned when his gig upset in Southampton Harbor.

In June 1860, with but thirty-six passengers aboard, the *Great Eastern* set out on her first transatlantic voyage. Her speed was reduced by difficulty in setting sails, defective safety valves on her engines, a heavily barnacle-laden bottom, and other causes, but she was off Sandy Hook in ten and one-half days. At New York she received a tremendous ovation. Within a month over 140,000 visitors paid their half dollars for the privilege of going over the ship. But whatever favor she had acquired (there had been many minor collisions between the public and her personnel) was canceled when, at the end of July, she made a two-day cruise to Cape May and return. Two thousand passengers had been taken aboard. There was a lack of sleeping accommodations, food, or even water for this number. Coffee sold for a dollar a cup, and a basin of hot water brought the same amount. Indignation meetings, fights, and near riots broke out on the great deck. American newspapers gave

which I will say a word further by-and-by—are joined to and in fact are a portion of the station of the Grand Trunk Railway, which runs from Portland up to Canada. So that passengers landing at Portland out of a vessel so large even as the Great Eastern can walk at once on shore, and goods can be passed on to the railway without any of the cost of removal. I will not say that there is no other harbour in the world that would allow of this, but I do not know any other that would do so.

From Portland a line of railway, called as a whole by the name of the Canada Grand Trunk line, runs across the State of Maine through the Northern parts of New Hampshire and Vermont, to Montreal, a branch striking from Richmond, a little within the limits of Canada, to Quebec, and down the St. Lawrence to Rivière du Loup. The main line is continued from Montreal, through Upper Canada to Toronto, and from thence to Detroit in the State of Michigan. The total distance thus traversed is in a direct line about 900 miles. From Detroit there is railway communication through the immense North-Western States of Michigan, Wisconsin, and Illinois, than which perhaps the surface of the globe affords no finer districts for purposes of agriculture. The produce of the two Canadas must be poured forth to the Eastern world, and the men of the Eastern world must throng into these lands, by means of this railroad,— and, as at present arranged, through the harbour of Portland. At present the line has been opened, and they who have opened are sorely suffering in pocket for what they have done. The question of the railway is rather one applying to Canada than to the State of Maine, and I will therefore leave it for the present.

But the Great Eastern has never been to Portland, and as far as I know has no intention of going there. She was, I believe, built with that object. At any rate it was proclaimed during her building that such was

---

the trip columns of lurid detail and roundly denounced the ship they had once hailed with florid praise.

In August the *Great Eastern* sailed for England with seventy-two passengers roaming her halls and decks. Engine trouble compelled her to lay to for some hours in mid-passage. Minor mishaps and ruinously slender passenger lists marked her crossings until the next spring, when she tore loose thirty yards of her hull on a rock. In September 1861, about the time Trollope reached the United States, she came close to foundering off the Irish coast when her patent steam-driven steering gears refused to function during a heavy storm. This incident marked the approximate end of the *Great Eastern's* career as a passenger ship. In 1866 she gained prestige by laying the first successful transatlantic cable, but her operating costs as a cable-layer were so huge that she paid meager dividends to her investors. In 1888, after two decades given mainly to rusting at anchor, she was sold to a shipbreaker for $80,000. The market for scrap iron happened to be flourishing, and the shipbreaker seems to have been one of the few people who, having had anything to do with the *Great Eastern*, came away the richer.

her destiny, and the Portlanders believed it with a perfect faith. They went to work and built wharves expressly for her; two wharves prepared to fit her two gangways, or ways of exit and entrance. They built a huge hotel to receive her passengers. They prepared for her advent with a full conviction that a millennium of trade was about to be wafted to their happy port. "Sir, the town has expended two hundred thousand dollars in expectation of that ship, and that ship has deceived us." So was the matter spoken of to me by an intelligent Portlander. I explained to that intelligent gentleman that two hundred thousand dollars would go a very little way towards making up the loss which the ill-fortuned vessel had occasioned on the other side of the water. He did not in words express gratification at this information, but he looked it. The matter was as it were a partnership without deed of contract between the Portlanders and the shareholders of the vessel, and the Portlanders, though they also have suffered their losses, have not had the worst of it.

But there are still good days in store for the town. Though the Great Eastern has not gone there, other ships from Europe, more profitable if less in size, must eventually find their way thither. At present the Canada line of packets runs to Portland only during those months in which it is shut out from the St. Lawrence and Quebec by ice. But the St. Lawrence and Quebec cannot offer the advantages which Portland enjoys, and that big hotel and those new wharves will not have been built in vain.

I have said that a good time is coming, but I would by no means wish to signify that the present times in Portland are bad. So far from it, that I doubt whether I ever saw a town with more evident signs of prosperity. It has about it every mark of ample means, and no mark of poverty. It contains about 27,000 people, and for that population covers a very large space of ground. The streets are broad and well built, the main streets not running in those absolutely straight parallels which are so common in American towns, and are so distressing to English eyes and English feelings. All these, except the streets devoted exclusively to business, are shaded on both sides by trees—generally, if I remember rightly, by the beautiful American elm, whose drooping boughs have all the grace of the willow without its fantastic melancholy. What the poorer streets of Portland may be like I cannot say. I saw no poor street. But in no town of 30,000 inhabitants did I ever see so many houses which must require an expenditure of from six to eight hundred a year to maintain them.

The place too is beautifully situated. It is on a long promontory,

which takes the shape of a peninsula;—for the neck which joins it to
the mainland is not above half a mile across. But though the town thus
stands out into the sea, it is not exposed and bleak. The harbour again
is surrounded by land, or so guarded and locked by islands as to form
a series of salt-water lakes running round the town. Of those islands
there are, of course, 365. Travellers who write their travels are constantly called upon to record that number, so that it may now be considered as a superlative in local phraseology, signifying a very great
many indeed. The town stands between two hills, the suburbs or outskirts running up on to each of them. The one looking out towards the
sea is called Mountjoy—though the obstinate Americans will write it
Munjoy on their maps. From thence the view out to the harbour and
beyond the harbour to the islands is, I may not say unequalled, or I
shall be guilty of running into superlatives myself; but it is, in its way,
equal to anything I have seen. Perhaps it is more like Cork harbour,
as seen from certain heights over Passage than anything else I can remember; but Portland harbour, though equally landlocked, is larger;
and then from Portland harbour there is as it were a river outlet, running through delicious islands, most unalluring to the navigator, but
delicious to the eyes of an uncommercial traveller. There are in all [,]
four outlets to the sea, one of which appears to have been made expressly for the Great Eastern. Then there is the hill looking inwards.
If it has a name I forget it. The view from this hill is also over the
water on each side, and though not so extensive is perhaps as pleasing
as the other.

The ways of the people seemed to be quiet, smooth, orderly, and
republican. There is nothing to drink in Portland of course, for, thanks
to Mr. Neal Dow, the Father Mathew of the State of Maine,[2] the Maine
Liquor Law is still in force in that State. There is nothing to drink, I
should say, in such orderly houses as that I selected. "People do drink
some in the town, they say," said my hostess to me; "and liquor is to be
got. But I never venture to sell any. An ill-natured person might turn
on me, and where should I be then?" I did not press her, and she was
good enough to put a bottle of porter at my right hand at dinner, for
which I observed she made no charge. "But they advertise beer in the

[2] Neal Dow was an eminent American champion of prohibition, ardent in the
cause but less remarkable than Father Theobald Mathew, a Capuchin priest who entered the United States in 1849 to promote abstinence among Irish-Americans. Before he left the country two years later, he had traveled 37,000 miles and persuaded
a half-million people to join the Sons of Temperance, a secret ritualistic organization for pledge-takers.
Maine had passed the first state-wide prohibition law in the Union in 1851.

shop-windows," I said to a man who was driving me—"Scotch ale, and bitter beer. A man can get drunk on them." "Wa'al, yes. If he goes to work hard, and drinks a bucketfull," said the driver, "perhaps he may." From which and other things I gathered that the men of Maine drank pottle deep before Mr. Neal Dow brought his exertions to a successful termination.

The Maine Liquor Law still stands in Maine, and is the law of the land throughout New England; but it is not actually put in force in the other States. By this law no man may retail wine, spirits, or, in truth, beer, except with a special license, which is given only to those who are presumed to sell them as medicines. A man may have what he likes in his own cellar for his own use—such at least is the actual working of the law—but may not obtain it at hotels and public-houses. This law, like all sumptuary laws, must fail. And it is fast failing even in Maine. But it did appear to me from such information as I could collect that the passing of it had done much to hinder and repress a habit of hard drinking which was becoming terribly common, not only in the towns of Maine, but among the farmers and hired labourers in the country.

But if the men and women of Portland may not drink they may eat, and it is a place, I should say, in which good living on that side of the question is very rife. It has an air of supreme plenty, as though the agonies of an empty stomach were never known there. The faces of the people tell of three regular meals of meat a day, and of digestive powers in proportion. Oh happy Portlanders, if they only knew their own good fortune! They get up early, and go to bed early. The women are comely and sturdy, able to take care of themselves without any fal-lal of chivalry; and the men are sedate, obliging, and industrious. I saw the young girls in the streets, coming home from their tea-parties at nine o'clock, many of them alone, and all with some basket in their hands which betokened an evening not passed absolutely in idleness. No fear there of unruly questions on the way, or of insolence from the ill-conducted of the other sex! All was, or seemed to be, orderly, sleek, and unobtrusive. Probably of all modes of life that are allotted to man by his Creator, life such as this is the most happy. One hint, however, for improvement I must give, even to Portland! It would be well if they could make their streets of some material harder than sand.

I must not leave the town without desiring those who may visit it to mount the Observatory. They will from thence get the best view of the harbour and of the surrounding land; and, if they chance to do so under the reign of the present keeper of the signals, they will find a man there able and willing to tell them everything needful about the

State of Maine in general, and the harbour in particular. He will come out in his shirt sleeves, and, like a true American, will not at first be very smooth in his courtesy; but he will wax brighter in conversation, and if not stroked the wrong way will turn out to be an uncommonly pleasant fellow. Such I believe to be the case with most of them.

From Portland we made our way up to the White Mountains, which lay on our route to Canada. Now I would ask any of my readers who are candid enough to expose their own ignorance whether they ever heard, or at any rate whether they know anything of the White Mountains. As regards myself I confess that the name had reached my ears; that I had an indefinite idea that they formed an intermediate stage between the Rocky Mountains and the Alleghenies, and that they were inhabited either by Mormons, Indians, or simply by black bears. That there was a district in New England containing mountain scenery superior to much that is yearly crowded by tourists in Europe, that this is to be reached with ease by railways and stage-coaches, and that it is dotted with huge hotels, almost as thickly as they lie in Switzerland, I had no idea. Much of this scenery, I say, is superior to the famed and classic lands of Europe. I know nothing, for instance, on the Rhine equal to the view from Mount Willard, down the mountain pass called the Notch.

Let the visitor of these regions be as late in the year as he can, taking care that he is not so late as to find the hotels closed. October, no doubt, is the most beautiful month among these mountains, but according to the present arrangement of matters here, the hotels are shut up by the end of September. With us, August, September, and October are the holiday months; whereas our rebel children across the Atlantic love to disport themselves in July and August. The great beauty of the autumn, or fall, is in the brilliant hues which are then taken by the foliage. The autumnal tints are fine with us. They are lovely and bright wherever foliage and vegetation form a part of the beauty of scenery. But in no other land do they approach the brilliancy of the fall in America. The bright rose colour, the rich bronze which is almost purple in its richness, and the glorious golden yellows must be seen to be understood. By me at any rate they cannot be described. These begin to show themselves in September, and perhaps I might name the latter half of that month as the best time for visiting the White Mountains.

I am not going to write a guide-book, feeling sure that Mr. Murray will do New England, and Canada, including Niagara and the Hudson river, with a peep into Boston and New York before many more seasons have passed by. But I cannot forbear to tell my countrymen that any enterprising individual with a hundred pounds to spend on his holiday,—a hundred and twenty would make him more comfortable in regard to wine, washing, and other luxuries,—and an absence of two months from his labours, may see as much and do as much here for the money as he can see or do elsewhere. In some respects he may do more; for he will learn more of American nature in such a journey than he can ever learn of the nature of Frenchmen or Americans by such an excursion among them. Some three weeks of the time, or perhaps a day or two over, he must be at sea, and that portion of his trip will cost him fifty pounds,—presuming that he chooses to go in the most comfortable and costly way;—but his time on board ship will not be lost. He will learn to know much of Americans there, and will perhaps form acquaintances of which he will not altogether lose sight for many a year. He will land at Boston, and staying a day or two there will visit Cambridge, Lowell, and Bunker Hill; and, if he be that way given, will remember that here live, and occasionally are to be seen alive, men such as Longfellow, Emerson, Hawthorne, and a host of others whose names and fames have made Boston the throne of Western Literature. He will then,—if he take my advice and follow my track,—go by Portland up into the White Mountains. At Gorham, a station on the Grand Trunk line, he will find an hotel as good as any of its kind, and from thence he will take a light waggon, so called in these countries;—and here let me presume that the traveller is not alone; he has his wife or friend, or perhaps a pair of sisters,—and in his waggon he will go up through primeval forests to the Glen House. When there he will ascend Mount Washington on a pony. That is *de rigueur,* and I do not, therefore, dare to recommend him to omit the ascent. I did not gain much myself by my labour. He will not stay at the Glen House, but will go on to—Jackson's I think they call the next hotel; at which he will sleep. From thence he will take his waggon on through the Notch to the Crawford House, sleeping there again; and when here let him of all things remember to go up Mount Willard. It is but a walk of two hours, up and down, if so much. When reaching the top he will be startled to find that he looks down into the ravine without an inch of foreground. He will come out suddenly on a ledge of rock, from whence, as it seems, he might leap down at once into the valley below. Then going on from the Crawford House he will be driven through the woods of Cherry Mount, passing, I fear without toll of custom, the house of my excellent friend Mr. Plaistead, who keeps an hotel at Jefferson. "Sir," said Mr. Plaistead. "I have everything here that a man ought to want; air, sir, that ain't to be got better nowhere; trout, chickens, beef, mutton, milk,—and all for a dollar a day. Atop of that hill, sir, there's a view that ain't to be beaten this side of the Atlantic, or I believe the other. And an echo, sir!—We've an echo that comes back to us six times, sir; floating on the light wind, and wafted about from rock to rock till you would think the angels were talking to you. If I could raise that echo, sir, every day at command I'd give a thousand dollars for it. It would be worth all the money to a house like this." And he waved his hand about from hill to hill, pointing out in graceful curves the lines which the sounds would take. Had destiny not called on Mr. Plaistead to keep an American hotel, he might have been a poet.

My traveller, however, unless time were plenty with him, would pass Mr. Plaistead, merely lighting a friendly cigar, or perhaps breaking the Maine Liquor Law if the weather be warm, and would return to Gorham on the railway. All this mountain district is in New Hampshire, and presuming him to be capable of going about the world with his mouth, ears, and eyes open, he would learn much of the way in which men are settling themselves in this still sparsely populated country. Here young farmers go into the woods, as they are doing far down west in the Territories, and buying some hundred acres at perhaps six shillings an acre, fell and burn the trees and build their huts, and take the first steps, as far as man's work is concerned, towards accomplishing the will of the Creator in those regions. For such pioneers of civilization there is still ample room even in the long settled States of New Hampshire and Vermont.

But to return to my traveller, whom having brought so far, I must send on. Let him go on from Gorham to Quebec, and the heights of Abraham, stopping at Sherbrooke that he might visit from thence the lake of Memphra Magog. As to the manner of travelling over this ground I shall say a little in the next chapter, when I come to the progress of myself and my wife. From Quebec he will go up the St. Lawrence to Montreal. He will visit Ottawa, the new capital, and Toronto. He will cross the Lake to Niagara, resting probably at the Clifton House on the Canada side. He will then pass on to Albany, taking the Trenton falls on his way. From Albany he will go down the Hudson to West-Point. He cannot stop at the Catskill Mountains, for the hotel will be closed. And then he will take the river boat, and in a few hours will find himself at New York. If he desires to go into American city society, he will find New York agreeable; but in that case he must exceed his two months. If he do not so desire, a short sojourn at New York will show him all that there is to be seen, and all that there is not to be seen in that great city. That the Cunard line of steamers will bring him safely back to Liverpool in about eleven days, I need not tell to any Englishman, or, as I believe, to any American. So much, in the spirit of a guide, I vouchsafe to all who are willing to take my counsel,— thereby anticipating Murray, and leaving these few pages as a legacy to him or to his collaborateurs.

I cannot say that I like the hotels in those parts, or indeed the mode of life at American hotels in general. In order that I may not unjustly defame them, I will commence these observations by declaring that they are cheap to those who choose to practise the economy which they encourage, that the viands are profuse in quantity and wholesome in quality, that the attendance is quick and unsparing, and that travellers are never annoyed by that grasping greedy hunger and thirst after francs and shillings which disgrace in Europe many English and many continental inns. All this is, as must be admitted, great praise; and yet I do not like the American hotels.

One is in a free country and has come from a country in which one has been brought up to hug one's chains,— so at least the English traveller is constantly assured—and yet in an American inn one can never do as one likes. A terrific gong sounds early in the morning, breaking one's sweet slumbers, and then a second gong sounding some thirty minutes later, makes you understand that you must proceed to breakfast, whether you be dressed or no. You certainly can go on with your toilet and obtain your meal after half an hour's delay. Nobody actually scolds you for so doing, but the breakfast is, as they say in this country, "through." You sit down alone, and the attendant stands immediately over you. Probably there are two so standing. They fill your cup the instant it is empty. They tender you fresh food before that which has disappeared from your plate has been swallowed. They begrudge you no amount that you can eat or drink; but they begrudge you a single moment that you sit there neither eating nor drinking. This is your fate if you're too late, and therefore as a rule you are not late. In that case you form one of a long row of eaters who proceed through their work with a solid energy that is past all praise. It is wrong to say that Americans will not talk at their meals. I never met but few who would not talk to me, at any rate till I got to the far west; but I have rarely found that they would address me first. Then the dinner comes early; at least it always does so in New England, and the ceremony is much of the same kind. You came there to eat, and the food is pressed on you almost *ad nauseam*. But as far as one can see there is no drinking. In these days, I am quite aware, that drinking has become improper, even in England. We are apt at home to speak of wine as a thing tabooed, wondering how our fathers lived and swilled. I believe that as a fact we drink as much as they did; but nevertheless that is our theory. I confess, however, that I like wine. It is very wicked, but it seems to me that my dinner goes down better with a glass of sherry than without it. As a rule I always did get it at hotels in America. But I had no comfort with it. Sherry they do not understand at all. Of course I am only speaking of hotels. Their claret they get exclusively from Mr. Gladstone, and looking at the quality, have a right to quarrel even with Mr. Gladstone's price. But it is not the quality of the wine that I hereby intend to subject to ignominy, so much as the want of any opportunity for drinking it. After dinner, if all that I hear be true, the gentlemen occasionally drop into the hotel bar and "liquor up." Or rather this is not done specially after dinner, but without prejudice to the hour at any time that may be found desirable. I also have "liquored up," but I cannot say that I enjoy the process. I do not intend hereby to accuse Americans of drinking much, but I maintain that what they do drink, they drink in the most uncomfortable manner that the imagination can devise.

The greatest luxury at an English inn is one's tea, one's fire, and one's book. Such an arrangement is not practicable at an American hotel. Tea, like breakfast, is a great meal, at which meat should be eaten, generally with the addition of much jelly, jam, and sweet preserve; but no person delays over his tea-cup. I love to have my tea-cup emptied and filled with gradual pauses, so that time for oblivion may accrue, and no exact record be taken. No such meal is known at American hotels. It is possible to hire a separate room and have one's meals served in it; but in doing so a man runs counter to all the institutions of the country, and a woman does so equally. A stranger does not wish to be viewed askance by all around him; and the rule which holds that men at Rome should do as Romans do, if true anywhere, is true in America. Therefore I say that in an American inn one can never do as one pleases.

In what I have here said I do not intend to speak of hotels in the largest cities, such as Boston or New York. At them meals are served in the public room separately, and pretty nearly at any or at all hours of the day; but at them also the attendant stands over the unfortunate eater, and drives him. The guest feels that he is controlled by laws adapted to the usages of the Medes and Persians. He is not the master on the occasion, but the slave; a slave well treated and fattened up to the full endurance of humanity; but yet a slave.

From Gorham we went on to Island Pond, a station on the same

Canada Trunk Railway, on a Saturday evening, and were forced by the circumstances of the line to pass a melancholy Sunday at the place. The cars do not run on Sundays, and run but once a day on other days over the whole line; so that in fact the impediment to travelling spreads over two days. Island Pond is a lake with an island in it, and the place which has taken the name is a small village, about ten years old, standing in the midst of uncut forests, and has been created by the railway. In ten years more there will no doubt be a spreading town at Island Pond; the forests will recede, and men rushing out from the crowded cities will find here food and space and wealth. For myself I never remain long in such a spot without feeling thankful that it has not been my mission to be a pioneer of civilization.

The farther that I got away from Boston the less strong did I find the feeling of anger against England. There, as I have said before, there was a bitter animosity against the mother country in that she had shown no open sympathy with the North. In Maine and New Hampshire I did not find this to be the case to any violent degree. Men spoke of the war as openly as they did at Boston, and in speaking to me generally connected England with the subject. But they did so simply to ask questions as to England's policy. What will she do for cotton when her operatives are really pressed? Will she break the blockade? Will she insist on a right to trade with Charlestown and New Orleans? I always answered that she would insist on no such right, if that right were denied to others and the denial enforced. England, I took upon myself to say, would not break a veritable blockade, let her be driven to what shifts she might in providing for her operatives. "Ah; that's what we fear," a very stanch patriot said to me, if words may be taken as a proof of stanchness. "If England allies herself with the Southerners, all our trouble is for nothing." It was impossible not to feel that all that was said was complimentary to England. It is her sympathy that the Northern men desire, to her co-operation that they would willingly trust, on her honesty that they would choose to depend. It is the same feeling whether it shows itself in anger or in curiosity. An American whether he be embarked in politics, in literature, or in commerce, desires English admiration, English appreciation of his energy, and English encouragement. The anger of Boston is but a sign of its affectionate friendliness. What feeling is so hot as that of a friend when his dearest friend refuses to share his quarrel or to sympathize in his wrongs? To my thinking the men of Boston are wrong and unreasonable in their anger; but were I a man of Boston I should be as wrong and as unreasonable as any of them. All that, however, will come right. I will not believe it possible that there should in very truth be a quarrel between England and the Northern States.

In the guidance of those who are not quite *au fait* at the details of American Government, I will here in a few words describe the outlines of State Government as it is arranged in New Hampshire. The States in this respect are not all alike, the modes of election of their officers and periods of service being different. Even the franchise is different in different States. Universal suffrage is not the rule throughout the United States; though it is I believe very generally thought in England that such is the fact. I need hardly say that the laws in the different States may be as various as the different legislatures may choose to make them.

In New Hampshire universal suffrage does prevail; which means that any man may vote who lives in the State, supports himself, and assists to support the poor by means of poor rates. A governor of the State is elected for one year only, but it is customary or at any rate not uncustomary to re-elect him for a second year. His salary is a thousand dollars a year, or 200*l.* It must be presumed therefore that glory and not money is his object. To him is appended a council, by whose opinions he must in a great degree be guided. His functions are to the State what those of the President are to the country, and for the short period of his reign he is as it were a Prime Minister of the State with certain very limited regal attributes. He however by no means enjoys the regal attribute of doing no wrong. In every State there is an Assembly, consisting of two houses of elected representatives; the Senate, or upper house, and the House of Representatives so called. In New Hampshire this Assembly, or Parliament, is styled The General Court of New Hampshire. It sits annually; whereas the legislature in many States sits only every other year. Both Houses are re-elected every year. This Assembly passes laws with all the power vested in our Parliament, but such laws apply of course only to the State in question. The Governor of the State has a veto on all bills passed by the two Houses. But, after receipt of his veto, any bill so stopped by the Governor can be passed by a majority of two thirds in each House. The General Court generally sits for about ten weeks. There are in the State eight judges, three Supreme who sit at Concord, the capital, as a court of appeal both in civil and criminal matters; and then five lesser judges, who go circuit through the State. The salaries of these lesser judges do not exceed from 250*l.* to 300*l.* a year; but they are, I believe, allowed to practise as lawyers in any counties except those in which they sit as judges,—being guided in this respect by the same law as that which regulates the work of assistant barristers in Ireland. The assistant barristers in Ireland are attached to the counties as judges at Quarter Sessions, but they practise or may practise as advocates in all counties except that to which they are so attached. The judges in New Hampshire are appointed by the Governor with the assistance of his Council. No judge in New Hampshire can hold his seat after he has reached seventy years of age.

So much at the present moment with reference to the Government of New Hampshire.

CHAPTER IV

LOWER CANADA

THE GRAND TRUNK RAILWAY runs directly from Portland to Montreal, which latter town is, in fact, the capital of Canada, though it never has been so exclusively, and, as it seems, never is to be so, as regards authority, government, and official name. In such matters authority and government often say one thing while commerce says another; but commerce always has the best of it and wins the game whatever Government may decree. Albany in this way is the capital of the State of New York, as authorized by the State Government; but New York has made herself the capital of America, and will remain so. So also Montreal has made herself the capital of Canada. The Grand Trunk Railway runs from Portland to Montreal; but there is a branch from Richmond, a township within the limits of Canada, to Quebec; so that travellers to Quebec, as we were, are not obliged to reach that place *viâ* Montreal.

Quebec is the present seat of Canadian Government, its turn for that honour having come round some two years ago; but it is about to be deserted in favour of Ottawa, a town which is, in fact, still to be built on the river of that name. The public edifices are, however, in a state of forwardness; and if all goes well the Governor, the two Councils, and the House of Representatives will be there before two years are over whether there be any town to receive them or no. Who can think of Ottawa without bidding his brothers to row, and reminding them that the stream runs fast, that the rapids are near and the daylight past? [1] I asked, as a matter of course, whether Quebec was much disgusted at the proposed change, and I was told that the feeling was not now very strong. Had it been determined to make Montreal the

---

[1] Trollope alludes to Tom Moore's *A Canadian Boat-Song*, which speaks of "Utawa's tide" as the place where the oarsmen are headed. The first stanza follows:

> *Faintly as tolls the evening chime,*
> *Our voices keep tune and our oars keep time.*
> *Soon as the woods on shore look dim,*
> *We'll sing at St Ann's our parting hymn.*
> *Row, brothers, row, the stream runs fast,*
> *The rapids are near, and the day-light's past!*

Moore had visited the United States and Canada in 1804.

permanent seat of government Quebec and Toronto would both have
been up in arms.

I must confess that in going from the States into Canada, an Englishman is struck by the feeling that he is going from a richer country
into one that is poorer, and from a greater country into one that is less.
An Englishman going from a foreign land into a land which is in one
sense his own, of course finds much in the change to gratify him. He
is able to speak as the master, instead of speaking as the visitor. His
tongue becomes more free, and he is able to fall back to his national
habits and national expressions. He no longer feels that he is admitted
on sufferance, or that he must be careful to respect laws which he does
not quite understand. This feeling was naturally strong in an Englishman in passing from the States into Canada at the time of my visit. English policy at that moment was violently abused by Americans, and was
upheld as violently in Canada. But, nevertheless, with all this, I could
not enter Canada without seeing, and hearing, and feeling that there
was less of enterprise around me there than in the States—less of general movement, and less of commercial success. To say why this is so
would require a long and very difficult discussion, and one which I am
not prepared to hold. It may be that a dependent country, let the feeling of dependence be ever so much modified by powers of self-governance, cannot hold its own against countries which are in all respects
their own masters. Few, I believe, would now maintain that the Northern States of America would have risen in commerce as they have risen,
had they still remained attached to England as colonies. If this be so,
that privilege of self-rule which they have acquired, has been the cause
of their success. It does not follow as a consequence that the Canadas
fighting their battle alone in the world could do as the States have done.
Climate, or size, or geographical position might stand in their way. But
I fear that it does follow, if not as a logical conclusion at least as a natural result, that they never will do so well unless some day they shall so
fight their battle. It may be argued that Canada has in fact the power
of self-governance; that she rules herself and makes her own laws as
England does; that the Sovereign of England has but a veto on those
laws, and stands in regard to Canada exactly as she does in regard to
England. This is so, I believe, by the letter of the Constitution, but is
not so in reality, and cannot, in truth, be so in any colony, even of
Great Britain. In England the political power of the Crown is nothing.
The Crown has no such power, and now-a-days makes no attempt at
having any. But the political power of the Crown, as it is felt in Canada, is everything. The Crown has no such power in England because

it must change its ministers whenever called upon to do so by the House of Commons. But the Colonial Minister in Downing Street is the Crown's Prime Minister as regards the Colonies, and he is changed not as any Colonial House of Assembly may wish, but in accordance with the will of the British Commons. Both the Houses in Canada— that, namely, of the Representatives, or Lower House, and of the Legislative Council, or Upper House—are now elective, and are filled without direct influence from the Crown. The power of self-government is as thoroughly developed as perhaps may be possible in a colony. But after all it is a dependent form of government, and as such may perhaps not conduce to so thorough a development of the resources of the country as might be achieved under a ruling power of its own, to which the welfare of Canada itself would be the chief if not the only object.

I beg that it may not be considered from this that I would propose to Canada to set up for itself at once and declare itself independent. In the first place I do not wish to throw over Canada; and in the next place I do not wish to throw over England. If such a separation shall ever take place, I trust that it may be caused, not by Canadian violence but by British generosity. Such a separation, however, never can be good till Canada herself shall wish it. That she does not wish it yet is certain. If Canada ever should wish it, and should ever press for the accomplishment of such a wish, she must do so in connection with Nova Scotia and New Brunswick. If at any future time there be formed such a separate political power, it must include the whole of British North America.

In the meantime, I return to my assertion, that in entering Canada from the States one clearly comes from a richer to a poorer country. When I have said so, I have heard no Canadian absolutely deny it; though in refraining from denying it, they have usually expressed a general conviction, that in settling himself for life, it is better for a man to set up his staff in Canada than in the States. "I do not know that we are richer," a Canadian says, "but on the whole we are doing better and are happier." Now, I regard the golden rules against the love of gold, the *"aurum irrepertum et sic melius situm,"* [2] and the rest of it, as very excellent when applied to individuals. Such teaching has not much effect, perhaps, in inducing men to abstain from wealth,— but such effect as it may have will be good. Men and women do, I suppose, learn to be happier when they learn to disregard riches. But such a doctrine is absolutely false as regards a nation. National wealth produces education and progress, and through them produces plenty of

[2] "the gold unfound, and so the better placed."—Horace: *Odes,* III, iii, 49.

food, good morals, and all else that is good. It produces luxury also, and certain evils attendant on luxury. But I think it may be clearly shown, and that it is universally acknowledged, that national wealth produces individual well-being. If this be so, the argument of my friend the Canadian is nought.

To the feeling of a refined gentleman, or of a lady whose eye loves to rest always on the beautiful, an agricultural population that touches its hat, eats plain victuals, and goes to church is more picturesque and delightful than the thronged crowd of a great city by which a lady and gentleman is hustled without remorse, which never touches its hat, and perhaps also never goes to church. And as we are always tempted to approve of that which we like, and to think that that which is good to us is good altogether, we—the refined gentlemen and ladies of England I mean—are very apt to prefer the hat-touchers to those who are not hat-touchers. In doing so we intend, and wish, and strive to be philanthropical. We argue to ourselves that the dear, excellent lower classes receive an immense amount of consoling happiness from that ceremony of hat-touching, and quite pity those who, unfortunately for themselves, know nothing about it. I would ask any such lady or gentleman whether he or she does not feel a certain amount of commiseration for the rudeness of the town-bred artisan, who walks about with his hands in his pockets as though he recognized a superior in no one.

But that which is good and pleasant to us, is often not good and pleasant altogether. Every man's chief object is himself; and the philanthropist should endeavour to regard this question, not from his own point of view, but from that which would be taken by the individuals for whose happiness he is anxious. The honest, happy rustic makes a very pretty picture; and I hope that honest rustics are happy. But the man who earns two shillings a day in the country would always prefer to earn five in the town. The man who finds himself bound to touch his hat to the squire would be glad to dispense with that ceremony, if circumstance would permit. A crowd of greasy-coated town artisans with grimy hands and pale faces, is not in itself delectable; but each of that crowd has probably more of the goods of life than any rural labourer. He thinks more, reads more, feels more, sees more, hears more, learns more, and lives more. It is through great cities that the civilization of the world has progressed, and the charms of life been advanced. Man in his rudest state begins in the country, and in his most finished state may retire there. But the battle of the world has to be fought in the cities; and the country that shows the greatest city population is ever the one that is going most ahead in the world's history.

If this be so, I say that the argument of my Canadian friend was nought. It may be that he does not desire crowded cities with dirty, independent artisans; that to his view small farmers, living sparingly but with content on the sweat of their brows, are surer signs of a country's prosperity than hives of men and smoking chimneys. He has, probably, all the upper classes of England with him in so thinking, and as far as I know the upper classes of all Europe. But the crowds themselves, the thick masses of which are composed those populations which we count by millions, are against him. Up in those regions which are watered by the great lakes, Lake Michigan, Lake Huron, Lake Erie, Lake Ontario,[3] and by the St. Lawrence, the country is divided between Canada and the States. The cities in Canada were settled long before those in the States. Quebec and Montreal were important cities before any of the towns belonging to the States had been founded. But taking the population of three of each, including the largest Canadian towns, we find they are as follows:—In Canada, Quebec has 60,000; Montreal, 85,000; Toronto, 55,000. In the States, Chicago has 120,000; Detroit, 70,000, and Buffalo, 80,000. If the population had been equal, it would have shown a great superiority in the progress of those belonging to the States, because the towns of Canada had so great a start. But the numbers are by no means equal, showing instead a vast preponderance in favour of the States. There can be no stronger proof that the States are advancing faster than Canada,—and in fact doing better than Canada.

Quebec is a very picturesque town,—from its natural advantages almost as much so as any town I know. Edinburgh, perhaps, and Innsbruck may beat it. But Quebec has very little to recommend it beyond the beauty of its situation. Its public buildings and works of art do not deserve a long narrative. It stands at the confluence of the St. Lawrence and St. Charles rivers; the best part of the town is built high upon the rock,—the rock which forms the celebrated plains of Abram; and the view from thence down to the mountains which shut in the St. Lawrence is magnificent. The best point of view is, I think, from the esplanade, which is distant some five minutes' walk from the hotels. When that has been seen by the light of the setting sun, and seen again, if possible, by moonlight, the most considerable lion of Quebec may be regarded as "done," and may be ticked off from the list.

3 Trollope omits Lake Superior in the manuscript also.

The most considerable lion according to my taste. Lions which roar merely by the force of association of ideas are not to me very valuable beasts. To many the rock over which Wolfe climbed to the plains of Abram, and on the summit of which he fell in the hour of victory, gives to Quebec its chiefest charm. But I confess to being somewhat dull in such matters. I can count up Wolfe, and realize his glory, and put my hand as it were upon his monument, in my own room at home as well as I can at Quebec. I do not say this boastingly or with pride; but truly acknowledging a deficiency. I have never cared to sit in chairs in which old kings have sat, or to have their crowns upon my head.

Nevertheless, and as a matter of course, I went to see the rock, and can only say, as so many have said before me, that it is very steep. It is not a rock which I think it would be difficult for any ordinarily active man to climb,—providing, of course, that he was used to such work. But Wolfe took regiments of men up there at night—and that in face of enemies who held the summits. One grieves that he should have fallen there and have never tasted the sweet cup of his own fame. For fame is sweet, and the praise of one's brother men the sweetest draught which a man can drain. But now, and for coming ages, Wolfe's name stands higher than it probably would have done had he lived to enjoy his reward.

But there is another very worthy lion near Quebec,—the Falls, namely, of Montmorency. They are eight miles from the town, and the road lies through the suburb of St. Roch, and the long straggling French village of Beauport. These are in themselves very interesting, as showing the quiet, orderly, unimpulsive manner in which the French Canadians live. Such is their character, although there have been such men as Papineau,[4] and although there have been times in which English rule has been unpopular with the French settlers. As far as I could learn there is no such feeling now. These people are quiet, contented; and as regards a sufficiency of the simple staples of living, sufficiently well to do. They are thrifty;—but they do not thrive. They do not advance, and push ahead, and become a bigger people from year to year as settlers in a new country should do. They do not even hold their own in comparison with those around them. But has not this always

[4] Louis Joseph Papineau (1786–1871), the "champion and embodiment of French Canadian nationalism," was speaker of the French-Canadian Assembly of Lower Canada as early as 1815. He wielded increasing power over his party until the rebellion of 1837, when he was forced to flee to the United States. He returned to Canada in 1847, resumed a part in politics, but never regained his former influence.

been the case with colonists out of France; and has it not always been the case with Roman Catholics when they have been forced to measure themselves against Protestants? As to the ultimate fate in the world of this people, one can hardly form a speculation. There are, as nearly as I could learn, about 800,000 of them in Lower Canada; but it seems that the wealth and commercial enterprise of the country is passing out of their hands. Montreal, and even Quebec are, I think, becoming less and less French every day; but in the villages and on the small farms the French remain, keeping up their language, their habits, and their religion. In the cities they are becoming hewers of wood and drawers of water. I am inclined to think that the same will ultimately be their fate in the country. Surely one may declare as a fact that a Roman Catholic population can never hold its ground against one that is Protestant. I do not speak of numbers, for the Roman Catholics will increase and multiply, and stick by their religion, although their religion entails poverty and dependence; as they have done and still do in Ireland. But in progress and wealth the Romanists have always gone to the wall when the two have been made to compete together. And yet I love their religion. There is something beautiful and almost divine in the faith and obedience of a true son of the Holy Mother. I sometimes fancy that I would fain be a Roman Catholic,—if I could; as also I would often wish to be still a child, if that were possible.

All this is on the way to the Falls of Montmorency. These falls are placed exactly at the mouth of the little river of the same name, so that it may be said absolutely to fall into the St. Lawrence. The people of the country, however, declare that the river into which the waters of the Montmorency fall is not the St. Lawrence, but the Charles. Without a map I do not know that I can explain this. The river Charles appears to, and in fact does, run into the St. Lawrence just below Quebec. But the waters do not mix. The thicker, browner stream of the lesser river still keeps the north-eastern bank till it comes to the island of Orleans, which lies in the river five or six miles below Quebec. Here or hereabouts are the Falls of the Montmorency, and then the great river is divided for twenty-five miles by the Isle of Orleans. It is said that the waters of the Charles and the St. Lawrence do not mix till they meet each other at the foot of this island.

I do not know that I am particularly happy at describing a waterfall, and what little capacity I may have in this way I would wish to keep for Niagara. One thing I can say very positively about Montmorency, and one piece of advice I can give to those who visit the falls. The place from which to see them is not the horrible little wooden

temple, which has been built immediately over them on that side
which lies nearest to Quebec. The stranger is put down at a gate
through which a path leads to this temple, and at which a woman
demands from him twenty-five cents for the privilege of entrance. Let
him by all means pay the twenty-five cents. Why should he attempt to
see the falls for nothing, seeing that this woman has a vested interest
in the showing of them? I declare that if I thought that I should hinder
this woman from her perquisites by what I write, I would leave it un-
written, and let my readers pursue their course to the temple—to their
manifest injury. But they will pay the twenty-five cents. Then let them
cross over the bridge, eschewing the temple, and wander round on the
open field till they get the view of the falls, and the view of Quebec
also, from the other side. It is worth the twenty-five cents, and the hire
of the carriage also. Immediately over the falls there was a suspension
bridge, of which the supporting, or rather non-supporting, pillars are
still to be seen. But the bridge fell down one day into the river; and,
alas, alas! with the bridge fell down an old woman, and a boy, and a
cart,—a cart and horse,—and all found a watery grave together in the
spray. No attempt has been made since that to renew the suspension
bridge; but the present wooden bridge has been built higher up, in
lieu of it.

Strangers naturally visit Quebec in summer or autumn, seeing that
a Canada winter is a season with which a man cannot trifle; but I
imagine that the mid-winter is the best time for seeing the Falls of
Montmorency. The water in its fall is dashed into spray, and that
spray becomes frozen, till a cone of ice is formed immediately under
the cataract, which gradually rises till the temporary glacier reaches
nearly half-way to the level of the higher river. Up this men climb,—
and ladies also, I am told,—and then descend with pleasant rapidity on
sledges of wood, sometimes not without an innocent tumble in the
descent. As we were at Quebec in September, we did not experience the
delights of this pastime.

As I was too early for the ice cone under the Montmorency Falls, so
also was I too late to visit the Saguenay river which runs into the St.
Lawrence, some hundred miles below Quebec. I presume that the
scenery of the Saguenay is the finest in Canada. During the summer
steamers run down the St. Lawrence and up the Saguenay, but I was
too late for them. An offer was made to us through the kindness of
Sir Edmund Head, who was then the Governor-General,[5] of the use of

---

[5] Sir Edmund Walker Head (1805–68) had become Governor-General of Canada in 1854 after serving seven years as Governor of New Brunswick. Trollope's ac-

a steam-tug belonging to a gentleman who carries on a large commercial enterprise at Chicoutimi, far up the Saguenay; but an acceptance of this offer would have entailed some delay at Quebec, and as we
were anxious to get into the North Western States before the winter
commenced, we were obliged with great regret to decline the journey.

I feel bound to say that a stranger regarding Quebec merely as a
town, finds very much of which he cannot but complain. The foot-
paths through the streets are almost entirely of wood, as indeed seems
to be general throughout Canada. Wood is of course the cheapest material, and though it may not be altogether good for such a purpose it
would not create animadversion if it were kept in tolerable order. But
in Quebec the paths are intolerably bad. They are full of holes. The
boards are rotten and worn in some places to dirt. The nails have gone,
and the broken planks go up and down under the feet, and in the dark
they are absolutely dangerous. But if the paths are bad the roadways
are worse. The street through the lower town along the quays is, I
think, the most disgraceful thoroughfare I ever saw in any town. I believe the whole of it, or at any rate a great portion, has been paved
with wood; but the boards have been worked into mud, and the
ground under the boards has been worked into holes, till the street is
more like the bottom of a filthy ditch than a roadway through one of
the most thickly populated parts of a city. Had Quebec in Wolfe's
time been as it is now, Wolfe would have stuck in the mud between
the river and the rock, before he reached the point which he desired
to climb. In the upper town the roads are not so bad as they are below,
but still they are very bad. I was told that this arose from disputes
among the municipal corporations. Everything in Canada relating to
roads, and a very great deal affecting the internal government of the
people, is done by these municipalities. It is made a subject of great
boast in Canada that the communal authorities do carry on so large
a part of the public business, and that they do it generally so well, and
at so cheap a rate. I have nothing to say against this, and as a whole
believe that the boast is true. I must protest, however, that the streets
of the greater cities,—for Montreal is nearly as bad as Quebec,—prove
the rule by a very sad exception. The municipalities of which I speak

count book shows that he dined with Sir Edmund on September 25, 1861. It was
probably a pleasant dinner; Sir Edmund and his guest were fellow alumni of Win-
chester, and the Governor-General was noted for his command of languages and
literature. He also had some reputation as the author of literary reviews, an essay
on grammar, and a handbook on painting.

He was to retire and return to England within a few weeks of the time when
Trollope dined with him.

extend, I believe, to all Canada; the two provinces being divided into counties, and the counties subdivided into townships to which, as a matter of course, the municipalities are attached.

From Quebec to Montreal there are two modes of travel. There are the steamers up the St. Lawrence which, as all the world knows, is, or at any rate hitherto has been, the high road of the Canadas; and there is the Grand Trunk Railway. Passengers choosing the latter go towards Portland as far as Richmond, and there join the main line of the road, passing from Richmond on to Montreal. We learned while at Quebec that it behoved us not to leave the colony till we had seen the lake and mountains of Memphra-Magog, and as we were clearly neglecting our duty with regard to the Saguenay, we felt bound to make such amends as lay in our power, by deviating from our way to the lake above named. In order to do this we were obliged to choose the railway, and to go back beyond Richmond to the station at Sherbrooke. Sherbrooke is a large village on the confines of Canada, and as it is on the railway will no doubt become a large town. It is very prettily situated on the meeting of two rivers, it has three or four different churches, and intends to thrive. It possesses two newspapers, of the prosperity of which I should be inclined to feel less assured. The annual subscription to such a newspaper published twice a week is ten shillings per annum. A sale of a thousand copies is not considered bad. Such a sale would produce 500*l.* a year, and this would, if entirely devoted to that purpose, give a moderate income to a gentleman qualified to conduct a newspaper. But the paper and printing must cost something, and the capital invested should receive its proper remuneration. And then,—such at least is the general idea,—the getting together of news and the framing of intelligence is a costly operation. I can only hope that all this is paid for by the advertisements, for I must trust that the editors do not receive less than the moderate sum above named. At Sherbrooke we are still in Lower Canada. Indeed, as regards distance, we are when there nearly as far removed from Upper Canada as at Quebec. But the race of people here is very different. The French population had made their way down into these townships before the English and American war broke out, but had not done so in great numbers. The country was then very unapproachable, being far to the south of the St. Lawrence, and far also from any great line of internal communication towards the Atlantic. But, nevertheless, many settlers made their way in here from the States; men who preferred to live under British rule, and perhaps doubted the stability of the new order of things. They or their children have remained here since, and as the whole country has been opened up by the railway many others have flocked in. Thus a better class of people than the French hold possession of the larger farms, and are on the whole doing well. I am told that many Americans are now coming here, driven over the borders from Maine, New Hampshire, and Vermont, by fears of the war and the weight of taxation. I do not think that fears of war or the paying of taxes drive many individuals away from home. Men who would be so influenced have not the amount of foresight which would induce them to avoid such evils; or, at any rate, such fears would act slowly. Labourers, however, will go where work is certain, where work is well paid, and where the wages to be earned will give plenty in return. It may be that work will become scarce in the States, as it has done with those poor jewellers at Attleborough, of whom we spoke, and that food will become dear. If this be so, labourers from the States will no doubt find their way into Canada.

From Sherbrooke we went with the mails on a pair-horse waggon to Magog. Cross country mails are not interesting to the generality of readers, but I have a professional liking for them myself. I have spent the best part of my life in looking after and I hope in improving such mails, and I always endeavour to do a stroke of work when I come across them. I learned on this occasion that the conveyance of mails with a pair of horses in Canada costs little more than half what is paid for the same work in England with one horse, and something less than what is paid in Ireland, also for one horse. But in Canada the average pace is only five miles an hour. In Ireland it is seven, and the time is accurately kept, which does not seem to be the case in Canada. In England the pace is eight miles an hour. In Canada and in Ireland these conveyances carry passengers; but in England they are prohibited from doing so. In Canada the vehicles are much better got up than they are in England, and the horses too look better. Taking Ireland as a whole they are more respectable in appearance there than in England. From all which it appears that pace is the article that costs the highest price, and that appearance does not go for much in the bill. In Canada the roads are very bad in comparison with the English or Irish roads; but to make up for this, the price of forage is very low.

I have said that the cross mail conveyances in Canada did not seem to be very closely bound as to time; but they are regulated by clockwork in comparison with some of them in the United States. "Are you going this morning?" I said to a mail-driver in Vermont. "I thought you always started in the evening." "Wa'll; I guess I do. But it rained some last night, so I jist stayed at home." I do not know that I ever felt more shocked in my life, and I could hardly keep my tongue off the man. The mails, however, would have paid no respect to me in Vermont, and I was obliged to walk away crestfallen.

We went with the mails from Sherbrooke to a village called Magog at the outlet of the lake, and from thence by a steamer up the lake to a solitary hotel called the Mountain House, which is built at the foot of the mountain on the shore, and which is surrounded on every side by thick forest. There is no road within two miles of the house. The lake therefore is the only highway, and that is frozen up for four months in the year. When frozen, however, it is still a road, for it is passable for sledges. I have seldom been in a house that seemed so remote from the world, and so little within reach of doctors, parsons, or butchers. Bakers in this country are not required, as all persons make their own bread. But in spite of its position the hotel is well kept, and on the whole we were more comfortable there than at any other inn in Lower Canada. The Mountain House is but five miles from the borders of Vermont, in which State the head of the lake lies. The steamer which brought us runs on to Newport,—or rather from Newport to Magog and back again. And Newport is in Vermont.

The one thing to be done at the Mountain House is the ascent of the mountain called the Owl's Head. The world there offers nothing else of active enterprise to the traveller, unless fishing be considered an active enterprise. I am not capable of fishing, therefore we resolved on going up the Owl's Head. To dine in the middle of the day is absolutely imperative at these hotels, and thus we were driven to select either the morning or the afternoon. Evening lights we declared were the best for all views, and therefore we decided on the afternoon. It is but two miles; but then, as we were told more than once by those who had spoken to us on the subject, those two miles are not like other miles. "I doubt if the lady can do it," one man said to me. I asked if ladies did not sometimes go up. "Yes; young women do, at times," he said. After that my wife resolved that she would see the top of the Owl's Head, or die in the attempt, and so we started. They never think of sending a guide with one in these places, whereas in Europe a traveller is not allowed to go a step without one. When I asked for one to show us the way up Mount Washington, I was told that there were no idle boys about that place. The path was indicated to us, and off we started with high hopes.

I have been up many mountains, and have climbed some that were perhaps somewhat dangerous in their ascent. In climbing the Owl's Head there is no danger. One is closed in by thick trees the whole way.

But I doubt if I ever went up a steeper ascent. It was very hard work, but we were not beaten. We reached the top, and there sitting down thoroughly enjoyed our victory. It was then half-past five o'clock, and the sun was not yet absolutely sinking. It did not seem to give us any warning that we should especially require its aid, and as the prospect below us was very lovely we remained there for a quarter of an hour. The ascent of the Owl's Head is certainly a thing to do, and I still think, in spite of our following misfortune, that it is a thing to do late in the afternoon. The view down upon the lakes and the forests around, and on the wooded hills below, is wonderfully lovely. I never was on a mountain which gave me a more perfect command of all the country round. But as we arose to descend we saw a little cloud coming towards us from over Newport.

The little cloud came on with speed, and we had hardly freed ourselves from the rocks of the summit before we were surrounded by rain. As the rain became thicker, we were surrounded by darkness also, or if not by darkness by so dim a light that it became a task to find our path. I still thought that the daylight had not gone, and that as we descended and so escaped from the cloud we should find light enough to guide us. But it was not so. The rain soon became a matter of indifference, and so also did the mud and briars beneath our feet. Even the steepness of the way was almost forgotten as we endeavoured to thread our path through the forest before it should become impossible to discern the track. A dog had followed us up, and though the beast would not stay with us so as to be our guide, he returned ever and anon and made us aware of his presence by dashing by us. I may confess now that I became much frightened. We were wet through, and a night out in the forest would have been unpleasant to us. At last I did utterly lose the track. It had become quite dark, so dark that we could hardly see each other. We had succeeded in getting down the steepest and worst part of the mountain, but we were still among dense forest-trees, and up to our knees in mud. But the people at the Mountain House were Christians, and men with lanterns were sent hallooing after us through the dark night. When we were thus found we were not many yards from the path, but unfortunately on the wrong side of a stream. Through that we waded and then made our way in safety to the inn. In spite of which misadventure I advise all travellers in Lower Canada to go up the Owl's Head.

On the following day we crossed the lake to Georgeville, and drove round another lake called the Massawhippi back to Sherbrooke. This was all very well, for it showed us a part of the country which is comparatively well tilled, and has been long settled; but the Massawhippi itself is not worth a visit. The route by which we returned occupies a longer time than the other, and is more costly as it must be made in a hired vehicle. The people here are quiet, orderly, and I should say a little slow. It is manifest that a strong feeling against the Northern States has lately sprung up. This is much to be deprecated, but I cannot but say that it is natural. It is not that the Canadians have any special Secession feelings, or that they have entered with peculiar warmth into the questions of American politics; but they have been vexed and acerbated by the braggadocio of the Northern States. They constantly hear that they are to be invaded, and translated into citizens of the Union: that British rule is to be swept off the Continent, and that the star-spangled banner is to be waved over them in pity. The star-spangled banner is in fact a fine flag, and has waved to some purpose; but those who live near it, and not under it, fancy that they hear too much of it. At the present moment the loyalty of both the Canadas to Great Britain is beyond all question. From all that I can hear I doubt whether this feeling in the Provinces was ever so strong, and under such circumstances American abuse of England and American braggadocio is more than usually distasteful. All this abuse and all this braggadocio comes to Canada from the Northern States, and therefore the Southern cause is at the present moment the more popular with them.

I have said that the Canadians hereabouts are somewhat slow. As we were driving back to Sherbrooke it became necessary that we should rest for an hour or so in the middle of the day, and for this purpose we stopped at a village inn. It was a large house, in which there appeared to be three public sitting-rooms of ample size, one of which was occupied as the bar. In this there were congregated some six or seven men, seated in arm-chairs round a stove, and among these I placed myself. No one spoke a word either to me or to any one else. No one smoked, and no one read, nor did they even whittle sticks. I asked a question first of one and then of another, and was answered with monosyllables. So I gave up any hope in that direction, and sat staring at the big stove in the middle of the room, as the others did. Presently another stranger entered, having arrived in a waggon as I had done. He entered the room and sat down, addressing no one, and addressed by no one. After a while, however, he spoke. "Will there be any chance of dinner here?" he said. "I guess there'll be dinner by-and-by," answered the landlord, and then there was silence for another ten minutes, during which the stranger stared at the stove. "Is that dinner any

way ready?" he asked again. "I guess it is," said the landlord. And
then the stranger went out to see after his dinner himself. When we
started at the end of an hour nobody said anything to us. The driver
"hitched" on the horses, as they call it, and we started on our way,
having been charged nothing for our accommodation. That some profit
arose from the horse provender is to be hoped.

On the following day we reached Montreal, which, as I have said
before, is the commercial capital of the two Provinces. This question of
the capitals is at the present moment a subject of great interest in
Canada, but as I shall be driven to say something on the matter when
I report myself as being at Ottawa, I will refrain now. There are two
special public affairs at the present moment to interest a traveller in
Canada. The first I have named, and the second is the Grand Trunk
Railway. I have already stated what is the course of this line. It runs
from the Western State of Michigan to Portland on the Atlantic in the
State of Maine, sweeping the whole length of Canada in its route. It
was originally made by three Companies. The Atlantic and St. Lawrence constructed it from Portland to Island Pond on the borders of the
States. The St. Lawrence and Atlantic took it from the South Eastern
side of the river at Montreal to the same point, viz., Island Pond. And
the Grand Trunk Company have made it from Detroit to Montreal,
crossing the river there with a stupendous tubular bridge, and have
also made the branch connecting the main line with Quebec and
Rivière du Loup. This latter company is now incorporated with the
St. Lawrence and Atlantic, but has only leased the portion of the line
running through the States. This they have done, guaranteeing the
shareholders an interest of six per cent. There never was a grander
enterprise set on foot. I will not say there never was one more unfortunate, for is there not the Great Eastern, which by the weight and
constancy of its failures demands for itself a proud pre-eminence of
misfortune? But surely the Grand Trunk comes next to it.[6] I presume
it to be quite out of the question that the shareholders should get any
interest whatever on their shares for years. The company when I was
at Montreal had not paid the interest due to the Atlantic and St. Law-

6 For the misfortunes of the *Great Eastern*, see the note on pages 34–5. The English contractors for the Grand Trunk Railway, the firm of Peto, Brassey, Betts &
Jackson, had gone bankrupt before the road was finished, after luring a large number of British investors with predictions of dividends of 11½ per cent. The English
public was ignorant of conditions in Canada; the London *Times*, for example, had
announced that the Grand Trunk was designed to connect Hudson Bay with the
St. Lawrence River, the rails to be laid over tree trunks cut eighteen inches from
the ground!

rence Company for the last year, and there was a doubt whether the lease would not be broken. No party that had advanced money to the undertaking was able to recover what had been advanced. I believe that one firm in London had lent nearly a million to the Company and is now willing to accept half the sum so lent in quittance of the whole debt. In 1860 the line could not carry the freight that offered, not having or being able to obtain the necessary rolling stock; and on all sides I heard men discussing whether the line would be kept open for traffic. The Government of Canada advanced to the Company three millions of money, with an understanding that neither interest nor principal should be demanded till all other debts were paid, and all shareholders in receipt of six per cent. interest. But the three millions were clogged with conditions which, though they have been of service to the country, have been so expensive to the Company that it is hardly more solvent with it than it would have been without it. As it is, the whole property seems to be involved in ruin; and yet the line is one of the grandest commercial conceptions that was ever carried out on the face of the globe, and in the process of a few years will do more to make bread cheap in England than any other single enterprise that exists.

I do not know that blame is to be attached to any one. I at least attach no such blame. Probably it might be easy now to show that the road might have been made with sufficient accommodation for ordinary purposes without some of the more costly details. The great tubular bridge on which was expended 1,300,000*l.* might, I should think, have been dispensed with. The Detroit end of the line might have been left for later time. As it stands now, however, it is a wonderful operation carried to a successful issue as far as the public are concerned, and one can only grieve that it should be so absolute a failure to those who have placed their money in it. There are schemes which seem to be too big for men to work out with any ordinary regard to profit and loss. The Great Eastern is one, and this is another. The national advantage arising from such enterprises is immense; but the wonder is that men should be found willing to embark their money where the risk is so great, and the return even hoped for is so small.

While I was in Canada some gentlemen were there from the Lower Provinces—Nova Scotia, that is, and New Brunswick—agitating the subject of another great line of railway from Quebec to Halifax. The project is one in favour of which very much may be said. In a national point of view an Englishman or a Canadian cannot but regret that there should be no winter mode of exit from, or entrance to, Canada, except through the United States. The St. Lawrence is blocked up for four or five months in winter, and the steamers which run to Quebec in the summer run to Portland during the season of ice. There is at present no mode of public conveyance between the Canadas and the Lower Provinces, and an immense district of country on the borders of Lower Canada, through New Brunswick and into Nova Scotia [,] is now absolutely closed against civilization, which by such a railway would be opened up to the light of day. We all know how much the want of such a road was felt when our troops were being forwarded to Canada during the last winter. It was necessary they should reach their destiny without delay; and as the river was closed, and the passing of troops through the States was of course out of the question, that long over-land journey across Nova Scotia and New Brunswick became a neces-sity. It would certainly be a very great thing for British interests if a direct line could be made from such a port as Halifax, a port which is open throughout the whole year, up into the Canadas. If these Colo-nies belonged to France or to any other despotic Government, the thing would be done. But the Colonies do not belong to any despotic Government.

Such a line would in fact be a continuance of the Grand Trunk; and who that looks at the present state of the finances of the Grand Trunk can think it to be on the cards that private enterprise should come forward with more money,—with more millions? The idea is that England will advance the money, and that the English House of Com-mons will guarantee the interest, with some counter-guarantee from the Colonies that this interest shall be duly paid. But it would seem that if such Colonial guarantee is to go for anything, the Colonies might raise the money in the money market without the intervention of the British House of Commons.

Montreal is an exceedingly good commercial town, and business there is brisk. It has now 85,000 inhabitants. Having said that of it, I do not know what more there is left to say. Yes; one word there is to say of Sir William Logan the creator of the Geological Museum there and the head of all matters geological throughout the Province.[7] While

---

[7] Sir William Edmond Logan (1798–1875), the "father of Canadian science," had been knighted by the Queen for his contributions to geology. His best-known work, *Geology of Canada,* was to be published in 1863.

Some of the lengthy and inescapable lectures on geology that Trollope later in the paragraph speaks of having been subjected to may well have come to him at an early age from his older brother Henry (1811–34). Henry had pursued the science with such enthusiasm that at the age of twenty-one he was elected a fellow of the Geological Society.

he was explaining to me with admirable perspicuity the result of investigations into which he had poured his whole heart, I stood by understanding almost nothing, but envying everything. That I understood almost nothing, I know he perceived. That, ever and anon, with all his graciousness became apparent. But I wonder whether he perceived also that I did envy everything. I have listened to geologists by the hour before—have had to listen to them, desirous simply of escape. I have listened and understood absolutely nothing, and have only wished myself away. But I could have listened to Sir William Logan for the whole day, if time allowed. I found even in that hour that some ideas found their way through to me, and I began to fancy that even I could become a geologist at Montreal.

Over and beyond Sir William Logan there is at Montreal for strangers the drive round the mountain, not very exciting; and there is the tubular bridge over the St. Lawrence. This, it must be understood, is not made in one tube, as is that over the Menai Straits, but is divided into, I think, thirteen tubes. To the eye there appear to be twenty-five tubes; but each of the six side tubes is supported by a pier in the middle. A great part of the expense of the bridge was incurred in sinking the shafts for these piers.

CHAPTER V

UPPER CANADA

OTTAWA is in Upper Canada, but crossing the suspension bridge from Ottawa into Hull the traveller is in Lower Canada. It is therefore exactly in the confines, and has been chosen as the site of the new Government capital very much for this reason. Other reasons have, no doubt, had a share in the decision. At the time when the choice was made Ottawa was not large enough to create the jealousy of the more populous towns. Though not on the main line of railway, it was connected with it by a branch railway, and it is also connected with the St. Lawrence by water communication. And then it stands nobly on a magnificent river, with high overhanging rock, and a natural grandeur of position which has perhaps gone far in recommending it to those whose voice in the matter has been potential. Having the world of Canada from whence to choose the site of a new town, the choosers have certainly chosen well. It is another question whether or no a new town should have been deemed necessary.

Perhaps it may be well to explain the circumstances under which it was thought expedient thus to establish a new Canadian capital. In 1841 when Lord Sydenham was Governor General of the Provinces, the two Canadas, separate till then, were united under one Government. At that time the people of Lower or French Canada, and the people of Upper or English Canada differed much more in their habits and language than they do now. I do not know that the English have become in any way Gallicized, but the French have been very materially Anglicized. But while this has been in progress, national jealousy has been at work; and even yet that national jealousy is not at an end. While the two provinces were divided there were, of course, two capitals, and two seats of Government. These were at Quebec for Lower Canada, and at Toronto for Upper Canada, both which towns are centrically situated as regards the respective provinces. When the union was effected, it was deemed expedient that there should be but one capital; and the small town of Kingstown was selected, which is situated on the lower end of Lake Ontario in the Upper Province. But Kingstown was found to be inconvenient, lacking space and accommodation for those who had to follow the Government, and the

Governor removed it and himself to Montreal. Montreal is in the Lower Province, but is very central to both the provinces; and it is, moreover, the chief town in Canada. This would have done very well, but for an unforeseen misfortune.

It will be remembered by most readers that in 1837 took place the Mackenzie-Papineau rebellion, of which those who were then old enough to be politicians heard so much in England. I am not going back to recount the history of the period, otherwise than to say that the English Canadians at that time, in withstanding and combating the rebels, did considerable injury to the property of certain French Canadians, and that when the rebellion had blown over and those in fault had been pardoned, a question arose whether or no the Government should make good the losses of those French Canadians who had been injured. The English Canadians protested that it would be monstrous that they should be taxed to repair damages suffered by rebels, and made necessary in the suppression of rebellion. The French Canadians declared that the rebellion had been only a just assertion of their rights, that if there had been crime on the part of those who took up arms that crime had been condoned, and that the damages had not fallen exclusively or even chiefly on those who had done so. I will give no opinion on the merits of the question, but simply say that blood ran very hot when it was discussed. At last the Houses of the Provincial Parliament, then assembled at Montreal, decreed that the losses should be made good by the public treasury; and the English mob in Montreal, when this decree became known, was roused to great wrath by a decision which seemed to be condemnatory of English loyalty. It pelted Lord Elgin, the Governor General, with rotten eggs, and burned down the Parliament House. Hence, there arose, not unnaturally, a strong feeling of anger on the part of the local Government against Montreal; and moreover there was no longer a House in which the Parliament could be held in that town. For these conjoint reasons it was decided to move the seat of Government again, and it was resolved that the Governor and the Parliament should sit alternately at Toronto in Upper Canada, and at Quebec in Lower Canada, remaining four years at each place. They went at first to Toronto for two years only, having agreed that they should be there on this occasion only for the remainder of the term of the then Parliament. After that they were at Quebec for four years; then at Toronto for four; and now are again at Quebec. But this arrangement has been found very inconvenient. In the first place there is a great national expenditure incurred in moving old records, and in keeping double records, in moving the library, and as I have been informed even the pictures. The Government clerks also are called on to move as the Government moves; and though an allowance is made to them from the national purse to cover their loss, the arrangement has nevertheless been felt by them to be a grievance, as may be well understood. The accommodation also for the ministers of the Government, and for members of the two Houses has been insufficient. Hotels, lodgings, and furnished houses could not be provided to the extent required, seeing that they would be left nearly empty for every alternate space of four years. Indeed it needs but little argument to prove that the plan adopted must have been a thoroughly uncomfortable plan, and the wonder is that it should have been adopted. Lower Canada had undertaken to make all her leading citizens wretched, providing Upper Canada would treat hers with equal severity. This has now gone on for some twelve years, and as the system was found to be an unendurable nuisance it has been at last admitted that some steps must be taken towards selecting one capital for the country.

I should here, in justice to the Canadians, state a remark made to me on this matter by one of the present leading politicians of the colony. I cannot think that the migratory scheme was good; but he defended it, asserting that it had done very much to amalgamate the people of the two provinces; that it had brought Lower Canadians into Upper Canada, and Upper Canadians into Lower Canada, teaching English to those who spoke only French before, and making each pleasantly acquainted with the other. I have no doubt that something, —perhaps much,—has been done in this way; but valuable as the result may have been, I cannot think it worth the cost of the means employed. The best answer to the above argument consists in the undoubted fact that a migratory Government would never have been established for such a reason. It was so established because Montreal, the central town, had given offence, and because the jealousy of the provinces against each other would not admit of the Government being placed entirely at Quebec, or entirely at Toronto.

But it was necessary that some step should be taken; and as it was found to be unlikely that any resolution should be reached by the joint provinces themselves, it was loyally and wisely determined to refer the matter to the Queen. That Her Majesty has constitutionally the power to call the Parliament of Canada at any town of Canada which she may select, admits, I conceive, of no doubt. It is, I imagine, within her prerogative to call the Parliament of England where she may please within that realm, though her lieges would be somewhat startled if it were called otherwhere than in London. It was therefore well done to ask Her Majesty to act as arbiter in the matter. But there are not wanting those in Canada who say that in referring the matter to the Queen it was in truth referring it to those by whom very many of the Canadians were least willing to be guided in the matter; to·the Governor General namely, and the Colonial Secretary. Many indeed in Canada now declare that the decision simply placed the matter in the hands of the Governor General.

Be that as it may, I do not think that any unbiassed traveller will doubt that the best possible selection has been made, presuming always, as we may presume in the discussion, that Montreal could not be selected. I take for granted that the rejection of Montreal was regarded as a *sine quâ non* in the decision. To me it appears grievous that this should have been so. It is a great thing for any country to have a large, leading, world-known city, and I think that the Government should combine with the commerce of the country in carrying out this object. But commerce can do a great deal more for Government than Government can do for commerce. Government has selected Ottawa as the capital of Canada; but commerce has already made Montreal the capital, and Montreal will be the chief city of Canada, let Government do what it may to foster the other town. The idea of spiting a town because there has been a row in it seems to me to be preposterous. The row was not the work of those who have made Montreal rich and respectable. Montreal is more centrical than Ottawa,—nay, it is as nearly centrical as any town can be. It is easier to get to Montreal from Toronto, than to Ottawa;—and if from Toronto, then from all that distant portion of Upper Canada, back of Toronto. To all Lower Canada Montreal is, as a matter of course, much easier of access than Ottawa. But having said so much in favour of Montreal, I will again admit that, putting aside Montreal, the best possible selection has been made.

When Ottawa was named, no time was lost in setting to work to prepare for the new migration. In 1859 the Parliament was removed to Quebec, with the understanding that it should remain there till the new buildings should be completed. These buildings were absolutely commenced in April 1860, and it was, and I believe still is, expected that they will be completed in 1863. I am now writing in the winter of 1861; and, as is necessary in Canadian winters, the works are suspended. But unfortunately they were suspended in the early part of October,—on the 1st of October,—whereas they might have been continued, as far as the season is concerned, up to the end of November. We reached Ottawa on the 3rd of October, and more than a thousand men had then been just dismissed. All the money in hand had been expended, and the Government,—so it was said,—could give no more money till Parliament should meet again. This was most unfortunate. In the first place the suspension was against the contract as made with the contractors for the building; in the next place there was the delay; and then, worst of all, the question again became agitated whether the colonial legislature were really in earnest with reference to Ottawa. Many men of mark in the colony were still anxious—I believe are still anxious,—to put an end to the Ottawa scheme, and think that there still exists for them a chance of success. And very many men who are not of mark are thus united, and a feeling of doubt on the subject has been created. 225,000*l.* has already been spent on these buildings, and I have no doubt myself that they will be duly completed, and duly used.

We went up to the new town by boat, taking the course of the river Ottawa. We passed St. Ann's, but no one at St. Ann's seemed to know anything of the brothers who were to rest there on their weary oars.[1] At Maxwellstown I could hear nothing of Annie Laurie or of her trysting place on the braes, and the turnpike man at Tara could tell me nothing of the site of the hall, and had never even heard of the harp. When I go down South I shall expect to find that the negro melodies have not yet reached "Old Virginie." This boat conveyance from Montreal to Ottawa is not all that could be wished in convenience, for it is allied too closely with railway travelling. Those who use it leave Montreal by a railway; after nine miles, they are changed into a steamboat. Then they encounter another railway, and at last reach Ottawa in a second steamboat. But the river is seen, and a better idea of the country is obtained than can be had solely from the railway cars. The scenery is by no means grand, nor is it strikingly picturesque; but it is in its way interesting. For a long portion of the river the old primeval forests come down close to the water's edge, and in the fall of the year the brilliant colouring is very lovely. It should not be imagined,—as I think it often is imagined,—that these forests are made up of splendid trees, or that splendid trees are even common. When timber grows on undrained ground, and when it is uncared for, it does not seem to approach nearer to its perfection than wheat and grass do un-

[1] Trollope either visited St. Anne's a few years too early or failed to meet the right people. By 1884, according to S. E. Dawson's *Hand-Book for the Dominion of Canada*, natives not only had heard of *A Canadian Boat-Song* but were in the habit of pointing out the house where Tom Moore had written it, thus triumphing over fact and the song's second title, *Written on the River St. Lawrence.* For further comment on the song, see page 47 and note.

der similar circumstances. Seen from a little distance the colour and
effect is good, but the trees themselves have shallow roots and grow up
tall, narrow, and shapeless. It necessarily is so with all timber that is
not thinned in its growth. When fine forest trees are found, and are
left standing alone by any cultivator who may have taste enough to
wish for such adornment, they almost invariably die. They are robbed
of the sickly shelter by which they have been surrounded; the hot sun
strikes the uncovered fibres of the roots, and the poor solitary invalid
languishes and at last dies.

As one ascends the river, which by its breadth forms itself into
lakes, one is shown Indian villages clustering down upon the bank.
Some years ago these Indians were rich, for the price of furs, in which
they dealt, was high; but furs have become cheaper, and the beavers
with which they used to trade are almost valueless. That a change in
the fashion of hats should have assisted to polish these poor fellows off
the face of creation must, one may suppose, be very unintelligible to
them; but nevertheless it is probably a subject of deep speculation. If
the reading world were to take to sermons again and eschew their
novels, Messrs. Thackeray, Dickens, and some others would look about
them and inquire into the causes of such a change with considerable
acuteness. They might not, perhaps, hit the truth, and these Indians
are much in that predicament. It is said that very few pure-blooded
Indians are now to be found in their villages, but I doubt whether this
is not erroneous. The children of the Indians are now fed upon baked
bread, and on cooked meat, and are brought up in houses. They are
nursed somewhat as the children of the white men are nursed; and
these practices no doubt have done much towards altering their appearance. The negroes who have been bred in the States, and whose
fathers have been so bred before them, differ both in colour and form
from their brothers who have been born and nurtured in Africa.

I said in the last chapter that the city of Ottawa was still to be
built; but I must explain, lest I should draw down on my head the
wrath of the Ottawaites, that the place already contains a population
of 15,000 inhabitants. As, however, it is being prepared for four times
that number—for eight times that number let us hope—and as it strag-
gles over a vast extent of ground, it gives one the idea of a city in an
active course of preparation. In England we know nothing about
unbuilt cities. With us four or five blocks of streets together never
assume that ugly, unfledged appearance which belongs to the half-
finished carcase of a house, as they do so often on the other side of the
Atlantic. Ottawa is preparing for itself broad streets, and grand thor-

oughfares. The buildings already extend over a length considerably exceeding two miles, and half a dozen hotels have been opened, which, if I were writing a guide-book in a complimentary tone, it would be my duty to describe as first-rate. But the half-dozen first-rate hotels, though open, as yet enjoy but a moderate amount of custom. All this justifies me, I think, in saying that the city has as yet to get itself built. The manner in which this is being done justifies me also in saying that the Ottawaites are going about their task with a worthy zeal.

To me I confess that the nature of the situation has great charms,—regarding it as the site for a town. It is not on a plain, and from the form of the rock overhanging the river, and of the hill that falls from thence down to the water, it has been found impracticable to lay out the place in right-angled parallelograms. A right-angled parallelogramical city, such as are Philadelphia and the new portion of New York, is from its very nature odious to me. I know that much may be said in its favour—that drainage and gas-pipes come easier to such a shape, and that ground can be better economized. Nevertheless I prefer a street that is forced to twist itself about. I enjoy the narrowness of Temple Bar, and the misshapen curvature of Pickett Street. The disreputable dinginess of Holywell Street is dear to me, and I love to thread my way up by the Olympic into Covent Garden. Fifth Avenue in New York is as grand as paint and glass can make it; but I would not live in a palace in Fifth Avenue if the corporation of the city would pay my baker's and butcher's bills.

The town of Ottawa lies between two waterfalls. The upper one, or Rideau Fall, is formed by the confluence of a small river with the larger one; and the lower fall—designated as lower because it is at the foot of the hill, though it is higher up the Ottawa river—is called the Chaudière, from its resemblance to a boiling kettle. This is on the Ottawa river itself. The Rideau fall is divided into two branches, thus forming an island in the middle as is the case at Niagara. It is pretty enough, and worth visiting, even were it further from the town than it is; but by those who have hunted out many cataracts in their travels it will not be considered very remarkable. The Chaudière fall I did think very remarkable. It is of trifling depth, being formed by fractures in the rocky bed of the river; but the waters have so cut the rock as to create beautiful forms in the rush which they make in their descent. Strangers are told to look at these falls from the suspension bridge; and it is well that they should do so. But in so looking at them they obtain but a very small part of their effect. On the Ottawa side of the bridge is a brewery, which brewery is surrounded by a huge timber-yard. This timber-yard I found to be very muddy, and the passing and repassing through it is a work of trouble; but nevertheless let the traveller by all means make his way through the mud, and scramble over the timber, and cross the plank bridges which traverse the streams of the sawmills, and thus take himself to the outer edge of the woodwork over the water. If he will then seat himself, about the hour of sunset, he will see the Chaudière fall aright.

But the glory of Ottawa will be—and, indeed, already is—the set of public buildings which is now being erected on the rock which guards as it were the town from the river. How much of the excellence of these buildings may be due to the taste of Sir Edmund Head, the late Governor, I do not know. That he has greatly interested himself in the subject is well known: and as the style of the different buildings is so much alike as to make one whole, though the designs of different architects were selected, and these different architects employed, I imagine that considerable alterations must have been made in the original drawings. There are three buildings, forming three sides of a quadrangle; but they are not joined, the vacant spaces at the corner being of considerable extent. The fourth side of the quadrangle opens upon one of the principal streets of the town. The centre building is intended for the Houses of Parliament, and the two side buildings for the Government offices. Of the first Messrs. Fuller and Jones are the architects, and of the latter Messrs. Stent and Laver. I did not have the pleasure of meeting any of these gentlemen; but I take upon myself to say that as regards purity of art and manliness of conception their joint work is entitled to the very highest praise. How far the buildings may be well arranged for the required purposes, how far they may be economical in construction, or specially adapted to the severe climate of the country, I cannot say; but I have no hesitation in risking my reputation for judgment in giving my warmest commendation to them as regards beauty of outline and truthful nobility of detail.

I will not attempt to describe them, for I should interest no one in doing so, and should certainly fail in my attempt to make any reader understand me. I know no modern Gothic purer of its kind, or less sullied with fictitious ornamentation. Our own Houses of Parliament are very fine, but it is, I believe, generally felt that the ornamentation is too minute; and, moreover, it may be questioned whether perpendicular Gothic is capable of the highest nobility which architecture can achieve. I do not pretend to say that these Canadian public buildings will reach that highest nobility. They must be finished before any final judgment can be pronounced; but I do feel very certain that that final judgment will be greatly in their favour. The total frontage of the quadrangle, including the side buildings, is 1,200 feet; that of the centre buildings is 475. As I have said before, £225,000 has already been expended, and it is estimated that the total cost, including the arrangement and decoration of the ground behind the building and in the quadrangle, will be half a million.

The buildings front upon what will, I suppose, be the principal street of Ottawa, and they stand upon a rock looking immediately down upon the river. In this way they are blessed with a site peculiarly happy. Indeed I cannot at this moment remember any so much so. The castle of Edinburgh stands very well; but then, like many other castles, it stands on a summit by itself, and can only be approached by a steep ascent. These buildings at Ottawa, though they look down from a grand eminence immediately on the river, are approached from the town without any ascent. The rock, though it falls almost precipitously down to the water, is covered with trees and shrubs, and then the river that runs beneath is rapid, bright, and picturesque in the irregularity of all its lines. The view from the back of the library, up to the Chaudière falls, and to the saw-mills by which they are surrounded, is very lovely. So that I will say again, that I know no site for such a set of buildings so happy as regards both beauty and grandeur. It is intended that the library, of which the walls were only ten feet above the ground when I was there, shall be an octagonal building, in shape and outward character like the chapter-house of a cathedral. This structure will, I presume, be surrounded by gravel walks and green sward. Of the library there is a large model showing all the details of the architecture; and if that model be ultimately followed, this building alone will be worthy of a visit from English tourists. To me it was very wonderful to find such an edifice in the course of erection on the banks of a wild river, almost at the back of Canada. But if ever I visit Canada again it will be to see those buildings when completed.

And now, like all friendly critics, having bestowed my modicum of praise, I must proceed to find fault. I cannot bring myself to administer my sugar-plum without adding to it some bitter morsel by way of antidote. The building to the left of the quadrangle as it is entered is deficient in length, and on that account appears mean to the eye. The two side buildings are brought up close to the street, so that each has a frontage immediately on the street. Such being the case they should be of equal length, or nearly so. Had the centre of one fronted the centre of the other, a difference of length might have been allowed; but in this case the side front of the smaller one would not have

reached the street. As it is, the space between the main building and
the smaller wing is disproportionably large, and the very distance at
which it stands will, I fear, give to it that appearance of meanness of
which I have spoken. The clerk of the works, who explained to me
with much courtesy the plan of the buildings, stated that the design
of this wing was capable of elongation, and had been expressly prepared with that object. If this be so, I trust that the defect will be
remedied.

The great trade of Canada is lumbering; and lumbering consists in
cutting down pine trees up in the far distant forests, in hewing or saw-
ing them into shape for market, and getting them down the rivers to
Quebec, from whence they are exported to Europe, and chiefly to England. Timber in Canada is called lumber; those engaged in the trade
are called lumberers, and the business itself is called lumbering. After
a lapse of time it must no doubt become monotonous to those engaged
in it, and the name is not engaging; but there is much about it that is
very picturesque. A saw-mill worked by water power is almost always a
pretty object, and stacks of new cut timber are pleasant to the smell,
and group themselves not amiss on the water's edge. If I had the time,
and were a year or two younger. I should love well to go up lumbering
into the woods. The men for this purpose are hired in the fall of the
year, and are sent up hundreds of miles away to the pine forests in
strong gangs. Everything is there found for them. They make log huts
for their shelter, and food of the best and the strongest is taken up for
their diet. But no strong drink of any kind is allowed, nor is any within
reach of the men. There are no publics, no shebeen houses, no grog-
shops. Sobriety is an enforced virtue; and so much is this considered by
the masters, and understood by the men, that very little contraband
work is done in the way of taking up spirits to these settlements. It
may be said that the work up in the forests is done with the assistance
of no stronger drink than tea; and it is very hard work. There cannot
be much work that is harder; and it is done amidst the snows and
forests of a Canadian winter. A convict in Bermuda cannot get through
his daily eight hours of light labour without an allowance of rum; but
a Canadian lumberer can manage to do his daily task on tea without
milk. These men, however, are by no means teetotallers. When they
come back to the towns they break out, and reward themselves for
their long enforced moderation. The wages I found to be very various,
running from thirteen or fourteen dollars a month to twenty-eight or
thirty, according to the nature of the work. The men who cut down
the trees receive more than those who hew them when down, and these

again more than the under class who make the roads and clear the ground. These money wages, however, are in addition to their diet. The operation requiring the most skill is that of marking the trees for the axe. The largest only are worth cutting; and form and soundness must also be considered.

But if I were about to visit a party of lumberers in the forest, I should not be disposed to pass a whole winter with them. Even of a very good thing one may have too much. I would go up in the spring, when the rafts are being formed in the small tributary streams, and I would come down upon one of them, shooting the rapids of the rivers as soon as the first freshets had left the way open. A freshet in the rivers is the rush of waters occasioned by melting snow and ice. The first freshets take down the winter waters of the nearer lakes and rivers. Then the streams become for a time navigable, and the rafts go down. After that comes the second freshet, occasioned by the melting of far-off snow and ice, up in the great northern lakes which are little known. These rafts are of immense construction, such as those which we have seen on the Rhone and Rhine, and often contain timber to the value of two, three, and four thousand pounds. At the rapids the large rafts are, as it were, unyoked, and divided into small portions, which go down separately. The excitement and motion of such transit must, I should say, be very joyous. I was told that the Prince of Wales desired to go down a rapid on a raft, but that the men in charge would not undertake to say that there was no possible danger.[2] Whereupon those

2 Albert Edward, Prince of Wales, visited Canada and the United States in the summer and fall of 1860. His tour created great excitement in both countries. Apparently Trollope uses the term *rapid* to refer to the lumber slides of the Chaudière, and if so, he was misinformed regarding the Prince's activities. The *Illustrated London News* (October 20, 1860) gives the following account:

"DESCENT OF A TIMBER-SLIDE BY HIS ROYAL HIGHNESS

"Shortly after the corner-stone of the Parliament Buildings had been laid the Royal party took horse and rode, in plain clothes, to the Chaudière, where they admired the suspension bridge and the beautiful lumberers' arch, containing no less than nineteen thousand feet of deal boards, which now forms a portal to it.

"A novel and exciting incident here occurred. Dismounting, the whole of the party, including the Earl of St. Germans, walked along a boom to a crib which was moored at the entrance of the timber-slide. A slide, everybody should know, is an inclined plane, with several feet of water rushing over it, forming a waterway down which the crib can pass without damage, thus avoiding waterfalls like the Chaudière, where they would be broken and the timber injured. A crib consists of sticks of timber of any length, forming a small raft twenty-five feet wide, the longitudinal sticks having pieces across them to tie them, as it were, together. The crib, when fairly launched, goes down the slide with great velocity, the water rushing over the forward part and sometimes dashing over the men upon it. On each side of the slide on this occasion were thousands of people, and the numerous bridges which

who accompanied the prince requested his Royal Highness to forbear. I fear that in these careful days crowned heads and their heirs must often find themselves in the position of Sancho at the banquet.[3] The sailor prince who came after his brother was allowed to go down a rapid, and got, as I was told, rather a rough bump as he did so.

Ottawa is a great place for these timber rafts. Indeed, it may, I think, be called the head-quarters of timber for the world. Nearly all the best pine wood comes down the Ottawa and its tributaries. The other rivers by which timber is brought down to the St. Lawrence are chiefly the St. Maurice, the Madawaska, and the Saguenay; but the Ottawa and its tributaries water 75,000 square miles; whereas the other three rivers with their tributaries water only 53,000. The timber from the Ottawa and St. Maurice finds its way down the St. Lawrence to Quebec, where, however, it loses the whole of its picturesque character. The Saguenay and the Madawaska fall into the St. Lawrence below Quebec.

From Ottawa we went by rail to Prescott, which is surely one of the most wretched little places to be found in any country. Immediately opposite to it, on the other side of the St. Lawrence, is the thriving town of Ogdensburgh. But Ogdensburgh is in the United States. Had we been able to learn at Ottawa any facts as to the hours of the river steamers and railways we might have saved time and have avoided Prescott; but this was out of the question. Had I asked the exact hour at which I might reach Calcutta by the quickest route, an accurate reply would not have been more out of the question. I was much struck at Prescott—and indeed all through Canada, though more

---

crossed it were alive with human beings. When the Royal crib got under way and shot past or below them these people cheered and waved their handkerchiefs, and the most intense excitement prevailed; for, although there is really little danger, yet accidents sometimes happen, and in every case the passengers who try this mode of locomotion for the first time have to brace their nerves and clench their lips and stand firm, lest the vibration and the shocks which the crib always receives should make them lose their footing. And when Albert Edward, Prince of Wales, was to undergo this experience, how much greater than usual was the interest taken in the running of the crib. Everything, luckily, went well, both with the Prince's raft and with that which was carrying the leading members of the press immediately following. The whole of both parties were delighted. After the rapid descent, the cribs floated into the centre of the bay at the foot of the Chaudière. . . .

"There they found themselves surrounded by a hundred birch canoes, manned by lumberers in scarlet shirts and white trousers. . . ."

[3] Early in his brief term as Governor of the island of Baratria, Sancho Panza sits down to what he assumes will be a sumptuous banquet worthy of his new dignity. But before he can eat it each successive dish that is brought to the table is whisked away by order of the court physician, who explains that such rich foods present a grave and avoidable peril to the welfare of the Governor.

in the upper than in the lower province—by the sturdy roughness, some would call it insolence, of those of the lower classes of the people with whom I was brought into contact. If the words "lower classes" give offence to any reader, I beg to apologize;—to apologize and to assert that I am one of the last of men to apply such a term in a sense of reproach to those who earn their bread by the labour of their hands. But it is hard to find terms which will be understood; and that term, whether it give offence or no, will be understood. Of course such a complaint as that I now make is very common as made against the States. Men in the States with horned hands and fustian coats are very often most unnecessarily insolent in asserting their independence. What I now mean to say is that precisely the same fault is to be found in Canada. I know well what the men mean when they offend in this manner. And when I think on the subject with deliberation, at my own desk, I cannot only excuse, but almost approve them. But when one personally encounters their corduroy braggadocio; when the man to whose services one is entitled answers one with determined insolence; when one is bidden to follow "that young lady," meaning the chambermaid, or desired, with a toss of the head, to wait for the "gentleman who is coming," meaning the boots, the heart is sickened, and the English traveller pines for the civility,—for the servility, if my American friends choose to call it so,—of a well-ordered servant. But the whole scene is easily construed, and turned into English. A man is asked by a stranger some question about his employment, and he replies in a tone which seems to imply anger, insolence, and a dishonest intention to evade the service for which he is paid. Or if there be no question of service or payment, the man's manner will be the same, and the stranger feels that he is slapped in the face and insulted. The translation of it is this. The man questioned, who is aware that as regards coat, hat, boots, and outward cleanliness he is below him by whom he is questioned, unconsciously feels himself called upon to assert his political equality. It is his shibboleth that he is politically equal to the best, that he is independent, and that his labour, though it earn him but a dollar a day by porterage, places him as a citizen on an equal rank with the most wealthy fellowman that may employ or accost him. But being so inferior in that coat, hat and boots matter, he is forced to assert his equality by some effort. As he improves in externals he will diminish the roughness of his claim. As long as the man makes his claim with any roughness, so long does he acknowledge within himself some feeling of external inferiority. When that has gone,—when the American has polished himself up by education and general well being to a feeling of external equality with gentlemen, he shows, I think, no more of that outward braggadocio of independence than a Frenchman.

But the blow at the moment of the stroke is very galling. I confess that I have occasionally all but broken down beneath it. But when it is thought of afterwards it admits of full excuse. No effort that a man can make is better than a true effort at independence. But this insolence is a false effort, it will be said. It should rather be called a false accompaniment to a life-long true effort. The man probably is not dishonest, does not desire to shirk any service which is due from him,—is not even inclined to insolence. Accept his first declaration of equality for that which it is intended to represent, and the man afterwards will be found obliging and communicative. If occasion offer he will sit down in the room with you, and will talk with you on any subject that he may choose; but having once ascertained that you show no resentment for this assertion of equality, he will do pretty nearly all that he is asked. He will at any rate do as much in that way as an Englishman. I say thus much on this subject now especially, because I was quite as much struck by the feeling in Canada as I was within the States.

From Prescott we went on by the Grand Trunk Railway to Toronto, and stayed there for a few days. Toronto is the capital of the province of Upper Canada, and I presume will in some degree remain so in spite of Ottawa and its pretensions. That is, the law courts will still be held there. I do not know that it will enjoy any other supremacy, unless it be that of trade and population. Some few years ago Toronto was advancing with rapid strides, and was bidding fair to rival Quebec, or even perhaps Montreal. Hamilton, also, another town of Upper Canada, was going a head in the true American style; but then reverses came in trade, and the towns were checked for a while. Toronto, with a neighbouring suburb which is a part of it, as Southwark is of London, contains now over 50,000 inhabitants. The streets are all parallelogramical, and there is not a single curvature to rest the eye. It is built down close upon Lake Ontario; and as it is also on the Grand Trunk Railway it has all the aid which facility of traffic can give it.

The two sights of Toronto are the Osgoode Hall and the University. The Osgoode Hall is to Upper Canada what the Four Courts are to Ireland. The law courts are all held there. Exteriorly little can be said for Osgoode Hall, whereas the exterior of the Four Courts in Dublin is very fine; but as an interior the temple of Themis at Toronto beats hollow that which the goddess owns in Dublin. In Dublin the Courts themselves are shabby, and the space under the dome is not so fine as the exterior seems to promise that it should be. In Toronto the Courts themselves are, I think, the most commodious that I ever saw, and the passages, vestibules, and hall are very handsome. In Upper Canada the common law judges and those in Chancery are divided as they are in England; but it is, as I was told, the opinion of Canadian lawyers that the work may be thrown together. Appeal is allowed in criminal cases; but as far as I could learn such power of appeal is held to be both troublesome and useless. In Lower Canada the old French laws are still administered.

But the University is the glory of Toronto. This is a Gothic building and will take rank after, but next to[,] the buildings at Ottawa. It will be the second piece of noble architecture in Canada, and as far as I know on the American continent. It is, I believe, intended to be purely Norman, though I doubt whether the received types of Norman architecture have not been departed from in many of the windows. Be this as it may the College is a manly, noble structure, free from false decoration, and infinitely creditable to those who projected it. I was informed by the head of the College that it has been open only two years, and here also I fancy that the colony has been much indebted to the taste of the late Governor, Sir Edmund Head.

Toronto as a city is not generally attractive to a traveller. The country around it is flat; and, though it stands on a lake, that lake has no attributes of beauty. Large inland seas such as are these great Northern lakes of America never have such attributes. Picturesque mountains rise from narrow valleys, such as form the beds of lakes in Switzerland, Scotland, and Northern Italy. But from such broad waters as those of Lake Ontario, Lake Erie, and Lake Michigan, the shores shelve very gradually, and have none of the materials of lovely scenery.

The streets in Toronto are framed with wood, or rather planked, as are those of Montreal and Quebec; but they are kept in better order. I should say that the planks are first used at Toronto, then sent down by the lake to Montreal, and when all but rotted out there, are again floated off by the St. Lawrence to be used in the thoroughfares of the old French capital. But if the streets of Toronto are better than those of the other towns, the roads round it are worse. I had the honour of meeting two distinguished members of the Provincial Parliament at dinner some few miles out of town, and, returning back a short while after they had left our host's house, was glad to be of use in picking them up from a ditch into which their carriage had been upset. To me it appeared all but miraculous that any carriage should make its way over that road without such misadventure. I may perhaps be allowed to hope that the discomfiture of those worthy legislators may lead to some improvement in the thoroughfare.

I had on a previous occasion gone down the St. Lawrence, through the thousand isles, and over the rapids in one of those large summer steamboats which ply upon the lake and river. I cannot say that I was much struck by the scenery, and therefore did not encroach upon my time by making the journey again. Such an opinion will be regarded as heresy by many who think much of the thousand islands. I do not believe that they would be expressly noted by any traveller who was not expressly bidden to admire them.

From Toronto we went across to Niagara, re-entering the States at Lewiston in New York.

CHAPTER VI

THE CONNEXION OF THE CANADAS WITH GREAT BRITAIN

W HEN the American war began troops were sent out to Canada, and when I was in the Provinces more troops were then expected. The matter was much talked of, as a matter of course, in Canada; and it had been discussed in England before I left. I had seen much said about it in the English papers since, and it also had become the subject of very hot question among the politicians of the Northern States. The measure had at that time given more umbrage to the North than anything else done or said by England from the beginning of the war up to that time, except the declaration made by Lord John Russell in the House of Commons as to the neutrality to be preserved by England between the two belligerents. The argument used by the Northern States was this. If France collects men and material of war in *the* neighbourhood of England, England considers herself injured, calls for an explanation, and talks of invasion. Therefore as England is now collecting men and material of war in our neighbourhood, we will consider ourselves injured. It does not suit us to ask for an explanation, because it is not our habit to interfere with other nations. We will not pretend to say that we think we are to be invaded. But as we clearly are injured, we will express our anger at that injury, and when the opportunity shall come will take advantage of having that new grievance.

As we all know, a very large increase of force was sent when we were still in doubt as to the termination of the Trent affair, and imagined that war was imminent. But the sending of that large force did not anger the Americans, as the first despatch of troops to Canada had angered them. Things had so turned out that measures of military precaution were acknowledged by them to be necessary. I cannot, however, but think that Mr. Seward might have spared that offer to send British troops across Maine; and so, also, have all his countrymen thought by whom I have heard the matter discussed.[1]

---

[1] Contrary to popular rumor, Seward had made no such offer. In January 1862, with the Trent affair but recently settled, he had merely refrained, despite some prodding by the Senate and the Governor of Maine, from putting any unusual barriers in the way of a body of British troops already on the seas bound for Portland.

As to any attempt at invasion of Canada by the Americans, or idea of punishing the alleged injuries suffered by the States from Great Britain by the annexation of those provinces, I do not believe that any sane-minded citizens of the States believe in the possibility of such retaliation. Some years since the Americans thought that Canada might shine in the Union firmament as a new star, but that delusion is, I think, over. Such annexation[,] if ever made, must have been made not only against the arms of England but must also have been made in accordance with the wishes of the people so annexed. It was then believed that the Canadians were not averse to such a change, and there may possibly have then been among them the remnant of such a wish. There is certainly no such desire now, not even a remnant of such a desire; and the truth on this matter is, I think, generally acknowledged. The feeling in Canada is one of strong aversion to the United States Government, and of predilection for self-government under the English Crown. A fainéant Governor and the prestige of British power is now the political aspiration of the Canadians in general; and I think that this is understood in the States. Moreover the States have a job of work on hand which, as they themselves are well aware, is taxing all their energies. Such being the case I do not think that England needs to fear any invasion of Canada, authorized by the States Government.

This feeling of a grievance on the part of the States was a manifest absurdity. The new reinforcement of the garrisons in Canada did not, when I was in Canada, amount as I believe to more than 2,000 men. But had it amounted to 20,000 the States would have had no just ground for complaint. Of all nationalities that in modern days have risen to power, they above all others have shown that they would do what they liked with their own, indifferent to foreign councils, and deaf to foreign remonstrance. "Do you go your way, and let us go ours. We will trouble you with no question, nor do you trouble us." Such has been their national policy, and it has obtained for them great respect. They have resisted the temptation of putting their fingers into the caldron of foreign policy; and foreign politicians, acknowledging their reserve in this respect, have not been offended at the bristles with which their Noli me tangere has been proclaimed. Their intelligence has been appreciated, and their conduct has been respected. But if

---

Maine, and due to cross a part of that state on their way to Canada. To refuse the customary privilege between nations would be to expose the troops to needless suffering in the ice and snow of Canada and quite possibly to invoke a new Anglo-American crisis.

this has been their line of policy, they must be entirely out of court in raising any question as to the position of British troops on British soil.

"It shows us that you doubt us," an American says, with an air of injured honour—or did say, before that Trent affair. "And it is done to express sympathy with the South. The Southerners understand it, and we understand it also. We know where your hearts are; nay, your very souls. They are among the slave-begotten cotton bales of the rebel South." Then comes the whole of the long argument, in which it seems so easy to an Englishman to prove that England in the whole of this sad matter has been true and loyal to her friend. She could not interfere when the husband and wife would quarrel. She could only grieve, and wish that things might come right and smooth for both parties. But the argument though so easy is never effectual.

It seems to me foolish in an American to quarrel with England for sending soldiers to Canada; but I cannot say that I thought it was well done to send them at the beginning of the war. The English Government did not, I presume, take this step with reference to any possible invasion of Canada by the Government of the States. We are fortifying Portsmouth, and Portland, and Plymouth, because we would fain be safe against the French army acting under a French Emperor. But we sent 2,000 troops to Canada, if I understand the matter rightly, to guard our provinces against the filibustering energies of a mass of unemployed American soldiers, when those soldiers should come to be disbanded. When this war shall be over—a war during which not much, if any, under a million of American citizens will have been under arms—it will not be easy for all who survive to return to their old homes and old occupations. Nor does a disbanded soldier always make a good husbandman, notwithstanding the great examples of Cincinnatus and Bird-o'-freedom Sawin.[2] It may be that a considerable amount of filibustering energy will be afloat, and that the then Government of those who neighbour us in Canada will have other matters in hand more important to them than the controlling of these unruly spirits. That, as I take it, was the evil against which we of Great Britain and of Canada desired to guard ourselves.

But I doubt whether 2,000 or 10,000 British soldiers would be any effective guard against such inroads, and I doubt more strongly whether any such external guarding will be necessary. If the Canadians were prepared to fraternize with filibusters from the States, neither three nor ten thousand soldiers would avail against such a feeling over

[2] For comment on Birdofredum Sawin, the unhappy warrior of James Russell Lowell's *The Biglow Papers*, see the note on page 246.

a frontier stretching from the State of Maine to the shores of Lake Huron and Lake Erie. If such a feeling did exist, if the Canadians wished the change, in God's name let them go. Is it for their sakes and not for our own that we would have them bound to us? But the Canadians are averse to such a change with a degree of feeling that amounts to national intensity. Their sympathies are with the Southern States, not becaue they care for cotton, not because they are antiabolitionists, not because they admire the hearty pluck of those who are endeavouring to work out for themselves a new revolution. They sympathize with the South from strong dislike to the aggression, the braggadocio, and the insolence they have felt upon their own borders. They dislike Mr. Seward's weak and vulgar joke with the Duke of Newcastle.[3] They dislike Mr. Everett's flattering hints to his countrymen as to the one nation that is to occupy the whole continent. They dislike the Monroe doctrine. They wonder at the meekness with which England has endured the vauntings of the Northern States, and are endued with no such meekness of their own. They would, I believe, be well prepared to meet and give an account of any filibusters who might visit them; and I am not sure that it is wisely done on our part to show any intention of taking the work out of their hands.

But I am led to this opinion in no degree by a feeling that Great Britain ought to grudge the cost of the soldiers. If Canada will be safer with them, in heaven's name let her have them. It has been argued in many places, not only with regard to Canada, but as to all our self-governed colonies, that military service should not be given at British expense and with British men to any colony which has its own representative government, and which levies its own taxes. "While Great Britain absolutely held the reins of government, and did as it pleased with the affairs of its dependencies," such politicians say, "it was just and right that she should pay the bill. As long as her government of a colony was paternal, so long was it right that the mother country should put herself in the place of a father, and enjoy a father's

---

[3] Late in 1860 Seward had sat next to the Duke of Newcastle, English Secretary of State for the Colonies, during festivities connected with the Prince of Wales's visit to the United States. Seward had remarked that as a high official in the administration about to take office it would be his duty to insult Great Britain. The Duke assumed that the remark had serious undertones. Seward seems, indeed, to have been half-serious, for he favored the idea that threat of foreign war might be the best means of bringing the North and the South together and thus averting the threat of a civil war. Seward's "joke" soon reached the English newspapers and raised wild conjectures and alarms.

For Everett's "flattering hints to his countrymen" mentioned in the next sentence, see page 237.

undoubted prerogative of putting his hand into his breeches pocket
to provide for all the wants of his child. But when the adult son set up
for himself in business, having received education from the parent,
and having had his apprentice fees duly paid, then that son should
settle his own bills, and look no longer to the paternal pocket." Such
is the law of the world all over, from little birds whose young fly away
when fledged, upwards to men and nations. Let the father work for
the child while he is a child, but when the child has become a man let
him lean no longer on his father's staff.

The argument is, I think, very good; but it proves, not that we are
relieved from the necessity of assisting our colonies with payments
made out of British taxes, but that we are still bound to give such
assistance; and that we shall continue to be so bound as long as we
allow these colonies to adhere to us, or as they allow us to adhere to
them. In fact the young bird is not yet fully fledged. That illustration
of the father and the child is a just one, but in order to make it just it
should be followed throughout. When the son is in fact established on
his own bottom, then the father expects that he will live without assistance. But when the son does so live he is freed from all paternal control. The father, while he expects to be obeyed, continues to fill the
paternal office of paymaster,—of paymaster, at any rate, to some extent.
And so, I think, it must be with our colonies. The Canadas at present
are not independent, and have not political power of their own apart
from the political power of Great Britain. England has declared herself neutral as regards the Northern and Southern States, and by that
neutrality the Canadas are bound; and yet the Canadas were not consulted in the matter. Should England go to war with France, Canada
must close her ports against French vessels. If England chooses to send
her troops to Canadian barracks, Canada cannot refuse to accept them.
If England should send to Canada an unpopular Governor, Canada
has no power to reject his services. As long as Canada is a colony, so
called, she cannot be independent, and should not be expected to walk
alone. It is exactly the same with the colonies of Australia, with New
Zealand, with the Cape of Good Hope, and with Jamaica. While England enjoys the prestige of her colonies, while she boasts that such large
and now populous territories are her dependencies, she must and
should be content to pay some portion of the bill. Surely it is absurd on
our part to quarrel with Caffre warfare, with New Zealand fighting, and
the rest of it. Such complaints remind one of an ancient paterfamilias,
who insists on having his children and his grandchildren under the old
paternal roof, and then grumbles because the butcher's bill is high.

Those who will keep large households and bountiful tables should not be afraid of facing the butcher's bill, or unhappy at the tonnage of the coal. It is a grand thing, that power of keeping a large table; but it ceases to be grand when the items heaped upon it cause inward groans and outward moodiness.

Why should the colonies remain true to us as children are true to their parents, if we grudge them the assistance which is due to a child? They raise their own taxes, it is said, and administer them. True; and it is well that the growing son should do something for himself. While the father does all for him the son's labour belongs to the father. Then comes a middle state in which the son does much for himself, but not all. In that middle state now stand our prosperous colonies. Then comes the time when the son shall stand alone by his own strength; and to that period of manly self-respected strength let us all hope that those colonies are advancing. It is very hard for a mother country to know when such a time has come; and hard also for the child-colony to recognize justly the period of its own maturity. Whether or no such severance may ever take place without a quarrel, without weakness on one side and pride on the other, is a problem in the world's history yet to be solved. The most successful child that ever yet has gone off from a successful parent and taken its own path into the world, is without doubt the nation of the United States. Their present troubles are the result and the proofs of their success. The people that were too great to be dependent on any nation have now spread till they are themselves too great for a single nationality. No one now thinks that that daughter should have remained longer subject to her mother. But the severance was not made in amity, and the shrill notes of the old family quarrel are still sometimes heard across the waters.

From all this the question arises whether that problem may ever be solved with reference to the Canadas. That it will never be their destiny to join themselves to the States of the Union, I feel fully convinced. In the first place it is becoming evident from the present circumstances of the Union,—if it had never been made evident by history before,—that different people with different habits living at long distances from each other cannot well be brought together on equal terms under one Government. That noble ambition of the Americans that all the continent north of the isthmus should be united under one flag, has already been thrown from its saddle. The North and South are virtually separated, and the day will come in which the West also will secede. As population increases and trades arise peculiar to those different climates, the interests of the people will differ, and a new secession will take place beneficial alike to both parties. If this be so, if even there be any tendency this way, it affords the strongest argument against the probability of any future annexation of the Canadas. And then, in the second place, the feeling of Canada is not American, but British. If ever she be separated from Great Britain, she will be separated as the States were separated. She will desire to stand alone, and to enter herself as one among the nations of the earth.

She will desire to stand alone;—alone, that is without dependence either on England or on the States. But she is so circumstanced geographically that she can never stand alone without amalgamation with our other North American provinces. She has an outlet to the sea at the Gulf of St. Lawrence, but it is only a summer outlet. Her winter outlet is by railway through the States, and no other winter outlet is possible for her except through the sister provinces. Before Canada can be nationally great, the line of railway which now runs for some hundred miles below Quebec to Rivière du Loup, must be continued on through New Brunswick and Nova Scotia to the port of Halifax.

When I was in Canada I heard the question discussed of a Federal Government between the provinces of the two Canadas, New Brunswick and Nova Scotia. To these were added, or not added, according to the opinion of those who spoke, the smaller outlying colonies of Newfoundland and Prince Edward's Island. If a scheme for such a Government were projected in Downing Street, all would no doubt be included, and a clean sweep would be made without difficulty. But the project as made in the colonies appears in different guises as it comes either from Canada or from one of the other provinces. The Canadian idea would be that the two Canadas should form two States of such a confederation, and the other provinces a third State. But this slight participation in power would hardly suit the views of New Brunswick and Nova Scotia. In speaking of such a Federal Government as this, I shall of course be understood as meaning a confederation acting in connection with a British Governor, and dependent upon Great Britain as far as the different colonies are now dependent.

I cannot but think that such a confederation might be formed with great advantage to all the colonies and to Great Britain. At present the Canadas are in effect almost more distant from Nova Scotia and New Brunswick than they are from England. The intercourse between them is very slight—so slight that it may almost be said that there is no intercourse. A few men of science or of political importance may from time to time make their way from one colony into the other, but even this is not common. Beyond that they seldom see each other. Though New

Brunswick borders, both with Lower Canada and with Nova Scotia, thus making one whole of the three colonies, there is neither railroad nor stage conveyance running from one to the other. And yet their interests should be similar. From geographical position their modes of life must be alike, and a close conjunction between them is essentially necessary to give British North America any political importance in the world. There can be no such conjunction, no amalgamation of interests, until a railway shall have been made joining the Canada Grand Trunk Line with the two outlying colonies. Upper Canada can feed all England with wheat, and could do so without any aid of railway through the States, if a railway were made from Quebec to Halifax. But then comes the question of the cost. The Canada Grand Trunk is at the present moment at the lowest ebb of commercial misfortune, and with such a fact patent to the world what company will come forward with funds for making four or five hundred miles of railway, through a district of which one half is not yet prepared for population? It would be, I imagine, out of the question that such a speculation should for many years give any fair commercial interest on the money, to be expended. But nevertheless to the colonies,—that is, to the enormous regions of British North America,—such a railroad would be invaluable. Under such circumstances it is for the Home Government and the colonies between them to see how such a measure may be carried out. As a national expenditure to be defrayed in the course of years by the territories interested, the sum of money required would be very small.

But how would this affect England? And how would England be affected by a union of the British North American colonies under one Federal Government? Before this question can be answered, he who prepares to answer it must consider what interest England has in her colonies, and for what purpose she holds them. Does she hold them for profit, or for glory, or for power; or does she hold them in order that she may carry out the duty which has devolved upon her of extending civilization, freedom, and well-being through the new uprising nations of the world? Does she hold them, in fact, for her own benefit, or does she hold them for theirs? I know nothing of the ethics of the Colonial Office, and not much perhaps of those of the House of Commons; but looking at what Great Britain has hitherto done in the way of colonization, I cannot but think that the national ambition looks to the welfare of the colonists, and not to home aggrandisement. That the two may run together is most probable. Indeed there can be no glory to a people so great or so readily recognized by mankind at large as that of spreading civilization from East to West, and from North to South. But the one object should be the prosperity of the colonists; and not profit, nor glory, nor even power to the parent country.

There is no virtue of which more has been said and sung than patriotism, and none which when pure and true has led to finer results. Dulce et decorum est pro patriâ mori.[4] To live for one's country also is a very beautiful and proper thing. But if we examine closely much patriotism, that is so called, we shall find it going hand in hand with a good deal that is selfish, and with not a little that is devilish. It was some fine fury of patriotic feeling which enabled the national poet to put into the mouth of every Englishman that horrible prayer with regard to our enemies, which we sing when we wish to do honour to our sovereign.[5] It did not seem to him that it might be well to pray that their hearts should be softened, and our own hearts softened also. National success was all that a patriotic poet could desire, and therefore in our national hymn have we gone on imploring the Lord to arise and scatter our enemies; to confound their politics, whether they be good or ill; and to expose their knavish tricks,—such knavish tricks being taken for granted. And then with a steady confidence we used to declare how certain we were that we should achieve all that was desirable, not exactly by trusting to our prayer to heaven, but by relying almost exclusively on George the Third or George the Fourth. Now I have always thought that that was rather a poor patriotism. Luckily for us our national conduct has not squared itself with our national anthem. Any patriotism must be poor which desires glory or even profit for a few at the expense of many, even though the few be brothers and the many aliens. As a rule patriotism is a virtue only because man's aptitude for good is so finite, that he cannot see and comprehend a wider humanity. He can hardly bring himself to understand that salvation should be extended to Jew and Gentile alike. The word philanthropy has become odious, and I would fain not use it; but the thing itself is as much higher than patriotism, as heaven is above the earth.

[4] "It is sweet and fitting to die for one's country."—Horace: *Odes*, III, ii, 13.

[5] The second stanza of *God Save the King*, doubtfully attributed to Henry Carey:

> O Lord our God, arise,
> Scatter his enemies,
> And make them fall.
> Confound their politics,
> Frustrate their knavish tricks;
> On Thee our hearts we fix,
> God save us all!

A wish that British North America should ever be severed from England, or that the Australian colonies should ever be so severed, will by many Englishmen be deemed unpatriotic. But I think that such severance is to be wished if it be the case that the colonies standing alone would become more prosperous than they are under British rule. We have before us an example in the United States of the prosperity which has attended such a rupture of old ties. I will not now contest the point with those who say that the present moment of an American civil war is ill chosen for vaunting that prosperity. There stand the cities which the people have built, and their power is attested by the world-wide importance of their present contest. And if the States have so risen since they left their parent's apron-string, why should not British North America rise as high? That the time has as yet come for such rising I do not think; but that it will soon come I do most heartily hope. The making of the railway of which I have spoken, and the amalgamation of the provinces would greatly tend to such an event. If, therefore, England desires to keep these colonies in a state of dependency; if it be more essential to her to maintain her own power with regard to them than to increase their influence; if her main object be to keep the colonies and not to improve the colonies, then I should say that an amalgamation of the Canadas with Nova Scotia and New Brunswick should not be regarded with favour by statesmen in Downing Street. But if, as I would fain hope, and do partly believe, such ideas of national power as these are now out of vogue with British statesmen, then I think that such an amalgamation should receive all the support which Downing Street can give it.

The United States severed themselves from Great Britain with a great struggle and after heartburnings and bloodshed. Whether Great Britain will ever allow any colony of hers to depart from out of her nest, to secede and start for herself, without any struggle or heartburnings, with all furtherance for such purpose which an old and powerful country can give to a new nationality then first taking its own place in the world's arena, is a problem yet to be solved. There is, I think, no more beautiful sight than that of a mother, still in all the glory of womanhood, preparing the wedding trousseau for her daughter. The child hitherto has been obedient and submissive. She has been one of a household in which she has held no command. She has sat at table as a child, fitting herself in all things to the behests of others. But the day of her power and her glory, and also of her cares and solicitude is at hand. She is to go forth, and do as she best may in the world under that teaching which her old home has given her. The hour of separation has come; and the mother, smiling through her tears, sends her forth decked with a bounteous hand and furnished with full stores, so that all may be well with her as she enters on her new duties. So is it that England should send forth her daughters. They should not escape from her arms with shrill screams and bleeding wounds, with ill-omened words which live so long, though the speakers of them lie cold in their graves.

But this sending forth of a child-nation to take its own political status in the world has never yet been done by Great Britain. I cannot remember that such has ever been done by any great power with reference to its dependency;—by any power that was powerful enough to keep such dependency within its grasp. But a man thinking on these matters cannot but hope that a time will come when such amicable severance may be effected. Great Britain cannot think that through all coming ages she is to be the mistress of the vast continent of Australia, lying on the other side of the globe's surface; that she is to be the mistress of all South Africa, as civilization shall extend northward; that the enormous territories of British North America are to be subject for ever to a veto from Downing Street. If the history of past empires does not teach her that this may not be so, at least the history of the United States might so teach her. "But we have learned a lesson from those United States," the patriot will argue who dares to hope that the glory and extent of the British Empire may remain unimpaired *in sæcula sæculorum.* "Since that day we have given political rights to our colonies, and have satisfied the political longings of their inhabitants. We do not tax their tea and stamps, but leave it to them to tax themselves as they may please." True. But in political aspirations the giving of an inch has ever created the desire for an ell. If the Australian colonies, even now,—with their scanty population and still young civilization, chafe against imperial interference, will they submit to it when they feel within their veins all the full blood of political manhood? What is the cry even of the Canadians—of the Canadians who are thoroughly loyal to England? Send us a fainéant Governor, a King Log,[6] who will not presume to interfere with us; a Governor who will spend his money and live like a gentleman and care little or nothing for politics. That is the Canadian *beau idéal* of a Governor. They are

---

6 According to Æsop, the frogs once became tired of living without a government and asked Jupiter for a king. Jupiter threw down a log, and this served as a satisfactory monarch until the frogs lost their fear of it. When the frogs asked for a new king, Jupiter sent them a stork. The stork ate them up.

to govern themselves; and he who comes to them from England is to sit among them as the silent representative of England's protection. If that be true—and I do not think that any who know the Canadas will deny it—must it not be presumed that they will soon also desire a fainéant minister in Downing Street? Of course they will so desire. Men do not become milder in their aspirations for political power, the more that political power is extended to them. Nor would it be well that they should be so humble in their desires. Nations devoid of political power have never risen high in the world's esteem. Even when they have been commercially successful, commerce has not brought to them the greatness which it has always given when joined with a strong political existence. The Greeks are commercially rich and active; but "Greece" and "Greek" are bye-words now for all that is mean. Cuba is a colony, and putting aside the cities of the States, the Havana is the richest town on the other side of the Atlantic and commercially the greatest; but the political villainy of Cuba, her daily importation of slaves, her breaches of treaty, and the bribery of her all but royal Governor are known to all men. But Canada is not dishonest; Canada is no bye-word for anything evil; Canada eats her own bread in the sweat of her brow, and fears a bad word from no man. True. But why does New York with its suburbs boast a million of inhabitants, while Montreal has 85,000? Why has that babe in years, Chicago, 120,000, while Toronto has not half the number? I do not say that Montreal and Toronto should have gone ahead abreast with New York and Chicago. In such races one must be first, and one last. But I do say that the Canadian towns will have no equal chance, till they are actuated by that feeling of political independence which has created the growth of the towns in the United States.

I do not think that the time has yet come in which Great Britain should desire the Canadians to start for themselves. There is the making of that railroad to be effected, and something done towards the union of those provinces. Canada could no more stand alone without New Brunswick and Nova Scotia, than could those latter colonies without Canada. But I think it would be well to be prepared for such a coming day; and that it would at any rate be well to bring home to ourselves and realize the idea of such secession on the part of our colonies, when the time shall have come at which such secession may be carried out with profit and security to them. Great Britain, should she ever send forth her child alone into the world, must of course guarantee her security. Such guarantees are given by treaties; and in the wording of them it is presumed that such treaties will last for ever. It will be argued that in starting British North America as a political power on its own bottom, we should bind ourself to all the expense of its defence, while we should give up all right to any interference in its concerns; and that from a state of things so unprofitable as this there would be no prospect of deliverance. But such treaties, let them be worded how they will, do not last for ever. For a time, no doubt, Great Britain would be so hampered—if indeed she would feel herself hampered by extending her name and prestige to a country bound to her by ties such as those which would then exist between her and this new nation. Such treaties are not everlasting, nor can they be made to last even for ages. Those who word them seem to think that powers and dynasties will never pass away. But they do pass away, and the balance of power will not keep itself fixed for ever on the same pivot. The time may come—that it may not come soon we will all desire—but the time may come when the name and prestige of what we call British North America will be as serviceable to Great Britain as those of Great Britain are now serviceable to her colonies.

But what shall be the new form of government for the new kingdom? That is a speculation very interesting to a politician; though one which to follow out at great length in these early days would be rather premature. That it should be a kingdom—that the political arrangement should be one of which a crowned hereditary king should form a part, nineteen out of every twenty Englishmen would desire; and, as I fancy, so would also nineteen out of every twenty Canadians. A king for the United States when they first established themselves was impossible. A total rupture from the Old World and all its habits was necessary for them. The name of a king, or monarch, or sovereign had become horrible to their ears. Even to this day they have not learned the difference between arbitrary power retained in the hand of one man, such as that now held by the Emperor over the French, and such hereditary headship in the State as that which belongs to the Crown in Great Britain. And this was necessary, seeing that their division from us was effected by strife, and carried out with war and bitter animosities. In those days also there was a remnant, though but a small remnant, of the power of tyranny left within the scope of the British Crown. That small remnant has been removed; and to me it seems that no form of existing government—no form of government that ever did exist, gives or has given so large a measure of individual freedom to all who live under it as a constitutional monarchy in which the Crown is divested of direct political power.

I will venture then to suggest a king for this new nation; and seeing that we are rich in princes there need be no difficulty in the selection. Would it not be beautiful to see a new nation established under such auspices, and to establish a people to whom their independence had been given,—to whom it had been freely surrendered as soon as they were capable of holding the position assigned to them?

CHAPTER VII

NIAGARA

OF all the sights on this earth of ours which tourists travel to see,—
at least of all those which I have seen,—I am inclined to give the palm
to the Falls of Niagara. In the catalogue of such sights I intend to include all buildings, pictures, statues, and wonders of art made by men's
hands, and also all beauties of nature prepared by the Creator for the
delight of his creatures. This is a long word; but as far as my taste and
judgment go, it is justified. I know no other one thing so beautiful, so
glorious, and so powerful. I would not by this be understood as saying
that a traveller wishing to do the best with his time should first of all
places seek Niagara. In visiting Florence he may learn almost all that
modern art can teach. At Rome he will be brought to understand the
cold hearts, correct eyes, and cruel ambition of the old Latin race. In
Switzerland he will surround himself with a flood of grandeur and
loveliness, and fill himself, if he be capable of such filling, with a flood
of romance. The Tropics will unfold to him all that vegetation in its
greatest richness can produce. In Paris he will find the supreme of
polish, the *ne plus ultra* of varnish according to the world's capability
of varnishing. And in London he will find the supreme of power, the
ne plus ultra of work according to the world's capability of working.
Any one of such journeys may be more valuable to a man,—nay, any
one such journey must be more valuable to a man, than a visit to Niagara. At Niagara there is that fall of waters alone. But that fall is more
graceful than Giotto's tower, more noble than the Apollo. The peaks
of the Alps are not so astounding in their solitude. The valleys of the
Blue Mountains in Jamaica are less green. The finished glaze of life
in Paris is less invariable; and the full tide of trade round the Bank
of England is not so inexorably powerful.

I came across an artist at Niagara who was attempting to draw the
spray of the waters. "You have a difficult subject," said I. "All subjects
are difficult," he replied, "to a man who desires to do well." "But
yours, I fear, is impossible," I said. "You have no right to say so till I
have finished my picture," he replied. I acknowledged the justice of
his rebuke, regretted that I could not remain till the completion of

his work should enable me to revoke my words, and passed on. Then
I began to reflect whether I did not intend to try a task as difficult in
describing the falls, and whether I felt any of that proud self-confidence which kept him happy at any rate while his task was in hand. I
will not say that it is as difficult to describe aright that rush of waters,
as it is to paint it well. But I doubt whether it is not quite as difficult
to write a description that shall interest the reader, as it is to paint a
picture of them that shall be pleasant to the beholder. My friend the
artist was at any rate not afraid to make the attempt, and I also will
try my hand.

That the waters of Lake Erie have come down in their courses
from the broad basins of Lake Michigan, Lake Superior, and Lake
Huron; that these waters fall into Lake Ontario by the short and rapid
river of Niagara, and that the Falls of Niagara are made by a sudden
break in the level of this rapid river, is probably known to all who will
read this book. All the waters of these huge northern inland seas run
over that breach in the rocky bottom of the stream; and thence it
comes that the flow is unceasing in its grandeur, and that no eye can
perceive a difference in the weight, or sound, or violence of the fall,
whether it be visited in the drought of autumn, amidst the storms of
winter, or after the melting of the upper worlds of ice in the days of
the early summer. How many cataracts does the habitual tourist visit
at which the waters fail him? But at Niagara the waters never fail.
There it thunders over its ledge in a volume that never ceases and is
never diminished;—as it has done from times previous to the life of
man, and as it will do till tens of thousands of years shall see the rocky
bed of the river worn away, back to the upper lake.

This stream divides Canada from the States, the western or farther-
most bank belonging to the British Crown, and the eastern or nearer
bank being in the State of New York. In visiting Niagara it always becomes a question on which side the visitor shall take up his quarters.
On the Canada side there is no town, but there is a large hotel, beautifully placed immediately opposite to the falls, and this is generally
thought to be the best locality for tourists. In the State of New York is
the town called Niagara Falls, and here there are two large hotels,
which, as to their immediate site, are not so well placed as that in
Canada. I first visited Niagara some three years since. I stayed then at
the Clifton House on the Canada side, and have since sworn by that
position. But the Clifton House was closed for the season when I was
last there, and on that account we went to the Cataract House in the
town on the other side. I now think that I should set up my staff on the

American side if I went again. My advice on the subject to any party starting for Niagara would depend upon their habits, or on their nationality. I would send Americans to the Canadian side, because they dislike walking; but English people I would locate on the American side, seeing that they are generally accustomed to the frequent use of their own legs. The two sides are not very easily approached, one from the other. Immediately below the falls there is a ferry, which may be traversed at the expense of a shilling; but the labour of getting up and down from the ferry is considerable, and the passage becomes wearisome. There is also a bridge, but it is two miles down the river, making a walk or drive of four miles necessary, and the toll for passing is four shillings or a dollar in a carriage, and one shilling on foot. As the greater variety of prospect can be had on the American side, as the island between the two falls is approachable from the American side and not from the Canadian, and as it is in this island that visitors will best love to linger and learn to measure in their minds the vast triumph of waters before them, I recommend such of my readers as can trust a little,—it need be but a little,—to their own legs, to select their hotel at Niagara Falls town.

It has been said that it matters much from what point the falls are first seen, but to this I demur. It matters, I think, very little, or not at all. Let the visitor first see it all, and learn the whereabouts of every point, so as to understand his own position and that of the waters; and then having done that in the way of business let him proceed to enjoyment. I doubt whether it be not the best to do this with all sight seeing. I am quite sure that it is the way in which acquaintance may be best and most pleasantly made with a new picture.

The falls are, as I have said, made by a sudden breach in the level of the river. All cataracts are, I presume, made by such breaches; but generally the waters do not fall precipitously as they do at Niagara, and never elsewhere, as far as the world yet knows, has a breach so sudden been made in a river carrying in its channel such or any approach to such a body of water. Up above the falls, for more than a mile, the waters leap and burst over rapids, as though conscious of the destiny that awaits them. Here the river is very broad, and comparatively shallow, but from shore to shore it frets itself into little torrents, and begins to assume the majesty of its power. Looking at it even here, in the expanse which forms itself over the greater fall, one feels sure that no strongest swimmer could have a chance of saving himself, if fate had cast him in even among those petty whirlpools. The waters, though so broken in their descent, are deliciously green. This colour as seen early in the morning, or just as the sun has set, is so bright as to give to the place of its chiefest charms.

This will be best seen from the further end of the island,—Goat Island, as it is called, which, as the reader will understand, divides the river immediately above the falls. Indeed the island is a part of that precipitously broken ledge over which the river tumbles; and no doubt in process of time will be worn away and covered with water. The time, however, will be very long. In the meanwhile it is perhaps a mile round, and is covered thickly with timber. At the upper end of the island the waters are divided, and coming down in two courses, each over its own rapids, form two separate falls. The bridge by which the island is entered is a hundred yards or more above the smaller fall. The waters here have been turned by the island, and make their leap into the body of the river below at a right angle with it,—about two hundred yards below the greater fall. Taken alone this smaller cataract would, I imagine, be the heaviest fall of water known, but taken in conjunction with the other it is terribly shorn of its majesty. The waters here are not green as they are at the larger cataract, and though the ledge has been hollowed and bowed by them so as to form a curve, that curve does not deepen itself into a vast abyss as it does at the horseshoe up above. This smaller fall is again divided, and the visitor passing down a flight of steps and over a frail wooden bridge finds himself on a smaller island in the midst of it.

But we will go at once on to the glory, and the thunder, and the majesty, and the wrath of that upper hell of waters. We are still, let the reader remember, on Goat Island, still in the States, and on what is called the American side of the main body of the river. Advancing beyond the path leading down to the lesser fall, we come to that point of the island at which the waters of the main river begin to descend. From hence across to the Canadian side the cataract continues itself in one unabated line. But the line is very far from being direct or straight. After stretching for some little way from the shore, to a point in the river which is reached by a wooden bridge at the end of which stands a tower upon the rock,—after stretching to this, the line of the ledge bends inwards against the flood,—in, and in, and in, till one is led to think that the depth of that horseshoe is immeasurable. It has been cut with no stinting hand. A monstrous cantle has been worn back out of the centre of the rock, so that the fury of the waters converges, and the spectator as he gazes into the hollow with wishful eyes fancies that he can hardly trace out the centre of the abyss.

Go down to the end of that wooden bridge, seat yourself on the rail, and there sit till all the outer world is lost to you. There is no grander spot about Niagara than this. The waters are absolutely around you. If you have that power of eye-control which is so necessary to the full enjoyment of scenery you will see nothing but the water. You will certainly hear nothing else; and the sound, I beg you to remember, is not an ear-cracking, agonizing crash and clang of noises; but is melodious, and soft withal, though loud as thunder. It fills your ears, and as it were envelopes them, but at the same time you can speak to your neighbour without an effort. But at this place, and in these moments, the less of speaking I should say the better. There is no grander spot than this. Here, seated on the rail of the bridge, you will not see the whole depth of the fall. In looking at the grandest works of nature, and of art too, I fancy, it is never well to see all. There should be something left to the imagination, and much should be half concealed in mystery. The greatest charm of a mountain range is the wild feeling that there must be strange unknown desolate worlds in those far-off valleys beyond. And so here, at Niagara, that converging rush of waters may fall down, down at once into a hell of rivers for what the eye can see. It is glorious to watch them in their first curve over the rocks. They come green as a bank of emeralds; but with a fitful flying colour, as though conscious that in one moment more they would be dashed into spray and rise into air, pale as driven snow. The vapour rises high into the air, and is gathered there, visible always as a permanent white cloud over the cataract; but the bulk of the spray which fills the lower hollow of that horse-shoe is like a tumult of snow. This you will not fully see from your seat on the rail. The head of it rises ever and anon out of that caldron below, but the caldron itself will be invisible. It is ever so far down,—far as your own imagination can sink it. But your eyes will rest full upon the curve of the waters. The shape you will be looking at is that of a horse-shoe, but of a horse-shoe miraculously deep from toe to heel;—and this depth becomes greater as you sit there. That which at first was only great and beautiful, becomes gigantic and sublime till the mind is at loss to find an epithet for its own use. To realize Niagara you must sit there till you see nothing else than that which you have come to see. You will hear nothing else, and think of nothing else. At length you will be at one with the tumbling river before you. You will find yourself among the waters as though you belonged to them. The cool liquid green will run through your veins, and the voice of the cataract will be the expression of your own heart. You will fall as the bright waters fall, rushing down into your new world with no hesitation and with no dismay;

and you will rise again as the spray rises, bright, beautiful, and pure. Then you will flow away in your course to the uncompassed, distant, and eternal ocean.

When this state has been reached and has passed away you may get off your rail and mount the tower. I do not quite approve of that tower, seeing that it has about it a gingerbread air, and reminds one of those well-arranged scenes of romance in which one is told that on the left you turn to the lady's bower, price sixpence; and on the right ascend to the knight's bed, price sixpence more, with a view of the hermit's tomb thrown in. But nevertheless the tower is worth mounting, and no money is charged for the use of it. It is not very high, and there is a balcony at the top on which some half dozen persons may stand at ease. Here the mystery is lost, but the whole fall is seen. It is not even at this spot brought so fully before your eye,—made to show itself in so complete and entire a shape, as it will do when you come to stand near to it on the opposite or Canadian shore. But I think that it shows itself more beautifully. And the form of the cataract is such, that, here in Goat Island, on the American side, no spray will reach you, although you are absolutely over the waters. But on the Canadian side, the road as it approaches the fall is wet and rotten with spray, and you, as you stand close upon the edge, will be wet also. The rainbows as they are seen through the rising cloud—for the sun's rays as seen through these waters show themselves in a bow as they do when seen through rain,—are pretty enough, and are greatly loved. For myself I do not care for this prettiness at Niagara. It is there, but I forget it,—and do not mind how soon it is forgotten.

But we are still on the tower; and here I must declare that though I forgive the tower, I cannot forgive the horrid obelisk which has latterly been built opposite to it, on the Canadian side, up above the fall; built apparently,—for I did not go to it,—with some camera obscura intention for which the projector deserves to be put in Coventry by all good Christian men and women. At such a place as Niagara tasteless buildings, run up in wrong places with a view to money making, are perhaps necessary evils. It may be that they are not evils at all;—that they give more pleasure than pain, seeing that they tend to the enjoyment of the multitude. But there are edifices of this description which cry aloud to the gods by the force of their own ugliness and malposition. As to such it may be said that there should somewhere exist a power capable of crushing them in their birth. This new obelisk or picture-building at Niagara is one of such.

And now we will cross the water, and with this object will return by the bridge out of Goat Island on the main land of the American side. But as we do so let me say that one of the great charms of Niagara consists in this,—that over and above that one great object of wonder and beauty, there is so much little loveliness;—loveliness especially of water I mean. There are little rivulets running here and there over little falls, with pendent boughs above them, and stones shining under their shallow depths. As the visitor stands and looks through the trees the rapids glitter before him, and then hide themselves behind islands. They glitter and sparkle in far distances under the bright foliage till the remembrance is lost, and one knows not which way they run. And then the river below, with its whirlpool;—but we shall come to that by-and-by, and to the mad voyage which was made down the rapids by that mad captain who ran the gauntlet of the waters at the risk of his own life, with fifty to one against him, in order that he might save another man's property from the Sheriff.

The readiest way across to Canada is by the ferry; and on the American side this is very pleasantly done. You go into a little house, pay 20 cents, take a seat on a wooden car of wonderful shape, and on the touch of a spring find yourself travelling down an inclined plane of terrible declivity and at a very fast rate. You catch a glance of the river below you, and recognize the fact that if the rope by which you are held should break, you would go down at a very fast rate indeed, —and find your final resting place in the river. As I have gone down some dozen times and have come to no such grief, I will not presume that you will be less lucky. Below there is a boat generally ready. If it be not there, the place is not chosen amiss for a rest of ten minutes, for the lesser fall is close at hand, and the larger one is in full view. Looking at the rapidity of the river you will think that the passage must be dangerous and difficult. But no accidents ever happen, and the lad who takes you over seems to do it with sufficient ease. The walk up the hill on the other side is another thing. It is very steep, and for those who have not good locomotive power of their own, will be found to be disagreeable. In the full season, however, carriages are generally waiting there. In so short a distance I have always been ashamed to trust to other legs than my own, but I have observed that Americans are always dragged up. I have seen single young men of from eighteen to twenty-five, from whose outward appearance no story of idle luxurious life can be read, carried about alone in carriages over distances which would be counted as nothing by any healthy English lady of fifty. None but the old and invalids should require the assistance of carriages in seeing Niagara, but the trade in carriages is to all appearance the most brisk trade there.

Having mounted the hill on the Canada side you will walk on towards the falls. As I have said before, you will from this side look directly into the full circle of the upper cataract, while you will have before you at your left hand the whole expanse of the lesser fall. For those who desire to see all at a glance, who wish to comprise the whole with their eyes, and to leave nothing to be guessed, nothing to be surmised, this, no doubt, is the best point of view.

You will be covered with spray as you walk up to the ledge of rocks, but I do not think that the spray will hurt you. If a man gets wet through going to his daily work, cold, catarrh, cough, and all their attendant evils may be expected; but these maladies usually spare the tourist. Change of air, plenty of air, excellence of air, and increased exercise make these things powerless. I should therefore bid you disregard the spray. If, however, you are yourself of a different opinion, you may hire a suit of oil-cloth clothes, for, I believe, a quarter of a dollar. They are nasty of course, and have this further disadvantage, that you become much more wet having them on than you would be without them.

Here, on this side, you walk on to the very edge of the cataract, and, if your tread be steady and your legs firm, you dip your foot into the water exactly at the spot where the thin outside margin of the current reaches the rocky edge and jumps to join the mass of the fall. The bed of white foam beneath is certainly seen better here than elsewhere, and the green curve of the water is as bright here as when seen from the wooden rail across. But nevertheless I say again that that wooden rail is the one point from whence Niagara may be best seen aright.

Close to the cataract, exactly at the spot from whence in former days the Table Rock used to project from the land over the boiling caldron below, there is now a shaft down which you will descend to the level of the river, and pass between the rock and the torrent. This Table Rock broke away from the cliff and fell, as up the whole course of the river the seceding rocks have split and fallen from time to time through countless years, and will continue to do till the bed of the upper lake is reached. You will descend this shaft, taking to yourself or not taking to yourself a suit of oil-clothes as you may think best. I have gone with and without the suit, and again recommend that they be left behind. I am inclined to think that the ordinary payment should be made for their use, as otherwise it will appear to those whose trade it is to prepare them that you are injuring them in their vested rights.

Some three years since I visited Niagara on my way back to England from Bermuda, and in a volume of travels which I then published I endeavoured to explain the impression made upon me by this passage between the rock and the waterfall. An author should not quote himself; but as I feel myself bound, in writing a chapter specially about Niagara, to give some account of this strange position, I will venture to repeat my own words.[1]

In the spot to which I allude the visitor stands on a broad safe path, made of shingles, between the rock over which the water rushes and the rushing water. He will go in so far that the spray rising back from the bed of the torrent does not incommode him. With this exception, the further he can go in the better; but circumstances will clearly show him the spot to which he should advance. Unless the water be driven in by a very strong wind, five yards make the difference between a comparatively dry coat and an absolute wet one. And then let him stand with his back to the entrance, thus hiding the last glimmer of the expiring day. So standing he will look up among the falling waters, or down into the deep misty pit, from which they reascend in almost as palpable a bulk. The rock will be at his right hand, high and hard, and dark and straight, like the wall of some huge cavern, such as children enter in their dreams. For the first five minutes he will be looking but at the waters of a cataract,—at the waters, indeed, of such a cataract as we know no other, and at their interior curves which elsewhere we cannot see. But by-and-by all this will change. He will no longer be on a shingly path beneath a waterfall; but that feeling of a cavern wall will grow upon him, of a cavern deep, below roaring seas, in which the waves are there, though they do not enter in upon him; or rather not the waves, but the very bowels of the ocean. He will feel as though the floods surrounded him, coming and going with their wild sounds, and he will hardly recognize that though among them he is not in them. And they, as they fall with a continual roar, not hurting the ear, but musical withal, will seem to move as the vast ocean waters may perhaps move in their internal currents. He will lose the sense of one continued descent, and think that they are passing round

---

[1] In the next paragraph Trollope does repeat, with only minor variations, a passage from *The West Indies and the Spanish Main* (1859). It begins with "And then let him stand with his back to the entrance . . ." and runs to the end of the paragraph. For an account of Trollope's first visit to America, see section I of our Introduction, and Appendix C.

him in their appointed courses. The broken spray that rises from the depth below, rises so strongly, so palpably, so rapidly, that the motion in every direction will seem equal. And, as he looks on, strange colours will show themselves through the mist; the shades of grey will become green or blue, with ever and anon a flash of white; and then, when some gust of wind blows in with greater violence, the sea-girt cavern will become all dark and black. Oh, my friend, let there be no one there to speak to thee then; no, not even a brother. As you stand there speak only to the waters.

Two miles below the falls the river is crossed by a suspension bridge of marvellous construction. It affords two thoroughfares, one above the other. The lower road is for carriages and horses, and the upper one bears a railway belonging to the Great Western Canada line. The view from hence both up and down the river is very beautiful, for the bridge is built immediately over the first of a series of rapids. One mile below the bridge these rapids end in a broad basin called the whirl-pool, and, issuing out of this, the current turns to the right through a narrow channel overhung by cliffs and trees, and then makes its way down to Lake Ontario with comparative tranquillity.

But I will beg you to take notice of those rapids from the bridge and to ask yourself what chance of life would remain to any ship, craft, or boat required by destiny to undergo navigation beneath the bridge and down into that whirlpool. Heretofore all men would have said that no chance of life could remain to so ill-starred a bark. The navi-gation, however, has been effected. But men used to the river still say that the chances would be fifty to one against any vessel which should attempt to repeat the experiment.

The story of that wondrous voyage was as follows. A small steamer called the Maid of the Mist was built upon the river, between the falls and the rapids, and was used for taking adventurous tourists up amidst the spray, as near to the cataract as was possible. The Maid of the Mist plied in this way for a year or two, and was, I believe, much patronized during the season. But in the early part of last summer an evil time had come. Either the Maid got into debt, or her owner had embarked in other and less profitable speculations. At any rate he became sub-ject to the law, and tidings reached him that the Sheriff would seize the Maid. On most occasions the Sheriff is bound to keep such inten-tions secret, seeing that property is moveable, and that an insolvent debtor will not always await the officers of justice. But with the poor Maid there was no need of such secrecy. There was but a mile or so of water on which she could ply, and she was forbidden by the nature of her properties to make any way upon land. The Sheriff's prey therefore was easy and the poor Maid was doomed.

In any country in the world but America such would have been the case, but an American would steam down Phlegethon to save his property from the Sheriff; he would steam down Phlegethon or get some one else to do it for him. Whether or no in this case the captain of the boat was the proprietor, or whether, as I was told, he was paid for the job, I do not know; [2] but he determined to run the rapids, and he procured two others to accompany him in the risk. He got up his steam, and took the Maid up amidst the spray according to his custom. Then suddenly turning on his course, he with one of his companions fixed himself at the wheel, while the other remained at his engine. I wish I could look into the mind of that man and understand what his thoughts were at that moment; what were his thoughts and what his beliefs. As to one of the men I was told that he was carried down, not knowing what he was about to do, but I am inclined to believe that all the three were joined together in the attempt.

I was told by a man who saw the boat pass under the bridge, that she made one long leap down as she came thither, that her funnel was at once knocked flat on the deck by the force of the blow, that the waters covered her from stem to stern, and that then she rose again and skimmed into the whirlpool a mile below. When there she rode with comparative ease upon the waters, and took the sharp turn round into the river below without a struggle. The feat was done, and the Maid was rescued from the Sheriff. It is said that she was sold below at the mouth of the river, and carried from thence over Lake Ontario and down the St. Lawrence to Quebec.

[2] Joel R. Robinson, the captain but not the owner of the *Maid of the Mist*, was the chief hero of this almost incredible exploit. Jones, the regular engineer, and McIntyre, a machinist volunteer, accompanied him. The ship, built in 1854, was 72 feet long with 17 feet breadth of beam and 8 feet depth of hold. She was heavily mortgaged, but the owner managed to strike up a deal that would yield him about half her value provided he could deliver her at Niagara, opposite the fort. The trip through the Whirlpool Rapids took place on June 6, 1861. Mrs. Robinson told George W. Holley (*The Falls of Niagara* [1883]) that her husband looked "twenty years older when he came home that day than when he went out." Somewhat later, however, he declared himself eager to make the voyage again if anyone would finance it and enter into an agreement with him to share the profits, for he believed a good deal of money could be made from the spectators.

CHAPTER VIII

NORTH AND WEST

FROM Niagara we determined to proceed north-west; as far to the
north-west as we could go with any reasonable hope of finding American citizens in a state of political civilization, and perhaps guided also
in some measure by our hopes as to hotel accommodation. Looking to
these two matters we resolved to get across to the Mississippi, and to
go up that river as far as the town of St. Paul and the falls of St. Anthony, which are some twelve miles above the town; then to descend
the river as far as the States of Iowa on the west, and Illinois on the
east; and to return eastwards through Chicago and the large cities on
the southern shores of Lake Erie, from whence we would go across to
Albany, the capital of New York State, and down the Hudson to New
York, the capital of the Western world. For such a journey, in which
scenery was one great object, we were rather late, as we did not leave
Niagara till the 10th of October; but though the winters are extremely
cold through all this portion of the American continent—15, 20, and
even 25 degrees below zero being an ordinary state of the atmosphere [1]
in latitudes equal to those of Florence, Nice, and Turin—nevertheless
the autumns are mild, the noon day being always warm, and the
colours of the foliage are then in all their glory. I was also very anxious
to ascertain, if it might be in my power to do so, with what spirit or
true feeling as to the matter, the work of recruiting for the now
enormous army of the States was going on in those remote regions.
That men should be on fire in Boston and New York, in Philadelphia,
and along the borders of secession, I could understand. I could understand also that they should be on fire throughout the cotton, sugar,
and rice plantations of the South. But I could hardly understand that
this political fervour should have communicated itself to the far-off
farmers who had thinly spread themselves over the enormous wheat-
growing districts of the North-West. St. Paul, the capital of Minne-

---

[1] It is hard to make out what Trollope means by "ordinary." Later, in Chapter ix, he implies that in Wisconsin, presumably in or near Milwaukee, the mercury in winter "is commonly 20 degrees below zero." All in all, his informants seem
to have given him a somewhat exaggerated notion of the severity of winter in the
Northern states.

sota, is 900 miles directly north of St. Louis, the most northern point
to which slavery extends in the Western States of the Union, and the
farming lands of Minnesota stretch away again for some hundreds of
miles north and west of St. Paul. Could it be that those scanty and
far-off pioneers of agriculture, those frontier farmers who are nearly
one half German and nearly the other half Irish, would desert their
clearings and ruin their chances of progress in the world for distant
wars of which the causes must, as I thought, be to them unintelligible?
I had been told that distance had but lent enchantment to the view,
and that the war was even more popular in the remote and newly
settled States than in those which have been longer known as great
political bodies. So I resolved that I would go and see.

It may be as well to explain here that that great political Union
hitherto called the United States of America may be more properly
divided into three than into two distinct interests. In England we
have long heard of North and South as pitted against each other, and
we have always understood that the southern politicians or democrats
have prevailed over the northern politicians or republicans, because
they were assisted in their views by northern men of mark who have
held southern principles;—that is, by northern men who have been
willing to obtain political power by joining themselves to the southern party. That as far as I can understand has been the general idea
in England, and in a broad way it has been true. But as years have
advanced and as the States have extended themselves westward, a
third large party has been formed, which sometimes rejoices to call
itself The Great West; and though at the present time the West and
the North are joined together against the South, the interests of the
North and the West are not, I think, more closely interwoven than are
those of the West and South; and when the final settlement of this
question shall be made, there will doubtless be great difficulty in satisfying the different aspirations and feelings of two great free soil populations. The North, I think, will ultimately perceive that it will gain
much by the secession of the South; but it will be very difficult to make
the West believe that secession will suit its views.

I will attempt in a rough way to divide the States, as they seem to
divide themselves, into these three parties. As to the majority of them
there is no difficulty in locating them; but this cannot be done with
absolute certainty as to some few that lie on the borders.

New England consists of six States, of which all of course belong
to the North. They are Maine, New Hampshire, Vermont, Massachusetts, Rhode Island, and Connecticut; the six States which should be

most dear to England, and in which the political success of the United States as a nation is to my eyes the most apparent. But even in them there was till quite of late a strong section so opposed to the republican party as to give a material aid to the South. This, I think, was particularly so in New Hampshire, from whence President Pierce came. He had been one of the senators from New Hampshire; and yet to him as President, is affixed the disgrace, whether truly affixed or not I do not say, of having first used his power in secretly organizing those arrangements which led to secession and assisted at its birth. In Massachusetts also itself there was a strong democratic party, of which Massachusetts now seems to be somewhat ashamed. Then, to make up the North, must be added the two great States of New York and Pennsylvania, and the small State of New Jersey. The West will not agree even to this absolutely, seeing that they claim all territory west of the Alleghenies, and that a portion of Pennsylvania, and some part also of New York lie westward of that range; but in endeavouring to make these divisions ordinarily intelligible I may say that the North consists of the nine States above named. But the North will also claim Maryland and Delaware, and the eastern half of Virginia. The North will claim them though they are attached to the South by joint participation in the great social institution of slavery, for Maryland, Delaware, and Virginia are slave States;—and I think that the North will ultimately make good its claim. Maryland and Delaware lie, as it were, behind the capital, and Eastern Virginia is close upon the capital. And these regions are not tropical in their climate or influences. They are and have been slave States; but will probably rid themselves of that taint and become a portion of the free North.

The southern or slave States, properly so called, are easily defined. They are Texas, Louisiana, Arkansas, Mississippi, Alabama, Florida, Georgia, South Carolina, and North Carolina. The South will also claim Tennessee, Kentucky, Missouri, Virginia, Delaware, and Maryland, and will endeavour to prove its right to the claim by the fact of the social institution being the law of the land in those States. Of Delaware, Maryland, and Eastern Virginia, I have already spoken. Western Virginia is, I think, so little tainted with slavery, that, as she stands even at present, she properly belongs to the West. As I now write the struggle is going on in Kentucky and Missouri. In Missouri the slave population is barely more than a tenth of the whole, while in South Carolina and Mississippi it is more than half. And, therefore, I venture to count Missouri among the western States, although slavery is still the law of the land within its borders. It is surrounded on three sides by free States of the West, and its soil, let us hope, must become free. Kentucky I must leave as doubtful, though I am inclined to believe that slavery will be abolished there also. Kentucky at any rate will never throw in its lot with the southern States. As to Tennessee, it seceded heart and soul, and I fear that it must be accounted as southern, although the northern army has now, in May 1862, possessed itself of the great part of the State.

To the great West remains an enormous territory, of which, however, the population is as yet but scanty; though perhaps no portion of the world has increased so fast in population as have these western States. The list is as follows: Ohio, Indiana, Illinois, Michigan, Wisconsin, Minnesota, Iowa, Kansas,—to which I would add Missouri, and probably the western half of Virginia. We have then to account for the two already admitted States on the Pacific, California and Oregon, and also for the unadmitted Territories, Dacotah, Nebraska, Washington, Utah, New Mexico, Colorado, and Nevada. I should be refining too much for my present very general purpose, if I were to attempt to marshal these huge but thinly populated regions in either rank. Of California and Oregon it may probably be said that it is their ambition to form themselves into a separate division;—a division which may be called the further West.

I know that all statistical statements are tedious, and I believe that but few readers believe them. I will, however, venture to give the populations of these States in the order I have named them, seeing that power in America depends almost entirely on population. The census of 1860 gave the following results:—

In the North.

Maine	619,000
New Hampshire	326,872
Vermont	325,827
Massachusetts	1,231,494
Rhode Island	174,621
Connecticut	460,670
New York	3,851,563
Pennsylvania	2,916,018
New Jersey	676,034
Total	10,582,099

In the South—the population of which must be divided into free and slave.

	FREE	SLAVE	TOTAL
Texas	415,999	184,956	600,955
Louisiana	354,245	312,186	666,431
Arkansas	331,710	109,065	440,775
Mississippi . . .	407,051	479,607	886,658
Alabama	520,444	435,473	955,917
Florida	81,885	63,809	145,694
Georgia	615,366	467,461	1,082,827
South Carolina .	308,186	407,185	715,371
North Carolina .	679,965	328,377	1,008,342
Tennessee . . .	859,578	287,112	1,146,690
Total . .	4,574,429	3,075,231	7,649,660

In the West.

Ohio	2,377,917
Indiana	1,350,802
Illinois	1,691,238
Michigan	754,291
Wisconsin	763,485
Minnesota	172,796
Iowa	682,002
Kansas	143,645
Missouri . . . . *	1,204,214
Total	9,140,390

* Of which number, in Missouri, 115,619 are slaves.

In the doubtful States.

Maryland .	646,183	85,382	731,565
Delaware . .	110,548	1,805	112,353
Virginia . .	1,097,373	495,826	1,593,199
Kentucky . .	920,077	225,490	1,145,567
Total .	2,774,181	808,503	3,582,684

To these must be added to make up the population of the United States, as it stood in 1860.

The separate district of Columbia, in
   which is included Washington, the
   seat of the Federal Government . . . 75,321
California 384,770
Oregon 52,566
The Territories of
   Dacotah 4,839
   Nebraska 28,892
   Washington 11,624
   Utah 49,000
   New Mexico 93,024
   Colorado 34,197
   Nevada. 6,857
      Total 741,090

And thus the total population may be given as follows:—

North 10,582,099
South 7,649,660
West 9,140,390
Doubtful 3,582,684
Outlying States and Territories . . . 741,090
      Total 31,695,923

Each of the three interests would consider itself wronged by the division above made, but the South would probably be the loudest in asserting its grievance. The South claims all the slave States, and would point to secession in Virginia to justify such claim,—and would point also to Maryland and Baltimore, declaring that secession would be as strong there as at New Orleans, if secession were practicable. Maryland and Baltimore lie behind Washington, and are under the heels of the northern troops, so that secession is not practicable; but, the South would say that they have seceded in heart. In this the South would have some show of reason for its assertion; but, nevertheless, I shall best convey a true idea of the position of these States by classing them as doubtful. When secession shall have been accomplished,—if ever it be accomplished,—it will hardly be possible that they should adhere to the South.

It will be seen by the above tables that the population of the West is nearly equal to that of the North, and that therefore western power is almost as great as northern. It is almost as great already, and as population in the West increases faster than it does in the North, the two will soon be equalized. They are already sufficiently on a par to enable them to fight on equal terms, and they will be prepared for fighting—political fighting, if no other—as soon as they have established their supremacy over a common enemy.

Whilst I am on the subject of population, I should 'explain—though the point is not one which concerns the present argument—that the numbers given, as they regard the South, include both the whites and blacks, the free men and the slaves. The political power of the South is of course in the hands of the white race only, and the total white population should therefore be taken as the number indicating the southern power. The political power of the South, however, as contrasted with that of the North, has, since the commencement of the Union, been much increased by the slave population. The slaves have been taken into account in determining the number of representatives which should be sent to Congress by each State. That number depends on the population, but it was decided in 1787, that in counting up the number of representatives to which each State should be held to be entitled, five slaves should represent three white men. A Southern population, therefore, of five thousand free men and five thousand slaves would claim as many representatives as a Northern population of eight thousand free men, although the voting would be confined to the free population. This has ever since been the law of the United States.

The western power is nearly equal to that of the North, and this fact, somewhat exaggerated in terms, is a frequent boast in the mouths of western men. "We ran Fremont for President," they say, "and had it not been for northern men with southern principles, we should have put him in the White House [2] instead of the traitor Buchanan. If that had been done, there would have been no secession." How things might have gone had Fremont been elected in lieu of Buchanan, I will not pretend to say; but the nature of the argument shows the difference that exists between northern and western feeling. At the time that I was in the West, General Fremont was the great topic of public interest. Every newspaper was discussing his conduct, his ability as a soldier, his energy, and his fate. At that time General Maclellan was in command at Washington on the Potomac, it being understood that

[2] In the election of 1856 Buchanan had secured 174 electoral votes to 114 for John C. Frémont, the Republican candidate, and 8 for Millard Fillmore, the Whig candidate; but he had less than an actual majority of the popular votes cast. Outside the South and the border states Buchanan carried only Illinois, Indiana, California, New Jersey, and Pennsylvania.

he held his power directly under the President,—free from the exercise of control on the part of the veteran General Scott, though at that time General Scott had not actually resigned his position as head of the army. And General Fremont, who some five years before had been "run" for President by the Western States, held another command of nearly equal independence in Missouri. He had been put over General Lyon in the western command, and directly after this General Lyon had fallen in battle at Springfield, in the first action in which the opposing armies were engaged in the West. General Fremont at once proceeded to carry matters with a very high hand. On the 30th of August, 1861, he issued a proclamation by which he declared martial law at St. Louis, the city at which he held his head quarters, and indeed throughout the State of Missouri generally. In this proclamation he declared his intention of exercising a severity beyond that ever threatened, as I believe, in modern warfare. He defines the region presumed to be held by his army of occupation, drawing his lines across the State, and then declares "that, all persons who shall be taken with arms in their hands within those lines shall be tried by Court Martial, and if found guilty will be shot." He then goes on to say that he will confiscate all the property of persons in the State who shall have taken up arms against the Union, or who shall have taken part with the enemies of the Union, and *that he will make free all slaves belonging to such persons.* This proclamation was not approved at Washington, and was modified by the order of the President. It was understood also that he issued orders for military expenditure, which were not recognized at Washington, and men began to understand that the army in the West was gradually assuming that irresponsible military position, which in disturbed countries and in times of civil war has so frequently resulted in a military dictatorship. Then there arose a clamour for the removal of General Fremont. A semi-official account of his proceedings, which had reached Washington from an officer under his command, was made public; and also the correspondence which took place on the subject between the President and General Fremont's wife. The officer in question was thereupon placed under arrest, but immediately released by orders from Washington. He then made official complaint of his General, sending forward a list of charges in which Fremont was accused of rashness, incompetency, want of fidelity to the interests of the Government, and disobedience to orders from head quarters. After a while the Secretary of War himself proceeded from Washington to the quarters of General Fremont at St. Louis, and remained there for a day or two, making or pretending to make inquiry into

the matter. But when he returned he left the General still in command. During the whole month of October the papers were occupied
in declaring in the morning that General Fremont had been recalled
from his command, and in the evening that he was to remain. In the
mean time they who befriended his cause, and this included the whole
West, were hoping from day to day that he would settle the matter for
himself and silence his accusers, by some great military success. General Price held the command opposed to him, and men said that Fremont would sweep General Price and his army down the valley of the
Mississippi into the sea. But General Price would not be so swept, and
it began to appear that a guerilla warfare would prevail; that General
Price, if driven southwards, would reappear behind the backs of his
pursuers, and that General Fremont would not accomplish all that
was expected of him with that rapidity for which his friends had given
him credit. So the newspapers still went on waging the war, and every
morning General Fremont was recalled, and every evening they who
had recalled him were shown up as having known nothing of the
matter.

"Never mind; he is a pioneer man, and will do a'most anything he
puts his hand too," his friends in the West still said. "He understands
the frontier." Understanding the frontier is a great thing in Western
America, across which the vanguard of civilization continues to march
on in advance from year to year. "And it's he that is bound to sweep
slavery from off the face of this Continent. He's the man, and he's
about the only man." I am not qualified to write the life of General
Fremont, and can at present only make this slight reference to the details of his romantic career. That it has been full of romance, and
that the man himself is indued with a singular energy and a high
romantic idea of what may be done by power and will, there is no
doubt. Five times he has crossed the continent of North America from
Missouri to Oregon and California, enduring great hardships in the
service of advancing civilization and knowledge. That he has considerable talent, immense energy, and strong self-confidence, I believe.
He is a frontier man; one of those who care nothing for danger, and
who would dare anything with the hope of accomplishing a great
career. But I have never heard that he has shown any practical knowledge of high military matters. It may be doubted whether a man of
this stamp is well fitted to hold the command of a nation's army for
great national purposes. May it not even be presumed that a man of
this class is of all men the least fitted for such a work? The officer required should be a man with two specialities—a speciality for military

tactics, and a speciality for national duty. The army in the West was far removed from head quarters in Washington, and it was peculiarly desirable that the General commanding it should be one possessing a strong idea of obedience to the control of his own Government. Those frontier capabilities, that self-dependent energy for which his friends gave Fremont,—and probably justly gave him,—such unlimited credit are exactly the qualities which are most dangerous in such a position.

I have endeavoured to explain the circumstances of the Western command in Missouri, as they existed at the time when I was in the North-Western States, in order that the double action of the North and West may be understood. I, of course, was not in the secret of any official persons, but I could not but feel sure that the Government in Washington would have been glad to have removed Fremont at once from the command, had they not feared that by doing so they would have created a schism, as it were, in their own camp, and have done much to break up the integrity or oneness of Northern loyalty. The western people almost to a man desired abolition. The States there were sending out their tens of thousands of young men into the army with a prodigality as to their only source of wealth which they hardly recognized themselves, because this to them was a fight against slavery. The western population has been increased to a wonderful degree by a German infusion;—so much so that the western towns appear to have been peopled with Germans. I found regiments of volunteers consisting wholly of Germans. And the Germans are all abolitionists. To all the men of the West the name of Fremont is dear. He is their hero, and their Hercules. He is to cleanse the stables of the southern king, and turn the waters of emancipation through the foul stalls of slavery. And, therefore, though the Cabinet in Washington would have been glad for many reasons to have removed Fremont in October last, it was at first scared from committing itself to so strong a measure. At last, however, the charges made against him were too fully substantiated to allow of their being set on one side, and early in November, 1861, he was superseded. I shall be obliged to allude again to General Fremont's career as I go on with my narrative.

At this time the North was looking for a victory on the Potomac; but they were no longer looking for it with that impatience which in the summer had led to the disgrace at Bull's Run. They had recognized the fact that their troops must be equipped, drilled, and instructed; and they had also recognized the perhaps greater fact, that their enemies were neither weak, cowardly, nor badly officered. I have always thought that the tone and manner with which the North bore the defeat at Bull's Run was creditable to it. It was never denied, never explained away, never set down as trifling. "We have been whipped!" was what all Northerners said,—"We've got an almighty whipping, and here we are." I have heard many Englishmen complain of this, saying that the matter was taken almost as a joke,—that no disgrace was felt, and the licking was owned by a people who ought never to have allowed that they had been licked. To all this, however, I demur. Their only chance of speedy success consisted in their seeing and recognizing the truth. Had they confessed the whipping and then sat down with their hands in their pockets,—had they done as second-rate boys at school will do, declare that they had been licked, and then feel that all the trouble is over,—they would indeed have been open to reproach. The old mother across the water would in such case have disowned her son. But they did the very reverse of this. "I have been whipped," Jonathan said, and he immediately went into training under a new system for another fight.

And so all through September and October the great armies on the Potomac rested comparatively in quiet, the Northern forces drawing to themselves immense levies. The general confidence in Maclellan was then very great, and the cautious measures by which he endeavoured to bring his vast untrained body of men under discipline were such as did at that time recommend themselves to most military critics. Early in September the northern party obtained a considerable advantage by taking the fort at Cape Hatteras, in North Carolina, situated on one of those long banks which lie along the shores of the Southern States; but towards the end of October they experienced a considerable reverse in an attack which was made on the Secessionists by General Stone, and in which Colonel Baker was killed. Colonel Baker had been senator for Oregon, and was well known as an orator. Taking all things together, however, nothing material had been done up to the end of October; and at that time northern men were waiting—not perhaps impatiently, considering the great hopes, and perhaps great fears which filled their hearts, but with eager expectation for some event of which they might talk with pride.

The man to whom they had trusted all their hopes was young for so great a command. I think that at this time (October 1861) General Maclellan was not yet thirty-five.[3] He had served early in life in the Mexican war, having come originally from Pennsylvania, and having been educated at the military college at West Point. During our war with Russia he was sent to the Crimea by his own Government in con-

[3] General George Brinton McClellan was born on December 3, 1826.

junction with two other officers of the United States army, that they might learn all that was to be learned there as to military tactics, and report especially as to the manner in which fortifications were made and attacked. I have been informed that a very able report was sent in by them to the Government, on their return, and that this was drawn up by Maclellan. But in America a man is not only a soldier or always a soldier; nor is he always a clergyman if once a clergyman. He takes a spell at anything suitable that may be going. And in this way Maclellan was for some years engaged on the Central Illinois Railway, and was for a considerable time the head manager of that concern. We all know with what suddenness he rose to the highest command in the army immediately after the defeat at Bull's Run.

I have endeavoured to describe what were the feelings of the West in the autumn of 1861 with regard to the war. The excitement and eagerness there were very great, and they were perhaps as great in the North. But in the North the matter seemed to me to be regarded from a different point of view. As a rule, the men of the North are not abolitionists. It is quite certain that they were not so before secession began. They hate slavery as we in England hate it; but they are aware, as also are we, that the disposition of four million of black men and women forms a question which cannot be solved by the chivalry of any modern Orlando. The property invested in these four million slaves forms the entire wealth of the South. If they could be wafted by a philanthropic breeze back to the shores of Africa,—a breeze of which the philanthropy would certainly not be appreciated by those so wafted,—the South would be a wilderness. The subject is one as full of difficulty as any with which politicians of these days are tormented. The Northerners fully appreciate this, and as a rule are not abolitionists in the western sense of the word. To them the war is recommended by precisely those feelings which animated us when we fought for our colonies,—when we strove to put down American independence. Secession is rebellion against the Government: and is all the more bitter to the North because that rebellion broke out at the first moment of northern ascendancy. "We submitted," the North says, "to southern Presidents, and southern statesmen, and southern councils, because we obeyed the vote of the people. But as to you—the voice of the people is nothing in your estimation! At the first moment in which the popular vote places at Washington a President with northern feelings, you rebel. We submitted in your days; and by heaven, you shall submit in ours! We submitted loyally; through love of the law and the Constitution. You have disregarded the law, and thrown over the Constitution. But you shall be made to submit, as a child is made to submit to its governor."

It must also be remembered that on commercial questions the North and the West are divided. The Morrill tariff is as odious to the West as it is to the South. The South and West are both agricultural productive regions, desirous of sending cotton and corn to foreign countries and of receiving back foreign manufactures on the best terms. But the North is a manufacturing country. A poor manufacturing country as regards excellence of manufacture—and therefore the more anxious to foster its own growth by protective laws. The Morrill tariff [4] is very injurious to the West, and is odious there. I might add that its folly has already been so far recognized even in the North, as to make it very generally odious there also.

So much I have said endeavouring to make it understood how far the North and West were united in feeling against the South in the autumn of 1861, and how far there existed between them a diversity of interests.

[4] This tariff, introduced by Justin S. Morrill of Vermont and passed in the last days of the Buchanan administration after Southern Democrats had withdrawn, was designed primarily to augment Federal revenue rather than to protect home industry. Though it caused a considerable increase over the low duties of 1857, it was not judged to be objectionably high in its levies even by low-tariff advocates.

CHAPTER IX

From Niagara to the Mississippi

From Niagara we went by the Canada Great Western Railway to Detroit, the big city of Michigan. It is an American institution that the States should have a commercial capital, or what I call their big city, as well as a political capital, which may as a rule be called the State's central city. The object in choosing the political capital is average nearness of approach from the various confines of the State; but commerce submits to no such Procrustean laws in selecting her capitals, and consequently she has placed Detroit on the borders of Michigan, on the shore of the neck of water which joins Lake Huron to Lake Erie through which all the trade must flow which comes down from Lakes Michigan, Superior, and Huron, on its way to the eastern States and to Europe. We had thought of going from Buffalo across Lake Erie to Detroit; but we found that the better class of steamers had been taken off the waters for the winter. And we also found that navigation among these lakes is a mistake whenever the necessary journey can be taken by railway. Their waters are by no means smooth; and then there is nothing to be seen. I do not know whether others may have a feeling, almost instinctive, that lake navigation must be pleasant,—that lakes must of necessity be beautiful. I have such a feeling; but not now so strongly as formerly. Such an idea should be kept for use in Europe, and never brought over to America with other travelling gear. The lakes in America are cold, cumbrous, uncouth, and uninteresting; intended by nature for the conveyance of cereal produce, but not for the comfort of travelling men and women. So we gave up our plan of traversing the lake, and passing back into Canada by the suspension bridge at Niagara, we reached the Detroit river at Windsor by the Great Western line, and passed thence by the ferry into the city of Detroit.

In making this journey at night we introduced ourselves to the thoroughly American institution of sleeping-cars;—that is, of cars in which beds are made up for travellers. The traveller may have a whole bed, or half a bed, or no bed at all as he pleases, paying a dollar or half a dollar extra should he choose the partial or full fruition of a couch. I confess I have always taken a delight in seeing these beds made up, and consider that the operations of the change are generally as well executed as the manœuvres of any pantomime at Drury Lane. The work is usually done by negroes or coloured men; and the domestic negroes of America are always light-handed and adroit. The nature of an American car is no doubt known to all men. It looks as far removed from all bedroom accommodation, as the baker's barrow does from the steam-engine into which it is to be converted by harlequin's wand. But the negro goes to work much more quietly than the harlequin, and for every four seats in the railway car he builds up four beds, almost as quickly as the hero of the pantomime goes through his performance. The great glory of the Americans is in their wondrous contrivances,—in their patent remedies for the usually troublous operations of life. In their huge hotels all the bell-ropes of each house ring on one bell only, but a patent indicator discloses a number, and the whereabouts of the ringer is shown. One fire heats every room, passage, hall, and cupboard,—and does it so effectually that the inhabitants are all but stifled. Soda-water bottles open themselves without any trouble of wire or strings. Men and women go up and down stairs without motive power of their own.[1] Hot and cold water are laid on to all the chambers;—though it sometimes happens that the water from both taps is boiling, and that when once turned on it cannot be turned off again by any human energy. Everything is done by a new and wonderful patent contrivance; and of all their wonderful contrivances that of their railroad beds is by no means the least.[2] For every four seats the

[1] Though the Otis elevator had been invented in 1852, it was still a novel device, installed in only a few hotels. An enthusiastic article on the Continental Hotel of Philadelphia in *Godey's Lady's Book* for May 1860 announces that this hotel is equipped with "a vertical railway, on a new and scientific plan," so that the most delicate lady, learning with some perturbation that her reservation is on the sixth floor, need only "sit in an easy-chair and be wafted to her room nearer the stars."

[2] Sleeping cars of one sort or another were in use in America as early as 1836. A fuller account of the type of car Trollope describes, with a double accommodation below and two single trays, one above the other, surmounting it, is given by an English traveler in *All the Year Round* for January 12, 1861:

"Now, as we are between Little Falls and Herkimer, the officer of the sleeping-cars enters and calls out, 'Now, then, misters, if you please, get up from your seats, and allow me to make up the beds!' Two by two we rise, and with neat trimness and quick hand the nimble Yankee turns over every other seat, so as to reverse the back, and make two seats, one facing the other. Nimbly he shuts the windows and pulls up the shutters, leaving for ventilation the slip of perforated zinc open at the top of each. Smartly he strips up the cushions, and unfastens from beneath each seat a light cane-bottomed frame there secreted. In a moment, opening certain ratchet-holes in the wall of the carriage, he has slided [*sic*] these in at a suitable height above, and covered each with cushions and sleeping-rugs. I go outside on the balcony to be out of the way, and when I come back the whole place is transformed—

V   The White Mountains—All Aboard

Harper's Weekly, III (*August* 13, 1859), 521

VI   Citadel of Quebec: "Nevertheless, and as a matter of course, I
went to see the rock, and can only say, as so many have said before me,
that it is very steep."

The Illustrated London News, XXXVII (August 4, 1860), 103

negro builds up four beds,—that is, four half-beds or accommodation
for four persons. Two are supposed to be below on the level of the
ordinary four seats, and two up above on shelves which are let down
from the roof. Mattresses slip out from one nook and pillows from another. Blankets are added, and the bed is ready. Any over particular
individual—an islander, for instance, who hugs his chains—will generally prefer to pay the dollar for the double accommodation. Looking
at the bed in the light of a bed,—taking as it were an abstract view of
it,—or comparing it with some other bed or beds with which the occu-
pant may have acquaintance, I cannot say that it is in all respects
perfect. But distances are long in America; and he who declines to
travel by night will lose very much time. He who does so travel will
find the railway bed a great relief. I must confess that the feeling of
dirt on the following morning is rather oppressive.

From Windsor on the Canada side we passed over to Detroit in the
State of Michigan by a steam ferry. But ferries in England and ferries
in America are very different. Here on this Detroit ferry, some hundred
of passengers who were going forward from the other side without delay, at once sat down to breakfast. I may as well explain the way in
which disposition is made of one's luggage as one takes these long
journeys. The traveller when he starts has his baggage checked. He
abandons his trunk—generally a box studded with nails, as long as a
coffin and as high as a linen chest,—and in return for this he receives an
iron ticket with a number on it. As he approaches the end of his first
instalment of travel, and while the engine is still working its hardest,
a man comes up to him, bearing with him suspended on a circular bar
an infinite variety of other checks. The traveller confides to this man
his wishes; and if he be going further without delay, surrenders his
checks and receives a counter-check in return. Then while the train is
still in motion, the new destiny of the trunk is imparted to it. But
another man, with another set of checks, also comes the way, walking

---

no longer an aisle of double seats, like a section of a proprietary chapel put on
wheels, but the cabin of a small steamer, snug for sleeping, with curtained berths
and closed portholes. . . .

"The bottom berths are singularly comfortable. There is room to wander and
explore, to roll and turn, and the curtains hush all sound, and keep off all inquisi-
tive rays from Zena's and Ezra's [the conductors'] portable lamps. . . .

"Now I mount my berth. . . . There are two berths to choose from; both
wicker trays, lodged in, cushioned, and rugged; one about half a foot higher than
the other [sic!]. I choose the top one, as being nearer the zinc ventilator."

By 1861 G. M. Pullman already had three remodeled coaches in service on the
Chicago & Alton line, and the first car fully of his own designing was put on the
rails three years later.

leisurely through the train as he performs his work. This is the minister of the hotel-omnibus institution. His business is with those who do not travel beyond the next terminus. To him, if such be your intention, you make your confidence, giving up your tallies and taking other tallies, by way of receipt; and your luggage is afterwards found by you in the hall of your hotel. There is undoubtedly very much of comfort in this; and the mind of the traveller is lost in amazement as he thinks of the futile efforts with which he would struggle to regain his luggage were there no such arrangement. Enormous piles of boxes are disclosed on the platform at all the larger stations, the numbers of which are roared forth with quick voice by some two or three railway denizens at once. A modest English voyager with six or seven small packages, would stand no chance of getting anything if he were left to his own devices. As it is I am bound to say that the thing is well done. I have had my desk with all my money in it lost for a day, and my black leather bag was on one occasion sent back over the line. They, however, were recovered; and on the whole I feel grateful to the check system of the American railways. And then, too, one never hears of extra luggage. Of weight they are quite regardless. On two or three occasions an overwrought official has muttered between his teeth that ten packages were a great many, and that some of those "light fixings" might have been made up into one. And when I came to understand that the number of every check was entered in a book, and re-entered at every change, I did whisper to my wife that she ought to do without a bonnet-box. The ten, however, went on, and were always duly protected. I must add, however, that articles requiring tender treatment will sometimes reappear a little the worse from the hardships of their journey.

I have not much to say of Detroit; not much, that is, beyond what I have to say of all the North. It is a large well-built half-finished city, lying on a convenient water way, and spreading itself out with promises of a wide and still wider prosperity. It has about it perhaps as little of intrinsic interest as any of those large western towns which I visited. It is not so pleasant as Milwaukee, nor so picturesque as St. Paul, nor so grand as Chicago, nor so civilized as Cleveland, nor so busy as Buffalo. Indeed Detroit is neither pleasant nor picturesque at all. I will not say that it is uncivilized, but it has a harsh, crude, unprepossessing appearance. It has some 70,000 inhabitants, and good accommodation for shipping. It was doing an enormous business before the war began, and when these troublous times are over will no doubt again go ahead. I do not, however, think it well to recommend any

Englishman to make a special visit to Detroit, who may be wholly un-commercial in his views and travel in search of that which is either beautiful or interesting.

From Detroit we continued our course westward across the State of Michigan through a country that was absolutely wild till the rail-way pierced it. Very much of it is still absolutely wild. For miles upon miles the road passes the untouched forest, showing that even in Michigan the great work of civilization has hardly more than been commenced. As one thinks of the all but countless population which is before long to be fed from these regions, of the cities which will grow here, and of the amount of government which in due time will be required, one can hardly fail to feel that the division of the United States into separate nationalities is merely a part of the ordained work of creation, as arranged for the well-being of mankind. The States already boast of thirty millions of inhabitants,—not of unnoticed and unnoticeable beings, requiring little, knowing little, and doing little, such as are the Eastern hordes which may be counted by tens of mil-lions; but of men and women who talk loudly and are ambitious, who eat beef, who read and write, and understand the dignity of manhood. But these thirty millions are as nothing to the crowds which will grow sleek and talk loudly, and become aggressive on these wheat and meat producing levels. The country is as yet but touched by the pioneering hand of population. In the old countries agriculture, following on the heels of pastoral patriarchal life, preceded the birth of cities. But in this young world the cities have come first. The new Jasons, blessed with the experience of the old world adventurers, have gone forth in search of their golden fleeces armed with all that the science and skill of the East had as yet produced, and in settling up their new Colchis have begun by the erection of first-class hotels and the fabrication of railroads. Let the old world bid them God speed in their work. Only it would be well if they could be brought to acknowledge from whence they have learned all that they know.

Our route lay right across the State to a place called Grand Haven on Lake Michigan, from whence we were to take boat for Milwaukee, a town in Wisconsin on the opposite or western shore of the lake. Michigan is sometimes called the Peninsular State from the fact that the main part of its territory is surrounded by Lakes Michigan and Huron, by the little Lake St. Clair, and by Lake Erie. It juts out to the northward from the main land of Indiana and Ohio, and is circum-navigable on the east, north, and west. These particulars refer, how-ever, to a part of the State only, for a portion of it lies on the other side of Lake Michigan, between that and Lake Superior. I doubt whether any large inland territory in the world is blessed with such facilities of water carriage.

On arriving at Grand Haven we found that there had been a storm on the lake, and that the passengers from the trains of the preceding day were still remaining there, waiting to be carried over to Milwaukee. The water, however,—or the sea as they all call it,—was still very high, and the captain declared his intention of remaining there that night. Whereupon all our fellow-travellers huddled themselves into the great lake steam-boat, and proceeded to carry on life there as though they were quite at home. The men took themselves to the bar-room and smoked cigars and talked about the war with their feet upon the counter, and the women got themselves into rocking-chairs in the saloon and sat there listless and silent, but not more listless and silent than they usually are in the big drawing-rooms of the big hotels. There was supper there, precisely at six o'clock, beefsteaks, and tea, and apple jam, and hot cakes, and light fixings, to all which luxuries an American deems himself entitled, let him have to seek his meal where he may. And I was soon informed with considerable energy, that let the boat be kept there as long as it might by stress of weather, the beefsteaks and apple jam, light fixings and heavy fixings, must be supplied at the cost of the owners of the ship. "Your first supper you pay for," my informant told me, "because you eat that on your own account. What you consume after that comes of their doing, because they don't start; and if it's three meals a day for a week, it's their look out." It occurred to me that under such circumstances a captain would be very apt to sail either in foul weather or in fair.

It was a bright moonlight night, moonlight such as we rarely have in England, and I started off by myself for a walk, that I might see of what nature were the environs of Grand Haven. A more melancholy place I never beheld. The town of Grand Haven itself is placed on the opposite side of a creek, and was to be reached by a ferry. On our side, to which the railway came and from which the boat was to sail, there was nothing to be seen but sandhills which stretched away for miles along the shore of the lake. There were great sand mountains, and sand valleys, on the surface of which were scattered the debris of dead trees, scattered logs white with age, and boughs half buried beneath the sand. Grand Haven itself is but a poor place, not having succeeded in catching much of the commerce which comes across the lake from Wisconsin, and which takes itself on eastwards by the railway. Altogether it is a dreary place, such as might break a man's heart, should he find that inexorable fate required him there to pitch his tent.

On my return I went down into the bar-room of the steamer, put my feet upon the counter, lit my cigar, and struck into the debate then proceeding on the subject of the war. I was getting West, and General Fremont was the hero of the hour. "He's a frontier man, and that's what we want. I guess he'll about go through. Yes, sir." "As for reliev-ing General Fre-mont,"—with the accent always strongly on the "mont,"—"I guess you may as well talk of relieving the whole West. They won't meddle with Fre-mont. They are beginning to know in Washington what stuff he's made of." "Why, sir; there are 50,000 men in these States who will follow Fre-mont, who would not stir a foot after any other man." From which, and the like of it in many other places, I began to understand how difficult was the task which the statesmen in Washington had in hand.

I received no pecuniary advantage whatever from that law as to the steam-boat meals which my new friend had revealed to me. For my one supper of course I paid, looking forward to any amount of subsequent gratuitous provisions. But in the course of the night the ship sailed, and we found ourselves at Milwaukee in time for break-fast on the following morning.

Milwaukee is a pleasant town, a very pleasant town, containing 45,000 inhabitants. How many of my readers can boast that they know anything of Milwaukee, or even have heard of it? To me its name was unknown until I saw it on huge railway placards stuck up in the smoking-rooms and lounging halls of all American hotels. It is the big town of Wisconsin, whereas Madison is the capital. It stands imme-diately on the western shore of Lake Michigan, and is very pleasant. Why it should be so, and why Detroit should be the contrary, I can hardly tell; only I think that the same verdict would be given by any English tourist. It must be always borne in mind that 10,000 or 40,000 inhabitants in an American town, and especially in any new western town, is a number which means much more than would be implied by any similar number as to an old town in Europe. Such a population in America consumes double the amount of beef which it would in England, wears double the amount of clothes, and demands double as much of the comforts of life. If a census could be taken of the watches it would be found, I take it, that the American population possessed among them nearly double as many as would the English; and I fear also that it would be found that many more of the Ameri cans were readers and writers by habit. In any large town in England

it is probable that a higher excellence of education would be found
than in Milwaukee, and also a style of life into which more of refine-
ment and more of luxury had found its way. But the general level of
these things, of material and intellectual well being—of beef, that is,
and book learning—is no doubt infinitely higher in a new American
than in an old European town. Such an animal as a beggar is as much
unknown as a mastodon. Men out of work and in want are almost
unknown. I do not say that there are none of the hardships of life,—
and to them I will come by-and-by; but want is not known as a hardship in these towns, nor is that dense ignorance in which so large a
proportion of our town populations is still steeped. And then the town
of 40,000 inhabitants is spread over a surface which would suffice in
England for a city of four times the size. Our towns in England,—and
the towns, indeed, of Europe generally,—have been built as they have
been wanted. No aspiring ambition as to hundreds of thousands of
people warmed the bosoms of their first founders. Two or three
dozen men required habitations in the same locality, and clustered
them together closely. Many such have failed and died out of the
world's notice. Others have thriven, and houses have been packed on
to houses till London and Manchester, Dublin and Glasgow have been
produced. Poor men have built, or have had built for them, wretched
lanes; and rich men have erected grand palaces. From the nature of
their beginnings such has, of necessity, been the manner of their creation. But in America, and especially in Western America, there has
been no such necessity and there is no such result. The founders of
cities have had the experience of the world before them. They have
known of sanitary laws as they began. That sewerage, and water, and
gas, and good air would be needed for a thriving community has been
to them as much a matter of fact as are the well understood combina-
tions between timber and nails, and bricks and mortar. They have
known that water carriage is almost a necessity for commercial success, and have chosen their sites accordingly. Broad streets cost as little,
while land by the foot is not as yet of value to be regarded, as those
which are narrow; and therefore the sites of towns have been prepared
with noble avenues, and imposing streets. A city at its commencement
is laid out with an intention that it shall be populous. The houses
are not all built at once, but there are the places allocated for them.
The streets are not made, but there are the spaces. Many an abortive
attempt at municipal greatness has so been made and then all but
abandoned. There are wretched villages with huge straggling parallel
ways which will never grow into towns. They are the failures,—failures

in which the pioneers of civilization, frontier men as they call themselves, have lost their tens of thousands of dollars. But when the success comes; when the happy hit has been made, and the ways of commerce have been truly foreseen with a cunning eye, then a great and
prosperous city springs up, ready made, as it were, from the earth.
Such a town is Milwaukee, now containing 45,000 inhabitants, but
with room apparently for double that number; with room for four
times that number, were men packed as closely there as they are
with us.

In the principal business streets of all these towns one sees vast
buildings. They are usually called blocks, and are often so denominated in large letters on their front, as Portland Block, Devereux
Block, Buel's Block. Such a block may face to two, three, or even four
streets, and, as I presume, has generally been a matter of one special
speculation. It may be divided into separate houses, or kept for a
single purpose, such as that of an hotel, or grouped into shops below,
and into various sets of chambers above. I have had occasion in various
towns to mount the stairs within these blocks, and have generally
found some portion of them vacant;—have sometimes found the greater
portion of them vacant. Men build on an enormous scale, three times,
ten times as much as is wanted. The only measure of size is an increase
on what men have built before. Monroe P. Jones, the speculator, is
very probably ruined, and then begins the world again, nothing
daunted. But Jones's block remains, and gives to the city in its aggregate a certain amount of wealth. Or the block becomes at once of
service and finds tenants. In which case Jones probably sells it and
immediately builds two others twice as big. That Monroe P. Jones will
encounter ruin is almost a matter of course; but then he is none the
worse for being ruined. It hardly makes him unhappy. He is greedy
of dollars with a terrible covetousness; but he is greedy in order that
he may speculate more widely. He would sooner have built Jones's
tenth block, with a prospect of completing a twentieth, than settle
himself down at rest for life as the owner of a Chatsworth or a Woburn.
As for his children he has no desire of leaving them money. Let the
girls marry. And for the boys,—for them it will be good to begin as he
began. If they cannot build blocks for themselves, let them earn their
bread in the blocks of other men. So Monroe P. Jones, with his million
of dollars accomplished, advances on to a new frontier, goes to work
again on a new city, and loses it all. As an individual I differ very
much from Monroe P. Jones. The first block accomplished, with an
adequate rent accruing to me as the builder, I fancy that I should

never try a second. But Jones is undoubtdly the man for the West. It is that love of money to come, joined to a strong disregard for money made, which constitutes the vigorous frontier mind, the true pioneering organization. Monroe P. Jones would be a great man to all posterity, if only he had a poet to sing of his valour.

It may be imagined how large in proportion to its inhabitants will be a town which spreads itself in this way. There are great houses left untenanted, and great gaps left unfilled. But if the place be successful,—if it promise success, it will be seen at once that there is life all through it. Omnibuses, or street cars working on rails run hither and thither. The shops that have been opened are well filled. The great hotels are thronged. The quays are crowded with vessels, and a general feeling of progress pervades the place. It is easy to perceive whether or no an American town is going ahead. The days of my visit to Milwaukee were days of civil war and national trouble, but in spite of civil war and national trouble Milwaukee looked healthy.

I have said that there was but little poverty,—little to be seen of real want in these thriving towns, but that they who laboured in them had nevertheless their own hardships. This is so. I would not have any man believe that he can take himself to the western States of America, —to those States of which I am now speaking,—Michigan, Wisconsin, Minnesota, Iowa, or Illinois, and there by industry escape the ills to which flesh is heir. The labouring Irish in these towns eat meat seven days a week, but I have met many a labouring Irishman among them who has wished himself back in his old cabin. Industry is a good thing, and there is no bread so sweet as that which is eaten in the sweat of a man's brow; but labour carried to excess wearies the mind as well as body, and the sweat that is ever running makes the bread bitter. There is, I think, no task-master over free labour so exacting as an American. He knows nothing of hours, and seems to have that idea of a man which a lady always has of a horse. He thinks that he will go for ever. I wish those masons in London who strike for nine hours' work with ten hours' pay could be driven to the labour market of Western America for a spell. And moreover, which astonished me, I have seen men driven and hurried,—as it were forced forward at their work, in a manner which to an English workman would be intolerable. This surprised me much, as it was at variance with our,—or perhaps I should say with my,—preconceived ideas as to American freedom. I had fancied that an American citizen would not submit to be driven; —that the spirit of the country if not the spirit of the individual would have made it impossible. I thought that the shoe would have pinched quite on the other foot. But I found that such driving did exist; and American masters in the West with whom I had an opportunity of discussing the subject all admitted it. "Those men 'll never half move unless they're driven," a foreman said to me once as we stood together over some twenty men who were at their work. "They kinder look for it, and don't well know how to get along when they miss it." It was not his business at this moment to drive;—nor was he driving. He was standing at some little distance from the scene with me, and speculating on the sight before him. I thought the men were working at their best; but their movements did not satisfy his practised eye, and he saw at a glance that there was no one immediately over them.

But there is worse even than this. Wages in these regions are what we should call high. An agricultural labourer will earn perhaps fifteen dollars a month and his board; and a town labourer will earn a dollar a day. A dollar may be taken as representing four shillings, though it is in fact more. Food in these parts is much cheaper than in England, and therefore the wages must be considered as very good. In making, however, a just calculation it must be borne in mind that clothing is dearer than in England and that much more of it is necessary. The wages nevertheless are high, and will enable the labourer to save money,—if only he can get them paid. The complaint that wages are held back and not even ultimately paid is very common. There is no fixed rule for satisfying all such claims once a week; and thus debts to labourers are contracted and when contracted are ignored. With us there is a feeling that it is pitiful, mean almost beyond expression, to wrong a labourer of his hire. We have men who go in debt to tradesmen perhaps without a thought of paying them;—but when we speak of such a one who has descended into the lowest mire of insolvency, we say that he has not paid his washerwoman. Out there in the West the washerwoman is as fair game as the tailor, the domestic servant as the wine merchant. If a man be honest he will not willingly take either goods or labour without payment; and it may be hard to prove that he who takes the latter is more dishonest than he who takes the former; but with us there is a prejudice in favour of one's washerwoman by which the western mind is not weakened. "They certainly have to be smart to get it," a gentleman said to me whom I taxed on the subject. "You see on the frontier a man is bound to be smart. If he ain't smart he'd better go back East;—perhaps as far as Europe. He'll do there." I had got my answer, and my friend had turned the question. But the fact was admitted by him as it had been by many others.

Why this should be so, is a question, to answer which thoroughly would require a volume in itself. As to the driving, why should men submit to it, seeing that labour is abundant, and that in all newly settled countries the labourer is the true hero of the age? In answer to this is to be alleged the fact that hired labour is chiefly done by fresh comers, by Irish and Germans, who have not as yet among them any combination sufficient to protect them from such usage. The men over them are new as masters,—masters who are rough themselves, who themselves have been roughly driven, and who have not learned to be gracious to those below them. It is a part of their contract that very hard work shall be exacted; and the driving resolves itself into this,—that the master looking after his own interest is constantly accusing his labourer of a breach of his part of the contract. The men no doubt do become used to it, and slacken probably in their endeavours when the tongue of the master or foreman is not heard. But as to that matter of non-payment of wages, the men must live; and here as elsewhere the master who omits to pay once, will hardly find labourers in future. The matter would remedy itself elsewhere, and does it not do so here? This of course is so, and it is not to be understood that labour as a rule is defrauded of its hire. But the relation of the master and the man admits of such fraud here much more frequently than in England. In England the labourer who did not get his wages on the Saturday could not go on for the next week. To him under such circumstances the world would be coming to an end. But in the Western States, the labourer does not live so completely from hand to mouth. He is rarely paid by the week, is accustomed to give some credit, and till hard pressed by bad circumstances generally has something by him. They do save money, and are thus fattened up to a state which admits of victimization. I cannot owe money to the little village cobbler who mends my shoes, because he demands and receives his payment when his job is done. But to my friend in Regent Street I extend my custom on a different system; and when I make my start for continental life, I have with him a matter of unsettled business to a considerable extent. The American labourer is in the condition of the Regent Street boot-maker;—excepting in this respect, that he gives his credit under com-pulsion. "But does not the law set him right? Is there no law against debtors?" The laws against debtors are plain enough as they are writ-ten down, but seem to be anything but plain when called into action. They are perfectly understood, and operations are carried on with the express purpose of evading them. If you proceed against a man, you find that his property is in the hands of some one else. You work in

fact for Jones who lives in the next street to you; but when you quarrel
with Jones about your wages, you find that according to law you have
been working for Smith in another State. In all countries such dodges
are probably practicable. But men will or will not have recourse to
such dodges according to the light in which they are regarded by the
community. In the Western States such dodges do not appear to be
regarded as disgraceful. "It behoves a frontier man to be smart, sir."

Honesty is the best policy. That is a doctrine which has been widely
preached, and which has recommended itself to many minds as being
one of absolute truth. It is not very ennobling in its sentiment, seeing
that it advocates a special virtue, not on the ground that that virtue
is in itself a thing beautiful, but on account of the immediate reward
which will be its consequence. Smith is enjoined not to cheat Jones,
because he will, in the long run, make more money by dealing with
Jones on the square. This is not teaching of the highest order; but it
is teaching well adapted to human circumstances, and has obtained
for itself a wide credit. One is driven, however, to doubt whether even
this teaching is not too high for the frontier man. Is it possible that
a frontier man should be scrupulous and at the same time successful?
Hitherto those who have allowed scruples to stand in their way have
not succeeded; and they who have succeeded and made for themselves
great names,—who have been the pioneers of civilization,—have not
allowed ideas of exact honesty to stand in their way. From General
Jason down to General Fremont there have been men of great aspirations but of slight scruples. They have been ambitious of power and
desirous of progress, but somewhat regardless how power and progress
shall be attained. Clive and Warren Hastings were great frontier men,
but we cannot imagine that they had ever realized the doctrine that
honesty is the best policy. Cortez, and even Columbus, the prince of
frontier men, are in the same category. The names of such heroes is
legion. But with none of them has absolute honesty been a favourite
virtue. "It behoves a frontier man to be smart, sir." Such, in that or
other language, has been the prevailing idea. Such is the prevailing
idea. And one feels driven to ask oneself whether such must not be
the prevailing idea with those who leave the world and its rules behind
them, and go forth with the resolve that the world and its rules shall
follow them.

Of filibustering, annexation, and polishing savages off the face of
creation there has been a great deal, and who can deny that humanity
has been the gainer? It seems to those who look widely back over
history, that all such works have been carried on in obedience to God's

laws. When Jacob by Rebecca's aid cheated his elder brother he was very smart; but we cannot but suppose that a better race was by this smartness put in possession of the patriarchal sceptre. Esau was polished off, and readers of Scripture wonder why heaven with its thunder did not open over the heads of Rebecca and her son. But Jacob with all his fraud was the chosen one. Perhaps the day may come when scrupulous honesty may be the best policy even on the frontier. I can only say that hitherto that day seems to be as distant as ever. I do not pretend to solve the problem, but simply record my opinion that under circumstances as they still exist I should not willingly select a frontier life for my children.

I have said that all great frontier men have been unscrupulous. There is, however, an exception in history which may perhaps serve to prove the rule. The Puritans who colonized New England were frontier men, and were, I think, in general scrupulously honest. They had their faults. They were stern, austere men, tyrannical at the backbone when power came in their way,—as are all pioneers;—hard upon vices for which they who made the laws had themselves no minds; but they were not dishonest.

At Milwaukee I went up to see the Wisconsin volunteers, who were then encamped on open ground in the close vicinity of the town. Of Wisconsin I had heard before,—and have heard the same opinion repeated since,—that it was more backward in its volunteering than its neighbour States in the West. Wisconsin has 760,000 inhabitants, and its tenth thousand of volunteers was not then made up; whereas Indiana with less than double its number had already sent out thirty-six thousand. Iowa, with a hundred thousand less of inhabitants, had then made up fifteen thousand. But nevertheless to me it seemed that Wisconsin was quite alive to its presumed duty in that respect. Wisconsin with its three quarters of a million of people is as large as England. Every acre of it may be made productive, but as yet it is not half cleared. Of such a country its young men are its heart's blood. Ten thousand men fit to bear arms carried away from such a land to the horrors of civil war is a sight as full of sadness as any on which the eye can rest. Ah me, when will they return, and with what altered hopes! It is, I fear, easier to turn the sickle into the sword, than to recast the sword back again into the sickle!

We found a completed regiment at Wisconsin consisting entirely of Germans. A thousand Germans had been collected in that State and brought together in one regiment, and I was informed by an officer on the ground that there are many Germans in sundry other of the Wisconsin regiments. It may be well to mention here that the number of Germans through all these western States is very great. Their number and well-being were to me astonishing. That they form a great portion of the population of New York, making the German quarter of that city the third largest German town in the world, I have long known; but I had no previous idea of their expansion westward. In Detroit nearly every third shop bore a German name, and the same remark was to be made at Milwaukee;—and on all hands I heard praises of their morals, of their thrift, and of their new patriotism. I was continually told how far they exceeded the Irish settlers. To me in all parts of the world an Irishman is dear. When handled tenderly he becomes a creature most loveable. But with all my judgment in the Irishman's favour, and with my prejudices leaning the same way, I feel myself bound to state what I heard and what I saw as to the Germans.

But this regiment of Germans, and another not completed regiment, called from the State generally, were as yet without arms, accoutrements, or clothing. There was the raw material of the regiment, but there was nothing else. Winter was coming on,—winter in which the mercury is commonly 20 degrees below zero,—and the men were in tents with no provision against the cold. These tents held each two men, and were just large enough for two to lie. The canvas of which they were made seemed to me to be thin, but was I think always double. At this camp there was a house in which the men took their meals, but I visited other camps in which there was no such accommodation. I saw the German regiment called to its supper by tuck of drum, and the men marched in gallantly, armed each with a knife and spoon. I managed to make my way in at the door after them, and can testify to the excellence of the provisions of which their supper consisted. A poor diet never enters into any combination of circumstances contemplated by an American. Let him be where he will, animal food is, with him, the first necessary of life, and he is always provided accordingly. As to those Wisconsin men whom I saw, it was probable that they might be marched off, down south to Washington, or to the doubtful glories of the western campaign under Fremont before the winter commenced. The same might have been said of any special regiment. But taking the whole mass of men who were collected under canvas at the end of the autumn of 1861, and who were so collected without arms or military clothing, and without protection from the weather, it did seem that the task taken in hand by the Commissariat of the Northern army was one not devoid of difficulty.

The view from Milwaukee over Lake Michigan is very pleasing. One looks upon a vast expanse of water to which the eye finds no bounds, and therefore there are none of the common attributes of lake beauty; but the colour of the lake is bright, and within a walk of the city the traveller comes to the bluffs or low round-topped hills from which he can look down upon the shores. These bluffs form the beauty of Wisconsin and Minnesota, and relieve the eye after the flat level of Michigan. Round Detroit there is no rising ground, and therefore, perhaps, it is that Detroit is uninteresting.

I have said that those who are called on to labour in these States have their own hardships, and I have endeavoured to explain what are the sufferings to which the town labourer is subject. To escape from this is the labourer's great ambition, and his mode of doing so consists almost universally in the purchase of land. He saves up money in order that he may buy a section of an allotment, and thus become his own master. All his savings are made with a view to this independence. Seated on his own land he will have to work probably harder than ever, but he will work for himself. No taskmaster can then stand over him and wound his pride with harsh words. He will be his own master; will eat the food which he himself has grown, and live in the cabin which his own hands have built. This is the object of his life; and to secure this position he is content to work late and early and to undergo the indignities of previous servitude. The Government price for land is about five shillings an acre—one dollar and a quarter—and the settler may get it for this price if he be contented to take it not only untouched as regards clearing, but also far removed from any completed road. The traffic in these lands has been the great speculating business of western men. Five or six years ago, when the rage for such purchases was at its height, land was becoming a scarce article in the market! Individuals or companies bought it up with the object of reselling it at a profit; and many no doubt did make money. Railway companies were, in fact, companies combined for the purchase of land. They purchased land, looking to increase the value of it fivefold by the opening of a railroad. It may easily be understood that a railway, which could not be in itself remunerative, might in this way become a lucrative speculation. No settler could dare to place himself absolutely at a distance from any thoroughfare. At first the margins of nature's highways, the navigable rivers and lakes, were cleared. But as the railway system grew and expanded itself, it became manifest that lands might be rendered quickly available which were not so circumstanced by nature. A company which had purchased an enormous territory from the United States Government at five shillings an acre might well repay itself all the cost of a railway through that territory, even though the receipts of the railway should do no more than maintain the current expenses. It is in this way that the thousands of miles of American railroads have been opened; and here again must be seen the immense advantages which the States as a new country have enjoyed. With us the purchase of valuable land for railways, together with the legal expenses which those compulsory purchases entailed, have been so great that with all our traffic railways are not remunerative. But in the States the railways have created the value of the land. The States have been able to begin at the right end, and to arrange that the districts which are benefited shall themselves pay for the benefit they receive.

The Government price of land is 125 cents, or about five shillings an acre; and even this need not be paid at once if the settler purchase directly from the Government.[3] He must begin by making certain improvements on the selected land,—clearing and cultivating some small portion, building a hut, and probably sinking a well. When this has been done,—when he has thus given a pledge of his intentions by depositing on the land the value of a certain amount of labour, he cannot be removed. He cannot be removed for a term of years, and then if he pays the price of the land it becomes his own with an indefeasible title. Many such settlements are made on the purchase of warrants for land. Soldiers returning from the Mexican wars were donated with warrants for land,—the amount being 160 acres, or the quarter of a section. The localities of such lands were not specified, but the privilege granted was that of occupying any quarter-section not hitherto tenanted. It will of course be understood that land favourably situated would be tenanted. Those contiguous to railways were of course so occupied, seeing that the lines were not made till the lands were in the hands of the companies. It may therefore be understood of what nature would be the traffic in these warrants. The owner of a single warrant might find it of no value to him. To go back utterly into the woods, away from river or road, and there to commence with 160 acres of forest, or even of prairie, would be a hopeless task even to an American settler. Some mode of transport for his produce must be found before his produce would be of value,—before indeed he could find the means of living. But a company buying up a large aggregate

3 The Homestead Act, giving a quarter section of land to any settler who held actual residence for five years, was not passed until May 20, 1862; but the government had been increasingly generous in fixing its price on Western lands.

of such warrants would possess the means of making such allotments valuable and of reselling them at greatly increased prices.

The primary settler, therefore,—who, however, will not usually have been the primary owner,—goes to work upon his land amidst all the wildness of nature. He levels and burns the first trees, and raises his first crop of corn amidst stumps still standing four or five feet above the soil; but he does not do so till some mode of conveyance has been found for him. So much I have said hoping to explain the mode in which the frontier speculator paves the way for the frontier agriculturist. But the permanent farmer very generally comes on the land as the third owner. The first settler is a rough fellow, and seems to be so wedded to his rough life that he leaves his land after his first wild work is done, and goes again further off to some untouched allotment. He finds that he can sell his improvements at a profitable rate and takes the price. He is a preparer of farms rather than a farmer. He has no love for the soil which his hand has first turned. He regards it merely as an investment; and when things about him are beginning to wear an aspect of comfort,—when his property has become valuable, he sells it, packs up his wife and little ones, and goes again into the woods. The western American has no love for his own soil, or his own house. The matter with him is simply one of dollars. To keep a farm which he could sell at an advantage from any feeling of affection,—from what we should call an association of ideas,—would be to him as ridiculous as the keeping of a family pig would be in an English farmer's establishment. The pig is a part of the farmer's stock in trade, and must go the way of all pigs. And so is it with house and land in the life of the frontier man in the western States.

But yet this man has his romance, his high poetic feeling, and above all his manly dignity. Visit him, and you will find him without coat or waistcoat, unshorn, in ragged blue trousers and old flannel shirt, too often bearing on his lantern jaws the signs of ague and sickness; but he will stand upright before you and speak to you with all the ease of a lettered gentleman in his own library. All the odious incivility of the republican servant has been banished. He is his own master, standing on his own threshold, and finds no need to assert his equality by rudeness. He is delighted to see you, and bids you sit down on his battered bench without dreaming of any such apology as an English cottier offers to a Lady Bountiful when she calls. He has worked out his independence, and shows it in every easy movement of his body. He tells you of it unconsciously in every tone of his voice. You will always find in his cabin some newspaper, some book, some token of advance in education. When he questions you about the old country he astonishes you by the extent of his knowledge. I defy you not to feel that he is superior to the race from whence he has sprung in England or in Ireland. To me I confess that the manliness of such a man is very charming. He is dirty and perhaps squalid. His children are sick and he is without comforts. His wife is pale, and you think you see shortness of life written in the faces of all the family. But over and above it all there is an independence which sits gracefully on their shoulders, and teaches you at the first glance that the man has a right to assume himself to be your equal. It is for this position that the labourer works, bearing hard words and the indignity of tyranny,—suffering also too often the dishonest ill-usage which his superior power enables the master to inflict.

"I have lived very rough," I heard a poor woman say, whose husband had ill-used and deserted her. "I have known what it is to be hungry and cold, and to work hard till my bones have ached. I only wish that I might have the same chance again. If I could have ten acres cleared two miles away from any living being, I could be happy with my children. I find a kind of comfort when I am at work from daybreak to sundown, and know that it is all my own." I believe that life in the backwoods has an allurement to those who have been used to it, that dwellers in cities can hardly comprehend.

From Milwaukee we went across Wisconsin and reached the Mississippi at La Crosse. From hence, according to agreement, we were to start by steamer at once up the river. But we were delayed again, as had happened to us before on Lake Michigan at Grand Haven.

CHAPTER X

THE UPPER MISSISSIPPI

IT had been promised to us that we should start from La Crosse by the river steamer immediately on our arrival there; but on reaching La Crosse we found that the vessel destined to take us up the river had not yet come down. She was bringing a regiment from Minnesota, and under such circumstances some pardon might be extended to irregularities. This plea was made by one of the boat clerks in a very humble tone, and was fully accepted by us. The wonder was that at such a period all means of public conveyance were not put absolutely out of gear. One might surmise that when regiments were constantly being moved for the purposes of civil war, when the whole North had but the one object of collecting together a sufficient number of men to crush the South, ordinary travelling for ordinary purposes would be difficult, slow, and subject to sudden stoppages. Such, however, was not the case either in the northern or western States. The trains ran much as usual, and those connected with the boats and railways were just as anxious as ever to secure passengers. The boat clerk at La Crosse apologised amply for the delay, and we sat ourselves down with patience to await the arrival of the second Minnesota regiment on its way to Washington.

During the four hours that we were kept waiting we were harboured on board a small steamer, and at about eleven the terribly harsh whistle that is made by the Mississippi boats informed us that the regiment was arriving. It came up to the quay in two steamers, 750 being brought in that which was to take us back, and 250 in a smaller one. The moon was very bright, and great flaming torches were lit on the vessel's side, so that all the operations of the men were visible. The two steamers had run close up, thrusting us away from the quay in their passage, but doing it so gently that we did not even feel the motion. These large boats—and their size may be understood from the fact that one of them had just brought down 750 men,—are moved so easily and so gently that they come gliding in among each other without hesitation and without pause. On English waters we do not willingly run ships against each other; and when we do so unwillingly, they bump and crush and crash upon each other, and timbers fly while men are swearing. But here there was neither crashing nor swearing, and the boats noiselessly pressed against each other as though they were cased in muslin and crinoline.

I got out upon the quay and stood close by the plank, watching each man as he left the vessel and walked across towards the railway. Those whom I had previously seen in tents were not equipped, but these men were in uniform and each bore his musket. Taking them all together they were as fine a set of men as I ever saw collected. No man could doubt on seeing them that they bore on their countenances the signs of higher breeding and better education than would be seen in a thousand men enlisted in England. I do not mean to argue from this that Americans are better than English. I do not mean to argue here that they are even better educated. My assertion goes to show that the men generally were taken from a higher level in the community than that which fills our own ranks. It was a matter of regret to me, here and on many subsequent occasions, to see men bound for three years to serve as common soldiers, who were so manifestly fitted for a better and more useful life. To me it is always a source of sorrow to see a man enlisted. I feel that the individual recruit is doing badly with himself —carrying himself and the strength and intelligence which belongs to him to a bad market. I know that there must be soldiers; but as to every separate soldier I regret that he should be one of them. And the higher is the class from which such soldiers are drawn, the greater the intelligence of the men so to be employed, the deeper with me is that feeling of regret. But this strikes one much less in an old country than in a country that is new. In the old countries population is thick, and food sometimes scarce. Men can be spared, and any employment may be serviceable, even though that employment be in itself so unproductive as that of fighting battles or preparing for them. But in the western States of America every arm that can guide a plough is of incalculable value. Minnesota was admitted as a State about three years before this time, and its whole population is not much above 150,000. Of this number perhaps 40,000 may be working men. And now this infant State with its huge territory and scanty population is called upon to send its heart's blood out to the war.

And it has sent its heart's best blood. Forth they came—fine, stalwart, well-grown fellows, looking to my eye as though they had as yet but faintly recognised the necessary severity of military discipline. To them hitherto the war had seemed to be an arena on which each might do something for his country, which that country would recognise. To themselves as yet—and to me also—they were a band of heroes, to be reduced by the compressing power of military discipline to the lower level, but more necessary position of a regiment of soldiers. Ah me! how terrible to them has been the breaking up of that delusion! When a poor yokel in England is enlisted with a shilling and a promise of unlimited beer and glory, one pities and if possible would save him. But with him the mode of life to which he goes may not be much inferior to that he leaves. It may be that for him soldiering is the best trade possible in his circumstances. It may keep him from the hen-roosts, and perhaps from his neighbours' pantries; and discipline may be good for him. Population is thick with us, and there are many whom it may be well to collect and make available under the strictest surveillance. But of these men whom I saw entering on their career upon the banks of the Mississippi, many were fathers of families, many were owners of lands, many were educated men capable of high aspirations,—all were serviceable members of their State. There were probably there not three or four of whom it would be well that the State should be rid. As soldiers fit, or capable of being made fit for the duties they had undertaken, I could find but one fault with them. Their average age was too high. There were men among them with grizzled beards, and many who had counted thirty, thirty-five, and forty years. They had, I believe, devoted themselves with a true spirit of patriotism. No doubt each had some ulterior hope as to himself,—as has every mortal patriot. Regulus when he returned hopeless to Carthage, trusted that some Horace would tell his story. Each of these men from Minnesota looked probably forward to his reward; but the reward desired was of a high class.

The first great misery to be endured by these regiments will be the military lesson of obedience which they must learn before they can be of any service. It always seemed to me when I came near them that they had not as yet recognized the necessary austerity of an officer's duty. Their idea of a captain was the stage idea of a leader of dramatic banditti, a man to be followed and obeyed as a leader, but to be obeyed with that free and easy obedience which is accorded to the reigning chief of the forty thieves. "Wa'll Captain," I have heard a private say to his officer, as he sat on one seat in a railway-car with his feet upon the back of another. And the captain has looked as though he did not like it. The captain did not like it, but the poor private was being fast carried to that destiny which he would like still less. From the first I have had faith in the northern army; but from the first I have felt that the suffering to be endured by these free and independent volunteers would be very great. A man to be available as a private soldier must be compressed and belted in till he be a machine.

As soon as the men had left the vessel we walked over the side of it and took possession. "I am afraid your cabin won't be ready for a quarter of an hour," said the clerk. "Such a body of men as that will leave some dirt after them." I assured him of course that our expectations under such circumstances were very limited, and that I was fully aware that the boat and the boat's company were taken up with matters of greater moment than the carriage of ordinary passengers. But to this he demurred altogether. "The regiments were very little to them, but occasioned much trouble. Everything, however, should be square in fifteen minutes." At the expiration of the time named the key of our state-room was given to us, and we found the appurtenances as clean as though no soldier had ever put his foot upon the vessel.

From La Crosse to St. Paul, the distance up the river is something over 200 miles, and from St. Paul down to Dubuque, in Iowa, to which we went on our return, the distance is 450 miles. We were therefore for a considerable time on board these boats; more so than such a journey may generally make necessary, as we were delayed at first by the soldiers, and afterwards by accidents, such as the breaking of a paddle-wheel, and other causes to which navigation on the Upper Mississippi seems to be liable. On the whole we slept on board four nights, and lived on board as many days. I cannot say that the life was comfortable, though I do not know that it could be made more so by any care on the part of the boat-owners. My first complaint would be against the great heat of the cabins. The Americans as a rule live in an atmosphere which is almost unbearable by an Englishman. To this cause, I am convinced, is to be attributed their thin faces, their pale skins, their unenergetic temperament,—unenergetic as regards physical motion,—and their early old age. The winters are long and cold in America, and mechanical ingenuity is far extended. These two facts together have created a system of stoves, hot-air pipes, steam chambers, and heating apparatus, so extensive that from autumn till the end of spring all inhabited rooms are filled with the atmosphere of a hot oven. An Englishman fancies that he is to be baked, and for a while finds it almost impossible to exist in the air prepared for him. How the heat is engendered on board the river steamers I do not know, but it is engendered to so great a degree that the sitting-cabins are unendurable. The patient is therefore driven out at all hours into the outside balconies of the boat, or on to the top roof,—for it is a roof rather than a deck,—and there as he passes through the air at the rate of twenty miles an hour, finds himself chilled to the very bones. That is my first complaint. But as the boats are made for Americans, and as Americans like hot air, I do not put it forward with any idea that a change ought to be effected. My second complaint is equally unreasonable, and is quite as incapable of a remedy as the first. Nine-tenths of the travellers carry children with them. They are not tourists engaged on pleasure excursions, but men and women intent on the business of life. They are moving up and down, looking for fortune, and in search of new homes. Of course they carry with them all their household gods. Do not let any critic say that I grudge these young travellers their right to locomotion. Neither their right to locomotion is grudged by me, nor any of those privileges which are accorded in America to the rising generation. The habits of their country and the choice of their parents give to them full dominion over all hours and over all places, and it would ill become a foreigner to make such habits and such choice a ground of serious complaint. But nevertheless the uncontrolled energies of twenty children round one's legs do not convey comfort or happiness, when the passing events are producing noise and storm rather than peace and sunshine. I must protest that American babies are an unhappy race. They eat and drink just as they please; they are never punished; they are never banished, snubbed, and kept in the back ground as children are kept with us; and yet they are wretched and uncomfortable. My heart has bled for them as I have heard them squalling by the hour together in agonies of discontent and dyspepsia. Can it be, I wonder, that children are happier when they are made to obey orders and are sent to bed at six o'clock, than when allowed to regulate their own conduct; that bread and milk is more favourable to laughter and soft childish ways than beef-steaks and pickles three times a day; that an occasional whipping, even, will conduce to rosy cheeks? It is an idea which I should never dare to broach to an American mother; but I must confess that after my travels on the western continent my opinions have a tendency in that direction. Beef-steaks and pickles certainly produce smart little men and women. Let that be taken for granted. But rosy laughter and winning childish ways are, I fancy, the produce of bread and milk. But there was a third reason why travelling on these boats was not as pleasant as I had expected. I could not get my fellow-travellers to talk to me. It must be understood that our fellow-travellers were not generally of that class which we Englishmen, in our pride, designate as gentlemen and ladies. They were people, as I have said, in search of new homes and new fortunes. But I protest that as such they would have been in those parts much more agreeable as companions to me than any gentlemen or any ladies, if only they would have talked to me. I do not accuse them of any incivility. If addressed, they answered me. If application was made by me for any special information, trouble was taken to give it me. But I found no aptitude, no wish for conversation; nay, even a disinclination to converse. In the western States I do not think that I was ever addressed first by an American sitting next to me at table. Indeed I never held any conversation at a public table in the West. I have sat in the same room with men for hours, and have not had a word spoken to me. I have done my very best to break through this ice, and have always failed. A western American man is not a talking man. He will sit for hours over a stove with his cigar in his mouth, and his hat over his eyes, chewing the cud of reflection. A dozen will sit together in the same way, and there shall not be a dozen words spoken between them in an hour. With the women one's chance of conversation is still worse. It seemed as though the cares of the world had been too much for them, and that all talking excepting as to business,—demands for instance on the servants for pickles for their children,—had gone by the board. They were generally hard, dry, and melancholy. I am speaking of course of aged females,— from five and twenty perhaps to thirty, who had long since given up the amusements and levities of life. I very soon abandoned any attempt at drawing a word from these ancient mothers of families; but not the less did I ponder in my mind over the circumstances of their lives. Had things gone with them so sadly, was the struggle for independence so hard, that all the softness of existence had been trodden out of them? In the cities too it was much the same. It seemed to me that a future mother of a family in those parts had left all laughter behind her when she put out her finger for the wedding ring.

For these reasons I must say that life on board these steam-boats was not as pleasant as I had hoped to find it, but for our discomfort in this respect we found great atonement in the scenery through which we passed. I protest that of all the river scenery that I know, that of the Upper Mississippi is by far the finest and the most continued. One thinks of course of the Rhine; but, according to my idea of beauty, the Rhine is nothing to the Upper Mississippi. For miles upon miles, for hundreds of miles, the course of the river runs through low hills, which are there called bluffs. These bluffs rise in every imaginable form, looking sometimes like large straggling unwieldy castles, and then throwing themselves into sloping lawns which stretch back away from the river till the eye is lost in their twists and turnings. Land-scape beauty, as I take it, consists mainly in four attributes: in water, in broken land, in scattered timber,—timber scattered as opposed to continuous forest timber,—and in the accident of colour. In all these particulars the banks of the Upper Mississippi can hardly be beaten. There are no high mountains; but high mountains themselves are grand rather than beautiful. There are no high mountains, but there is a succession of hills which group themselves for ever without monotony. It is perhaps the ever-variegated forms of these bluffs which chiefly constitute the wonderful loveliness of this river. The idea constantly occurs that some point on every hillside would form the most charming site ever yet chosen for a noble residence. I have passed up and down rivers clothed to the edge with continuous forest. This at first is grand enough, but the eye and feeling soon become weary. Here the trees are scattered so that the eye passses through them, and ever and again a long lawn sweeps back into the country, and up the steep side of a hill, making the traveller long to stay there and linger through the oaks, and climb the bluffs, and lie about on the bold but easy summits. The boat, however, steams quickly up against the current, and the happy valleys are left behind, one quickly after another. The river is very various in its breadth, and is constantly divided by islands. It is never so broad that the beauty of the banks is lost in the distance or injured by it. It is rapid, but has not the beauti-fully bright colour of some European rivers,—of the Rhine for in-stance, and the Rhone. But what is wanting in the colour of the water is more than compensated by the wonderful hues and lustre of the shores. We visited the river in October, and I must presume that they who seek it solely for the sake of scenery should go there in that month. It was not only that the foliage of the trees was bright with every imaginable colour, but that the grass was bronzed, and that the rocks were golden. And this beauty did not last only for a while and then cease. On the Rhine there are lovely spots and special morsels of scenery with which the traveller becomes duly enraptured. But on the Upper Mississippi there are no special morsels. The position of the sun in the heavens will, as it always does, make much difference in the degree of beauty. The hour before and the half-hour after sunset are always the loveliest for such scenes. But of the shores themselves one may declare that they are lovely throughout those 400 miles which run immediately south from St. Paul.

About half-way between La Crosse and St. Paul we came upon Lake Pepin, and continued our course up the lake for perhaps fifty or sixty miles. This expanse of water is narrow for a lake, and by those who know the lower courses of great rivers, would hardly be dignified by that name. But, nevertheless, the breadth here lessens the beauty. There are the same bluffs, the same scattered woodlands, and the same colours. But they are either at a distance, or else they are to be seen on one side only. The more that I see of the beauty of scenery, and the more I consider its elements, the stronger becomes my conviction that size has but little to do with it, and rather detracts from it than adds to it. Distance gives one of its greatest charms, but it does so by conceal-ing rather than displaying an expanse of surface. The beauty of dis-tance arises from the romance,—the feeling of mystery which it creates. It is like the beauty of woman which allures the more the more that it is veiled. But open, uncovered land and water, mountains which simply rise to great heights with long unbroken slopes, wide expanses of lake, and forests which are monotonous in their continued thickness, are never lovely to me. A landscape should always be partly veiled, and display only half its charms.

To my taste the finest stretch of the river was that immediately above Lake Pepin; but then, at this point, we had all the glory of the setting sun. It was like fairy land, so bright were the golden hues, so fantastic were the shapes of the hills, so broken and twisted the course of the waters! But the noisy steamer went groaning up the narrow passages with almost unabated speed, and left the fairy land behind all too quickly. Then the bell would ring for tea, and the children with the beef-steaks, the pickled onions, and the light fixings would all come over again. The care-laden mothers would tuck the bibs under the chins of their tyrant children, and some embryo senator of four years old would listen with concentrated attention, while the negro servant recapitulated to him the delicacies of the supper-table, in order that he might make his choice with due consideration. "Beef-steak," the embryo four-year old senator would lisp, "and stewed potato, and buttered toast, and corn cake, and coffee,—and—and—and—; mother, mind you get me the pickles."

St. Paul enjoys the double privilege of being the commercial and political capital of Minnesota. The same is the case with Boston in Massachusetts, but I do not remember another instance in which it is so. It is built on the eastern bank of the Mississippi, though the bulk of the State lies to the west of the river. It is noticeable as the spot up to which the river is navigable. Immediately above St. Paul there are narrow rapids up which no boat can pass. North of this, continuous navigation does not go; but from St. Paul down to New Orleans, and the Gulf of Mexico, it is uninterrupted. The distance to St. Louis in Missouri, a town built below the confluence of the three rivers, Mississippi, Missouri, and Illinois, is 900 miles; and then the navigable waters down to the gulf wash a southern country of still greater extent. No river on the face of the globe forms a highway for the produce of so wide an extent of agricultural land. The Mississippi with its tributaries carried to market, before the war, the produce of Wisconsin, Minnesota, Iowa, Illinois, Indiana, Ohio, Kentucky, Tennessee, Missouri, Kansas, Arkansas, Mississippi, and Louisiana. This country is larger than England, Ireland, Scotland, Holland, Belgium, France, Germany and Spain together, and is undoubtedly composed of much more fertile land. The States named comprise the great centre valley of the continent, and are the farming lands and garden grounds of the western world. He who has not seen corn on the ground in Illinois or Minnesota, does not know to what extent the fertility of land may go, or how great may be the weight of cereal crops. And for all this the Mississippi was the high road to market. When the crop of 1861 was garnered this high road was stopped by the war. What suffering this entailed on the South, I will not here stop to say, but on the West the effect was terrible. Corn was in such plenty, Indian corn that is or maize, that it was not worth the farmer's while to prepare it for market. When I was in Illinois the second quality of Indian corn when shelled was not worth more than from eight to ten cents a bushel. But the shelling and preparation are laborious, and in some instances it was found better to burn it for fuel than to sell it. Respecting the export of corn from the West, I must say a further word or two in the next chapter; but it seemed to be indispensable that I should point out here how great to the United States is the need of the Mississippi. Nor is it for corn and wheat only that its waters are needed. Timber, lead, iron, coal, pork, all find, or should find, their exit to the world at large by this road. There are towns on it, and on its tributaries, already holding more than one hundred and fifty thousand inhabitants. The number of Cincinnati exceeds that, as also does the number of St. Louis. Under these circumstances it is not wonderful that the States should wish to keep in their own hands the navigation of this river.

It is not wonderful. But it will not, I think, be admitted by the politicians of the world, that the navigation of the Mississippi need be closed against the West, even though the southern States should succeed in raising themselves to the power and dignity of a separate nationality. If the waters of the Danube be not open to Austria, it is through the fault of Austria. That the subject will be one of trouble no man can doubt; and of course it would be well for the North to avoid that, or any other trouble. In the meantime the importance of this right of way must be admitted; and it must be admitted also that whatever may be the ultimate resolve of the North, it will be very difficult to reconcile the West to a divided dominion of the Mississippi.

St. Paul contains about fourteen thousand inhabitants, and, like all other American towns, is spread over a surface of ground adapted to the accommodation of a very extended population. As it is belted on one side by the river, and on the other by the bluffs which accompany the course of the river, the site is pretty, and almost romantic. Here also we found a great hotel,—a huge square building, such as we in England might perhaps place near to a railway terminus, in such a city as Glasgow or Manchester; but on which no living Englishman would expend his money in a town even five times as big again as St. Paul. Everything was sufficiently good, and much more than sufficiently plentiful. The whole thing went on exactly as hotels do down in Massachusetts, or the State of New York. Look at the map, and see where St. Paul is. Its distance from all known civilization,—all civilization that has succeeded in obtaining acquaintance with the world at large, is very great. Even American travellers do not go up there in great numbers, excepting those who intend to settle there. A stray sportsman or two, American or English, as the case may be, makes his way into Minnesota for the sake of shooting, and pushes on up through St. Paul to the Red River. Some few adventurous spirits visit the Indian settlements, and pass over into the unsettled regions of Dacotah and Washington territory. But there is no throng of travelling. Nevertheless, an hotel has been built there capable of holding three hundred guests, and other hotels exist in the neighbourhood, one of which is even larger than that at St. Paul. Who can come to them, and create even a hope that such an enterprise may be remunerative? In America it is seldom more than hope, for one always hears that such enterprises fail.

When I was there the war was in hand, and it was hardly to be expected that any hotel should succeed. The landlord told me that he held it at the present time for a very low rent, and that he could just manage to keep it open without loss. The war which hindered people from travelling, and in that way injured the innkeepers, also hindered people from housekeeping, and reduced them to the necessity of boarding out,—by which the innkeepers were, of course, benefited. At St. Paul I found that the majority of the guests were inhabitants of the town, boarding at the hotel, and thus dispensing with the cares of a separate establishment. I do not know what was charged for such accommodation at St. Paul, but I have come across large houses at which a single man could get all that he required for a dollar a day. Now Americans are great consumers, especially at hotels, and all that a man requires includes three hot meals with a choice from about two dozen dishes at each.

From St. Paul there are two waterfalls to be seen, which we, of course, visited. We crossed the river at Fort Snelling, a ricketty, ill-conditioned building, standing at the confluence of the Minnesota and Mississippi rivers, built there to repress the Indians. It is, I take it, very necessary, especially at the present moment, as the Indians seem to require repressing. They have learned that the attention of the federal government has been called to the war, and have become bold in consequence. When I was at St. Paul I heard of a party of Englishmen who had been robbed of everything they possessed, and was informed that the farmers in the distant parts of the State were by no means secure. The Indians are more to be pitied than the farmers. They are turning against enemies who will neither forgive nor forget any injuries done. When the war is over they will be improved, and polished, and annexed, till no Indian will hold an acre of land in Minnesota. At present Fort Snelling is the nucleus of a recruiting camp. On the point between the bluffs of the two rivers there is a plain, immediately in front of the fort, and there we saw the newly-joined Minnesota recruits going through their first military exercises. They were in detachments of twenties, and were rude enough at their goose step. The matter which struck me most in looking at them was the difference of condition which I observed in the men. There were the country lads, fresh from the farms, such as we see following the recruiting sergeant through English towns; but there were also men in black coats and black trousers, with thin boots, and trimmed beards, —beards which had been trimmed till very lately; and some of them with beards which showed that they were no longer young. It was inexpressibly melancholy to see such men as these twisting and turning about at the corporal's word, each handling some stick in his hand in lieu of weapon. Of course they were more awkward than the boys, even though they were twice more assiduous in their efforts. Of course they were sad, and wretched. I saw men there that were very wretched, —all but heart-broken, if one might judge from their faces. They should not have been there handling sticks, and moving their unaccustomed legs in cramped paces. They were as razors, for which no better purpose could be found than the cutting of blocks. When such attempts are made the block is not cut, but the razor is spoilt. Most unfit for the commencement of a soldier's life were some that I saw there, but I do not doubt that they had been attracted to the work by the one idea of doing something for their country in its trouble.

From Fort Snelling we went on to the Falls of Minnehaha. Minnehaha, laughing water. Such I believe is the interpretation. The name in this case is more imposing than the fall. It is a pretty little cascade, and might do for a picnic in fine weather, but it is not a waterfall of which a man can make much when found so far away from home. Going on from Minnehaha we came to Minneapolis, at which place there is a fine suspension bridge across the river, just above the falls of St. Anthony and leading to the town of that name. Till I got there I could hardly believe that in these days there should be a living village called Minneapolis by living men. I presume I should describe it as a town, for it has a municipality, and a post-office, and, of course, a large hotel. The interest of the place however is in the saw-mills. On the opposite side of the water, at St. Anthony, is another very large hotel,—and also a smaller one. The smaller one may be about the size of the first-class hotels at Cheltenham or Leamington. They were both closed, and there seemed to be but little prospect that either would be opened till the war should be over. The saw-mills, however, were at full work, and to my eyes were extremely picturesque. I had been told that the beauty of the falls had been destroyed by the mills. Indeed all who had spoken to me about St. Anthony had said so. But I did not agree with them. Here, as at Ottawa, the charm in fact consists, not in an uninterrupted shoot of water, but in a succession of rapids over a bed of broken rocks. Among these rocks logs of loose timber are caught, which have escaped from their proper courses, and here they lie, heaped up in some places, and constructing themselves into bridges in others, till the freshets of the spring carry them off. The timber is generally brought down in logs to St. Anthony, is sawn there, and then sent down the Mississippi in large rafts. These rafts on other rivers are I think generally made of unsawn timber. Such logs as have escaped in the manner above described are recognized on their passage down the river by their marks, and are made up separately, the original owners receiving the value,—or not receiving it as the case may be. "There is quite a trade going on with the loose lumber," my informant told me. And from his tone I was led to suppose that he regarded the trade as sufficiently lucrative if not peculiarly honest.

There is very much in the mode of life adopted by the settlers in these regions which creates admiration. The people are all intelligent. They are energetic and speculative, conceiving grand ideas, and carrying them out almost with the rapidity of magic. A suspension bridge half a mile long is erected, while in England we should be fastening together a few planks for a foot passage. Progress, mental as well as material, is the demand of the people generally. Everybody understands everything, and everybody intends sooner or later to do everything. All this is very grand;—but then there is a terrible drawback. One hears on every side of intelligence, but one hears also on every side of dishonesty. Talk to whom you will, of whom you will, and you will hear some tale of successful or unsuccessful swindling. It seems to be the recognized rule of commerce in the Far West that men shall go into the world's markets prepared to cheat and to be cheated. It may be said that as long as this is acknowledged and understood on all sides, no harm will be done. It is equally fair for all. When I was a child there used to be certain games at which it was agreed in beginning either that there should be cheating or that there should not. It may be said that out there in the western States, men agree to play the cheating game; and that the cheating game has more of interest in it than the other. Unfortunately, however, they who agree to play this game on a large scale, do not keep outsiders altogether out of the playground. Indeed outsiders become very welcome to them;—and then it is not pleasant to hear the tone in which such outsiders speak of the peculiarities of the sport to which they have been introduced. When a beginner in trade finds himself furnished with a barrel of wooden nutmegs, the joke is not so good to him as to the experienced merchant who supplies him. This dealing in wooden nutmegs, this selling of things which do not exist, and buying of goods for which no price is ever to be given, is an institution which is much honoured in the West. We call it swindling;—and so do they. But it seemed to me that in the western States the word hardly seemed to leave the same impress on the mind that it does elsewhere.

On our return down the river we passed La Crosse, at which we had embarked, and went down as far as Dubuque in Iowa. On our way down we came to grief and broke one of our paddle-wheels to pieces. We had no special accident. We struck against nothing above or below water. But the wheel went to pieces, and we lay-to on the river side for the greater part of a day while the necessary repairs were being made. Delay in travelling is usually an annoyance, because it causes the unsettlement of a settled purpose. But the loss of the day did us no harm, and our accident had happened at a very pretty spot.

I climbed up to the top of the nearest bluff, and walked back till I came to the open country, and also went up and down the river banks, visiting the cabins of two settlers who live there by supplying wood to the river steamers. One of these was close to the spot at which we were lying; and yet though most of our passengers came on shore, I was the only one who spoke to the inmates of the cabin. These people must live there almost in desolation from one year's end to another. Once in a fortnight or so they go up to a market town in their small boats, but beyond that they can have little intercourse with their fellow-creatures. Nevertheless none of these dwellers by the river side came out to speak to the men and women who were lounging about from eleven in the morning till four in the afternoon; nor did one of the passengers except myself knock at the door or enter the cabin, or exchange a word with those who lived there.

I spoke to the master of the house, whom I met outside, and he at once asked me to come in and sit down. I found his father there and his mother, his wife, his brother, and two young children. The wife, who was cooking, was a very pretty, pale young woman, who, however, could have circulated round her stove more conveniently had her crinoline been of less dimensions. She bade me welcome very prettily, and went on with her cooking, talking the while, as though she were in the habit of entertaining guests in that way daily. The old woman sat in a corner knitting—as old women always do. The old man lounged with a grandchild on his knee, and the master of the house threw himself on the floor while the other child crawled over him. There was no stiffness or uneasiness in their manners, nor was there anything approaching to that republican roughness which so often operates upon a poor, well-intending Englishman like a slap on the cheek. I sat there for about an hour, and when I had discussed with them English politics and the bearing of English politics upon the American war, they told me of their own affairs. Food was very plenty, but life was very hard. Take the year through each man could not earn above half a dollar a day by cutting wood. This, however, they owned, did not take up all their time. Working on favourable wood on favourable days they could each earn to two dollars a day; but these favourable circumstances did not come together very often. They did not deal with the boats themselves, and the profits were eaten up by the middleman. He, the middleman, had a good thing of it, because he could cheat the captains of the boats in the measurement of the wood. The chopper was obliged to supply a genuine cord of logs,—true measure. But the man who took it off in the barge to the steamer could so pack it that fifteen true cords would make twenty-two false cords. "It cuts up into a fine trade, you see, sir," said the young man, as he stroked back the little girl's hair from her forehead. "But the captains of course must find it out," said I. This he acknowledged, but argued that the captains on this account insisted on buying the wood so much cheaper, and that the loss all came upon the chopper. I tried to teach him that the remedy lay in his own hands, and the three men listened to me quite patiently while I explained to them how they should carry on their own trade. But the young father had the last word. "I guess we don't get above the fifty cents a day any way." He knew at least where the shoe pinched him. He was a handsome, manly, noble-looking fellow, tall and thin, with black hair and bright eyes. But he had the hollow look about his jaws, and so had his wife, and so had his brother. They all owned to fever and ague. They had a touch of it most years, and sometimes pretty sharply. "It was a coarse place to live in," the old woman said, "but there was no one to meddle with them, and she guessed that it suited." They had books and newspapers, tidy delf, and clean glass upon their shelves, and undoubtedly provisions in plenty. Whether fever and ague yearly, and cords of wood stretched from fifteen to twenty-two are more than a set-off for these good things, I will leave every one to decide according to his own taste.

In another cabin I found women and children only, and one of the children was in the last stage of illness. But nevertheless the woman of the house seemed glad to see me, and talked cheerfully as long as I would remain. She inquired what had happened to the vessel, but it had never occurred to her to go out and see. Her cabin was neat and well furnished, and there also I saw newspapers and Harper's everlasting magazine. She said it was a coarse, desolate place for living, but that she could raise almost anything in her garden.

I could not then understand, nor can I now understand, why none of the numerous passengers out of the boat should have entered those cabins except myself; and why the inmates of the cabins should not have come out to speak to any one. Had they been surly, morose people, made silent by the specialties of their life, it would have been explicable; but they were delighted to talk and to listen. The fact, I take it, is, that the people are all harsh to each other. They do not care to go out of their way to speak to any one unless something is to be gained. They say that two Englishmen meeting in the desert would not speak unless they were introduced. The further I travel, the less true do I find this of Englishmen, and the more true of other people.

VII   Sleeping Cars Now in Use on the New York Central Railroad:
". . . and of all their wonderful contrivances that of their railroad
beds is by no means the least."

Frank Leslie's Illustrated Newspaper, V (*April* 30, 1859), 335

VIII   Going on Board

Harper's Weekly, II (*July* 17, 1858), 452

CHAPTER XI

CERES AMERICANA

WE stopped at the Julien House, Dubuque. Dubuque is a city in Iowa on the western shore of the Mississippi, and as the names both of the town and of the hotel sounded French in my ears, I asked for an explanation. I was then told that Julien Dubuque, a Canadian Frenchman, had been buried on one of the bluffs of the river within the precincts of the present town, that he had been the first white settler in Iowa, and had been the only man who had ever prevailed upon the Indians to work.[1] Among them he had become a great "Medicine," and seems for a while to have had absolute power over them. He died I think in 1800, and was buried on one of the hills over the river: "He was a bold bad man," my informant told me, "and committed every sin under heaven. But he made the Indians work."

Lead mines are the glory of Dubuque, and very large sums of money have been made from them. I was taken out to see one of them, and to go down it; but we found, not altogether to my sorrow, that the works had been stopped on account of the water. No effort has been made in any of these mines to subdue the water, nor has steam been applied to the working of them. The lodes have been so rich with lead that the speculators have been content to take out the metal that was easily reached, and to go off in search of fresh ground when disturbed by water. "And are wages here paid pretty punctually?" I asked. "Well; a man has to be smart, you know." And then my friend went on to acknowledge that it would be better for the country if smartness were not so essential.

[1] Julien Dubuque (1762–1810), born in the province of Quebec, was by 1785 settled at Prairie du Chien (now in Wisconsin). Discovering that a band of Fox Indians in the Iowa country had control of rich deposits of lead, he learned their language, gave them presents, and flattered them into granting him permission to work their mines. He brought in French-Canadian helpers, built a smelting furnace, opened more mines, and set up a store for trading with the Indians. Twice a year he brought his boatloads of pig lead and furs to St. Louis. These visits are said to have been periods of great rejoicing for both the merchants and the ladies of the town.

Dubuque did "prevail upon the Indians to work," but the man who told Trollope this would probably have been less awed by the feat had he known that even Dubuque was able to extract labor only from the squaws and the old men of the tribe.

Iowa has a population of 674,000 souls, and in October 1861 had already mustered eighteen regiments of 1000 men each. Such a population would give probably 170,000 men capable of bearing arms, and therefore the number of soldiers sent had already amounted to more than a decimation of the available strength of the State. When we were at Dubuque nothing was talked of but the army. It seemed that mines, coal-pits, and corn-fields, were all of no account in comparison with the war. How many regiments could be squeezed out of the State, was the one question which filled all minds; and the general desire was that such regiments should be sent to the Western army, to swell the triumph which was still expected for General Fremont, and to assist in sweeping slavery out into the Gulf of Mexico. The patriotism of the West has been quite as keen as that of the North, and has produced results as memorable; but it has sprung from a different source, and been conducted and animated by a different sentiment. National greatness and support of the law have been the ideas of the North; national greatness and abolition of slavery have been those of the West. How they are to agree as to terms when between them they have crushed the South,—that is the difficulty.

At Dubuque in Iowa, I ate the best apple that I ever encountered. I make that statement with the purpose of doing justice to the Americans on a matter which is to them one of considerable importance. Americans as a rule do not believe in English apples. They declare that there are none, and receive accounts of Devonshire cyder with manifest incredulity. "But at any rate there are no apples in England equal to ours." That is an assertion to which an Englishman is called upon to give an absolute assent; and I hereby give it. Apples so excellent as some which were given to us at Dubuque, I have never eaten in England. There is a great jealousy respecting all the fruits of the earth. "Your peaches are fine to look at," was said to me, "but they have no flavour." This was the assertion of a lady, and I made no answer. My idea had been that American peaches had no flavour; that French peaches had none; that those of Italy had none; that little as there might be of which England could boast with truth, she might at any rate boast of her peaches without fear of contradiction. Indeed my idea had been that good peaches were to be got in England only. I am beginning to doubt whether my belief on the matter has not been the product of insular ignorance, and idolatrous self-worship. It may be that a peach should be a combination of an apple and a turnip. "My great objection to your country, sir," said another, "is that you have got no vegetables." Had he told me that we had got no seaboard, or no coals, he would not have surprised me more. No vegetables in England! I could not restrain myself altogether, and replied by a confession "that we 'raised' no squash." Squash is the pulp of the pumpkin,[2] and is much used in the States, both as a vegetable and for pies. No vegetables in England! Did my surprise arise from the insular ignorance and idolatrous self-worship of a Britisher, or was my American friend labouring under a delusion? Is Covent Garden well supplied with vegetables, or is it not? Do we cultivate our kitchen gardens with success, or am I under a delusion on that subject? Do I dream, or is it true that out of my own little patches at home I have enough for all domestic purposes of peas, beans, brocoli, cauliflower, celery, beetroot, onions, carrots, parsnips, turnips, seakale, asparagus, French beans, artichokes, vegetable marrow, cucumber, tomatoes, endive, lettuce, as well as herbs of many kinds, cabbages throughout the year, and potatoes? No vegetables! Had the gentleman told me that England did not suit him because we had nothing but vegetables, I should have been less surprised.

From Dubuque, on the western shore of the river, we passed over to Dunleath in Illinois, and went on from thence by railway to Dixon. I was induced to visit this not very flourishing town by a desire to see the rolling prairie of Illinois, and to learn by eyesight something of the crops of corn or Indian maize which are produced upon the land. Had that gentleman told me that we knew nothing of producing corn in England he would have been nearer the mark; for of corn in the profusion in which it is grown here we do not know much. Better land than the prairies of Illinois for cereal crops the world's surface probably cannot show. And here there has been no necessity for the long previous labour of banishing the forest. Enormous prairies stretch across the State, into which the plough can be put at once. The earth is rich with the vegetation of thousands of years, and the farmer's return is given to him without delay. The land bursts with its own produce, and the plenty is such that it creates wasteful carelessness in the gathering of the crop. It is not worth a man's while to handle less than large quantities. Up in Minnesota I had been grieved by the loose manner in which wheat was treated. I have seen bags of it upset, and left upon the ground. The labour of collecting it was more than it was worth. There wheat is the chief crop, and as the lands become cleared and cultivation spreads itself, the amount coming down the Mississippi

[2] It would be interesting to know how Trollope came by this bit of misinformation. For his tilt with James Russell Lowell and Nathaniel Hawthorne over the relative merits of English and American fruits, see section V of our Introduction.

will be increased almost to infinity. The price of wheat in Europe will soon depend, not upon the value of the wheat in the country which grows it, but on the power and cheapness of the modes which may exist for transporting it. I have not been able to obtain the exact prices with reference to the carriage of wheat from St. Paul, the capital of Minnesota, to Liverpool, but I have done so as regards Indian corn from the State of Illinois. The following statement will show what proportion the value of the article at the place of its growth bears to the cost of the carriage; and it shows also how enormous an effect on the price of corn in England would follow any serious decrease in the cost of carriage.

> A bushel of Indian corn at Blooming-
> ton in Illinois cost in October, 1861 10 cents.
> Freight to Chicago . . . . 10 "
> Storeage . . . . 2 "
> Freight from Chicago to Buffalo . . . 22 "
> Elevating, and canal freight to New
> York . . . . 19 "
> Transfer in New York and insurance . 3 "
> Ocean freight . . . . 23 "
> Cost of a bushel of Indian corn at
> Liverpool . . . . 89 cents.

Thus corn which in Liverpool costs 3s. 10d. has been sold by the farmer who produced it for 5d.! It is probable that no great reduction can be expected in the cost of ocean transit; but it will be seen by the above figures that out of the Liverpool price of 3s. 10d. or 89 cents, considerably more than half is paid for carriage across the United States. All or nearly all this transit is by water, and there can, I think, be no doubt but that a few years will see it reduced by fifty per cent. In October last the Mississippi was closed, the railways had not rolling stock sufficient for their work, the crops of the two last years had been excessive, and there existed the necessity of sending out the corn before the internal navigation had been closed by frost. The parties who had the transit in their hands put their heads together and were able to demand any prices that they pleased. It will be seen that the cost of carrying a bushel of corn from Chicago to Buffalo, by the lakes, was within one cent of the cost of bringing it from New York to Liverpool. These temporary causes for high prices of transit will cease, a more perfect system of competition between the railways and the water transit will be organized, and the result must necessarily be both an increase of price to the producer and a decrease of price to the consumer. It certainly seems that the produce of cereal crops in the valleys of the Mississippi and its tributaries, increases at a faster rate than population increases. Wheat and corn are sown by the thousand acres in a piece. I heard of one farmer who had 10,000 acres of corn. Thirty years ago grain and flour were sent westward out of the State of New York to supply the wants of those who had emigrated into the prairies, and now we find that it will be the destiny of those prairies to feed the universe. Chicago is the main point of exportation north-westward from Illinois, and at the present time sends out from its granaries more cereal produce than any other town in the world. The bulk of this passes, in the shape of grain or flour, from Chicago to Buffalo, which latter place is as it were a gateway leading from the lakes or big waters to the canals or small waters. I give below the amount of grain and flour in bushels received into Buffalo for transit in the month of October during four consecutive years.

October, 1858	4,429,055	bushels.
" 1859	5,523,448	"
" 1860	6,500,864	"
" 1861	12,483,797	"

In 1860, from the opening to the close of navigation, 30,837,632 bushels of grain and flour passed through Buffalo. In 1861 the amount received up to the 31st of October, was 51,969,142 bushels. As the navigation would be closed during the month of November, the above figures may be taken as representing not quite the whole amount transported for the year. It may be presumed the 52,000,000 of bushels, as quoted above, will swell itself to 60,000,000. I confess that to my own mind statistical amounts do not bring home any enduring idea. Fifty million bushels of corn and flour simply seems to mean a great deal. It is a powerful form of superlative, and soon vanishes away, as do other superlatives in this age of strong words. I was at Chicago and at Buffalo in October 1861. I went down to the granaries, and climbed up into the elevators. I saw the wheat running in rivers from one vessel into another, and from the railroad vans up into the huge bins on the top stores of the warehouses;—for these rivers of food run up hill as easily as they do down. I saw the corn measured by the forty bushel measure with as much ease as we measure an ounce of cheese, and with greater rapidity. I ascertained that the work went on, week day and Sunday, day and night incessantly; rivers of wheat and rivers of maize ever running. I saw the men bathed in corn as they distributed it in its flow. I saw bins by the score laden with wheat, in each of which bins there was space for a comfortable residence. I breathed the flour, and drank the flour, and felt myself to be enveloped in a world of breadstuff. And then I believed, understood, and brought it home to myself as a fact, that here in the corn lands of Michigan, and amidst the bluffs of Wisconsin, and on the high table plains of Minnesota, and the prairies of Illinois, had God prepared the food for the increasing millions of the Eastern world, as also for the coming millions of the Western.

I do not find many minds constituted like my own, and therefore I venture to publish the above figures. I believe them to be true in the main, and they will show, if credited, that the increase during the last four years has gone on with more than fabulous rapidity. For myself I own that those figures would have done nothing unless I had visited the spot myself. A man cannot, perhaps, count up the results of such a work by a quick glance of his eye, nor communicate with precision to another the conviction which his own short experience has made so strong within himself;—but to himself seeing is believing. To me it was so at Chicago and at Buffalo. I began then to know what it was for a country to overflow with milk and honey, to burst with its own fruits, and be smothered by its own riches. From St. Paul down the Mississippi by the shores of Wisconsin and Iowa,—by the ports on Lake Pepin,—by La Crosse, from which one railway runs eastward,—by Prairie du Chien[,] the terminus of a second,—by Dunleath, Fulton, and Rock Island from whence three other lines run eastward, all through that wonderful State of Illinois—the farmers' glory,—along the ports of the great lakes,—through Michigan, Indiana, Ohio, and further Pennsylvania, up to Buffalo, the great gate of the western Ceres, the loud cry was this—"How shall we rid ourselves of our corn and wheat?" The result has been the passage of 60,000,000 bushels of breadstuffs through that gate in one year! Let those who are susceptible of statistics ponder that. For them who are not I can only give this advice:—Let them go to Buffalo next October, and look for themselves.

In regarding the above figures and the increase shown between the years 1860 and 1861, it must of course be borne in mind that during the latter autumn no corn or wheat was carried into the Southern States, and that none was exported from New Orleans or the mouth of the Mississippi. The States of Mississippi, Alabama, and Louisiana have for some time past received much of their supplies from the northwestern lands, and the cutting off of this current of consumption has tended to swell the amount of grain which has been forced into the narrow channel of Buffalo. There has been no southern exit allowed, and the southern appetite has been deprived of its food. But taking this item for all that it is worth,—or taking it, as it generally will be taken, for much more than it can be worth,—the result left will be materially the same. The grand markets to which the western States look and have looked are those of New England, New York, and Europe. Already corn and wheat are not the common crops of New England. Boston, and Hartford, and Lowell are fed from the great western States. The State of New York, which, thirty years ago, was famous chiefly for its cereal produce, is now fed from these States. New York city would be starved if it depended on its own State; and it will soon be as true that England would be starved if it depended on itself. It was but the other day that we were talking of free trade in corn as a thing desirable, but as yet doubtful;—but the other day that Lord Derby who may be Prime Minister to-morrow, and Mr. Disraeli who may be Chancellor of the Exchequer to-morrow, were stoutly of opinion that the corn laws might be and should be maintained;—but the other day that the same opinion was held with confidence by Sir Robert Peel, who, however, when the day for the change came, was not ashamed to become the instrument used by the people for their repeal.[3] Events in these days march so quickly that they leave men behind, and our dear old Protectionists at home will have grown sleek upon American flour before they have realized the fact that they are no longer fed from their own furrows.

I have given figures merely as regards the trade of Buffalo; but it must not be presumed that Buffalo is the only outlet from the great corn lands of Northern America. In the first place no grain of the produce of Canada finds its way to Buffalo. Its exit is by the St. Lawrence, or by the Grand Trunk Railway, as I have stated when speaking of Canada. And then there is the passage for large vessels from the Upper Lakes, Lake Michigan, Lake Huron, and Lake Erie, through the Welland Canal, into Lake Ontario, and out by the St. Lawrence. There is also the direct communication from Lake Erie, by the New York and

[3] The corn laws of 1815, designed to protect British farming, prohibited the importing of foreign wheat until the market price rose to ten shillings a bushel. In seasons of poor harvests these laws made the cost of bread so high as to work an acute hardship upon laborers. There was intense and widespread agitation for repeal. The Tories traditionally stood for Protection, but in 1846, when a succession of bad harvests in England and a potato blight in Ireland had created a crisis, it was a Tory Prime Minister, Sir Robert Peel, who secured abolition of the corn laws. "Rotten potatoes have done it," exclaimed that arch-Tory, the Duke of Wellington; "they put Peel in his damned fright."

Erie railway to New York. I have more especially alluded to the trade
of Buffalo, because I have been enabled to obtain a reliable return of
the quantity of grain and flour which passes through that town, and
because Buffalo and Chicago are the two spots which are becoming
most famous in the cereal history of the western States.

Everybody has a map of North America. A reference to such a map
will show the peculiar position of Chicago. It is at the south or head of
Lake Michigan, and to it converge railways from Wisconsin, Iowa,
Illinois, and Indiana. At Chicago is found the nearest water carriage
which can be obtained for the produce of a large portion of these States.
From Chicago there is direct water conveyance round through the
lakes to Buffalo at the foot of Lake Erie. At Milwaukee, higher up on
the lake, certain lines of railway come in, joining the lake to the Upper
Mississippi, and to the wheat-lands of Minnesota. Thence the passage
is round by Detroit which is the port for the produce of the greatest
part of Michigan, and still it all goes on towards Buffalo. Then on Lake
Erie there are the ports of Toledo, Cleveland, and Erie. At the bottom
of Lake Erie, there is this city of corn, at which the grain and flour is
transhipped into the canal boats and into the railway cars for New
York; and there is also the Welland Canal, through which large vessels
pass from the upper Lakes, without transhipment of their cargo.

I have said above that corn—meaning maize or Indian corn—was to
be bought at Bloomington in Illinois for 10 cents or fivepence a bushel.
I found this also to be the case at Dixon—and also that corn of inferior
quality might be bought for fourpence; but I found also that it was
not worth the farmer's while to shell it and sell it at such prices. I was
assured that farmers were burning their Indian corn in some places,
finding it more available to them as fuel, than it was for the market.
The labour of detaching a bushel of corn from the hulls or cobs is considerable, as is also the task of carrying it to market. I have known
potatoes in Ireland so cheap that they would not pay for digging and
carrying away for purposes of sale. There was then a glut of potatoes in
Ireland; and in the same way there was in the autumn of 1861 a glut of
corn in the western States. The best qualities would fetch a price,
though still a low price; but corn that was not of the best quality was
all but worthless. It did for fuel, and was burnt. The fact was that the
produce had re-created itself quicker than mankind had multiplied.
The ingenuity of man had not worked quick enough for its disposal.
The earth had given forth her increase so abundantly that the lap of
created humanity could not stretch itself to hold it. At Dixon in 1861
corn cost fourpence a bushel. In Ireland in 1848, it was sold for a penny

a pound, a pound being accounted sufficient to sustain life for a day,— and we all felt that at that price food was brought into the country cheaper than it had ever been brought before.

Dixon is not a town of much apparent prosperity. It is one of those places at which great beginnings have been made, but as to which the deities presiding over new towns have not been propitious. Much of it has been burnt down, and more of it has never been built up. It had a straggling, ill-conditioned, uncommercial aspect, very different from the look of Detroit, Milwaukee, or St. Paul. There was, however, a great hotel there, as usual, and a grand bridge over the Rock River, a tributary of the Mississippi which runs by or through the town. I found that life might be maintained on very cheap terms at Dixon. To me as a passing traveller the charges at the hotel were, I take it, the same as elsewhere. But I learned from an inmate there that he with his wife and horse were fed and cared for, and attended for two dollars or 8s. 4d. a day. This included a private sitting-room, coals, light, and all the wants of life—as my informant told me—except tobacco and whiskey. Feeding at such a house means a succession of promiscuous hot meals as often as the digestion of the patient can face them. Now I do not know any locality where a man can keep himself and his wife, with all material comforts, and the luxury of a horse and carriage, on cheaper terms than that. Whether or no it might be worth a man's while to live at all at such a place as Dixon is altogether another question.

We went there because it is surrounded by the prairie, and out into the prairie we had ourselves driven. We found some difficulty in getting away from the corn, though we had selected this spot as one at which the open rolling prairie was specially attainable. As long as I could see a corn-field or a tree I was not satisfied. Nor indeed was I satisfied at last. To have been thoroughly on the prairie and in the prairie I should have been a day's journey from tilled land. But I doubt whether that could now be done in the State of Illinois. I got out into various patches and brought away specimens of corn;—ears bearing sixteen rows of grain, with forty grains in each row; each ear bearing a meal for a hungry man.

At last we did find ourselves on the prairie, amidst the waving grass, with the land rolling on before us in a succession of gentle sweeps, never rising so as to impede the view, or apparently changing in its general level,—but yet without the monotony of flatness. We were on the prairie, but still I felt no satisfaction. It was private property— divided among holders and pastured over by private cattle. Salisbury plain is as wild, and Dartmoor almost wilder. Deer they told me were to be had within reach of Dixon; but for the buffalo one has to go much further afield than Illinois. The farmer may rejoice in Illinois, but the hunter and the trapper must cross the big rivers and pass away into the western territories before he can find lands wild enough for his purposes. My visit to the corn-fields of Illinois was in its way successful; but I felt as I turned my face eastward towards Chicago that I had no right to boast that I had as yet made acquaintance with a prairie.

All minds were turned to the war, at Dixon as elsewhere. In Illinois the men boasted that as regards the war, they were the leading State of the Union. But the same boast was made in Indiana, and also in Massachusetts; and probably in half the States of the North and West. They, the Illinoisians, call their country the war nest of the West. The population of the State is 1,700,000, and it had undertaken to furnish sixty volunteer regiments of 1000 men each. And let it be borne in mind that these regiments, when furnished, are really full,—absolutely containing the thousand men when they are sent away from the parent States. The number of souls above named will give 420,000 working men, and if out of these 60,000 are sent to the war, the State, which is almost purely agricultural, will have given more than one man in eight. When I was in Illinois, over forty regiments had already been sent—forty-six if I remember rightly,—and there existed no doubt whatever as to the remaining number. From the next State of Indiana, with a population of 1,350,000, giving something less than 350,000 working men, thirty-six regiments had been sent. I fear that I am mentioning these numbers usque ad nauseam; [4] but I wish to impress upon English readers the magnitude of the effort made by the States in mustering and equipping an army within six or seven months of the first acknowledgment that such an army would be necessary. The Americans have complained bitterly of the want of English sympathy, and I think they have been weak in making that complaint. But I would not wish that they should hereafter have the power of complaining of a want of English justice. There can be no doubt that a genuine feeling of patriotism was aroused throughout North and West, and that men rushed into the ranks actuated by that feeling—men for whom war and army life, a camp and fifteen dollars a month, would not of themselves have had any attraction. It came to that, that young men were ashamed not to go into the army. This feeling of course produced coercion, and the movement was in that way tyrannical. There is nothing more tyrannical than a strong popular feeling among a democratic people. During the period of en-

4 "even to the point of nausea."

listment this tyranny was very strong. But the existence of such a tyranny proves the passion and patriotism of the people. It got the better of the love of money, of the love of children, and of the love of progress. Wives who with their bairns were absolutely dependent on their husbands' labours, would wish their husbands to be at the war. Not to conduce, in some special way, towards the war,—to have neither father there, nor brother, nor son,—not to have lectured, or preached, or written for the war,—to have made no sacrifice for the war, to have had no special and individual interest in the war, was disgraceful. One sees at a glance the tyranny of all this in such a country as the States. One can understand how quickly adverse stories would spread themselves as to the opinion of any man who chose to remain tranquil at such a time. One shudders at the absolute absence of true liberty which such a passion throughout a democratic country must engender. But he who has observed all this must acknowledge that that passion did exist. Dollars, children, progress, education, and political rivalry all gave way to the one strong national desire for the thrashing and crushing of those who had rebelled against the authority of the Stars and Stripes.

When we were at Dixon they were getting up the Dement regiment. The attempt at the time did not seem to be prosperous, and the few men who had been collected had about them a forlorn, ill-conditioned look. But then, as I was told, Dixon had already been decimated and re-decimated by former recruiting colonels. Colonel Dement, from whom the regiment was to be named, and whose military career was only now about to commence, had come late into the field. I did not afterwards ascertain what had been his success, but I hardly doubt that he did ultimately scrape together his thousand men. "Why don't you go?" I said to a burly Irishman who was driving me. "I'm not a sound man, yer honour," said the Irishman. "I'm deficient in me liver." Taking the Irishmen, however, throughout the Union, they had not been found deficient in any of the necessaries for a career of war. I do not think that any men have done better than the Irish in the American army.

From Dixon we went to Chicago. Chicago is in many respects the most remarkable city among all the remarkable cities of the Union. Its growth has been the fastest and its success the most assured. Twenty-five years ago there was no Chicago, and now it contains 120,000 inhabitants. Cincinnati on the Ohio, and St. Louis at the junction of the Missouri and Mississippi, are larger towns; but they have not grown large so quickly nor do they now promise so excessive a development of commerce. Chicago may be called the metropolis of American corn

—the favourite city haunt of the American Ceres. The goddess seats herself there amidst the dust of her full barns, and proclaims herself a goddess ruling over things political and philosophical as well as agricultural. Not furrows only are in her thoughts, but free trade also, and brotherly love. And within her own bosom there is a boast that even yet she will be stronger than Mars. In Chicago there are great streets, and rows of houses fit to be the residences of a new Corn Exchange nobility. They look out on the wide lake which is now the highway for breadstuffs, and the merchant, as he shaves at his window, sees his rapid ventures as they pass away, one after the other, towards the East.

I went over one great grain store in Chicago possessed by gentlemen of the name of Sturgess and Buckenham.[5] It was a world in itself,—and the dustiest of all the worlds. It contained, when I was there, half a million bushels of wheat—or a very great many, as I might say in other language. But it was not as a storehouse that this great building was so remarkable, but as a channel or a river course for the flooding freshets of corn. It is so built that both railway vans and vessels come immediately under its claws, as I may call the great trunks of the elevators. Out of the railway vans the corn and wheat is clawed up into the building, and down similar trunks it is at once again poured out into the vessels. I shall be at Buffalo in a page or two, and then I will endeavour to explain more minutely how this is done. At Chicago the corn is bought and does change hands, and much of it, therefore, is stored there for some space of time,—shorter or longer as the case may be. When I was at Chicago, the only limit to the rapidity of its transit was set by the amount of boat accommodation. There were not bottoms enough to take the corn away from Chicago, nor indeed on the railway was there a sufficiency of rolling stock or locomotive power to bring it into Chicago. As I said before, the country was bursting with its own produce and smothered in its own fruits.

At Chicago the hotel was bigger than other hotels, and grander.[6] There were pipes without end for cold water which ran hot, and for hot water which would not run at all. The post-office also was grander and bigger than other post-offices;—though the postmaster confessed to me that that matter of the delivery of letters was one which could not

---

5 Sturgis, Buckingham & Company possessed two vast storehouses besides the Illinois Central Railroad Depot in Chicago. According to *Harper's Weekly* for September 10, 1859, each of these had a capacity of 700,000 bushels and was capable of storing 225,000 bushels in a single day.

6 The Sherman House, with accommodations for seven hundred guests, had been erected at Clark Street and Randolph in 1860 at a cost of nearly a half-million dollars.

be compassed. Just at that moment it was being done as a private speculation; but it did not pay, and would be discontinued. The theatre
too was large, handsome, and convenient; but on the night of my
attendance it seemed to lack an audience. A good comic actor it did
not lack, and I never laughed more heartily in my life.[7] There was
something wrong too just at that time—I could not make out what—in
the constitution of Illinois, and the present moment had been selected
for voting a new constitution. To us in England such a necessity would
be considered a matter of importance, but it did not seem to be much
thought of here. "Some slight alteration probably," I suggested. "No,"
said my informant—one of the judges of their courts—"it is to be a
thorough radical change of the whole constitution. They are voting
the delegates to-day." I went to see them vote the delegates; but unfortunately got into a wrong place—by invitation—and was turned out,
not without some slight tumult.[8] I trust that the new constitution was
carried through successfully.

From these little details it may perhaps be understood how a town
like Chicago goes on and prospers, in spite of all the drawbacks which
are incident to newness. Men in those regions do not mind failures,
and when they have failed, instantly begin again. They make their
plans on a large scale, and they who come after them fill up what has
been wanting at first. Those taps of hot and cold water will be made
to run by the next owner of the hotel, if not by the present owner. In

[7] McVicker's Theatre, on Madison Street between State and Dearborn, could
hold two thousand people. During Trollope's visit to Chicago the theater was fea-
turing "the celebrated artist and Shakespearian Comedian, Mr. Hackett." Since
Trollope found the entertainment so enormously funny, he must have attended on
Tuesday, October 22, 1861, which, as his account book shows, was the day of his arrival. The program for that night was uncannily suited to challenge the attention of
an Englishman in America who had spent much of his life as a post-office official.
The Yankee in England, a comedy in three acts, was followed by *Mons. Mallet; or,
The Post-Office Mistake*, a "serio comic sketch . . . founded on an incident at the
New York Post Office." On the following night, the only other night Trollope spent
in Chicago, he would have seen *Rip Van Winkle* and a farce dealing with mesmer-
ism entitled *His Last Legs*.

[8] What Trollope failed to grasp was that the Cook County elections were also
taking place. These, to judge from the newspapers, involved a fierce battle between
the "Court-House Clique" and the faction that was out of office. According to the
Chicago Evening Journal for October 24, 1861, there had been "a vast deal of buying up of men" and other shady proceedings. If, as seems likely, Trollope was invited into the polls to cast his ballot in the local election and was then discovered
to be no native of the county, it is understandable that he should have been turned
out with "some slight tumult."
  The new state constitution as an entirety was rejected by the delegates, though
a few of its provisions were approved.

another ten years the letters, I do not doubt, will all be delivered. Long before that time the theatre will probably be full. The new constitution is no doubt already at work; and if found deficient, another will succeed to it without any trouble to the State or any talk on the subject through the Union. Chicago was intended as a town of export for corn, and, therefore, the corn stores have received the first attention. When I was there, they were in perfect working order.

From Chicago we went on to Cleveland, a town in the State of Ohio on Lake Erie, again travelling by the sleeping cars. I found that these cars were universally mentioned with great horror and disgust by Americans of the upper class. They always declared that they would not travel in them on any account. Noise and dirt were the two objections. They are very noisy, but to us belonged the happy power of sleeping down noise. I invariably slept all through the night, and knew nothing about the noise. They are also very dirty,—extremely dirty,—dirty so as to cause much annoyance. But then they are not quite so dirty as the day cars. If dirt is to be a bar against travelling in America, men and women must stay at home. For myself I don't much care for dirt, having a strong reliance on soap and water and scrubbing brushes. No one regards poisons who carries antidotes in which he has perfect faith.

Cleveland is another pleasant town,—pleasant as Milwaukee and Portland. The streets are handsome, and are shaded by grand avenues of trees. One of these streets is over a mile in length, and throughout the whole of it, there are trees on each side—not little paltry trees as are to be seen on the boulevards of Paris, but spreading elms,—the beautiful American elm which not only spreads, but droops also, and makes more of its foliage than any other tree extant. And there is a square in Cleveland, well sized, as large as Russell Square I should say, with open paths across it, and containing one or two handsome buildings. I cannot but think that all men and women in London would be great gainers if the iron rails of the squares were thrown down, and the grassy enclosures thrown open to the public. Of course the edges of the turf would be worn, and the paths would not keep their exact shapes. But the prison look would be banished, and the sombre sadness of the squares would be relieved.

I was particularly struck by the size and comfort of the houses at Cleveland. All down that street of which I have spoken, they do not stand continuously together, but are detached and separate; houses which in England would require some fifteen or eighteen hundred a year for their maintenance. In the States, however, men commonly expend upon house rent a much greater proportion of their income than they do in England. With us it is, I believe, thought that a man should certainly not apportion more than a seventh of his spending income to his house rent,—some say not more than a tenth. But in many cities of the States a man is thought to live well within bounds if he so expends a fourth. There can be no doubt as to Americans living in better houses than Englishmen,—making the comparison of course between men of equal incomes. But the Englishman has many more incidental expenses than the American. He spends more on wine, on entertainments, on horses, and on amusements. He has a more numerous establishment, and keeps up the adjuncts and outskirts of his residence with a more finished neatness.

These houses in Cleveland were very good,—as indeed they are in most Northern towns; but some of them have been erected with an amount of bad taste that is almost incredible. It is not uncommon to see in front of a square brick house a wooden quasi-Greek portico, with a pediment and Ionic columns, equally high with the house itself. Wooden columns with Greek capitals attached to the doorways, and wooden pediments over the windows, are very frequent. As a rule these are attached to houses which, without such ornamentation, would be simple, unpretentious, square, roomy residences. An Ionic or Corinthian capital stuck on to a log of wood called a column, and then fixed promiscuously to the outside of an ordinary house, is to my eye the vilest of architectural pretences. Little turrets are better than this; or even brown battlements made of mortar. Except in America I do not remember to have seen these vicious bits of white timber,—timber painted white,—plastered on to the fronts and sides of red-brick houses.

Again we went on by rail,—to Buffalo. I have travelled some thousands of miles by railway in the States, taking long journeys by night and longer journeys by day; but I do not remember that while doing so I ever made acquaintance with an American. To an American lady in a railway car I should no more think of speaking than I should to an unknown female in the next pew to me at a London church. It is hard to understand from whence come the laws which govern societies in this respect; but there are different laws in different societies, which soon obtain recognition for themselves. American ladies are much given to talking, and are generally free from all *mauvaise honte*.[9] They are collected in manner, well instructed, and resolved to have their share of the social advantages of the world. In this phase of life they come out more strongly than English women. But on a railway journey,

9 "bashfulness."

be it ever so long, they are never seen speaking to a stranger. English
women, however, on English railways are generally willing to converse.
They will do so if they be on a journey; but will not open their mouths
if they be simply passing backwards and forwards between their homes
and some neighbouring town. We soon learn the rules on these subjects;—but who make the rules? If you cross the Atlantic with an
American lady you invariably fall in love with her before the journey
is over. Travel with the same woman in a railway car for twelve hours,
and you will have written her down in your own mind in quite other
language than that of love.

And now for Buffalo, and the elevators. I trust I have made it understood that corn [1] 'comes into Buffalo, not only from Chicago, of
which I have spoken specially, but from all the ports round the lakes;
Racine, Milwaukee, Grandhaven, Port Sarnia, Detroit, Toledo, Cleveland, and many others. At these ports the produce is generally bought
and sold; but at Buffalo it is merely passed through a gateway. It is
taken from vessels of a size fitted for the lakes, and placed in other
vessels fitted for the canal. This is the Erie Canal, which connects the
lakes with the Hudson River and with New York. The produce which
passes through the Welland Canal—the canal which connects Lake
Erie and the upper lakes with Lake Ontario and the St. Lawrence—is
not transhipped, seeing that the Welland Canal, which is less than
thirty miles in length, gives a passage to vessels of 500 tons. As I have
before said, 60,000,000 bushels of breadstuff were thus pushed through
Buffalo in the open months of the year 1861. These open months run
from the middle of April to the middle of November; but the busy
period is that of the last two months,—the time that is which inter-
venes between the full ripening of the corn and the coming of the ice.

An elevator is as ugly a monster as has been yet produced. In un-
couthness of form it outdoes those obsolete old brutes who used to
roam about the semiaqueous world, and live a most uncomfortable
life with their great hungering stomachs and huge unsatisfied maws.
The elevator itself consists of a big moveable trunk,—moveable as is
that of an elephant, but not pliable, and less graceful even than an
elephant's. This is attached to a huge granary or barn; but in order
to give altitude within the barn for the necessary moving up and down
of this trunk,—seeing that it cannot be curled gracefully to its purposes
as the elephant's is curled,—there is an awkward box erected on the
roof of the barn, giving some twenty feet of additional height, up into

[1] Of course Trollope, as an Englishman, uses the term to mean grain in general
rather than Indian maize in particular.

which the elevator can be thrust. It will be understood, then, that this big moveable trunk, the head of which, when it is at rest, is thrust up into the box on the roof, is made to slant down in an oblique direction from the building to the river. For the elevator is an amphibious institution, and flourishes only on the banks of navigable waters. When its head is ensconced within its box, and the beast of prey is thus nearly hidden within the building, the unsuspicious vessel is brought up within reach of the creature's trunk, and down it comes, like a mosquito's proboscis, right through the deck, in at the open aperture of the hole, and so into the very vitals and bowels of the ship. When there, it goes to work upon its food with a greed and an avidity that is disgusting to a beholder of any taste or imagination. And now I must explain the anatomical arrangement by which the elevator still devours and continues to devour, till the corn within its reach has all been swallowed, masticated, and digested. Its long trunk, as seen slanting down from out of the building across the wharf and into the ship, is a mere wooden pipe; but this pipe is divided within. It has two departments; and as the grain-bearing troughs pass up the one on a pliable band, they pass empty down the other. The system therefore is that of an ordinary dredging machine; only that corn, and not mud is taken away, and that the buckets or troughs are hidden from sight. Below, within the stomach of the poor bark, three or four labourers are at work, helping to feed the elevator. They shovel the corn up towards its maw, so that at every swallow he should take in all that he can hold. Thus the troughs, as they ascend, are kept full, and when they reach the upper building they empty themselves into a shoot, over which a porter stands guard, moderating the shoot by a door, which the weight of his finger can open and close. Through this doorway the corn runs into a measure, and is weighed. By measures of forty bushels each, the tale is kept. There stands the apparatus, with the figures plainly marked, over against the porter's eye; and as the sum mounts nearly up to forty bushels he closes the door till the grains run thinly through, hardly a handful at a time, so that the balance is exactly struck. Then the teller standing by marks down his figure, and the record is made. The exact porter touches the string of another door, and the forty bushels of corn run out at the bottom of the measure, disappear down another shoot, slanting also towards the water, and deposit themselves in the canal-boat. The transit of the bushels of corn from the larger vessel to the smaller will have taken less than a minute, and the cost of that transit will have been—a farthing.

But I have spoken of the rivers of wheat, and I must explain what are those rivers. In the working of the elevator, which I have just attempted to describe, the two vessels were supposed to be lying at the same wharf, on the same side of the building, in the same water, the smaller vessel inside the larger one. When this is the case the corn runs direct from the weighing measure into the shoot that communicates with the canal boat. But there is not room or time for confining the work to one side of the building. There is water on both sides, and the corn or wheat is elevated on the one side, and re-shipped on the other. To effect this the corn is carried across the breadth of the building; but, nevertheless, it is never handled or moved in its direction on trucks or carriages requiring the use of men's muscles for its motion. Across the floor of the building are two gutters, or channels, and through these small troughs on a pliable band circulate very quickly. They which run one way, in one channel, are laden; they which return by the other channel are empty. The corn pours itself into these, and they again pour it into the shoot which commands the other water. And thus rivers of corn are running through these buildings night and day. The secret of all the motion and arrangement consists of course in the elevation. The corn is lifted up; and when lifted up can move itself and arrange itself, and weigh itself, and load itself.

I should have stated that all this wheat which passes through Buffalo comes loose, in bulk. Nothing is known of sacks or bags. To any spectator at Buffalo this becomes immediately a matter of course; but this should be explained, as we in England are not accustomed to see wheat travelling in this open, unguarded, and plebeian manner. Wheat with us is aristocratic, and travels always in its private carriage.

Over and beyond the elevators there is nothing specially worthy of remark at Buffalo. It is a fine city, like all other American cities of its class. The streets are broad, the "blocks" are high, and cars on tramways run all day, and nearly all night as well.

CHAPTER XII

Buffalo to New York

W<small>E</small> had now before us only two points of interest before we should reach New York,—the Falls of Trenton, and West Point on the Hudson River. We were too late in the year to get up to Lake George, which lies in the State of New York, north of Albany, and is, in fact, the southern continuation of Lake Champlain. Lake George, I know, is very lovely, and I would fain have seen it; but visitors to it must have some hotel accommodation, and the hotel was closed when we were near enough to visit it. I was in its close neighbourhood three years since in June; but then the hotel was not yet opened. A visitor to Lake George must be very exact in his time. July and August are the months, —with perhaps the grace of a week in September.

The hotel at Trenton was also closed, as I was told. But even if there were no hotel at Trenton, it can be visited without difficulty. It is within a carriage drive of Utica, and there is moreover a direct railway from Utica, with a station at the Trenton Falls. Utica is a town on the line of railway from Buffalo to New York viâ Albany, and is like all the other towns we had visited. There are broad streets, and avenues of trees, and large shops, and excellent houses. A general air of fat prosperity pervades them all, and is strong at Utica as elsewhere.

I remember to have been told thirty years ago that a traveller might go far and wide in search of the picturesque, without finding a spot more romantic in its loveliness than Trenton Falls.[1] The name of the river is Canada Creek West; but as that is hardly euphonious, the course of the water which forms the falls has been called after the town or parish. This course is nearly two miles in length, and along the space of these two miles it is impossible to say where the greatest beauty exists. To see Trenton aright one must be careful not to have too much water. A sufficiency is no doubt desirable, and it may be that

---

[1] Anthony was the sixth of the Trollopes to view Trenton Falls. His father and his brother Tom had visited them in 1829 on their return from a brief stay in Cincinnati. Tom recorded in his autobiography that he had liked Trenton better than Niagara. In the spring of 1831 Frances Trollope and her two daughters saw Trenton Falls. They were delighted not only with the scenic splendor but also with finding, among the innumerable scrawls on the wall of a small building overlooking the whirlpool: "Trollope, England," surely the mark of Tom.

at the close of summer, before any of the autumnal rains have fallen, there may occasionally be an insufficiency. But if there be too much, the passage up the rocks along the river is impossible. The way on which the tourist should walk becomes the bed of the stream, and the great charm of the place cannot be enjoyed. That charm consists in descending into the ravine of the river, down amidst the rocks through which it has cut its channel, and in walking up the bed against the stream, in climbing the sides of the various falls, and sticking close to the river till an envious block is reached, which comes sheer down into the water, and prevents further progress. This is nearly two miles above the steps by which the descent is made; and not a foot of this distance but is wildly beautiful. When the river is very low there is a pathway even beyond that block; but when this is the case there can hardly be enough of water to make the fall satisfactory.

There is no one special cataract at Trenton which is in itself either wonderful or pre-eminently beautiful. It is the position, form, colour, and rapidity of the river which give the charm. It runs through a deep ravine, at the bottom of which the water has cut for itself a channel through the rocks, the sides of which rise sometimes with the sharpness of the walls of a stone sarcophagus. They are rounded too towards the bed, as I have seen the bottom of a sarcophagus. Along the side of the right bank of the river there is a passage, which when the freshets come is altogether covered. This passage is sometimes very narrow, but in the narrowest parts an iron chain is affixed into the rock. It is slippery and wet, and it is well for ladies when visiting the place to be provided with outside india-rubber shoes, which keep a hold upon the stone. If I remember rightly there are two actual cataracts, one not far above the steps by which the descent is made into the channel, and the other close under a summer-house, near to which the visitors reascend into the wood. But these cataracts, though by no means despicable as cataracts, leave comparatively a slight impression. They tumble down with sufficient violence, and the usual fantastic disposition of their forces; but simply as cataracts, within a day's journey of Niagara, they would be nothing. Up beyond the summer-house the passage along the river can be continued for another mile, but it is rough, and the climbing in some places rather difficult for ladies. Every man, however, who has the use of his legs, should do it, for the succession of rapids, and the twistings of the channels, and the forms of the rocks are as wild and beautiful as the imagination can desire. The banks of the river are closely wooded on each side; and though this circumstance does not at first seem to add much to the beauty, seeing that the ravine is so deep that the absence of wood above would hardly be noticed, still there are broken clefts ever and anon through which the colours of the foliage show themselves, and straggling boughs and rough roots break through the rocks here and there, and add to the wildness and charm of the whole.

The walk back from the summer-house through the wood is very lovely; but it would be a disappointing walk to visitors who had been prevented by a flood in the river from coming up the channel, for it indicates plainly how requisite it is that the river should be seen from below and not from above. The best view of the larger fall itself is that seen from the wood. And here again I would point out that any male visitor should walk the channel of the river up and down. The descent is too slippery and difficult for bipeds laden with petticoats. We found a small hotel open at Trenton, at which we got a comfortable dinner, and then in the evening were driven back to Utica.

Albany is the capital of the State of New York, and our road from Trenton to West Point lay through that town; but these political State capitals have no interest in themselves. The State legislature was not sitting, and we went on, merely remarking that the manner in which the railway cars are made to run backward and forward through the crowded streets of the town must cause a frequent loss of human life. One is led to suppose that children in Albany can hardly have a chance of coming to maturity. Such accidents do not become the subject of long-continued and strong comment in the States as they do with us; but, nevertheless, I should have thought that such a state of things as we saw there would have given rise to some remark on the part of the philanthropists. I cannot myself say that I saw anybody killed, and therefore should not be justified in making more than this passing remark on the subject.

When first the Americans of the Northern States began to talk much of their country, their claims as to fine scenery were confined to Niagara and the Hudson River. Of Niagara, I have spoken, and all the world has acknowledged that no claim made on that head can be regarded as exaggerated. As to the Hudson, I am not prepared to say so much generally, though there is one spot upon it which cannot be beaten for sweetness. I have been up and down the Hudson by water, and confess that the entire river is pretty. But there is much of it that is not pre-eminently pretty among rivers. As a whole it cannot be named with the Upper Mississippi, with the Rhine, with the Moselle, or with the Upper Rhone. The palisades just out of New York are pretty, and the whole passage through the mountains from West Point up to Catskill and Hudson is interesting. But the glory of the Hudson is at West Point itself; and thither on this occasion we went direct by railway, and there we remained for two days. The Catskill mountains should be seen by a detour off from the river. We did not visit them because, here again, the hotel was closed. I will leave them therefore for the new handbook which Mr. Murray will soon bring out.

Of West Point there is something to be said independently of its scenery. It is the Sandhurst of the States. Here is their military school, from which officers are drafted to their regiments, and the tuition for military purposes is, I imagine, of a high order. It must, of course, be borne in mind that West Point, even as at present arranged, is fitted to the wants of the old army, and not to that of the army now required. It can go but a little way to supply officers for 500,000 men; but would do much towards supplying them for 40,000. At the time of my visit to West Point the regular army of the northern States had not even then swelled itself to the latter number.

I found that there were 220 students at West Point; that about forty graduate every year, each of whom receives a commission in the army; that about 120 pupils are admitted every year; and that in the course of every year about eighty either resign, or are called upon to leave on account of some deficiency, or fail in their final examination. The result is simply this, that one third of those who enter succeeds, and that two thirds fail. The number of failures seemed to me to be terribly large,—so large as to give great ground of hesitation to a parent in accepting a nomination for the college. I especially inquired into the particulars of these dismissals and resignations, and was assured that the majority of them take place in the first year of the pupillage. It is soon seen whether or no a lad has the mental and physical capacities necessary for the education and future life required of him, and care is taken that those shall be removed early as to whom it may be determined that the necessary capacity is clearly wanting. If this is done,—and I do not doubt it,—the evil is much mitigated. The effect otherwise would be very injurious. The lads remain till they are perhaps one and twenty, and have then acquired aptitudes for military life, but no other aptitudes. At that age the education cannot be commenced anew, and, moreover, at that age the disgrace of failure is very injurious. The period of education used to be five years, but has now been reduced to four. This was done in order that a double class might be graduated in 1861 to supply the wants of the war. I believe it is considered that but for such necessity as that, the fifth year of education can be ill spared.

The discipline, to our English ideas, is very strict. In the first place no kind of beer, wine, or spirits is allowed at West Point. The law upon this point may be said to be very vehement, for it debars even the visitors at the hotel from the solace of a glass of beer. The hotel is within the bounds of the College, and as the lads might become purchasers at the bar, there is no bar allowed. Any breach of this law leads to instant expulsion; or, I should say rather, any detection of such breach. The officer who showed us over the College assured me that the presence of a glass of wine in a young man's room would secure his exclusion, even though there should be no evidence that he had tasted it. He was very firm as to this; but a little bird of West Point, whose information, though not official or probably accurate in words, seemed to me to be worthy of reliance in general, told me that eyes were wont to wink when such glasses of wine made themselves unnecessarily visible. Let us fancy an English mess of young men from seventeen to twenty-one, at which a mug of beer would be felony, and a glass of wine high treason! But the whole management of the young with the Americans differs much from that in vogue with us. We do not require so much at so early an age, either in knowledge, in morals, or even in manliness. In America, if a lad be under control, as at West Point, he is called upon for an amount of labour, and a degree of conduct, which would be considered quite transcendental and out of the question in England. But if he be not under control, if at the age of eighteen he be living at home, or be from his circumstances exempt from professorial power, he is a full-fledged man with his pipe apparatus and his bar acquaintances.

And then I was told at West Point how needful and yet how painful it was that all should be removed who were in any way deficient in credit to the establishment. "Our rules are very exact," my informant told me; "but the carrying out of our rules is a task not always very easy." As to this also I had already heard something from that little bird of West Point, but of course I wisely assented to my informant, remarking that discipline in such an establishment was essentially necessary. The little bird had told me that discipline at West Point had been rendered terribly difficult by political interference. "A young man will be dismissed by the unanimous voice of the Board, and will be sent away. And then, after a week or two, he will be sent back, with an order from Washington, that another trial shall be given him. The lad will march back into the college with all the honours of a victory, and will be conscious of a triumph over the superintendent and his officers." "And is that common?" I asked. "Not at the present moment,"

I was told. "But it was common before the war. While Mr. Buchanan, and Mr. Pierce, and Mr. Polk were Presidents, no officer or board of officers then at West Point was able to dismiss a lad whose father was a Southerner, and who had friends among the Government."

Not only was this true of West Point, but the same allegation is true as to all matters of patronage throughout the United States. During the three or four last Presidencies, and I believe back to the time of Jackson, there has been an organized system of dishonesty in the management of all beneficial places under the control of the Government. I doubt whether any despotic court of Europe has been so corrupt in the distribution of places,—that is in the selection of public officers,—as has been the assemblage of statesmen at Washington. And this is the evil which the country is now expiating with its blood and treasure. It has allowed its knaves to stand in the high places; and now it finds that knavish works have brought about evil results. But of this I shall be constrained to say something further hereafter.

We went into all the schools of the College, and made ourselves fully aware that the amount of learning imparted was far above our comprehension. It always occurs to me in looking through the new schools of the present day, that I ought to be thankful to persons who know so much for condescending to speak to me at all in plain English. I said a word to the gentleman who was with me about horses, seeing a lot of lads going to their riding lesson. But he was down upon me, and crushed me instantly beneath the weight of my own ignorance. He walked me up to the image of a horse, which he took to pieces bit by bit, taking off skin, muscle, flesh, nerves and bones, till the animal was a heap of atoms, and assured me that the anatomy of the horse throughout was one of the necessary studies of the place. We afterwards went to see the riding. The horses themselves were poor enough. This was accounted for by the fact that such of them as had been found fit for military service had been taken for the use of the army.

There is a gallery in the College in which are hung sketches and pictures by former students. I was greatly struck with the merit of many of these. There were some copies from well-known works of art of very high excellence, when the age is taken into account of those by whom they were done. I don't know how far the art of drawing, as taught generally and with no special tendency to military instruction, may be necessary for military training; but if it be necessary I should imagine that more is done in that direction at West Point than at Sandhurst. I found, however, that much of that in the gallery which was good had been done by lads who had not obtained their degree, and

who had shown an aptitude for drawing, but had not shown any aptitude for other pursuits necessary to their intended career.

And then we were taken to the chapel, and there saw, displayed as
trophies, two of our own dear old English flags. I have seen many a
banner hung up in token of past victory, and many a flag taken on the
field of battle mouldering by degrees into dust on some chapel's wall,
—but they have not been the flags of England. Till this day I had never
seen our own colours in any position but one of self-assertion and independent power. From the tone used by the gentleman who showed
them to me, I could gather that he would have passed them by had he
not foreseen that he could not do so without my notice. "I don't know
that we are right to put them there," he said. "Quite right," was my
reply, "as long as the world does such things." In private life it is vulgar
to triumph over one's friends, and malicious to triumph over one's
enemies. We have not got so far yet in public life, but I hope we are
advancing toward it. In the mean time I did not begrudge the Americans our two flags. If we keep flags and cannons taken from our enemies, and show them about as signs of our own prowess after those
enemies have become friends, why should not others do so as regards
us? It clearly would not be well for the world that we should always
beat other nations and never be beaten. I did not begrudge that chapel
our two flags. But nevertheless the sight of them made me sick in the
stomach and uncomfortable. As an Englishman I do not want to be
ascendant over any one. But it makes me very ill when any one tries to
be ascendant over me. I wish we could send back with our compliments
all the trophies that we hold, carriage paid, and get back in return
those two flags and any other flag or two of our own that may be doing
similar duty about the world. I take it that the parcel sent away would
be somewhat more bulky than that which would reach us in return.

The discipline at West Point seemed, as I have said, to be very
severe; but it seemed also that that severity could not in all cases be
maintained. The hours of study also were long, being nearly continuous throughout the day. "English lads of that age could not do it," I
said; thus confessing that English lads must have in them less power
of sustained work than those of America. "They must do it here," said
my informant, "or else leave us." And then he took us off to one of the
young gentleman's quarters, in order that we might see the nature of
their rooms. We found the young gentleman fast asleep on his bed, and
felt uncommonly grieved that we should have thus intruded on him. As
the hour was one of those allocated by my informant in the distribution
of the day to private study, I could not but take the present occupation

of the embryo warrior as an indication that the amount of labour required might be occasionally too much even for an American youth.
"The heat makes one so uncommonly drowsy," said the young man.
I was not the least surprised at the exclamation. The air of the apart-
ment had been warmed up to such a pitch by the hot-pipe apparatus
of the building that prolonged life to me would, I should have thought,
be out of the question in such an atmosphere. "Do you always have it
as hot as this?" I asked. The young man swore that it was so, and with
considerable energy expressed his opinion that all his health and spirits
and vitality were being baked out of him. He seemed to have a strong
opinion on the matter, for which I respected him; but it had never
occurred to him, and did not then occur to him, that anything could
be done to moderate that deathly flow of hot air which came up to
him from the neighbouring infernal regions. He was pale in the face,
and all the lads there were pale. American lads and lasses are all
pale. Men at thirty and women at twenty-five have had all semblance
of youth baked out of them. Infants even are not rosy, and the only
shades known on the cheeks of children are those composed of brown,
yellow, and white. All this comes of those damnable hot-air pipes
with which every tenement in America is infested. "We cannot do
without them," they say. "Our cold is so intense that we must heat
our houses throughout. Open fire-places in a few rooms would not
keep our toes and fingers from the frost." There is much in this. The
assertion is no doubt true, and thereby a great difficulty is created. It
is no doubt quite within the power of American ingenuity to moderate
the heat of these stoves, and to produce such an atmosphere as may
be most conducive to health. In hospitals no doubt this will be done;
perhaps is done at present,—though even in hospitals I have thought
the air hotter than it should be. But hot-air-drinking is like dram-
drinking. There is the machine within the house capable of supplying
any quantity, and those who consume it unconsciously increase their
draughts, and take their drams stronger and stronger, till a breath of
fresh air is felt to be a blast direct from Boreas.

West Point is at all points a military colony, and as such belongs
exclusively to the Federal Government as separate from the Government of any individual State. It is the purchased property of the United
States as a whole, and is devoted to the necessities of a military college.
No man could take a house there, or succeed in getting even permanent lodgings, unless he belonged to or were employed by the establishment. There is no intercourse by road between West Point and
other towns or villages on the river side, and any such intercourse even

by water is looked upon with jealousy by the authorities. The wish is that West Point should be isolated and kept apart for military instruction to the exclusion of all other purposes whatever,—especially love-making purposes. The coming over from the other side of the water of young ladies by the ferry is regarded as a great hindrance. They will come, and then the military students will talk to them. We all know to what such talking leads! A lad when I was there had been tempted to get out of barracks in plain clothes, in order that he might call on a young lady at the hotel;—and was in consequence obliged to abandon his commission and retire from the Academy. Will that young lady ever again sleep quietly in her bed? I should hope not. An opinion was expressed to me that there should be no hotel in such a place;—that there should be no ferry, no roads, no means by which the attention of the students should be distracted;—that these military Rasselases should live in a happy military valley from which might be excluded both strong drinks and female charms,—those two poisons from which youthful military ardour is supposed to suffer so much.

It always seems to me that such training begins at the wrong end. I will not say that nothing should be done to keep lads of eighteen from strong drinks. I will not even say that there should not be some line of moderation with reference to feminine allurements. But as a rule the restraint should come from the sense, good feeling, and education of him who is restrained. There is no embargo on the beer-shops either at Harrow or at Oxford,—and certainly none upon the young ladies. Occasional damage may accrue from habits early depraved, or a heart too early and too easily susceptible; but the injury so done is not, I think, equal to that inflicted by a Draconian code of morals, which will probably be evaded, and will certainly create a desire for its evasion.

Nevertheless, I feel assured that West Point taken as a whole, is an excellent military academy, and that young men have gone forth from it, and will go forth from it, fit for officers as far as training can make men fit. The fault, if fault there be, is that which is to be found in so many of the institutions of the United States; and is one so allied to a virtue that no foreigner has a right to wonder that it is regarded in the light of a virtue by all Americans. There has been an attempt to make the place too perfect. In the desire to have the establishment self-sufficient at all points, more has been attempted than human nature can achieve. The lad is taken to West Point, and it is presumed that from the moment of his reception, he shall expend every energy of his mind and body in making himself a soldier. At fifteen he is not to be a boy, at twenty he is not to be a young man. He is to be a gentleman, a soldier, and an officer. I believe that those who leave the College for the army are gentlemen, soldiers, and officers, and therefore the result is good. But they are also young men; and it seems that they have become so, not in accordance with their training, but in spite of it.

But I have another complaint to make against the authorities of West Point, which they will not be able to answer so easily as that already preferred. What right can they have to take the very prettiest spot on the Hudson—the prettiest spot on the continent—one of the prettiest spots which Nature, with all her vagaries, ever formed—and shut it up from all the world for purposes of war? Would not any plain, however ugly, do for military exercises? Cannot broadsword, goose-step, and double quick time be instilled into young hands and legs in any field of thirty, forty, or fifty acres? I wonder whether these lads appreciate the fact that they are studying fourteen hours a day amidst the sweetest river, rock, and mountain scenery that the imagination can conceive. Of course it will be said that the world at large is not excluded from West Point, that the ferry to the place is open, and that there is even a hotel there, closed against no man or woman who will consent to become a teetotaller for the period of his visit. I must admit that this is so; but still one feels that one is only admitted as a guest. I want to go and live at West Point, and why should I be prevented? The Government had a right to buy it of course, but Government should not buy up the prettiest spots on a country's surface. If I were an American I should make a grievance of this; but Americans will suffer things from their Government which no Englishmen would endure.

It is one of the peculiarities of West Point that every thing there is in good taste. The Point itself consists of a bluff of land so formed that the river Hudson is forced to run round three sides of it. It is consequently a peninsula, and as the surrounding country is mountainous on both sides of the river, it may be imagined that the site is good. The views both up and down the river are lovely, and the mountains behind break themselves so as to make the landscape perfect. But this is not all. At West Point there is much of buildings, much of military arrangement in the way of cannons, forts, and artillery yards. All these things are so contrived as to group themselves well into pictures. There is no picture of architectural grandeur; but everything stands well and where it should stand, and the eye is not hurt at any spot. I regard West Point as a delightful place, and was much gratified by the kindness I received there.

From West Point we went direct to New York.

CHAPTER XIII

AN APOLOGY FOR THE WAR

I THINK it may be received as a fact that the Northern States, taken together, sent a full tenth of their able-bodied men into the ranks of the army in the course of the summer and autumn of 1861. The South, no doubt, sent a much larger proportion; but the effect of such a drain upon the South would not be the same, because the slaves were left at home to perform the agricultural work of the country. I very much doubt whether any other nation ever made such an effort in so short a time. To a people who can do this it may well be granted that they are in earnest; and I do not think it should be lightly decided by any foreigner that they are wrong. The strong and unanimous impulse of a great people is seldom wrong. And let it be borne in mind that in this case both people may be right,—the people both of North and South. Each may have been guided by a just and noble feeling; though each was brought to its present condition by bad government and dishonest statesmen.

There can be no doubt that, since the commencement of the war, the American feeling against England has been very bitter. All Americans to whom I spoke on the subject admitted that it was so. I, as an Englishman, felt strongly the injustice of this feeling, and lost no opportunity of showing or endeavouring to show that the line of conduct pursued by England towards the States was the only line which was compatible with her own policy and just interests, and also with the dignity of the States' Government. I heard much of the tender sympathy of Russia. Russia sent a flourishing general message, saying that she wished the North might win, and ending with some good general advice, proposing peace.[1] It was such a message as strong nations send to those which are weaker. Had England ventured on such council the diplomatic paper would probably have been returned to her. It is, I think, manifest that an absolute and disinterested neu-

---

[1] In June 1861 Alexander II had informed the American Minister of his sympathy with the cause of emancipation. Earlier, at the outbreak of the war, the Russian Foreign Minister had intimated to the American Minister that Russia valued the United States as a counterpoise to England and had no desire to see the Union weakened or destroyed.

trality has been the only course which could preserve England from deserved rebuke,—a neutrality on which her commercial necessity for importing cotton or exporting her own manufactures should have no effect. That our Government would preserve such a neutrality I have always insisted, and I believe it has been done with a pure and strict disregard to any selfish views on the part of Great Britain. So far I think England may feel that she has done well in this matter. But I must confess that I have not been so proud of the tone of all our people at home, as I have been of the decisions of our statesmen. It seems to me that some of us never tire in abusing the Americans, and calling them names for having allowed themselves to be driven into this civil war. We tell them that they are fools and idiots; we speak of their doings as though there had been some plain course by which the war might have been avoided; and we throw it in their teeth that they have no capability for war. We tell them of the debt which they are creating, and point out to them that they can never pay it. We laugh at their attempt to sustain loyalty, and speak of them as a steady father of a family is wont to speak of some unthrifty prodigal who is throwing away his estate and hurrying from one ruinous debauchery to another. And alas! we too frequently allow to escape from us some expression of that satisfaction which one rival tradesman has in the downfall of another. "Here you are with all your boasting," is what we say. "You were going to whip all creation the other day; and it has come to this! Brag is a good dog, but Holdfast is a better. Pray remember that, if ever you find yourselves on your legs again." That little advice about the two dogs is very well, and was not altogether inapplicable. But this is not the time in which it should be given. Putting aside slight asperities, we will all own that the people of the States have been and are our friends, and that as friends we cannot spare them. For one Englishman who brings home to his own heart a feeling of cordiality for France—a belief in the affection of our French alliance— there are ten who do so with reference to the States. Now, in these days of their trouble, I think that we might have borne with them more tenderly.

And how was it possible that they should have avoided this war? I will not now go into the cause of it, or discuss the course which it has taken, but will simply take up the fact of the rebellion. The South rebelled against the North, and such being the case, was it possible that the North should yield without a war? It may very likely be well that Hungary should be severed from Austria, or Poland from Russia, or Venice from Austria. Taking Englishmen in a lump they think that such separation would be well. The subject people do not speak the language of those that govern them, or enjoy kindred interests. But yet when military efforts are made by those who govern Hungary, Poland, and Venice, to prevent such separation, we do not say that Russia and Austria are fools. We are not surprised that they should take up arms against the rebels, but would be very much surprised indeed if they did not do so. We know that nothing but weakness would prevent their doing so. But if Austria and Russia insist on tying to themselves a people who do not speak their language or live in accordance with their habits, and are not considered unreasonable in so insisting, how much more thoroughly would they carry with them the sympathy of their neighbours in preventing any secession by integral parts of their own nationalities? Would England let Ireland walk off by herself if she wished it? In 1843 she did wish it. Three-fourths of the Irish population would have voted for such a separation; but England would have prevented such secession *vi et armis* had Ireland driven her to the necessity of such prevention.[2]

I will put it to any reader of history whether, since government commenced, it has not been regarded as the first duty of government to prevent a separation of the territories governed, and whether also it has not been regarded as a point of honour with all nationalities to preserve uninjured each its own greatness and its own power? I trust that I may not be thought to argue that all governments or even all nationalities should succeed in such endeavours. Few kings have fallen in my day in whose fate I have not rejoiced; none, I take it, except that poor citizen King of the French. And I can rejoice that England lost her American colonies, and shall rejoice when Spain has been deprived of Cuba. But I hold that citizen King of the French in small esteem, seeing that he made no fight, and I know that England was bound to struggle when the Boston people threw her tea into the water. Spain keeps a tighter hand on Cuba than we thought she would some ten years since, and therefore she stands higher in the world's respect.

It may be well that the South should be divided from the North. I am inclined to think that it would be well—at any rate for the North; but the South must have been aware that such division could only be effected in two ways; either by agreement,—in which case the proposition must have been brought forward by the South and discussed by the North,—or by violence. They chose the latter way, as

---

[2] Trollope refers to O'Connell's "monster meetings" of 1843 demanding repeal of the union with England (see the note to page 12).

"*Vi et armis*": "by armed force."

being the readier and the surer, as most seceding nations have done. O'Connell, when struggling for the secession of Ireland, chose the other, and nothing came of it. The South chose violence, and prepared for it secretly and with great adroitness. If that be not rebellion there never has been rebellion since history began; and if civil war was ever justified in one portion of a nation by turbulence in another, it has now been justified in the northern States of America.

What was the North to do; this foolish North, which has been so liberally told by us that she has taken up arms for nothing, that she is fighting for nothing, and will ruin herself for nothing? When was she to take the first step towards peace? Surely every Englishman will remember that when the earliest tidings of the coming quarrel reached us on the election of Mr. Lincoln, we all declared that any division was impossible;—it was a mere madness to speak of it. The States, which were so great in their unity, would never consent to break up all their prestige and all their power by a separation! Would it have been well for the North then to say, "If the South wish it we will certainly separate?" After that, when Mr. Lincoln assumed the power to which he had been elected, and declared with sufficient manliness, and sufficient dignity also, that he would make no war upon the South, but would collect the customs and carry on the government, did we turn round and advise him that he was wrong? No. The idea in England then was that his message was, if anything, too mild. "If he means to be President of the whole Union," England said, "he must come out with something stronger than that." Then came Mr. Seward's speech, which was, in truth, weak enough. Mr. Seward had run Mr. Lincoln very hard for the President's chair on the republican interest, and was —most unfortunately, as I think—made Secretary of State by Mr. Lincoln, or by his party. The Secretary of State holds the highest office in the United States Government under the President. He cannot be compared to our Prime Minister, seeing that the President himself exercises political power, and is responsible for its exercise. Mr. Seward's speech simply amounted to a declaration that separation was a thing of which the Union would neither hear, speak, nor, if possible, think. Things looked very like it; but no; they could never come to that! The world was too good, and especially the American world. Mr. Seward had no specific against secession; but let every free man strike his breast, look up to heaven, determine to be good, and all would go right. A great deal had been expected from Mr. Seward, and when this speech came out, we in England were a little disappointed, and nobody presumed even then that the North would let the South go.

It will be argued by those who have gone into the details of American politics that an acceptance of the Crittenden compromise [3] at this point would have saved the war. What is or was the Crittenden compromise I will endeavour to explain hereafter; but the terms and meaning of that compromise can have no bearing on the subject. The republican party who were in power disapproved of that compromise, and could not model their course upon it. The republican party may have been right or may have been wrong; but surely it will not be argued that any political party elected to power by a majority should follow the policy of a minority, lest that minority should rebel. I can conceive of no government more lowly placed than one which deserts the policy of the majority which supports it, fearing either the tongues or arms of a minority.

As the next scene in the play, the State of South Carolina bombarded Fort Sumter. Was that to be the moment for a peaceable separation? Let us suppose that O'Connell had marched down to the Pigeon House at Dublin, and had taken it—in 1843, let us say—would that have been an argument to us for allowing Ireland to set up for herself? Is that the way of men's minds, or of the minds of nations? The powers of the President were defined by law, as agreed upon among all the States of the Union, and against that power and against that law, South Carolina raised her hand, and the other States joined her in rebellion. When circumstances had come to that, it was no longer possible that the North should shun the war. To my thinking the rights of rebellion are holy. When would the world have been, or where would the world hope to be, without rebellion? But let rebellion look the truth in the face, and not blanch from its own consequences. She has to judge her own opportunities and to decide on her own fitness. Success is the test of her judgment. But rebellion can never be successful except by overcoming the power against which she raises herself. She has no right to expect bloodless triumphs; and if she be not the stronger in the encounter which she creates, she must bear the penalty of her rashness. Rebellion is justified by being better served than constituted authority, but cannot be justified otherwise. Now and again it may happen that rebellion's cause is so good that constituted authority will fall to the ground at the first glance of her sword. This was so the other day in Naples, when Garibaldi blew away the king's armies with a breath. But this is not so often. Rebellion knows that it must fight, and the legalized power against which rebels rise must of necessity fight also.

3 Trollope discusses the Crittenden Compromise at some length on pages 283–5.

I cannot see at what point the North first sinned; nor do I think that had the North yielded, England would have honoured her for her meekness. Had she yielded without striking a blow she would have been told that she had suffered the Union to drop asunder by her supineness. She would have been twitted with cowardice, and told that she was no match for Southern energy. It would then have seemed to those who sat in judgment on her that she might have righted everything by that one blow from which she had abstained. But having struck that one blow, and having found that it did not suffice, could she then withdraw, give way, and own herself beaten? Has it been so usually with Anglo-Saxon pluck? In such case as that would there have been no mention of those two dogs, Brag and Holdfast? The man of the northern States knows that he has bragged,—bragged as loudly as his English forefathers. In that matter of bragging the British lion and the Star-spangled banner may abstain from throwing mud at each other. And now the northern man wishes to show that he can hold fast also. Looking at all this I cannot see that peace has been possible to the North.

As to the question of secession and rebellion being one and the same thing, the point to me does not seem to bear an argument. The confederation of States had a common army, a common policy, a common capital, a common government, and a common debt. If one might secede, any or all might secede, and where then would be their property, their debt, and their servants? A confederation with such a license attached to it would have been simply playing at national power. If New York had seceded—a State which stretches from the Atlantic to British North America—it would have cut New England off from the rest of the Union. Was it legally within the power of New York to place the six States of New England in such a position? And why should it be assumed that so suicidal a power of destroying a nationality should be inherent in every portion of the nation? The States are bound together by a written compact, but that compact gives each State no such power. Surely such a power would have been specified had it been intended that it should be given. But there are axioms in politics as in mathematics, which recommend themselves to the mind at once, and require no argument for their proof. Men who are not argumentative perceive at once that they are true. A part cannot be greater than the whole.

I think it is plain that the remnant of the Union was bound to take up arms against those States which had illegally torn themselves off from her; and if so, she could only do so with such weapons as were at her hand. The United States' army had never been numerous or well appointed; and of such officers and equipments as it possessed, the more valuable part was in the hands of the Southerners. It was clear enough that she was ill-provided, and that in going to war she was undertaking a work as to which she had still to learn many of the rudiments. But Englishmen should be the last to twit her with such ignorance. It is not yet ten years since we were all boasting that swords and guns were useless things, and that military expenditure might be cut down to any minimum figure that an economizing Chancellor of the Exchequer could name. Since that we have extemporized two, if not three armies. There are our volunteers at home; and the army which holds India can hardly be considered as one with that which is to maintain our prestige in Europe and the West. We made some natural blunders in the Crimea, but in making those blunders we taught ourselves the trade. It is the misfortune of the northern States that they must learn these lessons in fighting their own countrymen. In the course of our history we have suffered the same calamity more than once. The Roundheads, who beat the Cavaliers and created English liberty, made themselves soldiers on the bodies of their countrymen. But England was not ruined by that civil war; nor was she ruined by those which preceded it. From out of these she came forth stronger than she entered them,—stronger, better, and more fit for a great destiny in the history of nations. The northern States had nearly five hundred thousand men under arms when the winter of 1861 commenced, and for that enormous multitude all commissariat requirements were well supplied. Camps and barracks sprang up through the country as though by magic. Clothing was obtained with a rapidity that has, I think, never been equalled. The country had not been prepared for the fabrication of arms, and yet arms were put into the men's hands almost as quickly as the regiments could be mustered. The eighteen millions of the northern States lent themselves to the effort as one man. Each State gave the best it had to give. Newspapers were as rabid against each other as ever, but no newspaper could live which did not support the war. "The South has rebelled against the law, and the law shall be supported." This has been the cry and the heartfelt feeling of all men; and it is a feeling which cannot but inspire respect.

We have heard much of the tyranny of the present Government of the United States, and of the tyranny also of the people. They have both been very tyrannical. The "habeas corpus" has been suspended by the word of one man. Arrests have been made on men who have been hardly suspected of more than secession principles. Arrests have,

I believe, been made in cases which have been destitute even of any fair ground for such suspicion. Newspapers have been stopped for advocating views opposed to the feelings of the North, as freely as newspapers were ever stopped in France for opposing the Emperor. A man has not been safe in the streets who was known to be a Secessionist. It must be at once admitted that opinion in the northern States was not free when I was there. But has opinion ever been free anywhere on all subjects? In the best-built strongholds of freedom have there not always been questions on which opinion has not been free; and must it not always be so? When the decision of a people on any matter has become, so to say, unanimous,—when it has shown itself to be so general as to be clearly the expression of the nation's voice as a single chorus,—that decision becomes holy, and may not be touched. Could any newspaper be produced in England which advocated the overthrow of the Queen? And why may not the passion for the Union be as strong with the northern States, as the passion for the Crown is strong with us? The Crown with us is in no danger, and therefore the matter is at rest. But I think we must admit that in any nation, let it be ever so free, there may be points on which opinion must be held under restraint. And as to those summary arrests, and the suspension of the "habeas corpus," is there not something to be said for the States' Government on that head also? Military arrests are very dreadful, and the soul of a nation's liberty is that personal freedom from arbitrary interference which is signified to the world by those two unintelligible Latin words. A man's body shall not be kept in duress at any man's will; but shall be brought up into open court, with uttermost speed, in order that the law may say whether or no it should be kept in duress. That I take it is the meaning of "habeas corpus," and it is easy to see that the suspension of that privilege destroys all freedom, and places the liberty of every individual at the mercy of him who has the power to suspend it. Nothing can be worse than this; and such suspension, if extended over any long period of years, will certainly make a nation weak, mean-spirited, and poor. But in a period of civil war, or even of a widely-extended civil commotion, things cannot work in their accustomed grooves. A lady does not willingly get out of her bedroom-window with nothing on but her nightgown; but when her house is on fire she is very thankful for an opportunity of doing so. It is not long since the "habeas corpus" was suspended in parts of Ireland, and absurd arrests were made almost daily when that suspension first took effect. It was grievous that there should be necessity for such a step, and it is very grievous now that such necessity should be felt in the northern States. But I do not think that it becomes Englishmen to bear hardly upon Americans generally for what has been done in that matter. Mr. Seward, in an official letter to the British Minister at Washington—which letter, through official dishonesty, found its way to the press—claimed for the President the right of suspending the "habeas corpus" in the States whenever it might seem good to him to do so. If this be in accordance with the law of the land, which I think must be doubted, the law of the land is not favourable to freedom. For myself, I conceive that Mr. Lincoln and Mr. Seward have been wrong in their law, and that no such right is given to the President by the Constitution of the United States. This I will attempt to prove in some subsequent chapter. But I think it must be felt by all who have given any thought to the Constitution of the States, that let what may be the letter of the law, the Presidents of the United States have had no such power. It is because the States have been no longer united that Mr. Lincoln has had the power, whether it be given to him by the law or no.

And then as to the debt; it seems to me very singular that we in England should suppose that a great commercial people would be ruined by a national debt. As regards ourselves, I have always looked on our national debt as the ballast in our ship. We have a great deal of ballast, but then the ship is very big. The States also are taking in ballast at a rather rapid rate;—and we too took it in quickly when we were about it. But I cannot understand why their ship should not carry, without shipwreck, that which our ship has carried without damage, and, as I believe, with positive advantage to its sailing. The ballast, if carried honestly, will not, I think, bring the vessel to grief. The fear is lest the ballast should be thrown overboard.

So much I have said, wishing to plead the cause of the northern States before the bar of English opinion, and thinking that there is ground for a plea in their favour. But yet I cannot say that their bitterness against Englishmen has been justified, or that their tone towards England has been dignified. Their complaint is that they have received no sympathy from England; but it seems to me that a great nation should not require an expression of sympathy during its struggle. Sympathy is for the weak rather than for the strong. When I hear two powerful men contending together in argument, I do not sympathize with him who has the best of it; but I watch the precision of his logic, and acknowledge the effects of his rhetoric. There has been a whining weakness in the complaints made by Americans against England, which has done more to lower them as a people in my judgment than any other part of their conduct during the present crisis. When we were at war with Russia, the feeling of the States was strongly against us. All their wishes were with our enemies. When the Indian mutiny was at its worst, the feeling of France was equally adverse to us. The joy expressed by the French newspapers was almost ecstatic. But I do not think that on either occasion we bemoaned ourselves sadly on the want of sympathy shown by our friends. On each occasion we took the opinion expressed for what it was worth, and managed to live it down. We listened to what was said, and let it pass by. When in each case we had been successful, there was an end of our friends' croakings.

But in the northern States of America the bitterness against England has amounted almost to a passion. The players, those chroniclers of the time, have had no hits so sure as those which have been aimed at Englishmen as cowards, fools, and liars. No paper has dared to say that England has been true in her American policy. The name of an Englishman has been made a byword for reproach. In private intercourse private amenities have remained. I, at any rate, may boast that such has been the case as regards myself. But even in private life I have been unable to keep down the feeling that I have always been walking over smothered ashes.

It may be that, when the civil war in America is over, all this will pass by, and there will be nothing left of international bitterness but its memory. It is sincerely to be hoped that this may be so;—that even the memory of the existing feeling may fade away and become unreal. I for one cannot think that two nations, situated as are the States and England, should permanently quarrel and avoid each other. But words have been spoken which will, I fear, long sound in men's ears, and thoughts have sprung up which will not easily allow themselves to be extinguished.

CHAPTER XIV

New York

Speaking of New York as a traveller I have two faults to find with it. In the first place there is nothing to see; and in the second place there is no mode of getting about to see anything. Nevertheless New York is a most interesting city. It is the third biggest city in the known world;—for those Chinese congregations of unwinged ants are not cities in the known world. In no other city is there a population so mixed and cosmopolitan in their modes of life. And yet in no other city that I have seen are there such strong and ever-visible characteristics of the social and political bearings of the nation to which it belongs. New York appears to me as infinitely more American than Boston, Chicago, or Washington. It has no peculiar attribute of its own, as have those three cities; Boston in its literature and accomplished intelligence, Chicago in its internal trade, and Washington in its congressional and State politics. New York has its literary aspirations, its commercial grandeur, and,—heaven knows,—it has its politics also. But these do not strike the visitor as being specially characteristic of the city. That it is pre-eminently American is its glory or its disgrace,—as men of different ways of thinking may decide upon it. Free institutions, general education, and the ascendancy of dollars are the words written on every paving-stone along Fifth Avenue, down Broadway, and up Wall Street. Every man can vote, and values the privilege. Every man can read, and uses the privilege. Every man worships the dollar, and is down before his shrine from morning to night.

As regards voting and reading no American will be angry with me for saying so much of him; and no Englishman, whatever may be his ideas as to the franchise in his own country, will conceive that I have said aught to the dishonour of an American. But as to that dollar-worshipping, it will of course seem that I am abusing the New Yorkers. We all know what a wretchedly wicked thing money is! How it stands between us and heaven! How it hardens our hearts, and makes vulgar our thoughts! Dives has ever gone to the devil, while Lazarus has been laid up in heavenly lavender. The hand that employs itself in compelling gold to enter the service of man has always been stigmatized as the ravisher of things sacred. The world is agreed about that, and therefore the New Yorker is in a bad way. There are very few citizens in any town known to me which under this dispensation are in a good way, but the New Yorker is in about the worst way of all. Other men, the world over, worship regularly at the shrine with matins and vespers, nones and complines, and whatever other daily services may be known to the religious houses; but the New Yorker is always on his knees.

That is the amount of the charge which I bring against New York; and now having laid on my paint thickly, I shall proceed, like an unskilful artist, to scrape a great deal of it off again. New York has been a leading commercial city in the world for not more than fifty or sixty years. As far as I can learn, its population at the close of the last century did not exceed 60,000, and ten years later it had not reached 100,000. In 1860, it had reached nearly 800,000 in the city of New York itself. To this number must be added the numbers of Brooklyn, Williamsburgh, and the city of New Jersey, in order that a true conception may be had of the population of this American metropolis, seeing that those places are as much a part of New York as Southwark is of London. By this the total will be swelled to considerably above a million. It will no doubt be admitted that this growth has been very fast, and that New York may well be proud of it. Increase of population is, I take it, the only trustworthy sign of a nation's success or of a city's success. We boast that London has beaten the other cities of the world, and think that that boast is enough to cover all the social sins for which London has to confess her guilt. New York beginning with 60,000 sixty years since has now a million souls;—a million mouths, all of which eat a sufficiency of bread, all of which speak *ore rotundo*,[1] and almost all of which can read. And this has come of its love of dollars.

For myself I do not believe that Dives is so black as he is painted, or that his peril is so imminent. To reconcile such an opinion with holy writ might place me in some difficulty were I a clergyman. Clergymen in these days are surrounded by difficulties of this nature, finding it necessary to explain away many old-established teachings which narrowed the Christian Church, and to open the door wide enough to satisfy the aspirations and natural hopes of instructed men. The brethren of Dives are now so many and so intelligent that they will no longer consent to be damned, without looking closely into the matter themselves. I will leave them to settle the matter with the Church,

[1] "with finished grace." Horace (*Ars Poetica*, line 323) uses the phrase in referring to the talents of the Greeks.

merely assuring them of my sympathies in their little difficulties in any case in which mere money causes the hitch.

To eat his bread in the sweat of his brow was man's curse in Adam's day, but is certainly man's blessing in our day. And what is eating one's bread in the sweat of one's brow but making money? I will believe no man who tells me that he would not sooner earn two loaves than one;—and if two, then two hundred. I will believe no man who tells me that he would sooner earn one dollar a day than two;—and if two, then two hundred. That is, in the very nature of the argument,— *cæteris paribus*.[2] When a man tells me that he would prefer one honest loaf to two that are dishonest, I will, in all possible cases, believe him. So also a man may prefer one quiet loaf to two that are unquiet. But under circumstances that are the same, and to a man who is sane, a whole loaf is better than half, and two loaves are better than one. The preachers have preached well, but on this matter they have preached in vain. Dives has never believed that he will be damned because he is Dives. He has never even believed that the temptations incident to his position have been more than a fair counterpoise, or even so much as a fair counterpoise, to his opportunities for doing good. All men who work desire to prosper by their work, and they so desire by the nature given to them from God. Wealth and progress must go on hand in hand together, let the accidents which occasionally divide them for a time happen as often as they may. The progress of the Americans has been caused by their aptitude for money-making, and that continual kneeling at the shrine of the coined goddess has carried them across from New York to San Francisco. Men who kneel at that shrine are called on to have ready wits, and quick hands, and not a little aptitude for self-denial. The New Yorker has been true to his dollar, because his dollar has been true to him.

But not on this account can I, nor on this account will any Englishman, reconcile himself to the savour of dollars which pervades the atmosphere of New York. The *ars celare artem*[3] is wanting. The making of money is the work of man; but he need not take his work to bed with him, and have it ever by his side at table, amidst his family, in church, while he disports himself, as he declares his passion to the girl of his heart, in the moments of his softest bliss, and at the periods of his most solemn ceremonies. That many do so elsewhere than in New York,—in London, for instance, in Paris, among the mountains of Switzerland, and the steppes of Russia, I do not doubt. But there is

2 "other things being equal."
3 "the art of concealing art," a proverbial expression.

generally a veil thrown over the object of the worshipper's idolatry. In New York one's ear is constantly filled with the fanatic's voice as he prays, one's eyes are always on the familiar altar. The frankincense from the temple is ever in one's nostrils. I have never walked down Fifth Avenue alone without thinking of money. I have never walked there with a companion without talking of it. I fancy that every man there, in order to maintain the spirit of the place, should bear on his forehead a label stating how many dollars he is worth, and that every label should be expected to assert a falsehood.

I do not think that New York has been less generous in the use of its money than other cities, or that the men of New York generally are so. Perhaps I might go farther and say that in no city has more been achieved for humanity by the munificence of its richest citizens than in New York. Its hospitals, asylums, and institutions for the relief of all ailments to which flesh is heir, are very numerous, and beyond praise in the excellence of their arrangements. And this has been achieved in a great degree by private liberality. Men in America are not as a rule anxious to leave large fortunes to their children. The millionaire when making his will very generally gives back a considerable portion of the wealth which he has made to the city in which he made it. The rich citizen is always anxious that the poor citizen shall be relieved. It is a point of honour with him to raise the character of his municipality, and to provide that the deaf and dumb, the blind, the mad, the idiots, the old, and the incurable shall have such alleviation in their misfortune as skill and kindness can afford.

Nor is the New Yorker a hugger-mugger with his money. He does not hide up his dollars in old stockings and keep rolls of gold in hidden pots. He does not even invest it where it will not grow but only produce small though sure fruit. He builds houses, he speculates largely, he spreads himself in trade to the extent of his wings,—and not seldom somewhat further. He scatters his wealth broadcast over strange fields, trusting that it may grow with an increase of an hundred-fold, but bold to bear the loss should the strange field prove itself barren. His regret at losing his money is by no means commensurate with his desire to make it. In this there is a living spirit which to me divests the dollar-worshipping idolatry of something of its ugliness. The hand when closed on the gold is instantly reopened. The idolator is anxious to get, but he is anxious also to spend. He is energetic to the last, and has no comfort with his stock unless it breeds with transatlantic rapidity of procreation.

So much I say, being anxious to scrape off some of that daub of black paint with which I have smeared the face of my New Yorker; but not desiring to scrape it all off. For myself, I do not love to live amidst the clink of gold, and never have "a good time," as the Americans say, when the price of shares and percentages come up in conversation. That state of men's minds here which I have endeavoured to explain tends, I think, to make New York disagreeable. A stranger there who has no great interest in percentages soon finds himself anxious to escape. By degrees he perceives that he is out of his element, and had better go away. He calls at the bank, and when he shows himself ignorant as to the price at which his sovereigns should be done, he is conscious that he is ridiculous. He is like a man who goes out hunting for the first time at forty years of age. He feels himself to be in the wrong place, and is anxious to get out of it. Such was my experience of New York, at each of the visits that I paid to it.

But, yet, I say again, no other American city is so intensely American as New York. It is generally considered that the inhabitants of New England, the Yankees properly so called, have the American characteristics of physiognomy in the fullest degree. The lantern jaws, the thin and lithe body, the dry face on which there has been no tint of the rose since the baby's long-clothes were first abandoned, the harsh, thick hair, the thin lips, the intelligent eyes, the sharp voice with the nasal twang—not altogether harsh, though sharp and nasal,— all these traits are supposed to belong especially to the Yankee. Perhaps it was so once, but at present they are, I think, more universally common in New York than in any other part of the States. Go to Wall Street, the front of the Astor House, and the regions about Trinity Church, and you will find them in their fullest perfection.

What circumstances of blood or food, of early habit or subsequent education, have created for the latter-day American his present physiognomy? It is as completely marked, as much his own, as is that of any race under the sun that has bred in and in for centuries. But the American owns a more mixed blood than any other race known. The chief stock is English, which is itself so mixed that no man can trace its ramifications. With this are mingled the bloods of Ireland, Holland, France, Sweden, and Germany. All this has been done within but a few years, so that the American may be said to have no claim to any national type of face. Nevertheless, no man has a type of face so clearly national as the American. He is acknowledged by it all over the continent of Europe, and on his own side of the water is gratified by knowing that he is never mistaken for his English visitor. I think it comes from the hot-air pipes and from dollar worship.[4] In the Jesuit his mode of dealing with things divine has given a peculiar cast of countenance; and why should not the American be similarly moulded by his special aspirations? As to the hot-air pipes, there can, I think be no doubt that to them is to be charged the murder of all rosy cheeks throughout the States. If the effect was to be noticed simply in the dry faces of the men about Wall Street, I should be very indifferent to the matter. But the young ladies of Fifth Avenue are in the same category. The very pith and marrow of life is baked out of their young bones by the hot-air chambers to which they are accustomed. Hot air is the great destroyer of American beauty.

In saying that there is very little to be seen in New York, I have also said that there is no way of seeing that little. My assertion amounts to this,—that there are no cabs. To the reading world at large this may not seem to be much, but let the reading world go to New York, and it will find out how much the deficiency means. In London, in Paris, in Florence, in Rome, in the Havana, or at Grand Cairo, the cab-driver or attendant does not merely drive the cab or belabour the donkey, but he is the visitor's easiest and cheapest guide. In London, the Tower, Westminster Abbey, and Madame Tussaud are found by the stranger without difficulty, and almost without a thought, because the cab-driver knows the whereabouts and the way. Space is moreover annihilated, and the huge distances of the English metropolis are brought within the scope of mortal power. But in New York there is no such institution.

In New York there are street omnibuses as we have,—there are street cars such as last year we declined to have,[5]—and there are very excellent public carriages; but none of these give you the accommoda-

---

[4] Anthony Trollope's mother, in *Domestic Manners of the Americans*, had traced the singularity of the American countenance to another cause:

"I am inclined to think this most vile and universal habit of chewing tobacco is the cause of a remarkable peculiarity of the male physiognomy of Americans; their lips are almost uniformly thin and compressed. At first I accounted for this upon Lavater's theory, and attributed it to the arid temperament of the people; but it is too universal to be so explained; whereas the habit above mentioned, which pervades all classes (excepting the literary) well accounts for it, as the act of expressing the juices of this loathsome herb, enforces exactly that position of the lips, which gives this remarkable peculiarity to the American countenance."

[5] London had already decided upon an underground system. In 1861 the first four and a half miles of subway were completed. The coal-burning locomotive invented by John Fowler made travel in the tunnels feasible. His engine condensed its own steam and damped its flues so efficiently that "not the least smell of smoke was given off."

tion of a cab, nor can all of them combined do so. The omnibuses, though clean and excellent, were to me very unintelligible. They have no conductor to them. To know their different lines and usages a man should have made a scientific study of the city. To those going up and down Broadway I became accustomed, but in them I was never quite at my ease. The money has to be paid through a little hole behind the driver's back, and should, as I learned at last, be paid immediately on entrance. But in getting up to do this I always stumbled about, and it would happen that when with considerable difficulty I had settled my own account, two or three ladies would enter, and would hand me, without a word, some coins with which I had no life-long familiarity in order that I might go through the same ceremony on their account. The change I would usually drop into the straw, and then there would arise trouble and unhappiness. Before I became aware of that law as to instant payment, bells used to be rung at me which made me uneasy. I knew I was not behaving as a citizen should behave, but could not compass the exact points of my delinquency. And then when I desired to escape, the door being strapped up tight, I would halloo vainly at the driver through the little hole; whereas, had I known my duty, I should have rung a bell, or pulled a strap, according to the nature of the omnibus in question. In a month or two all these things may possibly be learned;—but the visitor requires his facilities for locomotion at the first moment of his entrance into the city. I heard it asserted by a lecturer in Boston, Mr. Wendell Phillips, whose name is there a household word, that citizens of the United States carried brains in their fingers as well as in their heads, whereas "common people," by which Mr. Phillips intended to designate the remnant of mankind beyond the United States, were blessed with no such extended cerebral development. Having once learned this fact from Mr. Phillips, I understood why it was that a New York omnibus should be so disagreeable to me, and at the same time so suitable to the wants of the New Yorkers.

And then there are streets cars—very long omnibuses—which run on rails but are dragged by horses. They are capable of holding forty passengers each, and as far as my experience goes carry an average load of sixty. The fare of the omnibus is six cents or three pence. That of the street car five cents or two pence half-penny. They run along the different avenues, taking the length of the city. In the upper or new part of the town their course is simple enough, but as they descend to the Bowery, Peckslip, and Pearl Street, nothing can be conceived more difficult or devious than their courses. The Broadway omnibus, on the other hand, is a straightforward honest vehicle in the lower part of the town, becoming, however, dangerous and miscellaneous when it ascends to Union Square and the vicinities of fashionable life.

The street cars are manned with conductors, and therefore are free from many of the perils of the omnibus, but they have perils of their own. They are always quite full. By that I mean that every seat is crowded, that there is a double row of men and women standing down the centre, and that the driver's platform in front is full, and also the conductor's platform behind. That is the normal condition of a street car in the Third Avenue. You, as a stranger in the middle of the car, wish to be put down at, let us say, 89th Street. In the map of New York now before me the cross streets running from east to west are numbered up northwards as far as 154th Street. It is quite useless for you to give the number as you enter. Even an American conductor, with brains all over him, and an anxious desire to accommodate as is the case with all these men, cannot remember. You are left therefore in misery to calculate the number of the street as you move along, vainly endeavouring through the misty glass to decipher the small numbers which after a day or two you perceive to be written on the lamp posts.

But I soon gave up all attempts at keeping a seat in one of these cars. It became my practice to sit down on the outside iron rail behind, and as the conductor generally sat in my lap I was in a measure protected. As for the inside of these vehicles, the women of New York, were, I must confess, too much for me. I would no sooner place myself on a seat, than I would be called on by a mute, unexpressive, but still impressive stare into my face, to surrender my place. From cowardice if not from gallantry I would always obey; and as this led to discomfort and an irritated spirit, I preferred nursing the conductor on the hard bar in the rear.

And here if I seem to say a word against women in America, I beg that it may be understood that I say that word only against a certain class; and even as to that class I admit that they are respectable, intelligent, and, as I believe, industrious. Their manners, however, are to me more odious than those of any other human beings that I ever met elsewhere. Nor can I go on with that which I have to say without carrying my apology further, lest perchance I should be misunderstood by some American women whom I would not only exclude from my censure, but would include in the very warmest eulogium which words of mine could express as to those of the female sex whom I love and admire the most. I have known, do know, and mean to continue to know as far as in me may lie, American ladies as bright, as beautiful, as graceful, as sweet, as mortal limits for brightness, beauty, grace, and sweetness will permit. They belong to the aristocracy of the land, by whatever means they may have become aristocrats. In America one does not inquire as to their birth, their training, or their old names. The fact of their aristocratic power comes out in every word and look. It is not only so with those who have travelled or with those who are rich. I have found female aristocrats with families and slender means, who have as yet made no grand tour across the ocean. These women are charming beyond expression. It is not only their beauty. Had he been speaking of such, Wendell Phillips would have been right in saying that they have brains all over them. So much for those who are bright and beautiful; who are graceful and sweet! And now a word as to those who to me are neither bright nor beautiful; and who can be to none either graceful or sweet.

It is a hard task that of speaking ill of any woman, but it seems to me that he who takes upon himself to praise incurs the duty of dispraising also where dispraise is, or to him seems to be, deserved. The trade of a novelist is very much that of describing the softness, sweetness, and loving dispositions of women; and this he does, copying as best he can from nature. But if he only sings of that which is sweet, whereas that which is not sweet too frequently presents itself, his song will in the end be untrue and ridiculous. Women are entitled to much observance from men, but they are entitled to no observance which is incompatible with truth. Women, by the conventional laws of society, are allowed to exact much from men, but they are allowed to exact nothing for which they should not make some adequate return. It is well that a man should kneel in spirit before the grace and weakness of a woman, but it is not well that he should kneel either in spirit or body if there be neither grace or weakness. A man should yield everything to a woman for a word, for a smile,—to one look of entreaty. But if there be no look of entreaty, no word, no smile, I do not see that he is called upon to yield much.

The happy privileges with which women are at present blessed, have come to them from the spirit of chivalry. That spirit has taught men to endure in order that women may be at their ease; and has generally taught women to accept the ease bestowed on them with grace and thankfulness. But in America the spirit of chivalry has sunk deeper among men than it has among women. It must be borne in mind that in that country material well-being and education are more extended than with us; and that, therefore, men there have learned to be chivalrous who with us have hardly progressed so far. The conduct of men to women throughout the States is always gracious. They have learned the lesson. But it seems to me that the women have not advanced as far as the men have done. They have acquired a sufficient perception of the privileges which chivalry gives them, but no perception of that return which chivalry demands from them. Women of the class to which I allude are always talking of their rights; but seem to have a most indifferent idea of their duties. They have no scruple at demanding from men everything that a man can be called on to relinquish in a woman's behalf, but they do so without any of that grace which turns the demand made into a favour conferred.

I have seen much of this in various cities of America, but much more of it in New York than elsewhere. I have heard young Americans complain of it, swearing that they must change the whole tenor of their habits towards women. I have heard American ladies speak of it with loathing and disgust. For myself, I have entertained on sundry occasions that sort of feeling for an American woman which the close vicinity of an unclean animal produces. I have spoken of this with reference to street cars, because in no position of life does an unfortunate man become more liable to these anti-feminine atrocities than in the centre of one of these vehicles.[6] The woman, as she enters, drags after her a misshapen, dirty mass of battered wirework, which she calls her crinoline, and which adds as much to her grace and comfort as a log of wood does to a donkey when tied to the animal's leg in a paddock. Of this she takes much heed, not managing it so that it may be conveyed up the carriage with some decency, but striking it about against men's legs, and heaving it with violence over people's knees. The touch of a real woman's dress is in itself delicate; but these blows from a harpy's fins are loathsome. If there be two of them they talk loudly together, having a theory that modesty has been put out of court by women's rights. But, though not modest, the woman I describe is ferocious in her propriety. She ignores the whole world around her, and as she sits with raised chin and face flattened by affectation, she pretends to declare aloud that she is positively not aware that any man is even near her. She speaks as though to her, in her womanhood, the neighbourhood of men was the same as that of dogs or cats. They are there, but she does not hear them, see them, or even acknowledge

6 "The worst of it is that his picture is a true one. We all know the woman who comes flaunting into the cars, swinging her crinoline, accepting every courtesy as though it were a covert insult; we know her in the streets, sweeping along as though the world owed her a vast debt for exhibiting her wonders to the public eye; we know her and her daughter at the hotel table, with her fantastic wriggle. . . . We ought to be greatly obliged to Mr. Trollope, who faithfully daguerreotypes the species."—*Harper's New Monthly Magazine* for June 1862.

them by any courtesy of motion. But her own face always gives her the
lie. In her assumption of indifference she displays her nasty consciousness, and in each attempt at a would-be propriety is guilty of an im-
modesty. Who does not know the timid retiring face of the young girl
who when alone among men unknown to her feels that it becomes her
to keep herself secluded? As many men as there are around her, so
many knights has such a one, ready bucklered for her service, should
occasion require such services. Should it not, she passes on unmolested,
—but not, as she herself will wrongly think, unheeded. But as to her
of whom I am speaking, we may say that every twist of her body, and
every tone of her voice is an unsuccessful falsehood. She looks square
at you in the face, and you rise to give her your seat. You rise from a
deference to your own old convictions, and from that courtesy which
you have ever paid to a woman's dress, let it be worn with ever such
hideous deformities. She takes the place from which you have moved
without a word or a bow. She twists herself round, banging your shins
with her wires, while her chin is still raised, and her face is still flattened, and she directs her friend's attention to another seated man, as
though that place were also vacant, and necessarily at her disposal. Perhaps the man opposite has his own ideas about chivalry. I have seen
such a thing, and have rejoiced to see it.

    You will meet these women daily, hourly,—everywhere in the
streets. Now and again you will find them in society, making themselves
even more odious there than elsewhere. Who they are, whence they
come, and why they are so unlike that other race of women of which I
have spoken, you will settle for yourself. Do we not all say of our chance
acquaintances after half an hour's conversation,—nay, after half an
hour spent in the same room without conversation,—that this woman
is a lady, and that that other woman is not? They jostle each other
even among us, but never seem to mix. They are closely allied; but
neither imbues the other with her attributes. Both shall be equally
well-born, or both shall be equally ill-born; but still it is so. The contrast exists in England; but in America it is much stronger. In England women become ladylike or vulgar. In the States they are either
charming or odious.

    See that female walking down Broadway. She is not exactly such a
one as her I have attempted to describe on her entrance into the street
car; for this lady is well-dressed, if fine clothes will make well-dressing.
The machinery of her hoops is not battered, and altogether she is a
personage much more distinguished in all her expenditures. But yet
she is a copy of the other woman. Look at the train which she drags

behind her over the dirty pavement, where dogs have been, and chewers of tobacco, and everything concerned with filth except a scavenger. At every hundred yards some unhappy man treads upon the silken swab which she trails behind her,—loosening it dreadfully at the girth one would say; and then see the style of face and the expression of features with which she accepts the sinner's half-muttered apology. The world, she supposes, owes her everything because of her silken train,—even room enough in a crowded thoroughfare to drag it along unmolested. But, according to her theory, she owes the world nothing in return. She is a woman with perhaps a hundred dollars on her back, and having done the world the honour of wearing them in the world's presence, expects to be repaid by the world's homage and chivalry. But chivalry owes her nothing,—nothing, though she walk about beneath a hundred times a hundred dollars,—nothing even though she be a woman. Let every woman learn this,—that chivalry owes her nothing unless she also acknowledge her debt to chivalry. She must acknowledge it and pay it; and then chivalry will not be backward in making good her claims upon it.

All this has come of the street cars. But as it was necessary that I should say it somewhere, it is as well said on that subject as on any other. And now to continue with the street cars. They run, as I have said, the length of the town, taking parallel lines. They will take you from the Astor House, near the bottom of the town, for miles and miles northward,—half way up the Hudson river,—for, I believe, five pence. They are very slow, averaging about five miles an hour; but they are very sure. For regular inhabitants, who have to travel five or six miles perhaps to their daily work, they are excellent. I have nothing really to say against the street cars. But they do not fill the place of cabs.

There are, however, public carriages, roomy vehicles dragged by two horses, clean and nice, and very well suited to ladies visiting the city. But they have none of the attributes of the cab. As a rule they are not to be found standing about. They are very slow. They are very dear. A dollar an hour is the regular charge; but one cannot regulate one's motion by the hour. Going out to dinner and back costs two dollars, over a distance which in London would cost two shillings. As a rule, the cost is four times that of a cab; and the rapidity half that of a cab. Under these circumstances I think I am justified in saying that there is no mode of getting about in New York to see anything.

And now as to the other charge against New York, of there being nothing to see. How should there be anything there to see of general interest? In other large cities, cities as large in name as New York, there are works of art, fine buildings, ruins, ancient churches, picturesque costumes, and the tombs of celebrated men. But in New York there are none of these things. Art has not yet grown up there. One or two fine figures by Crawford are in the town,—especially that of the sorrowing Indian at the rooms of the Historical Society; but art is a luxury in a city which follows but slowly on the heels of wealth and civilization. Of fine buildings,—which indeed are comprised in art,— there are none deserving special praise or remark. It might well have been that New York should ere this have graced herself with something grand in architecture; but she has not done so. Some good architectural effect there is, and much architectural comfort. Of ruins of course there can be none; none at least of such ruins as travellers admire, though perhaps some of that sort which disgraces rather than decorates. Churches there are plenty, but none that are ancient. The costume is the same as our own; and I need hardly say that it is not picturesque. And the time for the tombs of celebrated men has not yet come. A great man's ashes are hardly of value till they have all but ceased to exist.

The visitor to New York must seek his gratification and obtain his instruction from the habits and manners of men. The American, though he dresses like an Englishman, and eats roast beef with a silver fork,—or sometimes with a steel knife,—as does an Englishman, is not like an Englishman in his mind, in his aspirations, in his tastes, or in his politics. In his mind he is quicker, more universally intelligent, more ambitious of general knowledge, less indulgent of stupidity and ignorance in others, harder, sharper, brighter with the surface brightness of steel, than is an Englishman; but he is more brittle, less enduring, less malleable, and I think less capable of impressions. The mind of the Englishman has more imagination, but that of the American more incision. The American is a great observer, but he observes things material rather than things social or picturesque. He is a constant and ready speculator; but all speculations, even those which come of philosophy, are with him more or less material. In his aspirations the American is more constant than an Englishman,—or I should rather say he is more constant in aspiring. Every citizen of the United States intends to do something. Every one thinks himself capable of some effort. But in his aspirations he is more limited than an Englishman. The ambitious American never soars so high as the ambitious Englishman. He does not even see up to so great a height; and when he has raised himself somewhat above the crowd becomes sooner dizzy with his own altitude. An American of mark, though always anxious to show his mark, is always fearful of a fall. In his tastes the American imitates the Frenchman. Who shall dare to say that he is wrong, seeing that in general matters of design and luxury the French have won for themselves the foremost name? I will not say that the American is wrong, but I cannot avoid thinking that he is so. I detest what is called French taste; but the world is against me. When I complained to a landlord of an hotel out in the West that his furniture was useless; that I could not write at a marble table whose outside rim was curved into fantastic shapes; that a gold clock in my bedroom which did not go would give me no aid in washing myself; that a heavy, immoveable curtain shut out the light; and that *papier-maché* chairs with small fluffy velvet seats were bad to sit on,—he answered me completely by telling me that his house had been furnished not in accordance with the taste of England, but with that of France. I acknowledged the rebuke, gave up my pursuits of literature and cleanliness, and hurried out of the house as quickly as I could. All America is now furnishing itself by the rules which guided that hotel-keeper. I do not merely allude to actual household furniture,—to chairs, tables, and detestable gilt clocks. The taste of America is becoming French in its conversation, French in its comforts and French in its discomforts, French in its eating, and French in its dress, French in its manners, and will become French in its art. There are those who will say that English taste is taking the same direction. I do not think so. I strongly hope that it is not so. And therefore I say that an Englishman and an American differ in their tastes.

But of all differences between an Englishman and an American that in politics is the strongest, and the most essential. I cannot here, in one paragraph, define that difference with sufficient clearness to make my definition satisfactory; but I trust that some idea of that difference may be conveyed by the general tenor of my book. The American and the Englishman are both republicans. The governments of the States and of England are probably the two purest republican governments in the world. I do not, of course, here mean to say that the governments are more pure than others, but that the systems are more absolutely republican. And yet no men can be much further asunder in politics than the Englishman and the American. The American of the present day puts a ballot-box into the hands of every citizen and takes his stand upon that and that only. It is the duty of an American citizen to vote, and when he has voted he need trouble himself no further till the time for voting shall come round again. The candidate for whom he has voted represents his will, if he have voted with the majority, and in that case he has no right to look for further influence. If he have voted with the minority, he has no right to look for any influence at all. In either case he has done his political work, and may go about his business till the next year or the next two or four years shall have come round. The Englishman, on the other hand, will have no ballot-box, and is by no means inclined to depend exclusively upon voters or upon voting. As far as voting can show it, he desires to get the sense of the country; but he does not think that that sense will be shown by universal suffrage. He thinks that property amounting to a thousand pounds will show more of that sense than property amounting to a hundred; but he will not on that account go to work and apportion votes to wealth. He thinks that the educated can show more of that sense than the uneducated; but he does not therefore lay down any rule about reading, writing, and arithmetic, or apportion votes to learning. He prefers that all these opinions of his shall bring themselves out and operate by their own intrinsic weight. Nor does he at all confine himself to voting in his anxiety to get the sense of the country. He takes it in any way that it will show itself, uses it for what it is worth, —or perhaps for more than it is worth,—and welds it into that gigantic lever by which the political action of the country is moved. Every man in Great Britain, whether he possess any actual vote or no, can do that which is tantamount to voting every day of his life, by the mere expression of his opinion. Public opinion in America has hitherto been nothing, unless it has managed to express itself by a majority of ballot-boxes. Public opinion in England is everything, let votes go as they may. Let the people want a measure, and there is no doubt of their obtaining it. Only the people must want it;—as they did want Catholic emancipation, reform, and corn-law repeal;—and as they would want war if it were brought home to them that their country was insulted.

In attempting to describe this difference in the political action of the two countries, I am very far from taking all praise for England or throwing any reproach on the States. The political action of the States is undoubtedly the more logical and the clearer. That indeed of England is so illogical and so little clear that it would be quite impossible for any other nation to assume it, merely by resolving to do so. Whereas the political action of the States might be assumed by any nation to-morrow, and all its strength might be carried across the water in a few written rules as are the prescriptions of a physician or the regulations of an infirmary. With us the thing has grown of habit, has been fostered by tradition, has crept up uncared for and in some parts unnoticed. It can be written in no book, can be described in no words, can be copied by no statesmen, and I almost believe can be understood by no people but that to whose peculiar uses it has been adapted.

In speaking as I have here done of American taste and American politics I must allude to a special class of Americans who are to be met more generally in New York than elsewhere,—men who are educated, who have generally travelled, who are almost always agreeable, but who as regards their politics are to me the most objectionable of all men. As regards taste they are objectionable to me also. But that is a small thing; and as they are quite as likely to be right as I am I will say nothing against their taste. But in politics it seems to me that these men have fallen into the bitterest and perhaps into the basest of errors. Of the man who begins his life with mean political ideas, having sucked them in with his mother's milk, there may be some hope. The evil is at any rate the fault of his forefathers rather than of himself. But who can have hope of him who having been thrown by birth and fortune into the running river of free political activity, has allowed himself to be drifted into the stagnant level of general political servility? There are very many such Americans. They call themselves republicans, and sneer at the idea of a limited monarchy, but they declare that there is no republic so safe, so equal for all men, so purely democratic as that now existing in France. Under the French empire all men are equal. There is no aristocracy; no oligarchy; no overshadowing of the little by the great. One superior is admitted;—admitted on earth, as a superior is also admitted in heaven. Under him everything is level, and—provided he be not impeded—everything is free. He knows how to rule, and the nation, allowing him the privilege of doing so, can go along its course safely;—can eat, drink, and be merry. If few men can rise high, so also can few men fall low. Political equality is the one thing desirable in a commonwealth, and by this arrangement political equality is obtained. Such is the modern creed of many an educated republican of the States.

To me it seems that such a political state is about the vilest to which a man can descend. It amounts to a tacit abandonment of the struggle which men are making for political truth and political beneficence, in order that bread and meat may be eaten in peace during the score of years or so that are at the moment passing over us. The politicians of this class have decided for themselves that the *summum bonum* is to be found in bread and the circus games. If they be free to eat, free to rest, free to sleep, free to drink little cups of coffee while the world passes before them on a boulevard, they have that freedom which they covet. But equality is necessary as well as freedom. There must be no towering trees in this parterre to overshadow the clipped shrubs, and destroy the uniformity of a growth which should never mount more than two feet above the earth. The equality of this politician would forbid any to rise above him instead of inviting all to rise up to him. It is the equality of fear and of selfishness, and not the equality of courage and philanthropy. And brotherhood too must be invoked,—fraternity as we may better call it in the jargon of the school. Such politicians tell one much of fraternity, and define it too. It consists in a general raising of the hat to all mankind; in a daily walk that never hurries itself into a jostling trot, inconvenient to passengers on the pavement;—in a placid voice, a soft smile, and a small cup of coffee on a boulevard. It means all this, but I could never find that it meant any more. There is a nation for which one is almost driven to think that such political aspirations as these are suitable; but that nation is certainly not the States of America.

And yet one finds many American gentlemen who have allowed themselves to be drifted into such a theory. They have begun the world as republican citizens, and as such they must go on. But in their travels and their studies, and in the luxury of their life, they have learned to dislike the rowdiness of their country's politics. They want things to be soft and easy;—as republican as you please, but with as little noise as possible. The President is there for four years. Why not elect him for eight, for twelve, or for life?—for eternity if it were possible to find one who could continue to live? It is to this way of thinking that Americans are driven, when the polish of Europe has made the roughness of their own elections odious to them.

"Have you seen any of our great institootions, sir?" That of course is a question, which is put to every Englishman who has visited New York, and the Englishman who intends to say that he has seen New York, should visit many of them. I went to schools, hospitals, lunatic asylums, institutes for deaf and dumb, water works, historical societies, telegraph offices, and large commercial establishments. I rather think that I did my work in a thorough and conscientious manner, and I owe much gratitude to those who guided me on such occasions. Perhaps I ought to describe all these institutions; but were I to do so, I fear that I should inflict fifty or sixty very dull pages on my readers. If I could make all that I saw as clear and intelligible to others as it was made to me who saw it, I might do some good. But I know that I should fail.

I marvelled much at the developed intelligence of a room full of deaf and dumb pupils, and was greatly astonished at the performance of one special girl, who seemed to be brighter and quicker, and more rapidly easy with her pen than girls generally are who can hear and talk; but I cannot convey my enthusiasm to others. On such a subject a writer may be correct, may be exhaustive, may be statistically great; but he can hardly be entertaining, and the chances are that he will not be instructive.

In all such matters, however, New York is pre-eminently great. All through the States suffering humanity receives so much attention that humanity can hardly be said to suffer. The daily recurring boast of "our glorious institootions, sir," always provokes the ridicule of an Englishman. The words have become ridiculous, and it would, I think, be well for the nation if the term "Institution" could be excluded from its vocabulary. But, in truth, they are glorious. The country in this respect boasts, but it has done that which justifies a boast. The arrangements for supplying New York with water are magnificent. The drainage of the new part of the city is excellent. The hospitals are almost alluring. The lunatic asylum which I saw was perfect,—though I did not feel obliged to the resident physician for introducing me to all the worst patients as countrymen of my own. "An English lady, Mr. Trollope. I'll introduce you. Quite a hopeless case. Two old women. They've been here fifty years. They're English. Another gentleman from England, Mr. Trollope. A very interesting case! Confirmed inebriety."

And as to the schools, it is almost impossible to mention them with too high a praise. I am speaking here specially of New York, though I might say the same of Boston, or of all New England. I do not know any contrast that would be more surprising to an Englishman, up to that moment ignorant of the matter, than that which he would find by visiting first of all a free school in London, and then a free school in New York. If he would also learn the number of children that are educated gratuitously in each of the two cities, and also the number in each which altogether lack education, he would, if susceptible of statistics, be surprised also at that. But seeing and hearing are always more effective than mere figures. The female pupil at a free school in London is, as a rule, either a ragged pauper, or a charity girl, if not degraded at least stigmatized by the badges and dress of the Charity. We Englishmen know well the type of each, and have a fairly correct idea of the amount of education which is imparted to them. We see the result afterwards when the same girls become our servants, and the wives of our grooms and porters. The female pupil at a free school in New York is neither a pauper nor a charity girl. She is dressed with the utmost decency. She is perfectly cleanly. In speaking to her, you cannot in any degree guess whether her father has a dollar a day, or three thousand dollars a year. Nor will you be enabled to guess by the manner in which her associates treat her. As regards her own manner to you, it is always the same as though her father were in all respects your equal. As to the amount of her knowledge, I fairly confess that it is terrific. When, in the first room which I visited, a slight slim creature was had up before me to explain to me the properties of the hypothenuse I fairly confess that, as regards education, I backed down, and that I resolved to confine my criticisms to manner, dress, and general behaviour. In the next room I was more at my ease, finding that ancient Roman history was on the tapis. "Why did the Romans run away with the Sabine women?" asked the mistress, herself a young woman of about three-and-twenty. "Because they were pretty," simpered out a little girl with a cherry mouth. The answer did not give complete satisfaction; and then followed a somewhat abstruse explanation on the subject of population. It was all done with good faith and a serious intent, and showed what it was intended to show,—that the girls there educated had in truth reached the consideration of important subjects, and that they were leagues beyond that terrible repetition of A B C, to which, I fear, that most of our free metropolitan schools are still necessarily confined. You and I, reader, were we called on to superintend the education of girls of sixteen, might not select as favourite points either the hypothenuse, or the ancient methods of populating young colonies. There may be, and to us on the European side of the Atlantic there will be, a certain amount of absurdity in the transatlantic idea that all knowledge is knowledge, and that it should be imparted if it be not knowledge of evil. But as to the general result, no fair-minded man or woman can have a doubt. That the lads and girls in these schools are excellently educated comes home as a fact to the mind of any one who will look into the subject. That girl could not have got as far as the hypothenuse without a competent and abiding knowledge of much that is very far beyond the outside limits of what such girls know with us. It was at least manifest in the other examination that the girls knew as well as I did who were the Romans, and who were the Sabine women. That all this is of use, was shown in the very gestures and bearings of the girl. *Emollit mores,*

as Colonel Newcombe used to say.[7] That young woman whom I had
watched while she cooked her husband's dinner upon the banks of the
Mississippi, had doubtless learned all about the Sabine women, and I
feel assured that she cooked her husband's dinner all the better for that
knowledge,—and faced the hardships of the world with a better front
than she would have done had she been ignorant on the subject.

In order to make a comparison between the schools of London and
those of New York, I have called them both free schools. They are in
fact more free in New York than they are in London, because in New
York every boy and girl, let his parentage be what it may, can attend
these schools without any payment. Thus an education as good as the
American mind can compass, prepared with every care, carried on by
highly paid tutors, under ample surveillance, provided with all that
is most excellent in the way of rooms, desks, books, charts, maps, and
implements, is brought actually within the reach of everybody. I need
not point out to Englishmen how different is the nature of schools in
London. It must not, however, be supposed that these are charity
schools. Such is not their nature. Let us say what we may as to the
beauty of charity as a virtue, the recipient of charity in its customary
sense among us is ever more or less degraded by the position. In the
States that has been fully understood, and the schools to which I allude,
are carefully preserved from any such taint. Throughout the States a
separate tax is levied for the maintenance of these schools, and as the
tax-payer supports them, he is of course entitled to the advantage which
they confer. The child of the non-tax-payer is also entitled, and to him
the boon, if strictly analysed, will come in the shape of a charity. But
under the system as it is arranged, this is not analysed. It is understood
that the school is open to all in the ward to which it belongs, and no
inquiry is made whether the pupil's parent has or has not paid anything towards the school's support. I found this theory carried out so
far that at the deaf and dumb school, where some of the poorer children are wholly provided by the institution, care is taken to clothe
them in dresses of different colours and different make, in order that
nothing may attach to them which has the appearance of a badge. Po-

---

[7] Colonel Newcome shows less command of Latin than Trollope grants him. In
Chapter v of Thackeray's *The Newcomes* (1853-5) , he says *"emollunt mores"* and
makes other slips trying to recall the tag from Ovid (*Epistulæ ex Ponto*, II, ix,
47-8) :

> . . . *ingenuas didicisse fideliter artes*
> *Emollit mores nec sinit esse feros*

("". . . a faithful study of the liberal arts humanizes character **and** does not allow it **to be** cruel"") .

litical economists will see something of evil in this. But philanthropists will see very much that is good.

It is not without a purpose that I have given this somewhat glowing account of a girls' school in New York so soon after my little picture of New York women, as they behave themselves in the streets and street cars. It will, of course, be said that those women of whom I have spoken, by no means in terms of admiration, are the very girls whose education has been so excellent. This of course is so; but I beg to remark that I have by no means said that an excellent school education will produce all female excellences. The fact, I take it is this,—that seeing how high in the scale these girls have been raised, one is anxious that they should be raised higher. One is surprised at their pert vulgarity and hideous airs, not because they are so low in our general estimation but because they are so high. Women of the same class in London are humble enough, and therefore rarely offend us who are squeamish. They show by their gestures that they hardly think themselves good enough to sit by us; they apologise for their presence; they conceive it to be their duty to be lowly in their gestures. The question is which is best, the crouching and crawling or the impudent unattractive self-composure. Not, my reader, which action on her part may the better conduce to my comfort or to yours! That is by no means the question. Which is the better for the woman herself? That I take it is the point to be decided. That there is something better than either we shall all agree;—but to my thinking the crouching and crawling is the lowest type of all.

At that school I saw some five or six hundred girls collected in one room, and heard them sing. The singing was very pretty, and it was all very nice; but I own that I was rather startled, and to tell the truth somewhat abashed, when I was invited to "say a few words to them." No idea of such a suggestion had dawned upon me, and I felt myself quite at a loss. To be called up before five hundred men is bad enough, but how much worse before that number of girls! What could I say but that they were all very pretty. As far as I can remember I did say that and nothing else. Very pretty they were, and neatly dressed, and attractive; but among them all there was not a pair of rosy cheeks. How should there be, when every room in the building was heated up to the condition of an oven by those damnable hot-air pipes!

In England a taste for very large shops has come up during the last twenty years. A firm is not doing a good business, or at any rate a distinguished business, unless he can assert in his trade card that he occupies at least half a dozen houses—Nos. 105, 106, 107, 108, 109, and

110. The old way of paying for what you want over the counter is gone; and when you buy a yard of tape or a new carriage,—for either of which articles you will probably visit the same establishment,—you go through about the same amount of ceremony as when you sell a thousand pounds out of the stocks in *propriâ personâ*. But all this is still further exaggerated in New York. Mr. Stewart's store there is perhaps the handsomest institution in the city,[8] and his hall of audience for new carpets is a magnificent saloon. "You have nothing like that in England," my friend said to me as he walked me through it in triumph. "I wish we had nothing approaching to it," I answered. For I confess to a liking for the old-fashioned private shops. Harper's establishment for the manufacture and sale of books is also very wonderful. Everything is done on the premises, down to the very colouring of the paper which lines the covers, and places the gilding on their backs. The firm prints, engraves, electroplates, sews, binds, publishes, and sells wholesale and retail. I have no doubt that the authors have rooms in the attics where the other slight initiatory step is taken towards the production of literature.

New York is built upon an island, which is I believe about ten miles long, counting from the southern point at the battery up to Carmansville, to which place the city is presumed to extend northwards. This island is called Manhattan,—a name which I have always thought would have been more graceful for the city than that of New York. It is formed by the Sound or East river, which divides the continent from Long Island, by the Hudson river which runs into the Sound or rather joins it at the city foot, and by a small stream called the Haarlem river which runs out of the Hudson and meanders away into the Sound at the north of the city, thus cutting the city off from the main land. The breadth of the island does not much exceed two miles, and therefore the city is long, and not capable of extension in point of breadth. In its old days it clustered itself round about the Point, and stretched itself up from there along the quays of the two waters. The streets down in this part of the town are devious enough, twisting themselves about with delightful irregularity; but as the city grew there came the taste for parallelograms, and the upper streets are rectangular and numbered. Broadway, the street of New York with which the world is generally best acquainted, begins at the southern

8 Alexander Turney Stewart (1803–76) had perhaps already exchanged his six-story marble emporium built in 1848 for the eight-story building of stone and steel completed in 1862. The new building covered an entire city block (Ninth and Tenth Streets, Broadway and Fourth Avenue). Stewart's was the largest retail store in the world, with an employment list of two thousand persons.

point of the town and goes northward through it. For some two miles and a half it walks away in a straight line, and then it turns to the left towards the Hudson, and becomes in fact a continuation of another street called the Bowery, which comes up in a devious course from the south-east extremity of the island. From that time Broadway never again takes a straight course, but crosses the various Avenues in an oblique direction till it becomes the Bloomingdale road, and under that name takes itself out of town. There are eleven so-called Avenues, which descend in absolutely straight lines from the northern, and at present unsettled, extremity of the new town, making their way southward till they lose themselves among the old streets. These are called First Avenue, Second Avenue, and so on. The town had already progressed two miles up northwards from the Battery before it had caught the parallelogrammic fever from Philadelphia, for at about that distance we find "First Street." First Street runs across the Avenues from water to water, and then Second Street. I will not name them all, seeing that they go up to 154th Street! They do so at least on the map, and I believe on the lamp-posts. But the houses are not yet built in order beyond 50th or 60th Street. The other hundred streets, each of two miles long, with the Avenues which are mostly unoccupied for four or five miles, is the ground over which the young New Yorkers are to spread themselves. I do not in the least doubt that they will occupy it all, and that 154th Street will find itself too narrow a boundary for the population.

I have said that there was some good architectural effect in New York, and I alluded chiefly to that of the Fifth Avenue. The Fifth Avenue is the Belgrave Square, the Park Lane, and the Pall Mall of New York. It is certainly a very fine street. The houses in it are magnificent, not having that aristocratic look which some of our detached London residences enjoy, or the palatial appearance of an old-fashioned hotel in Paris, but an air of comfortable luxury and commercial wealth which is not excelled by the best houses of any other town that I know. They are houses, not hotels or palaces; but they are very roomy houses, with every luxury that complete finish can give them. Many of them cover large spaces of ground, and their rent will sometimes go up as high as 800*l.* and 1000*l.* a year. Generally the best of these houses are owned by those who live in them, and rent is not therefore paid. But this is not always the case, and the sums named above may be taken as expressing their value. In England a man should have a very large income indeed who could afford to pay 1000*l.* a year for his house in London. Such a one would as a matter of course have an establish-

ment in the country, and be an Earl or a Duke or a millionaire. But it
is different in New York. The resident there shows his wealth chiefly
by his house, and though he may probably have a villa at Newport or
a box somewhere up the Hudson he has no second establishment.
Such a house therefore will not represent a total expenditure of above
4,000*l.* a year.

There are churches on each side of Fifth Avenue,—perhaps five or
six within sight at one time,—which add much to the beauty of the
street. They are well-built, and in fairly good taste. These, added to
the general well-being and splendid comfort of the place, give it an
effect better than the architecture of the individual houses would seem
to warrant. I own that I have enjoyed the vista as I have walked up and
down Fifth Avenue, and have felt that the city had a right to be proud
of its wealth. But the greatness and beauty and glory of wealth have on
such occasions been all in all with me. I know no great man, no celebrated statesman, no philanthropist of peculiar note who has lived in
Fifth Avenue. That gentleman on the right made a million of dollars
by inventing a shirt-collar; this one on the left electrified the world by
a lotion; as to the gentleman at the corner there,—there are rumours
about him and the Cuban slave-trade; but my informant by no means
knows that they are true. Such are the aristocracy of Fifth Avenue. I
can only say that if I could make a million dollars by a lotion, I should
certainly be right to live in such a house as one of those.

The suburbs of New York are, by the nature of the localities,
divided from the city by water. New Jersey and Hoboken are on the
other side of the Hudson, and in another State. Williamsburgh and
Brooklyn are in Long Island, which is a part of the State of New York.
But these places are as easily reached as Lambeth is reached from
Westminster. Steam ferries ply every three or four minutes, and into
these boats coaches, carts, and waggons of any size or weight are driven.
In fact they make no other stoppage to the commerce than that occasioned by the payment of a few cents. Such payment no doubt is a
stoppage, and therefore it is that New Jersey, Brooklyn, and Williamsburgh, are, at any rate in appearance, very dull and uninviting. They
are, however, very populous. Many of the quieter citizens prefer to live
there; and I am told that the Brooklyn tea-parties consider themselves
to be, in æsthetic feeling, very much ahead of anything of the kind in
the more opulent centres of the city. In beauty of scenery Staten Island
is very much the prettiest of the suburbs of New York. The view from
the hill side in Staten Island down upon New York harbour is very
lovely. It is the only really good view of that magnificent harbour which

I have been able to find. As for appreciating such beauty when one is entering a port from sea, or leaving it for sea, I do not believe in any such power. The ship creeps up or creeps out while the mind is engaged on other matters. The passenger is uneasy either with hopes or fears; and then the grease of the engines offends one's nostrils. But it is worth the tourist's while to look down upon New York harbour from the hill side in Staten Island. When I was there Fort Lafayette looked black in the centre of the channel, and we knew that it was crowded with the victims of secession. Fort Tomkins was being built, to guard the pass, —worthy of a name of richer sound; and Fort something else was bristling with new cannon. Fort Hamilton, on Long Island, opposite, was frowning at us; and immediately around us a regiment of volunteers was receiving regimental stocks and boots from the hands of its officers. Everything was bristling with war; and one could not but think that not in this way had New York raised herself so quickly to her present greatness.

But the glory of New York is the Central Park;—its glory in the mind of all New Yorkers of the present day. The first question asked of you is whether you have seen the Central Park, and the second is as to what you think of it. It does not do to say simply that it is fine, grand, beautiful, and miraculous. You must swear by cock and pie that it is more fine, more grand, more beautiful, more miraculous than anything else of the kind anywhere. Here you encounter, in its most annoying form, that necessity for eulogium which presses you everywhere. For, in truth, taken as it is at present, the Central Park is not fine, nor grand, nor beautiful. As to the miracle, let that pass. It is perhaps as miraculous as some other great latter-day miracles.

But the Central Park is a very great fact, and affords a strong additional proof of the sense and energy of the people. It is very large, being over three miles long, and about three quarters of a mile in breadth. When it was found that New York was extending itself, and becoming one of the largest cities of the world, a space was selected between Fifth and Seventh Avenues, immediately outside the limits of the city as then built, but nearly in the centre of the city as it is intended to be built. The ground around it became at once of great value; and I do not doubt that the present fashion of the fifth Avenue about Twentieth Street will in course of time move itself up to the Fifth Avenue as it looks, or will look, over the Park at Seventieth, Eightieth, and Ninetieth Streets. The great waterworks of the city bring the Croton River, whence New York is supplied, by an aqueduct over the Haarlem river into an enormous reservoir just above the

Park; and hence it has come to pass that there will be water not only for sanitary and useful purposes, but also for ornament. At present the Park, to English eyes, seems to be all road. The trees are not grown up, and the new embankments, and new lakes, and new ditches, and new paths give to the place anything but a picturesque appearance. The Central Park is good for what it will be, rather than for what it is. The summer heat is so very great that I doubt much whether the people of New York will ever enjoy such verdure as our parks show. But there will be a pleasant assemblage of walks and water-works, with fresh air, and fine shrubs and flowers, immediately within the reach of the citizens. All that art and energy can do will be done, and the Central Park doubtless will become one of the great glories of New York. When I was expected to declare that St. James's Park, Green Park, Hyde Park, and Kensington Gardens, altogether, were nothing to it, I confess that I could only remain mute.

Those who desire to learn what are the secrets of society in New York, I would refer to the Potiphar Papers.[9] The Potiphar Papers are perhaps not as well known in England as they deserve to be. They were published, I think, as much as seven or eight years ago; but are probably as true now as they were then. What I saw of society in New York was quiet and pleasant enough; but doubtless I did not climb into that circle in which Mrs. Potiphar held so distinguished a position. It may be true that gentlemen habitually throw fragments of their

[9] *The Potiphar Papers* (1853), by George William Curtis, satirizes New York society in a manner patterned after Thackeray, whom Curtis (and Trollope) greatly admired. As Trollope implies later in the paragraph, the parties of the newly rich and socially ambitious Mrs. Potiphar were lavish but somewhat chaotic:

"Hal could come, eat Potiphar's supper, drink his wines, spoil his carpets, laugh at his fashionable struggles, and affect the puppyism of a foreign lord, because he disgraced the name of a man who had done some service somewhere, while Potiphar was only an honest man who made a fortune.

"The supper-room was a pleasant place. The table was covered with a chaos of supper. Everything sweet and rare, and hot and cold, solid and liquid, was there. It was the very apotheosis of gilt and gingerbread. There was a universal rush and struggle. The charge of the guards at Waterloo was nothing to it. Jellies, custard, oyster-soup, ice-cream, wine and water, gushed in profuse cascades over transparent precipices of *tulle*, muslin, gauze, silk, and satin. Clumsy boys tumbled against costly dresses and smeared them with preserves; when clean plates failed, the contents of plates already used were quietly 'chucked' under the table—heel-taps of champagne were poured into the oyster tureens or overflowed upon plates to clear the glasses—wine of all kinds flowed in torrents, particularly down the throats of very young men, who evinced their manhood by becoming noisy, troublesome, and disgusting, and were finally either led, sick, into the hatroom, or carried out of the way, drunk."

supper and remnants of their wine on to their host's carpets; but if so
I did not see it.

As I progress in my work I feel that duty will call upon me to write
a separate chapter on hotels in general, and I will not, therefore, here
say much about those in New York. I am inclined to think that few
towns in the world, if any, afford on the whole better accommodation,
but there are many in which the accommodation is cheaper. Of the
railways also I ought to say something. The fact respecting them which
is most remarkable is that of their being continued into the centre of
the town through the streets. The cars are not dragged through the
city by locomotive engines, but by horses; the pace therefore is slow,
but the convenience to travellers in being brought nearer to the centre
of trade must be much felt. It is as though passengers from Liverpool
and passengers from Bristol were carried on from Euston Square and
Paddington along the New Road, Portland Place, and Regent Street
to Pall Mall, or up the City Road to the Bank. As a general rule, however, the railways, railway cars, and all about them are ill-managed.
They are monopolies, and the public, through the press, has no restraining power upon them as it has in England. A parcel sent by
express over a distance of forty miles will not be delivered within
twenty-four hours. I once made my plaint on this subject at the bar or
office of an hotel, and was told that no remonstrance was of avail. "It
is a monopoly," the man told me, "and if we say anything, we are told
that if we do not like it we need not use it." In railway matters and
postal matters time and punctuality are not valued in the States as they
are with us, and the public seem to acknowledge that they must put
up with defects,—that they must grin and bear them in America, as the
public no doubt do in Austria where such affairs are managed by a
government bureau.

In the beginning of this chapter I spoke of the population of New
York, and I cannot end it without remarking that out of that population more than one-eighth is composed of Germans. It is, I believe,
computed that there are about 120,000 Germans in the city, and that
only two other German cities in the world, Vienna and Berlin, have a
larger German population than New York. The Germans are good
citizens and thriving men, and are to be found prospering all over the
northern and western parts of the Union. It seems that they are excellently well adapted to colonization, though they have in no instance
become the dominant people in a colony, or carried with them their
own language or their own laws. The French have done so in Algeria,

in some of the West India islands, and quite as essentially into Lower Canada, where their language and laws still prevail. And yet it is, I think, beyond doubt that the French are not good colonists, as are the Germans.

Of the ultimate destiny of New York as one of the ruling commercial cities of the world, it is, I think, impossible to doubt. Whether or no it will ever equal London in population I will not pretend to say. Even should it do so, should its numbers so increase as to enable it to say that it had done so, the question could not very well be settled. When it comes to pass that an assemblage of men in one so-called city have to be counted by millions, there arises the impossibility of defining the limits of that city, and of saying who belong to it and who do not. An arbitrary line may be drawn, but that arbitrary line, though perhaps false when drawn as including too much, soon becomes more false as including too little. Ealing, Acton, Fulham, Putney, Norwood, Sydenham, Blackheath, Woolwich, Greenwich, Stratford, Highgate, and Hampstead, are, in truth, component parts of London, and very shortly Brighton will be as much so.

CHAPTER XV

BOSTON

From New York we returned to Boston by Hartford, the capital, or one of the capitals of Connecticut. This proud little State is composed of two old provinces, of which Hartford and Newhaven were the two metropolitan towns. Indeed there was a third colony called Saybrook, which was joined to Hartford. As neither of the two could of course give way when Hartford and Newhaven made into one, the houses of legislature and the seat of government are changed about, year by year. Connecticut is a very proud little State, and has a pleasant legend of its own stanchness in the old colonial days. In 1662 the colonies were united, and a charter was given to them by Charles II. But some years later, in 1686, when the bad days of James II. had come, this charter was considered to be too liberal, and order was given that it should be suspended. One Sir Edmund Andros had been appointed governor of all New England, and sent word from Boston to Connecticut that the charter itself should be given up to him. This the men of Connecticut refused to do. Whereupon Sir Edmund with a military following presented himself at their assembly, declared their governing powers to be dissolved, and after much palaver caused the charter itself to be laid upon the table before him. The discussion had been long, having lasted through the day into the night, and the room had been lighted with candles. On a sudden each light disappeared, and Sir Edmund with his followers were in the dark. As a matter of course, when the light was restored the charter was gone, and Sir Edmund, the governor-general, was baffled, as all governors-general and all Sir Edmunds always are in such cases. The charter was gone, a gallant Captain Wadsworth having carried it off and hidden it in an oak tree. The charter was renewed when William III. came to the throne, and now hangs triumphantly in the State House at Hartford. The charter oak has, alas! succumbed to the weather, but was standing a few years since. The men of Hartford are very proud of their charter, and regard it as the parent of their existing liberties quite as much as though no national revolution of their own had intervened.

And indeed the Northern States of the Union, especially those of New England, refer all their liberties to the old charters which they held from the mother-country. They rebelled, as they themselves would seem to say, and set themselves up as a separate people, not because the mother-country had refused to them by law sufficient liberty and sufficient self-control, but because the mother-country infringed the liberties and powers of self-control which she herself had given. The mother-country, so these States declare, had acted the part of Sir Edmund Andros, had endeavoured to take away their charters. So they also put out the lights, and took themselves to an oak tree of their own,—which is still standing, though winds from the infernal regions are now battering its branches. Long may it stand!

Whether the mother-country did or did not infringe the charters she had given, I will not here inquire. As to the nature of those alleged infringements, are they not written down to the number of twenty-seven in the Declaration of Independence? I have taken the liberty of appending this Declaration to the end of my book,[1] and the twenty-seven paragraphs may all be seen. They mostly begin with He. "He" has done this, and "He" has done that. The "He" is poor George III., whose twenty-seven mortal sins against his transatlantic colonies are thus recapitulated. It would avail nothing to argue now whether those deeds were sins or virtues; nor would it have availed then. The child had grown up and was strong, and chose to go alone into the world. The young bird was fledged, and flew away. Poor George III. with his cackling was certainly not efficacious in restraining such a flight. But it is gratifying to see how this new people, when they had it in their power to change all their laws, to throw themselves upon any Utopian theory that the folly of a wild philanthropy could devise, to discard as abominable every vestige of English rule and English power,—it is gratifying to see that when they could have done all this, they did not do so, but preferred to cling to things English. Their old colonial limits were still to be the borders of their States. Their old charters were still to be regarded as the sources from whence their State powers had come. The old laws were to remain in force. The precedents of the English courts were to be held as legal precedents in the courts of the new nation,—and are now so held. It was still to be England,—but England without a King making his last struggle for political power. This was the idea of the people, and this was their feeling; and that idea has been carried out, and that feeling has remained.

In the constitution of the State of New York nothing is said about the religion of the people. It was regarded as a subject with which the constitution had no concern whatever. But as soon as we come among

[1] Omitted in the present edition. See Appendix A.

the stricter people of New England we find that the constitution-makers have not been able absolutely to ignore the subject. In Connecticut it is enjoined that as it is the duty of all men to worship the Supreme Being, and their right to render that worship in the mode most consistent with their consciences, no person shall be by law compelled to join or be classed with any religious association. The line of argument is hardly logical, the conclusion not being in accordance with, or hanging on the first of the two premises. But nevertheless the meaning is clear. In a free country no man shall be made to worship after any special fashion; but it is decreed by the constitution that every man is bound by duty to worship after some fashion. The article then goes on to say how they who do worship are to be taxed for the support of their peculiar church. I am not quite clear whether the New Yorkers have not managed this difficulty with greater success. When we come to the old Bay State,—to Massachusetts,—we find the Christian religion spoken of in the Constitution as that which in some one of its forms should receive the adherence of every good Christian.

Hartford is a pleasant little town, with English-looking houses, and an English-looking country around it. Here, as everywhere through the States, one is struck by the size and comfort of the residences. I sojourned there at the house of a friend, and could find no limit to the number of spacious sitting-rooms which it contained. The modest dining-room and drawing-room which suffice with us for men of seven or eight hundred a year would be regarded as very mean accommodation by persons of similar incomes in the States.

I found that Hartford was all alive with trade, and that wages were high, because there are there two factories for the manufacture of arms. Colt's pistols [2] come from Hartford, as do also Sharpe's rifles. Wherever arms can be prepared, or gunpowder; where clothes or blankets fit for soldiers can be made, or tents or standards, or things appertaining in any way to warfare, there trade was still brisk. No being is more costly in his requirements than a soldier, and no soldier so costly as the American. He must eat and drink of the best, and have good boots and warm bedding, and good shelter. There were during the Christmas of 1861 above half a million of soldiers so to be provided,—the President, in his message made in December to Congress, declared the number to be above six hundred thousand—and therefore in such places as Hartford trade was very brisk. I went over the rifle factory, and was shown everything, but I do not know that I brought away

[2] Samuel Colt's factory, established at Hartford in the early 1850's, had already become the largest producer of firearms in the world.

much with me that was worth any reader's attention. The best of rifles, I have no doubt, were being made with the greatest rapidity, and all were sent to the army as soon as finished. I saw some murderous-looking weapons, with swords attached to them instead of bayonets, but have since been told by soldiers that the old-fashioned bayonet is thought to be more serviceable.

Immediately on my arrival in Boston I heard that Mr. Emerson was going to lecture at the Tremont Hall on the subject of the war, and I resolved to go and hear him. I was acquainted with Mr. Emerson, and by reputation knew him well. Among us in England he is regarded as transcendental, and perhaps even as mystic in his philosophy. His "Representative Men" is the work by which he is best known on our side of the water, and I have heard some readers declare that they could not quite understand Mr. Emerson's "Representative Men." For myself, I confess that I had broken down over some portions of that book.[3] Since I had become acquainted with him I had read others of his writings, especially his book on England, and had found that he improved greatly on acquaintance. I think that he has confined his mysticism to the book above named. In conversation he is very clear, and by no means above the small practical things of the world. He would, I fancy, know as well what interest he ought to receive for his money as though he were no philosopher; and I am inclined to think that if he held land he would make his hay while the sun shone, as might any common farmer. Before I had met Mr. Emerson, when my idea of him was formed simply on the "Representative Men," I should have thought that a lecture from him on the war would have taken his hearers all among the clouds. As it was, I still had my doubts, and was inclined to fear that a subject which could only be handled usefully at such a time before a large audience by a combination of common sense, high principles, and eloquence, would hardly be safe in Mr. Emerson's hands. I did not doubt the high principles, but feared much that there would be a lack of common sense. So many have talked on that subject, and

---

[3] *Representative Men* (1850) is not a book one would expect Trollope to find easy or congenial. It deals with six leaders of mankind (Plato, Swedenborg, Montaigne, Shakespeare, Napoleon, Goethe) in a manner not unlike that of Carlyle in *Heroes and Hero-Worship*, emphasizing the idea that humanity is pervaded by the spirit of the Deity and the leader is great through the power of the divine essence within him.

English Traits (1856), which Trollope mentions in the sentence following, describes Emerson's visits to Coleridge, Wordsworth, and Carlyle, but is in the main an admiring study of the characteristics of the English people.

have shown so great a lack of common sense! As to the eloquence, that might be there, or might not.

Mr. Emerson is a Massachusetts man, very well known in Boston, and a great crowd was collected to hear him. I suppose there were some three thousand persons in the room. I confess that when he took his place before us my prejudices were against him. The matter in hand required no philosophy. It required common sense, and the very best of common sense. It demanded that he should be impassioned, for of what interest can any address be on a matter of public politics without passion? But it demanded that the passion should be winnowed, and free from all rhodomontade. I fancied what might be said on such a subject as to that overlauded star-spangled banner, and how the star-spangled flag would look when wrapped in a mist of mystic Platonism.

But from the beginning to the end there was nothing mystic—no Platonism; and, if I remember rightly, the star-spangled banner was altogether omitted. To the national eagle he did allude. "Your American eagle," he said, "is very well. Protect it here and abroad. But beware of the American peacock." [4] He gave an account of the war from the beginning, showing how it had arisen, and how it had been conducted; and he did so with admirable simplicity and truth. He thought the North were right about the war; and as I thought so also, I was not called upon to disagree with him. He was terse and perspicuous in his sentences, practical in his advice, and, above all things, true in what he said to his audience of themselves. They who know America will understand how hard it is for a public man in the States to practise such truth in his addresses. Fluid compliments and high-flown national eulogium are expected. In this instance none were forthcoming. The North had risen with patriotism to make this effort, and it was now

[4] Emerson delivered this lecture, entitled *American Nationality*, at Tremont Temple November 12, 1861. A summary of the lecture printed next day in the *Boston Daily Transcript* gives Emerson's remark about the peacock and its setting as follows:

"He spoke of the city of Washington, saying that if the capital were removed to any other city, very few associations would be lost. The spread eagle must fold his foolish wings and become less of a peacock. It is a proud illusion which led us to call ourselves the American nation; we must now lose that empty compliment. We were really two nations; why not acknowledge it? . . . the country is relieved in the thought that it has a government at last. . . . The war brings together the politics of different states. . . ."

Emerson used the figure of the peacock again, with phrasing identical with that of the sentence in the summary just quoted, in a lecture of 1863 entitled *The Fortune of the Republic*. Trollope, essaying to quote from memory, seems to have coined his own epigram.

warned that in doing so it was simply doing its national duty. And
then came the subject of slavery. I had been told that Mr. Emerson
was an abolitionist, and knew that I must disagree with him on that
head, if on no other. To me it has always seemed that to mix up the
question of general abolition with this war must be the work of a man
too ignorant to understand the real subject of the war, or too false to
his country to regard it. Throughout the whole lecture I was waiting
for Mr. Emerson's abolition doctrine, but no abolition doctrine came.
The words abolition and compensation were mentioned, and then
there was an end of the subject. If Mr. Emerson be an abolitionist he
expressed his views very mildly on that occasion. On the whole the lecture was excellent, and that little advice about the peacock was in itself
worth an hour's attention.

That practice of lecturing is "quite an institution" in the States.
So it is in England, my readers will say. But in England it is done in
a different way, with a different object and with much less of result.
With us, if I am not mistaken, lectures are mostly given gratuitously
by the lecturer. They are got up here and there with some philanthropical object, and in the hope that an hour at the disposal of young
men and women may be rescued from idleness. The subjects chosen
are social, literary, philanthropic, romantic, geographical, scientific, religious,—anything rather than political. The lecture-rooms are not
usually filled to overflowing, and there is often a question whether
the real good achieved is worth the trouble taken. The most popular
lectures are given by big people, whose presence is likely to be attractive; and the whole thing, I fear we must confess, is not pre-eminently
successful. In the northern States of America the matter stands on a
very different footing. Lectures there are more popular than either
theatres or concerts. Enormous halls are built for them. Tickets for
long courses are taken with avidity. Very large sums are paid to popular lecturers, so that the profession is lucrative,—more so, I am given to
understand, than is the cognate profession of literature. The whole
thing is done in great style. Music is introduced. The lecturer stands
on a large raised platform, on which sit around him the bald and hoary-
headed and superlatively wise. Ladies come in large numbers; especially
those who aspire to soar above the frivolities of the world. Politics is
the subject most popular, and most general. The men and women of
Boston could no more do without their lectures, than those of Paris
could without their theatres. It is the decorous diversion of the best
ordered of her citizens. The fast young men go to clubs, and the fast
young women to dances, as fast young men and women do in other

places that are wicked; but lecturing is the favourite diversion of the steady-minded Bostonian. After all, I do not know that the result is very good. It does not seem that much will be gained by such lectures on either side of the Atlantic,—except that respectable killing of an evening which might otherwise be killed less respectably. It is but an industrious idleness, an attempt at a royal road to information, that habit of attending lectures. Let any man or woman say what he has brought away from any such attendance. It is attractive, that idea of being studious without any of the labour of study; but I fear it is illusive. If an evening can be so passed without ennui, I believe that that may be regarded as the best result to be gained. But then it so often happens that the evening is not passed without ennui! Of course in saying this, I am not alluding to lectures given in special places as a course of special study. Medical lectures, no doubt, are a necessary part of medical education. As many as two or three thousand often attend these political lectures in Boston, but I do not know whether on that account the popular subjects are much better understood. Nevertheless I resolved to hear more, hoping that I might in that way teach myself to understand what were the popular politics in New England. Whether or no I may have learned this in any other way I do not perhaps know; but at any rate I did not learn it in this way.

The next lecture which I attended was also given in the Tremont Hall, and on this occasion also the subject of the war was to be treated. The special treachery of the rebels was, I think, the matter to be taken in hand.[5] On this occasion also the room was full, and my hopes of a pleasant hour ran high. For some fifteen minutes I listened, and I am bound to say that the gentleman discoursed in excellent English. He was master of that wonderful fluency which is peculiarly the gift of an American. He went on from one sentence to another with rhythmic tones and unerring pronunciation. He never faltered, never repeated his words, never fell into those vile half-muttered hems and haws by which an Englishman in such a position so generally betrays his timidity. But during the whole time of my remaining in the room he did not give expression to a single thought. He went on from one soft platitude to another, and uttered words from which I would defy any one of his audience to carry away with them anything. And yet it seemed to me that his audience was satisfied. I was not satisfied, and managed to escape out of the room.

[5] Trollope refers almost certainly to the address by William R. Alger, who followed Emerson in the course of weekly lectures at Tremont Temple. Alger chose as his title *Judas Iscariot and His Family*.

The next lecturer to whom I listened was Mr. Everett.[6] Mr. Everett's reputation as an orator is very great, and I was especially anxious to hear him. I had long since known that his power of delivery was very marvellous; that his tones, elocution, and action were all great; and that he was able to command the minds and sympathies of his audience in a remarkable manner. His subject also was the war;— or rather the causes of the war, and its qualification. Had the North given to the South cause of provocation? Had the South been fair and honest in its dealings to the North? Had any compromise been possible by which the war might have been avoided, and the rights and dignity of the North preserved? Seeing that Mr. Everett is a Northern man and was lecturing to a Boston audience, one knew well how these questions would be answered, but the manner of the answering would be everything. This lecture was given at Roxboro', one of the suburbs of Boston. So I went out to Roxboro' with a party, and found myself honoured by being placed on the platform among the bald-headed ones and the superlatively wise. This privilege is naturally gratifying, but it entails on him who is so gratified the inconvenience of sitting at the lecturer's back, whereas it is perhaps better for the listener to be before his face.

I could not but be amused by one little scenic incident. When we all went upon the platform, some one proposed that the clergymen should lead the way out of the waiting-room in which we bald-headed ones and superlatively wise were assembled. But to this the manager of the affair demurred. He wanted the clergymen for a purpose, he said. And so the profane ones led the way, and the clergymen, of whom there might be some six or seven, clustered in around the lecturer at last. Early in his discourse Mr. Everett told us what it was that the country needed at this period of her trial. Patriotism, courage, the bravery of the men, the good wishes of the women, the self-denial of all,—"and," continued the lecturer, turning to his immediate neighbours, "the prayers of these holy men whom I see around me." It had not been for nothing that the clergymen were detained.

Mr. Everett lectures without any book or paper before him, and continues from first to last as though the words came from him on the spur of the moment. It is known, however, that it is his practice to prepare his orations with great care and commit them entirely to memory, as does an actor. Indeed he repeats the same lecture over and over again, I am told, without the change of a word or of an action. I did not like Mr. Everett's lecture. I did not like what he said, or the seem-

[6] Both here and earlier (see page 21 and note) Trollope treats this old friend of his mother's rather roughly.

ing spirit in which it was framed. But I am bound to admit that his power of oratory is very wonderful. Those among his countrymen who have criticised his manner in my hearing have said that he is too florid, that there is an affectation in the motion of his hands, and that the intended pathos of his voice sometimes approaches too near the precipice over which the fall is so deep and rapid, and at the bottom of which lies absolute ridicule. Judging for myself, I did not find it so. My position for seeing was not good, but my ear was not offended. Critics also should bear in mind that an orator does not speak chiefly to them or for their approval. He who writes, or speaks, or sings for thousands, must write, speak, or sing as those thousands would have him. That to a dainty connoisseur will be false music, which to the general ear shall be accounted as the perfection of harmony. An eloquence altogether suited to the fastidious and hypercritical, would probably fail to carry off the hearts and interest the sympathies of the young and eager. As regards manners, tone, and choice of words, I think that the oratory of Mr. Everett places him very high. His skill in his work is perfect. He never falls back upon a word. He never repeats himself. His voice is always perfectly under command. As for hesitation or timidity, the days for those failings have long passed by with him. When he makes a point, he makes it well, and drives it home to the intelligence of every one before him. Even that appeal to the holy men around him sounded well,—or would have done so had I not been present at that little arrangement in the anteroom. On the audience at large it was manifestly effective.

But nevertheless the lecture gave me but a poor idea of Mr. Everett as a politician, though it made me regard him highly as an orator. It was impossible not to perceive that he was anxious to utter the sentiments of the audience rather than his own;—that he was making himself an echo, a powerful and harmonious echo of what he conceived to be public opinion in Boston at that moment;—that he was neither leading nor teaching the people before him, but allowing himself to be led by them, so that he might best play his present part for their delectation. He was neither bold nor honest, as Emerson had been, and I could not but feel that every tyro of a politician before him would thus recognize his want of boldness and of honesty. As a statesman, or as a critic of statecraft and of other statesmen, he is wanting in backbone. For many years Mr. Everett has been not even inimical to southern politics and southern courses, nor was he among those who, during the last eight years previous to Mr. Lincoln's election, fought the battle for northern principles. I do not say that on this account he is now false to advocate the war. But he cannot carry men with him when, at his age, he advocates it by arguments opposed to the tenour of his long political life. His abuse of the South and of southern ideas was as virulent as might be that of a young lad now beginning his political career, or of one who had through life advocated abolition principles. He heaped reproaches on poor Virginia, whose position as the chief of the border States has given to her hardly the possibility of avoiding a Scylla of ruin on the one side, or a Charybdis of rebellion on the other. When he spoke as he did of Virginia, ridiculing the idea of her sacred soil, even I, Englishman as I am, could not but think of Washington, of Jefferson, of Randolph, and of Madison. He should not have spoken of Virginia as he did speak; for no man could have known better Virginia's difficulties. But Virginia was at a discount in Boston, and Mr. Everett was speaking to a Boston audience. And then he referred to England and to Europe. Mr. Everett has been minister to England, and knows the people. He is a student of history, and must, I think, know that England's career has not been unhappy or unprosperous. But England also was at a discount in Boston, and Mr. Everett was speaking to a Boston audience. They are sending us their advice across the water, said Mr. Everett. And what is their advice to us? that we should come down from the high place we have built for ourselves, and be even as they are. They screech at us from the low depths in which they are wallowing in their misery, and call on us to join them in their wretchedness. I am not quoting Mr. Everett's very words, for I have not them by me; but I am not making them stronger, nor so strong as he made them. As I thought of Mr. Everett's reputation, and of his years of study,—of his long political life and unsurpassed sources of information,—I could not but grieve heartily when I heard such words fall from him. I could not but ask myself whether it were impossible that under the present circumstances of her constitution this great nation of America should produce an honest, high-minded statesman. When Lincoln and Hamlin, the existing President and Vice-President of the States, were in 1860 as yet but the candidates of the Republican party, Bell and Everett also were the candidates of the old Whig, conservative party. Their express theory was this,—that the question of slavery should not be touched. Their purpose was to crush agitation and restore harmony by an impartial balance between the North and South: a fine purpose,—the finest of all purposes, had it been practicable. But such a course of compromise was now at a discount in Boston, and Mr. Everett was speaking to a Boston audience.

As an orator, Mr. Everett's excellence is, I think, not to be questioned; but as a politician I cannot give him a high rank.

After that I heard Mr. Wendell Phillips. Of him, too, as an orator all the world of Massachusetts speaks with great admiration, and I have no doubt so speaks with justice. He is, however, known as the hottest and most impassioned advocate of abolition. Not many months since the cause of abolition as advocated by him, was so unpopular in Boston, that Mr. Phillips was compelled to address his audience surrounded by a guard of policemen. Of this gentlemen, I may at any rate say that he is consistent, devoted, and disinterested. He is an abolitionist by profession, and seeks to find in every turn of the tide of politics some stream on which he may bring himself nearer to his object. In the old days, previous to the selection of Mr. Lincoln, in days so old that they are now nearly eighteen months past, Mr. Phillips was an anti-Union man. He advocated strongly the disseverance of the Union, so that the country to which he belonged might have hands clean from the taint of slavery. He had probably acknowledged to himself, that while the North and South were bound together no hope existed of emancipation, but that if the North stood alone the South would become too weak to foster and keep alive the "social institution." In which, if such were his opinions, I am inclined to agree with him. But now he is all for the Union, thinking that a victorious North can compel the immediate emancipation of southern slaves. As to which I beg to say that I am bold to differ from Mr. Phillips altogether.

It soon became evident to me that Mr. Phillips was unwell, and lecturing at a disadvantage. His manner was clearly that of an accustomed orator, but his voice was weak, and he was not up to the effect which he attempted to make. His hearers were impatient, repeatedly calling upon him to speak out, and on that account I tried hard to feel kindly towards him and his lecture. But I must confess that I failed. To me it seemed that the doctrine he preached was one of rapine, bloodshed, and social destruction. He would call upon the Government and upon Congress to enfranchise the slaves at once,—now during the war,—so that the Southern power might be destroyed by a concurrence of misfortunes. And he would do so at once, on the spur of the moment, fearing lest the South should be before him, and themselves emancipate their own bondsmen. I have sometimes thought that there is no being so venomous, so bloodthirsty as a professed philanthropist; and that when the philanthropist's ardour lies negro-wards, it then assumes the deepest die of venom and bloodthirstiness. There are four millions of slaves in the southern States, none of whom have any capacity for self-maintenance or self-control. Four millions of slaves, with the necessities of children, with the passions of men, and the ignorance of savages! And Mr. Phillips would emancipate these at a blow; would, were it possible for him to do so, set them loose upon the soil to tear their masters, destroy each other, and make such a hell upon the earth as has never even yet come from the uncontrolled passions and unsatisfied wants of men. But Congress cannot do this. All the members of Congress put together cannot, according to the constitution of the United States, emancipate a single slave in South Carolina; not if they were all unanimous. No emancipation in a Slave State can come otherwise than by the legislative enactment of that State. But it was then thought that in this coming winter of 1860–61 the action of Congress might be set aside. The North possessed an enormous army under the control of the President. The South was in rebellion, and the President could pronounce, and the army perhaps enforce the confiscation of all property held in slaves. If any who held them were not disloyal, the question of compensation might be settled afterwards. How those four million slaves should live, and how white men should live among them, in some States or parts of States not equal to the blacks in number;— as to that Mr. Phillips did not give us his opinion.

And Mr. Phillips also could not keep his tongue away from the abominations of Englishmen and the miraculous powers of his own countrymen. It was on this occasion that he told us more than once how Yankees carried brains in their fingers, whereas "common people" —alluding by that name to Europeans—had them only, if at all, inside their brain-pans. And then he informed us that Lord Palmerston had always hated America. Among the Radicals there might be one or two who understood and valued the institutions of America, but it was a well-known fact that Lord Palmerston was hostile to the country. Nothing but hidden enmity,—enmity hidden or not hidden,—could be expected from England. That the people of Boston, or of Massachusetts, or of the North generally, should feel sore against England is to me intelligible. I know how the minds of men are moved in masses to certain feelings, and that it ever must be so. Men in common talk are not bound to weigh their words, to think, and speculate on their results, and be sure of the premises on which their thoughts are founded. But it is different with a man who rises before two or three thousand of his countrymen to teach and instruct them. After that I heard no more political lectures in Boston.

Of course I visited Bunker's Hill, and went to Lexington and Con-

cord. From the top of the monument on Bunker's Hill there is a fine
view of Boston Harbour, and seen from thence the harbour is picturesque. The mouth is crowded with islands and jutting necks and
promontories; and though the shores are in no place rich enough to
make the scenery grand, the general effect is good. The monument,
however, is so constructed that one can hardly get a view through the
windows at the top of it, and there is no outside gallery round it. Immediately below the monument is a marble figure of Major Warren,
who fell there,—not from the top of the monument, as some one was
led to believe when informed that on that spot the Major had fallen.
Bunker's Hill, which is little more than a mound, is at Charleston,—
a dull, populous, respectable, and very unattractive suburb of Boston.

Bunker's Hill has obtained a considerable name, and is accounted
great in the annals of American history. In England we have all heard
of Bunker's Hill, and some of us dislike the sound as much as Frenchmen do that of Waterloo. In the States men talk of Bunker's Hill as
we may, perhaps, talk of Agincourt and such favourite fields. But, after
all, little was done at Bunker's Hill, and, as far as I can learn, no victory was gained there by either party. The road from Boston to the
town of Concord, on which stands the village of Lexington, is the true
scene of the earliest and greatest deeds of the men of Boston. The
monument at Bunker's Hill stands high and commands attention, while
those at Lexington and Concord are very lowly and command no attention. But it is of that road and what was done on it that Massachusetts
should be proud. When the colonists first began to feel that they were
oppressed, and a half resolve was made to resist that oppression by
force, they began to collect a few arms and some gunpowder at Concord, a small town about eighteen miles from Boston. Of this preparation the English Governor received tidings, and determined to send a
party of soldiers to seize the arms. This he endeavoured to do secretly;
but he was too closely watched, and word was sent down over the waters
by which Boston was then surrounded that the colonists might be prepared for the soldiers. At that time Boston Neck, as it was and is still
called, was the only connection between the town and the main land,
and the road over Boston Neck did not lead to Concord. Boats therefore were necessarily used, and there was some difficulty in getting the
soldiers to the nearest point. They made their way, however, to the
road, and continued their route as far as Lexington without interruption. Here, however, they were attacked, and the first blood of that
war was shed. They shot three or four of the—rebels, I suppose I should
in strict language call them, and then proceeded on to Concord. But

at Concord they were stopped and repulsed, and along the road back from Concord to Lexington they were driven with slaughter and dismay. And thus the rebellion was commenced which led to the establishment of a people which, let us Englishmen say and think what we may of them at this present moment, has made itself one of the five great nations of the earth, and has enabled us to boast that the two out of the five who enjoy the greatest liberty and the widest prosperity, speak the English language and are known by English names. For all that has come and is like to come, I say again, long may that honour remain. I could not but feel that that road from Boston to Concord deserves a name in the world's history greater, perhaps, than has yet been given to it.

Concord is at present to be noted as the residence of Mr. Emerson and of Mr. Hawthorne, two of those many men of letters of whose presence Boston and its neighbourhood have reason to be proud. Of Mr. Emerson I have already spoken. The author of the "Scarlet Letter" I regard as certainly the first of American novelists. I know what men will say of Mr. Cooper,—and I also am an admirer of Cooper's novels.[7] But I cannot think that Mr. Cooper's powers were equal to those of Mr. Hawthorne, though his mode of thought may have been more genial, and his choice of subjects more attractive in their day. In point of imagination, which, after all, is the novelist's greatest gift, I hardly know any living author who can be accounted superior to Mr. Hawthorne.

Very much has, undoubtedly, been done in Boston to carry out that theory of Colonel Newcome's—*Emollit mores*,[8] by which the Colonel meant to signify his opinion that a competent knowledge of reading, writing, and arithmetic, with a taste for enjoying those accomplishments, goes very far towards the making of a man, and will by no means mar a gentleman. In Boston nearly every man, woman, and child has had his or her manners so far softened; and though they may still occasionally be somewhat rough to the outer touch, the inward effect is plainly visible. With us, especially among our agricultural population, the absence of that inner softening is as visible.

I went to see a public library in the city, which, if not founded by

[7] Trollope's first acquaintance with Cooper dated back to the bleak months of his childhood spent at Harrow Weald while his mother was still in America. "In the old house," Anthony recalls in *An Autobiography*, "were the two first volumes of Cooper's novel, called *The Prairie*, a relic—probably a dishonest relic—of some subscription to Hookham's library. . . . I wonder how many dozen times I read those two first volumes."

[8] See the note on page 210.

Mr. Bates whose name is so well known in London as connected with the house of Messrs. Baring, has been greatly enriched by him.[9] It is by his money that it has been enabled to do its work. In this library there is a certain number of thousands of volumes—a great many volumes, as there are in most public libraries. There are books of all classes, from ponderous unreadable folios, of which learned men know the title-pages, down to the lightest literature. Novels are by no means eschewed,—are rather, if I understood aright, considered as one of the staples of the library. From this library any book, excepting such rare volumes as in all libraries are considered holy, is given out to any inhabitant of Boston, without any payment, on presentation of a simple request on a prepared form. In point of fact, it is a gratuitous circulating library open to all Boston, rich or poor, young or old. The books seemed in general to be confided to young children, who came as messengers from their fathers and mothers, or brothers and sisters. No question whatever is asked, if the applicant is known or the place of his residence undoubted. If there be no such knowledge, or there be any doubt as to the residence, the applicant is questioned, the object being to confine the use of the library to the *bonâ fide* inhabitants of the city. Practically the books are given to those who ask for them, whoever they may be. Boston contains over 200,000 inhabitants, and all those 200,000 are entitled to them. Some twenty men and women are kept employed from morning to night in carrying on this circulating library; and there is, moreover, attached to the establishment a large reading-room supplied with papers and magazines, open to the public of Boston on the same terms.

Of course I asked whether a great many of the books were not lost, stolen, and destroyed; and of course I was told that there were no losses, no thefts, and no destruction. As to thefts, the librarian did not seem to think that any instance of such an occurrence could be found. Among the poorer classes a book might sometimes be lost when they were changing their lodgings, but anything so lost was more than replaced by the fines. A book is taken out for a week, and if not brought back at the end of that week, when the loan can be renewed if the reader wishes, a fine, I think of two cents, is incurred. The children, when too late with the books, bring in the two cents as a matter of course, and the sum so collected fully replaces all losses. It was all *couleur de rose*; the librarianesses looked very pretty and learned, and, if I remember

9 Joshua Bates had made the largest single contribution of money to the Boston Public Library, a gift of fifty thousand dollars. The library had been established in 1854.

aright, mostly wore spectacles; the head librarian was enthusiastic; the nice instructive books were properly dog's-eared; my own productions were in enormous demand; the call for books over the counter was brisk, and the reading-room was full of readers.

It has, I dare say, occurred to other travellers to remark that the proceedings at such institutions, when visited by them on their travels, are always rose coloured. It is natural that the bright side should be shown to the visitor. It may be that many books are called for and returned unread, that many of those taken out are so taken by persons who ought to pay for their novels at circulating libraries, that the librarian and librarianesses get very tired of their long hours of attendance, —for I found that they were very long;—and that many idlers warm themselves in that reading-room: nevertheless the fact remains,—the library is public to all the men and women in Boston, and books are given out without payment to all who may choose to ask for them. Why should not the great Mr. Mudie [1] emulate Mr. Bates, and open a library in London on the same system?

The librarian took me into one special room, of which he himself kept the key, to show me a present which the library had received from the English Government. The room was filled with volumes of two sizes, all bound alike, containing descriptions and drawings of all the patents taken out in England. According to this librarian such a work would be invaluable as to American patents; but he conceived that the subject had become too confused to render any such an undertaking possible. "I never allow a single volume to be used for a moment without the presence of myself or one of my assistants," said the librarian; and then he explained to me, when I asked him why he was so particular, that the drawings would, as a matter of course, be cut out and stolen if he omitted his care. "But they may be copied," I said. "Yes; but if Jones merely copies one, Smith may come after him and copy it also. Jones will probably desire to hinder Smith from having any evidence of such a patent." As to the ordinary borrowing and returning of books, the poorest labourer's child in Boston might be trusted as honest; but when a question of trade came up, of commercial competition, then the librarian was bound to bethink himself that his countrymen are very smart. "I hope," said the librarian, "you will let them know in England how grateful we are for their present." And I hereby execute that librarian's commission.

---

1 By 1861 Charles Edward Mudie, proprietor of the famous Mudie's Select Library, offered persons in all parts of England the loan of his 800,000 volumes. His institution was conducted for profit, however, and available only to paid subscribers.

I shall always look back to social life in Boston with great pleasure. I met there many men and women whom to know is a distinction, and with whom to be intimate is a great delight. It was a Puritan city, in which strict old Roundhead sentiments and laws used to prevail; but now-a-days ginger is hot in the mouth there, and in spite of the war there were cakes and ale. There was a law passed in Massachusetts in the old days that any girl should be fined and imprisoned who allowed a young man to kiss her. That law has now, I think, fallen into abeyance, and such matters are regulated in Boston much as they are in other large towns further eastward. It still, I conceive, calls itself a Puritan city, but it has divested its Puritanism of austerity, and clings rather to the politics and public bearing of its old fathers than to their social manners and pristine severity of intercourse. The young girls are, no doubt, much more comfortable under the new dispensation,— and the elderly men also, as I fancy. Sunday, as regards the outer streets, is sabbatical. But Sunday evenings within doors I always found to be, what my friends in that country call "quite a good time." It is not the thing in Boston to smoke in the streets during the day; but the wisest, the sagest, and the most holy,—even those holy men whom the lecturer saw around him,—seldom refuse a cigar in the dining-room as soon as the ladies have gone. Perhaps even the wicked weed would make its appearance before that sad eclipse, thereby postponing, or perhaps absolutely annihilating, the melancholy period of widowhood to both parties, and would light itself under the very eyes of those who in sterner cities will lend no countenance to such lightings. Ah me, it was very pleasant! I confess I like this abandonment of the stricter rules of the more decorous world. I fear that there is within me an aptitude to the milder debaucheries which makes such deviations pleasant. I like to drink and I like to smoke, but I do not like to turn women out of the room. Then comes the question whether one can have all that one likes together. In some small circles in New England I found people simple enough to fancy that they could. In Massachusetts the Maine Liquor Law is still the law of the land, but, like that other law to which I have alluded, it has fallen very much out of use. At any rate it had not reached the houses of the gentlemen with whom I had the pleasure of making acquaintance. But here I must guard myself from being misunderstood. I saw but one drunken man through all New England, and he was very respectable. He was, however, so uncommonly drunk that he might be allowed to count for two or three. The Puritans of Boston are, of course, simple in their habits and simple in their expenses. Champagne and canvas-back ducks I found to be the provisions most in vogue among those who desired to adhere closely to the manners of their forefathers. Upon the whole I found the ways of life which had been brought over in the "Mayflower" from the stern sects of England, and preserved through the revolutionary war for liberty, to be very pleasant ways, and I made up my mind that a Yankee Puritan can be an uncommonly pleasant fellow. I wish that some of them did not dine so early; for when a man sits down at half-past two, that keeping up of the after-dinner recreations till bedtime becomes hard work.

In Boston the houses are very spacious and excellent, and they are always furnished with those luxuries which it is so difficult to introduce into an old house. They have hot and cold water pipes into every room, and baths attached to the bed-chambers. It is not only that comfort is increased by such arrangements, but that much labour is saved. In an old English house it will occupy a servant the best part of the day to carry water up and down for a large family. Everything also is spacious, commodious, and well lighted. I certainly think that in house building the Americans have gone beyond us, for even our new houses are not commodious as are theirs. One practice which they have in their cities would hardly suit our limited London spaces. When the body of the house is built, they throw out the dining-room behind. It stands alone, as it were, with no other chamber above it, and removed from the rest of the house. It is consequently behind the double drawing-rooms which form the ground-floor, and is approached from them, and also from the back of the hall. The second entrance to the dining-room is thus near the top of the kitchen stairs, which no doubt is its proper position. The whole of the upper part of the house is thus kept for the private uses of the family. To me this plan of building recommended itself as being very commodious.

I found the spirit for the war quite as hot at Boston now (in November), if not hotter than it was when I was there ten weeks earlier; and I found also, to my grief, that the feeling against England was as strong. I can easily understand how difficult it must have been, and still must be, to Englishmen at home to understand this, and see how it has come to pass. It has not arisen, as I think, from the old jealousy of England. It has not sprung from that source which for years has induced certain newspapers, especially the "New York Herald" to vilify England. I do not think that the men of New England have ever been, as regards this matter, in the same boat with the "New York Herald." But when this war between the North and South first broke out, even before there was as yet a war, the Northern men had taught themselves to expect what they called British sympathy, meaning British encouragement. They regarded, and properly regarded, the action of the South as a rebellion, and said among themselves that so staid and conservative a nation as Great Britain would surely countenance them in quelling rebels. If not,—should it come to pass that Great Britain should show no such countenance and sympathy for Northern law, if Great Britain did not respond to her friend as she was expected to respond, then it would appear that Cotton was king, at least in British eyes. The war did come, and Great Britain regarded the two parties as belligerents, standing, as far as she was concerned, on equal grounds. This it was that first gave rise to that fretful anger against England which has gone so far towards ruining the northern cause. We know how such passions are swelled by being ventilated, and how they are communicated from mind to mind till they become national. Politicians—American politicians I here mean—have their own future careers ever before their eyes, and are driven to make capital where they can. Hence it is that such men as Mr. Seward in the cabinet, and Mr. Everett out of it, can reconcile it to themselves to speak as they have done of England. It was but the other day that Mr. Everett spoke in one of his orations of the hope that still existed that the flag of the United States might still float over the whole continent of North America. What would he say of an English statesman who should speak of putting up the Union Jack on the State House in Boston? Such words tell for the moment on the hearers, and help to gain some slight popularity; but they tell for more than a moment on those who read them and remember them.

And then came the capture of Messrs. Slidell and Mason. I was at Boston when those men were taken out of the "Trent" by the "San Jacinto," and brought to Fort Warren in Boston Harbour. Captain Wilkes was the officer who had made the capture, and he immediately was recognized as a hero.[2] He was invited to banquets and fêted. Speeches were made to him as speeches are commonly made to high officers who come home after many perils victorious from the wars. His health was drunk with great applause, and thanks were voted to him by one of the Houses of Congress. It was said that a sword was to be given to him, but I do not think that the gift was consummated. Should it not have been a policeman's truncheon? Had he at the best done anything beyond a policeman's work? Of Captain Wilkes no one would

[2] Trollope had met Captain Charles Wilkes, perhaps at Washington, and found him unpleasant company. He was the sole American, Trollope wrote later, who continued to abuse England after he was aware that he was in the presence of an Englishman. (See Trollope's "The Present Condition of the Northern States of the American Union," *Four Lectures,* edited by Morris L. Parrish [London, 1938]).

complain for doing policeman's duty. If his country were satisfied with
the manner in which he did it, England, if she quarrelled at all, would
not quarrel with him. It may now and again become the duty of a
brave officer to do work of so low a calibre. It is a pity that an ambitious sailor should find himself told off for so mean a task, but the
world would know that it is not his fault. No one could blame Captain
Wilkes for acting policeman on the seas. But who ever before heard of
giving a man glory for achievements so little glorious? How Captain
Wilkes must have blushed when those speeches were made to him,
when that talk about the sword came up, when the thanks arrived to
him from Congress! An officer receives his country's thanks when he
has been in great peril, and has borne himself gallantly through his
danger; when he has endured the brunt of war, and come through it
with victory; when he has exposed himself on behalf of his country
and singed his epaulets with an enemy's fire. Captain Wilkes tapped
a merchantman on the shoulder in the high seas, and told him that his
passengers were wanted. In doing this he showed no lack of spirit, for
it might be his duty; but where was his spirit when he submitted to be
thanked for such work?

And then there arose a clamour of justification among the lawyers;
judges and ex-judges flew to Wheaton, Phillimore, and Lord Stowell.
Before twenty-four hours were over, every man and every woman in
Boston were armed with precedents. Then there was the burning of the
"Caroline." England had improperly burned the "Caroline" on Lake
Erie, or rather in one of the American ports on Lake Erie, and had then
begged pardon.[3] If the States had been wrong, they would beg pardon;
but whether wrong or right, they would not give up Slidell and Mason.
But the lawyers soon waxed stronger. The men were manifestly ambassadors, and as such contraband of war. Wilkes was quite right, only
he should have seized the vessel also. He was quite right, for though
Slidell and Mason might not be ambassadors, they were undoubtedly
carrying despatches. In a few hours there began to be a doubt whether
the men could be ambassadors, because if called ambassadors, then the
power that sent the embassy must be presumed to be recognized. That
Captain Wilkes had taken no despatches was true; but the Captain

[3] During the Canadian Rebellion of 1837, a small American-owned steamer, the
Caroline, had been carrying men and supplies from Buffalo to the rebel encamp-
ment on Navy Island in Lake Erie. On the night of December 29 a small Canadian
Loyalist force took the *Caroline* from her moorings at Fort Schlosser, New York, set
fire to her, and sent her over Niagara Falls. The incident created intense resentment
in the United States, and diplomatic negotiations went on for five years before the
matter was finally settled.

suggested a way out of this difficulty by declaring that he had regarded the two men themselves as an incarnated embodiment of despatches. At any rate, they were clearly contraband of war. They were going to do an injury to the North. It was pretty to hear the charming women of Boston, as they became learned in the law of nations: "Wheaton is quite clear about it," one young girl said to me. It was the first I had ever heard of Wheaton, and so far was obliged to knock under. All the world, ladies and lawyers, expressed the utmost confidence in the justice of the seizure, but it was clear that all the world was in a state of the profoundest nervous anxiety on the subject. To me it seemed to be the most suicidal act that any party in a life-and-death struggle ever committed. All Americans on both sides had felt, from the beginning of the war, that any assistance given by England to one or the other would turn the scale. The Government of Mr. Lincoln must have learned by this time that England was at least true in her neutrality; that no desire for cotton would compel her to give aid to the South as long as she herself was not ill-treated by the North. But it seemed as though Mr. Seward, the President's prime minister, had no better work on hand than that of showing in every way his indifference as to courtesy with England. Insults offered to England would, he seemed to think, strengthen his hands. He would let England know that he did not care for her. When our minister, Lord Lyons, appealed to him regarding the suspension of the habeas corpus, Mr. Seward not only answered him with insolence, but instantly published his answer in the papers. He instituted a system of passports, especially constructed so as to incommode Englishmen proceeding from the States across the Atlantic. He resolved to make every Englishman in America feel himself in some way punished because England had not assisted the North. And now came the arrest of Slidell and Mason out of an English mail-steamer; and Mr. Seward took care to let it be understood that, happen what might, those two men should not be given up.

Nothing during all this time astonished me so much as the estimation in which Mr. Seward was then held by his own party. It is, perhaps, the worst defect in the Constitution of the States, that no incapacity on the part of a minister, no amount of condemnation expressed against him by the people or by Congress, can put him out of office during the term of the existing Presidency. The President can dismiss him; but it generally happens that the President is brought in on a "platform," which has already nominated for him his Cabinet as thoroughly as they have nominated him. Mr. Seward ran Mr. Lincoln very hard for the position of candidate for the Presidency on the Republican interest. On the second voting of the Republican delegates at the Convention at Chicago, Mr. Seward polled 184 to Mr. Lincoln's 181. But as a clear half of the total number of votes was necessary—that is 233 out of 465—there was necessarily a third polling, and Mr. Lincoln won the day. On that occasion Mr. Chase and Mr. Cameron, both of whom became members of Mr. Lincoln's Cabinet, were also candidates for the White House on the Republican side. I mention this here to show, that though the President can in fact dismiss his Ministers, he is in a great manner bound to them, and that a Minister in Mr. Seward's position is hardly to be dismissed. But from the 1st of November, 1861, till the day on which I left the States, I do not think that I heard a good word spoken of Mr. Seward as a Minister even by one of his own party. The Radical or Abolitionist Republicans all abused him. The Conservative or Anti-abolition Republicans, to whose party he would consider himself as belonging, spoke of him as a mistake. He had been prominent as Senator from New York, and had been Governor of the State of New York, but had none of the aptitudes of a statesman. He was there, and it was a pity. He was not so bad as Mr. Cameron, the Minister for War; that was the best his own party could say for him, even in his own State of New York. As to the Democrats, their language respecting him was as harsh as any that I have heard used towards the Southern leaders. He seemed to have no friend, no one who trusted him;—and yet he was the President's chief minister, and seemed to have in his own hands the power of mismanaging all foreign relations as he pleased. But, in truth, the States of America, great as they are, and much as they have done, have not produced Statesmen. That theory of governing by the little men rather than by the great, has not been found to answer, and such follies as those of Mr. Seward have been the consequence.

At Boston, and indeed elsewhere, I found that there was even then, —at the time of the capture of Mason and Slidell, no true conception of the neutrality of England with reference to the two parties. When any argument was made, showing that England who had carried those messengers from the South, would undoubtedly have also carried messengers from the North, the answer always was—"But the Southerners are all rebels. Will England regard us who are by treaty her friend, as she does a people that is in rebellion against its own government?" That was the old story over again, and as it was a very long story, it was hardly of use to go back through all its details. But the fact was that unless there had been such absolute neutrality—such equality between the parties in the eyes of England—even Captain Wilkes would not have thought of stopping the "Trent," or the Government at Washington of justifying such a proceeding. And it must be remembered that the Government at Washington had justified that proceeding. The Secretary of the Navy had distinctly done so in his official report; and that report had been submitted to the President and published by his order. It was because England was neutral between the North and South that Captain Wilkes claimed to have the right of seizing those two men. It had been the President's intention, some month or so before this affair, to send Mr. Everett and other gentlemen over to England with objects as regards the North, similar to those which had caused the sending of Slidell and Mason with reference to the South. What would Mr. Everett have thought had he been refused a passage from Dover to Calais, because the carrying of him would have been towards the South a breach of neutrality? It would never have occurred to him that he could become subject to such stoppage. How should we have been abused for Southern sympathies had we so acted? We, forsooth, who carry passengers about the world, from China and Australia, round to Chili and Peru, who have the charge of the world's passengers and letters, and as a nation incur out of our pocket annually a loss of some half-million of pounds sterling for the privilege of doing so, are to inquire the business of every American traveller before we let him on board, and be stopped in our work if we take anybody on one side whose journeyings may be conceived by the other side to be to them prejudicial! Not on such terms will Englishmen be willing to spread civilization across the ocean! I do not pretend to understand Wheaton and Phillimore, or even to have read a single word of any international law. I have refused to read any such, knowing that it would only confuse and mislead me. But I have my common sense to guide me. Two men living in one street, quarrel and shy brickbats at each other, and make the whole street very uncomfortable. Not only is no one to interfere with them, but they are to have the privilege of deciding that their brickbats have the right of way, rather than the ordinary intercourse of the neighbourhood! If that be national law, national law must be changed. It might do for some centuries back, but it cannot do now. Up to this period my sympathies had been with the North. I thought, and still think, that the North had no alternative, that the war had been forced upon them, and that they had gone about their work with patriotic energy. But this stopping of an English mail-steamer was too much for me.

What will they do in England? was now the question. But for any knowledge as to that, I had to wait till I reached Washington.

CHAPTER XVI

CAMBRIDGE AND LOWELL

THE TWO places of most general interest in the vicinity of Boston are Cambridge and Lowell. Cambridge is to Massachusetts, and, I may almost say, is to all the northern States, what Cambridge and Oxford are to England. It is the seat of the University which gives the highest education to be attained by the highest classes in that country. Lowell also is in little to Massachusetts and to New England what Manchester is to us in so great a degree. It is the largest and most prosperous cotton-manufacturing town in the States.

Cambridge is not above three or four miles from Boston. Indeed, the town of Cambridge properly so called begins where Boston ceases. The Harvard College—that is its name, taken from one of its original founders—is reached by horse-cars in twenty minutes from the city. An Englishman feels inclined to regard the place as a suburb of Boston; but if he so expresses himself, he will not find favour in the eyes of the men of Cambridge.

The University is not so large as I had expected to find it. It consists of Harvard College, as the undergraduates' department, and of professional schools of law, medicine, divinity, and science. In the few words that I will say about it I will confine myself to Harvard College proper, conceiving that the professional schools connected with it have not in themselves any special interest. The average number of under-graduates does not exceed 450, and these are divided into four classes. The average number of degrees taken annually by bachelors of art is something under 100. Four years' residence is required for a degree, and at the end of that period a degree is given as a matter of course if the candidate's conduct has been satisfactory. When a young man has pursued his studies for that period, going through the required examinations and lectures, he is not subjected to any final examination as is the case with a candidate for a degree at Oxford and Cambridge. It is, perhaps, in this respect that the greatest difference exists between the English Universities and Harvard College. With us a young man may, I take it, still go through his three or four years with a small amount of study. But his doing so does not insure him his degree. If he have utterly wasted his time he is plucked, and late but heavy punishment comes upon him. At Cambridge in Massachusetts the daily work of the men is made more obligatory; but if this be gone through with such diligence as to enable the student to hold his own during the four years, he has his degree as a matter of course. There are no degrees conferring special honour. A man cannot go out "in honours" as he does with us. There are no "firsts" or "double firsts"; no "wranglers"; no "senior opts" or "junior opts." Nor are there prizes of fellowships and livings to be obtained. It is, I think, evident from this that the greatest incentives to high excellence are wanting at Harvard College. There is neither the reward of honour nor of money. There is none of that great competition which exists at our Cambridge for the high place of Senior Wrangler; and, consequently, the degree of excellence attained is no doubt lower than with us.[1] But I conceive that the general level of the University education is higher there than with us; that a young man is more sure of getting his education, and that a smaller percentage of men leaves Harvard College utterly uneducated than goes in that condition out of Oxford or Cambridge. The education at Harvard College is more diversified in its nature, and study is more absolutely the business of the place than it is at our Universities.

The expense of education at Harvard College is not much lower than at our colleges; with us there are, no doubt, more men who are absolutely extravagant than at Cambridge, Massachusetts. The actual authorized expenditure in accordance with the rules is only 50*l.* per annum, *i.e.,* 249 dollars; but this does not, by any means, include everything. Some of the richer young men may spend as much as 300*l.* per annum, but the largest number vary their expenditure from 100*l.* to 180*l.* per annum; and I take it the same thing may be said of our Universities. There are many young men at Harvard College of very small means. They will live on 70*l.* per annum, and will earn a great portion of that by teaching in the vacations. There are thirty-six scholarships attached to the University varying in value from 20*l.* to 60*l.* per annum; and there is also a beneficiary fund for supplying poor scholars with assistance during their collegiate education. Many are thus brought up at Cambridge who have no means of their own, and I think I may say that the consideration in which they are held among their brother

1 "In most respects Mr. Trollope's criticism on the American collegiate system as seen at Harvard is just; but he is entirely mistaken in saying that 'the greatest incentives to high excellence are wanting.' It is true that there are no 'prizes of fellowships and livings to be obtained'; but although Harvard cannot offer to her successful students 'the reward of money,' she does give 'the reward of honor,' and her first places are striven for with as much zeal as the 'double-firsts' at Oxford, or the 'wranglers' at the English Cambridge."—*North American Review,* October 1862.

students is in no degree affected by their position. I doubt whether we can say so much of the sizars and bible clerks at our Universities.

At Harvard College there is, of course, none of that old-fashioned, time-honoured, delicious, mediæval life which lends so much grace and beauty to our colleges. There are no gates, no porter's lodges, no butteries, no halls, no battels, and no common rooms. There are no proctors, no bulldogs, no bursers, no deans, no morning and evening chapel, no quads, no surplices, no caps and gowns. I have already said that there are no examinations for degrees and no honours; and I can easily conceive that in the absence of all these essentials many an Englishman will ask what right Harvard College has to call itself a University.

I have said that there are no honours,—and in our sense there are none. But I should give offence to my American friends if I did not explain that there are prizes given—I think, all in money, and that they vary from 50 to 10 dollars. These are called *deturs*. The degrees are given on Commencement Day, at which occasion certain of the expectant graduates are selected to take parts in a public literary exhibition. To be so selected seems to be tantamount to taking a degree in honours. There is also a dinner on Commencement Day,—at which, however, "no wine or other intoxicating drink shall be served."

It is required that every student shall attend some place of Christian worship on Sundays; but he, or his parents for him, may elect what denomination of church he shall attend. There is a University chapel on the University grounds which belongs, if I remember right, to the Episcopalian Church. The young men for the most part live in College, having rooms in the College buildings; but they do not board in those rooms. There are establishments in the town under the patronage of the University, at which dinner, breakfast, and supper are provided; and the young men frequent one of these houses or another as they, or their friends for them, may arrange. Every young man not belonging to a family resident within a hundred miles of Cambridge, and whose parents are desirous to obtain the protection thus provided, is placed, as regards his pecuniary management, under the care of a patron, and this patron acts by him as a father does in England by a boy at school. He pays out his money for him and keeps him out of debt. The arrangement will not recommend itself to young men at Oxford quite so powerfully as it may do to the fathers of some young men who have been there. The rules with regard to the lodging and boarding-houses are very stringent. Any festive entertainment is to be reported to the President. No wine or spirituous liquors may be used, &c. It is not a picturesque system, this; but it has its advantages.

There is a handsome library attached to the College, which the young men can use; but it is not as extensive as I had expected. The University is not well off for funds by which to increase it. The new museum in the College is also a handsome building. The edifices used for the undergraduates' Chambers and for the lecture-rooms are by no means handsome. They are very ugly red-brick houses standing here and there without order. There are seven such, and they are called Brattle House, College House, Divinity Hall, Hollis Hall, Holsworthy Hall, Massachusetts Hall, and Stoughton Hall. It is almost astonishing that buildings so ugly should have been erected for such a purpose. These, together with the library, the museum, and the chapel, stand on a large green, which might be made pretty enough if it were kept well mown like the gardens of our Cambridge colleges; but it is much neglected. Here, again, the want of funds—the *res angusta domi* [2]—must be pleaded as an excuse. On the same green, but at some little distance from any other building, stands the President's pleasant house.

The immediate direction of the College is of course mainly in the hands of the President, who is supreme. But for the general management of the Institution there is a Corporation, of which he is one. It is stated in the laws of the University that the Corporation of the University and its Overseers constitute the Government of the University. The Corporation consists of the President, five Fellows, so called, and a Treasurer. These Fellows are chosen, as vacancies occur, by themselves, subject to the concurrence of the Overseers. But these Fellows are in nowise like to the Fellows of our colleges, having no salaries attached to their offices. The Board of Overseers consists of the State Governor, other State officers, the President and Treasurer of Harvard College, and thirty other persons,—men of note, chosen by vote. The Faculty of the College, in which is vested the immediate care and government of the undergraduates, is composed of the President and the Professors. The Professors answer to the tutors of our colleges, and upon them the education of the place depends. I cannot complete this short notice of Harvard College without saying that it is happy in the possession of that distinguished natural philosopher, Professor Agassiz. M. Agassiz has collected at Cambridge a museum of such things as natural philosophers delight to show, which I am told is all but invaluable. As my ignorance on all such matters is of a depth which the Professor can hardly imagine, and which it would have shocked him to behold, I did not visit the museum. Taking the University of Harvard College as a whole, I should say that it is most remarkable in this,—

2 "the narrow means at home."—Juvenal: *Satires.*

that it does really give to its pupils that education which it professes to give. Of our own Universities other good things may be said, but that one special good thing cannot always be said.

Cambridge boasts itself as the residence of four or five men well known to fame on the American, and also on the European side of the ocean. President Felton's * name is very familiar to us, and wherever Greek scholarship is held in repute, that is known. So also is the name of Professor Agassiz, of whom I have spoken. Russell Lowell is one of the Professors of the College,—that Russell Lowell who sang of Birdo'-fredum Sawin, and whose Biglow Papers were edited with such an ardour of love by our Tom Brown. Birdo'fredum is worthy of all the ardour.[3] Mr. Dana is also a Cambridge man,—he who was "two years before the mast," and who since that has written to us of Cuba. But Mr. Dana, though residing at Cambridge, is not of Cambridge, and, though a literary man, he does not belong to literature.[4] He is,—could he help it?—a special attorney. I must not, however, degrade him, for in the States barristers and attorneys are all one. I cannot but think that he could help it, and that he should not give up to law what was meant for mankind. I fear, however, that successful law has caught him

---

* Since these words were written President Felton has died. I, as I returned on my way homewards, had the melancholy privilege of being present at his funeral. I feel bound to record here the great kindness with which Mr. Felton assisted me in obtaining such information as I needed respecting the Institution over which he presided.

[3] Birdofredum Sawin in the first series of James Russell Lowell's The Biglow Papers (1846–8) serves as a "Private in the Massachusetts Regiment" during the Mexican War. He writes three rhymed epistles home to his friend Hosea Biglow. The realities of a soldier's life have filled Birdofredum's soul with disillusion:

O, would n't I be off, quick time, ef't wornt thet I wuz sartin
They'd let the daylight into me to pay me fer desartin!

In his opinion,

Ninepunce a day fer killin folks comes kind o' low fer murder.

Birdofredum figures also in two parts of the second series of The Biglow Papers, which were appearing in the Atlantic Monthly while Trollope was in the United States. In these Birdofredum has settled in the South and become a gull of Confederate propaganda. Thomas Hughes, Lowell's editor, wrote Tom Brown's Schooldays.

[4] To judge from the tone of this passage and Trollope's letters to him, Richard Henry Dana, Jr. (1815–82), was one of the new friends whom Trollope found most congenial during his stay in Boston. Dana's Two Years before the Mast had first been published in 1840. During the Civil War he was United States attorney for the district of Massachusetts. Since 1840 he had given his prime energies to diplomacy and the law. He never attained the high offices he seems to have been qualified to hold. As an old man he said: "My great success—my book—was a boy's work, done before I came to the Bar," and at another time: "My life has been a failure compared with what I might and ought to have done." His travel book, To Cuba and Back, a work of much lower caliber than Two Years before the Mast, was published in 1859.

in her intolerant clutches, and that literature, who surely would be the nobler mistress, must wear the willow. Last and greatest is the poet-laureat of the West; for Mr. Longfellow also lives at Cambridge.

I am not at all aware whether the nature of the manufacturing corporation of Lowell is generally understood by Englishmen. I confess that until I made personal acquaintance with the plan, I was absolutely ignorant on the subject. I knew that Lowell was a manufacturing town at which cotton is made into calico, and at which calico is printed,— as is the case at Manchester; but I conceived this was done at Lowell, as it is done at Manchester, by individual enterprise,—that I or any one else could open a mill at Lowell, and that the manufacturers there were ordinary traders, as they are at other manufacturing towns. But this is by no means the case.

That which most surprises an English visitor on going through the mills at Lowell is the personal appearance of the men and woman who work at them. As there are twice as many women as there are men, it is to them that the attention is chiefly called. They are not only better dressed, cleaner, and better mounted in every respect than the girls employed at manufactories in England, but they are so infinitely superior as to make a stranger immediately perceive that some very strong cause must have created the difference. We all know the class of young women whom we generally see serving behind counters in the shops of our larger cities. They are neat, well dressed, careful, especially about their hair, composed in their manner, and sometimes a little supercilious in the propriety of their demeanour. It is exactly the same class of young women that one sees in the factories at Lowell. They are not sallow, nor dirty, nor ragged, nor rough. They have about them no signs of want, or of low culture. Many of us also know the appearance of those girls who work in the factories in England; and I think it will be allowed that a second glance at them is not wanting to show that they are in every respect inferior to the young women who attend our shops. The matter, indeed, requires no argument. Any young woman at a shop would be insulted by being asked whether she had worked at a factory. The difference with regard to the men at Lowell is quite as strong, though not so striking. Working men do not show their status in the world by their outward appearance as readily as women; and, as I have said before, the number of the women greatly exceeded that of the men.

One would of course be disposed to say that the superior condition of the workers must have been occasioned by superior wages; and this, to a certain extent, has been the cause. But the higher payment is not the chief cause. Women's wages, including all that they receive at the Lowell factories, average about 14s. a week, which is, I take it, fully a third more than women can earn in Manchester, or did earn before the loss of the American cotton began to tell upon them. But if wages at Manchester were raised to the Lowell standard, the Manchester women would not be clothed, fed, cared for, and educated like the Lowell women. The fact is, that the workmen and the workwomen at Lowell are not exposed to the chances of an open labour market. They are taken in, as it were, to a philanthropical manufacturing college, and then looked after and regulated more as girls and lads at a great seminary, than as hands by whose industry profit is to be made out of capital. This is all very nice and pretty at Lowell, but I am afraid it could not be done at Manchester.

There are at present twelve different manufactories at Lowell, each of which has what is called a separate corporation. The Merrimack manufacturing company was incorporated in 1822, and thus Lowell was commenced. The Lowell machine-shop was incorporated in 1845, and since that no new establishment has been added. In 1821 a certain Boston manufacturing company, which had mills at Waltham, near Boston, was attracted by the water-power of the river Merrimack, on which the present town of Lowell is situated. A canal, called the Pawtucket Canal, had been made for purposes of navigation from one reach of the river to another, with the object of avoiding the Pawtucket Falls; and this canal, with the adjacent water-power of the river, was purchased for the Boston Company. The place was then called Lowell, after one of the partners in that company.

It must be understood that water-power alone is used for preparing the cotton and working the spindles and looms of the cotton mills. Steam is applied in the two establishments in which the cottons are printed, for the purposes of printing, but I think nowhere else. When the mills are at full work, about two-and-a-half million yards of cotton goods are made every week, and nearly a million pounds of cotton are consumed per week (*i.e.* 842,000 lbs.), but the consumption of coal is only 30,000 tons in the year. This will give some idea of the value of the water-power. The Pawtucket Canal was, as I say, bought, and Lowell was commenced. The town was incorporated in 1826, and the railway between it and Boston was opened in 1835, under the superintendence of Mr. Jackson, the gentleman by whom the purchase of the canal had in the first instance been made. Lowell now contains about 40,000 inhabitants.

The following extract is taken from the hand-book to Lowell:—

IX New York Street Railroad Cars—an Interior: "The woman, as she enters, drags after her a misshapen, dirty mass of battered wirework, which she calls her crinoline. . . . Of this she takes much heed, not managing it so that it may be conveyed up the carriage with some decency, but striking it about against men's legs, and heaving it with violence over people's knees."

Harper's Weekly, XI (*March* 23, 1867), 189

X Skating at Boston

Harper's Weekly, III (*March* 12, 1859) , 173

"Mr. F. C. Lowell [5] had in his travels abroad observed the effect of large manufacturing establishments on the character of the people, and in the establishment at Waltham the founders looked for a remedy for these defects. They thought that education and good morals would even enhance the profit, and that they could compete with Great Britain by introducing a more cultivated class of operatives. For this purpose they built boarding-houses, which, under the direct supervision of the agent, were kept by discreet matrons"—I can answer for the discreet matrons at Lowell—"mostly widows, no boarders being allowed except operatives. Agents and overseers of high moral character were selected; regulations were adopted at the mills and boarding-houses, by which only respectable girls were employed. The mills were nicely painted and swept,"—I can also answer for the painting and sweeping at Lowell,—"trees set out in the yards and along the streets, habits of neatness and cleanliness encouraged; and the result justified the expenditure. At Lowell the same policy has been adopted and extended; more spacious mills and elegant boarding-houses have been erected";— as to the elegance, it may be a matter of taste, but as to the comfort there is no question,—"the same care as to the classes employed; more capital has been expended for cleanliness and decoration; a hospital has been established for the sick, where, for a small price, they have an experienced physician and skilful nurses. An institute, with an extensive library, for the use of the mechanics, has been endowed. The agents have stood forward in the support of schools, churches, lectures, and lyceums, and their influence contributed highly to the elevation of the moral and intellectual character of the operatives. Talent has been encouraged, brought forward, and recommended."—For some considerable time the young women wrote, edited, and published a newspaper among themselves, called the Lowell Offering.[6]—"And Lowell has supplied agents and mechanics for the later manufacturing places who have given tone to society, and extended the beneficial influence of Lowell through the United States. Girls from the country, with a

[5] Francis Cabot Lowell (1774–1817) was the original conceiver of the enlightened system employed at the mills; he was also the main promoter of the Boston Manufacturing Company, the parent organization located at Waltham, Massachusetts, up to the time of his death. Patrick Tracy Jackson (1780–1847), his brother-in-law, was one of the men who joined him in the Boston Manufacturing Company and who, some years after Lowell's death, established the mills at the new town, naming it Lowell in honor of him.

[6] *The Lowell Offering*, the first periodical in the world to be written exclusively by women, found subscribers all over the country. Harriet Martineau wrote a glowing review of it for the *Athenæum*, and Dickens praised it in *American Notes*. Between 1840 and 1849 it extended to seven volumes.

true Yankee spirit of independence, and confident in their own powers, pass a few years here, and then return to get married with a dower secured by their exertions, with more enlarged ideas and extended means of information, and their places are supplied by younger relatives. A larger proportion of the female population of New England has been employed at some time in manufacturing establishments, and they are not on this account less good wives, mothers, or educators of families." Then the account goes on to tell how the health of the girls has been improved by their attendance at the mills, how they put money into the savings-banks, and buy railway shares and farms; how there are thirty churches in Lowell, a library, banks, and insurance offices; how there is a cemetery, and a park, and how everything is beautiful, philanthropic, profitable, and magnificent.

Thus Lowell is the realization of a commercial Utopia. Of all the statements made in the little book which I have quoted I cannot point out one which is exaggerated, much less false. I should not call the place elegant; in other respects I am disposed to stand by the book. Before I had made any inquiry into the cause of the apparent comfort, it struck me at once that some great effort at excellence was being made. I went into one of the discreet matrons' residences; and perhaps may give but an indifferent idea of her discretion when I say that she allowed me to go into the bedrooms. If you want to ascertain the inner ways or habits of life of any man, woman, or child, see, if it be practicable to do so, his or her bedroom. You will learn more by a minute's glance round that holy of holies, than by any conversation. Looking-glasses and such like, suspended dresses, and toilet-belongings, if taken without notice, cannot lie or even exaggerate. The discreet matron at first showed me rooms only prepared for use, for at the period of my visit Lowell was by no means full; but she soon became more intimate with me, and I went through the upper part of the house. My report must be altogether in her favour and in that of Lowell. Everything was cleanly, well-ordered, and feminine. There was not a bed on which any woman need have hesitated to lay herself if occasion required it. I fear that this cannot be said of the lodgings of the manufacturing classes at Manchester. The boarders all take their meals together. As a rule, they have meat twice a-day. Hot meat for dinner is with them as much a matter of course, or probably more so, than with any English man or woman who may read this book. For in the States of America regulations on this matter are much more rigid than with us. Cold meat is rarely seen, and to live a day without meat would be as great a privation as to pass a night without bed.

The rules for the guidance of these boarding-houses are very rigid. The houses themselves belong to the corporations or different manufacturing establishments, and the tenants are altogether in the power of the managers. None but operatives are to be taken in. The tenants are answerable for improper conduct. The doors are to be closed at ten o'clock. Any boarders who do not attend divine worship are to be reported to the managers. The yards and walks are to be kept clean, and snow removed at once; and the inmates must be vaccinated, &c., &c., &c. It is expressly stated by the Hamilton Company,—and I believe by all the companies,—that no one shall be employed who is habitually absent from public worship on Sunday, or who is known to be guilty of immorality. It is stated that the average wages of the women are two dollars, or eight shillings, a week, besides their board. I found when I was there that from three dollars to three-and-a-half a week were paid to the women, of which they paid one dollar and twenty-five cents for their board. As this would not fully cover the expense of their keep, twenty-five cents a week for each was also paid to the boarding-house keepers by the mill agents. This substantially came to the same thing, as it left the two dollars a week, or eight shillings, with the girls over and above their cost of living. The board included washing, lights, food, bed, and attendance,—leaving a surplus of eight shillings a week for clothes and saving. Now let me ask any one acquainted with Manchester and its operatives, whether that is not Utopia realized. Factory girls, for whom every comfort of life is secured, with 21*l.* a year over for saving and dress! One sees the failing, however, at a moment. It is Utopia.[7] Any Lady Bountiful can tutor three or four peasants and make

[7] When Trollope inspected it in 1861, Utopia was already in its decline. During the 1830's and 1840's, Lowell had been filled with high-minded, agile-witted girls from the New England countryside. Encouraged by an altruistic management, they had followed a fairly leisurely pace in their work, saved money for the future, eaten, lodged, and dressed well, studied science and literature, published their magazine, organized debating and lecture societies, and in general led a life that brought respect and even prestige to the American factory girl. By 1850 the former altruistic managers of Lowell were giving place to absentee owners, and the corporations were already finding means of getting more work for less outlay. By the time of Trollope's visit the Yankee girls of Lowell's heyday, finding better wages elsewhere, had with few exceptions left the mills; immigrant labor was rapidly taking their place. By 1881 the old atmosphere had almost completely vanished. The mill girls now put in shorter hours, but they were obliged to do a much greater amount of work. "They are always on the jump," Harriet H. Robinson reported (*Early Factory Labor in New England* [1889]). "They have no time to improve themselves." New waves of immigrant labor from Europe and Asia, settling in family groups, made the corporation boarding-house system unfeasible, and Lowell became the crowded mill town depressingly anatomized in George F. Kenngott's *The Record of a City* (1912).

them luxuriously comfortable. But no Lady Bountiful can give luxurious comfort to half-a-dozen parishes. Lowell is now nearly forty years old, and contains but 40,000 inhabitants. From the very nature of its corporations it cannot spread itself. Chicago, which has grown out of nothing in a much shorter period, and which has no factories,[8] has now 120,000 inhabitants. Lowell is a very wonderful place and shows what philanthropy can do; but I fear it also shows what philanthropy cannot do.

There are, however, other establishments, conducted on the same principle as those at Lowell, which have had the same amount, or rather the same sort, of success. Lawrence is now a town of about 15,000 inhabitants, and Manchester of about 24,000,—if I remember rightly; —and at those places the mills are also owned by corporations and conducted as are those at Lowell. But it seems to me that as New England takes her place in the world as a great manufacturing country—which place she undoubtedly will take sooner or later—she must abandon the hot-house method of providing for her operatives with which she has commenced her work. In the first place, Lowell is not open as a manufacturing town to the capitalists even of New England at large. Stock may, I presume, be bought in the corporations, but no interloper can establish a mill there. It is a close manufacturing community, bolstered up on all sides, and has none of that capacity for providing employment for a thickly-growing population which belongs to such places as Manchester and Leeds. That it should under its present system have been made in any degree profitable reflects great credit on the managers; but the profit does not reach an amount which in America can be considered as remunerative. The total capital invested by the twelve corporations is thirteen million and a half of dollars, or about two million seven hundred thousand pounds. In only one of the corporations, that of the Merrimack Company, does the profit amount to 12 per cent. In one, that of the Boott Company, it falls below 7 per cent. The average profit of the various establishments is something below 9 per cent. I am of course speaking of Lowell as it was previous to the war. American capitalists are not, as a rule, contented with so low a rate of interest as this.

The States in these matters have had a great advantage over England. They have been able to begin at the beginning. Manufactories have grown up among us as our cities grew;—from the necessities and

8 A shaky generalization. As early as 1855 Chicago had 6,288 employees in its factories; by 1860 the number and size of her manufacturing concerns had greatly increased. McCormick's reaper factory alone employed several hundred workmen.

chances of the times. When labour was wanted it was obtained in the ordinary way; and so when houses were built they were built in the ordinary way. We had not the experience, and the results either for good or bad, of other nations to guide us. The Americans, in seeing and resolving to adopt our commercial successes, have resolved also, if possible, to avoid the evils which have attended those successes. It would be very desirable that all our factory girls should read and write, wear clean clothes, have decent beds, and eat hot meat every day. But that is now impossible. Gradually, with very up-hill work, but still I trust with sure work, much will be done to improve their position and render their life respectable; but in England we can have no Lowells. In our thickly populated island any commercial Utopia is out of the question. Nor can, as I think, Lowell be taken as a type of the future manufacturing towns of New England. When New England employs millions in her factories, instead of thousands,—the hands employed at Lowell, when the mills are at full work, are about 11,000,—she must cease to provide for them their beds and meals, their church-going proprieties and orderly modes of life. In such an attempt she has all the experience of the world against her. But nevertheless I think she will have done much good. The tone which she will have given will not altogether lose its influence. Employment in a factory is now considered reputable by a farmer and his children, and this idea will remain. Factory work is regarded as more respectable than domestic service, and this prestige will not wear itself altogether out. Those now employed have a strong conception of the dignity of their own social position, and their successors will inherit much of this, even though they may find themselves excluded from the advantages of the present Utopia. The thing has begun well, but it can only be regarded as a beginning. Steam, it may be presumed, will become the motive power of cotton mills in New England as it is with us; and when it is so, the amount of work to be done at any one place will not be checked by any such limit as that which now prevails at Lowell. Water-power is very cheap, but it cannot be extended; and it would seem that no place can become large as a manufacturing town which has to depend chiefly upon water. It is not improbable that steam may be brought into general use at Lowell, and that Lowell may spread itself. If it should spread itself widely, it will lose its Utopian characteristics.

One cannot but be greatly struck by the spirit of philanthropy in which the system of Lowell was at first instituted. It may be presumed that men who put their money into such an undertaking did so with the object of commercial profit to themselves; but in this case that was not their first object. I think it may be taken for granted that when Messrs. Jackson and Lowell went about their task, their grand idea was to place factory work upon a respectable footing,—to give employment in mills which should not be unhealthy, degrading, demoralizing, or hard in its circumstances. Throughout the northern States of America the same feeling is to be seen. Good and thoughtful men have been active to spread education, to maintain health, to make work compatible with comfort and personal dignity, and to divest the ordinary lot of man of the sting of that curse which was supposed to be uttered when our first father was ordered to eat his bread in the sweat of his brow. One is driven to contrast this feeling, of which on all sides one sees such ample testimony, with that sharp desire for profit, that anxiety to do a stroke of trade at every turn, that acknowledged necessity of being smart, which we must own is quite as general as the nobler propensity. I believe that both phases of commercial activity may be attributed to the same characteristic. Men in trade in America are not more covetous than tradesmen in England, nor probably are they more generous or philanthropical. But that which they do, they are more anxious to do thoroughly and quickly. They desire that every turn taken shall be a great turn,—or at any rate that it shall be as great as possible. They go ahead either for bad or good with all the energy they have. In the institutions at Lowell I think we may allow that the good has very much prevailed.

I went over two of the mills, those of the Merrimack corporation, and of the Massachusetts. At the former the printing establishment only was at work; the cotton mills were closed. I hardly know whether it will interest any one to learn that something under half-a-million yards of calico are here printed annually. At the Lowell bleachery fifteen million yards are dyed annually. The Merrimack cotton-mills were stopped, and so had the other mills at Lowell been stopped, till some short time before my visit. Trade had been bad, and there had of course been a lack of cotton. I was assured that no severe suffering had been created by this stoppage. The greater number of hands had returned into the country,—to the farms from whence they had come; and though a discontinuance of work and wages had of course produced hardship, there had been no actual privation,—no hunger and want. Those of the workpeople who had no homes out of Lowell to which to betake themselves, and no means at Lowell of living, had received relief before real suffering had begun. I was assured, with something of a smile of contempt at the question, that there had been nothing like hunger. But, as I said before, visitors always see a great deal of rose colour, and should endeavour to allay the brilliancy of the tint with the proper amount of human shading. But do not let any visitor mix in the browns with too heavy a hand!

At the Massachusetts cotton-mills they were working with about two-thirds of their full number of hands, and this, I was told, was about the average of the number now employed throughout Lowell. Working at this rate they had now on hand a supply of cotton to last them for six months. Their stocks had been increased lately, and on asking from whence, I was informed that that last received had come to them from Liverpool. There is, I believe, no doubt but that a considerable quantity of cotton has been shipped back from England to the States since the civil war began. I asked the gentleman, to whose care at Lowell I was consigned, whether he expected to get cotton from the South,—for at that time Beaufort in South Carolina had just been taken by the naval expedition. He had, he said, a political expectation of a supply of cotton, but not a commercial expectation. That at least was the gist of his reply, and I found it to be both intelligent and intelligible. The Massachusetts mills, when at full work, employ 1300 females and 400 males, and turn out 540,000 yards of calico per week.

On my return from Lowell in the smoking car, an old man came and squeezed in next to me. The place was terribly crowded, and as the old man was thin and clean and quiet I willingly made room for him, so as to avoid the contiguity of a neighbour who might be neither thin, nor clean, nor quiet. He began talking to me in whispers about the war, and I was suspicious that he was a Southerner and a Secessionist. Under such circumstances his company might not be agreeable, unless he could be induced to hold his tongue. At last he said, "I come from Canada, you know, and you,—you're an Englishman, and therefore I can speak to you openly"; and he gave me an affectionate grip on the knee with his old skinny hand. I suppose I do look more like an Englishman than an American, but I was surprised at his knowing me with such certainty. "There is no mistaking you," he said, "with your round face and your red cheeks. They don't look like that here," and he gave me another grip. I felt quite fond of the old man, and offered him a cigar.

CHAPTER XVII

THE RIGHTS OF WOMEN

W<small>E</small> all know that the subject which appears above as the title of this chapter is a very favourite subject in America.[1] It is, I hope, a very favourite subject in England also, and I am inclined to think has been so for many years past. The rights of women, as contradistinguished from the wrongs of women, has perhaps been the most precious of the legacies left to us by the feudal ages. How amidst the rough darkness of old Teuton rule women began to receive that respect which is now their dearest right, is one of the most interesting studies of history. It came, I take it, chiefly from their own conduct. The women of the old classic races seem to have enjoyed but a small amount of respect or of rights, and to have deserved as little. It may have been very well for one Cæsar to have said that his wife should be above suspicion; but his wife was put away, and therefore either did not have her rights, or else had justly forfeited them. The daughter of the next Cæsar lived in Rome the life of a Messalina, and did not on that account seem to have lost her "position in society," till she absolutely declined to throw any veil whatever over her propensities. But as the Roman empire fell, chivalry began. For a time even chivalry afforded but a dull time to the women. During the musical period of the troubadours, ladies, I fancy, had but little to amuse them save the music. But that was the beginning, and from that time downwards the rights of women have progressed very favourably. It may be that they have not yet all that should belong to them. If that be the case, let the men lose no time in making

[1] Trollope apparently had no doubts about the relevancy to a book entitled *North America* of a chapter on women's rights. Americans had been conspicuous in the cause even in the decade before 1840, in which year Lucretia Mott and Elizabeth Cady Stanton were sent as delegates from the United States to attend the World's Anti-Slavery Conference in London. They were denied active participation but were allowed to watch the proceedings from behind a screen in the gallery. Thereupon, as a sweeping gesture of protest, William Lloyd Garrison refused to give his scheduled speech to the convention and joined his sister delegates in the gallery. Since that time, Caroline Dall, Lucy Stone, Dr. Elizabeth Blackwell, and other leaders, including the two woman delegates of 1840, had kept before the American public such varied issues as divorce-law reform, woman suffrage, liquor-control, the right of women to study and practice medicine, and their right to more practicable clothing (the bloomer costume had enjoyed a period of some popularity and much publicity in the years 1851–3) .

up the difference. But it seems to me that the women who are now making their claims may perhaps hardly know when they are well off. It will be an ill movement if they insist on throwing away any of the advantages they have won. As for the women in America especially, I must confess that I think they have a "good time." I make them my compliments on their sagacity, intelligence, and attractions, but I utterly refuse to them any sympathy for supposed wrongs. *O fortunatos sua si bona nôrint!* [2] Whether or no, were I an American married man and father of a family, I should not go in for the rights of man—that is altogether another question.

This question of the rights of women divides itself into two heads, —one of which is very important, worthy of much consideration, capable perhaps of much philanthropic action, and at any rate affording matter for grave discussion. This is the question of women's work; how far the work of the world, which is now borne chiefly by men, should be thrown open to women further than is now done. The other seems to me to be worthy of no consideration, to be capable of no action, to admit of no grave discussion. This refers to the political rights of women; how far the political working of the world, which is now entirely in the hands of men, should be divided between them and women. The first question is being debated on our side of the Atlantic as keenly perhaps as on the American side. As to that other question, I do not know that much has ever been said about it in Europe.

"You are doing nothing in England towards the employment of females," a lady said to me in one of the States soon after my arrival in America. "Pardon me," I answered. "I think we are doing much, perhaps too much. At any rate we are doing something." I then explained to her how Miss Faithfull had instituted a printing establishment in London; how all the work in that concern was done by females, except such heavy tasks as those for which women could not be fitted, and I handed to her one of Miss Faithfull's cards.[3] "Ah," said my American friend, "poor creatures! I have no doubt their very flesh will be worked

---

[2] "Ah, happy [husbandmen], if they but knew their own good fortune!"—Virgil: *Eclogues*, line 458.

[3] Miss Emily Faithfull, a philanthropist and lecturer on women's rights, had established a Fund for Destitute Gentlewomen to aid them in obtaining employment for self-support. The Victoria Press, which was one part of her plan, grew into a publishing firm of considerable size. In 1863 Trollope helped Miss Faithfull in her capacity as editor by contributing a short story, "Miss Ophelia Gledd," to *A Welcome: Original Contributions in Poetry and Prose,* a gift volume celebrating the marriage of the Prince of Wales.

Miss Faithfull was herself a writing tourist. Her *Three Visits to America* was published in 1884.

off their bones." I thought this a little unjust on her part; but never-theless it occurred to me as an answer not unfit to be made by some other lady,—by some woman who had not already advocated the in-creased employment of women. Let Miss Faithfull look to that. Not that she will work the flesh off her young women's bones, or allow such terrible consequences to take place in Coram-street; not that she or that those connected with her in that enterprise will do aught but good to those employed therein. It will not even be said of her individually, or of her partners, that they have worked the flesh off women's bones; but may it not come to this, that when the tasks now done by men have been shifted to the shoulders of women, women themselves will so complain. May it not go further, and come even to this, that women will have cause for such complaint. I do not think that such a result will come, because I do not think that the object desired by those who are active in the matter will be attained. Men, as a general rule among civilized nations, have elected to earn their own bread and the bread of the women also, and from this resolve on their part I do not think that they will be beaten off.

We know that Mrs. Dall,[4] an American lady, has taken up this subject, and has written a book on it, in which great good sense and honesty of purpose are shown. Mrs. Dall is a strong advocate for the increased employment of women, and I, with great deference, disagree with her. I allude to her book now because she has pointed out, I think very strongly, the great reason why women do not engage themselves advantageously in trade pursuits. She by no means overpraises her own sex, and openly declares that young women will not consent to place themselves in fair competition with men. They will not undergo the labour and servitude of long study at their trades. They will not give themselves up to an apprenticeship. They will not enter upon their tasks as though they were to be the tasks of their lives. They may have the same physical and mental aptitudes for learning a trade as men, but they have not the same devotion to the pursuit, and will not bind themselves to it thoroughly as men do. In all which I quite agree with Mrs. Dall; and the English of it is,—that the young women want to get married.

God forbid that they should not so want. Indeed God has forbidden in a very express way that there should be any lack of such a desire on the part of women. There has of late years arisen a feeling among masses of the best of our English ladies that this feminine propensity

---

[4] Caroline Wells Healey Dall (1822–1912), preacher, lecturer, and writer on women's rights, had published *Woman's Right to Labor* in 1860.

should be checked. We are told that unmarried women may be respectable, which we always knew; that they may be useful, which we also acknowledge,—thinking still that if married they would be more useful; and that they may be happy, which we trust,—feeling confident however that they might in another position be more happy. But the question is not only as to the respectability, usefulness, and happiness of womankind, but as to that of men also. If women can do without marriage, can men do so? And if not, how are the men to get wives if the women elect to remain single?

It will be thought that I am treating the subject as though it were simply jocose, but I beg to assure my reader that such is not my intention. It certainly is the fact that that disinclination to an apprenticeship and unwillingness to bear the long training for a trade, of which Mrs. Dall complains on the part of young women, arise from the fact, that they have other hopes with which such apprenticeships would jar; and it is also certain that if such disinclination be overcome on the part of any great number, it must be overcome by the destruction or banishment of such hopes. The question is, whether would good or evil result from such a change? It is often said that whatever difficulty a woman may have in getting a husband, no man need encounter difficulty in finding a wife. But in spite of this seeming fact, I think it must be allowed that if women are withdrawn from the marriage market, men must be withdrawn from it also to the same extent.

In any broad view of this matter we are bound to look, not on any individual case, and the possible remedies for such cases, but on the position in the world occupied by women in general; on the general happiness and welfare of the aggregate feminine world, and perhaps also a little on the general happiness and welfare of the aggregate male world. When ladies and gentlemen advocate the right of women to employment, they are taking very different ground from that on which stand those less extensive philanthropists who exert themselves for the benefit of distressed needlewomen, for instance, or for the alleviation of the more bitter misery of governesses. The two questions are in fact absolutely antagonistic to each other. The rights-of-women advocate is doing his best to create that position for women, from the possible misfortunes of which the friend of the needlewomen is struggling to relieve them. The one is endeavouring to throw work from off the shoulders of men on to the shoulders of women, and the other is striving to lessen the burden which women are already bearing. Of course it is good to relieve distress in individual cases. That Song of the Shirt, which I regard as poetry of the immortal kind, has done an amount of good infinitely wider than poor Hood ever ventured to hope.[5] Of all such efforts I would speak not only with respect, but with loving admiration. But of those whose efforts are made to spread work more widely among women, to call upon them to make for us our watches, to print our books, to sit at our desks as clerks, and to add up our accounts; much as I may respect the individual operators in such a movement, I can express no admiration for their judgment.

I have seen women with ropes round their necks drawing a harrow over ploughed ground. No one will, I suppose, say that they approve of that. But it would not have shocked me to see men drawing a harrow. I should have thought it slow, unprofitable work, but my feelings would not have been hurt. There must, therefore, be some limit; but if we men teach ourselves to believe that work is good for women, where is the limit to be drawn, and who shall draw it? It is true that there is now no actually defined limit. There is much work that is commonly open to both sexes. Personal domestic attendance is so, and the attendance in shops. The use of the needle is shared between men and women, and few, I take it, know where the sempstress ends and where the tailor begins. In many trades a woman can be, and very often is, the owner and manager of the business. Painting is as much open to women as to men; as also is literature. There can be no defined limit; but nevertheless there is at present a quasi limit, which the rights-of-women advocates wish to move, and so to move that women shall do more work and not less. A woman now could not well be a cab-driver in London; but are these advocates sure that no woman will be a cab-driver when success has attended their efforts? And would they like to see a woman driving a cab? For my part I confess I do not like to see a woman acting as roadkeeper on a French railway. I have seen a woman acting as ostler at a public stage in Ireland. I knew the circumstances,—how her husband had become ill and incapable, and how she had been allowed to earn the wages; but nevertheless the sight was to me disagreeable, and seemed, as far as it went, to degrade the sex. Chivalry has been very active in raising women from the hard and hardening tasks of the world, and through this action they have become soft, tender, and virtuous. It seems to me that they of whom I am now speaking are desirous of undoing what chivalry has done.

The argument used is of course plain enough. It is said that women

[5] Tom Hood's *Song of the Shirt* attained an enormous popularity. It was printed on penny broadsheets and on cheap pocket handkerchiefs. When this song of the overworked and half-starved sempstress made its first appearance, in the Christmas number of *Punch* for 1843, it is said to have trebled the circulation of the magazine.

are left destitute in the world,—destitute unless they can be self-dependent, and that to women should be given the same open access to wages
that men possess, in order that they may be as self-dependent as men.
Why should a young woman, for whom no father is able to provide, not
enjoy those means of provision which are open to a young man so
circumstanced? But I think the answer is very simple. The young man
under the happiest circumstances which may befall him is bound to
earn his bread. The young woman is only so bound when happy circumstances do not befall her. Should we endeavour to make the recurrence of unhappy circumstances more general or less so? What does
any tradesman, any professional man, any mechanic wish for his children? Is it not this, that his sons shall go forth and earn their bread, and
that his daughters shall remain with him till they are married? Is not
that the mother's wish? Is it not notorious that such is the wish of us
all as to our daughters? In advocating the rights of women it is of other
men's girls that we think, never of our own.

But, nevertheless, what shall we do for those women who must earn
their bread by their own work? Whatever we do, do not let us wilfully
increase their number. By opening trades to women, by making them
printers, watchmakers, accountants, or what not, we shall not simply
relieve those who must now earn their bread by some such work or else
starve. It will not be within our power to stop ourselves exactly at a
certain point; to arrange that those women who under existing circumstances may now be in want, shall be thus placed beyond want,
but that no others shall be affected. Men, I fear, will be too willing to
relieve themselves of some portion of their present burden, should the
world's altered ways enable them to do so. At present a lawyer's clerk
may earn perhaps his two guineas a week, and he with his wife lives on
that in fair comfort. But if his wife, as well as he, has been brought up
as a lawyer's clerk, he will look to her also for some amount of wages.
I doubt whether the two guineas would be much increased, but I do
not doubt at all that the woman's position would be injured.

It seems to me that in discussing this subject, philanthropists fail
to take hold of the right end of the argument. Money returns from
work are very good, and work itself is good, as bringing such returns
and occupying both body and mind; but the world's work is very hard,
and workmen are too often overdriven. The question seems to me to be
this,—of all this work have the men got on their own backs too heavy a
share for them to bear, and should they seek relief by throwing more
of it upon women? It is the rights of man that we are in fact debating.
These watches are weary to make, and this type is troublesome to set.

We have battles to fight and speeches to make, and our hands altogether are too full. The women are idle,—many of them. They shall
make the watches for us and set the type; and when they have done
that, why should they not make nails as they do sometimes in Worces-
tershire, or clean horses, or drive the cabs? They have had an easy time
of it for these years past, but we'll change that. And then it would come
to pass that with ropes round their necks the women would be drawing
harrows across the fields.

I don't think this will come to pass. The women generally do know
when they are well off, and are not particularly anxious to accept the
philanthropy proffered to them;—as Mrs. Dall says, they do not wish to
bind themselves as apprentices to independent money-making. This
cry has been louder in America than with us, but even in America it
has not been efficacious for much. There is in the States, no doubt, a
sort of hankering after increased influence, a desire for that promi-
nence of position which men attain by loud voices and brazen fore-
heads, a desire in the female heart to be up and doing something, if
the female heart only knew what; but even in the States it has hardly
advanced beyond a few feminine lectures. In many branches of work
women are less employed than in England. They are not so frequent
behind counters in the shops, and are rarely seen as servants in hotels.
The fires in such houses are lighted and the rooms swept by men. But
the American girls may say they do not desire to light fires and sweep
rooms. They are ambitious of the higher classes of work. But those
higher branches of work require study, apprenticeship, a devotion of
youth; and that they will not give. It is very well for a young man to
bind himself for four years, and to think of marrying four years after
that apprenticeship is over. But such a prospectus will not do for a girl.
While the sun shines the hay must be made, and her sun shines earlier
in the day than that of him who is to be her husband. Let him go
through the apprenticeship and the work, and she will have sufficient
on her hands if she looks well after his household. Under nature's
teaching she is aware of this, and will not bind herself to any other
apprenticeship, let Mrs. Dall preach as she may.

I remember seeing, either at New York or Boston, a wooden figure
of a neat young woman, as large as life, standing at a desk with a
ledger before her, and looking as though the beau ideal of human bliss
were realized in her employment. Under the figure there was some
notice respecting female accountants. Nothing could be nicer than the
lady's figure, more flowing than the broad lines of her drapery, or more
attractive than her auburn ringlets. There she stood at work, earning

her bread without any impediment to the natural operation of her female charms, and adjusting the accounts of some great firm with as much facility as grace. I wonder whether he who designed that figure had ever sat or stood at a desk for six hours,—whether he knew the dull hum of the brain which comes from long attention to another man's figures; whether he had ever soiled his own fingers with the everlasting work of office hours, or worn his sleeves threadbare as he leaned weary in body and mind upon his desk? Work is a grand thing,—the grandest thing we have; but work is not picturesque, graceful, and in itself alluring. It sucks the sap out of men's bones, and bends their backs, and sometimes breaks their hearts; but though it be so, I for one would not wish to throw any heavier share of it on to a woman's shoulders. It was pretty to see those young women with spectacles at the Boston library, but when I heard that they were there from eight in the morning till nine at night, I pitied them their loss of all the softness of home, and felt that they would not willingly be there if necessity were less stern.

Say that by advocating the rights of women, philanthropists succeed in apportioning more work to their share, will they eat more, wear better clothes, lie softer, and have altogether more of the fruits of work than they do now? That some would do so there can be no doubt, but as little that some would have less. If on the whole they would not have more, for what good result is the movement made? The first question is, whether at the present time they have less than their proper share. There are, unquestionably, terrible cases of female want, and so there are also of want among men. Alas! do we not all feel that it must be so, let the philanthropists be ever so energetic? And if a woman be left destitute, without the assistance of father, brother, or husband, it would be hard if no means of earning subsistence were open to her. But the object now sought is not that of relieving such distress. It has a much wider tendency, or at any rate a wider desire. The idea is that women will ennoble themselves by making themselves independent, by working for their own bread instead of eating bread earned by men. It is in that that these new philosophers seem to me to err so greatly. Humanity and chivalry have succeeded after a long struggle in teaching the man to work for the woman; and now the woman rebels against such teaching,—not because she likes the work, but because she desires the influence which attends it. But in this I wrong the woman,—even the American woman. It is not she who desires it, but her philanthropical philosophical friends who desire it for her.

If work were more equally divided between the sexes some women would, of course, receive more of the good things of the world. But women generally would not do so. The tendency then would be to force young women out upon their own exertions. Fathers would soon learn to think that their daughters should be no more dependent on them than their sons; men would expect their wives to work at their own trades; brothers would be taught to think it hard that their sisters should lean on them; and thus women, driven upon their own re-sources, would hardly fare better than they do at present.

After all it is a question of money, and a contest for that power and influence which money gives. At present men have the position of the Lower House of Parliament. They have to do the harder work, but they hold the purse. Even in England there has grown up a feeling that the old law of the land gives a married man too much power over the joint pecuniary resources of him and his wife, and in America this feeling is much stronger, and the old law has been modified. Why should a married woman be able to possess nothing? And if such be the law of the land, is it worth a woman's while to marry and put herself in such a position? Those are the questions asked by the friends of the rights of women. But the young women do marry, and the men pour their earnings into their wives' laps.

If little has as yet been done in extending the rights of women by giving them a greater share of the work of the world, still less has been done towards giving them their portion of political influence. In the States there are many men of mark, and women of mark also, who think that women should have votes for public elections. Mr. Wendell Phillips, the Boston lecturer who advocates abolition, is an apostle in this cause also; and while I was at Boston I read the provisions of a will lately left by a millionaire, in which he bequeathed some very large sums of money to be expended in agitation on this subject. A woman is subject to the law; why then should she not help to make the law? A child is subject to the law, and does not help to make it; but the child lacks that discretion which the woman enjoys equally with the man. That I take it is the amount of the argument in favour of the political rights of women. The logic of this is so conclusive, that I am prepared to acknowledge that it admits of no answer. I will only say that the mutual good relations between men and women, which are so indispensable to our happiness, require that men and women should not take to voting at the same time and on the same result. If it be de-cided that women shall have political power, let them have it all to themselves for a season. If that be so resolved, I think we may safely leave it to them to name the time at which they will begin.

I confess that in the States I have sometimes been driven to think that chivalry has been carried too far;—that there is an attempt to make women think more of the rights of their womanhood than is needful. There are ladies' doors at hotels, and ladies' drawing-rooms, ladies' sides on the ferry-boats, ladies' windows at the post office for the delivery of letters;—which, by-the-by, is an atrocious institution, as anybody may learn who will look at the advertisements called personal in some of the New York papers. Why should not young ladies have their letters sent to their houses, instead of getting them at a private window? The post-office clerks can tell stories about those ladies' windows. But at every turn it is necessary to make separate provision for ladies. From all this it comes to pass that the baker's daughter looks down from a great height on her papa, and by no means thinks her brother good enough for her associate. Nature, the great restorer, comes in and teaches her to fall in love with the butcher's son. Thus the evil is mitigated; but I cannot but wish that the young woman should not see herself denominated a lady so often, and should receive fewer lessons as to the extent of her privileges. I would save her if I could from working at the oven; I would give to her bread and meat earned by her father's care and her brother's sweat; but when she has received these good things, I would have her proud of the one and by no means ashamed of the other.

Let women say what they will of their rights, or men who think themselves generous say what they will for them, the question has all been settled both for them and for us men by a higher power. They are the nursing mothers of mankind, and in that law their fate is written with all its joys and all its privileges. It is for men to make those joys as lasting and those privileges as perfect as may be. That women should have their rights no man will deny. To my thinking neither increase of work nor increase of political influence are among them. The best right a woman has is the right to a husband, and that is the right to which I would recommend every young woman here and in the States to turn her best attention. On the whole, I think that my doctrine will be more acceptable than that of Mrs. Dall or Mr. Wendell Phillips.

CHAPTER XVIII

EDUCATION AND RELIGION

THE ONE matter in which, as far as my judgment goes, the people of the United States have excelled us Englishmen, so as to justify them in taking to themselves praise which we cannot take to ourselves or refuse to them, is the matter of Education. In saying this I do not think that I am proclaiming anything disgraceful to England, though I am proclaiming much that is creditable to America. To the Americans of the States was given the good fortune of beginning at the beginning. The French at the time of their revolution endeavoured to reorganize everything, and to begin the world again with new habits and grand theories; but the French as a people were too old for such a change, and the theories fell to the ground. But in the States, after their revolution, an Anglo-Saxon people had an opportunity of making a new State, with all the experience of the world before them; and to this matter of education they were from the first aware that they must look for their success. They did so; and unrivalled population, wealth, and intelligence have been the results; and with these, looking at the whole masses of the people,—I think I am justified in saying,—unrivalled comfort and happiness. It is not that you, my reader, to whom in this matter of education fortune and your parents have probably been bountiful, would have been more happy in New York than in London. It is not that I, who, at any rate, can read and write, have cause to wish that I had been an American. But it is this;—if you and I can count up in a day all those on whom our eyes may rest, and learn the circumstances of their lives, we shall be driven to conclude that nine-tenths of that number would have had a better life as Americans than they can have in their spheres as Englishmen. The States are at a discount with us now, in the beginning of this year of grace 1862; and Englishmen were not very willing to admit the above statement, even when the States were not at a discount. But I do not think that a man can travel through the States with his eyes open and not admit the fact. Many things will conspire to induce him to shut his eyes and admit no conclusion favourable to the Americans. Men and women will sometimes be impudent to him;—the better his coat, the greater the impudence. He will be pelted with the braggadocio of equality. The corns of his

Old-World conservatism will be trampled on hourly by the purposely vicious herd of uncouth democracy. The fact that he is paymaster will go for nothing, and will fail to insure civility. I shall never forget my agony as I saw and heard my desk fall from a porter's hand on a railway station, as he tossed it from him seven yards off on to the hard pavement. I heard its poor weak intestines rattle in their death-struggle, and knowing that it was smashed I forgot my position on American soil and remonstrated. "It's my desk, and you've have utterly destroyed it," I said. "Ha! ha! ha!" laughed the porter. "You've destroyed my property," I rejoined, "and it's no laughing matter." And then all the crowd laughed. "Guess you'd better get it glued," said one. So I gathered up the broken article and retired mournfully and crestfallen into a coach. This was very sad, and for the moment I deplored the ill-luck which had brought me to so savage a country. Such and such like are the incidents which make an Englishman in the States unhappy, and rouse his gall against the institutions of the country;—these things and the continued appliance of the irritating ointment of American braggadocio with which his sores are kept open. But though I was badly off on that railway platform,—worse off than I should have been in England,—all that crowd of porters round me were better off than our English porters. They had a "good time" of it. And this, O my English brother who hast travelled through the States and returned disgusted, is the fact throughout. Those men whose familiarity was so disgusting to you are having a good time of it. "They might be a little more civil," you say, "and yet read and write just as well." True; but they are arguing in their minds that civility to you will be taken by you for subservience, or for an acknowledgment of superiority; and looking at your habits of life,—yours and mine together,—I am not quite sure that they are altogether wrong. Have you ever realized to yourself as a fact that the porter who carries your box has not made himself inferior to you by the very act of carrying that box? If not, that is the very lesson which the man wishes to teach you.

If a man can forget his own miseries in his journeyings, and think of the people he comes to see rather than of himself, I think he will find himself driven to admit that education has made life for the million in the Northern States better than life for the million is with us. They have begun at the beginning, and have so managed that every one may learn to read and write,—have so managed that almost every one does learn to read and write. With us this cannot now be done. Population had come upon us in masses too thick for management before we had as yet acknowledged that it would be a good thing that these masses should be educated. Prejudices, too, had sprung up, and habits, and strong sectional feelings, all antagonistic to a great national system of education. We are, I suppose, now doing all that we can do; but comparatively it is little. I think I saw some time since that the cost for gratuitous education, or education in part gratuitous, which had fallen upon the nation had already amounted to the sum of 800,-000*l*.; and I think also that I read in the document which revealed to me this fact, a very strong opinion that Government could not at present go much further. But if this matter were regarded in England as it is regarded in Massachusetts,—or rather, had it from some prosperous beginning been put upon a similar footing, 800,000*l*. would not have been esteemed a great expenditure for free education simply in the city of London. In 1857 the public schools of Boston cost 70,000*l*., and these schools were devoted to a population of about 180,000 souls. Taking the population of London at two-and-a-half millions, the whole sum now devoted to England would, if expended in the metropolis, make education there even cheaper than it is in Boston. In Boston during 1857 there were above 24,000 pupils at these public schools, giving more than one-eighth of the whole population. But I fear it would not be practicable for us to spend 800,000*l*. on the gratuitous education of London. Rich as we are, we should not know where to raise the money. In Boston it is raised by a separate tax. It is a thing understood, acknowledged, and made easy by being habitual,—as is our national debt. I do not know that Boston is peculiarly blessed, but I quote the instance as I have a record of its schools before me. At the three high schools in Boston at which the average of pupils is 526, about 13*l*. per head is paid for free education. The average price per annum of a child's schooling throughout these schools in Boston is about 3*l*. per annum. To the higher schools any boy or girl may attain without any expense, and the education is probably as good as can be given, and as far advanced. The only question is, whether it is not advanced further than may be necessary. Here, as at New York, I was almost startled by the amount of knowledge around me, and listened, as I might have done, to an examination in theology among young Brahmins. When a young lad explained in my hearing all the properties of the different levers as exemplified by the bones of the human body, I bowed my head before him in unaffected humility. We, at our English schools, never got beyond the use of those bones which he described with such accurate scientific knowledge. In one of the girls' schools they were reading Milton, and when we entered were discussing the nature of the pool in which the Devil is described as wallowing.

The question had been raised by one of the girls. A pool, so called, was supposed to contain but a small amount of water, and how could the Devil, being so large, get into it? Then came the origin of the word pool,—from "palus," a marsh, as we were told, some dictionary attesting to the fact,—and such a marsh might cover a large expanse. The "Palus Mæotis" [1] was then quoted. And so we went on till Satan's theory of political liberty,

"Better to reign in hell than serve in heaven," [2]

was thoroughly discussed and understood. These girls of sixteen and seventeen got up one after another and gave their opinions on the subject,—how far the Devil was right and how far he was manifestly wrong. I was attended by one of the directors or guardians of the schools, and the teacher, I thought, was a little embarrassed by her position. But the girls themselves were as easy in their demeanour as though they were stitching handkerchiefs at home.

It is impossible to refrain from telling all this, and from making a little innocent fun out of the super-excellencies of these schools; but the total result on my mind was very greatly in their favour. And indeed the testimony came in both ways. Not only was I called on to form an opinion of what the men and women would become from the education which was given to the boys and girls, but also to say what must have been the education of the boys and girls from what I saw of the men and women. Of course it will be understood that I am not here speaking of those I met in society, or of their children, but of the working people,—of that class who find that a gratuitous education for their children is needful, if any considerable amount of education is to be given. The result is to be seen daily in the whole intercourse of life. The coachman who drives you, the man who mends your window, the boy who brings home your purchases, the girl who stitches your wife's dress,—they all carry with them sure signs of education, and show it in every word they utter.

It will of course be understood that this is, in the separate States, a matter of State law; indeed I may go further and say that it is in most of the States a matter of State constitution. It is by no means a matter of Federal constitution. The United States as a nation takes no heed of the education of its people. All that is left to the judgment of the separate States. In most of the thirteen original States provision is made in

[1] The teacher may have quoted Herodotus (iv, 86) or Pliny (iv, 24) regarding the *Palus Mæotis*, an inland sea north of the Black Sea on the borders of Europe and Asia.

[2] *Paradise Lost*, Book I, line 263.

the written constitution for the general education of the people; but this is not done in all. I found that it was more frequently done in the Northern or Freesoil States than in those which admitted slavery,—as might have been expected. In the constitutions of South Carolina and Virginia I find no allusion to the public provision for education, but in those of North Carolina and Georgia it is enjoined. The forty-first section of the constitution for North Carolina enjoins that "schools shall be established by the legislature for the convenient instruction of youth, with such salaries to the masters, paid by the public, as may enable them to instruct *at low prices*"; showing that the intention here was to assist education, and not provide it altogether gratuitously. I think that provision for public education is enjoined in the constitutions of all the States admitted into the Union since the first federal knot was tied, except in that of Illinois. Vermont was the first so admitted, in 1791, and Vermont declares that "a competent number of schools ought to be maintained in each town for the convenient instruction of youth." Ohio was the second, in 1802, and Ohio enjoins that "the general assembly shall make such provisions by taxation or otherwise as, with the income arising from the school trust fund, will secure a thorough and efficient system of common schools throughout the State; but no religious or other sect or sects shall ever have any exclusive right or control of any part of the school funds of this State." In Indiana, admitted in 1816, it is required that "the general assembly shall provide by law for a general and uniform system of common schools." Illinois was admitted next, in 1818; but the constitution of Illinois is silent on the subject of education. It enjoins, however, in lieu of this, that no person shall fight a duel or send a challenge! If he do he is not only to be punished, but to be deprived for ever of the power of holding any office of honour or profit in the State. I have no reason, however, for supposing that education is neglected in Illinois, or that duelling has been abolished. In Maine it is demanded that the towns—the whole country is divided into what are called towns—shall make suitable provision at their own expense for the support and maintenance of public schools.

Some of these constitutional enactments are most magniloquently worded, but not always with precise grammatical correctness. That for the famous Bay State of Massachusetts runs as follows:—"Wisdom and knowledge, as well as virtue, diffused generally among the body of the people, being necessary for the preservation of their rights and liberties, and as these depend on spreading the opportunities and advantages of education in the various parts of the country, and among the different orders of the people, it shall be the duty of the legislatures and magistrates, in all future periods of this commonwealth, to cherish the interest of literature and the sciences, and of all seminaries of them, especially the University at Cambridge, public schools, and grammar schools in the towns; to encourage private societies and public institutions, by rewards, and immunities for the promotion of agriculture, arts, sciences, commerce, trades, manufactures, and a natural history of the country; to countenance and inculcate the principles of humanity and general benevolence, public and private charity, industry and frugality, honesty and punctuality in all their dealings; sincerity, good humour, and all social affections and generous sentiments among the people." I must confess, that had the words of that little constitutional enactment been made known to me before I had seen its practical results, I should not have put much faith in it. Of all the public schools I have ever seen,—by public schools I mean schools for the people at large maintained at public cost,—those of Massachusetts are, I think, the best. But of all the educational enactments which I ever read, that of the same State is, I should say, the worst. In Texas now, of which as a State the people of Massachusetts do not think much, they have done it better. "A general diffusion of knowledge being essential to the preservation of the rights and liberties of the people, it shall be the duty of the legislature of this State to make suitable provision for the support and maintenance of public schools." So say the Texians; but then the Texians had the advantage of a later experience than any which fell in the way of the constitution-makers of Massachusetts.

There is something of the magniloquence of the French style,—of the liberty, equality, and fraternity mode of eloquence in the preambles of most of these constitutions, which, but for their success, would have seemed to have prophesied loudly of failure. Those of New York and Pennsylvania are the least so, and that of Massachusetts by far the most violently magniloquent. They generally commence by thanking God for the present civil and religious liberty of the people, and by declaring that all men are born free and equal. New York and Pennsylvania, however, refrain from any such very general remarks.

I am well aware that all these constitutional enactments are not likely to obtain much credit in England. It is not only that grand phrases fail to convince us, but that they carry to our senses almost an assurance of their own inefficiency. When we hear that a people have declared their intention of being henceforward better than their neighbours, and going upon a new theory that shall lead them direct to a terrestrial paradise, we button up our pockets and lock up our spoons. And that is what we have done very much as regards the Americans.

We have walked with them and talked with them, and bought with them and sold with them; but we have mistrusted them as to their internal habits and modes of life, thinking that their philanthropy was pretentious and that their theories were vague. Many cities in the States are but skeletons of towns, the streets being there, and the houses numbered,—but not one house built out of ten that have been so counted up. We have regarded their institutions as we regard those cities, and have been specially willing so to consider them because of the fine language in which they have paraded before us. They have been regarded as the skeletons of philanthropical systems, to which blood and flesh and muscle, and even skin are wanting. But it is at least but fair to inquire how far the promise made has been carried out. The elaborate wordings of the constitutions made by the French politicians in the days of their great revolution have always been to us no more than so many written grimaces; but we should not have continued so to regard them had the political liberty which they promised followed upon the promises so magniloquently made. As regards education in the States,—at any rate in the northern and western States,—I think that the assurances put forth in the various written constitutions have been kept. If this be so, an American citizen, let him be ever so arrogant, ever so impudent if you will, is at any rate a civilized being, and on the road to that cultivation which will sooner or later divest him of his arrogance. *Emollit mores.* We quote here our old friend the Colonel again.[3] If a gentleman be compelled to confine his classical allusions to one quotation, he cannot do better than hang by that.

But has education been so general, and has it had the desired result? In the city of Boston, as I have said, I found that in 1857 about one-eighth of the whole population were then on the books of the free public schools as pupils, and that about one-ninth of the population formed the average daily attendance. To these numbers of course must be added all pupils of the richer classes,—those for whose education their parents chose to pay. As nearly as I can learn, the average duration of each pupil's schooling is six years, and if this be figured out statistically, I think it will show that education in Boston reaches a very large majority—I must almost say the whole—of the population. That the education given in other towns of Massachusetts is not so good as that given in Boston I do not doubt, but I have reason to believe that it is quite as general.

I have spoken of one of the schools of New York. In that city the

[3] For Colonel Newcome's erratic handling of the tag from Ovid, see the note on page 210.

public schools are apportioned to the wards, and are so arranged that in each ward of the city there are public schools of different standing for the gratuitous use of the children. The population of the city of New York in 1857 was about 650,000, and in that year it is stated that there were 135,000 pupils in the schools. By this it would appear that one person in five throughout the city was then under process of education,—which statement, however, I cannot receive with implicit credence. It is, however, also stated that the daily attendances averaged something less than 50,000 a day—and this latter statement probably implies some mistake in the former one. Taking the two together for what they are worth, they show, I think, that school teaching is not only brought within the reach of the population generally, but is used by almost all classes. At New York there are separate free schools for coloured children. At Philadelphia I did not see the schools, but I was assured that the arrangements there were equal to those at New York and Boston. Indeed I was told that they were infinitely better;—but then I was so told by a Philadelphian. In the State of Connecticut the public schools are certainly equal to those in any part of the Union. As far as I could learn, education—what we should called advanced education— is brought within the reach of all classes in the northern and western States of America,—and, I would wish to add here, to those of the Canadas also.

So much for the schools, and now for the results. I do not know that anything impresses a visitor more strongly with the amount of books sold in the States, than the practice of selling them as it has been adopted in the railway cars. Personally the traveller will find the system very disagreeable,—as is everything connected with these cars. A young man enters during the journey,—for the trade is carried out while the cars are travelling, as is also a very brisk trade in lollipops, sugar-candy, apples, and ham sandwiches,[4]—the young tradesman enters the car

[4] Judging from the account of another English traveler (in *All the Year Round* for January 12, 1861), Trollope's list of vendibles is far from complete:

"No want can arise in the traveller's mind that there is not some one in an American railway train ready to administer to. Every town you pass, pelts you with its daily papers. If you stop for ten minutes at a central station, a lean expounding sort of quack missionary, standing erect at the door, informs the whole carriageful that 'the dead-shot worm candy' is now selling at twenty-five cents the packet; that 'Vestris's bloom,' the finest cosmetic in the known world, is to be had for half a dollar the quarter of a pound, and dirt cheap at the money; or that 'Knickerbocker's corn exterminator' makes life's path easy, at a dime the ounce packet. . . . Anon, shouts a huge fellow with enormous apples, two cents each, peaches in their season, hickory nuts, 'pecans,' or maple sugar cakes. To them succeed sellers of ivory combs, parched corn, packets of mixed sweetmeats. . . ."

firstly with a pile of magazines or of novels bound like magazines. These are chiefly the "Atlantic," published at Boston, "Harper's Magazine," published at New York, and a cheap series of novels published at Philadelphia. As he walks along he flings one at every passenger. An Englishman, when he is first introduced to this manner of trade, becomes much astonished. He is probably reading, and on a sudden he finds a fat, fluffy magazine, very unattractive in its exterior, dropped on to the page he is perusing. I thought at first that it was a present from some crazed philanthropist, who was thus endeavouring to disseminate literature. But I was soon undeceived. The bookseller, having gone down the whole car and the next, returned, and beginning again where he had begun before, picked up either his magazine or else the price of it. Then, in some half-hour, he came again, with an armful or basket of books, and distributed them in the same way. They were generally novels, but not always. I do not think that any endeavour is made to assimilate the book to the expected customer. The object is to bring the book and the man together, and in this way a very large sale is effected. The same thing is done with illustrated newspapers. The sale of political newspapers goes on so quickly in these cars that no such enforced distribution is necessary. I should say that the average consumption of newspapers by an American must amount to about three a day. At Washington I begged the keeper of my lodgings to let me have a paper regularly,—one American newspaper being much the same to me as another,—and my host supplied me daily with four.

But the numbers of the popular books of the day, printed and sold, afford the most conclusive proof of the extent to which education is carried in the States. The readers of Tennyson, Thackeray, Dickens, Bulwer, Collins, Hughes, and—Martin Tupper, are to be counted by tens of thousand in the States, to the thousands by which they may be counted in our own islands. I do not doubt that I had fully fifteen copies of the "Silver Cord," [5] thrown at my head in different railway cars on the continent of America. Nor is the taste by any means confined to the literature of England. Longfellow, Curtis, Holmes, Hawthorne, Lowell, Emerson,—and Mrs. Stowe, are almost as popular as their English rivals. I do not say whether or no the literature is well chosen, but there it is. It is printed, sold, and read. The disposal of ten thousand copies of a work is no large sale in America of a book pub-

[5] *The Silver Cord, a Story*, by Shirley Brooks, editor of *Punch*, had been published in 1861 and was being puffed in America as "the most entertaining piece of fictitious literature that has made its appearance since the appearance of [Wilkie Collins's] 'The Woman in White.'"

lished at a dollar; but in England it is a large sale of a book brought out at five shillings.

I do not remember that I ever examined the rooms of an American without finding books or magazines in them. I do not speak here of the houses of my friends, as of course the same remark would apply as strongly in England, but of the houses of persons presumed to earn their bread by the labour of their hands. The opportunity for such examination does not come daily; but when it has been in my power I have made it, and have always found signs of education. Men and women of the classes to which I allude talk of reading and writing as of arts belonging to them as a matter of course, quite as much as are the arts of eating and drinking. A porter or a farmer's servant in the States is not proud of reading and writing. It is to him quite a matter of course. The coachmen on their boxes and the boots as they sit in the halls of the hotels, have newspapers constantly in their hands. The young women have them also, and the children. The fact comes home to one at every turn, and at every hour, that the people are an educated people. The whole of this question between North and South is as well understood by the servants as by their masters, is discussed as vehemently by the private soldiers as by the officers. The politics of the country and the nature of its constitution are familiar to every labourer. The very wording of the Declaration of Independence is in the memory of every lad of sixteen. Boys and girls of a younger age than that know why Slidell and Mason were arrested, and will tell you why they should have been given up, or why they should have been held in durance. The question of the war with England is debated by every native paviour and hodman of New York.

I know what Englishmen will say in answer to this. They will declare that they do not want their paviours and hodmen to talk politics; that they are as well pleased that their coachmen and cooks should not always have a newspaper in their hands; that private soldiers will fight as well, and obey better, if they are not trained to discuss the causes which have brought them into the field. An English gentleman will think that his gardener will be a better gardener without than with any excessive political ardour; and the English lady will prefer that her housemaid shall not have a very pronounced opinion of her own as to the capabilities of the cabinet ministers. But I would submit to all Englishmen and Englishwomen who may look at these pages whether such an opinion or feeling on their part bears much, or even at all, upon the subject. I am not saying that the man who is driven in the coach is better off because his coachman reads the paper, but that the coachman himself who reads the paper is better off than the coachman who does not and cannot. I think that we are too apt, in considering the ways and habits of any people, to judge of them by the effect of those ways and habits on us, rather than by their effects on the owners of them. When we go among garlic-eaters, we condemn them because they are offensive to us; but to judge of them properly we should ascertain whether or no the garlic be offensive to them. If we could imagine a nation of vegetarians hearing for the first time of our habits as flesh-eaters, we should feel sure that they would be struck with horror at our blood-stained banquets; but when they came to argue with us, we should bid them inquire whether we flesh-eaters did not live longer and do more than the vegetarians. When we express a dislike to the shoeboy reading his newspaper, I fear we do so because we fear that the shoeboy is coming near our own heels. I know there is among us a strong feeling that the lower classes are better without politics, as there is also that they are better without crinoline and artificial flowers; but if politics and crinoline and artificial flowers are good at all, they are good for all who can honestly come by them and honestly use them. The political coachman is perhaps less valuable to his master as a coachman than he would be without his politics, but he with his politics is more valuable to himself. For myself, I do not like the Americans of the lower orders. I am not comfortable among them. They tread on my corns and offend me. They make my daily life unpleasant. But I do respect them. I acknowledge their intelligence and personal dignity. I know that they are men and women worthy to be so called; I see that they are living as human beings in possession of reasoning faculties; and I perceive that they owe this to the progress that education has made among them.

After all, what is wanted in this world? Is it not that men should eat and drink, and read and write, and say their prayers? Does not that include everything, providing that they eat and drink enough, read and write without restraint, and say their prayers without hypocrisy? When we talk of the advances of civilization, do we mean anything but this, that men who now eat and drink badly shall eat and drink well, and that those who cannot read and write now shall learn to do so,— the prayers following, as prayers will follow upon such learning? Civilization does not consist in the eschewing of garlic or the keeping clean of a man's finger-nails. It may lead to such delicacies, and probably will do so. But the man who thinks that civilization cannot exist without them imagines that the church cannot stand without the spire. In the States of America men do eat and drink, and do read and write.

But as to saying their prayers? That, as far as I can see, has come also, though perhaps not in a manner altogether satisfactory, or to a degree which should be held to be sufficient. Englishmen of strong religious feeling will often be startled in America by the freedom with which religious subjects are discussed, and the ease with which the matter is treated; but he will very rarely be shocked by that utter absence of all knowledge on the subject,—that total darkness, which is still so common among the lower orders in our own country. It is not a common thing to meet an American who belongs to no denomination of Christian worship, and who cannot tell you why he belongs to that which he has chosen.

"But," it will be said, "all the intelligence and education of this people have not saved them from falling out among themselves and their friends, and running into troubles by which they will be ruined. Their political arrangements have been so bad, that in spite of all their reading and writing they must go to the wall." I venture to express an opinion that they will by no means go to the wall, and that they will be saved from such a destiny, if in no other way, then by their education. Of their political arrangements, as I mean before long to rush into that perilous subject, I will say nothing here. But no political convulsions, should such arise,—no revolution in the constitution, should such be necessary,—will have any wide effect on the social position of the people to their serious detriment. They have the great qualities of the Anglo-Saxon race,—industry, intelligence, and self-confidence; and if these qualities will no longer suffice to keep such a people on their legs, the world must be coming to an end.

I have said that it is not a common thing to meet an American who belongs to no denomination of Christian worship. This I think is so; but I would not wish to be taken as saying that religion on that account stands on a satisfactory footing in the States. Of all subjects of discussion, this is the most difficult. It is one as to which most of us feel that to some extent we must trust to our prejudices rather than our judgments. It is a matter on which we do not dare to rely implicitly on our own reasoning faculties, and therefore throw ourselves on the opinions of those whom we believe to have been better men and deeper thinkers than ourselves. For myself, I love the name of State and Church, and believe that much of our English well-being has depended on it. I have made up my mind to think that union good, and not to be turned away from that conviction. Nevertheless I am not prepared to argue the matter. One does not always carry one's proofs at one's finger-ends.

But I feel very strongly that much of that which is evil in the structure of American politics is owing to the absence of any national religion, and that something also of social evil has sprung from the same cause. It is not that men do not say their prayers. For aught I know, they may do so as frequently and as fervently, or more frequently and more fervently, than we do; but there is a rowdiness, if I may be allowed to use such a word, in their manner of doing so which robs religion of that reverence which is, if not its essence, at any rate its chief protection. It is a part of their system that religion shall be perfectly free, and that no man shall be in any way constrained in that matter. Consequently, the question of a man's religion is regarded in a free-and-easy way. It is well, for instance, that a young lad should go somewhere on a Sunday; but a sermon is a sermon, and it does not much concern the lad's father whether his son hear the discourse of a freethinker in the music-hall, or the eloquent but lengthy outpouring of a preacher in a Methodist chapel. Everybody is bound to have a religion, but it does not much matter what it is.

The difficulty in which the first fathers of the Revolution found themselves on this question, is shown by the constitutions of the different States. There can be no doubt that the inhabitants of the New England States were, as things went, a strictly religious community. They had no idea of throwing over the worship of God, as the French had attempted to do at their Revolution. They intended that the new nation should be pre-eminently composed of a God-fearing people; but they intended also that they should be a people free in everything,—free to choose their own forms of worship. They intended that the nation should be a Protestant people; but they intended also that no man's conscience should be coerced in the matter of his own religion. It was hard to reconcile these two things, and to explain to the citizens that it behoved them to worship God,—even under penalties for omission; but that it was at the same time open to them to select any form of worship that they pleased, however that form might differ from the practices of the majority. In Connecticut it is declared that it is the duty of all men to worship the Supreme Being, the Creator and Preserver of the universe, but that it is their right to render that worship in the mode most consistent with the dictates of their consciences. And when a few lines further down the article skips the great difficulty in a manner somewhat disingenuous, and declares that each and every society of Christians in the State shall have and enjoy the same and equal privileges. But it does not say whether a Jew shall be divested of those privileges, or, if he be divested, how that treatment of him is to be reconciled with the assurance that it is every man's right to worship the Supreme Being in the mode most consistent with the dictates of his own conscience.

In Rhode Island they were more honest. It is there declared that every man shall be free to worship God according to the dictates of his own conscience, and to profess and by argument to maintain his opinion in matters of religion; and that the same shall in nowise diminish, enlarge, or affect his civil capacity. Here it is simply presumed that every man will worship a God, and no allusion is made even to Christianity.

In Massachusetts they are again hardly honest. "It is the right," says the constitution, "as well as the duty of all men in society publicly and at stated seasons to worship the Supreme Being, the great Creator and Preserver of the universe." And then it goes on to say that every man may do so in what form he pleases; but further down it declares that "every denomination of Christians, demeaning themselves peaceably and as good subjects of the commonwealth, shall be equally under the protection of the law." But what about those who are not Christians? In New Hampshire it is exactly the same. It is enacted that—"Every individual has a natural and unalienable right to worship God according to the dictates of his own conscience and reason." And that—"Every denomination of Christians, demeaning themselves quietly and as good citizens of the State, shall be equally under the protection of the law." From all which it is, I think, manifest that the men who framed these documents, desirous above all things of cutting themselves and their people loose from every kind of trammel, still felt the necessity of enforcing religion,—of making it to a certain extent a matter of State duty. In the first constitution of North Carolina it is enjoined,—"That no person who shall deny the being of God, or the truth of the Protestant religion, shall be capable of holding any office or place of trust or profit." But this was altered in the year 1836, and the words "Christian religion" were substituted for "Protestant religion."

In New England the Congregationalists are, I think, the dominant sect. In Massachusetts, and I believe in the other New England States, a man is presumed to be a Congregationalist if he do not declare himself to be anything else; as with us the Church of England counts all who do not specially have themselves counted elsewhere. The Congregationalist, as far as I can learn, is very near to a Presbyterian. In New England I think the Unitarians would rank next in number; but a Unitarian in America is not the same as a Unitarian with us. Here, if

I understand the nature of his creed, a Unitarian does not recognize the divinity of our Saviour.[6] In America he does do so, but throws over the doctrine of the Trinity. The Protestant Episcopalians muster strong in all the great cities, and I fancy that they would be regarded as taking the lead of the other religious denominations in New York. Their tendency is to high-church doctrines. I wish they had not found it necessary to alter the forms of our prayer-book in so many little matters, as to which there was no national expediency for such changes. But it was probably thought necessary that a new people should show their independence in all things. The Roman Catholics have a very strong party—as a matter of course—seeing how great has been the immigration from Ireland; but here, as in Ireland—and as indeed is the case all the world over—the Roman Catholics are the hewers of wood and drawers of water. The Germans, who have latterly flocked into the States in such swarms that they have almost Germanized certain States, have of course their own churches. In every town there are places of worship for Baptists, Presbyterians, Methodists, Anabaptists, and every denomination of Christianity; and the meeting-houses prepared for these sects are not, as with us, hideous buildings contrived to inspire disgust by the enormity of their ugliness, nor are they called Salem, Ebenezer, and Sion, nor do the ministers within them look in any way like the Deputy-Shepherd. The churches belonging to those sects are often handsome. This is especially the case in New York; and the pastors are not unfrequently among the best educated and most agreeable men whom the traveller will meet. They are for the most part well paid; and are enabled by their outward position to hold that place in the world's ranks which should always belong to a clergyman. I have not been able to obtain information from which I can state with anything like correctness what may be the average income of ministers of the Gospel in the northern States, but that it is much higher than the average income of our parish clergymen, admits, I think, of no doubt. The stipends of clergymen in the American towns are higher than those paid in the country. The opposite to this, I think as a rule, is the case with us.

I have said that religion in the States is rowdy. By that I mean to imply that it seems to me to be divested of that reverential order and

[6] Unitarian readers of *North America* on the two sides of the Atlantic must have been amazed by Trollope's offhand division between them. American followers of the faith, under the leadership of Emerson and Theodore Parker, seem to have felt the attraction of German idealism more strongly than their English brethren, but the problem is a complicated one that does not lend itself to clear-cut distinctions.

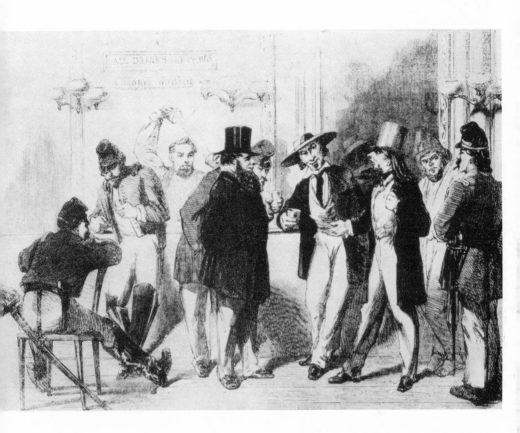

XI The Slidell and Mason Case Argued at the American Bar: "All the legal acumen of New England declared the seizure of Slidell and Mason to be right. The legal acumen of Old England had declared it to be wrong; and I have no doubt that the ladies of Old England can prove it to be wrong out of Vattel, Puffendorff, Stowell, Phillimore, and Wheaton."

Illustrated London News, XL (*January* 4, 1862) , 4

XII   Balloon View of Washington, D. C.: "It was, I suppose, intended that the streets to the eastward should be noble and populous, but hitherto they have come to nothing."

Harper's Weekly, V (*July* 27, 1861), 476

strictness of rule which, according to our ideas, should be attached to matters of religion. One hardly knows where the affairs of this world end, or where those of the next begin. When the holy men were had in at the lecture, were they doing stage-work or church-work? On hearing sermons, one is often driven to ask oneself whether the discourse from the pulpit be in its nature political or religious. I heard an Episcopalian Protestant clergyman talk of the scoffing nations of Europe,— because at that moment he was angry with England and France about Slidell and Mason. I have heard a chapter of the Bible read in Congress at the desire of a member, and very badly read. After which the chapter itself and the reading of it became the subject of a debate, partly jocose and partly acrimonious. It is a common thing for a clergyman to change his profession and follow any other pursuit. I know two or three gentlemen who were once in that line of life, but have since gone into other trades. There is, I think, an unexpressed determination on the part of the people to abandon all reverence, and to regard religion from an altogether worldly point of view. They are willing to have religion, as they are willing to have laws; but they choose to make it for themselves. They do not object to pay for it, but they like to have the handling of the article for which they pay. As the descendants of Puritans and other godly Protestants, they will submit to religious teaching, but as Republicans they will have no priestcraft. The French at their Revolution had the latter feeling without the former, and were therefore consistent with themselves in abolishing all worship. The Americans desire to do the same thing politically, but infidelity has had no charms for them. They say their prayers, and then seem to apologize for doing so, as though it were hardly the act of a free and enlightened citizen, justified in ruling himself as he pleases. All this to me is rowdy. I know no other word by which I can so well describe it.

Nevertheless the nation is religious in its tendencies, and prone to acknowledge the goodness of God in all things. A man there is expected to belong to some church, and is not, I think, well looked on if he profess that he belongs to none. He may be a Swedenborgian, a Quaker, a Muggletonian; [7]—anything will do. But it is expected of him that he shall place himself under some flag, and do his share in supporting the flag to which he belongs. This duty is, I think, generally fulfilled.

[7] Ludowick Muggleton, an English tailor, claimed that he had received divine inspiration. About 1651, with the aid of John Reeve, he founded a new sect that denied the Trinity and held that God has a human body.

CHAPTER XIX

FROM BOSTON TO WASHINGTON

FROM Boston, on the 27th of November, my wife returned to England, leaving me to prosecute my journey southward to Washington by myself. I shall never forget the political feeling which prevailed in Boston at that time, or the discussions on the subject of Slidell and Mason, in which I felt myself bound to take a part. Up to that period I confess that my sympathies had been strongly with the northern side in the general question; and so they were still, as far as I could divest the matter of its English bearings. I had always thought, and do think, that a war for the suppression of the southern rebellion could not have been avoided by the North without an absolute loss of its political prestige. Mr. Lincoln was elected President of the United States in the autumn of 1860, and any steps taken by him or his party towards a peaceable solution of the difficulties which broke out immediately on his election, must have been taken before he entered upon his office. South Carolina threatened secession as soon as Mr. Lincoln's election was known, while yet there were four months left of Mr. Buchanan's Government. That Mr. Buchanan might, during those four months, have prevented secession, few men, I think, will doubt when the history of the time shall be written. But instead of doing so he consummated secession. Mr. Buchanan is a northern man, a Pennsylvanian; but he was opposed to the party which had brought in Mr. Lincoln, having thriven as a politician by his adherence to southern principles. Now, when the struggle came, he could not forget his party in his duty as President. General Jackson's position was much the same when Mr. Calhoun, on the question of the tariff, endeavoured to produce secession in South Carolina thirty years ago, in 1832,—excepting in this, that Jackson was himself a southern man. But Jackson had a strong conception of the position which he held as President of the United States. He put his foot on secession and crushed it, forcing Mr. Calhoun, as senator from South Carolina, to vote for that compromise as to the tariff which the Government of the day proposed. South Carolina was as eager in 1832 for secession as she was in 1859–1860; but the Government was in the hands of a strong man and an honest one. Mr. Calhoun would have been hung had he carried out his threats. But

Mr. Buchanan had neither the power nor the honesty of General Jackson, and thus secession was in fact consummated during his Presidency.

But Mr. Lincoln's party, it is said—and I believe truly said—might have prevented secession by making overtures to the South, or accepting overtures from the South, before Mr. Lincoln himself had been inaugurated. That is to say,—if Mr. Lincoln and the band of politicians who with him had pushed their way to the top of their party, and were about to fill the offices of State, chose to throw overboard the political convictions which had bound them together and insured their success, —if they could bring themselves to adopt on the subject of slavery the ideas of their opponents,—then the war might have been avoided, and secession also avoided. I do believe that had Mr. Lincoln at that time submitted himself to a compromise in favour of the Democrats, promising the support of the Government to certain acts which would in fact have been in favour of slavery, South Carolina would again have been foiled for the time. For it must be understood, that though South Carolina and the Gulf States might have accepted certain compromises, they would not have been satisfied in so accepting them. They desired secession, and nothing short of secession would, in truth, have been acceptable to them. But in doing so Mr. Lincoln would have been the most dishonest politician even in America. The North would have been in arms against him; and any true spirit of agreement between the cotton-growing slave States and the manufacturing States of the North, or the agricultural States of the West, would have been as far off and as improbable as it is now. Mr. Crittenden, who proffered his compromise to the Senate in December, 1860, was at that time one of the two senators from Kentucky, a slave State. He now sits in the Lower House of Congress as a member from the same State. Kentucky is one of those border States which has found it impossible to secede, and almost equally impossible to remain in the Union. It is one of the States into which it was most probable that the war would be carried;—Virginia, Kentucky, and Missouri being the three States which have suffered the most in this way. Of Mr. Crittenden's own family, some have gone with secession and some with the Union. His name had been honourably connected with American politics for nearly forty years, and it is not surprising that he should have desired a compromise. His terms were in fact these,—a return to the Missouri compromise, under which the Union pledged itself that no slavery should exist north of 36.30 N. lat. unless where it had so existed prior to the date of that compromise; a pledge that Congress would not interfere with slavery in the individual States,—which under the constitution it cannot do; and a pledge that the Fugitive Slave Law should be carried out by the northern States. Such a compromise might seem to make very small demand on the forbearance of the Republican party, which was now dominant. The repeal of the Missouri compromise had been to them a loss, and it might be said that its re-enactment would be a gain. But since that compromise had been repealed, vast territories south of the line in question, had been added to the Union, and the re-enactment of that compromise would hand those vast regions over to absolute slavery, as had been done with Texas. This might be all very well for Mr. Critten-den in the slave State of Kentucky—for Mr. Crittenden, although a slave-owner, desired to perpetuate the Union; but it would not have been well for New England or for the West. As for the second proposi-tion, it is well understood that under the constitution Congress cannot interfere in any way in the question of slavery in the individual States. Congress has no more constitutional power to abolish slavery in Mary-land than she has to introduce it into Massachusetts. No such pledge, therefore, was necessary on either side. But such a pledge given by the North and West would have acted as an additional tie upon them, binding them to the finality of a constitutional enactment to which, as was of course well known, they strongly object. There was no question of Congress interfering with slavery, with the purport of extending its area by special enactment, and therefore by such a pledge the North and West could gain nothing; but the South would in prestige have gained much.

But that third proposition as to the Fugitive Slave Law and the faithful execution of that law by the northern and western States would, if acceded to by Mr. Lincoln's party, have amounted to an un-conditional surrender of everything. What! Massachusetts and Con-necticut carry out the Fugitive Slave Law! Ohio carry out the Fugitive Slave Law after the "Dred Scott" decision and all its consequences! Mr. Crittenden might as well have asked Connecticut, Massachusetts, and Ohio to introduce slavery within their own lands. The Fugitive Slave Law was then, as it is now, the law of the land; it was the law of the United States as voted by Congress and passed by the President, and acted on by the Supreme Judge of the United States' Court. But it was a law to which no free State had submitted itself, or would submit itself. "What!" the English reader will say,—"sundry States in the Union refuse to obey the laws of the Union,—refuse to submit to the constitu-tional action of their own Congress!" Yes. Such has been the position of this country! To such a dead lock has it been brought by the at-tempted but impossible amalgamation of North and South. Mr. Crittenden's compromise was moonshine. It was utterly out of the question that the free States should bind themselves to the rendition of escaped slaves,—or that Mr. Lincoln, who had just been brought in by their voices, should agree to any compromise which should attempt so to bind them. Lord Palmerston might as well attempt to re-enact the Corn Laws.

Then comes the question whether Mr. Lincoln or his Government could have prevented the war after he had entered upon his office in March, 1861. I do not suppose that any one thinks that he could have avoided secession and avoided the war also;—that by any ordinary effort of Government he could have secured the adhesion of the Gulf States to the Union after the first shot had been fired at Fort Sumter. The general opinion in England is, I take it, this,—that secession then was manifestly necessary, and that all the bloodshed and money-shed, and all this destruction of commerce and of agriculture might have been prevented by a graceful adhesion to an indisputable fact. But there are some facts, even some indisputable facts, to which a graceful adherence is not possible. Could King Bomba [1] have welcomed Garibaldi to Naples? Can the Pope shake hands with Victor Emmanuel? Could the English have surrendered to their rebel colonists peaceable possession of the colonies? The indisputability of a fact is not very easily settled while the circumstances are in course of action by which the fact is to be decided. The men of the northern States have not believed in the necessity of secession, but have believed it to be their duty to enforce the adherence of these States to the Union. The American Governments have been much given to compromises, but had Mr. Lincoln attempted any compromise by which any one southern State could have been let out of the Union, he would have been impeached. In all probability the whole constitution would have gone to ruin, and the presidency would have been at an end. At any rate, his presidency would have been at an end. When secession, or in other words, rebellion was once commenced, he had no alternative but the use of coercive measures for putting it down;—that is, he had no alternative but war. It is not to be supposed that he or his ministry contemplated such a war as has existed,—with 600,000 men in arms on one side, each man with his whole belongings maintained at a cost of 150*l.* per annum, or ninety millions sterling per annum for the army. Nor

---

[1] King Bomba was the nickname acquired by Ferdinand II of Naples after his bombardment of Messina. Garibaldi had dethroned him in September 1859. In the same month the troops of Victor Emmanuel had invaded the Pope's dominions and vanquished the papal troops at Castelfidardo.

did we, when we resolved to put down the French revolution, think of such a national debt as we now owe. These things grow by degrees, and the mind also grows in becoming used to them; but I cannot see that there was any moment at which Mr. Lincoln could have stayed his hand and cried Peace! It is easy to say now that acquiescence in secession would have been better than war, but there has been no moment when he could have said so with any avail. It was incumbent on him to put down rebellion, or to be put down by it. So it was with us in America in 1776.

I do not think that we in England have quite sufficiently taken all this into consideration. We have been in the habit of exclaiming very loudly against the war, execrating its cruelty and anathematizing its results, as though the cruelty were all superfluous and the results unnecessary. But I do not remember to have seen any statement as to what the northern States should have done,—what they should have done, that is, as regards the South, or when they should have done it. It seems to me that we have decided as regards them that civil war is a very bad thing, and that therefore civil war should be avoided. But bad things cannot always be avoided. It is this feeling on our part that has produced so much irritation in them against us,—reproducing, of course, irritation on our part against them. They cannot understand that we should not wish them to be successful in putting down a rebellion; nor can we understand why they should be outrageous against us for standing aloof, and keeping our hands, if it be only possible, out of the fire.

When Slidell and Mason were arrested, my opinions were not changed, but my feelings were altered. I seemed to acknowledge to myself that the treatment to which England had been subjected, and the manner in which that treatment was discussed, made it necessary that I should regard the question as it existed between England and the States, rather than in its reference to the North and South. I had always felt that as regarded the action of our Government we had been sans reproche; that in arranging our conduct we had thought neither of money or political influence, but simply of the justice of the case,—promising to abstain from all interference and keeping that promise faithfully. It had been quite clear to me that the men of the North, and the women also, had failed to appreciate this, looking, as men in a quarrel always do look, for special favour on their side. Everything that England did was wrong. If a private merchant, at his own risk, took a cargo of rifles to some southern port, that act to northern eyes was an act of English interference,—of favour shown to the South by

England as a nation; but twenty shiploads of rifles sent from England to the North merely signified a brisk trade and a desire for profit. The "James Adger," a northern man-of-war, was refitted at Southampton as a matter of course. There was no blame to England for that. But the "Nashville," belonging to the Confederates, should not have been allowed into English waters! It was useless to speak of neutrality. No Northerner would understand that a rebel could have any mutual right. The South had no claim in his eyes as a belligerent, though the North claimed all those rights which he could only enjoy by the fact of there being a recognized war between him and his enemy the South. The North was learning to hate England, and day by day the feeling grew upon me that, much as I wished to espouse the cause of the North, I should have to espouse the cause of my own country. Then Slidell and Mason were arrested, and I began to calculate how long I might remain in the country. "There is no danger. We are quite right," the lawyers said. "There are Vattel and Puffendorff and Stowell and Phillimore and Wheaton," said the ladies. "Ambassadors are contraband all the world over,—more so than gunpowder; and if taken in a neutral bottom, &c." I wonder why ships are always called bottoms when spoken of with legal technicality? But neither the lawyers nor the ladies convinced me. I know that there are matters which will be read not in accordance with any written law, but in accordance with the bias of the reader's mind. Such laws are made to be strained any way. I knew how it would be. All the legal acumen of New England declared the seizure of Slidell and Mason to be right. The legal acumen of Old England has declared it to be wrong; and I have no doubt that the ladies of Old England can prove it to be wrong out of Vattel, Puffendorff, Stowell, Phillimore, and Wheaton.

"But there's Grotius," I said, to an elderly female at New York, who had quoted to me some half-dozen writers on international law, thinking thereby that I should trump her last card. "I've looked into Grotius too," said she, "and as far as I can see," &c., &c., &c. So I had to fall back again on the convictions to which instinct and common sense had brought me. I never doubted for a moment that those convictions would be supported by English lawyers.

I left Boston with a sad feeling at my heart that a quarrel was imminent between England and the States, and that any such quarrel must be destructive to the cause of the North. I had never believed that the States of New England and the Gulf States would again become parts of one nation, but I had thought that the terms of separation would be dictated by the North, and not by the South. I had felt assured that South Carolina and the Gulf States, across from the Atlantic to Texas, would succeed in forming themselves into a separate confederation; but I had still hoped that Maryland, Virginia, Kentucky, and Missouri might be saved to the grander empire of the North, and that thus a great blow to slavery might be the consequence of this civil war. But such ascendancy could only fall to the North by reason of their command of the sea. The northern ports were all open, and the southern ports were all closed. But if this should be reversed. If by England's action the southern ports should be opened, and the northern ports closed, the North could have no fair expectation of success. The ascendancy in that case would all be with the South. Up to that moment,—the Christmas of 1861,—Maryland was kept in subjection by the guns which General Dix had planted over the city of Baltimore. Two-thirds of Virginia were in active rebellion, coerced originally into that position by her dependence for the sale of her slaves on the cotton States. Kentucky was doubtful, and divided. When the federal troops prevailed, Kentucky was loyal; when the Confederate troops prevailed, Kentucky was rebellious. The condition in Missouri was much the same. Those four States, by two of which the capital, with its district of Columbia, is surrounded, might be gained, or might be lost. And these four States are susceptible of white labour,—as much so as Ohio and Illinois,—are rich in fertility, and rich also in all associations which must be dear to Americans. Without Virginia, Maryland, and Kentucky, without the Potomac, the Chesapeake, and Mount Vernon, the North would indeed be shorn of its glory! But it seemed to be in the power of the North to say under what terms secession should take place, and where should be the line. A senator from South Carolina could never again sit in the same chamber with one from Massachusetts; but there need be no such bar against the border States. So much might at any rate be gained, and might stand hereafter as the product of all that money spent on 600,000 soldiers. But if the Northerners should now elect to throw themselves into a quarrel with England, if in the gratification of a shameless braggadocio they should insist on doing what they liked, not only with their own, but with the property of all others also, it certainly did seem as though utter ruin must await their cause. With England, or one might say with Europe, against them, secession must be accomplished, not on northern terms, but on terms dictated by the South. The choice was then for them to make; and just at that time it seemed as though they were resolved to throw away every good card out of their hand. Such had been the ministerial wisdom of Mr. Seward. I remember hearing the matter discussed in easy terms by one of the United States senators. "Remember, Mr. Trollope," he said to me, "we don't want a war with England. If the choice is given to us, we had rather not fight England. Fighting is a bad thing. But remember this also, Mr. Trollope—that if the matter is pressed on us, we have no great objection. We had rather not, but we don't care much one way or the other." What one individual may say to another is not of much moment, but this senator was expressing the feelings of his constituents, who were the legislature of the State from whence he came. He was expressing the general idea on the subject of a large body of Americans. It was not that he and his State had really no objection to the war. Such a war loomed terribly large before the minds of them all. They knew it to be fraught with the saddest consequences. It was so regarded in the mind of that senator. But the braggadocio could not be omitted. Had he omitted it, he would have been untrue to his constituency.

When I left Boston for Washington nothing was as yet known of what the English Government or the English lawyers might say. This was in the first week in December, and the expected voice from England could not be heard till the end of the second week. It was a period of great suspense, and of great sorrow also to the more sober-minded Americans. To me the idea of such a war was terrible. It seemed that in these days all the hopes of our youth were being shattered. That poetic turning of the sword into a sickle, which gladdened our hearts ten or twelve years since, had been clean banished from men's minds. To belong to a peace-party was to be either a fanatic, an idiot, or a driveller. The arts of war had become everything. Armstrong guns,[2] themselves indestructible, but capable of destroying everything within sight, and most things out of sight, were the only recognized results of man's inventive faculties. To build bigger, stronger, and more ships than the French was England's glory. To hit a speck with a rifle bullet at 800 yards' distance was an Englishman's first duty. The proper use for a young man's leisure hours was the practice of drilling. All this had come upon us with very quick steps, since the beginning of the Russian war. But if fighting must needs be done, one did not feel special grief at fighting a Russian. That the Indian mutiny should be put down was a matter of course. That those Chinese rascals should be forced into the harness of civilization was a good thing. That England

[2] By "Armstrong guns," Trollope, like many other people, probably meant new-fashioned guns in general. The Armstrong gun proper, invented by Sir William George Armstrong and first patented in 1857, was the pioneer among breech-loading artillery pieces with rifled barrel.

should be as strong as France,—or perhaps, if possible, a little stronger, —recommended itself to an Englishman's mind as a State necessity. But a war with the States of America! In thinking of it I began to believe that the world was going backwards. Over sixty millions sterling of stock —railway stock and such like—are held in America by Englishmen, and the chances would be that before such a war could be finished the whole of that would be confiscated. Family connections between the States and the British isles are almost as close as between one of those islands and another. The commercial intercourse between the two countries has given bread to millions of Englishmen, and a break in it would rob millions of their bread. These people speak our language, use our prayers, read our books, are ruled by our laws, dress themselves in our image, are warm with our blood. They have all our virtues; and their vices are our own too, loudly as we call out against them. They are our sons and our daughters, the source of our greatest pride, and as we grow old they should be the staff of our age. Such a war as we should now wage with the States would be an unloosing of hell upon all that is best upon the world's surface. If in such a war we beat the Americans, they with their proud stomachs would never forgive us. If they should be victors, we should never forgive ourselves. I certainly could not bring myself to speak of it with the equanimity of my friend the senator.

I went through New York to Philadelphia and made a short visit to the latter town. Philadelphia seems to me to have thrown off its Quaker garb, and to present itself to the world in the garments ordinarily assumed by large cities; by which I intend to express my opinion that the Philadelphians are not in these latter days any better than their neighbours. I am not sure whether in some respects they may not perhaps be worse. Quakers,—Quakers absolutely in the very flesh of close bonnets and brown knee-breeches,—are still to be seen there; but they are not numerous, and would not strike the eye if one did not specially look for a Quaker at Philadelphia. It is a large town, with a very large hotel,—there are no doubt half-a-dozen large hotels, but one of them is specially great,[3]—with long straight streets, good shops and markets, and decent comfortable-looking houses. The houses of Philadelphia generally are not so large as those of other great cities in the States. They are more modest than those of New York, and less com-

---

[3] The luxuriously appointed Continental Hotel, opened in February 1860, was six stories high, with six hundred rooms, and accommodations for a thousand guests. It is glowingly described in "Palace Homes for the Traveller," Godey's Lady's Book for August 1860.

modious than those of Boston. Their most striking appendage is the marble steps at the front doors. Two doors as a rule enjoy one set of steps, on the other edges of which there is generally no parapet or raised curb-stone. This, to my eye, gave the houses an unfinished appearance,—as though the marble ran short, and no further expenditure could be made. The frost came when I was there, and then all these steps were covered up in wooden cases.

The city of Philadelphia lies between the two rivers, the Delaware and the Schuylkill. Eight chief streets run from river to river, and twenty-four cross-streets bisect the eight at right angles. The long streets are, with the exception of Market Street, called by the names of trees,—chesnut, walnut, pine, spruce, mulberry, vine, and so on. The cross-streets are called by their numbers. In the long streets the number of the houses are not consecutive, but follow the numbers of the cross-streets; so that a person living in Chestnut Street between Tenth Street and Eleventh Street, and ten doors from Tenth Street, would live at No. 1010. The opposite house would be No. 1011. It thus follows that the number of the house indicates the exact block of houses in which it is situated. I do not like the right-angled building of these towns, nor do I like the sound of Twentieth Street and Thirtieth Street; but I must acknowledge that the arrangement in Philadelphia has its convenience. In New York I found it by no means an easy thing to arrive at the desired locality.

They boast in Philadelphia that they have half a million inhabitants. If this be taken as a true calculation, Philadelphia is in size the fourth city in the world,—putting out of the question the cities of China, as to which we have heard so much and believe so little. But in making this calculation the citizens include the population of a district on some sides ten miles distant from Philadelphia. It takes in other towns connected with it by railway, but separated by large spaces of open country. American cities are very proud of their population, but if they all counted in this way, there would soon be no rural population left at all. There is a very fine bank at Philadelphia,—and Philadelphia is a town somewhat celebrated in its banking history. My remarks here, however, apply simply to the external building, and not to its internal honesty and wisdom, or to its commercial credit.

In Philadelphia also stands the old house of Congress,—the house in which the Congress of the United States was held previous to 1800, when the Government, and the Congress with it, were moved to the new city of Washington. I believe, however, that the first Congress, properly so called, was assembled at New York in 1789, the date of the

inauguration of the first President. It was, however, here, in this building at Philadelphia, that the independence of the Union was declared
in 1776, and that the constitution of the United States was framed.

Pennsylvania, with Philadelphia for its capital, was once the leading State of the Union,—leading by a long distance. At the end of the
last century it beat all the other States in population, but has since been
surpassed by New York in all respects,—in population, commerce,
wealth, and general activity. Of course it is known that Pennsylvania
was granted to William Penn, the Quaker, by Charles II. I cannot completely understand what was the meaning of such grants,—how far they
implied absolute possession in the territory, or how far they confirmed
simply the power of settling and governing a colony. In this case a very
considerable property was confirmed, as the claim made by Penn's
children after Penn's death were bought up by the commonwealth of
Pennsylvania for 130,000*l.*; which in those days was a large price for
almost any landed estate on the other side of the Atlantic.

Pennsylvania lies directly on the borders of slave land, being immediately north of Maryland. Mason and Dixon's line, of which we
hear so often, and which was first established as the division between
slave soil and free soil, runs between Pennsylvania and Maryland. The
little State of Delaware, which lies between Maryland and the Atlantic,
is also tainted with slavery; but the stain is not heavy nor indelible. In
a population of a hundred and twelve thousand there are not two
thousand slaves, and of these the owners generally would willingly rid
themselves if they could. It is, however, a point of honour with these
owners, as it is also in Maryland, not to sell their slaves; and a man
who cannot sell his slaves must keep them. Were he to enfranchise
them and send them about their business, they would come back upon
his hands. Were he to enfranchise them and pay them wages for work,
they would get the wages but he would not get the work. They would
get the wages, but at the end of three months they would still fall back
upon his hands in debt and distress, looking to him for aid and comfort as a child looks for it. It is not easy to get rid of a slave in a slave
State. That question of enfranchising slaves is not one to be very
readily solved.

In Pennsylvania the right of voting is confined to free white men.
In New York the coloured free men have the right to vote, providing
they have a certain small property qualification, and have been citizens
for three years in the State;—whereas a white man need have been a
citizen but for ten days, and need have no property qualification; from
which it is seen that the position of the negro becomes worse, or less

like that of a white man, as the border of slave land is more nearly reached. But in the teeth of this embargo on coloured men, the constitution of Pennsylvania asserts broadly that all men are born equally free and independent. One cannot conceive how two clauses can have found their way into the same document so absolutely contradictory to each other. The first clause says that white men shall vote, and that black men shall not, which means that all political action shall be confined to white men. The second clause says that all men are born equally free and independent!

In Philadelphia I for the first time came across live secessionists,— secessionists who pronounced themselves to be such. I will not say that I had met in other cities men who falsely declared themselves true to the Union; but I had fancied, in regard to some, that their words were a little stronger than their feelings. When a man's bread,—and much more, when the bread of his wife and children—depends on his professing a certain line of political conviction, it is very hard for him to deny his assent to the truth of the argument. One feels that a man under such circumstances is bound to be convinced, unless he be in a position which may make a stanch adherence to opposite politics a matter of grave public importance. In the North I had fancied that I could sometimes read a secessionist tendency under a cloud of unionist protestations. But in Philadelphia men did not seem to think it necessary to have recourse to such a cloud. I generally found in mixed society, even there, that the discussion of secession was not permitted; but in society that was not mixed, I heard very strong opinions expressed on each side. With the unionists nothing was so strong as the necessity of keeping Slidell and Mason. When I suggested that the English Government would probably require their surrender, I was talked down and ridiculed. "Never that; come what may." Then, within half an hour, I would be told by a secessionist that England must demand reparation if she meant to retain any place among the great nations of the world; but he also would declare that the men would not be surrendered. "She must make the demand," the secessionist would say, "and then there will be war; and after that we shall see whose ports will be blockaded!" The Southerner has ever looked to England for some breach of the blockade, quite as strongly as the North has looked to England for sympathy and aid in keeping it.

The railway from Philadelphia to Baltimore passes along the top of Chesapeake Bay and across the Susquehanna River; at least the railway cars do so. On one side of that river they are run on to a huge ferryboat, and are again run off at the other side. Such an operation would seem to be one of difficulty to us under any circumstances; but as the Susquehanna is a tidal river, rising and falling a considerable number of feet, the natural impediment in the way of such an enterprise would, I think, have staggered us. We should have built a bridge costing two or three millions sterling, on which no conceivable amount of traffic would pay a fair dividend. Here, in crossing the Susquehanna, the boat is so constructed that its deck shall be level with the line of the railway at half tide, so that the inclined plane from the shore down to the boat, or from the shore up to the boat, shall never exceed half the amount of the rise or fall. One would suppose that the most intricate machinery would have been necessary for such an arrangement; but it was all rough and simple, and apparently managed by two negroes. We should employ a small corps of engineers to conduct such an operation, and men and women would be detained in their carriages under all manner of threats as to the peril of life and limb; but here everybody was expected to look out for himself. The cars were dragged up the inclined plane by a hawser attached to an engine, which hawser, had the stress broken it, as I could not but fancy probable, would have flown back and cut to pieces a lot of us who were standing in front of the car. But I do not think that any such accident would have caused very much attention. Life and limbs are not held to be so precious here as they are in England. It may be a question whether with us they are not almost too precious. Regarding railways in America generally, as to the relative safety of which, when compared with our own, we have not in England a high opinion, I must say that I never saw any accident or in any way became conversant with one. It is said that large numbers of men and women are slaughtered from time to time on different lines; but if it be so, the newspapers make very light of such cases. I myself have seen no such slaughter, nor have I even found myself in the vicinity of a broken bone. Beyond the Susquehanna we passed over a creek of Chesapeake Bay on a long bridge. The whole scenery here is very pretty, and the view up the Susquehanna is fine. This is the bay which divides the State of Maryland into two parts, and which is blessed beyond all other bays by the possession of canvas-back ducks. Nature has done a great deal for the State of Maryland, but in nothing more than in sending thither these web-footed birds of Paradise.

Nature has done a great deal for Maryland; and Fortune also has done much for it in these latter days in directing the war from its territory. But for the peculiar position of Washington as the capital, all that is now being done in Virginia would have been done in Maryland,

and I must say that the Marylanders did their best to bring about such a result. Had the presence of the war been regarded by the men of Baltimore as an unalloyed benefit, they could not have made a greater struggle to bring it close to them. Nevertheless fate has so far spared them.

As the position of Maryland and the course of events as they took place in Baltimore on the commencement of secession had considerable influence both in the North and in the South, I will endeavour to explain how that State was affected, and how the question was affected by that State. Maryland, as I have said before, is a slave State lying immediately south of Mason and Dixon's line. Small portions both of Virginia and of Delaware do run north of Maryland, but practically Maryland is the frontier State of the slave States. It was therefore of much importance to know which way Maryland would go in the event of secession among these slave States becoming general; and of much also to ascertain whether it could secede if desirous of doing so. I am inclined to think that as a State it was desirous of following Virginia, though there are many in Maryland who deny this very stoutly. But it was at once evident that if loyalty to the North could not be had in Maryland of its own free will, adherence to the North must be enforced upon Maryland. Otherwise the city of Washington could not be maintained as the existing capital of the nation.

The question of the fidelity of the State to the Union was first tried by the arrival at Baltimore of a certain Commissioner from the State of Mississippi, who visited that city with the object of inducing secession. It must be understood that Baltimore is the commercial capital of Maryland, whereas Annapolis is the seat of Government and the legislature—or is, in other terms, the political capital. Baltimore is a city containing 230,000 inhabitants, and is considered to have as strong and perhaps as violent a mob as any city in the Union. Of the above number 30,000 are negroes and 2000 are slaves. The Commissioner made his appeal, telling his tale of southern grievances, declaring, among other things, that secession was not intended to break up the Government but to perpetuate it, and asked for the assistance and sympathy of Maryland. This was in December, 1860. The Commissioner was answered by Governor Hicks, who was placed in a somewhat difficult position. The existing legislature of the State was presumed to be secessionist, but the legislature was not sitting, nor in the ordinary course of things would that legislature have been called on to sit again. The legislature of Maryland is elected every other year, and in the ordinary course sits only once in the two years. That session had been held, and the existing legislature was therefore exempt from further work,—unless specially summoned for an extraordinary session. To do this is within the power of the Governor. But Governor Hicks, who seems to have been mainly anxious to keep things quiet, and whose individual politics did not come out strongly, was not inclined to issue the summons. "Let us show moderation as well as firmness," he said; and that was about all he did say to the Commissioner from Mississippi. The Governor after that was directly called on to convene the legislature; but this he refused to do, alleging that it would not be safe to trust the discussion of such a subject as secession to—"excited politicians, many of whom having nothing to lose from the destruction of the Government, may hope to derive some gain from the ruin of the State!" I quote these words, coming from the head of the executive of the State and spoken with reference to the legislature of the State, with the object of showing in what light the political leaders of a State may be held in that very State to which they belong! If we are to judge of these legislators from the opinion expressed by Governor Hicks, they could hardly have been fit for their places. That plan of governing by the little men has certainly not answered. It need hardly be said that Governor Hicks having expressed such an opinion of his State's legislature, refused to call them to an extraordinary session.

On the 18th of April, 1860, Governor Hicks issued a proclamation to the people of Maryland, begging them to be quiet, the chief object of which, however, was that of promising that no troops should be sent out from their State, unless with the object of guarding the neighbouring city of Washington,—a promise which he had no means of fulfilling, seeing that the President of the United States is the Commander-in-Chief of the army of the nation and can summon the militia of the several States. This proclamation by the Governor to the State was immediately backed up by one from the Mayor of Baltimore to the city, in which he congratulates the citizens on the Governor's promise that none of their troops are to be sent to another State; and then he tells them that they shall be preserved from the horrors of civil war.

But on the very next day the horrors of civil war began in Baltimore.[4] By this time President Lincoln was collecting troops at Washington for the protection of the capital; and that army of the Potomac, which has ever since occupied the Virginian side of the river, was in course of construction. To join this, certain troops from Massachusetts were sent down by the usual route, *viâ* New York, Philadelphia, and

4 For further details of the Baltimore Riot and some minor corrections, see the note to page 25.

Baltimore; but on their reaching Baltimore by railway, the mob of that town refused to allow them to pass through,—and a fight began. Nine citizens were killed and two soldiers, and as many more were wounded. This, I think, was the first blood spilt in the civil war; and the attack was first made by the mob of the first slave city reached by the northern soldiers. This goes far to show, not that the border States desired secession, but that, when compelled to choose between secession and union,—when not allowed by circumstances to remain neutral,— their sympathies were with their sister slave States rather than with the North.

Then there was a great running about of official men between Baltimore and Washington, and the President was besieged with entreaties that no troops should be sent through Baltimore. Now this was hard enough upon President Lincoln, seeing that he was bound to defend his capital, that he could get no troops from the South, and that Baltimore is on the high road from Washington, both to the West and to the North; but, nevertheless, he gave way. Had he not done so, all Baltimore would have been in a blaze of rebellion, and the scene of the coming contest must have been removed from Virginia to Maryland, and Congress and the Government must have travelled from Washington north to Philadelphia. "They shall not come through Baltimore," said Mr. Lincoln. "But they shall come through the State of Maryland. They shall be passed over Chesapeake Bay by water to Annapolis, and shall come up by rail from thence." This arrangement was as distasteful to the State of Maryland as the other; but Annapolis is a small town without a mob, and the Marylanders had no means of preventing the passage of the troops. Attempts were made to refuse the use of the Annapolis branch railway, but General Butler had the arranging of that. General Butler was a lawyer from Boston, and by no means inclined to indulge the scruples of the Marylanders who had so roughly treated his fellow-citizens from Massachusetts. The troops did therefore pass through Annapolis, much to the disgust of the State. On the 27th of April Governor Hicks, having now had a sufficiency of individual responsibility, summoned the legislature of which he had expressed so bad an opinion; but on this occasion he omitted to repeat that opinion, and submitted his views in very proper terms to the wisdom of the senators and representatives. He entertained, as he said, an honest conviction that the safety of Maryland lay in preserving a neutral position between the North and the South. Certainly, Governor Hicks, if it were only possible! The legislature again went to work to prevent, if it might be prevented, the passage of troops through their

State; but luckily for them, they failed. The President was bound to defend Washington, and the Marylanders were denied their wish of having their own fields made the fighting ground of the civil war.

That which appears to me to be the most remarkable feature in all this is the antagonism between United States law and individual State feeling. Through the whole proceeding the Governor and the State of Maryland seemed to have considered it legal and reasonable to oppose the constitutional power of the President and his Government. It is argued in all the speeches and written documents that were produced in Maryland at the time, that Maryland was true to the Union; and yet she put herself in opposition to the constitutional military power of the President! Certain commissioners went from the State legislature to Washington, in May, and from their report, it appears that the President had expressed himself of opinion that Maryland might do this or that, as long "as she had not taken and was not about to take a hostile attitude to the Federal Government!" From which we are to gather that a denial of that military power given to the President by the constitution was not considered as an attitude hostile to the Federal Government. At any rate, it was direct disobedience of Federal law. I cannot but revert from this to the condition of the fugitive slave law. Federal law, and indeed the original constitution, plainly declare that fugitive slaves shall be given up by the free-soil States. Massachusetts proclaims herself to be specially a federal, law-loving State. But every man in Massachusetts knows that no judge, no sheriff, no magistrate, no policeman in that State would at this time, or then, when that civil war was beginning, have lent a hand in any way to the rendition of a fugitive slave. The Federal law requires the State to give up the fugitive, but the State law does not require judge, sheriff, magistrate, or policeman to engage in such work, and no judge, sheriff, or magistrate will do so; consequently that Federal law is dead in Massachusetts, as it is also in every free-soil State,—dead, except inasmuch as there was life in it to create ill-blood as long as the North and South remained together, and would be life in it for the same effect if they should again be brought under the same flag.

On the 10th May the Maryland legislature, having received the report of their Commissioners above-mentioned, passed the following resolution:—

"Whereas the war against the Confederate States is unconstitutional and repugnant to civilization, and will result in a bloody and shameful overthrow of our constitution, and whilst recognizing the obligations of Maryland to the Union, we sympathize with the South in the struggle for their rights; for the sake of humanity, we are for peace and reconciliation, and solemnly protest against this war, and will take no part in it.

"Resolved,—That Maryland implores the President, in the name of God, to cease this unholy war, at least until Congress assembles"— a period of above six months. "That Maryland desires and consents to the recognition of the independence of the Confederate States. The military occupation of Maryland is unconstitutional and she protests against it, though the violent interference with the transit of the Federal troops is discountenanced. That the vindication of her rights be left to time and reason, and that a convention under existing circumstances is inexpedient."

From which it is plain that Maryland would have seceded as effectually as Georgia seceded, had she not been prevented by the interposition of Washington between her and the Confederate States,—the happy intervention, seeing that she has thus been saved from becoming the battle-ground of the contest. But the legislature had to pay for its rashness. On the 13th of September thirteen of its members were arrested, as were also two editors of newspapers presumed to be secessionists. A member of Congress was also arrested at the same time, and a candidate for Governor Hicks's place, who belonged to the secessionist party. Previously, in the last days of June and beginning of July, the chief of the police at Baltimore and the member of the Board of Police had been arrested by General Banks, who then held Baltimore in his power.

I should be sorry to be construed as saying that republican institutions, or what may more properly be called democratic institutions, have been broken down in the States of America. I am far from thinking that they have broken down. Taking them and their work as a whole, I think that they have shown, and still show, vitality of the best order. But the written constitution of the United States and of the several States, as bearing upon each other, are not equal to the requirements made upon them. That, I think, is the conclusion to which a spectator should come. It is in that doctrine of finality that our friends have broken down,—a doctrine not expressed in their constitutions, and indeed expressly denied in the constitution of the United States, which provides the mode in which amendments shall be made—but appearing plainly enough in every word of self-gratulation which comes from them. Political finality has ever proved a delusion,—as has the idea of finality in all human institutions. I do not doubt but that the republican form of government will remain and make progress in

North America; but such prolonged existence and progress must be based on an acknowledgment of the necessity for change, and must in part depend on the facilities for change which shall be afforded.

I have described the condition of Baltimore as it was early in May, 1861. I reached that city just seven months later, and its condition was considerably altered. There was no question then whether troops should pass through Baltimore, or by an awkward round through Annapolis, or not pass at all through Maryland. General Dix, who had succeeded General Banks, was holding the city in his grip, and martial law prevailed. In such times as those, it was bootless to inquire as to that promise that no troops should pass southward through Baltimore. What have such assurances ever been worth in such days! Baltimore was now a military depôt in the hands of the northern army, and General Dix was not a man to stand any trifling. He did me the honour to take me to the top of Federal Hill, a suburb of the city, on which he had raised great earthworks and planted mighty cannons, and built tents and barracks for his soldiery, and to show me how instantaneously he could destroy the town from his exalted position. "This hill was made for the very purpose," said General Dix; and no doubt he thought so. Generals when they have fine positions and big guns and prostrate people lying under their thumbs, are inclined to think that God's providence has specially ordained them and their points of vantage. It is a good thing in the mind of a general so circumstanced that 200,000 men should be made subject to a dozen big guns. I confess that to me, having had no military education, the matter appeared in a different light, and I could not work up my enthusiasm to a pitch which would have been suitable to the General's courtesy. That hill, on which many of the poor of Baltimore had lived, was desecrated in my eyes by those columbiads.[5] The neat earthworks were ugly, as looked upon by me; and though I regarded General Dix as energetic, and no doubt skilful in the work assigned to him, I could not sympathize with his exultation.

Previously to the days of secession Baltimore had been guarded by Fort MacHenry, which lies on a spit of land running out into the bay just below the town. Hither I went with General Dix, and he explained to me how the cannon had heretofore been pointed solely towards the sea; that, however, now was all changed, and the mouths

5 Trollope probably intends the term to mean simply big guns. The Columbiad proper was a type of large cannon, usually of eight- or ten-inch bore. By the end of 1861, one twelve-inch and one sensational fifteen-inch Columbiad had been cast. The fifteen-inch, which fired a 320-pound shell over three miles with but slight lateral deviation, was set up at Fortress Monroe.

of his bombs and great artillery were turned all the other way. The commandant of the fort was with us, and other officers, and they all spoke of this martial tenure as a great blessing. Hearing them, one could hardly fail to suppose that they had lived their forty, fifty, or sixty years of life in full reliance on the powers of a military despotism. But not the less were they American republicans, who, twelve months since, would have dilated on the all-sufficiency of their republican institutions, and on the absence of any military restraint in their country, with that peculiar pride which characterizes the citizens of the States. There are, however, some lessons which may be learned with singular rapidity!

Such was the state of Baltimore when I visited that city. I found, nevertheless, that cakes and ale still prevailed there. I am inclined to think that cakes and ale prevail most freely in times that are perilous, and when sources of sorrow abound. I have seen more reckless joviality in a town stricken by pestilence than I ever encountered elsewhere. There was General Dix seated on Federal Hill with his cannon; and there, beneath his artillery, were gentlemen hotly professing themselves to be secessionists, men whose sons and brothers were in the southern army, and women!—alas whose brothers would be in one army, and their sons in another. That was the part of it which was most heart-rending in this border land. In New England and New York men's minds at any rate were bent all in the same direction,—as doubtless they were also in Georgia and Alabama. But here fathers were divided from sons, and mothers from daughters. Terrible tales were told of threats uttered by one member of a family against another. Old ties of friendship were broken up. Society had so divided itself, that one side could hold no terms of courtesy with the other. "When this is over," one gentleman said to me, "every man in Baltimore will have a quarrel to the death on his hands with some friend whom he used to love." The complaints made on both sides were eager and open-mouthed against the other.

Late in the autumn an election for a new legislature of the State had taken place, and the members returned were all supposed to be unionist. That they were prepared to support the Government is certain. But no known or presumed secessionist was allowed to vote without first taking the oath of allegiance. The election therefore, even if the numbers were true, cannot be looked upon as a free election. Voters were stopped at the poll and not allowed to vote unless they would take an oath which would, on their parts, undoubtedly have been false. It was also declared in Baltimore that men engaged to promote the northern party. were permitted to vote five or six times over, and the enormous number of votes polled on the Government side gave some colouring to the statement. At any rate an election carried under General Dix's guns cannot be regarded as an open election. It was out of the question that any election taken under such circumstances should be worth anything as expressing the minds of the people. Red and white had been declared to be the colours of the Confederates, and red and white had of course become the favourite colours of the Baltimore ladies. Then it was given out that red and white would not be allowed in the streets. Ladies wearing red and white were requested to return home. Children decorated with red and white ribbons were stripped of their bits of finery,—much to their infantine disgust and dismay. Ladies would put red and white ornaments in their windows, and the police would insist on the withdrawal of the colours. Such was the condition of Baltimore during the past winter. Nevertheless cakes and ale abounded; and though there was deep grief in the city, and wailing in the recesses of many houses, and a feeling that the good times were gone, never to return within the days of many of them, still there existed an excitement and a consciousness of the importance of the crisis which was not altogether unsatisfactory. Men and women can endure to be ruined, to be torn from their friends, to be overwhelmed with avalanches of misfortune, better than they can endure to be dull.

Baltimore is, or at any rate was, an aspiring city, proud of its commerce and proud of its society. It has regarded itself as the New York of the South, and to some extent has forced others so to regard it also. In many respects it is more like an English town than most of its transatlantic brethren, and the ways of its inhabitants are English. In old days a pack of fox-hounds was kept here,—or indeed in days that are not yet very old, for I was told of their doings by a gentleman who had long been a member of the hunt. The country looks as a hunting country should look, whereas no man that ever crossed a field after a pack of hounds would feel the slightest wish to attempt that process in New England or New York. There is in Baltimore an old inn with an old sign, standing at the corner of Eutaw and Franklin Streets, just such as may still be seen in the towns of Somersetshire, and before it are to be seen old wagons, covered and soiled and battered, about to return from the city to the country, just as the wagons do in our own agricultural counties. I have found nothing so thoroughly English in any other part of the Union.

But canvas-back ducks and terrapins are the great glories of Baltimore. Of the nature of the former bird I believe all the world knows something. It is a wild duck which obtains the peculiarity of its flavour from the wild celery on which it feeds. This celery grows on the Chesapeake Bay, and I believe on the Chesapeake Bay only. At any rate Baltimore is the head-quarters of the canvas-backs, and it is on the Chesapeake Bay that they are shot. I was kindly invited to go down on a shooting-party; but when I learned that I should have to ensconce myself alone for hours in a wet wooden box on the water's edge, waiting there for the chance of a duck to come to me, I declined. The fact of my never having as yet been successful in shooting a bird of any kind conduced somewhat perhaps to my decision. I must acknowledge that the canvas-back duck fully deserves all the reputation it has acquired. As to the terrapin, I have not so much to say. The terrapin is a small turtle, found on the shores of Maryland and Virginia, out of which a very rich soup is made. It is cooked with wines and spices, and is served in the shape of a hash, with heaps of little bones mixed through it. It is held in great repute, and the guest is expected as a matter of course to be helped twice. The man who did not eat twice of terrapin would be held in small repute, as the Londoner is held who at a city banquet does not partake of both thick and thin turtle. I must, however, confess that the terrapin for me had no surpassing charms.

Maryland was so called from Henrietta Maria, the wife of Charles I., by which king in 1632 the territory was conceded to the Roman Catholic Lord Baltimore. It was chiefly peopled by Roman Catholics, but I do not think that there is now any such speciality attaching to the State. There are in it two or three old Roman Catholic families, but the people have come down from the North, and have no peculiar religious tendencies. Some of Lord Baltimore's descendants remained in the State up to the time of the revolution. From Baltimore I went on to Washington.

CHAPTER XX

WASHINGTON

THE SITE of the present city of Washington was chosen with three special views; firstly, that being on the Potomac it might have the full advantage of water-carriage and a sea-port; secondly, that it might be so far removed from the seaboard as to be safe from invasion; and, thirdly, that it might be central alike to all the States. It was presumed when Washington was founded that these three advantages would be secured by the selected position. As regards the first, the Potomac affords to the city but few of the advantages of a sea-port. Ships can come up, but not ships of large burthen. The river seems to have dwindled since the site was chosen; and at present it is, I think, evident that Washington can never be great in its shipping. *Statio bene-fida carinis* [1] can never be its motto. As regards the second point, singularly enough Washington is the only city of the Union that has been in an enemy's possession since the United States became a nation. In the war of 1812 it fell into our hands, and we burnt it. As regards the third point, Washington, from the lie of the land, can hardly have been said to be centrical at any time. Owing to the irregularities of the coast it is not easy of access by railways from different sides. Baltimore would have been far better. But as far as we can now see, and as well as we can now judge, Washington will soon be on the borders of the nation to which it belongs, instead of at its centre. I fear, therefore, that we must acknowledge that the site chosen for his country's capital by George Washington has not been fortunate.

I have a strong idea, which I expressed before in speaking of the capital of the Canadas, that no man can ordain that on such a spot shall be built a great and thriving city. No man can so ordain even though he leave behind him, as was the case with Washington, a prestige sufficient to bind his successors to his wishes. The political leaders of the country have done what they could for Washington. The pride of the nation has endeavoured to sustain the character of its chosen metropolis. There has been no rival, soliciting favour on the strength of other charms. The country has all been agreed on the point since the father of the country first commenced the work. Florence and

---

[1] "Safe harborage for ships," a Latin motto.

Rome in Italy have each their pretensions; but in the States no other city has put itself forward for the honour of entertaining Congress. And yet Washington has been a failure. It is commerce that makes great cities, and commerce has refused to back the General's choice.[2] New York and Philadelphia, without any political power, have become great among the cities of the earth. They are beaten by none except by London and Paris. But Washington is but a ragged, unfinished collection of unbuilt broad streets, as to the completion of which there can now, I imagine, be but little hope.

Of all places that I know it is the most ungainly and most unsatisfactory;—I fear I must also say the most presumptuous in its pretensions. There is a map of Washington accurately laid down; and taking that map with him in his journeyings a man may lose himself in the streets, not as one loses oneself in London between Shoreditch and Russell Square, but as one does so in the deserts of the Holy Land, between Emmaus and Arimathea. In the first place no one knows where the places are, or is sure of their existence, and then between their presumed localities the country is wild, trackless, unbridged, uninhabited, and desolate. Massachusetts Avenue runs the whole length of the city, and is inserted on the maps as a full-blown street, about four miles in length. Go there, and you will find yourself not only out of town, away among the fields, but you will find yourself beyond the fields, in an uncultivated, undrained wilderness. Tucking your trousers up to your knees you will wade through the bogs, you will lose yourself among rude hillocks, you will be out of the reach of humanity. The unfinished dome of the Capitol will loom before you in the distance, and you will think that you approach the ruins of some western Palmyra. If you are a sportsman, you will desire to shoot snipe within sight of the President's house. There is much unsettled land within the States of America, but I think none so desolate in its state of nature as three-fourths of the ground on which is supposed to stand the city of Washington.

The city of Washington is something more than four miles long, and is something more than two miles broad. The land apportioned to it is nearly as compact as may be, and it exceeds in area the size of a parallelogram four miles long by two broad. These dimensions are adequate for a noble city, for a city to contain a million of inhabitants.

---

[2] It is true that George Washington chose the specific site of the city, but the placing of Washington in its general setting on the Potomac was the result of intricate and lengthy political maneuvering among conflicting state interests, nothing that the First President "ordained."

It is impossible to state with accuracy the actual population of Washington, for it fluctuates exceedingly. The place is very full during Congress, and very empty during the recess. By which I mean it to be understood that those streets, which are blessed with houses, are full when Congress meets. I do not think that Congress makes much difference to Massachusetts Avenue. I believe that the city never contains as many as eighty thousand, and that its permanent residents are less than sixty thousand.

But, it will be said,—was it not well to prepare for a growing city? Is it not true that London is choked by its own fatness, not having been endowed at its birth or during its growth, with proper means for accommodating its own increasing proportions? Was it not well to lay down fine avenues and broad streets, so that future citizens might find a city well prepared to their hand?

There is no doubt much in such an argument, but its correctness must be tested by its success. When a man marries it is well that he should make provision for a coming family. But a Benedict, who early in his career shall have carried his friends with considerable self-applause through half-a-dozen nurseries and at the end of twelve years shall still be the father of one ricketty baby, will incur a certain amount of ridicule. It is very well to be prepared for good fortune, but one should limit one's preparation within a reasonable scope. Two miles by one might perhaps have done for the skeleton sketch of a new city. Less than half that would contain much more than the present population of Washington; and there are, I fear, few towns in the Union so little likely to enjoy any speedy increase.

Three avenues sweep the whole length of Washington;—Virginia Avenue, Pennsylvania Avenue, and Massachusetts Avenue. But Pennsylvania Avenue is the only one known to ordinary men, and the half of that only is so known. This avenue is the backbone of the city, and those streets which are really inhabited cluster round that half of it which runs westward from the Capitol. The eastern end, running from the front of the Capitol, is again a desert. The plan of the city is somewhat complicated. It may truly be called "a mighty maze, but not without a plan." [3] The Capitol was intended to be the centre of the city. It faces eastward, away from the Potomac,—or rather from the main branch of the Potomac, and also unfortunately from the main body of the town. It turns its back upon the chief thoroughfare, upon the Treasury buildings, and upon the President's house; and indeed upon the whole place. It was, I suppose, intended that the streets to the east-

[3] Pope's *An Essay on Man*, Epistle I, line 6.

ward should be noble and populous, but hitherto they have come to nothing. The building therefore is wrong side foremost, and all mankind who enter it, senators, representatives, and judges included, go in at the back-door. Of course it is generally known that in the Capitol is the Chamber of the Senate, that of the House of Representatives, and the Supreme Judicial Court of the Union. It may be said that there are two centres in Washington, this being one and the President's house the other. At these centres the main avenues are supposed to cross each other, which avenues are called by the names of the respective States. At the Capitol, Pennsylvania Avenue, New Jersey Avenue, Delaware Avenue, and Maryland Avenue converge. They come from one extremity of the city to the square of the Capitol on one side, and run out from the other side of it to the other extremity of the city. Pennsylvania Avenue, New York Avenue, Vermont Avenue, and Connecticut Avenue do the same at what is generally called President's Square. In theory, or on paper, this seems to be a clear and intelligible arrangement; but it does not work well. These centre depôts are large spaces, and consequently one portion of a street is removed a considerable distance from the other. It is as though the same name should be given to two streets, one of which entered St. James's Park at Buckingham Gate, while the other started from the Park at Marlborough House. To inhabitants the matter probably is not of much moment, as it is well known that this portion of such an avenue and that portion of such another avenue are merely myths,—unknown lands away in the wilds. But a stranger finds himself in the position of being sent across the country knee-deep into the mud, wading through snipe grounds, looking for civilization where none exists.

All these avenues have a slanting direction. They are so arranged that none of them run north and south or east and west; but the streets, so called, all run in accordance with the points of the compass. Those from east to west, are A Street, B Street, C Street, and so on,—counting them away from the Capitol on each side, so that there are two A streets, and two B streets. On the map these streets run up to V Street, both right and left,—V Street North and V Street South. Those really known to mankind are, E, F, G, H, I, and K Streets North. Then those streets which run from north to south are numbered First Street, Second Street, Third Street, and so on, on each front of the Capitol, running to Twenty-fourth or Twenty-fifth Streets on each side. Not very many of these have any existence, or I might perhaps more properly say, any vitality in their existence.

Such is the plan of the city, that being the arrangement and those

the dimensions intended by the original architects and founders of
Washington; but the inhabitants have hitherto confined themselves
to Pennsylvania Avenue West, and to the streets abutting from it or
near to it. Whatever address a stranger may receive, however perplex-
ing it may seem to him, he may be sure that the house indicated is near
Pennsylvania Avenue. If it be not, I should recommend him to pay no
attention to the summons. Even in those streets with which he will become best acquainted, the houses are not continuous. There will be a
house, and then a blank; then two houses, and then a double blank.
After that a hut or two, and then probably an excellent, roomy, handsome family mansion. Taken altogether, Washington as a city is most
unsatisfactory, and falls more grievously short of the thing attempted
than any other of the great undertakings of which I have seen anything
in the States. San José, the capital of the republic of Costa Rica in
Central America, has been prepared and arranged as a new city in the
same way. But even San José comes nearer to what was intended than
does Washington.

For myself, I do not believe in cities made after this fashion. Commerce, I think, must select the site of all large congregations of mankind. In some mysterious way she ascertains what she wants, and having acquired that, draws men in thousands round her properties.
Liverpool, New York, Lyons, Glasgow, Venice, Marseilles, Hamburg,
Calcutta, Chicago, and Leghorn, have all become populous, and are
or have been great, because trade found them to be convenient for its
purposes. Trade seems to have ignored Washington altogether. Such
being the case, the Legislature and the Executive of the country together have been unable to make of Washington anything better than
a straggling congregation of buildings in a wilderness. We are now
trying the same experiment at Ottawa in Canada, having turned our
back upon Montreal in dudgeon. The site of Ottawa is more interesting than that of Washington, but I doubt whether the experiment
will be more successful. A new town for art, fashion, and politics has
been built at Munich, and there it seems to answer the expectation
of the builders; but at Munich there is an old city as well, and commerce had already got some considerable hold on the spot before the
new town was added to it.

The streets of Washington, such as exist, are all broad. Throughout the town there are open spaces,—spaces, I mean, intended to be
open by the plan laid down for the city. At the present moment it is
almost all open space. There is also a certain nobility about the proposed dimensions of the avenues and squares. Desirous of praising it

in some degree, I can say that the design is grand. The thing done, however, falls so infinitely short of that design, that nothing but disappointment is felt. And I fear that there is no look-out into the future which can justify a hope that the design will be fulfilled. It is therefore a melancholy place. The society into which one falls there consists mostly of persons who are not permanently resident in the capital; but of those who were permanent residents I found none who spoke of their city with affection. The men and women of Boston think that the sun shines nowhere else;—and Boston Common is very pleasant. The New Yorkers believe in Fifth Avenue with an unswerving faith; and Fifth Avenue is calculated to inspire a faith. Philadelphia to a Philadelphian is the centre of the universe, and the progress of Philadelphia, perhaps, justifies the partiality. The same thing may be said of Chicago, of Buffalo, and of Baltimore. But the same thing cannot be said in any degree of Washington. They who belong to it turn up their noses at it. They feel that they live surrounded by a failure. Its grand names are as yet false, and none of the efforts made have hitherto been successful. Even in winter, when Congress is sitting, Washington is melancholy;—but Washington in summer must surely be the saddest spot on earth.

There are six principal public buildings in Washington, as to which no expense seems to have been spared, and in the construction of which a certain amount of success has been obtained. In most of these this success has been more or less marred by an independent deviation from recognized rules of architectural taste. These are the Capitol, the Post-office, the Patent-office, the Treasury, the President's house, and the Smithsonian Institute. The five first are Grecian, and the last in Washington is called—Romanesque. Had I been left to classify it by my own unaided lights, I should have called it bastard Gothic.

The Capitol is by far the most imposing; and though there is much about it with which I cannot but find fault, it certainly is imposing. The present building was, I think, commenced in 1815, the former Capitol having been destroyed by the English in the war of 1812–13. It was then finished according to the original plan, with a fine portico and well-proportioned pediment above it,—looking to the east. The outer flight of steps, leading up to this from the eastern approach, is good and in excellent taste. The expanse of the building to the right and left, as then arranged, was well proportioned, and, as far as we can now judge, the then existing dome was well proportioned also. As seen from the east the original building must have been in itself very fine. The stone is beautiful, being bright almost as marble, and I do not know that there was any great architectural defect to offend the eye. The figures in the pediment are mean. There is now in the Capitol a group apparently prepared for a pediment, which is by no means mean. I was informed that they were intended for this position; but they, on the other hand, are too good for such a place, and are also too numerous. This set of statues is by Crawford. Most of them are well known, and they are very fine. They now stand within the old chamber of the Representative House, and the pity is, that if elevated to such a position as that indicated, they can never be really seen. There are models of them all at West Point, and some of them I have seen at other places in marble. The Historical Society at New York has one or two of them. In and about the front of the Capitol there are other efforts of sculpture,—imposing in their size, and assuming, if not affecting, much in the attitudes chosen. Statuary at Washington runs too much on two subjects, which are repeated perhaps almost ad nauseam; one is that of a stiff, steady-looking, healthy, but ugly individual, with a square jaw and big jowl, which represents the great General; he does not prepossess the beholder, because he appears to be thoroughly ill-natured. And the other represents a melancholy, weak figure without any hair, but often covered with feathers, and is intended to typify the red Indian. The red Indian is generally supposed to be receiving comfort; but it is manifest that he never enjoys the comfort ministered to him. There is a gigantic statue of Washington, by Greenough, out in the grounds in front of the building. The figure is seated and holding up one of its arms towards the city. There is about it a kind of weighty magnificence; but it is stiff, ungainly, and altogether without life.

But the front of the original building is certainly grand. The architect who designed it must have had skill, taste, and nobility of conception; but even this was spoilt, or rather wasted, by the fact that the front is made to look upon nothing, and is turned from the city. It is as though the *façade* of the London Post-office had been made to face the Goldsmiths' Hall. The Capitol stands upon the side of a hill, the front occupying a much higher position than the back; consequently they who enter it from the back—and everybody does so enter it—are first called on to rise to the level of the lower floor by a stiff ascent of exterior steps, which are in no way grand or imposing, and then, having entered by a mean back-door, are instantly obliged to ascend again by another flight,—by stairs sufficiently appropriate to a back entrance, but altogether unfitted for the chief approach to such a building. It may, of course, be said that persons who are particular in such matters should go in at the front door and not at the back; but one must take these things as one finds them. The entrance by which the Capitol is approached is such as I have described. There are mean little brick chimneys at the left hand as one walks in, attached to modern bakeries which have been constructed in the basement for the use of the soldiers; and there is on the other hand the road by which waggons find their way to the underground region with fuel, stationery, and other matters desired by senators and representatives,—and at present by bakers also.

In speaking of the front I have spoken of it as it was originally designed and built. Since that period very heavy wings have been added to the pile; wings so heavy that they are or seem to be much larger than the original structure itself. This, to my thinking, has destroyed the symmetry of the whole. The wings, which in themselves are by no means devoid of beauty, are joined to the centre by passages so narrow that from exterior points of view the light can be seen through them. This robs the mass of all oneness, of all entirety as a whole, and gives a scattered straggling appearance where there should be a look of massiveness and integrity. The dome also has been raised, a double drum having been given to it. This is unfinished and should not therefore yet be judged; but I cannot think that the increased height will be an improvement. This again, to my eyes, appears to be straggling rather than massive. At a distance it commands attention, and to one journeying through the desert places of the city gives that idea of Palmyra which I have before mentioned.

Nevertheless, and in spite of all that I have said, I have had pleasure in walking backwards and forwards, and through the grounds which lie before the eastern front of the Capitol. The space for the view is ample, and the thing to be seen has points which are very grand. If the Capitol were finished and all Washington were built around it, no man would say that the house in which Congress sat disgraced the city.

Going west, but not due west, from the Capitol, Pennsylvania Avenue stretches in a right line to the Treasury Chambers. The distance is beyond a mile, and men say, scornfully, that the two buildings have been put so far apart in order to save the Secretaries who sit in the bureaux from a too rapid influx of members of Congress. This statement I by no means indorse; but it is undoubtedly the fact that both senators and representatives are very diligent in their calls upon gentlemen high in office. I have been present on some such occasions, and it has always seemed to me that questions of patronage have been paramount. This reach of Pennsylvania Avenue is the quarter for the best shops of Washington,—that is to say, the frequented side of it is so,—that side which is on your right as you leave the Capitol. Of the other side the world knows nothing. And very bad shops they are. I doubt whether there be any town in the world at all equal in importance to Washington, which is in such respects so ill provided. The shops are bad and dear. In saying this I am guided by the opinions of all whom I heard speak on the subject. The same thing was told me of the hotels. Hearing that the city was very full at the time of my visit—full to overflowing—I had obtained private rooms through a friend before I went there. Had I not done so, I might have lain in the streets, or have made one with three or four others in a small room at some third-rate inn. There had never been so great a throng in the town. I am bound to say that my friend did well for me. I found myself put up at the house of one Wormley, a coloured man, in I Street, to whose attention I can recommend any Englishman who may chance to want quarters in Washington. He has an hotel on one side of the street, and private lodging-houses on the other in which I found myself located. From what I heard of the hotels I conceived myself to be greatly in luck. Willard's is the chief of these, and the everlasting crowd and throng of men with which the halls and passages of the house were always full, certainly did not seem to promise either privacy or comfort. But then there are places in which privacy and comfort are not expected,—are hardly even desired,—and Washington is one of them.

The Post-office and the Patent-office lie a little away from Pennsylvania Avenue in F Street, and are opposite to each other. The Post-office is certainly a very graceful building. It is square, and hardly can be said to have any settled front or any grand entrance. It is not approached by steps, but stands flush on the ground, alike on each of the four sides. It is ornamented with Corinthian pilasters, but is not over ornamented. It is certainly a structure creditable to any city. The streets around it are all unfinished, and it is approached through seas of mud and sloughs of despond, which have been contrived, as I imagine, to lessen, if possible, the crowd of callers, and lighten in this way the overtasked officials within. That side by which the public in general were supposed to approach was, during my sojourn, always guarded by vast mountains of flour-barrels. Looking up at the windows of the building I perceived also that barrels were piled within, and then I knew that the Post-office had become a provision depôt for the army. The official arrangements here for the public were so bad, as to be absolutely barbarous. I feel some remorse in saying this, for I was myself treated with the utmost courtesy by gentlemen holding high positions in the office,—to which I was specially attracted by my own connection with the Post-office in England. But I do not think that such courtesy should hinder me from telling what I saw that was bad,—seeing that it would not hinder me from telling what I saw that was good. In Washington there is but one Post-office. There are no iron pillars or wayside letter-boxes, as are to be found in other towns of the Union;—no subsidiary offices at which stamps can be bought and letters posted. The distances of the city are very great, the means of transit through the city very limited, the dirt of the city ways un-rivalled in depth and tenacity; and yet there is but one Post-office. Nor is there any established system of letter-carriers. To those who desire it, letters are brought out and delivered by carriers who charge a separate porterage for that service; but the rule is that letters shall be delivered from the window. For strangers this is of course a necessity of their position; and I found that when once I had left instructions that my letters should be delivered, those instructions were carefully followed. Indeed nothing could exceed the civility of the officials within;—but so also nothing can exceed the barbarity of the arrange-ments without. The purchase of stamps I found to be utterly imprac-ticable. They were sold at a window in a corner, at which newspapers were also delivered, to which there was no regular ingress, and from which there was no egress. It would generally be deeply surrounded by a crowd of muddy soldiers, who would wait there patiently till time should enable them to approach the window. The delivery of letters was almost more tedious, though in that there was a method. The aspirants stood in a long line, *en cue,* as we are told by Carlyle that the bread-seekers used to approach the bakers' shops at Paris during the Revolution. This "cue" would sometimes project out into the street. The work inside was done very slowly. The clerk had no facility, by use of a desk or otherwise, for running through the letters under the initials denominated, but turned letter by letter through his hand. To one questioner out of ten would a letter be given. It no doubt may be said in excuse for this that the presence of the army round Washing-ton caused at that period special inconvenience; and that plea should of course be taken, were it not that a very trifling alteration in the management within would have remedied all the inconvenience. As a building the Washington Post-office is very good; as the centre of a most complicated and difficult department, I believe it to be well managed: but as regards the special accommodation given by it to the city in which it stands, much cannot, I think, be said in its favour.

Opposite to that which is, I presume, the back of the Post-office, stands the Patent-office. This also is a grand building, with a fine portico of Doric pillars at each of its three fronts. These are approached by flights of steps, more gratifying to the eye than to the legs. The whole structure is massive and grand, and, if the streets round it were finished, would be imposing. The utilitarian spirit of the nation has, however, done much toward marring the appearance of the building, by piercing it with windows altogether unsuited to it, both in number and size. The walls, even under the porticoes, have been so pierced, in order that the whole space might be utilized without loss of light; and the effect is very mean. The windows are small and without ornament,—something like a London window of the time of George III. The effect produced by a dozen such at the back of a noble Doric porch, looking down among the pillars, may be imagined.

In the interior of this building the Minister of the Interior holds his court, and of course also the Commissioners of Patents. Here is, in accordance with the name of the building, a museum of models of all patents taken out. I wandered through it, gazing with listless eye, now upon this, and now upon that; but to me, in my ignorance, it was no better than a large toy-shop. When I saw an ancient dusty white hat, with some peculiar appendange to it which was unintelligible, it was no more to me than any other old white hat. But had I been a man of science, what a tale it might have told! Wandering about through the Patent-office I also found a hospital for soldiers. A British officer was with me who pronounced it to be, in its kind, very good. At any rate it was sweet, airy, and large. In these days the soldiers had got hold of everything.

The Treasury Chambers is as yet an unfinished building. The front to the south has been completed; but that to the north has not been built. Here at the north stands as yet the old Secretary of State's office. This is to come down, and the Secretary of State is to be located in the new building, which will be added to the Treasury. This edifice will probably strike strangers more forcibly than any other in the town, both from its position and from its own character. It stands with its side to Pennsylvania Avenue, but the avenue here has turned round, and runs due north and south, having taken a twist, so as to make way for the Treasury and for the President's house, through both of which it must run had it been carried straight on throughout. These public offices stand with their side to the street, and the whole length is orna-

mented with an exterior row of Ionic columns raised high above the
footway. This is perhaps the prettiest thing in the city, and when the
front to the north has been completed, the effect will be still better.
The granite monoliths which have been used, and which are to be
used, in this building are very massive. As one enters by the steps to
the south there are two flat stones, one on each side of the ascent, the
surface of each of which is about 20 feet by 18. The columns are, I
think, all monoliths. Of those which are still to be erected, and which
now lie about in the neighbouring streets, I measured one or two—one
which was still in the rough I found to be 32 feet long by 5 feet broad,
and 4½ deep. These granite blocks have been brought to Washington
from the State of Maine. The finished front of this building, looking
down to the Potomac, is very good; but to my eyes this also has been
much injured by the rows of windows which look out from the building into the space of the portico.

The President's house—or the White House as it is now called all
the world over—is a handsome mansion fitted for the chief officer of a
great Republic, and nothing more. I think I may say that we have
private houses in London considerably larger. It is neat and pretty,
and with all its immediate outside belongings calls down no adverse
criticism. It faces on to a small garden, which seems to be always accessible to the public, and opens out upon that everlasting Pennsylvania
Avenue, which has now made another turn. Here in front of the White
House is President's Square, as it is generally called. The technical
name is, I believe, La Fayette Square. The houses round it are few in
number,—not exceeding three or four on each side, but they are
among the best in Washington, and the whole place is neat and well
kept. President's Square is certainly the most attractive part of the
city. The garden of the square is always open, and does not seem to
suffer from any public ill-usage; by which circumstance I am again
led to suggest that the gardens of our London squares might be thrown
open in the same way. In the centre of this one at Washington, immediately facing the President's house, is an equestrian statue of General Jackson. It is very bad; but that it is not nearly as bad as it might
be is proved by another equestrian statue,[4]—of General Washington,

4 Trollope may not have been aware that the two statues were created by the
same artist and that he was damning in one breath the two proudest works of
Clark Mills (1810–83), self-taught American sculptor and bronze-founder. Starting
life as a poor orphan boy, Mills had labored successively as a farm hand, a cabinet-
maker's apprentice, and a worker in plaster and concrete. From the last occupation
he learned to shape figures out of plastic materials and was thereby led to the decision to become a sculptor. Mills possessed a pioneer's resourcefulness and temer-

—erected in the centre of a small garden-plat at the end of Pennsylvania Avenue, near the bridge leading to Georgetown. Of all the statues on horseback which I ever saw, either in marble or bronze, this is by far the worst and most ridiculous. The horse is most absurd, but the man sitting on the horse is manifestly drunk. I should think the time must come when this figure at any rate will be removed.

I did not go inside the President's house, not having had while at Washington an opportunity of paying my personal respects to Mr. Lincoln. I had been told that this was to be done without trouble, but when I inquired on the subject I found that this was not exactly the case. I believe there are times when anybody may walk into the President's house without an introduction; but that, I take it, is not considered to be the proper way of doing the work. I found that something like a favour would be incurred, or that some disagreeable trouble would be given, if I made a request to be presented,—and therefore I left Washington without seeing the great man.

The President's house is nice to look at, but it is built on marshy ground, not much above the level of the Potomac, and is very unhealthy. I was told that all who live there become subject to fever and ague, and that few who now live there have escaped it altogether. This comes of choosing the site of a new city, and decreeing that it shall be

---

ity. Before he ever beheld a statue, he had cut a bust of John C. Calhoun from Carolina marble and sold it to the city of Charleston. In 1848 the national Jackson Monument Committee asked him to submit a design for an equestrian statue of the hero of the Battle of New Orleans. Although Mills had never seen either Jackson or an equestrian statue, he took the challenge and contrived a model that the committee decided was acceptable. Congress found the completed statue so pleasing that it voted the sculptor twenty thousand dollars beyond the twelve thousand agreed upon and awarded him a fifty-thousand-dollar contract for an equestrian representation of Washington.

The second statue was dedicated with ambitious ceremonies on Washington's birthday, 1860. The newspapers applauded Mills's new sculpture and his method of conveying "meaning" in his work. Though Trollope thought the horse merely absurd and the rider drunk, *Harper's Weekly* (February 25, 1860), possibly with some prompting from the sculptor himself, read the artist's purpose aright:

"The crowning figure in this great historical representation is the statue of the Father of his Country, represented as he appeared at the battle of Princeton, where, after attempting several times in vain to rally his troops, he put spurs to his horse and dashes [sic] up to the cannon's mouth. His terror-stricken horse stops and recoils, while the balls tear up the earth beneath his feet; but Washington, cool, calm, collected, and dignified, believing himself simply an instrument in the hands of Providence to work out the great problem of liberty, remains firmly seated, like a god upon his throne. The repose of the hero at this moment of imminent peril to his life contrasts admirably with the fearful agitation manifested by his noble but unreasoning steed, who is sustained by none of the considerations which impart courage to the hero and the Christian."

built on this or on that spot. Large cities, especially in these latter days, do not collect themselves in unhealthy places. Men desert such localities,—or at least do not congregate at them when their character is once known. But the poor President cannot desert the White House. He must make the most of the residence which the nation has prepared for him.

Of the other considerable public building of Washington, called the Smithsonian Institution, I have said that its style was bastard Gothic; by this, I mean that its main attributes are Gothic, but that liberties have been taken with it, which, whether they may injure its beauty or no, certainly are subversive of architectural purity. It is built of red stone, and is not ugly in itself. There is a very nice Norman porch to it, and little bits of Lombard Gothic have been well copied from Cologne. But windows have been fitted in with stilted arches, of which the stilts seem to crack and bend, so narrow are they and so high. And then the towers with high pinnacled roofs are a mistake,—unless indeed they be needed to give to the whole structure that name of Romanesque which it has assumed. The building is used for museums and lectures, and was given to the city by one James Smithson, an Englishman.[5] I cannot say that the city of Washington seems to be grateful, for all to whom I spoke on the subject hinted that the Institution was a failure. It is to be remarked that nobody in Washington, is proud of Washington, or of anything in it. If the Smithsonian Institution were at New York or at Boston, one would have a different story to tell.

There has been an attempt made to raise at Washington a vast obelisk to the memory of Washington,—the first in war and first in peace, as the country is proud to call him. This obelisk is a fair type of the city. It is unfinished,—not a third of it having as yet been erected,— and in all human probability ever will remain so. If finished it would be the highest monument of its kind standing on the face of the globe, —and yet, after all, what would it be even then as compared with one of the great pyramids? Modern attempts cannot bear comparison with those of the old world in simple vastness. But in lieu of simple vastness, the modern world aims to achieve either beauty or utility. By the Washington monument, if completed, neither would be achieved. An obelisk with the proportions of a needle may be very graceful; but an

[5] James Smithson, himself author of twenty-four scientific treatises mainly on mineral chemistry, made a bequest of more than a half-million dollars "to found at Washington . . . an establishment for the increase and diffusion of knowledge among men." The bequest was accepted by Congress in 1836.

obelisk which requires an expanse of flat-roofed, sprawling buildings for its base, and of which the shaft shall be as big as a cathedral tower, cannot be graceful. At present some third portion of the shaft has been built, and there it stands. No one has a word to say for it. No one thinks that money will ever again be subscribed for its completion. I saw somewhere a box of plate-glass kept for contribution for this purpose, and looking in perceived that two half-dollar pieces had been given;—but both of them were bad. I was told also that the absolute foundation of the edifice is bad;—that the ground, which is near the river and swampy, would not bear the weight intended to be imposed on it.

A sad and saddening spot was that marsh, as I wandered down on it all alone one Sunday afternoon. The ground was frozen and I could walk dry-shod, but there was not a blade of grass. Around me on all sides were cattle in great numbers—steers and big oxen—lowing in their hunger for a meal. They were beef for the army, and never again I suppose would it be allowed to them to fill their big maws and chew the patient cud. There, on the brown, ugly, undrained field, within easy sight of the President's house, stood the useless, shapeless, gracious pile of stones. It was as though I were looking on the genius of the city. It was vast, pretentious, bold, boastful with a loud voice, already taller by many heads than other obelisks, but nevertheless still in its infancy,—ugly, unpromising, and false. The founder of the monument had said, Here shall be the obelisk of the world! and the founder of the city had thought of his child somewhat in the same strain. It is still possible that both city and monument shall be completed; but at the present moment nobody seems to believe in the one or in the other. For myself I have much faith in the American character, but I cannot believe either in Washington city or in the Washington monument. The boast made has been too loud, and the fulfilment yet accomplished has been too small!

Have I as yet said that Washington was dirty in that winter of 1861–1862? Or, I should rather ask, have I made it understood that in walking about Washington one waded as deep in mud as one does in floundering through an ordinary ploughed field in November? There were parts of Pennsylvania Avenue which would have been considered heavy ground by most hunting-men, and through some of the remoter streets none but light weights could have lived long. This was the state of the town when I left it in the middle of January. On my arrival in the middle of December, everything was in a cloud of dust. One walked through an atmosphere of floating mud; for the dirt was ponderous and thick, and very palpable in its atoms. Then came a severe frost and a little snow; and if one did not fall while walking, it was very well. After that we had the thaw; and Washington assumed its normal winter condition. I must say that, during the whole of this time, the atmosphere was to me exhilarating; but I was hardly out of the doctor's hands while I was there,[6] and he did not support my theory as to the goodness of the air. "It is poisoned by the soldiers," he said, "and everybody is ill." But then my doctor was perhaps a little tinged with southern proclivities.

On the Virginian side of the Potomac stands a country-house called Arlington Heights, from which there is a fine view down upon the city. Arlington Heights is a beautiful spot,—having all the attractions of a fine park in our country. It is covered with grand timber. The ground is varied and broken, and the private roads about sweep here into a dell and then up a brae-side, as roads should do in such a domain. Below it was the Potomac, and immediately on the other stands the city of Washington. Any city seen thus is graceful; and the white stones of the big buildings when the sun gleams on them, showing the distant rows of columns, seem to tell something of great endeavour and of achieved success. It is a place from whence Washington should be seen by those who wish to think well of the present city and of its future prosperity. But is it not the case that every city is beautiful from a distance?

The house at Arlington Heights is picturesque, but neither large nor good. It has before it a high Greek colonnade, which seems to be almost bigger than the house itself. Had such been built in a city,—and many such a portico does stand in cities through the States,—it would be neither picturesques nor graceful; but here it is surrounded by timber, and as the columns are seen through the trees, they gratify the eye rather than offend it. The place did belong, and as I think does still belong, to the family of the Lees,—if not already confiscated. General Lee, who is or would be the present owner, bears high command in the army of the Confederalists, and knows well by what tenure he holds, or is likely to hold, his family property. The family were friends of General Washington, whose seat, Mount Vernon, stands about twelve miles lower down the river; and here, no doubt, Washington often stood, looking on the site he had chosen. If his spirit could stand there now and look around upon the masses of soldiers by which his capital is surrounded, how would it address the

---

[6] Trollope's personal afflictions at Washington probably had something to do with his dour outlook on the nation's capital. See section V of our Introduction.

city of his hopes? When he saw that every foot of the neighbouring soil was desecrated by a camp, or torn into loathsome furrows of mud by cannon and army waggons,—that agriculture was gone, and that every effort both of North and South was concentrated on the art of killing; when he saw that this was done on the very spot chosen by himself for the centre temple of an everlasting union, what would he then say as to that boast made on his behalf by his countrymen that he was first in war and first in peace? Washington was a great man, and I believe a good man. I, at any rate, will not belittle him. I think that he had the firmness and audacity necessary for a revolutionary leader, that he had honesty to preserve him from the temptations of ambition and ostentation, and that he had the good sense to be guided in civil matters by men who had studied the laws of social life and the theories of free government. He was *justus et tenax propositi;* [7] and in periods that might well have dismayed a smaller man, he feared neither the throne to which he opposed himself, nor the changing voices of the fellow-citizens for whose welfare he had fought. But sixty or seventy years will not suffice to give to a man the fame of having been first among all men. Washington did much, and I for one do not believe that his work will perish. But I have always found it difficult,—I may say impossible,—to sound his praises in his own land. Let us suppose that a courteous Frenchman ventures an opinion among Englishmen that Wellington was a great general, would he feel disposed to go on with his eulogium when encountered on two or three sides at once with such observations as the following:—"I should rather calculate he was; about the first that ever did live or ever will live. Why, he whipped your Napoleon everlasting whenever he met him. He whipped everybody out of the field. There warn't anybody ever lived was able to stand nigh him, and there won't come any like him again. Sir, I guess our Wellington never had his likes on your side of the water. Such men can't grow in a down-trodden country of slaves and paupers." Under such circumstances the Frenchman would probably be shut up. And when I strove to speak of Washington I generally found myself shut up also.

Arlington Heights, when I was at Washington, was the head-quarters of General M'Dowell, the General to whom is attributed—I believe most wrongfully—the loss of the battle of Bull's Run. The whole place was then one camp. The fences had disappeared. The gardens were trodden into mud. The roads had been cut to pieces, and new tracks made everywhere through the grounds. But the timber still

7 "just and firm of purpose."—Horace: *Odes,* III, iii, 1.

remained. Some no doubt had fallen, but enough stood for the ample
ornamentation of the place. I saw placards up, prohibiting the destruction of the trees, and it is to be hoped that they have been spared. Very
little in this way has been spared in the country all around.

Mount Vernon, Washington's own residence, stands close over the
Potomac, above six miles below Alexandria. It will be understood that
the capital is on the eastern, or Maryland side of the river, and that
Arlington Heights, Alexandria, and Mount Vernon are in Virginia.
The river Potomac divided the two old colonies, or States as they afterwards became; but when Washington was to be built, a territory, said
to be ten miles square, was cut out of the two States and was called the
district of Columbia. The greater portion of this district was taken
from Maryland, and on that the city was built. It comprised the
pleasant town of Georgetown, which is now a suburb—and the only
suburb—of Washington. The portion of the district on the Virginian
side included Arlington Heights, and went so far down the river as to
take in the Virginian city of Alexandria. This was the extreme western
point of the district; but since that arrangement was made, the State
of Virginia petitioned to have their portion of Columbia back again,
and this petition was granted. Now it is felt that the land on both
sides of the river should belong to the city, and the Government is
anxious to get back the Virginian section. The city and the immediate
vicinity are freed from all State allegiance, and are under the immediate rule of the United States Government,—having of course its own
municipality; but the inhabitants have no political power, as power is
counted in the States. They vote for no political officer, not even for
the President, and return no member to Congress, either as a senator or
as a representative. Mount Vernon was never within the district of
Columbia.

When I first made inquiry on the subject I was told that Mount
Vernon at that time was not to be reached;—that though it was not in
the hands of the rebels, neither was it in the hands of Northerners,
and that therefore strangers could not go there; but this, though it was
told to me and others by those who should have known the facts, was
not the case. I had gone down the river with a party of ladies, and we
were opposite to Mount Vernon; but on that occasion we were assured
we could not land. The rebels, we were told, would certainly seize the
ladies, and carry them off into Secessia. On hearing which the ladies
were of course doubly anxious to be landed. But our stern commander,
for we were on a Government boat, would not listen to their prayers,
but carried us instead on board the "Pensacola," a sloop-of-war which

was now lying in the river, ready to go to sea, and ready also to run the gauntlet of the rebel batteries which lined the Virginian shore of the river for many miles down below Alexandria and Mount Vernon. A sloop-of-war in these days means a large man-of-war, the guns of which are so big that they only stand on one deck, whereas a frigate would have them on two decks, and a line-of-battle ship on three. Of line-of-battle ships there will, I suppose, soon be none, as the 'Warrior' is only a frigate. We went over the "Pensacola," and I must say she was very nice, pretty, and clean. I have always found American sailors on their men-of-war to be clean and nice-looking,—as much so I should say as our own; but nothing can be dirtier, more untidy, or apparently more ill-preserved than all the appurtenances of their soldiers.

We landed also on this occasion at Alexandria, and saw as melancholy and miserable a town as the mind of man can conceive. Its ordinary male population, counting by the voters, is 1500, and of these 700 were in the southern army. The place had been made a hospital for northern soldiers, and no doubt the site for that purpose had been well chosen. But let any woman imagine what would be the feelings of her life while living in a town used as a hospital for the enemies against whom her absent husband was then fighting! Her own man would be away ill,—wounded, dying, for what she knew, without the comfort of any hospital attendance, without physic, with no one to comfort him; but those she hated, with a hatred much keener than his, were close to her hand, using some friend's house that had been forcibly taken, crawling out into the sun under her eyes, taking the bread from her mouth! Life in Alexandria at this time must have been sad enough. The people were all secessionists, but the town was held by the northern party. Through the lines, into Virginia, they could not go at all. Up to Washington they could not go without a military pass, not to be obtained without some cause given. All trade was at an end. In no town at that time was trade very flourishing; but here it was killed altogether,—except that absolutely necessary trade of bread. Who would buy boots or coats, or want new saddles, or waste money on books, in such days as these, in such a town as Alexandria? And then out of 1500 men, one-half had gone to fight the southern battles! Among the women of Alexandria secession would have found but few opponents.

It was here that a hot-brained young man, named Ellsworth, was killed in the early days of the rebellion. He was a colonel in the northern volunteer army, and on entering Alexandria found a secession flag flying at the chief hotel. Instead of sending up a corporal's guard to remove it, he rushed up and pulled it down with his own hand. As he descended, the landlord shot him dead, and one of his soldiers shot the landlord dead. It was a pity that so brave a lad, who had risen so high, should fall so vainly; but they have made a hero of him in America;—have inscribed his name on marble monuments, and counted him up among their great men. In all this their mistake is very great.[8] It is bad for a country to have no names worthy of monumental brass; but it is worse for a country to have monumental brasses covered with names which have never been made worthy of such honour. Ellsworth had shown himself to be brave and foolish. Let his folly be pardoned on the score of his courage, and there, I think, should have been an end of it.

I found afterwards that Mount Vernon was accessible, and I rode thither with some officers from the staff of General Heintzleman, whose outside pickets were stationed beyond the old place. I certainly should not have been well pleased had I been forced to leave the country without seeing the house in which Washington had lived and died. Till lately this place was owned and inhabited by one of the family, a Washington, descended from a brother of the General's; but it has now become the property of the country, under the auspices of Mr.

[8] Ephraim Elmer Ellsworth (1837–61) had at least showed industry and organizing ability of no common sort. Born a poor boy at Mechanicsville, New York, he had worked and studied his way to a lucrative business as a patent-solicitor in Chicago before he was twenty-one. When this business failed through the fraud of an associate, he studied law, supporting himself meanwhile by copying legal papers at night. Sensing the coming conflict, he turned to the study of military tactics and formed a Zouave corps in Chicago, thereby becoming, it is said, the introducer of the Zouave drill and organization into the United States. Ellsworth held the men of his corps to a rigid discipline, forbidding the use of spirituous liquors or tobacco and putting them through the severest gymnastic drills. The corps became nationally famous, winning signal honors through competitive exhibitions in various Eastern cities. Their young commander next organized an entire Zouave regiment and offered it to the Governor of Illinois for defense of the state in the event of war.

Ellsworth entered heartily into the campaign for Lincoln and by way of reward was apparently destined for a position in the War Department. With the fall of Fort Sumter, however, he left Washington for New York and there organized a Zouave regiment from the fire department. According to Appleton's *American Annual Cyclopædia* for 1861, he "drilled his regiment assiduously, and more than any other man could have done, tamed and controlled those restless and ungovernable spirits." On May 24, 1861, a day after his regiment had arrived in Alexandria, Ellsworth saw the Confederate flag flying above the Marshall House of that city. With two of his men he ascended to the roof, tore down the flag, and wrapped it about his body. The proprietor of the hotel, James W. Jackson, had concealed himself in a dark passageway. As Ellsworth came down the stairs, Jackson shot him through the breast. Funeral services were held at the White House, with the President as chief mourner.

Everett, by whose exertions was raised the money with which it was purchased. It is a long house, of two stories, built, I think, chiefly of wood, with a verandah, or rather long portico, attached to the front, which looks upon the river. There are two wings, or sets of outhouses, containing the kitchen and servants' rooms, which were joined by open wooden verandahs to the main building; but one of these verandahs has gone, under the influence of years. By these a semicircular sweep is formed before the front door, which opens away from the river, and towards the old prim gardens, in which, we were told, General Washington used to take much delight. There is nothing very special about the house. Indeed, as a house, it would now be found comfortless and inconvenient. But the ground falls well down to the river, and the timber, if not fine, is plentiful and picturesque. The chief interest of the place, however, is in the tomb of Washington and his wife. It must be understood that it was a common practice throughout the States to make a family burying-ground in any secluded spot on the family property. I have not unfrequently come across these in my rambles, and in Virginia I have encountered small, unpretending gravestones under a shady elm, dated as lately as eight or ten years back. At Mount Vernon there is now a cemetery of the Washington family; and there, in an open vault—a vault open, but guarded by iron grating—is the great man's tomb, and by his side the tomb of Martha his wife. As I stood there alone, with no one by to irritate me by assertion of the man's absolute supremacy, I acknowledged that I had come to the final resting-place of a great and good man,—of a man whose patriotism was, I believe, an honest feeling, untinged by any personal ambition of a selfish nature. That he was pre-eminently a successful man may have been due chiefly to the excellence of his cause, and the blood and character of the people who put him forward as their right arm in their contest; but that he did not mar that success by arrogance, or destroy the brightness of his own name by personal aggrandisement, is due to a noble nature and to the calm individual excellence of the man.

Considering the circumstances and history of the place, the position of Mount Vernon, as I saw it, was very remarkable. It lay exactly between the lines of the two armies. The pickets of the Northern army had been extended beyond it, not improbably with the express intention of keeping a spot so hallowed within the power of the northern Government. But since the war began it had been in the hands of the seceders. In fact, it stood there in the middle of the battle-field, on the very line of division between loyalism and secession. And this was the spot which Washington had selected as the heart and centre, and safest rallying homestead of the united nation which he left behind him. But Washington, when he resolved to found his capital on the banks of the Potomac, knew nothing of the glories of the Mississippi. He did not dream of the speedy addition to his already gathered constellations of those Western stars, of Wisconsin, Illinois, Minnesota, and Iowa; nor did he dream of Texas conquered, Louisiana purchased, and Missouri and Kansas rescued from the wilderness.

I have said that Washington was at that time,—the Christmas of 1861–1862,—a melancholy place. This was partly owing to the despondent tone in which so many Americans then spoke of their own affairs. It was not that the northern men thought that they were to be beaten, or that the southern men feared that things were going bad with their party across the river; but that nobody seemed to have any faith in anybody. Maclellan had been put up as the true man—exalted perhaps too quickly, considering the limited opportunities for distinguishing himself which fortune had thrown in his way; but now belief in Maclellan seemed to be slipping away. One felt that it was so from day to day, though it was impossible to define how or whence the feeling came. And then the character of the ministry fared still worse in public estimation. That Lincoln, the President, was honest, and that Chase, the Secretary of the Treasury, was able, was the only good that one heard spoken. At this time two Jonahs were specially pointed out as necessary sacrifices, by whose immersion into the comfortless ocean of private life the ship might perhaps be saved. These were Mr. Cameron, the Secretary of War, and Mr. Welles, the Secretary of the Navy. It was said that Lincoln, when pressed to rid his Cabinet of Cameron, had replied, that when a man was crossing a stream the moment was hardly convenient for changing his horse; but it came to that at last, that he found he must change his horse, even in the very sharpest run of the river. Better that than sit an animal on whose exertions he knew that he could not trust. So Mr. Cameron went, and Mr. Stanton became Secretary of War in his place. But Mr. Cameron, though put out of the Cabinet, was to be saved from absolute disgrace by being sent as Minister to Russia. I do not know that it would become me here to repeat the accusations made against Mr. Cameron, but it had long seemed to me that the maintenance in such a position, at such a time, of a gentleman who had to sustain such a universal absence of public confidence, must have been most detrimental to the army and the Government.

Men whom one met in Washington were not unhappy about the state of things, as I had seen men unhappy in the North and in the West. They were mainly indifferent, but with that sort of indifference which arises from a break down of faith in anything. "There was the army! Yes, the army! But what an army! Nobody obeyed anybody. Nobody did anything! Nobody thought of advancing! There were, perhaps, two hundred thousand men assembled round Washington; and now the effort of supplying them with food and clothing was as much as could be accomplished! But the contractors, in the meantime, were becoming rich. And then as to the Government! Who trusted it? Who would put their faith in Seward and Cameron? Cameron was now gone, it was true; and in that way the whole of the Cabinet would soon be broken up. As to Congress, what could Congress do? Ask questions which no one would care to answer, and finally get itself packed up and sent home." The President and the constitution fared no better in men's mouths. The former did nothing,—neither harm nor good; and as for the latter, it had broken down and shown itself to be inefficient. So men ate, and drank, and laughed, waiting till chaos should come, secure in the belief that the atoms into which their world would resolve itself, would connect themselves again in some other form without trouble on their part.

And at Washington I found no strong feeling against England and English conduct towards America. "We men of the world," a Washington man might have said, "know very well that everybody must take care of himself first. We are very good friends with you,—of course, and are very glad to see you at our table whenever you come across the water; but as for rejoicing at your joys, or expecting you to sympathize with our sorrows, we know the world too well for that. We are splitting into pieces, and of course that is gain to you. Take another cigar." This polite, fashionable, and certainly comfortable way of looking at the matter had never been attained at New York or Philadelphia, at Boston or Chicago. The northern provincial world of the States had declared to itself that those who were not with it were against it; that its neighbours should be either friends or foes; that it would understand nothing of neutrality. This was often mortifying to me, but I think I liked it better on the whole than the *laisser-aller* indifference of Washington.

Everybody acknowledged that society in Washington had been almost destroyed by the loss of the southern half of the usual sojourners in the city. The senators and members of Government, who heretofore had come from the southern States, had no doubt spent more money in the capital than their northern brethren. They and their families had been more addicted to social pleasures. They are the descendants of the old English Cavaliers, whereas the northern men have come from the old English Roundheads. Or if, as may be the case, the blood of the races has now been too well mixed to allow of this being said with absolute truth, yet something of the manners of the old forefathers has been left. The southern gentleman is more genial, less dry,—I will not say more hospitable, but more given to enjoy hospitality than his northern brother; and this difference is quite as strong with the women as with the men. It may therefore be understood that secession would be very fatal to the society of Washington. It was not only that the members of Congress were not there. As to very many of the representatives, it may be said that they do not belong sufficiently to Washington to make a part of its society. It is not every representative that is, perhaps, qualified to do so. But secession had taken away from Washington those who held property in the South—who were bound to the South by any ties, whether political or other; who belonged to the South by blood, education, and old habits. In very many cases—nay, in most such cases—it had been necessary that a man should select whether he would be a friend to the South, and therefore a rebel; or else an enemy to the South, and therefore untrue to all the predilections and sympathies of his life. Here has been the hardship. For such people there has been no neutrality possible. Ladies even have not been able to profess themselves simply anxious for peace and goodwill, and so to remain tranquil. They who are not for me are against me, has been spoken by one side and by the other. And I suppose that in all civil war it is necessary that it should be so. I heard of various cases in which father and son had espoused different sides in order that property might be retained both in the North and in the South. Under such circumstances it may be supposed that society in Washington would be considerably cut up. All this made the place somewhat melancholy.

CHAPTER XXI

CONGRESS

Iɴ the interior of the Capitol much space is at present wasted, but this arises from the fact of great additions to the original plan having been made. The two chambers,—that of the Senate and of the Representatives, are in the two new wings, on the middle, or what we call the first-floor. The entrance is made under a dome, to a large circular hall, which is hung around with surely the worst pictures by which a nation ever sought to glorify its own deeds. There are yards of paintings at Versailles which are bad enough; but there is nothing at Versailles comparable in villainy to the huge daubs which are preserved in this hall at the Capitol. It is strange that even self-laudatory patriotism should desire the perpetuation of such rubbish. When I was there the new dome was still in progress, and an ugly column of woodwork, required for internal support and affording a staircase to the top, stood in this hall. This of course was a temporary and necessary evil; but even this was hung around with the vilest of portraits.

From the hall, turning to the left, if the entrance be made at the front door, one goes to the new Chamber of Representatives, passing through that which was the old chamber. This is now dedicated to the exposition of various new figures by Crawford, and to the sale of tarts and gingerbread,—of very bad tarts and gingerbread. Let that old woman look to it, or let the House dismiss her. In fact this chamber is now but a vestibule to a passage, a second hall as it were, and thus thrown away. Changes probably will be made which will bring it into some use, or some scheme of ornamentation. From this a passage runs to the Representative Chamber, passing between those tell-tale windows, which, looking to the right and left, proclaim the tenuity of the building. The windows on one side, that looking to the east or front, should, I think, be closed. The appearance, both from the inside and from the outside, would be thus improved.

The Representative Chamber itself—which of course answers to our House of Commons—is a handsome, commodious room, admirably fitted for the purposes required. It strikes one as rather low, but I doubt if it were higher whether it would be better adapted for hearing. Even at present it is not perfect in this respect as regards the listeners in the gallery. It is a handsome, long chamber, lighted by skylights from the roof, and is amply large enough for the number to be accommodated. The Speaker sits opposite to the chief entrance, his desk being fixed against the opposite wall. He is thus brought nearer to the body of the men before him than is the case with our Speaker. He sits at a marble table, and the clerks below him are also accommodated with marble. Every representative has his own arm-chair, and his own desk before it. This may be done for a house consisting of about 240 members, but could hardly be contrived with us. These desks are arranged in a semicircular form, or in a broad horseshoe, and every member as he sits faces the Speaker. A score or so of little boys are always running about the floor, ministering to the members' wishes, carrying up petitions to the chair, bringing water to long-winded legislators, delivering and carrying out letters, and running with general messages. They do not seem to interrupt the course of business, and yet they are the liveliest little boys I ever saw. When a member claps his hands, indicating a desire for attendance, three or four will jockey for the honour. On the whole, I thought the little boys had a good time of it.

But not so the Speaker. It seemed to me that the amount of work falling upon the Speaker's shoulders was cruelly heavy. His voice was always ringing in my ears, exactly as does the voice of the croupier at a gambling-table who goes on declaring and explaining the results of the game, and who generally does so in sharp, loud, ringing tones, from which all interest in the proceeding itself seems to be excluded. It was just so with the Speaker in the House of Representatives. The debate was always full of interruptions; but on every interruption the Speaker asked the gentleman interrupted whether he would consent to be so treated. "The gentleman from Indiana has the floor." "The gentleman from Ohio wishes to ask the gentleman from Indiana a question." "The gentleman from Indiana gives permission." "The gentleman from Ohio!"—these last words being a summons to him of Ohio to get up and ask his question. "The gentleman from Pennsylvania rises to order." "The gentleman from Pennsylvania is in order." And then the House seems always to be voting, and the Speaker is always putting the question. "The gentlemen who agree to the amendment will say, Ay." Not a sound is heard. "The gentlemen who oppose the amendment will say, No." Again not a sound. "The Ayes have it," says the Speaker, and then he goes on again. All this he does with amazing rapidity, and is always at it with the same hard, quick, ringing, uninterested voice. The gentleman whom I saw in the chair was very clever, and quite up to the task. But as for dignity—! Perhaps it might be found that any great accession of dignity would impede the celerity of the work to be done, and that a closer copy of the British model might not on the whole increase the efficiency of the American machine.

When any matter of real interest occasioned a vote, the ayes and noes would be given aloud; and then, if there were a doubt arising from the volume of sound, the Speaker would declare that the "ayes" or the "noes" would seem to have it! And upon this a poll would be demanded. In such cases the Speaker calls on two members, who come forth and stand fronting each other before the chair, making a gangway. Through this the ayes walk like sheep, the tellers giving them an accelerating poke when they fail to go on with rapidity. Thus they are counted, and the noes are counted in the same way. It seemed to me that it would be very possible in a dishonest legislator to vote twice on any subject of great interest; but it may perhaps be the case that there are no dishonest legislators in the House of Representatives.

According to a list which I obtained, the present number of members is 173, and there are 63 vacancies occasioned by secession. New York returns 33 members, Pennsylvania 25, Ohio 21, Virginia 13, Massachusetts and Indiana 11, Tennessee and Kentucky 10, South Carolina 6, and so on, till Delaware, Kansas, and Florida return only 1 each. When the constitution was framed, Pennsylvania returned 8, and New York only 6; whereas Virginia returned 10, and South Carolina 5. From which may be gathered the relative rate of increase in population of the Free-soil States and the Slave States. All these States return two senators each to the other House, Kansas sending as many as New York. The work in the House begins at 12 noon, and is not often carried on late into the evening. Indeed this, I think, is never done till towards the end of the session.

The Senate House is in the opposite wing of the building, the position of the one house answering exactly to that of the other. It is somewhat smaller, but is, as a matter of course, much less crowded. There are 34 States, and therefore 68 seats and 68 desks only are required. These also are arranged in a horse-shoe form, and face the President; but there was a sad array of empty chairs when I was in Washington, nineteen or twenty seats being vacant in consequence of secession. In this house the Vice-President of the United States acts as President, but has by no means so hard a job of work as his brother on the other side of the way. Mr. Hannibal Hamlin, from Maine, now fills this chair. I was driven, while in Washington, to observe something amounting almost to a peculiarity in the Christian names of the gentlemen who were then administrating the Government of the country. Mr. Abraham Lincoln was the President, Mr. Hannibal Hamlin the Vice-President, Mr. Galusha Grow the Speaker of the Representatives, Mr. Salmon Chase the Secretary of the Treasury, Mr. Caleb Smith the Attorney-General, Mr. Simon Cameron the Secretary of War, and Mr. Gideon Welles the Secretary of the Navy.

In the Senate House, as in the other house, there are very commodious galleries for strangers, running round the entire chambers, and these galleries are open to all the world. As with all such places in the States, a large portion of them is appropriated to ladies. But I came at last to find that the word lady signified a female or a decently dressed man. Any arrangement for classes is in America impossible; the seats intended for gentlemen must as a matter of course be open to all men; but by giving up to the rougher sex half the amount of accommodation nominally devoted to ladies, the desirable division is to a certain exent made. I generally found that I could obtain admittance to the ladies' gallery if my coat were decent and I had gloves with me.

All the adjuncts of both these chambers are rich and in good keeping. The staircases are of marble, and the outside passages and lobbies are noble in size and in every way convenient. One knows well the trouble of getting into the House of Lords and House of Commons, and the want of comfort which attends one there; and an Englishman cannot fail to make comparisons injurious to his own country. It would not, perhaps, be possible to welcome all the world in London as is done in Washington, but there can be no good reason why the space given to the public with us should not equal that given in Washington. But, so far are we from sheltering the public, that we have made our House of Commons so small, that it will not even hold all its own members.

I had an opportunity of being present at one of their field-days in the Senate. Slidell and Mason had just then been sent from Fort Warren across to England in the Rinaldo. And here I may as well say what further there is for me to say about those two heroes. I was in Boston when they were taken, and all Boston was then full of them. I was at Washington when they were surrendered, and at Washington for a time their names were the only household words in vogue. To me it had, from the first, been a matter of certainty that England would demand the restitution of the men. I had never attempted to argue the matter on the legal points, but I felt, as though by instinct, that it would be so. First of all there reached us, by telegram, from Cape

Race, rumours of what the press in England was saying;—rumours of a meeting in Liverpool, and rumours of the feeling in London. And then the papers followed, and we got our private letters. It was some days before we knew what was actually the demand made by Lord Palmerston's cabinet; and during this time, through the five or six days which were thus passed, it was clear to be seen that the American feeling was undergoing a great change—or if not the feeling, at any rate the purpose. Men now talked of surrendering these Commissioners as though it were a line of conduct which Mr. Seward might find convenient; and then men went further, and said that Mr. Seward would find any other line of conduct very inconvenient. The newspapers, one after another, came round. That, under all the circumstances, the States Government behaved well in the matter no one, I think, can deny; but the newspapers, taken as a whole, were not very consistent and, I think, not very dignified. They had declared with throats of brass that these men should never be surrendered to perfidious Albion; but when it came to be understood that in all probability they would be so surrendered, they veered round without an excuse, and spoke of their surrender as of a thing of course. And thus, in the course of about a week, the whole current of men's minds was turned. For myself, on my first arrival at Washington, I felt certain that there would be war, and was preparing myself for a quick return to England; but from the moment that the first whisper of England's message reached us, and that I began to hear how it was received and what men said about it, I knew that I need not hurry myself. One met a minister here, and a senator there, and anon some wise diplomatic functionary. By none of these grave men would any secret be divulged; none of them had any secret ready for divulging. But it was to be read in every look of the eye, in every touch of the hand, and in every fall of the foot of each of them, that Mason and Slidell would go to England.

Then we had, in all the fulness of diplomatic language, Lord Russell's demand and Mr. Seward's answer. Lord Russell's demand was worded in language so mild, was so devoid of threat, was so free from anger, that at the first reading it seemed to ask for nothing. It almost disappointed by its mildness. Mr. Seward's reply, on the other hand, by its length of argumentation, by a certain sharpness of diction to which that gentleman is addicted in his State papers, and by a tone of satisfaction inherent through it all, seemed to demand more than he conceded. But, in truth, Lord Russell had demanded everything, and the United States Government had conceded everything.

I have said that the American Government behaved well in its mode of giving the men up, and I think that so much should be allowed to them on a review of the whole affair. That Captain Wilkes had no instructions to seize the two men is a known fact. He did seize them and brought them into Boston harbour, to the great delight of his countrymen. This delight I could understand, though of course I did not share it. One of these men had been the parent of the Fugitive Slave Law; [1] the other had been great in fostering the success of fili- bustering. Both of them were hot secessionists, and undoubtedly rebels. No two men on the continent were more grievous by their antecedents and present characters to all northern feeling. It is impossible to deny that they were rebels against the Government of their country. That Captain Wilkes was not on this account justified in seizing them is now a matter of history, but that the people of the loyal States should re- joice in their seizure was a matter of course. Wilkes was received with an ovation, which as regarded him was ill-judged and undeserved, but which in its spirit was natural. Had the President's Government at that moment disowned the deed done by Wilkes, and declared its in- tention of giving up the men unasked, the clamour raised would have been very great, and perhaps successful. We were told that the Ameri- can lawyers were against their doing so; and indeed there was such a shout of triumph that no ministry in a country so democratic could have ventured to go at once against it, and to do so without any ex- ternal pressure.

Then came the one ministerial blunder. The President put forth his message, in which he was cunningly silent on the Slidell and Mason affair; but to his message was appended, according to custom, the re- port from Mr. Welles, the Secretary of the Navy. In this report ap- proval was expressed of the deed done by Captain Wilkes. Captain Wilkes was thus in all respects indemnified, and the blame, if any, was taken from his shoulders and put on to the shoulders of that officer who was responsible for the Secretary's letter. It is true that in that letter the Secretary declared that in case of any future seizure the vessel seized must be taken into port, and so declared in animadverting on the fact that Captain Wilkes had not brought the "Trent" into port. But, nevertheless, Secretary Welles approved of Captain Wilkes's con- duct. He allowed the reasons to be good which Wilkes had put forward for leaving the ship, and in all respects indemnified the captain. Then

---

[1] James Murray Mason, as Senator for Virginia, had fostered the stringent Fu- gitive Slave Law of 1850. This law required not only Federal marshals but all good citizens of any state in the Union to aid in catching runaway slaves. Any person obstructing the capture of a slave was made liable to a fine of one thousand dollars.

the responsibility shifted itself to Secretary Welles; but I think it must be clear that the President, in sending forward that report, took that responsibility upon himself. That he is not bound to send forward the reports of his Secretaries as he receives them;—that he can disapprove them and require alteration, was proved at the very time by the fact that he had in this way condemned Secretary Cameron's report, and caused a portion of it to be omitted. Secretary Cameron had unfortunately allowed his entire report to be printed, and it appeared in a New York paper. It contained a recommendation with reference to the slave question most offensive to a part of the Cabinet, and to the majority of Mr. Lincoln's party. This, by order of the President, was omitted in the official way. It was certainly a pity that Mr. Welles's paragraph respecting the 'Trent' was not omitted also. The President was dumb on the matter, and that being so the Secretary should have been dumb also.

But when the demand was made the States Government yielded at once, and yielded without bluster. I cannot say I much admired Mr. Seward's long letter. It was full of smart special pleading, and savoured strongly, as Mr. Seward's productions always do, of the personal author. Mr. Seward was making an effort to place a great State paper on record, but the *ars celare artem* was altogether wanting; and, if I am not mistaken, he was without the art itself. I think he left the matter very much where he found it. The men however were to be surrendered, and the good policy consisted in this,—that no delay was sought, no diplomatic ambiguities were put into request. It was the opinion of very many that some two or three months might be gained by correspondence, and that at the end of that time things might stand on a different footing. If during that time the North should gain any great success over the South, the States might be in a position to disregard England's threats. No such game was played. The illegality of the arrest was at once acknowledged, and the men were given up,—with a tranquillity that certainly appeared marvellous after all that had so lately occurred.

Then came Mr. Sumner's field day. Mr. Charles Sumner is a senator from Massachusetts, known as a very hot abolitionist and as having been the victim of an attack made upon him in the Senate House by Senator Brookes.[2] He was also at the time of which I am writing Chair-

[2] On May 19 and 20, 1856 Charles Sumner gave the Senate a protracted speech, afterward entitled *The Crime against Kansas*. His language was extremely abusive, and he had aimed a good part of his attack at Andrew P. Butler of South Carolina, a senior Senator generally esteemed by both sides for his courtliness and his moderation. Senator Butler's nephew, Preston S. Brooks, a member of the House (not the

man of the Committee on Foreign Affairs, which position is as near akin to that of a British minister in Parliament as can be attained under the existing constitution of the States. It is not similar, because such chairman is by no means bound to the Government; but he has ministerial relations, and is supposed to be specially conversant with all questions relating to foreign affairs. It was understood that Mr. Sumner did not intend to find fault either with England or with the Government of his own country as to its management of this matter; or that, at least, such fault-finding was not his special object, but that he was desirous to put forth views which might lead to a final settlement of all difficulties with reference to the right of international search.

On such an occasion, a speaker gives himself very little chance of making a favourable impression on his immediate hearers if he reads his speech from a written manuscript. Mr. Sumner did so on this occasion, and I must confess that I was not edified. It seemed to me that he merely repeated, at greater length, the arguments which I had heard fifty times during the last thirty or forty days. I am told that the discourse is considered to be logical, and that it "reads" well. As regards the gist of it, or that result which Mr. Sumner thinks to be desirable, I fully agree with him, as I think will all the civilized world before many years have passed. If international law be what the lawyers say it is, international law must be altered to suit the requirements of modern civilization. By those laws, as they are construed, everything is to be done for two nations at war with each other; but nothing is to be done for all the nations of the world that can manage to maintain the peace. The belligerents are to be treated with every delicacy, as we treat our heinous criminals; but the poor neutrals are to be handled with unjust rigour, as we handle our unfortunate witnesses in order that the murderer may, if possible, be allowed to escape. Two men living in the same street choose to pelt each other across the way with brickbats, and the other inhabitants are denied the privileges

---

Senate), felt it his duty to avenge the slanders against his kinsman. On May 22 he caught Sumner writing letters at his desk in the Senate Chamber after that body had adjourned for the day, and struck a succession of blows on Sumner's bare head with a gutta-percha cane. Sumner was so severely injured that it took him over three years to recover.

While Brooks's action was generally approved in the South and several groups presented him with ornamental canes, the North was fiercely aroused. Indignation meetings were the order of the day. In New York five thousand people jammed the Tabernacle to hear an address and pass resolutions; Sumner's speech was sold as a pamphlet in tens of thousands of copies. Sumner became the martyr of the North and served more effectively in that capacity than he had ever done as an orator.

of the footpath lest they should interfere with the due prosecution of the quarrel! It is, I suppose, the truth, that we English have insisted on this right of search with more pertinacity than any other nation. Now in this case of Slidell and Mason we have felt ourselves aggrieved, and have resisted. Luckily for us there was no doubt of the illegality of the mode of seizure in this instance; but who will say that if Captain Wilkes had taken the "Trent" into the harbour of New York, in order that the matter might have been adjudged there, England would have been satisfied? Our grievance was, that our mail-packet was stopped on the seas while doing its ordinary beneficent work. And our resolve is, that our mail-packets shall not be so stopped with impunity. As we were high-handed in old days in insisting on this right of search, and as we are high-handed now in resisting a right of search, it certainly behoves us to see that we be just in our modes of proceeding. Would Captain Wilkes have been right according to the existing law if he had carried the "Trent" away to New York? If so, we ought not to be content with having escaped from such a trouble merely through a mistake on his part. Lord Russell says that the "Trent's" voyage was an innocent voyage. That is the fact that should be established;—not only that the voyage was, in truth, innocent, but that it should not be made out to be guilty by any international law. Of its real innocency all thinking men must feel themselves assured. But it is not only of the seizure that we complain, but of the search also. An honest man is not to be handled by a policeman while on his daily work, lest by chance a stolen watch should be in his pocket. If international law did give such power to all belligerents, international law must give it no longer. In the beginning of these matters, as I take it, the object was when two powerful nations were at war to allow the smaller fry of nations to enjoy peace and quiet, and to avoid if possible the general scuffle. Thence arose the position of a neutral. But it was clearly not fair that any such nation, having proclaimed its neutrality, should, after that, fetch and carry for either of the combatants to the prejudice of the other. Hence came the right of search, in order that unjust falsehood might be prevented. But the seas were not then bridged with ships as they are now bridged, and the laws as written were, perhaps, then practical and capable of execution. Now they are impracticable and not capable of execution. It will not, however, do for us to ignore them if they exist; and therefore they should be changed. It is, I think, manifest that our own pretensions as to the right of search must be modified after this. And now I trust I may finish my book without again naming Messrs. Slidell and Mason.

The working of the Senate bears little or no analogy to that of our House of Lords. In the first place, the senator's tenure there is not hereditary, nor is it for life. They are elected, and sit for six years. Their election is not made by the people of their States, but by the State legislature. The two Houses, for instance, of the State of Massachusetts meet together and elect by their joint vote to the vacant seat for their State. It is so arranged that an entirely new senate is not elected every sixth year. Instead of this a third of the number is elected every second year. It is a common thing for senators to be re-elected, and thus to remain in the House for twelve and sixteen years. In our Parliament the House of Commons has greater political strength and wider political action than the House of Lords; but in Congress the Senate counts for more than the House of Representatives in general opinion. Money bills must originate in the House of Representatives, but that is, I think, the only special privilege attaching to the public purse which the lower House enjoys over the upper. Amendments to such bills can be moved in the Senate; and all such bills must pass the Senate before they become law. I am inclined to think that individual members of the Senate work harder than individual representatives. More is expected of them, and any prolonged absence from duty would be more remarked in the Senate than in the other House. In our Parliament this is reversed. The payment made to members of the Senate is 3000 dollars, or 600l. per annum, and to a representative, 500l. per annum. To this is added certain mileage allowance for travelling backwards and forwards, between their own State and the Capitol. A senator, therefore, from California or Oregon has not altogether a bad place; but the halcyon days of mileage allowances are, I believe, soon to be brought to an end. It is quite within rule that the senator of to-day should be the representative of to-morrow. Mr. Crittenden, who was senator from Kentucky, is now a member of the Lower House from an electoral district in that State. John Quincy Adams went into the House of Representatives after he had been President of the United States.

Divisions in the Senate do not take place as in the House of Representatives. The ayes and noes are called for in the same way; but if a poll be demanded, the clerk of the House calls out the names of the different senators, and makes out lists of the votes according to the separate answers given by the members. The mode is certainly more dignified than that pursued in the other House, where during the ceremony of voting the members look very much like sheep being passed into their pens.

I heard two or three debates in the House of Representatives, and that one especially in which, as I have said before, a chapter was read out of the book of Joshua. The manner in which the Creator's name and the authority of His Word was bandied about the house on that occasion, did not strike me favourably. The question originally under debate was the relative power of the civil and military authority. Congress had desired to declare its ascendancy over military matters; but the army and the Executive generally had demurred to this,—not with an absolute denial of the rights of Congress, but with those civil and almost silent generalities with which a really existing Power so well knows how to treat a nominal Power. The ascendant wife seldom tells her husband in so many words that his opinion in the house is to go for nothing; she merely resolves that such shall be the case, and acts accordingly. An observer could not but perceive that in those days Congress was taking upon itself the part, not exactly of an obedient husband, but of a husband vainly attempting to assert his supremacy. "I have got to learn," said one gentleman after another, rising indignantly on the floor, "that the military authority of our generals is above that of this House." And then one gentleman relieved the difficulty of the position by branching off into an eloquent discourse against slavery, and by causing a chapter to be read out of the book of Joshua.

On that occasion the gentleman's diversion seemed to have the effect of relieving the House altogether from the embarrassment of the original question; but it was becoming manifest, day by day, that Congress was losing its ground, and that the army was becoming indifferent to its thunders:—that the army was doing so, and also that ministers were doing so. In the States, the President and his ministers are not in fact subject to any parliamentary responsibility. The President may be impeached, but the member of an opposition does not always wish to have recourse to such an extreme measure as impeachment. The ministers are not in the houses, and cannot therefore personally answer questions. Different large subjects, such as Foreign affairs, Financial affairs, and Army matters, are referred to Standing Committees in both houses; and these Committees have relations with the ministers. But they have no constitutional power over the ministers; nor have they the much more valuable privilege of badgering a minister hither and thither by *vivâ voce* questions on every point of his administration. The minister sits safe in his office—safe there for the term of the existing Presidency if he can keep well with the President; and therefore, even under ordinary circumstances, does not care much for the printed or written messages of Congress. But under circumstances so little ordinary as those of 1861–62, while Washington was surrounded by hundreds of thousands of soldiers, Congress was absolutely impotent. Mr. Seward could snap his fingers at Congress, and he did so. He could not snap his fingers at the army; but then he could go with the army,—could keep the army on his side by remaining on the same side with the army; and this, as it seemed, he resolved to do. It must be understood that Mr. Seward was not Prime Minister. The President of the United States has no Prime Minister,—or hitherto has had none. The Minister for Foreign Affairs has usually stood highest in the Cabinet, and Mr. Seward, as holding that position, was not inclined to lessen its authority. He was gradually assuming for that position the prerogatives of a Premier, and men were beginning to talk of Mr. Seward's ministry. It may easily be understood that at such a time the powers of Congress would be undefined, and that ambitious members of Congress would rise and assert on the floor, with that peculiar voice of indignation so common in parliamentary debate, "that they had got to learn," &c., &c., &c. It seemed to me that the lesson which they had yet to learn was then in the process of being taught to them. They were anxious to be told all about the mischance at Ball's Bluff,[3] but nobody would tell them anything about it. They wanted to know something of that blockade on the Potomac; but such knowledge was not good for them. "Pack them up in boxes, and send them home," one military gentleman said to me. And I began to think that something of the kind would be done, if they made themselves troublesome. I quote here the manner in which their questions, respecting the affair at Ball's Bluff, were answered by the Secretary of War. "The Speaker laid before the House a letter from the Secretary at War, in which he says that he has the honour to acknowledge the receipt of the resolution adopted on the 6th instant, to the effect that the answer of the department to the resolution passed on the second day of the session, is not responsive and satisfactory to the House, and requesting a further

[3] The disaster at Ball's Bluff (October 21, 1861) was a minor affair as battles go, resulting in less than a thousand Union casualties; but several circumstances, including the proximity to Washington, made Congress carry on an extended investigation. The result did not bear out Trollope's comments on the impotency of Congressional inquiries. Though the colonel who seems to have been responsible for the disaster died in the action, Congress made a scapegoat of Brigadier General Charles P. Stone. He was arrested and imprisoned without trial for 189 days. When finally faced with the charges against him, he cleared himself and was restored to his command. But the defamation of character that he had undergone had destroyed his usefulness to the army. He resigned his commission and later became chief of staff to the Khedive of Egypt.

answer. The Secretary has now to state that measures have been taken to ascertain who is responsible for the disastrous movement at Ball's Bluff, but that it is not compatible with the public interest to make known those measures at the present time."

In truth the days are evil for any Congress of debaters, when a great army is in camp on every side of them. The people had called for the army, and there it was. It was of younger birth than Congress, and had thrown its elder brother considerably out of favour, as has been done before by many a new-born baby. If Congress could amuse itself with a few set speeches, and a field-day or two, such as those afforded by Mr. Sumner, it might all be very well,—provided that such speeches did not attack the army. Over and beyond this, let them vote the supplies and have done with it. Was it probable that General Maclellan should have time to answer questions about Ball's Bluff,—and he with such a job of work on his hands? Congress could of course vote what committees of military inquiry it might please, and might ask questions without end; but we all know to what such questions lead, when the questioner has no power to force an answer by a penalty. If it might be possible to maintain the semblance of respect for Congress, without too much embarrassment to military secretaries, such semblance should be maintained; but if Congress chose to make itself really disagreeable, then no semblance could be kept up any longer. That, as far as I could judge, was the position of Congress in the early months of 1862; and that, under existing circumstances, was perhaps the only possible position that it could fill.

All this to me was very melancholy. The streets of Washington were always full of soldiers. Mounted sentries stood at the corners of all the streets with drawn sabres,—shivering in the cold and besmeared with mud. A military law came out that civilians might not ride quickly through the street. Military riders galloped over one at every turn, splashing about through the mud, and reminding one not unfrequently of John Gilpin.[4] Why they always went so fast, destroying

---

[4] By trade a "linen-draper bold," the hero of William Cowper's *The Diverting History of John Gilpin* was less than an accomplished horseman:

> So stooping down, as needs he must
> Who cannot sit upright,
> He grasped the mane with both his hands,
> And eke with all his might.

> His horse, who never in that sort
> Had handled been before,
> What thing upon his back had got
> Did wonder more and more.

their horses' feet on the rough stones, I could never learn. But I, as a civilian, given, as Englishmen are, to trotting, and furnished for the time with a nimble trotter, found myself harried from time to time by muddy men with sabres, who would dash after me, rattling their trappings, and bid me go at a slower pace. There is a building in Washington, built by private munificence and devoted, according to an inscription which it bears, "To the Arts." [5] It has been turned into an army clothing establishment. The streets of Washington, night and day, were thronged with army waggons. All through the city military huts and military tents were to be seen, pitched out among the mud and in the desert places. Then there was the chosen locality of the teamsters and their mules and horses—a wonderful world in itself; and all within the city! Here horses and mules lived,—or died,— *sub dio,*[6] with no slightest apology for a stable over them, eating their provender from off the waggons to which they were fastened. Here, there, and everywhere large houses were occupied as the head-quarters of some officer, or the bureau of some military official. At Washington and round Washington the army was everything. While this was so, is it to be conceived that Congress should ask questions about military matters with success?

All this, as I say, filled me with sorrow. I hate military belongings, and am disgusted at seeing the great affairs of a nation put out of their regular course. Congress to me is respectable. Parliamentary debates, be they ever so prosy,—as with us, or even so rowdy, as sometimes they have been with our cousins across the water,—engage my sympathies. I bow inwardly before a Speaker's chair, and look upon the elected representatives of any nation, as the choice men of the age. Those muddy, clattering dragoons, sitting at the corners of the streets with dirty woollen comforters round their ears, were to me hideous in the extreme. But there at Washington, at the period of which I am writing, I was forced to acknowledge that Congress was at a discount, and that the rough-shod generals were the men of the day. "Pack them up and send them in boxes to their several States." It would come to that, I thought, or to something like that unless Congress would consent to be submissive. "I have yet to learn—!" said indignant members, stamping with their feet on the floor of the house. One would have said that by that time the lesson might almost have been understood.

Up to the period of this civil war Congress has certainly worked well for the United States. It might be easy to pick holes in it;—to show

5 Probably the gallery of W. W. Corcoran.
6 "beneath the open sky."

that some members have been corrupt, others quarrelsome, and others
again impracticable. But when we look at the circumstances under
which it has been from year to year elected,—when we remember the
position of the newly-populated States from which the members have
been sent, and the absence throughout the country of that old tradi-
tionary class of Parliament men on whom we depend in England;
when we think how recent has been the elevation in life of the majority of those who are and must be elected,—it is impossible to deny
them praise for intellect, patriotism, good sense, and diligence. They
began but sixty years ago, and for sixty years Congress has fully answered the purpose for which it was established. With no antecedents
of grandeur, the nation, with its Congress, has made itself one of the
five great nations of the world. And what living English politician will
say even now, with all its troubles thick upon it, that it is the smallest
of the five? When I think of this, and remember the position in Europe
which an American has been able to claim for himself, I cannot but
acknowledge that Congress on the whole has been conducted with
prudence, wisdom, and patriotism.

The question now to be asked is this,—Have the powers of Congress been sufficient, or are they sufficient, for the continued maintenance of free government in the States under the constitution? I think
that the power given by the existing constitution to Congress can no
longer be held to be sufficient; and that if the Union be maintained
at all, it must be done by a closer assimilation of its congressional
system to that of our Parliament. But to that matter I must allude
again, when speaking of the existing constitution of the States.[7]

[7] The chapter is omitted in the present edition. See Appendix A.

CHAPTER XXII

THE CAUSES OF THE WAR

I HAVE seen various essays purporting to describe the causes of this civil war between the North and South; but they have generally been written with the view of vindicating either one side or the other, and have spoken rather of causes which should, according to the ideas of their writers, have produced peace, than of those which did, in the course of events, actually produce war. This has been essentially the case with Mr. Everett, who in his lecture at New York, on the 4th of July, 1860, recapitulated all the good things which the North has done for the South, and who proved—if he has proved anything—that the South should have cherished the North instead of hating it. And this was very much the case also with Mr. Motley in his letter to the "London Times" [1] That letter is good in its way, as is everything that comes from Mr. Motley, but it does not tell us why the war has existed. Why is it that eight millions of people have desired to separate themselves from a rich and mighty empire,—from an empire which was apparently on its road to unprecedented success, and which had already achieved wealth, consideration, power, and internal well-being?

One would be led to imagine from the essays of Mr. Everett and of Mr. Motley, that slavery has had little or nothing to do with it. I must acknowledge it to be my opinion that slavery in its various bearings has been the single and necessary cause of the war;—that slavery being there in the South, this war was only to be avoided by a voluntary division,—secession voluntary both on the part of North and South;—that in the event of such voluntary secession being not asked for, or if asked for not conceded, revolution and civil war became necessary,—were not to be avoided by any wisdom or care on the part of the North.

The arguments used by both the gentlemen I have named prove very clearly that South Carolina and her sister States had no right to secede under the constitution; that is to say, that it was not open to them peaceably to take their departure, and to refuse further alle-

[1] This letter by John Lothrop Motley (1814–77), American novelist, diplomat, and historian, was published as a thirty-six-page pamphlet in 1861. It was entitled *The Causes of the Civil War, a Letter to the London Times.*

giance to the President and Congress without a breach of the laws by which they were bound. For a certain term of years, namely, from 1781 to 1787, the different States endeavoured to make their way in the world, simply leagued together by certain articles of confederation. It was declared that each State retained its sovereignty, freedom, and independence; and that the said States then entered severally into a firm league of friendship with each other for their common defence. There was no President, no Congress taking the place of our Parliament, but simply a congress of delegates or ambassadors, two or three from each State, who were to act in accordance with the policy of their own individual States. It is well that this should be thoroughly understood, not as bearing on the question of the present war, but as showing that a loose confederation, not subversive of the separate independence of the States, and capable of being partially dissolved at the will of each separate State, was tried, and was found to fail. South Carolina took upon herself to act as she might have acted had that confederation remained in force; but that confederation was an acknowledged failure. National greatness could not be achieved under it, and individual enterprise could not succeed under it. Then in lieu of that, by the united consent of the thirteen States the present constitution was drawn up and sanctioned, and to that every State bound itself in allegiance. In that constitution no power of secession is either named or presumed to exist. The individual sovereignty of the States had, in the first instance, been thought desirable. The young republicans hankered after the separate power and separate name which each might then have achieved; but that dream had been found vain,— and therefore the States, at the cost of some fond wishes, agreed to seek together for national power, rather than run the risks entailed upon separate existence. I append to this volume the articles of confederation and the constitution of the United States,[2] as they who desire to look into this matter may be anxious to examine them without reference to other volumes. The latter alone is clear enough on the subject, but is strengthened by the former in proving that under the latter no State could possess the legal power of seceding.

But they who created the constitution, who framed the clauses, and gave to this terribly important work what wisdom they possessed, did not presume to think that it could be final. The mode of altering the constitution is arranged in the constitution. Such alterations must be proposed either by two-thirds of both the houses of the general Congress, or by the legislatures of two-thirds of the States; and must, when

---

[2] Omitted in the present edition. See Appendix A.

so proposed, be ratified by the legislatures of three-fourths of the States— (Article V). There can, I think, be no doubt that any alteration so carried would be valid; even though that alteration should go to the extent of excluding one or any number of States from the Union. Any division so made would be made in accordance with the constitution.

South Carolina and the southern States no doubt felt that they would not succeed in obtaining secession in this way, and therefore they sought to obtain the separation which they wanted by revolution, —by revolution and rebellion, as Naples has lately succeeded in her attempt to change her political status; as Hungary is looking to do; as Poland has been seeking to do any time since her subjection; as the revolted colonies of Great Britain succeeded in doing in 1776, whereby they created this great nation which is now undergoing all the sorrows of a civil war. The name of secession claimed by the South for this movement is a misnomer. If any part of a nationality or empire ever rebelled against the government established on behalf of the whole, South Carolina so rebelled when, on the 20th November, 1860, she put forth her ordinance of so-called secession; and the other southern States joined in that rebellion when they followed her lead. As to that fact, there cannot, I think, much longer be any doubt in any mind. I insist on this especially, repeating perhaps unnecessarily, opinions expressed in my first volume, because I still see it stated by English writers that the secession ordinance of South Carolina should have been accepted as a political act by the government of the United States. It seems to me that no government can in this way accept an act of rebellion without declaring its own functions to be beyond its own power.

But what if such rebellion be justifiable, or even reasonable? what if the rebels have cause for their rebellion? For no one will now deny that rebellion may be both reasonable and justifiable; or that every subject in the land may be bound in duty to rebel. In such case the government will be held to have brought about its own punishment by its own fault. But as government is a wide affair, spreading itself gradually, and growing in virtue or in vice from small beginnings,— from seeds slow to produce their fruits, it is much easier to discern the incidence of the punishment than the perpetration of the fault. Government goes astray by degrees, or sins by the absence of that wisdom which should teach rulers how to make progress, as progress is made by those whom they rule. The fault may be absolutely negative and have spread itself over centuries; may be, and generally has been, attributable to dull good men;—but not the less does the punishment come at a blow. The rebellion exists and cannot be put down,—will put down all that opposes it; but the government is not the less bound to make its fight. That is the punishment that comes on governing men or on a governing people, that govern not well or not wisely.

As Mr. Motley says in the paper to which I have alluded, "No man, on either side of the Atlantic, with Anglo-Saxon blood in his veins, will dispute the right of a people, or of any portion of a people, to rise against oppression, to demand redress of grievances, and in case of denial of justice to take up arms to vindicate the sacred principle of liberty. Few Englishmen or Americans will deny that the source of government is the consent of the governed, or that every nation has the right to govern itself according to its will. When the silent consent is changed to fierce remonstrance, revolution is impending. The right of revolution is indisputable. It is written on the whole record of our race. British and American history is made up of rebellion and revolution. Hampden, Pym, and Oliver Cromwell; Washington, Adams, and Jefferson, all were rebels." Then comes the question whether South Carolina and the Gulf States had so suffered as to make rebellion on their behalf justifiable or reasonable; or if not, what cause had been strong enough to produce in them so strong a desire for secession,—a desire which has existed for fully half the term through which the United States has existed as a nation, and so firm a resolve to rush into rebellion with the object of accomplishing that which they deemed not to be accomplished on other terms.

It must, I think, be conceded that the Gulf States have not suffered at all by their connection with the northern States; that in lieu of any such suffering, they owe all their national greatness to the northern States; that they have been lifted up by the commercial energy of the Atlantic States and by the agricultural prosperity of the western States, to a degree of national consideration and respect through the world at large, which never could have belonged to them standing alone. I will not trouble my readers with statistics which few would care to follow, but let any man of ordinary every-day knowledge turn over in his own mind his present existing ideas of the wealth and commerce of New York, Boston, Philadelphia, Chicago, Pittsburgh, and Cincinnati, and compare them with his ideas as to New Orleans, Charleston, Savannah, Mobile, Richmond, and Memphis. I do not name such towns as Baltimore and St. Louis, which stand in slave States, but which have raised themselves to prosperity by northern habits. If this be not sufficient, let him refer to population tables and tables of shipping and tonnage.

And of those southern towns which I have named the commercial wealth is of northern creation. The success of New Orleans as a city can be no more attributed to Louisianians than can that of the Havana to the men of Cuba, or of Calcutta to the natives of India. It has been a repetition of the old story, told over and over again through every century since commerce has flourished in the world; the tropics can produce,—but the men from the North shall sow and reap, and garner and enjoy. As the Creator's work has progressed, this privilege has extended itself to regions further removed and still further from southern influences. If we look to Europe, we see that this has been so in Greece, Italy, Spain, France, and the Netherlands; in England and Scotland; in Prussia and in Russia; and the Western world shows us the same story. Where is now the glory of the Antilles? where the riches of Mexico, and the power of Peru? They still produce sugar, guano, gold, cotton, coffee, almost whatever we may ask them,—and will continue to do so while held to labour under sufficient restraint; but where are their men, where are their books, where are their learning, their art, their enterprise? I say it with sad regret at the decadence of so vast a population; but I do say that the southern States of America have not been able to keep pace with their northern brethren;—that they have fallen behind in the race, and feeling that the struggle is too much for them, have therefore resolved to part.

The reasons put forward by the South for secession have been trifling almost beyond conception. Northern tariffs have been the first, and perhaps foremost. Then there has been a plea that the national exchequer has paid certain bounties to New England fishermen, of which the South has paid its share,—getting no part of such bounty in return. There is also a complaint as to the navigation laws,—meaning, I believe, that the laws of the States increase the cost of coast traffic by forbidding foreign vessels to engage in the trade, thereby increasing also the price of goods and confining the benefit to the North, which carries on the coasting trade of the country, and doing only injury to the South which has none of it. Then last, but not least, comes that grievance as to the Fugitive Slave Law. The law of the land as a whole, —the law of the nation,—requires the rendition from free States of all fugitive slaves. But the free States will not obey this law. They even pass State laws in opposition to it. "Catch your own slaves," they say, "and we will not hinder you; at any rate we will not hinder you officially. Of non-official hindrance you must take your chance. But we absolutely decline to employ our officers to catch your slaves." That list comprises, as I take it, the amount of southern official grievances.

Southern people will tell you privately of others. They will say that they cannot sleep happy in their beds, fearing lest insurrection should be roused among their slaves. They will tell you of domestic comfort invaded by northern falsehood. They will explain to you how false has been Mrs. Beecher Stowe. Ladies will fill your ears and your hearts too with tales of the daily efforts they make for the comfort of their "people," and of the ruin to those efforts which arises from the malice of the abolitionists. To all this you make some answer with your tongue that is hardly true,—for in such a matter courtesy forbids the plain truth. But your heart within answers truly, "Madam,—dear madam, your sorrow is great; but that sorrow is the necessary result of your position."

As to those official reasons, in what fewest words I can use I will endeavour to show that they come to nothing. The tariff—and a monstrous tariff it then was—was the ground put forward by South Carolina for secession, when General Jackson was President, and Mr. Calhoun was the hero of the South. Calhoun bound himself and his State to take certain steps towards secession at a certain day if that tariff were not abolished. The tariff was so absurd that Jackson and his Government were forced to abandon it,—would have abandoned it without any threat from Calhoun; but under that threat it was necessary that Calhoun should be defied. General Jackson proposed a compromise tariff, which was odious to Calhoun,—not on its own behalf, for it yielded nearly all that was asked, but as being subversive of his desire for secession. The President, however, not only insisted on his compromise, but declared his purpose of preventing its passage into law unless Calhoun himself, as senator, would vote for it. And he also declared his purpose, not, we may presume, officially, of hanging Calhoun if he took that step towards secession which he had bound himself to take in the event of the tariff not being repealed. As a result of all this Calhoun voted for the compromise, and secession for the time was beaten down. That was in 1832, and may be regarded as the commencement of the secession movement. The tariff was then a convenient reason, a ground to be assigned with a colour of justice, because it was a tariff admitted to be bad. But the tariff has been modified again and again since that; and the tariff existing when South Carolina seceded in 1860 had been carried by votes from South Carolina. The absurd Morrill tariff could not have caused secession, for it was passed without a struggle in the collapse of Congress occasioned by secession.

The bounty to fishermen was given to create sailors, so that a marine might be provided for the nation. I need hardly show that the national benefit would accrue to the whole nation for whose protection such sailors were needed. Such a system of bounties may be bad, but if so it was bad for the whole nation. It did not affect South Carolina otherwise than it affected Illinois, Pennsylvania, or even New York.

The navigation laws may also have been bad. According to my thinking such protective laws are bad; but they created no special hardship on the South. By any such a theory of complaint all sections of all nations have ground of complaint against any other section which receives special protection under any law. The drinkers of beer in England should secede because they pay a tax, whereas the consumers of paper pay none. The navigation laws of the States are no doubt injurious to the mercantile interests of the States. I at least have no doubt on the subject. But no one will think that secession is justified by the existence of a law of questionable expediency. Bad laws will go by the board if properly handled by those whom they pinch, as the navigation laws went by the board with us in England.

As to that Fugitive Slave Law, it should be explained that the grievance has not arisen from the loss of slaves. I have heard it stated that South Carolina, up to the time of the secession, had never lost a slave in this way—that is, by northern opposition to the Fugitive Slave Law; and that the total number of slaves escaping successfully into the northern States, and there remaining through the non-operation of this law, did not amount to five in the year. It has not been a question of property but of feeling. It has been a political point, and the South has conceived—and probably conceived truly—that this resolution on the part of northern States to defy the law with reference to slaves, even though in itself it might not be immediately injurious to southern property, was an insertion of the narrow end of the wedge. It was an action taken against slavery,—an action taken by men of the North against their fellow-countrymen in the South. Under such circumstances the sooner such countrymen should cease to be their fellows the better it would be for them. That, I take it, was the argument of the South; or at any rate that was its feeling.

I have said that the reasons given for secession have been trifling, and among them have so estimated this matter of the Fugitive Slave Law. I mean to assert that the ground actually put forward is trifling; —the loss, namely, of slaves to which the South has been subjected. But the true reason pointed at in this—the conviction, namely, that the North would not leave slavery alone, and would not allow it to remain as a settled institution—was by no means trifling. It has been this conviction on the part of the South, that the North would not live in amity with slavery, would continue to fight it under this banner or under that, would still condemn it as disgraceful to man and rebuke it as impious before God, which has produced rebellion and civil war —and will ultimately produce that division for which the South is fighting, and against which the North is fighting; and which, when accomplished, will give the North new wings, and will leave the South without political greatness or commercial success.

Under such circumstances I cannot think that rebellion on the part of the South was justified by wrongs endured or made reasonable by the prospect of wrongs to be inflicted. It is disagreeable, that having to live with a wife who is always rebuking one for some special fault; but the outside world will not grant a divorce on that account, especially if the outside world is well aware that the fault so rebuked is of daily occurrence. "If you do not choose to be called a drunkard by your wife," the outside world will say, "it will be well that you should cease to drink." Ah! but that habit of drinking when once acquired cannot easily be laid aside. The brain will not work, the organs of the body will not perform their functions, the blood will not run. The drunkard must drink till he dies. All that may be a good ground for divorce, the outside world will say; but the plea should be put in by the sober wife, not by the intemperate husband. But what if the husband takes himself off without any divorce and takes with him also his wife's property, her earnings, that on which he has lived and his children? It may be a good bargain still for her, the outside world will say; but she, if she be a woman of spirit, will not willingly put up with such wrongs. The South has been the husband drunk with slavery, and the North has been the ill-used wife.

Rebellion, as I have said, is often justifiable, but it is, I think, never justifiable on the part of a paid servant of that Government against which it is raised. We must at any rate feel that this is true of men in high places,—as regards those men to whom by reason of their offices it should specially belong to put down rebellion. Had Washington been the Governor of Virginia, had Cromwell been a minister of Charles, had Garibaldi held a marshal's baton under the Emperor of Austria or the King of Naples, those men would have been traitors as well as rebels. Treason and rebellion may be made one under the law, but the mind will always draw the distinction. I, if I rebel against the Crown, am not on that account necessarily a traitor. A betrayal of trust is, I take it, necessary to treason. I am not aware that Jefferson Davis is a traitor; but that Buchanan was a traitor admits, I think, of no doubt.[3]

3 See the note to page 9.

Under him and with his connivance, the rebellion was allowed to make its way. Under him and by his officers arms and ships, and men and money, were sent away from those points at which it was known that they would be needed if it were intended to put down the coming rebellion, and to those points at which it was known that they would be needed if it were intended to foster the coming rebellion. But Mr. Buchanan had no eager feeling in favour of secession. He was not of that stuff of which are made Davis and Toombs and Slidell. But treason was easier to him than loyalty. Remonstrance was made to him, pointing out the misfortunes which his action, or want of action, would bring upon the country. "Not in my time," he answered. "It will not be in my time." So that he might escape unscathed out of the fire, this chief ruler of a nation of thirty million of men was content to allow treason and rebellion to work their way! I venture to say so much here as showing how impossible it was that Mr. Lincoln's government, on its coming into office, should have given to the South,—not what the South had asked, for the South had not asked,—but what the South had taken; what the South had tried to filch. Had the South waited for secession till Mr. Lincoln had been in his chair, I could understand that England should sympathize with her. For myself I cannot agree to that scuttling of the ship by the captain on the day which was to see the transfer of his command to another officer.

The southern States were driven into rebellion by no wrongs inflicted on them; but their desire for secession is not on that account matter for astonishment. It would have been surprising had they not desired secession. Secession of one kind, a very practical secession, had already been forced upon them by circumstances. They had become a separate people, dissevered from the North by habits, morals, institutions, pursuits, and every conceivable difference in their modes of thought and action. They still spoke the same language, as do Austria and Prussia; but beyond that tie of language they had no bond but that of a meagre political union in their Congress at Washington. Slavery, as it had been expelled from the North, and as it had come to be welcomed in the South, had raised such a wall of difference, that true political union was out of the question. It would be juster, perhaps, to say that those physical characteristics of the South which had induced this welcoming of slavery, and those other characteristics of the North which had induced its expulsion, were the true causes of the difference. For years and years this has been felt by both, and the fight has been going on. It has been continued for thirty years, and almost always to the detriment of the South. In 1845 Florida and Texas were admitted into the Union as slave States. I think that no State had then been admited, as a free State, since Michigan, in 1836.[4] In 1846 Iowa was admitted as a free State, and from that day to this Wisconsin, California, Minnesota, Oregon, and Kansas have been brought into the Union; all as free States. The annexation of another slave State to the existing Union had become, I imagine, impossible—unless such object were gained by the admission of Texas. We all remember that fight about Kansas, and what sort of a fight it was! Kansas lies alongside of Missouri, a slave State, and is contiguous to no other State. If the free-soil party could, in the days of Pierce and Buchanan, carry the day in Kansas, it is not likely that they would be beaten on any new ground under such a President as Lincoln. We have all heard in Europe how southern men have ruled in the White House, nearly from the days of Washington downwards; or if not southern men, northern men, such as Pierce and Buchanan, with southern politics; and therefore we have been taught to think that the South has been politically the winning party. They have, in truth, been the losing party as regards national power. But what they have so lost they have hitherto recovered by political address and individual statecraft. The leading men of the South have seen their position, and have gone to their work with the exercise of all their energies. They organized the Democrat party so as to include the leaders among the northern politicians. They never begrudged to these assistants a full share of the good things of official life. They have been aided by the fanatical abolitionism of the North by which the Republican party has been divided into two sections. It has been fashionable to be a Democrat, that is, to hold southern politics, and unfashionable to be a Republican, or to hold anti-southern politics. In that way the South has lived and struggled on against the growing will of the population; but at last that will became too strong, and when Mr. Lincoln was elected, the South knew that its day was over.

It is not surprising that the South should have desired secession. It is not surprising that it should have prepared for it. Since the days of Mr. Calhoun its leaders have always understood its position with a fair amount of political accuracy. Its only chance of political life lay in prolonged ascendancy at Washington. The swelling crowds of Germans, by whom the western States were being filled, enlisted themselves to a man in the ranks of abolition. What was the acquisition of Texas

---

[4] Michigan was not formally admitted to the Union until January 26, 1837, after the settling of a boundary dispute with Ohio, but she had been organized as a state since 1835.

against such hosts as these? An evil day was coming on the southern politicians, and it behoved them to be prepared. As a separate nation, —a nation trusting to cotton, having in their hands, as they imagined, a monopoly of the staple of English manufacture, with a tariff of their own, and those rabid curses on the source of all their wealth no longer ringing in their ears, what might they not do as a separate nation? But as a part of the Union, they were too weak to hold their own if once their political finesse should fail them. That day came upon them, not unexpected, in 1860, and therefore they cut the cable.

And all this has come from slavery. It is hard enough, for how could the South have escaped slavery? How, at least, could the South have escaped slavery any time during these last thirty years? And is it, moreover, so certain that slavery is an unmitigated evil, opposed to God's will, and producing all the sorrows which have ever been produced by tyranny and wrong? It is here, after all, that one comes to the difficult question. Here is the knot which the fingers of men cannot open, and which admits of no sudden cutting with the knife. I have likened the slave-holding States to the drunken husband, and in so doing have pronounced judgment against them. As regards the state of the drunken man, his unfitness for partnership with any decent, diligent, well-to-do wife, his ruined condition, and shattered prospects, the simile, I think, holds good. But I refrain from saying, that as the fault was originally with the drunkard in that he became such, so also has the fault been with the slave States. At any rate I refrain from so saying here, on this page. That the position of a slave-owner is terribly prejudicial, not to the slave of whom I do not here speak, but to the owner; —of so much at any rate I feel assured. That the position is therefore criminal and damnable, I am not now disposed to take upon myself to assert.

The question of slavery in America cannot be handled fully and fairly by any one who is afraid to go back upon the subject, and take its whole history since one man first claimed and exercised the right of forcing labour from another man. I certainly am afraid of any such task; but I believe that there has been no period yet, since the world's work began, which such a practice has not prevailed in a large portion, probably in the largest portion of the world's work-fields. As civilization has made its progress, it has been the duty and delight, as it has also been the interest of the men at the top of affairs, not to lighten the work of the men below, but so to teach them that they should recognize the necessity of working without coercion. Emancipation of serfs and thralls, of bondsmen and slaves, has always meant this,—that men having been so taught, should then work without coercion. As men become educated and aware of the nature of the tenure on which they hold their life, they learn the fact that work is a necessity for them, and that it is better to work without coercion than with it. When men have learned this they are fit for emancipation, but they are hardly fit till they have learned so much.

In talking or writing of slaves, we always now think of the negro slave. Of us Englishmen it must at any rate be acknowledged that we have done what in us lay to induce him to recognize this necessity for labour. At any rate we acted on the presumption that he would do so, and gave him his liberty throughout all our lands at a cost which has never yet been reckoned up in pounds, shillings, and pence.[5] The cost never can be reckoned up, nor can the gain which we achieved in purging ourselves from the degradation and demoralization of such employment. We come into court with clean hands, having done all that lay with us to do to put down slavery both at home and abroad. But when we enfranchised the negroes, we did so with the intention, at least, that they should work as free men. Their share of the bargain in that respect they have declined to keep, wherever starvation has not been the result of such resolve on their part; and from the date of our emancipation, seeing the position which the negroes now hold with us, the southern States of America have learned to regard slavery as a permanent institution, and have taught themselves to regard it as a blessing, and not as a curse.

Negroes were first taken over to America because the white man could not work under the tropical heats, and because the native Indian would not work. The latter people has been, or soon will be, exterminated,—polished off the face of creation, as the Americans say,—which fate must, I should say in the long run, attend all non-working people. As the soil of the world is required for increasing population, the non-working people must go. And so the Indians have gone. The negroes under compulsion did work, and work well; and under their hands vast regions of the western tropics became fertile gardens. The fact that they were carried up into northern regions which from their nature did not require such aid, that slavery prevailed in New York and Massachusetts, does not militate against my argument. The exact limits of any great movement will not be bounded by its purpose. The heated wax which you drop on your letter spreads itself beyond the necessities of your seal. That these negroes would not have come to the

[5] Slavery was abolished in the British colonies by a bill passed in 1833. The planters were given compensation to a total sum of £20,000,000.

western world without compulsion, or having come, would not have worked without compulsion, is, I imagine, acknowledged by all. That they have multiplied in the western world and have there become a race happier, at any rate in all the circumstances of their life, than their still untamed kinsmen in Africa, must also be acknowledged. Who, then, can dare to wish that all that has been done by the negro immigration should have remained undone?

The name of slave is odious to me. If I know myself I would not own a negro though he could sweat gold on my behoof. I glory in that bold leap in the dark which England took with regard to her own West Indian slaves. But I do not see the less clearly the difficulty of that position in which the southern States have been placed; and I will not call them wicked, impious, and abominable, because they now hold by slavery, as other nations have held by it at some period of their career. It is their misfortune that they must do so now,—now, when so large a portion of the world has thrown off the system, spurning as base and profitless all labour that is not free. It is their misfortune, for henceforth they must stand alone, with small rank among the nations, whereas their brethren of the North will still "flame in the forehead of the morning sky."

When the present constitution of the United States was written,— the merit of which must probably be given mainly to Madison and Hamilton, Madison finding the French democratic element, and Hamilton the English conservative element,—this question of slavery was doubtless a great trouble. The word itself is not mentioned in the constitution. It speaks not of a slave, but of a "person held to service or labour." It neither sanctions, nor forbids slavery. It assumes no power in the matter of slavery; and under it, at the present moment, all Congress voting together, with the full consent of the legislatures of thirty-three States, could not constitutionally put down slavery in the remaining thirty-fourth State. In fact the constitution ignored the subject.

But nevertheless Washington, and Jefferson from whom Madison received his inspiration, were opposed to slavery. I do not know that Washington ever took much action in the matter, but his expressed opinion is on record. But Jefferson did so throughout his life. Before the declaration of independence he endeavoured to make slavery illegal in Virginia. In this he failed, but long afterwards, when the United States was a nation, he succeeded in carrying a law by which the further importation of slaves into any of the States was prohibited after a certain year—1820. When this law was passed, the framers of it considered that the gradual abolition of slavery would be secured. Up to that period the negro population in the States had not been self-maintained. As now in Cuba, the numbers had been kept up by new importations, and it was calculated that the race, when not recruited from Africa, would die out. That this calculation was wrong we now know, and the breeding-grounds of Virginia have been the result.

At that time there were no cotton-fields. Alabama and Mississippi were outlying territories. Louisiana had been recently purchased, but was not yet incorporated as a State. Florida still belonged to Spain, and was all but unpopulated. Of Texas no man had yet heard. Of the slave States, Virginia, the two Carolinas, and Georgia were alone wedded to slavery. Then the matter might have been managed. But under the constitution as it had been framed, and with the existing powers of the separate States, there was not even then open any way by which slavery could be abolished other than by the separate action of the States; nor has there been any such way opened since. With slavery these southern States have grown and become fertile. The planters have thriven, and the cotton-fields have spread themselves. And then came emancipation in the British islands. Under such circumstances and with such a lesson, could it be expected that the southern States should learn to love abolition?

It is vain to say that slavery has not caused secession, and that slavery has not caused the war. That, and that only has been the real cause of this conflict, though other small collateral issues may now be put forward to bear the blame. Those other issues have arisen from this question of slavery, and are incidental to it and a part of it. Massachusetts, as we all know, is democratic in its tendencies, but South Carolina is essentially aristocratic. This difference has come of slavery. A slave country, which has progressed far in slavery, must be aristocratic in its nature,—aristocratic and patriarchal. A large slave-owner from Georgia may call himself a democrat,—may think that he reveres republican institutions, and may talk with American horror of the thrones of Europe; but he must in his heart be an aristocrat. We, in England, are apt to speak of republican institutions, and of universal suffrage which is perhaps the chief of them, as belonging equally to all the States. In South Carolina there is not and has not been any such thing. The electors for the President there are chosen not by the people, but by the legislature; and the votes for the legislature are limited by a high property qualification. A high property qualification is required for a member of the House of Representatives in South Carolina;—four hundred freehold acres of land and ten negroes is one qualification. Five hundred pounds clear of debt is another qualification;—for, where a sum of money is thus named, it is given in English money. Russia and England are not more unlike in their political and social feelings than are the real slave States and the real free-soil States. The gentlemen from one and from the other side of the line have met together on neutral ground, and have discussed political matters without flying frequently at each other's throats, while the great question on which they differed was allowed to slumber. But the awakening has been coming by degrees, and now the South had felt that it was come. Old John Brown, who did his best to create a servile insurrection at Harper's Ferry, has been canonized through the North and West, to the amazement and horror of the South. The decision in the "Dred Scott" case, given by the Chief Justice of the Supreme Court of the United States, has been received with shouts of execration through the North and West. The southern gentry have been Uncle-tommed into madness. It is no light thing to be told daily by your fellow-citizens, by your fellow-representatives, by your fellow-senators, that you are guilty of the one damning sin that cannot be forgiven. All this they could partly moderate, partly rebuke, and partly bear as long as political power remained in their hands; but they have gradually felt that that was going, and were prepared to cut the rope and run as soon as it was gone.

Such, according to my ideas, have been the causes of the war. But I cannot defend the South. As long as they could be successful in their schemes for holding the political power of the nation, they were prepared to hold by the nation. Immediately those schemes failed, they were prepared to throw the nation overboard. In this, there has undoubtedly been treachery as well as rebellion. Had these politicians been honest,—though the political growth of Washington has hardly admitted of political honesty,—but had these politicians been even ordinarily respectable in their dishonesty, they would have claimed secession openly before Congress, while yet their own President was at the White House. Congress would not have acceded. Congress itself could not have acceded under the constitution; but a way would have been found, had the southern States been persistent in their demand. A way, indeed, has been found; but it has lain through fire and water, through blood and ruin, through treason and theft, and the downfall of national greatness. Secession will, I think, be accomplished, and the southern Confederation of States will stand something higher in the world than Mexico and the republics of Central America. Her cotton monopoly will have vanished, and her wealth will have been wasted.

I think that history will agree with me in saying that the northern States had no alternative but war. What concession could they make? Could they promise to hold their peace about slavery? And had they so promised, would the South have believed them? They might have conceded secession; that is, they might have given all that would have been demanded. But what individual chooses to yield to such demands; and if not an individual,—then what people will do so? But in truth they could not have yielded all that was demanded. Had secession been granted to South Carolina and Georgia, Virginia would have been coerced to join those States by the nature of her property, and with Virginia Maryland would have gone, and Washington, the capital. What may be the future line of division between the North and the South I will not pretend to say; but that line will probably be dictated by the North. It may still be hoped that Missouri, Kentucky, Virginia, and Maryland will go with the North, and be rescued from slavery. But had secession been yielded, had the prestige of success fallen to the lot of the South, those States must have become southern.

While on this subject of slavery—for in discussing the cause of the war, slavery is the subject that must be discussed—I cannot forbear to say a few words about the negroes of the North American States. The republican party of the North is divided into two sections, of which one may be called abolitionist, and the other non-abolitionist. Mr. Lincoln's government presumes itself to belong to the latter, though its tendencies towards abolition are very strong. The abolition party is growing in strength daily. It is but a short time since Wendell Phillips could not lecture in Boston without a guard of police. Now, at this moment of my writing, he is a popular hero. The very men who, five years since, were accustomed to make speeches, strong as words could frame them, against abolition, are now turning round, and if not preaching abolition, are patting the backs of those who do so. I heard one of Mr. Lincoln's cabinet declare old John Brown to be a hero and a martyr. All the Protestant Germans are abolitionists,— and they have become so strong a political element in the country that many now declare that no future President can be elected without their aid. The object is declared boldly. No long political scheme is asked for, but instant abolition is wanted; abolition to be declared while yet the war is raging. Let the slaves of all rebels be declared free; and all slave-owners in the seceding States are rebels!

One cannot but ask what abolition means, and to what it would lead. Any ordinance of abolition now pronounced would not effect the emancipation of the slaves, but might probably effect a servile insurrection. I will not accuse those who are preaching this crusade of any desire for so fearful a scourge on the land. They probably calculate that an edict of abolition once given would be so much done towards the ultimate winning of the battle. They are making their hay while their sun shines. But if they could emancipate those four million slaves, in what way would they then treat them? How would they feed them? In what way would they treat the ruined owners of the slaves, and the acres of land which would lie uncultivated? Of all subjects with which a man can be called on to deal, it is the most difficult. But a New England abolitionist talks of it as though no more were required than an open path for his humanitarian energies. "I could arrange it all to-morrow morning," a gentleman said to me, who is well known for his zeal in this cause!

Arrange it all to-morrow morning,—abolition of slavery having become a fact during the night! I should not envy that gentleman his morning's work. It was bad enough with us, but what were our numbers compared with those of the southern States? We paid a price for the slaves, but no price is to be paid in this case. The value of the property would probably be lowly estimated at 100*l.* a piece for men, women, and children, or four hundred million pounds for the whole population. They form the wealth of the South; and if they were bought, what should be done with them? They are like children. Every slave-owner in the country,—every man who has had aught to do with slaves,—will tell the same story. In Maryland and Delaware are men who hate slavery, who would be only too happy to enfranchise their slaves; but the negroes who have been slaves are not fit for freedom. In many cases, practically, they cannot be enfranchised. Give them their liberty, starting them well in the world at what expense you please, and at the end of six months they will come back upon your hands for the means of support. Everything must be done for them. They expect food and clothes, and instruction as to every simple act of life, as do children. The negro domestic servant is handy at his own work; no servant more so; but he cannot go beyond that. He does not comprehend the object and purport of continued industry. If he have money he will play with it,—will amuse himself with it. If he have none, he will amuse himself without it. His work is like a schoolboy's task; he knows it must be done, but never comprehends that the doing of it is the very end and essence of his life. He is a child in all things, and the extent of prudential wisdom to which he ever attains is to disdain emancipation, and cling to the security of his bondage. It is true enough that slavery has been a curse. Whatever may have been its effect on the negroes, it has been a deadly curse upon the white masters.

The preaching of abolition during the war is to me either the deadliest of sins or the vainest of follies. Its only immediate result possible would be servile insurrection. That is so manifestly atrocious, —a wish for it would be so hellish, that I do not presume the preachers of abolition to entertain it. But if that be not meant, it must be intended that an act of emancipation should be carried throughout the slave Sates,—either in their separation from the North, or after their subjection and consequent reunion with the North. As regards the States while in secession, the North cannot operate upon their slaves any more than England can operate on the slaves of Cuba. But if a reunion is to be a precursor of emancipation, surely that reunion should be first effected. A decision in the northern and western mind on such a subject cannot assist in obtaining that reunion,—but must militate against the practicability of such an object. This is so well understood, that Mr. Lincoln and his government do not care to call themselves abolitionists.*

Abolition, in truth, is a political cry. It is the banner of defiance opposed to secession. As the differences between the North and South have grown with years, and have swelled to the proportions of national antipathy, southern nullification has amplified itself into secession, and northern free-soil principles have burst into this growth of abolition. Men have not calculated the results. Charming pictures are drawn for you of the negro in a state of Utopian bliss, owning his own hoe and eating his own hog; in a paradise, where everything is bought and sold, except his wife, his little ones, and himself. But the enfranchised negro has always thrown away his hoe, has eaten any man's hog but his own,—and has too often sold his daughter for a dollar when any such market has been open to him.

I confess that this cry of abolition has been made peculiarly displeasing to me, by the fact that the northern abolitionist is by no means willing to give even to the negro who is already free that position in

* President Lincoln has proposed a plan for the emancipation of slaves in the border States, and for compensation to the owners. His doing so proves that he regards present emancipation in the Gulf States as quite out of the question. It also proves that he looks forward to the recovery of the border States for the North, but that he does not look forward to the recovery of the Gulf States.

[Lincoln, who had for some time been advocating such a plan, induced Congress on April 10, 1862 to pass a resolution that "the United States ought to coöperate with any State which may adopt gradual abolishment of slavery, giving to such State pecuniary aid." The definitive proclamation of emancipation freeing all slaves in the Union was not issued until January 1, 1863.—EDS.]

the world which alone might tend to raise him in the scale of human beings,—if anything can so raise him and make him fit for freedom. The abolitionists hold that the negro is the white man's equal. I do not. I see, or think that I see, that the negro is the white man's inferior through laws of nature. That he is not mentally fit to cope with white men,—I speak of the full-blooded negro,—and that he must fill a position simply servile. But the abolitionist declares him to be the white man's equal. But yet, when he has him at his elbow, he treats him with a scorn which even the negro can hardly endure. I will give him political equality, but not social equality, says the abolitionist. But even in this he is untrue. A black man may vote in New York, but he cannot vote under the same circumstances as a white man. He is subjected to qualifications which in truth debar him from the poll. A white man votes by manhood suffrage, providing he has been for one year an inhabitant of his State; but a man of colour must have been for three years a citizen of the State, and must own a property qualification of 50l. free of debt. But political equality is not what such men want, nor indeed is it social equality. It is social tolerance and social sympathy; and these are denied to the negro. An American abolitionist would not sit at table with a negro. He might do so in England at the house of an English duchess; but in his own country the proposal of such a companion would be an insult to him. He will not sit with him in a public carriage if he can avoid it. In New York I have seen special street-cars for coloured people. The abolitionist is struck with horror when he thinks that a man and a brother should be a slave; but when the man and the brother has been made free, he is regarded with loathing and contempt. All this I cannot see with equanimity. There is falsehood in it from the beginning to the end. The slave as a rule is well treated,—gets all he wants and almost all he desires. The free negro as a rule is ill treated, and does not get that consideration which alone might put him in the worldly position for which his advocate declares him to be fit. It is false throughout,—this preaching. The negro is not the white man's equal by nature. But to the free negro in the northern States this inequality is increased by the white man's hardness to him.

In a former book, which I wrote some few years since, I expressed an opinion as to the probable destiny of this race in the West Indies.[6] I will not now go over that question again. I then divided the inhabitants of those islands into three classes,—the white, the black, and the

[6] Trollope had written on this subject at considerable length in Chapters iv and v of *The West Indies and the Spanish Main* (1859).

coloured, taking a nomenclature which I found there prevailing. By coloured men I alluded to mulattoes, and all those of mixed European and African blood. The word "coloured," in the States, seems to apply to the whole negro race, whether full-blooded or half-blooded. I allude to this now because I wish to explain that, in speaking of what I conceive to be the intellectual inferiority of the negro race, I allude to those of pure negro descent,—or of descent so nearly pure as to make the negro element manifestly predominant. In the West Indies, where I had more opportunity of studying the subject, I always believed myself able to tell a negro from a coloured man. Indeed the classes are to a great degree distinct there, the greater portion of the retail trade of the country being in the hands of the coloured people. But in the States I have been able to make no such distinction. One sees generally neither the rich yellow of the West Indian mulatto, nor the deep oily black of the West Indian negro. The prevailing hue is a dry, dingy brown,—almost dusty in its dryness. I have observed but little difference made between the negro and the half-caste,—and no difference in the actual treatment. I have never met in American society any man or woman in whose veins there can have been presumed to be any taint of African blood. In Jamaica they are daily to be found in society.

Every Englishman probably looks forward to the accomplishment of abolition of slavery at some future day. I feel as sure of it as I do of the final judgment. When or how it shall come I will not attempt to foretell. The mode which seems to promise the surest success and the least present or future inconvenience, would be an edict enfranchising all female children born after a certain date, and all their children. Under such an arrangement the negro population would probably die out slowly,—very slowly. What might then be the fate of the cotton-fields of the Gulf States, who shall dare to say? It may be that coolies from India and from China will then have taken the place of the negro there, as they probably will have done also in Guiana and the West Indies.

CHAPTER XXIII

WASHINGTON TO ST. LOUIS

THOUGH I had felt Washington to be disagreeable as a city, yet I was almost sorry to leave it when the day of my departure came. I had allowed myself a month for my sojourn in the capital, and I had stayed a month to the day. Then came the trouble of packing up, the necessity of calling on a long list of acquaintances one after another, the feeling that bad as Washington might be, I might be going to places that were worse, a conviction that I should get beyond the reach of my letters, and a sort of affection which I had acquired for my rooms. My landlord, being a coloured man, told me that he was sorry I was going. Would I not remain? Would I come back to him? Had I been comfortable? Only for so and so or so and so, he would have done better for me. No white American citizen, occupying the position of landlord, would have condescended to such comfortable words. I knew the man did not in truth want me to stay, as a lady and gentlemen were waiting to go in the moment I went out; but I did not the less value the assurance. One hungers and thirsts after such civil words among American citizens of this class. The clerks and managers at hotels, the officials at railway stations, the cashiers at banks, the women in the shops;—ah! they are the worst of all. An American woman who is bound by her position to serve you,—who is paid in some shape to supply your wants, whether to sell you a bit of soap or bring you a towel in your bedroom at an hotel,—is, I think, of all human creatures, the most insolent. I certainly had a feeling of regret at parting with my coloured friend,—and some regret also as regards a few that were white.

As I drove down Pennsylvania Avenue, through the slush and mud, and saw, perhaps for the last time, those wretchedly dirty horse sentries who had refused to allow me to trot through the streets, I almost wished that I could see more of them. How absurd they looked, with a whole kit of rattletraps strapped on their horses' backs behind them, —blankets, coats, canteens, coils of rope, and, always at the top of everything else, a tin pot! No doubt these things are all necessary to a mounted sentry, or they would not have been there; but it always seemed as though the horse had been loaded gipsy-fashion, in a manner that I may perhaps best describe as higgledy-piggledy, and that there was a want of military precision in the packing. The man would have looked more graceful, and the soldier more warlike, had the pannikin been made to assume some rigidly fixed position, instead of dangling among the ropes. The drawn sabre, too, never consorted well with the dirty outside woollen wrapper which generally hung loose from the man's neck. Heaven knows, I did not begrudge him his comforter in that cold weather, or even his long, uncombed shock of hair; but I think he might have been made more spruce, and I am sure that he could not have looked more uncomfortable. As I went, however, I felt for him a sort of affection, and wished in my heart of hearts that he might soon be enabled to return to some more congenial employment.

I went out by the Capitol, and saw that also, as I then believed, for the last time. With all its faults it is a great building, and, though unfinished, is effective; its very size and pretension give it a certain majesty. What will be the fate of that vast pile, and of those other costly public edifices at Washington, should the South succeed wholly in their present enterprise? If Virginia should ever become a part of the southern republic, Washington cannot remain the capital of the northern republic. In such case it would be almost better to let Maryland go also, so that the future destiny of that unfortunate city may not be a source of trouble, and a stumbling block of opprobrium. Even if Virginia be saved, its position will be most unfortunate.

I fancy that the railroads in those days must have been doing a very prosperous business. From New York to Philadelphia, thence on to Baltimore, and again to Washington, I had found the cars full; so full that sundry passengers could not find seats. Now, on my return to Baltimore, they were again crowded. The stations were all crowded. Luggage-trains were going in and out as fast as the rails could carry them. Among the passengers almost half were soldiers. I presume that these were men going on furlough, or on special occasions; for the regiments were of course not received by ordinary passenger trains. About this time a return was called for by Congress of all the moneys paid by the government, on account of the army, to the lines between New York and Washington. Whether or no it was ever furnished I did not hear; but it was openly stated that the colonels of regiments received large gratuities from certain railway companies for the regiments passing over their lines. Charges of a similar nature were made against officers, contractors, quartermasters, paymasters, generals, and cabinet ministers. I am not prepared to say that any of these men had dirty hands. It was not for me to make inquiries on such matters. But the continuance and universality of the accusations were dreadful. When everybody is suspected of being dishonest, dishonesty almost ceases to be regarded as disgraceful.

I will allude to a charge made against one member of the cabinet, because the circumstances of the case were all acknowledged and proved.[1] This gentleman employed his wife's brother-in-law to buy ships, and the agent so employed pocketed about 20,000*l.* by the transaction in six months. The excuse made was that this profit was in accordance with the usual practice of the ship-dealing trade, and that it was paid by the owners who sold, and not by the government which bought. But in so vast an agency the ordinary rate of profit on such business became an enormous sum; and the gentleman who made the plea must surely have understood that that 20,000*l.* was in fact paid by the government. It is the purchaser, and not the seller, who in fact pays all such fees. The question is this,—Should the government have paid so vast a sum for one man's work for six months? And if so, was it well that that sum should go into the pocket of a near relative of the Minister whose special business it was to protect the government?

American private soldiers are not pleasant fellow-travellers. They are loud and noisy, and swear quite as much as the army could possibly have sworn in Flanders. They are, moreover, very dirty; and each man, with his long, thick great-coat, takes up more space than is intended to be allotted to him. Of course I felt that if I chose to travel in a country while it had such a piece of business on its hands, I could not expect that everything should be found in exact order. The matter for wonder, perhaps, was that the ordinary affairs of life were so little disarranged, and that any travelling at all was practicable. Nevertheless the fact remains that American private soldiers are not agreeable fellow-travellers.

It was my present intention to go due west across the country into Missouri, skirting, as it were, the line of the war which had now extended itself from the Atlantic across into Kansas. There were at this time three main armies,—that of the Potomac, as the army of Virginia was called, of which Maclellan held the command; that of Kentucky, under General Buell, who was stationed at Louisville on the Ohio; and the army on the Mississippi, which had been under Fremont, and of which General Halleck now held the command. To these were opposed the three rebel armies of Beauregard, in Virginia; of Johnston, on the borders of Kentucky and Tennessee; and of Price, in Missouri. There was also a fourth army in Kansas, west of Missouri, under General

[1] Trollope returns to this matter, and names names, in pages 437-8.

Hunter; and while I was in Washington another general, supposed by some to be the "coming man," was sent down to Kansas to participate in General Hunter's command. This was General Jim Lane, who resigned a seat in the Senate in order that he might undertake this military duty. When he reached Kansas, having on his route made sundry violent abolition speeches, and proclaimed his intention of sweeping slavery out of the southwestern States, he came to loggerheads with his superior officer respecting their relative positions.

On my arrival at Baltimore, I found the place knee-deep in mud and slush and half-melted snow. It was then raining hard,—raining dirt, not water, as it sometimes does. Worse weather for soldiers out in tents could not be imagined,—nor for men who were not soldiers, but who nevertheless were compelled to leave their houses. I only remained at Baltimore one day, and then started again, leaving there the greater part of my baggage. I had a vague hope,—a hope which I hardly hoped to realize,—that I might be able to get through to the South. At any rate I made myself ready for the chance by making my travelling impediments as light as possible, and started from Baltimore, prepared to endure all the discomfort which lightness of baggage entails. My route lay over the Alleghanies by Pittsburg and Cincinnati, and my first stopping-place was at Harrisburg, the political capital of Pennsylvania. There is nothing special at Harrisburg to arrest any traveller; but the local legislature of the State was then sitting, and I was desirous of seeing the Senate and Representatives of at any rate one State, during its period of vitality.

In Pennsylvania the General Assembly, as the joint legislature is called, sits every year, commencing their work early in January, and continuing till it be finished. The usual period of sitting seems to be about ten weeks. In the majority of States, the legislature only sits every other year. In this State it sits every year, and the representatives are elected annually. The senators are elected for three years, a third of the body being chosen each year. The two chambers were ugly, convenient rooms, arranged very much after the fashion of the halls of Congress at Washington. Each member had his own desk, and his own chair. They were placed in the shape of a horse-shoe, facing the chairman, before whom sat three clerks. In neither house did I hear any set speech. The voices of the Speaker and of the clerks of the houses were heard more frequently than those of the members; and the business seemed to be done in a dull, serviceable, methodical manner, likely to be useful to the country, and very uninteresting to the gentlemen engaged. Indeed, at Washington also, in Congress, it seemed to me that there was much less of set speeches than in our House of Commons. With us there are certain men whom it seems impossible to put down, and by whom the time of Parliament is occupied from night to night, with advantage to no one and with satisfaction to none but themselves. I do not think that the evil prevails to the same extent in America, either in Congress or in the State legislatures. As regards Washington, this good result may be assisted by a salutary practice which, as I was assured, prevails there. A member gets his speech printed at the government cost, and sends it down free by post to his constituents, without troubling either the house with hearing it, or himself with speaking it. I cannot but think that the practice might be copied with success on our side of the water.

The appearance of the members of the legislature of Pennsylvania did not impress me very favourably. I do not know why we should wish a legislator to be neat in his dress, and comely, in some degree, in his personal appearance. There is no good reason, perhaps, why they should have cleaner shirts than their outside brethren, or have been more particular in the use of soap and water, and brush and comb. But I have an idea that if ever our own Parliament becomes dirty, it will lose its prestige; and I cannot but think that the Parliament of Pennsylvania would gain an accession of dignity by some slightly increased devotion to the Graces. I saw in the two houses but one gentleman, a senator, who looked like a Quaker; but even he was a very untidy Quaker.

I paid my respects to the Governor,[2] and found him briskly employed in arranging the appointments of officers. All the regimental appointments to the volunteer regiments,—and that is practically to the whole body of the army,*—are made by the State in which the regiments are mustered. When the affair commenced, the captains and lieutenants were chosen by the men; but it was found that this would not do. When the skeleton of a State militia only was required, such an arrangement was popular and not essentially injurious; but now that war had become a reality, and that volunteers were required to obey discipline, some other mode of promotion was found necessary. As far as I could understand, the appointments were in the hands of the State Governor, who however was expected in the selection of the superior officers to be guided by the expressed wishes of the regiment,

---

[2] Andrew Gregg Curtin (1815?-94), one of the most eminent of the "war governors."

* The army at this time consisted nominally of 660,000 men, of whom only 20,000 were regulars.

when no objection existed to such a choice. In the present instance the Governor's course was very thorny. Certain unfinished regiments were in the act of being amalgamated;—two perfect regiments being made up from perhaps five imperfect regiments, and so on. But though the privates had not been forthcoming to the full number for each expected regiment, there had been no such dearth of officers, and consequently the present operation consisted in reducing their number.

Nothing can be much uglier than the State House at Harrisburg, but it commands a magnificent view of one of the valleys into which the Alleghany mountains is broken. Harrisburg is immediately under the range, probably at its finest point, and the railway running west from the town to Pittsburg, Cincinnati, and Chicago passes right over the chain. The line has been magnificently engineered, and the scenery is very grand. I went over the Alleghanies in mid-winter when they were covered with snow, but even when so seen they were very fine. The view down the valley from Altoona, a point near the summit, must in summer be excessively lovely. I stopped at Altoona one night with the object of getting about among the hills, and making the best of the winter view; but I found it impossible to walk. The snow had become frozen and was like glass. I could not progress a mile in any way. With infinite labour I climbed to the top of one little hill, and when there became aware that the descent would be very much more difficult. I did get down, but should not choose to describe the manner in which I accomplished the descent.

In running down the mountains to Pittsburg an accident occurred which in any other country would have thrown the engine off the line, and have reduced the carriages behind the engine to a heap of ruins. But here it had no other effect that that of delaying us for three or four hours. The tire of one of the heavy driving wheels flew off, and in the shock the body of the wheel itself was broken, one spoke and a portion of the circumference of the wheel was carried away, and the steam-chamber was ripped open. Nevertheless the train was pulled up, neither the engine nor any of the carriage got off the line, and the men in charge of the train seemed to think very lightly of the matter. I was amused to see how little was made of the affair by any of the passengers. In England a delay of three hours would in itself produce a great amount of grumbling, or at least many signs of discomfort and temporary unhappiness. But here no one said a word. Some of the younger men got out and looked at the ruined wheel; but most of the passengers kept their seats, chewed their tobacco, and went to sleep.

In all such matters an American is much more patient than an Englishman. To sit quiet, without speech, and ruminate in some contorted position of body comes to him by nature. On this occasion I did not hear a word of complaint—nor yet a word of surprise or thankfulness that the accident had been attended with no serious result. "I have got a furlough for ten days," one soldier said to me. "And I have missed every connection all through from Washington here. I shall have just time to turn round and go back when I get home." But he did not seem to be in any way dissatisfied. He had not referred to his relatives when he spoke of "missing his connections," but to his want of good fortune as regarded railway travelling. He had reached Baltimore too late for the train on to Harrisburg, and Harrisburg too late for the train on to Pittsburg. Now he must again reach Pittsburg too late for his further journey. But nevertheless he seemed to be well pleased with his position.

Pittsburg is the Merthyr-Tydvil of Pennsylvania,—or perhaps I should better describe it as an amalgamation of Swansea, Merthyr-Tydvil, and South Shields. It is without exception the blackest place which I ever saw. The three English towns which I have named are very dirty, but all their combined soot and grease and dinginess do not equal that of Pittsburg. As regards scenery it is beautifully situated, being at the foot of the Alleghany mountains, and at the juncture of the two rivers Monongahela and Alleghany. Here, at the town, they come together and form the river Ohio. Nothing can be more picturesque than the site; for the spurs of the mountains come down close round the town, and the rivers are broad and swift, and can be seen for miles from heights which may be reached in a short walk. Even the filth and wondrous blackness of the place are picturesque when looked down upon from above. The tops of the churches are visible, and some of the larger buildings may be partially traced through the thick, brown, settled smoke. But the city itself is buried in a dense cloud. The atmosphere was especially heavy when I was there, and the effect was probably increased by the general darkness of the weather. The Monongahela is crossed by a fine bridge, and on the other side the ground rises at once, almost with the rapidity of a precipice; so that a commanding view is obtained down upon the town and the two rivers and the different bridges, from a height immediately above them. I was never more in love with smoke and dirt than when I stood here and watched the darkness of night close in upon the floating soot which hovered over the housetops of the city. I cannot say that I saw the sun

set, for there was no sun. I should say that the sun never shone at Pittsburg,—as foreigners who visit London in November declare that the
sun never shines there.

Walking along the river-side I counted thirty-two steamers, all
beached upon the shore with their bows towards the land,—large boats,
capable probably of carrying from one to two hundred passengers
each, and about 300 tons of merchandise. On inquiry I found that
many of these were not now at work. They were resting idle, the trade
down the Mississippi below St. Louis having been cut off by the war.
Many of them, however, were still running, the passage down the river
being open to Wheeling in Virginia, to Portsmouth, Cincinnati and
the whole of South Ohio, to Louisville in Kentucky, and to Cairo in
Illinois, where the Ohio joins the Mississippi. The amount of traffic
carried on by these boats while the country was at peace within itself
was very great, and conclusive as to the increasing prosperity of the
people. It seems that everybody travels in America, and that nothing is
thought of distance. A young man will step into a car and sit beside
you, with that easy, careless air which is common to a railway passenger in England who is passing from one station to the next; and on con-
versing with him you will find that he is going seven or eight hundred
miles. He is supplied with fresh newspapers three or four times a day
as he passes by the towns at which they are published; he eats a large
assortment of gum-drops and apples, and is quite as much at home as
in his own house. On board the river boats it is the same with him,
with this exception, that when there he can get whisky when he wants
it. He knows nothing of the ennui of travelling, and never seems to
long for the end of his journey, as travellers do with us. Should his
boat come to grief upon the river, and lie by for a day or a night, it
does not in the least disconcert him. He seats himself upon three chairs,
takes a bite of tobacco, thrusts his hands into his trousers pockets and
revels in an elysium of his own.

I was told that the stockholders in these boats were in a bad way
at the present time. There were no dividends going. The same story
was repeated as to many and many an investment. Where the war
created business, as it had done on some of the main lines of railroad
and in some special towns, money was passing very freely; but away
from this, ruin seemed to have fallen on the enterprise of the country.
Men were not broken-hearted, nor were they even melancholy; but
they were simply ruined. That is nothing in the States, so long as the
ruined man has the means left to him of supplying his daily wants till
he can start himself again in life. It is almost the normal condition of

the American man in business; and therefore I am inclined to think that when this war is over, and things begin to settle themselves into new grooves, commerce will recover herself more quickly there than she would do among any other people. It is so common a thing to hear of an enterprise that has never paid a dollar of interest on the original outlay,—of hotels, canals, railroads, banks, blocks of houses, &c., that never paid even in the happy days of peace,—that one is tempted to disregard the absence of dividends, and to believe that such a trifling accident will not act as any check on future speculation. In no country has pecuniary ruin been so common as in the States; but then in no country is pecuniary ruin so little ruinous. "We are a recuperative people," a west-country gentleman once said to me. I doubted the propriety of his word, but I acknowledged the truth of his assertion.

Pittsburg and Alleghany, which latter is a town similar in its nature to Pittsburg on the other side of the river of the same name, regard themselves as places apart; but they are in effect one and the same city. They live under the same blanket of soot, which is woven by the joint efforts of the two places. Their united population is 135,-000, of which Alleghany owns about 50,000. The industry of the towns is of that sort which arises from a union of coal and iron in the vicinity. The Pennsylvania coalfields are the most prolific in the Union; and Pittsburg is therefore great, exactly as Merthyr-Tydvil and Birmingham are great. But the foundry-work at Pittsburg is more nearly allied to the heavy, rough works of the Welsh coal metropolis than to the finish and polish of Birmingham.

"Why cannot you consume your own smoke?" I asked a gentleman there. "Fuel is so cheap that it would not pay," he answered. His idea of the advantage of consuming smoke was confined to the question of its paying as a simple operation in itself. The consequent cleanliness and improvement in the atmosphere had not entered into his calculations. Any such result might be a fortuitous benefit, but was not of sufficient importance to make any effort in that direction expedient on its own account. "Coal was burned," he said, "in the foundries at something less than two dollars a ton; while that was the case, it could not answer the purpose of any iron-founder to put up an apparatus for the consumption of smoke." I did not pursue the argument any further, as I perceived that we were looking at the matter from two different points of view.

Everything in the hotel was black; not black to the eye, for the eye teaches itself to discriminate colours even when loaded with dirt, but black to the touch. On coming out of a tub of water my foot took an

impress from the carpet exactly as it would have done had I trod bare-
footed on a path laid with soot. I thought that I was turning negro
upwards, till I put my wet hand upon the carpet, and found that the
result was the same. And yet the carpet was green to the eye,—a dull,
dingy green, but still green. "You shouldn't damp your feet," a man
said to me, to whom I mentioned the catastrophe. Certainly Pittsburg
is the dirtiest place I ever saw, but it is, as I said before, very picturesque in its dirt when looked at from above the blanket.

From Pittsburg I went on by train to Cincinnati, and was soon in
the State of Ohio. I confess that I have never felt any great regard for
Pennsylvania. It has always had in my estimation a low character for
commercial honesty, and a certain flavour of pretentious hypocrisy.
This probably has been much owing to the acerbity and pungency of
Sydney Smith's witty denunciations against the drab-coloured State.[3]
It is noted for repudiation of its own debts, and for sharpness in exac-
tion of its own bargains. It has been always smart in banking. It has
given Buchanan as a President to the country, and Cameron as a
Secretary at War to the Government! When the battle of Bull's Run
was to be fought, Pennsylvanian soldiers were the men who, on that
day, threw down their arms because the three months' term for which
they had been enlisted was then expired! Pennsylvania does not in my
mind stand on a par with Massachusetts, Connecticut, New York, or
Illinois, or Virginia. We are apt to connect the name of Benjamin
Franklin with Pennsylvania, but Franklin was a Boston man. Nevertheless, Pennsylvania is rich and prosperous. Indeed it bears all those
marks which Quakers generally leave behind them.

I had some little personal feeling in visiting Cincinnati, because
my mother had lived there for some time, and had there been concerned in a commercial enterprise, by which no one, I believe, made
any great sum of money. Between thirty and forty years ago she built
a bazaar in Cincinnati, which I was assured by the present owner of
the house, was at the time of its erection considered to be the great
building of the town. It has been sadly eclipsed now, and by no means
rears its head proudly among the great blocks around it. It had become
a "Physico-medical Institute" when I was there, and was under the
dominion of a quack doctor on one side, and of a college of rights-of-

[3] The last literary work of Sydney Smith (1771–1845), the celebrated English
wit and canon of St. Paul's, was addressed to the United States Congress in the
form of a complaint against the state of Pennsylvania for suspending interest on its
bonds. The original petition and several letters following up the subject created
some sensation in England and the United States during the year 1843. Pennsylvania resumed payments two years later, shortly after Smith's death.

women female medical professors on the other. "I believe, sir, no man or woman ever yet made a dollar in that building; and as for rent, I don't even expect it." Such was the account given of the unfortunate bazaar by the present proprietor.

Cincinnati has long been known as a great town,—conspicuous among all towns for the number of hogs which are there killed, salted, and packed. It is the great hog metropolis of the western States; but Cincinnati has not grown with the rapidity of other towns. It has now 170,000 inhabitants, but then it got an early start. St. Louis, which is west of it again, near the confluence of the Missouri and Mississippi, has gone ahead of it. Cincinnati stands on the Ohio river, separated by a ferry from Kentucky, which is a slave State. Ohio itself is a free-soil State. When the time comes for arranging the line of division, if such time shall ever come, it will be very hard to say where northern feeling ends and where southern wishes commence. Newport and Covington, which are in Kentucky, are suburbs of Cincinnati; and yet in these places slavery is rife. The domestic servants are mostly slaves, though it is essential that those so kept should be known as slaves who will not run away. It is understood that a slave who escapes into Ohio will not be caught and given up by the intervention of the Ohio police; and from Covington or Newport any slave can escape into Ohio with ease. But when that division takes place, no river like the Ohio can form the boundary between the divided nations. Such rivers are the highways, round which in this country people have clustered themselves. A river here is not a natural barrier, but a connecting street. It would be as well to make a railway a division, or the centre line of a city a national boundary. Kentucky and Ohio States are joined together by the Ohio river, with Cincinnati on one side and Louisville on the other; and I do not think that man's act can upset these ties of nature. But between Kentucky and Tennessee there is no such bond of union. There a mathematical line has been simply drawn, a continuation of that line which divides Virginia from North Carolina, to which two latter States Kentucky and Tennessee belonged when the thirteen original States first formed themselves into a union. But that mathematical line has offered no peculiar advantages to population. No great towns cluster there, and no strong social interests would be dissevered should Kentucky throw in her lot with the North, and Tennessee with the South; but Kentucky owns a quarter of million of slaves, and those slaves must either be emancipated or removed before such a junction can be firmly settled.

The great business of Cincinnati is hog-killing now, as it used to be in the old days of which I have so often heard.[4] It seems to be an established fact, that in this portion of the world the porcine genus are all hogs. One never hears of a pig. With us a trade in hogs and pigs is subject to some little contumely. There is a feeling, which has perhaps never been expressed in words, but which certainly exists, that these animals are not so honourable in their bearings as sheep and oxen. It is a prejudice which by no means exists in Cincinnati. There hog killing and salting and packing are very honourable, and the great men in the trade are the merchant princes of the city. I went to see the performance, feeling it to be a duty to inspect everywhere that which I found to be of most importance; but I will not describe it. There were a crowd of men operating, and I was told that the point of honour was to "put through" a hog a minute. It must be understood that the animal enters upon the ceremony alive, and comes out in that cleanly, disembowelled guise in which it may sometimes be seen hanging up previous to the operation of the pork-butcher's knife. To one special man was appointed a performance which seemed to be specially disagreeable, so that he appeared despicable in my eyes; but when on inquiry I learned that he earned five dollars, or a pound sterling, a day, my judgment as to his position was reversed. And after all what matters the ugly nature of such an occupation when a man is used to it?

Cincinnati is like all other American towns, with second, third, and fourth streets, seventh, eighth, and ninth streets, and so on. Then the cross-streets are named chiefly from trees. Chestnut, walnut, locust, &c. I do not know whence has come this fancy for naming streets after trees in the States, but it is very general. The town is well built, with good fronts to many of the houses, with large shops and larger stores; —of course also with an enormous hotel, which has never paid anything

---

[4] From Frances Trollope's *Domestic Manners of the Americans:*

"It seems hardly fair to quarrel with a place because its staple commodity is not pretty, but I am sure I should have liked Cincinnati much better if the people had not dealt so very largely in hogs. The immense quantity of business done in this line would hardly be believed by those who had not witnessed it. . . .

"But the annoyance came nearer than this; if I determined upon a walk up Main-street, the chances were five hundred to one against my reaching the shady side without brushing by a snout fresh dripping from the kennel; when we had screwed our courage to the enterprise of mounting a certain noble-looking sugar-loaf hill, that promised pure air and a fine view, we found the brook we had to cross, at its foot, red with the stream from a pig slaughter-house; while our noses, instead of meeting 'the thyme that loves the green hill's breast,' were greeted by odours that I will not describe, and which I heartily hope my readers cannot imagine; our feet, that on leaving the city had expected to press the flowery sod, literally got entangled in pig's tails and jawbones: and thus the prettiest walk in the neighborhood was interdicted for ever."

like a proper dividend to the speculator who built it. It is always the same story. But these towns shame our provincial towns by their breadth and grandeur. I am afraid that speculators with us are trammelled by an "ignorant impatience of ruin." I should not myself like to live in Cincinnati or in any of these towns. They are slow, dingy, and uninteresting; but they all possess an air of substantial, civic dignity. It must however be remembered that the Americans live much more in towns than we do. All with us that are rich and aristocratic and luxurious live in the country, frequenting the metropolis for only a portion of the year. But all that are rich and aristocratic and luxurious in the States live in the towns. Our provincial towns are not generally chosen as the residences of our higher classes.

Cincinnati has 170,000 inhabitants, and there are 14,000 children at the free schools,—which is about one in twelve of the whole population. This number gives the average of scholars throughout the year ended 30th June, 1861. But there are other schools in Cincinnati,— parish schools and private schools, and it is stated to me that there were in all 32,000 children attending school in the city throughout the year. The education at the State schools is very good. Thirty-four teachers are employed, at an average salary of 92*l.* each, ranging from 260*l.* to 60*l.* per annum. It is in this matter of education that the cities of the free States of America have done so much for the civilization and welfare of their population. This fact cannot be repeated in their praise too often. Those who have the management of affairs, who are at the top of the tree, are desirous of giving to all an opportunity of raising themselves in the scale of human beings. I dislike universal suffrage; I dislike vote by ballot; I dislike above all things the tyranny of democracy. But I do like the political feeling—for it is a political feeling— which induces every educated American to lend a hand to the education of his fellow-citizens. It shows, if nothing else does so, a germ of truth in that doctrine of equality. It is a doctrine to be forgiven when he who preaches it is in truth striving to raise others to his own level; —though utterly unpardonable when the preacher would pull down others to his level.

Leaving Cincinnati I again entered a slave State, namely, Kentucky. When the war broke out Kentucky took upon itself to say that it would be neutral, as if neutrality in such a position could by any means have been possible! Neutrality on the borders of secession, on the battle-field of the coming contest, was of course impossible. Tennessee, to the south, had joined the South by a regular secession ordinance. Ohio, Illinois, and Indiana to the north were of course true to the Union.

Under these circumstances it became necessary that Kentucky should choose her side. With the exception of the little State of Delaware, in which from her position secession would have been impossible, Kentucky was, I think, less inclined to rebellion, more desirous of standing by the North, than any other of the slave States. She did all she could, however, to put off the evil day of so evil a choice. Abolition within her borders was held to be abominable as strongly as it was so held in Georgia. She had no sympathy and could have none with the teachings and preachings of Massachusetts. But she did not wish to belong to a Confederacy of which the northern States were to be the declared enemy, and be the border State of the South under such circumstances. She did all she could for personal neutrality. She made that effort for general reconciliation of which I have spoken as the Crittenden compromise. But compromises and reconciliation were not as yet possible, and therefore it was necessary that she should choose her part. Her Governor declared for secession; and at first also her legislature was inclined to follow the Governor. But no overt act of secession by the State was committed, and at last it was decided that Kentucky should be declared to be loyal. It was in fact divided. Those on the southern border joined the secessionists, whereas the greater portion of the State, containing Frankfort the capital and the would-be secessionist Governor who lived there, joined the North. Men in fact became unionists or secessionists, not by their own conviction, but through the necessity of their positions; and Kentucky, through the necessity of her position, became one of the scenes of civil war.

I must confess that the difficulty of the position of the whole country seems to me to have been underestimated in England. In common life it is not easy to arrange the circumstances of a divorce between man and wife, all whose belongings and associations have for many years been in common. Their children, their money, their house, their friends, their secrets, have been joint property and have formed bonds of union. But yet such quarrels may arise, such mutual antipathy, such acerbity and even ill-usage, that all who know them admit that a separation is needed. So it is here in the States. Free-soil and slave-soil could, while both were young and unused to power, go on together,—not without many jars and unhappy bickerings; but they did go on together. But now they must part; and how shall the parting be made? With which side shall go this child, and who shall remain in possession of that pleasant homestead? Putting secession aside, there were in the United States two distinct political doctrines, of which the extremes were opposed to each other as pole is opposed to pole. We have no such variance of creed, no such radical difference as to the essential rules of life between parties in our country. We have no such cause for personal rancour in our Parliament as has existed for some years past in both Houses of Congress. These two extreme parties were the slave-owners of the South and the abolitionists of the North and West. Fifty years ago the former regarded the institution of slavery as a necessity of their position,—generally as an evil necessity,—and generally also as a custom to be removed in the course of years. Gradually they have learned to look upon slavery as good in itself, and to believe that it has been the source of their wealth and the strength of their position. They have declared it to be a blessing inalienable,—that should remain among them for ever,—as an inheritance not to be touched, and not to be spoken of with hard words. Fifty years ago the abolitionists of the North differed only in opinion from the slave-owners of the South in hoping for a speedier end to this stain upon the nation; and in thinking that some action should be taken towards the final emancipation of the bondsmen. But they also have progressed; and as the southern masters have called the institution blessed, they have called it accursed. Their numbers have increased, and with their numbers their power and their violence. In this way two parties have been formed who could not look on each other without hatred. An intermediate doctrine has been held by men who were nearer in their sympathies to the slave-owners than to the abolitionists; but who were not disposed to justify slavery as a thing apart. These men have been aware that slavery has existed in accordance with the constitution of their country, and have been willing to attach the stain which accompanies the institution to the individual State which entertains it, and not to the national Government, by which the question has been constitutionally ignored. The men who have participated in the Government have naturally been inclined towards the middle doctrine; but as the two extremes have retreated further from each other, the power of this middle-class of politicians has decreased. Mr. Lincoln, though he does not now declare himself an abolitionist, was elected by the abolitionists; and when, as a consequence of that election, secession was threatened, no step which he could have taken would have satisfied the South which had opposed him, and been at the same time true to the North which had chosen him. But it was possible that his Government might save Maryland, Virginia, Kentucky, and Missouri. As Radicals in England become simple Whigs when they are admitted into public offices, so did Mr. Lincoln with his government become anti-abolitionist when he entered on his functions. Had he combated secession with emancipation of the slaves, no slave State would or could have held by the Union. Abolition for a lecturer may be a telling subject. It is easy to bring down rounds of applause by tales of the wrongs of bondage. But to men in office, abolition was too stern a reality. It signified servile insurrection, absolute ruin to all southern slave-owners, and the absolute enmity of every slave State.

But that task of steering between the two has been very difficult. I fear that the task of so steering with success is almost impossible. In England it is thought that Mr. Lincoln might have maintained the Union by compromising matters with the South,—or if not so, that he might have maintained peace by yielding to the South. But no such power was in his hands. While we were blaming him for opposition to all southern terms, his own friends in the North were saying that all principle and truth was abandoned for the sake of such States as Kentucky and Missouri. "Virginia is gone; Maryland cannot go. And slavery is endured and the new virtue of Washington is made to tamper with the evil one, in order that a show of loyalty may be preserved in one or two States which after all are not truly loyal!" That is the accusation made against the government by the abolitionists; and that made by us on the other side is the reverse. I believe that Mr. Lincoln had no alternative but to fight, and that he was right also not to fight with abolition as his battle-cry. That he may be forced by his own friends into that cry, is, I fear, still possible. Kentucky at any rate did not secede in bulk. She still sent her senators to Congress, and allowed herself to be reckoned among the stars in the American firmament. But she could not escape the presence of the war. Did she remain loyal or did she secede, that was equally her fate.

The day before I entered Kentucky a battle was fought in that State, which gave to the northern arms their first actual victory. It was at a place called Mill Spring, near Somerset, towards the south of the State. General Zollicoffer, with a Confederate army, numbering, it was supposed, some eight thousand men, had advanced upon a smaller Federal force, commanded by General Thomas, and had been himself killed, while his army was cut to pieces and dispersed; the cannon of the Confederates were taken, and their camp seized and destroyed. Their rout was complete; but in this instance again the advancing party had been beaten, as had, I believe, been the case in all the actions hitherto fought throughout the war. Here, however, had been an actual victory, and it was not surprising that in Kentucky loyal men should rejoice greatly, and begin to hope that the Confederates would be beaten out of the State. Unfortunately, however, General Zollicoffer's army had only been an offshoot from the main rebel army in Kentucky. Buell, commanding the Federal troops at Louisville, and Sydney Johnston, the Confederate General, at Bowling Green, as yet remained opposite to each other, and the work was still to be done.

I visited the little towns of Lexington and Frankfort, in Kentucky. At the former I found in the hotel to which I went seventy-five teamsters belonging to the army. They were hanging about the great hall when I entered, and clustering round the stove in the middle of the chamber;—a dirty, rough, quaint set of men, clothed in a wonderful variety of garbs, but not disorderly or loud. The landlord apologized for their presence, alleging that other accommodation could not be found for them in the town. He received, he said, a dollar a day for feeding them, and for supplying them with a place in which they could lie down. It did not pay him,—but what could he do? Such an apology from an American landlord was in itself a surprising fact. Such high functionaries are, as a rule, men inclined to tell a traveller that if he does not like the guests among whom he finds himself, he may go elsewhere. But this landlord had as yet filled the place for not more than two or three weeks, and was unused to the dignity of his position. While I was at supper, the seventy-five teamsters were summoned into the common eating-room by a loud gong, and sat down to their meal at the public table. They were very dirty; I doubt whether I ever saw dirtier men; but they were orderly and well-behaved, and but for their extreme dirt might have passed as the ordinary occupants of a well-filled hotel in the West. Such men, in the States, are less clumsy with their knives and forks, less astray in an unused position, more intelligent in adapting themselves to a new life than are Englishmen of the same rank. It is always the same story. With us there is no level of society. Men stand on a long staircase, but the crowd congregates near the bottom, and the lower steps are very broad. In America men stand upon a common platform, but the platform is raised above the ground, though it does not approach in height the top of our staircase. If we take the average altitude in the two countries, we shall find that the American heads are the more elevated of the two. I conceived rather an affection for those dirty teamsters; they answered me civilly when I spoke to them, and sat in quietness, smoking their pipes, with a dull and dirty, but orderly demeanour.

The country about Lexington is called the Blue Grass Region, and boasts itself as of peculiar fecundity in the matter of pasturage. Why the grass is called blue, and or in what way or at what period it becomes blue, I did not learn; but the country is very lovely and very fertile. Between Lexington and Frankfort a large stock farm,[5] extending over three thousand acres, is kept by a gentleman, who is very well known as a breeder of horses, cattle, and sheep. He has spent much money on it, and is making for himself a Kentucky elysium. He was kind enough to entertain me for a while, and showed me something of country life in Kentucky. A farm in that part of the State depends, and must depend, chiefly on slave-labour. The slaves are a material part of the estate, and as they are regarded by the law as real property —being actually adstricti glebæ [6]—an inheritor of land has no alternative but to keep them. A gentleman in Kentucky does not sell his slaves. To do so is considered to be low and mean, and is opposed to the aristocratic traditions of the country. A man who does so willingly, puts himself beyond the pale of good-fellowship with his neighbours. A sale of slaves is regarded as a sign almost of bankruptcy. If a man cannot pay his debts, his creditors can step in and sell his slaves; but he does not himself make the sale. When a man owns more slaves than he needs, he hires them out by the year; and when he requires more than he owns, he takes them on hire by the year. Care is taken in such hirings not to remove a married man away from his home. The price paid for a negro's labour at the time of my visit was about a hundred dollars, or twenty pounds, for the year; but this price was then extremely low in consequence of the war disturbances. The usual price had been about fifty or sixty per cent. above this. The man who takes the negro on hire feeds him, clothes him, provides him with a bed, and supplies him with medical attendance. I went into some of their cottages on the estate which I visited, and was not in the least surprised to find them preferable in size, furniture, and all material comforts to the dwellings of most of our own agricultural labourers. Any comparison between the material comfort of a Kentucky slave and an English ditcher and delver would be preposterous. The Kentucky slave never wants for clothing fitted to the weather. He eats meat twice a day, and has three good meals; he knows no limit but his own appetite; his work is light; he has many varieties of amusement; he has instant medical assistance at all periods of necessity for himself, his wife, and his children. Of course he pays no rent, fears no baker, and knows no hunger. I would not have it supposed that I conceive slavery with all these comforts to be equal to freedom without them; nor do I conceive that the negro can be made equal to the white man. But in discussing

---

[5] Identified in Trollope's account book under entry of January 22, 1861 as the Woodford Stud Farm.
[6] "bound to the land."

the condition of the negro, it is necessary that we should understand what are the advantages of which abolition would deprive him, and in what condition he has been placed by the daily receipt of such advantages. If a negro slave wants new shoes, he asks for them, and receives them, with the undoubting simplicity of a child. Such a state of things has its picturesquely patriarchal side; but what would be the state of such a man if he were emancipated to-morrow?

The natural beauty of the place which I was visiting was very great. The trees were fine and well-scattered over the large, park-like pastures, and the ground was broken on every side into hills. There was perhaps too much timber, but my friend seemed to think that that fault would find a natural remedy only too quickly. "I do not like to cut down trees if I can help it," he said. After that I need not say that my host was quite as much an Englishman as an American. To the purely American farmer a tree is simply an enemy to be trodden under foot, and buried underground, or reduced to ashes and thrown to the winds with what most economical despatch may be possible. If water had been added to the landscape here it would have been perfect, regarding it as ordinary English park-scenery. But the little rivers at this place have a dirty trick of burying themselves under the ground. They go down suddenly into holes, disappearing from the upper air, and then come up again at the distance of perhaps half a mile. Unfortunately their periods of seclusion are more prolonged than those of their upper-air distance. There were three or four such ascents and descents about the place.

My host was a breeder of race-horses, and had imported sires from England; of sheep also, and had imported famous rams; of cattle too, and was great in bulls. He was very loud in praise of Kentucky and its attractions, if only this war could be brought to an end. But I could not obtain from him an assurance that the speculation in which he was engaged had been profitable. Ornamental farming in England is a very pretty amusement for a wealthy man, but I fancy,—without intending any slight on Mr. Mechi,[7]—that the amusement is expensive. I believe that the same thing may be said of it in a slave State.

Frankfort is the capital of Kentucky, and is as quietly dull a little town as I ever entered. It is on the river Kentucky, and as the grounds

7 John Joseph Mechi (1802–80) began life in London as the son of a poor Italian immigrant. After accumulating a large fortune from promoting Mechi's Magic Razor Strop and other ingenious mechanical devices, he turned his talents to agricultural science. He made his Tiptree Farm, located among the notoriously poor lands of Essex, yield handsome profits. His book How to Farm Profitably, published in 1857, was widely read.

about it on every side rise in wooded hills, it is a very pretty place. In January it was very pretty, but in summer it must be lovely. I was taken up to the cemetery there by a path along the river, and am inclined to say that it is the sweetest resting-place for the dead that I have ever visited. Daniel Boone lies there. He was the first white man who settled in Kentucky; or rather, perhaps, the first who entered Kentucky with a view to a white man's settlement. Such frontier men as was Daniel Boone never remained long contented with the spots they opened. As soon as he had left his mark in that territory he went again further west over the big rivers into Missouri, and there he died. But the men of Kentucky are proud of Daniel Boone, and so they have buried him in the loveliest spot they could select, immediately over the river. Frankfort is worth a visit, if only that this grave and graveyard may be seen. The legislature of the State was not sitting when I was there, and the grass was growing in the streets.

Louisville is the commercial city of the State, and stands on the Ohio. It is another great town, like all the others, built with high stores, and great houses and stone-faced blocks. I have no doubt that all the building speculations have been failures, and that the men engaged in them were all ruined. But there as the result of their labour, stands a fair great city on the southern banks of the Ohio. Here General Buell held his head-quarters, but his army lay at a distance. On my return from the West I visited one of the camps of this army, and will speak of it as I speak of my backward journey. I had already at this time begun to conceive an opinion that the armies in Kentucky and in Missouri would do at any rate as much for the northern cause, as that of the Potomac of which so much more had been heard in England.

While I was at Louisville the Ohio was flooded. It had begun to rise when I was at Cincinnati, and since then had gone on increasing hourly, rising inch by inch up into the towns upon its bank. I visited two suburbs of Louisville, both of which were submerged, as to the streets and ground-floors of the houses. At Shipping Port, one of these suburbs, I saw the women and children clustering in the up-stairs room, while the men were going about in punts and wherries, collecting drift wood from the river for their winter's firing. In some places bedding and furniture had been brought over to the high ground, and the women were sitting, guarding their little property. That village, amidst the waters, was a sad sight to see; but I heard no complaints. There was no tearing of hair and no gnashing of teeth; no bitter tears or moans of sorrow. The men who were not at work in the boats stood loafing about in clusters, looking at the still rising river; but each seemed to be personally indifferent to the matter. When the house of an American is carried down the river, he builds himself another;—as he would get himself a new coat when his old coat became unserviceable. But he never laments or moans for such a loss. Surely there is no other people so passive under personal misfortune!

Going from Louisville up to St. Louis, I crossed the Ohio river and passed through parts of Indiana and of Illinois, and striking the Mississippi opposite St. Louis, crossed that river also, and then entered the State of Missouri. The Ohio was, as I have said, flooded, and we went over it at night. The boat had been moored at some unaccustomed place. There was no light. The road was deep in mud up to the axletree, and was crowded with waggons and carts, which in the darkness of the night seemed to have stuck there. But the man drove his four horses through it all, and into the ferry-boat, over its side. There were three or four such omnibuses, and as many waggons, as to each of which I predicted in my own mind some fatal catastrophe. But they were all driven on to the boat in the dark, the horses mixing in through each other in a chaos which would have altogether incapacitated any English coachman. And then the vessel laboured across the flood, going sideways, and hardly keeping her own against the stream. But we did get over, and were all driven out again, up to the railway station in safety. On reaching the Mississippi about the middle of the next day, we found it frozen over, or rather covered from side to side with blocks of ice which had forced its way down the river, so that the steam ferry could not reach its proper landing. I do not think that we in England would have attempted the feat of carrying over horses and carriages under stress of such circumstances. But it was done here. Huge plankings were laid down over the ice, and omnibuses and waggons were driven on. In getting out again, these vehicles, each with four horses, had to be twisted about, and driven in and across the vessel, and turned in spaces to look at which would have broken the heart of an English coachman. And then with a spring they were driven up a bank as steep as a ladder! Ah me! under what mistaken illusions have I not laboured all the days of my youth, in supposing that no man could drive four horses well but an English stage-coachman? I have seen performances in America,—and in Italy and France also, but above all in America, which would have made the hair of any English professional driver stand on end. And in this way I entered St. Louis.

CHAPTER XXIV

MISSOURI

MISSOURI is a slave State lying to the west of the Mississippi and to the north of Arkansas. It forms a portion of the territory ceded by France to the United States in 1803. Indeed, it is difficult to say how large a portion of the continent of North America is supposed to be included in that territory. It contains the States of Louisiana, Arkansas, Missouri, and Kansas, as also the present Indian territory; but it also is said to have contained all the land lying back from them to the Rocky Mountains, Utah, Nebraska, and Dacotah, and forms no doubt the widest dominion ever ceded by one nationality to another.

Missouri lies exactly north of the old Missouri compromise line, that is, 36·30 north. When the Missouri compromise was made it was arranged that Missouri should be a slave State, but that no other State north of the 36·30 line should ever become slave soil. Kentucky and Virginia, as also of course Maryland and Delaware, four of the old slave States, were already north of that line; but the compromise was intended to prevent the advance of slavery in the north-west. The compromise has been since annulled, on the ground, I believe, that Congress had not constitutionally the power to declare that any soil should be free, or that any should be slave soil. That is a question to be decided by the States themselves, as each individual State may please. So the compromise was repealed. But slavery has not on that account advanced. The battle has been fought in Kansas, and after a long and terrible struggle, Kansas has come out of the fight as a free State. Kansas is in the same parallel of latitude as Virginia, and stretches west as far as the Rocky Mountains.

When the census of the population of Missouri was taken in 1860, the slaves amounted to 10 per cent. of the whole number. In the Gulf States the slave population is about 45 per cent. of the whole. In the three border States of Kentucky, Virginia, and Maryland, the slaves amount to 30 per cent. of the whole population. From these figures it will be seen that Missouri, which is comparatively a new slave State, has not gone a head with slavery as the old slave States have done, although from its position and climate, lying as far south as Virginia, it might seem to have had the same reasons for doing so. I think there is every reason to believe that slavery will die out in Missouri. The institution is not popular with the people generally; and as white labour becomes abundant,—and before the war it was becoming abundant,—men recognize the fact that the white man's labour is the more profitable. The heat in this State, in midsummer, is very great, especially in the valleys of the rivers. At St. Louis, on the Mississippi, it reaches commonly to 90, and very frequently goes above that. The nights moreover are nearly as hot as the days; but this great heat does not last for any very long period, and it seems that white men are able to work throughout the year. If correspondingly severe weather in winter affords any compensation to the white man for what of heat he endures during the summer, I can testify that such compensation is to be found in Missouri. When I was there we were afflicted with a combination of snow, sleet, frost, and wind, with a mixture of ice and mud, that makes me regard Missouri as the most inclement land into which I ever penetrated.

St. Louis, on the Mississippi, is the great town of Missouri, and is considered by the Missourians to be the star of the West. It is not to be beaten in population, wealth, or natural advantages by any other city so far west; but it has not increased with such rapidity as Chicago, which is considerably to the north of it on Lake Michigan. Of the great western cities I regard Chicago as the most remarkable, seeing that St. Louis was a large town before Chicago had been founded.

The population of St. Louis is 170,000. Of this number only 2000 are slaves. I was told that a large proportion of the slaves of Missouri are employed near the Missouri river in breaking hemp. The growth of hemp is very profitably carried on in that valley, and the labour attached to it is one which white men do not like to encounter. Slaves are not generally employed in St. Louis for domestic service, as is done almost universally in the towns of Kentucky. This work is chiefly in the hands of Irish and Germans. Considerably above one-third of the population of the whole city is made up of these two nationalities. So much is confessed; but if I were to form an opinion from the language I heard in the streets of the town, I should say that nearly every man was either an Irishman or a German.

St. Louis has none of the aspects of a slave city. I cannot say that I found it an attractive place, but then I did not visit it at an attractive time. The war had disturbed everything, given a special colour of its own to men's thoughts and words, and destroyed all interest except that which might proceed from itself. The town is well built, with good shops, straight streets, never-ending rows of excellent houses, and every sign of commercial wealth and domestic comfort,—of commercial wealth and domestic comfort in the past, for there was no present appearance either of comfort or of wealth. The new hotel here was to be bigger than all the hotels of all other towns. It is built, and is an enormous pile,[1] and would be handsome but for a terribly ambitious Grecian doorway. It is built, as far as the walls and roof are concerned, but in all other respects is unfinished. I was told that the shares of the original stockholders were now worth nothing. A shareholder, who so told me, seemed to regard this as the ordinary course of business.

The great glory of the town is the "levée," as it is called, or the long river beach up to which the steamers are brought with their bows to the shore. It is an esplanade looking on to the river, not built with quays or wharves, as would be the case with us, but with a sloping bank running down to the water. In the good days of peace a hundred vessels were to be seen here, each with its double funnels. The line of them seemed to be never ending even when I was there, but then a very large proportion of them were lying idle. They resemble huge wooden houses, apparently of frail architecture, floating upon the water. Each has its double row of balconies running round it, and the lower or ground floor is open throughout. The upper stories are propped and supported on ugly sticks and ricketty-looking beams; so that the first appearance does not convey any great idea of security to a stranger. They are always painted white and the paint is always very dirty. When they begin to move, they moan and groan in melancholy tones which are subversive of all comfort; and as they continue on their courses they puff and bluster, and are for ever threatening to burst and shatter themselves to pieces. There they lie in a continuous line nearly a mile in length along the levee of St. Louis, dirty, dingy, and now, alas, mute. They have ceased to groan and puff, and if this war be continued for six months longer, will become rotten and useless as they lie.

They boast at St. Louis that they command 46,000 miles of navigable river water, counting the great rivers up and down from that place. These rivers are chiefly the Mississippi, the Missouri and Ohio which fall into the Mississippi near St. Louis, the Platte and Kansas rivers—tributaries of the Missouri, the Illinois, and the Wisconsin. All these are open to steamers, and all of them traverse regions rich in

---

[1] The Lindell Hotel was recognized as "the largest building for purposes of accommodation ever erected in America." It was six stories high, not counting attic or basement, and had 530 rooms, one of which measured 116 by 44 feet. A half-million dollars' worth of furniture for it had been imported from Europe. The building was destroyed by fire in 1867.

corn, in coal, in metals, or in timber. These ready-made highways of the world centre, as it were, at St. Louis, and make it the depôt of the carrying trade of all that vast country. Minnesota is 1500 miles above New Orleans, but the wheat of Minnesota can be brought down the whole distance without change of the vessel in which it is first deposited. It would seem to be impossible that a country so blessed should not become rich. It must be remembered that these rivers flow through lands that have never yet been surpassed in natural fertility. Of all countries in the world one would say that the States of America should have been the last to curse themselves with a war; but now the curse has fallen upon them with a double vengeance. It would seem that they could never be great in war: their very institutions forbid it; their enormous distances forbid it; the price of labour forbids it; and it is forbidden also by the career of industry and expansion which has been given to them. But the curse of fighting has come upon them, and they are showing themselves to be as eager in the works of war as they have shown themselves capable in the works of peace. Men and angels must weep as they behold the things that are being done, as they watch the ruin that has come and is still coming, as they look on commerce killed and agriculture suspended. No sight so sad has come upon the earth in our days. They were a great people; feeding the world, adding daily to the mechanical appliances of mankind, increasing in population beyond all measures of such increase hitherto known, and extending education as fast as they extended their numbers. Poverty had as yet found no place among them, and hunger was an evil of which they had read, but were themselves ignorant. Each man among their crowds had a right to be proud of his manhood. To read and write,—I am speaking here of the North,—was as common as to eat and drink. To work was no disgrace, and the wages of work were plentiful. To live without work was the lot of none. What blessing above these blessings was needed to make a people great and happy? And now a stranger visiting them would declare that they are wallowing in a very slough of despond. The only trade open is the trade of war. The axe of the woodsman is at rest; the plough is idle; the artificer has closed his shop. The roar of the foundry is still heard because cannon are needed, and the river of molten iron comes out as an implement of death. The stone-cutter's hammer and the mason's trowel are never heard. The gold of the country is hiding itself as though it had returned to its mother-earth, and the infancy of a paper currency has been commenced. Sick soldiers, who have never seen a battlefield, are dying by hundreds in the squalid dirt of their unaccustomed camps. Men and women talk of war, and of war only. Newspapers full of the war are alone read. A contract for war stores,— too often a dishonest contract,—is the one path open for commercial enterprise. The young man must go to the war or he is disgraced. The war swallows everything, and as yet has failed to produce even such bitter fruits as victory or glory. Must it not be said that a curse has fallen upon the land?

And yet I still hope that it may ultimately be for good. Through water and fire must a nation be cleansed of its faults. It has been so with all nations, though the phases of their trials have been different. It did not seem to be well with us in Cromwell's early days; nor was it well with us afterwards in those disgraceful years of the later Stuarts. We know how France was bathed in blood in her effort to rid herself of her painted sepulchre of an ancient throne; how Germany was made desolate, in order that Prussia might become a nation. Ireland was poor and wretched, till her famine came. Men said it was a curse, but that curse has been her greatest blessing. And so will it be here in the West. I could not but weep in spirit as I saw the wretchedness around me,—the squalid misery of the soldiers, the inefficiency of their officers, the bickerings of their rulers, the noise and threats, the dirt and ruin, the terrible dishonesty of those who were trusted! These are things which made a man wish that he were anywhere but there. But I do believe that God is still over all, and that everything is working for good. These things are the fire and water through which this nation must pass. The course of this people had been too straight, and their ways had been too pleasant. That which to others had been ever difficult had been made easy for them. Bread and meat had come to them as things of course, and they hardly remembered to be thankful. "We ourselves have done it," they declared aloud. "We are not as other men. We are gods upon the earth. Whose arm shall be long enough to stay us, or whose bolt shall be strong enough to strike us?"

Now they are stricken sore, and the bolt is from their own bow. Their own hands have raised the barrier that has stayed them. They have stumbled in their running, and are lying hurt upon the ground; while they who have heard their boastings turn upon them with ridicule, and laugh at them in their discomforture. They are rolling in the mire, and cannot take the hand of any man to help them. Though the hand of the bystander may be stretched to them, his face is scornful and his voice full of reproaches. Who has not known that hour of misery when in the sullenness of the heart all help has been refused, and misfortune has been made welcome to do her worst? So is it now with those once United States. The man who can see without inward tears the self-inflicted wounds of that American people can hardly have within his bosom the tenderness of an Englishman's heart.

But the strong runner will rise again to his feet, even though he be stunned by his fall. He will rise again, and will have learned something by his sorrow. His anger will pass away, and he will again brace himself for his work. What great race has ever been won by any man, or by any nation, without some such fall during its course? Have we not all declared that some check to that career was necessary? Men in their pursuit of intelligence had forgotten to be honest; in struggling for greatness they had discarded purity. The nation has been great, but the statesmen of the nation have been little. Men have hardly been ambitious to govern, but they have coveted the wages of governers. Corruption has crept into high places,—into places that should have been high,—till of all holes and corners in the land they have become the lowest. No public man has been trusted for ordinary honesty. It is not by foreign voices, by English newspapers or in French pamphlets, that the corruption of American politicians has been exposed, but by American voices and by the American press. It is to be heard on every side. Ministers of the cabinet, senators, representatives, State legislatures, officers of the army, officials of the navy, contractors of every grade,—all who are presumed to touch, or to have the power of touching public money, are thus accused. For years it has been so. The word politician has stunk in men's nostrils. When I first visited New York, some three years since, I was warned not to know a man, because he was a "politician." We in England define a man of a certain class as a black-leg. How has it come about that in American ears the word politician has come to bear a similar signification?

The material growth of the States has been so quick, that the political growth has not been able to keep pace with it. In commerce, in education, in all municipal arrangements, in mechanical skill, and also in professional ability, the country has stalked on with amazing rapidity; but in the art of governing, in all political management and detail, it has made no advance. The merchants of our country and of that country have for many years met on terms of perfect equality, but it has never been so with their statesmen and our statesmen, with their diplomatists and our diplomatists. Lombard Street and Wall Street can do business with each other on equal footing, but it is not so between Downing Street and the State-office at Washington. The science of statemanship has yet to be learned in the States,—and certainly the highest lesson of that science, which teaches that honesty is the best policy.

I trust that the war will have left such a lesson behind it. If it do so, let the cost in money be what it may, that money will not have been wasted. If the American people can learn the necessity of employing their best men for their highest work—if they can recognize these honest men and trust them when they are so recognized,—then they may become as great in politics as they have become great in commerce and in social institutions.

St. Louis, and indeed the whole State of Missouri, was at the time of my visit under martial law. General Halleck was in command, holding his head-quarters at St. Louis, and carrying out, at any rate as far as the city was concerned, what orders he chose to issue. I am disposed to think that, situated as Missouri then was, martial law was the best law. No other law could have had force in a town surrounded by soldiers, and in which half of the inhabitants were loyal to the existing government, and half of them were in favour of rebellion. The necessity for such power is terrible, and the power itself in the hands of one man must be full of danger; but even that is better than anarchy. I will not accuse General Halleck of abusing his power, seeing that it is hard to determine what is the abuse of such power and what its proper use. When we were at St. Louis a tax was being gathered of 100*l.* a head from certain men presumed to be secessionists, and as the money was not of course very readily paid, the furniture of these suspected secessionists was being sold by auction.[2] No doubt such a measure was by them regarded as a great abuse. One gentleman informed me that, in addition to this, certain houses of his had been taken by the government at a fixed rent, and that the payment of the rent was now refused unless he would take the oath of allegiance. He no doubt thought that an abuse of power! But the worst abuse of such power comes not at first, but with long usage.

Up to the time however at which I was at St. Louis, martial law

2 General Henry W. Halleck's avowed purpose was to raise ten thousand dollars for the relief of refugees who had fled to St. Louis from the South and the West. According to Galusha Anderson (*A Border City during the Civil War* [1908]), this levy created unparalleled excitement; it struck hard at the "first families" of St. Louis. Many of these were openly sympathetic to the South—some had even mounted Confederate flags on their carriages. When any of the assessed refused to pay, property to the amount of the levy plus twenty-five per cent was confiscated. Beginning with such groups as railroad directors, licensed attorneys, university officials, and jurors, Halleck eventually required every voter in Missouri to take the oath of allegiance to the United States on pain of disfranchisement.

had chiefly been used in closing grog-shops and administering the oath
of allegiance to suspected secessionists. Something also had been done
in the way of raising money by selling the property of convicted secessionists; and while I was there eight men were condemned to be shot
for destroying railway bridges. "But will they be shot?" I asked of one of
the officers. "Oh, yes. It will be done quietly, and no one will know
anything about it. We shall get used to that kind of thing presently."
And the inhabitants of Missouri were becoming used to martial law.
It is surprising how quickly a people can reconcile themselves to altered circumstances, when the change comes upon them without the
necessity of any expressed opinion on their own part. Personal freedom
has been considered as necessary to the American of the States as the
air he breathes. Had any suggestion been made to him of a suspension
of the privilege of habeas corpus, of a censorship of the press, or of
martial law, the American would have declared his willingness to die
on the floor of the House of Representatives, and have proclaimed
with ten million voices his inability to live under circumstances so subversive of his rights as a man. And he would have thoroughly believed
the truth of his own assertions. Had a chance been given of an argument on the matter, of stump speeches, and caucus meetings, these
things could never have been done. But as it is, Americans are, I think,
rather proud of the suspension of the habeas corpus. They point with
gratification to the uniformly loyal tone of the newspapers, remarking
that any editor who should dare to give even a secession squeak, would
immediately find himself shut up. And now nothing but good is spoken
of martial law. I thought it a nuisance when I was prevented by soldiers from trotting my horse down Pennsylvania Avenue in Washington, but I was assured by Americans that such restrictions were very
serviceable in a community. At St. Louis martial law was quite popular. Why should not General Halleck be as well able to say what was
good for the people as any law or any lawyer? He had no interest in
the injury of the State, but every interest in its preservation. "But
what," I asked, "would be the effect were he to tell you to put out all
your fires at eight o'clock?" "If he were so to order, we should do it;
but we know that he will not." But who does know to what General
Halleck or other generals may come; or how soon a curfew-bell may
be ringing in American towns? The winning of liberty is long and
tedious, but the losing it is a downhill easy journey.

It was here, in St. Louis, that General Fremont had held his military court. He was a great man here during those hundred days
through which his command lasted. He lived in a great house, had a

bodyguard, was inaccessible as a great man should be, and fared sump-
tuously every day. He fortified the city,—or rather, he began to do so.
He constructed barracks here, and instituted military prisons. The
fortifications have been discontinued as useless, but the barracks and
the prisons remain. In the latter there were 1200 secessionist soldiers
who had been taken in the State of Missouri. "Why are they not exchanged?" I asked. "Because they are not exactly soldiers," I was informed. "The secessionists do not acknowledge them." "Then would
it not be cheaper to let them go?" "No," said my informant; "because
in that case we should have to catch them again." And so the 1200
remain in their wretched prison,—thinned from week to week and
from day to day by prison disease and prison death.

I went out twice to Benton barracks, as the camp of wooden huts
was called, which General Fremont had erected near the fair-ground
of the city. This fair-ground, I was told, had been a pleasant place. It
had been constructed for the recreation of the city, and for the purpose of periodical agricultural exhibitions. There is still in it a pretty
ornamented cottage, and in the little garden a solitary Cupid stood
dismayed by the dirt and ruin around him. In the fair-green are the
round buildings intended for show cattle and agricultural implements,
but now given up to cavalry horses and Parrott guns.[3] But Benton
barracks are outside the fair-green. Here on an open space, some half-
mile in length, two long rows of wooden sheds have been built, opposite to each other, and behind them are other sheds used for stabling
and cooking-places. Those in front are divided, not into separate huts,
but into chambers capable of containing nearly two hundred men
each. They were surrounded on the inside by great wooden trays, in
three tiers,—and on each tray four men were supposed to sleep. I went
into one or two while the crowd of soldiers was in them, but found it
inexpedient to stay there long. The stench of those places was foul beyond description. Never in my life before had I been in a place so horrid to the eyes and nose as Benton barracks. The path along the front
outside was deep in mud. The whole space between the two rows of
sheds was one field of mud, so slippery that the foot could not stand.
Inside and outside every spot was deep in mud. The soldiers were mud-
stained from foot to sole. These volunteer soldiers are in their nature
dirty, as must be all men brought together in numerous bodies without
special appliances for cleanliness, or control and discipline as to their
personal habits. But the dirt of the men in the Benton barracks sur-

[3] The Parrott gun, usually a "ten-pounder," was widely used as a fieldpiece or
siege gun.

passed any dirt that I had hitherto seen. Nor could it have been otherwise with them. They were surrounded by a sea of mud, and the foul
hovels in which they were made to sleep and live were fetid with
stench and reeking with filth. I had at this time been joined by another
Englishman, and we went through this place together. When we inquired as to the health of the men, we heard the saddest tales,—of three
hundred men gone out of one regiment, of whole companies that had
perished, of hospitals crowded with fevered patients. Measles had
been the great scourge of the soldiers here,—as it had also been in the
army of the Potomac. I shall not soon forget my visits to Benton barracks. It may be that our own soldiers were as badly treated in the
Crimea; or that French soldiers were treated worse on their march
into Russia. It may be that dirt, and wretchedness, disease and listless
idleness, a descent from manhood to habits lower than those of the
beasts, are necessary in warfare. I have sometimes thought that it is
so; but I am no military critic and will not say. This I say,—that the
degradation of men to the state in which I saw the American soldiers
in Benton barracks, is disgraceful to humanity.

General Halleck was at this time commanding in Missouri, and
was himself stationed at St. Louis; but his active measures against the
rebels were going on to the right and to the left. On the left shore of
the Mississippi, at Cairo, in Illinois, a fleet of gun-boats was being prepared to go down the river, and on the right an army was advancing
against Springfield, in the south-western district of Missouri, with the
object of dislodging Price, the rebel guerilla leader there, and, if possible, of catching him. Price had been the opponent of poor General
Lyon who was killed at Wilson's Creek, near Springfield, and of General Fremont, who during his hundred days had failed to drive him
out of the State. This duty had now been intrusted to General Curtis,
who had for some time been holding his head-quarters at Rolla, half-
way between St. Louis and Springfield. Fremont had built a fort at
Rolla, and it had become a military station. Over 10,000 men had been
there at one time, and now General Curtis was to advance from Rolla
against Price with something above that number of men. Many of
them, however, had already gone on, and others were daily being sent
up from St. Louis. Under these circumstances my friend and I, fortified with a letter of introduction to General Curtis, resolved to go and
see the army at Rolla.

On our way down by the railway we encountered a young German
officer, an aide-de-camp of the Federals, and under his auspices we saw
Rolla to advantage. Our companions in the railway were chiefly sol-

diers and teamsters. The car was crowded and filled with tobacco smoke, apple peel, and foul air. In these cars during the winter there is always a large lighted stove, a stove that might cook all the dinners for a French hotel, and no window is ever opened. Among our fellow-travellers there was here and there a west-country Missouri farmer going down, under the protection of the advancing army, to look after the remains of his chattels,—wild, dark, uncouth, savage-looking men. One such hero I specially remember, as to whom the only natural remark would be that one would not like to meet him alone on a dark night. He was burly and big, unwashed and rough, with a black beard, shorn some two months since. He had sharp, angry eyes, and sat silent, picking his teeth with a bowie knife. I met him afterwards at the Rolla hotel, and found that he was a gentleman of property near Springfield. He was mild and meek as a sucking dove, asked my advice as to the state of his affairs, and merely guessed that things had been pretty rough with him. Things had been pretty rough with him. The rebels had come upon his land. House, fences, stock, and crop were all gone. His homestead had been made a ruin, and his farm had been turned into a wilderness. Everything was gone. He had carried his wife and children off to Illinois, and had now returned, hoping that he might get on in the wake of the army till he could see the débris of his property. But even he did not seem disturbed. He did not bemoan himself or curse his fate. "Things were pretty rough," he said; and that was all that he did say.

It was dark when we got into Rolla. Everything had been covered with snow, and everywhere the snow was frozen. We had heard that there was an hotel, and that possibly we might get a bedroom there. We were first taken to a wooden building, which we were told was the head-quarters of the army, and in one room we found a colonel with a lot of soldiers loafing about, and in another a provost-marshal attended by a newspaper correspondent. We were received with open arms, and a suggestion was at once made that we were no doubt picking up news for European newspapers. "Air you a son of the Mrs. Trollope?" said the correspondent. "Then, sir, you are an accession to Rolla." Upon which I was made to sit down, and invited to "loaf about" at the head-quarters as long as I might remain at Rolla. Shortly, however, there came on a violent discussion about waggons. A general had come in and wanted all the colonel's waggons, but the colonel swore that he had none, declared how bitterly he was impeded with sick men, and became indignant and reproachful. It was Brutus and Cassius again; and as we felt ourselves in the way, and anxious moreover to ascertain what might be the nature of the Rolla hotel, we took up our heavy portmanteaux—for they were heavy—and with a guide to show us the way, started off through the dark and over the hill up to our inn. I shall never forget that walk. It was up hill and down hill, with an occasional half-frozen stream across it. My friend was impeded with an enormous cloak lined with fur, which in itself was a burden for a coal-heaver. Our guide, who was a clerk out of the colonel's office, carried an umbrella and a small dressing-bag, but we ourselves manfully shouldered our portmanteaux. Sydney Smith declared that an Englishman only wasted his time in training himself for gymnastic aptitudes, seeing that for a shilling he could always hire a porter. Had Sydney Smith ever been at Rolla he would have written differently. I could tell at great length how I fell on my face in the icy snow, how my friend stuck in the frozen mud when he essayed to jump the stream, and how our guide walked on easily in advance, encouraging us with his voice from a distance. Why is it that a stout Englishman bordering on fifty finds himself in such a predicament as that? No Frenchman, no Italian, no German, would so place himself, unless under the stress of insurmountable circumstances. No American would do so under any circumstances. As I slipped about on the ice and groaned with that terrible fardle on my back, burdened with a dozen shirts, and a suit of dress clothes, and three pair of boots, and four or five thick volumes, and a set of maps, and a box of cigars, and a washing-tub, I confessed to myself that I was a fool. What was I doing in such a galley as that? Why had I bought all that useless lumber down to Rolla? Why had I come to Rolla, with no certain hope even of shelter for a night? But we did reach the hotel; we did get a room between us with two bedsteads. And, pondering over the matter in my mind, since that evening, I have been inclined to think that the stout Englishman is in the right of it. No American of my age and weight will ever go through what I went through then; but I am not sure that he does not in his accustomed career go through worse things even than that. However, if I go to Rolla again during the war, I will at any rate leave the books behind me.

What a night we spent in that inn! They who know America will be aware that in all hotels there is a free admixture of different classes. The traveller in Europe may sit down to dinner with his tailor and shoemaker; but if so, his tailor and shoemaker have dressed themselves as he dresses, and are prepared to carry themselves according to a certain standard, which in exterior does not differ from his own. In the large Eastern cities of the States, such as Boston, New York, and Washington, a similar practice of life is gradually becoming prevalent. There are various hotels for various classes, and the ordinary traveller does not find himself at the same table with a butcher fresh from the shambles. But in the West there are no distinctions whatever. "A man's a man for a' that" in the West, let the "a' that" comprise what it may of coarse attire and unsophisticated manners. One soon gets used to it. In that inn at Rolla was a public room, heated in the middle by a stove, and round that we soon found ourself seated in a company of soldiers, farmers, labourers, and teamsters. But there was among them a general;—not a fighting, or would-be fighting general of the present time, but one of the old-fashioned local generals,—men who held, or had once held, some fabulous generalship in the State militia. There we sat, cheek by jowl with our new friends, till nearly twelve o'clock, talking politics and discussing the war. The General was a stanch Unionist, having, according to his own showing, suffered dreadful things from secessionist persecutors since the rebellion commenced. As a matter of course everybody present was for the Union. In such a place one rarely encounters any difference of opinion. The General was very eager about the war, advocating the immediate abolition of slavery, not as a means of improving the condition of the southern slaves, but on the ground that it would ruin the southern masters. We all sat by, edging in a word now and then, but the General was the talker of the evening. He was very wrathy, and swore at every other word. "It was pretty well time," he said, "to crush out this rebellion, and by —— it must and should be crushed out; General Jim Lane was the man to do it, and by —— General Jim Lane would do it!" and so on. In all such conversations the time for action has always just come, and also the expected man. But the time passes by as other weeks and months have passed before it, and the new General is found to be no more successful than his brethren. Our friend was very angry against England. "When we've polished off these accursed rebels, I guess we'll take a turn at you. You had your turn when you made us give up Mason and Slidell, and we'll have our turn by-and-by." But in spite of his dislike to our nation he invited us warmly to come and see him at his home on the Missouri river. It was, according to his showing, a new Eden,—a Paradise upon earth. He seemed to think that we might perhaps desire to buy a location, and explained to us how readily we could make our fortunes. But he admitted in the course of his eulogiums that it would be as much as his life was worth for him to ride out five miles from his own house. In the meantime the teamsters greased their boots, the soldiers snored, those who were wet took off their shoes and stockings, hanging them to dry round the stove, and the western farmers chewed tobacco in silence and ruminated. At such a house all the guests go in to their meals together. A gong is sounded on a sudden, close behind your ears; accustomed as you may probably be to the sound you jump up from your chair in the agony of the crash, and by the time that you have collected your thoughts the whole crowd is off in a general stampede into the eating room. You may as well join them; if you hesitate as to feeding with so rough a lot of men, you will have to sit down afterwards with the women and children of the family, and your lot will then be worse. Among such classes in the western States the men are always better than the women. The men are dirty and civil, the women are dirty and uncivil.

On the following day we visited the camp, going out in an ambulance and returning on horseback. We were accompanied by the General's aide-de-camp, and also, to our great gratification, by the General's daughter. There had been a hard frost for some nights, but though the cold was very great there was always heat enough in the middle of the day to turn the surface of the ground into glutinous mud; consequently we had all the roughness induced by frost, but none of the usually attendant cleanliness. Indeed, it seemed that in these parts nothing was so dirty as frost. The mud stuck like paste and encompassed everything. We heard that morning that from sixty to seventy baggage-waggons had "broken through," as they called it, and stuck fast near a river in their endeavour to make their way on to Lebanon. We encountered two generals of brigade, General Siegel, a German, and General Ashboth, an Hungarian,[4] both of whom were waiting till the weather should allow them to advance. They were extremely courteous, and warmly invited us to go on with them to Lebanon and Springfield, promising to us such accommodation as they might be able to obtain for themselves. I was much tempted to accept the offer; but I found that day after day might pass before any forward movement was commenced, and that it might be weeks before Springfield or even Lebanon could be reached. It was my wish, moreover, to see what I could of the people, rather than to scrutinize the ways of the army. We dined at the tent of General Ashboth, and afterwards rode his horses through the camp back to Rolla. I was greatly taken with this Hungarian gentleman. He was a tall, thin, gaunt man of fifty, a

4 Both Franz Sigel (1824–1902) and Alexander Sandor Asboth (1811–68) had distinguished careers in the Northern army and rose to the rank of major general. Both had led armies in Europe, Sigel serving under Hecker in the insurrection of 1848 in Baden, and Asboth under Kossuth in the Hungarian insurrection of 1848–9.

pure-blooded Magyar as I was told, who had come from his own country with Kossuth to America. His camp circumstances were not very
luxurious, nor was his table very richly spread; but he received us with
the ease and courtesy of a gentleman. He showed us his sword, his rifle,
his pistols, his chargers, and a daguerreotype of a friend he had loved
in his own country. They were all the treasures that he carried with
him,—over and above a chess-board and a set of chessmen which sorely
tempted me to accompany him in his march.

In my next chapter, which will, I trust, be very short, I purport to
say a few words as to what I saw of the American army, and therefore
I will not now describe the regiments which we visited. The tents were
all encompassed by snow, and the ground on which they stood was a
bed of mud; but yet the soldiers out here were not so wretchedly forlorn, or apparently so miserably uncomfortable, as those at Benton
barracks. I did not encounter that horrid sickly stench, nor were the
men so pale and wobegone. On the following day we returned to St.
Louis, bringing back with us our friend the German aide-de-camp. I
stayed two days longer in that city, and then I thought that I had seen
enough of Missouri;—enough of Missouri at any rate under the present
circumstances of frost and secession. As regards the people of the West,
I must say that they were not such as I expected to find them. With
the Northerns we are all more or less intimately acquainted. Those
Americans whom we meet in our own country, or on the Continent,
are generally from the North, or if not so they have that type of
American manners which has become familiar to us. They are talka-
tive, intelligent, inclined to be social, though frequently not sympa-
thetically social with ourselves; somewhat *soi-disant*,[5] but almost
invariably companionable. As the traveller goes southward into Maryland and Washington, the type is not altered to any great extent. The
hard intelligence of the Yankee gives place gradually to the softer, and
perhaps more polished manner of the Southern. But the change thus
experienced is not so great as is that between the American of the
western and the American of the Atlantic States. In the West I found
the men gloomy and silent,—I might almost say sullen. A dozen of
them will sit for hours round a stove, speechless. They chew tobacco
and ruminate. They are not offended if you speak to them, but they
are not pleased. They answer with monosyllables, or, if it be practicable, with a gesture of the head. They care nothing for the graces,—
or shall I say, for the decencies of life? They are essentially a dirty
people. Dirt, untidiness, and noise, seem in nowise to afflict them.

[5] "affected, pretentious."

Things are constantly done before your eyes, which should be done and might be done behind your back. No doubt we daily come into the closest contact with matters which, if we saw all that appertains to them, would cause us to shake and shudder. In other countries we do not see all this, but in the western States we do. I have eaten in Bedouin tents, and have been ministered to by Turks and Arabs. I have sojourned in the hotels of old Spain and of Spanish America. I have lived in Connaught, and have taken up my quarters with monks of different nations. I have, as it were, been educated to dirt, and taken out my degree in outward abominations. But my education had not reached a point which would enable me to live at my ease in the western States. A man or woman who can do that may be said to have graduated in the highest honours, and to have become absolutely invulnerable, either through the sense of touch, or by the eye, or by the nose. Indifference to appearances is there a matter of pride. A foul shirt is a flag of triumph. A craving for soap and water is as the wail of the weak and the confession of cowardice. This indifference is carried into all their affairs, or rather this manifestation of indifference. A few pages back, I spoke of a man whose furniture had been sold to pay a heavy tax raised on him specially as a secessionist; the same man had also been refused the payment of rent due to him by the government, unless he would take a false oath. I may presume that he was ruined in his circumstances by the strong hand of the northern army. But he seemed in nowise to be unhappy about his ruin. He spoke with some scorn of the martial law in Missouri, but I felt that it was esteemed a small matter by him that his furniture was seized and sold. No men love money with more eager love than these western men, but they bear the loss of it as an Indian bears his torture at the stake. They are energetic in trade, speculating deeply whenever speculation is possible; but nevertheless they are slow in motion, loving to loaf about. They are slow in speech, preferring to sit in silence, with the tobacco between their teeth. They drink, but are seldom drunk to the eye; they begin at it early in the morning, and take it in a solemn, sullen, ugly manner, standing always at a bar; swallowing their spirits, and saying nothing as they swallow it. They drink often, and to great excess; but they carry it off without noise, sitting down and ruminating over it with the everlasting cud within their jaws. I believe that a stranger might go into the West, and passing from hotel to hotel through a dozen of them, might sit for hours at each in the large everlasting public hall, and never have a word addressed to him. No stranger should travel in the western States, or indeed in any of the States, without letters of

introduction. It is the custom of the country, and they are easily procured. Without them everything is barren; for men do not travel in
the States of America as they do in Europe, to see scenery and visit the
marvels of old cities which are open to all the world. The social and
political life of the Americans must constitute the interest of the
traveller, and to these he can hardly make his way without intro-
ductions.

I cannot part with the West without saying in its favour that there
is a certain manliness about its men, which gives them a dignity of
their own. It is shown in that very indifference of which I have spoken.
Whatever turns up the man is still there,—still unsophisticated and
still unbroken. It has seemed to me that no race of men requires less
outward assistance than these pioneers of civilization. They rarely
amuse themselves. Food, newspapers, and brandy-smashes suffice for
life; and while these last, whatever may occur, the man is still there in
his manhood. The fury of the mob does not shake him, nor the stern
countenance of his present martial tyrant. Alas! I cannot stick to my
text by calling him a just man. Intelligence, energy, and endurance are
his virtues. Dirt, dishonesty, and morning drinks are his vices.

All native American women are intelligent. It seems to be their
birthright. In the eastern cities they have, in their upper classes, super-
added womanly grace to this intelligence, and consequently they are
charming as companions. They are beautiful also, and, as I believe,
lack nothing that a lover can desire in his love. But I cannot fancy
myself much in love with a western lady, or rather with a lady in the
West. They are as sharp as nails, but then they are also as hard. They
know, doubtless, all that they ought to know, but then they know so
much more than they ought to know. They are tyrants to their parents,
and never practise the virtue of obedience till they have half-grown-up
daughters of their own. They have faith in the destiny of their country, if in nothing else; but they believe that that destiny is to be worked
out by the spirit and talent of the young women. I confess that for me
Eve would have had no charms had she not recognized Adam as her
lord. I can forgive her in that she tempted him to eat the apple. Had
she come from the West country she would have ordered him to make
his meal, and then I could not have forgiven her.

St. Louis should be, and still will be, a town of great wealth. To no
city can have been given more means of riches. I have spoken of the
enormous mileage of water-communication of which she is the centre.
The country around her produces Indian corn, wheat, grasses, hemp,
and tobacco. Coal is dug even within the boundaries of the city, and

iron-mines are worked at a distance from it of a hundred miles. The iron is so pure, that it is broken off in solid blocks, almost free from alloy; and as the metal stands up on the earth's surface in the guise almost of a gigantic metal pillar, instead of lying low within its bowels, it is worked at a cheap rate, and with great certainty. Nevertheless, at the present moment, the iron-works of Pilot Knob, as the place is called, do not pay. As far as I could learn, nothing did pay, except government contracts.

CHAPTER XXV

Cairo and Camp Wood

To whatever period of life my days may be prolonged, I do not think that I shall ever forget Cairo. I do not mean Grand Cairo, which is also memorable in its way, and a place not to be forgotten,—but Cairo in the State of Illinois, which by native Americans is always called Caaro. An idea is prevalent in the States, and I think I have heard the same broached in England, that a popular British author had Cairo, State of Illinois, in his eye when under the name of Eden he depicted a chosen, happy spot on the Mississippi river, and told us how certain English emigrants fixed themselves in that locality, and there made light of those little ills of life which are incident to humanity even in the garden of the valley of the Mississippi. But I doubt whether that author ever visited Cairo in mid-winter, and I am sure that he never visited Cairo when Cairo was the seat of an American army. Had he done so, his love of truth would have forbidden him to presume that even Mark Tapley could have enjoyed himself in such an Eden.[1]

I had no wish myself to go to Cairo, having heard it but indifferently spoken of by all men; but my friend with whom I was travelling was peremptory in the matter. He had heard of gun-boats and mortar-

---

[1] Most readers, including indignant citizens of Cairo, judge that Dickens's picture is the darker:

"At last they stopped. At Eden too. The waters of the Deluge might have left it but a week before: so choked with slime and matted growth was the hideous swamp which bore that name. . . . There were a few log-houses visible among dark trees: the best, a cow-shed or a rude stable. . . . There were not above a score of cabins in the whole; half of these appeared untenanted; all were rotten and decayed. The most tottering, abject, and forlorn among them, was called, with great propriety, the Bank, and National Credit Office. . . . In some quarters, a snake or zigzag fence had been begun, but in no instance had it been completed; and the fallen logs, half hidden in the soil, lay mouldering away. Three or four meagre dogs, wasted and vexed with hunger; some long-legged pigs, wandering away into the woods in search of food; some children, nearly naked, gazing at him [Mark Tapley] from the huts, were all the living things he saw. A fetid vapour hot and sickening . . . rose up from the earth, and hung on everything around; and as his foot-prints sunk into the marshy ground, a black ooze started forth to blot them out. . . .

" 'Here's a ugly old tree in the way, sir,' he observed, 'which will be all the better down. We can build the oven in the afternoon. There never was such a handy spot for clay as Eden is. That's convenient, anyhow.' "—*Martin Chuzzlewit* (1843–4), Chapter xxiii.

boats, of forts built upon the river, of Columbiads, Dahlgrens, and Parrotts, of all the pomps and circumstance of glorious war, and entertained an idea that Cairo was the nucleus or pivot of all really strategic movements in this terrible national struggle. Under such circumstances I was as it were forced to go to Cairo, and bore myself, under the circumstances, as much like Mark Tapley as my nature would permit. I was not jolly while I was there certainly, but I did not absolutely break down and perish in its mud.

Cairo is the southern terminus of the Illinois Central Railway. There is but one daily arrival there, namely, at half-past four in the morning, and but one despatch, which is at half-past three in the morning. Everything is thus done to assist that view of life which Mark Tapley took when he resolved to ascertain under what possible worst circumstances of existence he could still maintain his jovial character. Why anybody should ever arrive at Cairo at half-past four A.M., I cannot understand. The departure at any hour is easy of comprehension. The place is situated exactly at the point at which the Ohio and the Mississippi meet, and is, I should say, merely guessing on the matter, some ten or twelve feet lower than the winter level of the two rivers. This gives it naturally a depressed appearance, which must have much aided Mark Tapley in his endeavours. Who were the founders of Cairo I have never ascertained. They are probably buried fathoms deep in the mud, and their names will no doubt remain a mystery to the latest ages. They were brought thither, I presume, by the apparent water privileges of the place; but the water privileges have been too much for them, and by the excess of their powers have succeeded in drowning all the capital of the early Cairovians, and in throwing a wet blanket of thick, moist, glutinous dirt over all their energies.

The free State of Illinois runs down far south between the slave States of Kentucky to the east, and of Missouri to the west, and is the most southern point of the continuous free-soil territory of the Northern States. This point of it is a part of a district called Egypt, which is fertile as the old country from whence it has borrowed a name; but it suffers under those afflictions which are common to all newly-settled lands which owe their fertility to the vicinity of great rivers. Fever and ague universally prevail. Men and women grow up with their lantern faces like spectres. The children are prematurely old; and the earth which is so fruitful is hideous in its fertility. Cairo and its immediate neighbourhood must, I suppose, have been subject to yearly inundation before it was "settled up." At present it is guarded on the shores of each river by high mud banks, built so as to protect the point of land. These are called the levees, and do perform their duty by keeping out the body of the waters. The shore between the banks is, I believe, never above breast deep with the inundation; and from the circumstances of the place, and the soft, half-liquid nature of the soil, this inundation generally takes the shape of mud instead of water.

Here, at the very point, has been built a town. Whether the town existed during Mr. Tapley's time I have not been able to learn. At the period of my visit, it was falling quickly into ruin; indeed I think I may pronounce it to have been on its last legs. At that moment a galvanic motion had been pumped into it by the war movements of General Halleck, but the true bearings of the town, as a town, were not less plainly to be read on that account. Every street was absolutely impassable from mud. I mean that in walking down the middle of any street in Cairo a moderately framed man would soon stick fast and not be able to move. The houses are generally built at considerable intervals and rarely face each other, and along one side of each street a plank boarding was laid, on which the mud had accumulated only up to one's ankles. I walked all over Cairo with big boots, and with my trousers tucked up to my knees; but at the crossings I found considerable danger, and occasionally had my doubts as to the possibility of progress. I was alone in my work, and saw no one else making any such attempt. A few only were moving about, and they moved in wretched carts, each drawn by two miserable, floundering horses. These carts were always empty, but were presumed to be engaged in some way on military service. No faces looked out at the windows of the houses, no forms stood in the doorways. A few shops were open, but only in the drinking shops did I see customers. In these silent, muddy men were sitting,—not with drink before them, as men sit with us,—but with the cud within their jaws, ruminating. Their drinking is always done on foot. They stand silent at a bar, with two small glasses before them. Out of one they swallow the whisky, and from the other they take a gulp of water, as though to rinse their mouths. After that, they again sit down and ruminate. It was thus that men enjoyed themselves at Cairo.

I cannot tell what was the existing population of Cairo.[2] I asked

[2] The census of 1860 gives the total population of Cairo as 2,188. By 1865, however, Cairo had become the largest city in southern Illinois, with over eight thousand inhabitants. It contained a brass foundry, a steamboat factory, a steam-engine factory, a vinegar factory, two boiler works, two planing-mills, and two machine shops. It supported five white and five Negro churches and published five newspapers.—*Cairo Guide* (1938) .

one resident; but he only shook his head and said that the place was about "played out." And a miserable play it must have been. I tried to walk round the point on the levees, but I found that the mud was so deep and slippery on that which protected the town from the Mississippi, that I could not move on it. On the other, which forms the bank of the Ohio, the railway runs, and here was gathered all the life and movement of the place. But the life was galvanic in its nature, created by a war-galvanism of which the shocks were almost neutralized by mud.

As Cairo is of all towns in America the most desolate, so is its hotel the most forlorn and wretched. Not that it lacked custom. It was so full that no room was to be had on our first entry from the railway cars at five A.M., and we were reduced to the necessity of washing our hands and faces in the public washroom. When I entered it the barber and his assistants were asleep there, and four or five citizens from the railway were busy at the basins. There is a fixed resolution in these places that you shall be drenched with dirt and drowned in abominations, which is overpowering to a mind less strong than Mark Tapley's. The filth is paraded and made to go as far as possible. The stranger is spared none of the elements of nastiness. I remember how an old woman once stood over me in my youth, forcing me to swallow the gritty dregs of her terrible medicine-cup. The treatment I received in the hotel at Cairo reminded me of that old woman. In that room I did not dare to brush my teeth lest I should give offence; and I saw at once that I was regarded with suspicion when I used my own comb instead of that provided for the public.

At length we got a room, one room for the two. I had become so depressed in spirits that I did not dare to object to this arrangement. My friend could not complain much, even to me, feeling that these miseries had been produced by his own obstinacy. "It is a new phase of life," he said. That, at any rate, was true. If nothing more be necessary for pleasurable excitement than a new phase of life, I would recommend all who require pleasurable excitement to go to Cairo. They will certainly find a new phase of life. But do not let them remain too long, or they may find something beyond a new phase of life. Within a week of that time my friend was taking quinine, looking hollow about the eyes, and whispering to me of fever and ague. To say that there was nothing eatable or drinkable in that hotel, would be to tell that which will be understood without telling. My friend, however, was a cautious man, carrying with him comfortable tin pots, hermetically sealed, from

Fortnum & Mason's; [3] and on the second day of our sojourn we were invited by two officers to join their dinner at a Cairo eating-house. We ploughed our way gallantly through the mud to a little shanty, at the door of which we were peremptorily demanded by the landlord to scrub ourselves before we entered with the stump of an old broom. This we did, producing on our nether persons the appearance of bread which has been carefully spread with treacle by an economic house-keeper. And the proprietor was right, for had we not done so, the treacle would have run off through the whole house. But after this we fared royally. Squirrel soup and prairie chickens regaled us. One of our new friends had laden his pockets with champagne and brandy, the other with glasses and a corkscrew; and as the bottle went round, I began to feel something of the spirit of Mark Tapley in my soul.

But our visit to Cairo had been made rather with reference to its present warlike character, than with any eye to the natural beauties of the place. A large force of men had been collected there, and also a fleet of gun-boats. We had come there fortified with letters to generals and commodores, and were prepared to go through a large amount of military inspection. But the bird had flown before our arrival; or rather the body and wings of the bird, leaving behind only a draggled tail and a few of its feathers. There were only a thousand soldiers at Cairo when we were there;—that is, a thousand stationed in the Cairo sheds. Two regiments passed through the place during the time, getting out of one steamer on to another, or passing from the railway into boats. One of these regiments passed before me down the slope of the river-bank, and the men as a body seemed to be healthy. Very many were drunk, and all were mud-clogged up to their shoulders and very caps. In other respects they appeared to be in good order. It must be understood that these soldiers, the volunteers, had never been made subject to any discipline as to cleanliness. They wore their hair long. Their hats or caps, though all made in some military form and with some military appendance, were various and ill-assorted. They all were covered with loose, thick, blue-gray great-coats, which no doubt were warm and wholesome, but which from their looseness and colour seemed to be peculiarly susceptible of receiving and showing a very large amount of mud. Their boots were always good; but each man was shod as he liked. Many wore heavy over-boots coming up the leg;

---

[3] "Tin cans" for preserving foods had already been in use for many years. By 1848 S. S. Pierce of Boston was doing a thriving business providing sailors with canned corn, and five years later Gail Borden produced his first tins of condensed milk. Fortnum & Mason's still offer a remarkable range of rare foods and spices to London and the world at large.

—boots of excellent manufacture, and from their cost, if for no other reason, quite out of the reach of an English soldier; boots in which a man would be not at all unfortunate to find himself hunting; but from these, or from their high-lows, shoes, or whatever they might wear, the mud had never been even scraped. These men were all warmly clothed, but clothed apparently with an endeavour to contract as much mud as might be possible.

The generals and commodores were gone up the Ohio river and up the Tennessee in an expedition with gun-boats, which turned out to be successful, and of which we have all read in the daily history of this war.[4] They had departed the day before our arrival, and though we still found at Cairo a squadron of gun-boats,—if gun-boats go in squadrons,—the bulk of the army had been moved. There was left there one regiment and one colonel, who kindly described to us the battles he had fought, and gave us permission to see everything that was to be seen. Four of these gun-boats were still lying in the Ohio, close under the terminus of the railway with their flat, ugly noses against the muddy bank, and we were shown over two of them. They certainly seemed to be formidable weapons for river warfare, and to have been "got up quite irrespective of expense." [5] So much, indeed, may be said for the Americans throughout the war. They cannot be accused of parsimony. The largest of these vessels, called the "Benton," had cost 36,000l. These boats are made with sides sloping inwards, at an angle of 45 degrees. The iron is two-and-a-half inches thick, and it has not, I believe, been calculated that this will resist cannon shot of great weight, should it be struck in a direct line. But the angle of the sides of the boat makes it improbable that any such shot should strike them; and the iron, bedded as it is upon oak, is supposed to be sufficient to turn a shot that does not hit it in a direct line. The boats are also roofed in with iron, and the pilots who steer the vessel stand encased, as it were, under an iron cupola. I imagine that these boats are well calculated for the river service, for which they have been built. Six or seven of them had gone up the Tennessee river the day before we reached Cairo, and while we were there they succeeded in knocking down Fort Henry, and in carrying off the soldiers stationed there and the officer in command. One of the boats, however, had been penetrated by a shot which made its way into the boiler, and the men on deck, six, I think, in number, were scalded to death by the escaping steam. The two pilots up in the cupola were destroyed in this terrible

---

4 Trollope gives particulars of this expedition later in the chapter.
5 A stock phrase in Victorian theatrical advertisements.

manner. As they were altogether closed in by the iron roof and sides, there was no escape for the steam. The boats, however, were well made and very powerfully armed, and will, probably, succeed in driving the secessionist armies away from the great river banks. By what machinery the secessionist armies are to be followed into the interior is altogether another question.

But there was also another fleet at Cairo, and we were informed that we were just in time to see the first essay made at testing the utility of this armada. It consisted of no less than thirty-eight mortar-boats, each of which had cost 1700*l.* These mortar-boats were broad, flat-bottomed rafts, each constructed with a deck raised three feet above the bottom. They were protected by high iron sides, supposed to be proof against rifle balls, and when supplied had been furnished each with a little boat, a rope, and four rough sweeps or oars. They had no other furniture or belongings, and were to be moved either by steam tugs or by the use of the long oars which were sent with them. It was intended that one 13-inch mortar, of enormous weight, should be put upon each, that these mortars should be fired with twenty-three pounds of powder, and that the shell thrown should, at a distance of three miles, fall with absolute precision into any devoted town which the rebels might hold on the river banks. The grandeur of the idea is almost sublime. So large an amount of powder had, I imagine, never then been used for the single charge in any instrument of war; and when we were told that thirty-eight of them were to play at once on a city, and that they could be used with absolute precision, it seemed as though the fate of Sodom and Gomorrah could not be worse than the fate of that city. Could any city be safe when such implements of war were about upon the waters?

But when we came to inspect the mortar-boats, our misgivings as to any future destination for this fleet were relieved, and our admiration was given to the smartness of the contractor who had secured to himself the job of building them. In the first place they had all leaked till the spaces between the bottoms and the decks were filled with water. This space had been intended for ammunition, but now seemed hardly to be fitted for that purpose. The officer who was about to test them by putting a mortar into one and by firing it off with twenty-three pounds of powder, had the water pumped out of a selected raft, and we were towed by a steam-tug from their moorings a mile up the river, down to the spot where the mortar lay ready to be lifted in by a derrick. But as we turned on the river, the tug-boat which had brought us down, was unable to hold us up against the force of the

XIII   Embarkation of General M'Clernand's Brigade at Cairo: "The generals and commodores were gone up the Ohio river and up the Tennessee in an expedition with gun-boats. . . ."

Harper's Weekly, VI (*February* 1, 1862), 72

XIV   Sleighing in Boston
Frank Leslie's Illustrated Newspaper, III *(February 7, 1857)*, 160

stream. A second tug-boat was at hand, and with one on each side we were just able, in half-an-hour, to recover the 100 yards which we had lost down the river. The pressure against the stream was so great, owing partly to the weight of the raft, and partly to the fact that its flat head buried itself in the water, that it was almost immovable against the stream, although the mortar was not yet on it.

It soon became manifest that no trial could be made on that day, and so we were obliged to leave Cairo without having witnessed the firing of the great gun. My belief is that very little evil to the enemy will result from those mortar-boats, and that they cannot be used with much effect. Since that time they have been used on the Mississippi, but as yet we do not know with what result. Island No. 10 has been taken, but I do not know that the mortar-boats contributed much to that success. The enormous cost of moving them against the stream of the river is in itself a barrier to their use. When we saw them—and then they were quite new—many of the rivets were already gone. The small boats had been stolen from some of them, and the ropes and oars from others. There they lay, thirty-eight in number, up against the mud-banks of the Ohio, under the boughs of the half-clad, melancholy forest trees, as sad a spectacle of reckless prodigality as the eye ever beheld. But the contractor who made them no doubt was a smart man.

This armada was moored on the Ohio against the low, reedy bank, a mile above the levee, where the old unchanged forest of nature came down to the very edge of the river, and mixed itself with the shallow overflowing waters. I am wrong in saying that it lay under the boughs of the trees, for such trees do not spread themselves out with broad branches. They stand thickly together, broken, stunted, spongy with rot, straight and ugly, with ragged tops and shattered arms, seemingly decayed, but still ever renewing themselves with the rapid moist life of luxuriant forest vegetation. Nothing to my eyes is sadder than the monotonous desolation of such scenery. We, in England, when we read and speak of the primeval forests of America, are apt to form pictures in our minds of woodland glades, with spreading oaks and green mossy turf beneath—of scenes than which nothing that God has given us is more charming. But these forests are not after that fashion; they offer no allurement to the lover, no solace to the melancholy man of thought. The ground is deep with mud, or overflown with water. The soil and the river have no defined margins. Each tree, though full of the forms of life, has all the appearance of death. Even to the outward eye they seem to be laden with ague, fever, sudden chills, and pestilential malaria.

When we first visited the spot we were alone, and we walked across from the railway line to the place at which the boats were moored. They lay in treble rank along the shore, and immediately above them an old steam-boat was fastened against the bank. Her back was broken, and she was given up to ruin,—placed there that she might rot quietly into her watery grave. It was mid-winter, and every tree was covered with frozen sleet and small particles of snow which had drizzled through the air; for the snow had not fallen in hearty, honest flakes. The ground beneath our feet was crisp with frost, but traitorous in its crispness; not frozen manfully so as to bear a man's weight, but ready at every point to let him through into the fat, glutinous mud below. I never saw a sadder picture, or one which did more to awaken pity for those whose fate had fixed their abodes in such a locality. And yet there was a beauty about it too,—a melancholy, death-like beauty. The disordered ruin and confused decay of the forest was all gemmed with particles of ice. The eye reaching through the thin underwood could form for itself picturesque shapes and solitary bowers of broken wood, which were bright with the opaque brightness of the hoar-frost. The great river ran noiselessly along, rapid, but still with an apparent lethargy in its waters. The ground beneath our feet was fertile beyond compare, but as yet fertile to death rather than to life. Where we then trod man had not yet come with his axe and his plough; but the railroad was close to us, and within a mile of the spot thousands of dollars had been spent in raising a city which was to have been rich with the united wealth of the rivers and the land. Hitherto fever and ague, mud and malaria, had been too strong for man, and the dollars had been spent in vain. The day, however, will come when this promontory between the two great rivers will be a fit abode for industry. Men will settle there, wandering down from the North and East, and toil sadly, and leave their bones among the mud. Thin, pale-faced, joyless mothers will come there, and grow old before their time; and sickly children will be born, struggling up with wan faces to their sad life's labour. But the work will go on, for it is God's work; and the earth will be prepared for the people, and the fat rottenness of the still living forest will be made to give forth its riches.

We found that two days at Cairo were quite enough for us. We had seen the gun-boats and the mortar-boats, and gone through the sheds of the soldiers. The latter were bad, comfortless, damp, and cold; and certain quarters of the officers, into which we were hospitably taken, were wretched abodes enough; but the sheds of Cairo did not stink like those of Benton barracks at St. Louis, nor had illness been prevalent there to the same degree. I do not know why this should have been so, but such was the result of my observation. The locality of Benton barracks must, from its nature, have been the more healthy, but it had become by art the foulest place I ever visited. Throughout the army it seemed to be the fact, that the men under canvas were more comfortable, in better spirits, and also in better health than those who were lodged in sheds. We had inspected the Cairo army and the Cairo navy, and had also seen all that Cairo had to show us of its own. We were thoroughly disgusted with the hotel, and retired on the second night to bed, giving positive orders that we might be called at half-past two, with reference to that terrible start to be made at half-past three. As a matter of course we kept dozing and waking till past one, in our fear lest neglect on the part of the watcher should entail on us another day at this place; of course we went fast asleep about the time at which we should have roused ourselves; and of course we were called just fifteen minutes before the train started. Everybody knows how these things always go. And then the pair of us, jumping out of bed in that wretched chamber, went through the mockery of washing and packing which always takes place on such occasions;—a mockery indeed of washing, for there was but one basin between us! And a mockery also of packing, for I left my hair-brushes behind me! Cairo was avenged in that I had declined to avail myself of the privileges of free citizenship which had been offered to me in that barber's shop. And then, while we were in our agony, pulling at the straps of our portmanteaux and swearing at the faithlessness of the boots, up came the clerk of the hotel—the great man from behind the bar—and scolded us prodigiously for our delay. "Called! We had been called an hour ago!" Which statement, however, was decidedly untrue, as we remarked, not with extreme patience. "We should certainly be late," he said; "it would take us five minutes to reach the train, and the cars would be off in four." Nobody who has not experienced them can understand the agonies of such moments,—of such moments as regards travelling in general; but none who have not been at Cairo can understand the extreme agony produced by the threat of a prolonged sojourn in that city. At last we were out of the house, rushing through the mud, slush, and half-melted snow, along the wooden track to the railway, laden with bags and coats, and deafened by that melancholy, wailing sound, as though of a huge polar she-bear in the pangs of travail upon an iceberg, which proceeds from an American railway-engine before it commences its work. How we slipped and stumbled, and splashed and swore, rushing along in the dark night, with buttons loose, and our

clothes half on! And how pitilessly we were treated! We gained our
cars, and even succeeded in bringing with us our luggage; but we did
not do so with the sympathy, but amidst the derision of the bystanders.
And then the seats were all full, and we found that there was a lower
depth even in the terrible deep of a railway train in a western State.
There was a second-class carriage, prepared, I presume, for those who
esteemed themselves too dirty for association with the aristocracy of
Cairo; and into this we flung ourselves. Even this was a joy to us, for
we were being carried away from Eden. We had acknowledged ourselves to be no fitting colleagues for Mark Tapley, and would have
been glad to escape from Cairo even had we worked our way out of
the place as assistant-stokers to the engine-driver. Poor Cairo! unfortunate Cairo! "It is about played out!" said its citizen to me. But in
truth the play was commenced a little too soon. Those players have
played out; but another set will yet have their innings, and make a
score that shall perhaps be talked of far and wide in the western world.

We were still bent upon army inspection, and with this purpose
went back from Cairo to Louisville in Kentucky. I had passed through
Louisville before, as told in my last chapter, but had not gone south
from Louisville towards the Green River, and had seen nothing of
General Buell's soldiers. I should have mentioned before that when
we were at St. Louis, we asked General Halleck, the officer in command
of the northern army of Missouri, whether he could allow us to pass
through his lines to the South. This he assured us he was forbidden to
do, at the same time offering us every facility in his power for such an
expedition if we could obtain the consent of Mr. Seward, who at that
time had apparently succeeded in engrossing into his own hands, for
the moment, supreme authority in all matters of government. Before
leaving Washington we had determined not to ask Mr. Seward, having
but little hope of obtaining his permission, and being unwilling to
encounter his refusal. Before going to General Halleck we had considered the question of visiting the land of Dixie without permission
from any of the men in authority. I ascertained that this might easily
have been done from Kentucky to Tennessee, but that it could only be
done on foot. There are very few available roads running North and
South through these States. The railways came before roads; and even
where the railways are far asunder, almost all the traffic of the country
takes itself to them, preferring a long circuitous conveyance with
steam, to short distances without. Consequently such roads as there
are run laterally to the railways, meeting them at this point or that,
and thus maintaining the communication of the country. Now the

railways were of course in the hands of the armies. The few direct roads leading from North to South were in the same condition, and the bye-roads were impassable from mud. The frontier of the North therefore, though very extended, was not very easily to be passed, unless, as I have said before, by men on foot. For myself I confess that I was anxious to go South; but not to do so without my coats and trousers, or shirts and pocket-handkerchiefs. The readiest way of getting across the line,—and the way which was I believe the most frequently used,—was from below Baltimore in Maryland by boat across the Potomac. But in this there was a considerable danger of being taken, and I had no desire to become a state-prisoner in the hands of Mr. Seward under circumstances which would have justified our Minister in asking for my release only as a matter of favour. Therefore when at St. Louis, I gave up all hopes of seeing "Dixie" during my present stay in America. I presume it to be generally known that Dixie is the negro's heaven,[6] and that the southern slave States, in which it is presumed that they have found a Paradise, have since the beginning of the war been so named.

We remained a few days at Louisville, and were greatly struck with the natural beauty of the country around it. Indeed, as far as I was enabled to see, Kentucky has superior attractions as a place of rural residence for an English gentleman, to any other State in the Union. There is nothing of landscape there equal to the banks of the upper Mississippi, or to some parts of the Hudson river. It has none of the wild grandeur of the White Mountains of New Hampshire, nor does it break itself into valleys equal to those of the Alleghanies in Pennsylvania. But all those are beauties for the tourist rather than for the resident. In Kentucky the land lies in knolls and soft sloping hills. The trees stand apart, forming forest openings. The herbage is rich, and the soil, though not fertile like the prairies of Illinois, or the river bottoms of the Mississippi and its tributaries, is good, steadfast, wholesome farming ground. It is a fine country for a resident gentleman farmer, and in its outward aspect reminds me more of England in its rural aspects, than any other State which I visited. Round Louisville there are beautiful sites for houses, of which advantage in some instances has been taken. But, nevertheless, Louisville though a well-built, handsome city, is not now a thriving city. I liked it because the hotel was above par, and because the country round it was good for walking; but it has not advanced as Cincinnati and St. Louis have

[6] The standard derivation is from *dixie,* a ten-dollar note issued by the Citizens' Bank of Louisiana with a large *dix* (French for *ten*) on the reverse; hence *land of dixies;* hence *Dixie Land.*

advanced. And yet its position on the Ohio is favourable, and it is well circumstanced as regards the wants of its own State. But it is not a free-soil city. Nor indeed is St. Louis; but St. Louis is tending that way, and has but little to do with the "domestic institution." At the hotels in Cincinnati and St. Louis you are served by white men, and are very badly served. At Louisville the ministration is black men, "bound to labour." The difference in the comfort is very great. The white servants are noisy, dirty, forgetful, indifferent, and sometimes impudent. The negroes are the very reverse of all this; you cannot hurry them; but in all other respects,—and perhaps even in that respect also,—they are good servants. This is the work for which they seem to have been intended. But nevertheless where they are, life and energy seem to languish, and prosperity cannot make any true advance. They are symbols of the luxury of the white men who employ them, and as such are signs of decay and emblems of decreasing power. They are good labourers themselves, but their very presence makes labour dishonourable. That Kentucky will speedily rid herself of the institution I believe firmly. When she has so done, the commercial city of that State may perhaps go a head again like her sisters.

At this very time the Federal army was commencing that series of active movements in Kentucky and through Tennessee which led to such important results, and gave to the North the first solid victories which they had gained since the contest began. On the 19th of January one wing of General Buell's army, under General Thomas, had defeated the secessionists near Somerset, in the south-eastern district of Kentucky, under General Zollicoffer, who was there killed. But in that action the attack was made by Zollicoffer and the secessionists. When we were at Louisville we heard of the success of that gun-boat expedition up the Tennessee river by which Fort Henry was taken. Fort Henry had been built by the Confederates on the Tennessee,— exactly on the confines of the States of Tennessee and Kentucky. They had also another fort, Fort Donnelson, on the Cumberland river, which at that point runs parallel to the Tennessee, and is there distant from it but a very few miles. Both these rivers run into the Ohio. Nashville, which is the capital of Tennessee, is higher up on the Cumberland; and it was now intended to send the gun-boats down the Tennessee back into the Ohio, and thence up the Cumberland, there to attack Fort Donnelson, and afterwards to assist General Buell's army in making its way down to Nashville. The gun-boats were attached to General Halleck's army, and received their directions from St. Louis. General Buell's head-quarters were at Louisville, and his advanced position was on the Green River, on the line of the railway from Louis-ville to Nashville. The secessionists had destroyed the railway bridge over the Green River, and were now lying at Bowling Green, between the Green River and Nashville. This place it was understood that they had fortified.

Matters were in this position when we got a military pass to go down by the railway to the army on the Green River,—for the railway was open to no one without a military pass;—and we started, trusting that Providence would supply us with rations and quarters. An officer attached to General Buell's staff, with whom however our acquaint-ance was of the very slightest, had telegraphed down to say that we were coming. I cannot say that I expected much from the message, see-ing that it simply amounted to a very thin introduction to a general officer to whom we were strangers even by name, from a gentleman to whom we had brought a note from another gentleman whose acquaint-ance we had chanced to pick up on the road. We manifestly had no right to expect much; but to us, expecting very little, very much was given. General Johnson was the officer to whose care we were confided,[7] he being a brigadier under General M'Cook, who commanded the ad-vance. We were met by an aide-de-camp and saddle-horses, and soon found ourselves in the General's tent, or rather in a shanty formed of solid upright wooden logs, driven into the ground with the bark still on, and having the interstices filled in with clay. This was roofed with canvas, and altogether made a very eligible military residence. The General slept in a big box about nine feet long and four broad which occupied one end of the shanty, and he seemed in all his fixings to be as comfortably put up as any gentleman might be when out on such a picnic as this. We arrived in time for dinner, which was brought in, table and all, by two negroes. The party was made up by a doctor, who carved, and two of the staff, and a very nice dinner we had. In half-an-hour we were intimate with the whole party, and as familiar with the things around us as though we had been living in tents all our lives. Indeed I had by this time been so often in the tents of the northern army, that I almost felt entitled to make myself at home. It has seemed to me that an Englishman has always been made welcome in these camps. There has been and is at this moment a terribly bitter feeling among Americans against England, and I have heard this expressed

---

[7] Entertaining an English novelist did not apparently strike General Rich-ard W. Johnson as an incident of any great moment in his life. In his memoirs (*Reminiscences in Peace and War* [1886]) he dismisses this period of his career in a half sentence: ". . . and here for long, weary weeks we floundered around in a sea of mud, which for military purposes was called Camp Wood."

quite as loudly by men in the army as by civilians; but I think I may
say that this has never been brought to bear upon individual intercourse. Certainly we have said some very sharp things of them,—words
which, whether true or false, whether deserved or undeserved, must
have been offensive to them. I have known this feeling of offence to
amount almost to an agony of anger. But nevertheless I have never
seen any falling off in the hospitality and courtesy generally shown by
a civilized people to passing visitors. I have argued the matter of England's course throughout the war, till I have been hoarse with as-
severating the rectitude of her conduct and her national unselfishness.
I have met very strong opponents on the subject, and have been coerced into loud strains of voice; but I never yet met one American who
was personally uncivil to me as an Englishman, or who seemed to be
made personally angry by my remarks. I found no coldness in that
hospitality to which as a stranger I was entitled, because of the national
ill-feeling which circumstances have engendered. And while on this
subject I will remark, that when travelling I have found it expedient
to let those with whom I might chance to talk know at once that I was
an Englishman. In fault of such knowledge things would be said which
could not but be disagreeable to me; but not even from any rough
western enthusiast in a railway carriage have I ever heard a word
spoken insolently to England, after I had made my nationality known.
I have learned that Wellington was beaten at Waterloo; that Lord
Palmerston was so unpopular that he could not walk alone in the
streets; that the House of Commons was an acknowledged failure; that
starvation was the normal condition of the British people, and that
the Queen was a bloodthirsty tyrant. But these assertions were not
made with the intention that they should be heard by an Englishman.
To us as a nation they are at the present moment unjust almost beyond
belief; but I do not think that the feeling has ever taken the guise of
personal discourtesy.

We spent two days in the camp close upon the Green River, and I
do not know that I enjoyed any days of my trip more thoroughly than
I did these. In truth for the last month, since I had left Washington,
my life had not been one of enjoyment. I had been rolling in mud and
had been damp with filth. Camp Wood, as they called this military
settlement on the Green River, was also muddy; but we were excellently well-mounted; the weather was very cold, but peculiarly fine,
and the soldiers around us, as far as we could judge, seemed to be better
off in all respects than those we had visited at St. Louis, at Rolla, or at
Cairo. They were all in tents, and seemed to be light-spirited and

happy. Their rations were excellent;—but so much may, I think, be said of the whole northern army from Alexandria on the Potomac to Springfield in the west of Missouri. There was very little illness at that time in the camp in Kentucky, and the reports made to us led us to think that on the whole this had been the most healthy division of the army. The men, moreover, were less muddy than their brethren either east or west of them,—at any rate this may be said of them as regards the infantry.

But perhaps the greatest charm of the place to me was the beauty of the scenery. The Green River at this spot is as picturesque a stream as I ever remember to have seen in such a country. It lies low down between high banks, and curves hither and thither, never keeping a straight line. Its banks are wooded; but not, as is so common in America, by continuous, stunted, uninteresting forest, but by large single trees standing on small patches of meadow by the water-side, with the high banks rising over them, with glades through them open for the horseman. The rides here in summer must be very lovely. Even in winter they were so, and made me in love with the place in spite of that brown, dull, barren aspect which the presence of an army always creates. I have said that the railway bridge which crossed the Green River at this spot had been destroyed by the secessionists. This had been done effectually as regarded the passage of trains, but only in part as regarded the absolute fabric of the bridge. It had been, and still was when I saw it, a beautifully light construction, made of iron and supported over a valley, rather than over a river, on tall stone piers. One of these piers had been blown up; but when we were there, the bridge had been repaired with beams and wooden shafts. This had just been completed, and an engine had passed over it. I must confess that it looked to me most perilously insecure; but the eye uneducated in such mysteries is a bad judge of engineering work. I passed with a horse backwards and forwards on it, and it did not tumble down then; but I confess that on the first attempt I was glad enough to lead the horse by the bridle.

That bridge was certainly a beautiful fabric, and built in a most lovely spot. Immediately under it there was also a pontoon bridge. The tents of General M'Cook's division were immediately at the northern end of it, and the whole place was alive with soldiers, nailing down planks, pulling up temporary rails at each side, carrying over straw for the horses, and preparing for the general advance of the troops. It was a glorious day. There had been heavy frost at night; but the air was dry, and the sun though cold was bright. I do not know when I

saw a prettier picture. It would perhaps have been nothing without
the loveliness of the river scenery; but the winding of the stream at the
spot, the sharp wooded hills on each side, the forest openings, and the
busy, eager, strange life together filled the place with no common interest. The officers of the army at the spot spoke with bitterest condemnation of the vandalism of their enemy in destroying the bridge.
The justice of the indignation, I ventured very strongly to question.
"Surely you would have destroyed their bridge?" I said. "But they are
rebels," was the answer. It has been so throughout the contest; and the
same argument has been held by soldiers and by non-soldiers,—by
women and by men. "Grant that they are rebels," I have answered.
"But when rebels fight they cannot be expected to be more scrupulous
in their mode of doing so than their enemies who are not rebels." The
whole population of the North has from the beginning of this war considered themselves entitled to all the privileges of belligerents; but
have called their enemies Goths and Vandals for even claiming those
privileges for themselves. The same feeling was at the bottom of their
animosity against England. Because the South was in rebellion, England should have consented to allow the North to assume all the rights
of a belligerent, and should have denied all those rights to the South!
Nobody has seemed to understand that any privilege which a belligerent can claim must depend on the very fact of his being in encounter
with some other party having the same privilege. Our press has animad-
verted very strongly on the States' government for the apparent untruth-
fulness of their arguments on this matter; but I profess that I believe
that Mr. Seward and his colleagues,—and not they only but the whole
nation,—have so thoroughly deceived themselves on this subject, have
so talked and speechified themselves into a misunderstanding of the
matter, that they have taught themselves to think that the men of the
South could be entitled to no consideration from any quarter. To have
rebelled against the Stars and Stripes seems to a northern man to be a
crime putting the criminal altogether out of all courts,—a crime which
should have armed the hands of all men against him, as the hands of
all men are armed at a dog that is mad, or a tiger that has escaped from
its keeper. It is singular that such a people, a people that has founded
itself on rebellion, should have such a horror of rebellion; but, as far
as my observation may have enabled me to read their feelings rightly,
I do believe that it has been as sincere as it is irrational.

We were out riding early on the morning of the second day of our
sojourn in the camp, and met the division of General Mitchell, a de-
tachment of General Buell's army, which had been in camp between

the Green River and Louisville, going forward to the bridge which was then being prepared for their passage. This division consisted of about 12,000 men, and the road was crowded throughout the whole day with them and their waggons. We first passed a regiment of cavalry, which appeared to be endless. Their cavalry regiments are, in general, more numerous than those of the infantry, and on this occasion we saw, I believe, about 1200 men pass by us. Their horses were strong and serviceable, and the men were stout and in good health; but the general appearance of everything about them was rough and dirty. The American cavalry have always looked to me like brigands. A party of them would, I think, make a better picture than an equal number of our dragoons; but if they are to be regarded in any other view than that of the picturesque, it does not seem to me that they have been got up successfully. On this occasion they were forming themselves into a picture for my behoof, and as the picture was, as a picture, very good, I at least have no reason to complain.

We were taken to see one German regiment, a regiment of which all the privates were German and all the officers save one,—I think the surgeon. We saw the men in their tents, and the food which they eat, and were disposed to think that hitherto things were going well with them. In the evening the colonel and lieutenant-colonel, both of whom had been in the Prussian service, if I remember rightly, came up to the general's quarters, and we spent the evening together in smoking cigars and discussing slavery round the stove. I shall never forget that night, or the vehement abolition enthusiasm of the two German colonels. Our host had told us that he was a slave-owner; and as our wants were supplied by two sable ministers, I concluded that he had brought with him a portion of his domestic institution. Under such circumstances I myself should have avoided such a subject, having been taught to believe that southern gentlemen did not generally take delight in open discussions on the subject. But had we been arguing the question of the population of the planet Jupiter, or the final possibility of the transmutation of metals, the matter could not have been handled with less personal feeling. The Germans, however, spoke the sentiments of all the Germans of the western States,—that is, of all the Protestant Germans, and to them is confined the political influence held by the German immigrants. They all regard slavery as an evil, holding on the matter opinions quite as strong as ours have ever been. And they argue that as slavery is an evil, it should therefore be abolished at once. Their opinions are as strong as ours have ever been, and they have not had our West Indian experience. Any one desiring to understand the pres-

ent political position of the States should realize the fact of the present
German influence on political questions. Many say that the present
President was returned by German voters. In one sense this is true, for
he certainly could not have been returned without them; but for them,
or for their assistance, Mr. Breckenridge would have been President,[8]
and this civil war would not have come to pass. As abolitionists they
are much more powerful than the Republicans of New England, and
also more in earnest. In New England the matter is discussed politically; in the great western towns, where the Germans congregate by
thousands, they profess to view it philosophically. A man, as a man, is
entitled to freedom. That is their argument, and it is a very old one.
When you ask them what they would propose to do with 4,000,000 of
enfranchised slaves and with their ruined masters,—how they would
manage the affairs of those 12,000,000 of people, all whose wealth and
work and very life have hitherto been hinged and hung upon slavery,
they again ask you whether slavery is not in itself bad, and whether
anything acknowledged to be bad should be allowed to remain.

But the American Germans are in earnest, and I am strongly of
opinion that they will so far have their way, that the country which
for the future will be their country, will exist without the taint of
slavery. In the northern nationality, which will reform itself after this
war is over, there will, I think, be no slave State. That final battle of
abolition will have to be fought among a people apart; and I must
fear that while it lasts their national prosperity will not be great.

[8] John C. Breckinridge, the candidate of the Southern Democrats in the 1860
presidential election, was nominated at their Baltimore convention after they had
walked out of the regular Democratic convention at Charleston, refusing to support
the Douglas platform. In the election of 1860 Lincoln drew 180 electoral votes;
Breckinridge, 72; Bell (the Know-Nothing candidate), 39; Douglas, 12.

CHAPTER XXVI

THE ARMY OF THE NORTH

I TRUST that it may not be thought that in this chapter I am going to take upon myself the duties of a military critic. I am well aware that I have no capacity for such a task, and that my opinion on such matters would be worth nothing. But it is impossible to write of the American States as they were when I visited them, and to leave that subject of the American army untouched. It was all but impossible to remain for some months in the northern States without visiting the army. It was impossible to join in any conversation in the States without talking about the army. It was impossible to make inquiry as to the present and future condition of the people without basing such inquiries more or less upon the doings of the army. If a stranger visit Manchester with the object of seeing what sort of place Manchester is, he must visit the cotton mills and printing establishments, though he may have no taste for cotton and no knowledge on the subject of calicoes. Under pressure of this kind I have gone about from one army to another, looking at the drilling of regiments, at the manœuvres of cavalry, at the practice of artillery, and at the inner life of the camps. I do not feel that I am in any degree more fitted to take the command of a campaign than I was before I began, or even more fitted to say who can and who cannot do so. But I have obtained on my own mind's eye a tolerably clear impression of the outward appearance of the northern army; I have endeavoured to learn something of the manner in which it was brought together, and of its cost as it now stands; and I have learned—as any man in the States may learn, without much trouble or personal investigation—how terrible has been the peculation of the contractors and officers by whom that army has been supplied. Of these things, writing of the States at this moment, I must say something. In what I shall say as to that matter of peculation I trust that I may be believed to have spoken without personal ill-feeling or individual malice.

While I was travelling in the States of New England and in the North-west, I came across various camps at which young regiments were being drilled and new regiments were being formed. These lay in our way as we made our journeys, and therefore we visited them; but they were not objects of any very great interest. The men had not acquired even any pretence of soldierlike bearing. The officers for the most part had only just been selected, having hardly as yet left their civil occupations, and anything like criticism was disarmed by the very nature of the movement which had called the men together. I then thought, as I still think, that the men themselves were actuated by proper motives, and often by very high motives, in joining the regiments. No doubt they looked to the pay offered. It is not often that men are able to devote themselves to patriotism without any reference to their personal circumstances. A man has got before him the necessity of earning his bread, and very frequently the necessity of earning the bread of others besides himself. This comes before him not only as his first duty, but as the very law of his existence. His wages are his life, and when he proposes to himself to serve his country that subject of payment comes uppermost as it does when he proposes to serve any other master. But the wages given, though very high in comparison with those of any other army, have not been of a nature to draw together from their distant homes at so short a notice, so vast a cloud of men, had no other influence been at work. As far as I can learn, the average rate of wages in the country since the war began has been about 65 cents a day over and beyond the workmen's diet. I feel convinced that I am putting this somewhat too low, taking the average of all the markets from which the labour has been withdrawn. In large cities labour has been higher than this, and a considerable proportion of the army has been taken from large cities. But taking 65 cents a day as the average, labour has been worth about 17 dollars a month over and above the labourers' diet. In the army the soldier receives 13 dollars a month, and also receives his diet and clothes; in addition to this, in many States, 6 dollars a month have been paid by the State to the wives and families of those soldiers who have left wives and families in the States behind them. Thus for the married men the wages given by the army have been 2 dollars a month, or less than 5l. a year, more than his earnings at home, and for the unmarried man they have been 4 dollars a month, or less than 10l. a year below his earnings at home. But the army also gives clothing to the extent of 3 dollars a month. This would place the unmarried soldier, in a pecuniary point of view, worse off by one dollar a month, or 2l. 10s. a year, than he would have been at home; and would give the married man 5 dollars a month, or 12l. a year more than his ordinary wages for absenting himself from his family. I cannot think therefore that the pecuniary attractions have been very great.

Our soldiers in England enlist at wages which are about one half that paid in the ordinary labour market to the class from whence they come. But labour in England is uncertain, whereas in the States it is certain. In England the soldier with his shilling gets better food than the labourer with his two shillings; and the Englishman has no objection to the rigidity of that discipline which is so distasteful to an American. Moreover, who in England ever dreamed of raising 600,000 new troops in six months, out of a population of thirty million? But this has been done in the northern States out of a population of eighteen million. If England were invaded, Englishmen would come forward in the same way, actuated, as I believe, by the same high motives. My object here is simply to show that the American soldiers have not been drawn together by the prospect of high wages, as has been often said since the war began.

They who inquire closely into the matter will find that hundreds and thousands have joined the army as privates, who in doing so have abandoned all their best worldly prospects, and have consented to begin the game of life again, believing that their duty to their country has now required their services. The fact has been that in the different States a spirit of rivalry has been excited. Indiana has endeavoured to show that she was as forward as Illinois; Pennsylvania has been unwilling to lag behind New York; Massachusetts, who has always struggled to be foremost in peace, has desired to boast that she was first in war also; the smaller States have resolved to make their names heard, and those which at first were backward in sending troops have been shamed into greater earnestness by the public voice. There has been a general feeling throughout the people that the thing should be done; —that the rebellion must be put down, and that it must be put down by arms. Young men have been ashamed to remain behind; and their elders, acting under that glow of patriotism which so often warms the hearts of free men, but which perhaps does not often remain there long in all its heat, have left their wives and have gone also. It may be true that the voice of the majority has been coercive on many;—that men have enlisted partly because the public voice required it of them, and not entirely through the promptings of individual spirit. Such public voice in America is very potent; but it is not, I think, true that the army has been gathered together by the hope of high wages.

Such was my opinion of the men when I saw them from State to State clustering into their new regiments. They did not look like soldiers; but I regarded them as men earnestly intent on a work which they believed to be right. Afterwards when I saw them in their camps, amidst all the pomps and circumstances of glorious war, positively converted into troops, armed with real rifles and doing actual military service, I believed the same of them,—but cannot say that I then liked them so well. Good motives had brought them there. They were the same men, or men of the same class that I had seen before. They were doing just that which I knew they would have to do. But still I found that the more I saw of them the more I lost of that respect for them which I had once felt. I think it was their dirt that chiefly operated upon me. Then, too, they had hitherto done nothing, and they seemed to be so terribly intent upon their rations! The great boast of this army was that they eat meat twice a day, and that their daily supply of bread was more than they could consume.

When I had been two or three weeks in Washington, I went over to the army of the Potomac and spent a few days with some of the officers. I had on previous occasions ridden about the camps, and had seen a review at which General Maclellan trotted up and down the lines with all his numerous staff at his heels. I have always believed reviews to be absurdly useless as regards the purpose for which they are avowedly got up,—that, namely, of military inspection. And I believed this especially of this review. I do not believe that any Commander-in-chief ever learns much as to the excellence or deficiencies of his troops by watching their manœuvres on a vast open space; but I felt sure that General Maclellan had learned nothing on this occasion. If before his review he did not know whether his men were good as soldiers, he did not possess any such knowledge after the review. If the matter may be regarded as a review of the general;—if the object was to show him off to the men, that they might know how well he rode, and how grand he looked with his staff of forty or fifty officers at his heels, then this review must be considered as satisfactory. General Maclellan does ride very well. So much I learned, and no more.

It was necessary to have a pass for crossing the Potomac either from one side or from the other, and such a pass I procured from a friend in the War-office, good for the whole period of my sojourn in Washington. The wording of the pass was more than ordinarily long, as it recommended me to the special courtesy of all whom I might encounter; but in this respect it was injurious to me rather than otherwise, as every picket by whom I was stopped found it necessary to read it to the end. The paper was almost invariably returned to me without a word; but the musket which was not unfrequently kept extended across my horse's nose by the reader's comrade would be withdrawn, and then I would ride on to the next barrier. It seemed to me that these passes were so numerous and were signed by so many officers, that there could have been no risk in forging them. The army of the Potomac into which they admitted the bearer lay in quarters which were extended over a length of twenty miles up and down on the Virginian side of the river, and the river could be traversed at five different places. Crowds of men and women were going over daily, and no doubt all the visitors who so went with innocent purposes were provided with proper passports; but any whose purposes were not innocent, and who were not so provided, could have passed the pickets with counterfeited orders. This, I have little doubt, was done daily. Washington was full of secessionists, and every movement of the Federal army was communicated to the Confederates at Richmond, at which city was now established the Congress and headquarters of the Confederacy. But no such tidings of the Confederate army reached those in command at Washington. There were many circumstances in the contest which led to this result, and I do not think that General Maclellan had any power to prevent it. His system of passes certainly did not do so.

I never could learn from any one what was the true number of this army on the Potomac. I have been informed by those who professed to know that it contained over 200,000 men, and by others who also professed to know, that it did not contain 100,000. To me the soldiers seemed to be innumerable, hanging like locusts over the whole country,—a swarm desolating everything around them. Those pomps and circumstances are not glorious in my eyes. They affect me with a melancholy which I cannot avoid. Soldiers gathered together in a camp are uncouth and ugly when they are idle; and when they are at work their work is worse than idleness. When I have seen a thousand men together, moving their feet hither at one sound and thither at another, throwing their muskets about awkwardly, prodding at the air with their bayonets, trotting twenty paces here and backing ten paces there, wheeling round in uneven lines, and looking, as they did so, miserably conscious of the absurdity of their own performances, I have always been inclined to think how little the world can have advanced in civilization, while grown-up men are still forced to spend their days in such grotesque performances. Those to whom the "pomps and circumstances" are dear—nay, those by whom they are considered simply necessary—will be able to confute me by a thousand arguments. I readily own myself confuted. There must be soldiers, and soldiers must be taught. But not the less pitiful is it to see men of thirty undergoing the goose-step, and tortured by orders as to the proper mode of handling a long instrument which is half-gun and half-spear. In the days of Hector and Ajax, the thing was done in a more picturesque manner, and the songs of battle should, I think, be confined to those ages.

The ground occupied by the divisions on the further, or south-western side of the Potomac was, as I have said, about twenty miles in length and perhaps seven in breadth. Through the whole of this district the soldiers were everywhere. The tents of the various brigades were clustered together in streets, the regiments being divided; and the divisions, combining the brigades, lay apart at some distance from each other. But everywhere, at all points, there were some signs of military life. The roads were continually thronged with waggons, and tracks were opened for horses wherever a shorter way might thus be made available. On every side the trees were falling, or had fallen. In some places whole woods had been felled with the express purpose of rendering the ground impracticable for troops, and firs and pines lay one over the other, still covered with their dark rough foliage, as though a mighty forest had grown there along the ground, without any power to raise itself towards the heavens. In other places the trees had been chopped off from their trunks about a yard from the ground, so that the soldier who cut it should have no trouble in stooping, and the tops had been dragged away for firewood, or for the erection of screens against the wind. Here and there in solitary places there were outlying tents, looking as though each belonged to some military recluse; and in the neighbourhood of every division was to be found a photo-graphing-establishment upon wheels, in order that the men might send home to their sweethearts pictures of themselves in their martial costumes.

I wandered about through these camps both on foot and on horse-back day after day, and every now and then I would come upon a farm-house that was still occupied by its old inhabitants. Many of such houses had been deserted, and were now held by the senior officers of the army; but some of the old families remained, living in the midst of this scene of war in a condition most forlorn. As for any tillage of their land, that under such circumstances might be pronounced as hopeless. Nor could there exist encouragement for farm-work of any kind. Fences had been taken down and burned; the ground had been overrun in every direction. The stock had of course disappeared; it had not been stolen, but had been sold in a hurry for what under such circumstances it might fetch. What farmer could work or have any hope for his land in the middle of such a crowd of soldiers? But yet there were the families. The women were in their houses, and the children playing at their doors, and the men, with whom I sometimes spoke, would stand around with their hands in their pockets. They knew that they were ruined; they expected no redress. In nine cases out of ten they were inimical in spirit to the soldiers around them. And yet it seemed that their equanimity was never disturbed. In a former chapter I have spoken of a certain general,—not a fighting general of the army, but a local farming general,[1]—who spoke loudly and with many curses of the injury inflicted on him by the secessionists. With that exception, I heard no loud complaint of personal suffering. These Virginian farmers must have been deprived of everything,—of the very means of earning bread. They still held by their houses, though they were in the very thick of the war, because there they had shelter for their families, and elsewhere they might seek it in vain. A man cannot move his wife and children if he have no place to which to move them, even though his house be in the midst of disease, of pestilence, or of battle. So it was with them then, but it seemed as though they were already used to it.

But there was a class of inhabitants in that same country to whom fate had been even more unkind than to those whom I saw. The lines of the northern army extended perhaps seven or eight miles from the Potomac, and the lines of the Confederate army were distant some four miles from those of their enemies. There was, therefore, an intervening space or strip of ground about four miles broad, which might be said to be no man's land. It was no man's land as to military possession, but it was still occupied by many of its old inhabitants. These people were not allowed to pass the lines either of one army or of the other; or if they did so pass they were not allowed to return to their homes. To these homes they were forced to cling, and there they remained. They had no market, no shops at which to make purchases even if they had money to buy; no customers with whom to deal even if they had produced to sell. They had their cows, if they could keep them from the Confederate soldiers, their pigs and their poultry; and on them they were living—a most forlorn life. Any advance made by either party must be over their homesteads. In the event of battle they would be in the midst of it; and in the meantime they could see no one, hear of nothing, go no whither beyond the limits of that miserable strip of ground!

The earth was hard with frost when I paid my visit to the camp, and the general appearance of things around my friend's quarters was on that account cheerful enough. It was the mud which made things sad and wretched. When the frost came it seemed as though the army had overcome one of its worst enemies. Unfortunately cold weather did not last long. I have been told in Washington that they rarely

[1] See page 396.

have had so open a season. Soon after my departure that terrible enemy, the mud, came back upon them, but during my stay the ground was hard and the weather very sharp. I slept in a tent, and managed to keep my body warm by an enormous overstructure of blankets and coats; but I could not keep my head warm. Throughout the night, I had to go down, like a fish beneath the water, for protection, and come up for air at intervals, half-smothered. I had a stove in my tent, but the heat of that when lighted was more terrible than the severity of the frost.

The tents of the brigade with which I was staying had been pitched not without an eye to appearances. They were placed in streets as it were, each street having its name, and between them screens had been erected of fir-poles and fir-branches, so as to keep off the wind. The outside boundaries of the nearest regiment was ornamented with arches, crosses, and columns constructed in the same way; so that the quarters of the men were reached, as it were, through gateways. The whole thing was pretty enough, and while the ground was hard the camp was picturesque, and a visit to it was not unpleasant. But unfortunately the ground was in its nature soft and deep, composed of red clay, and as the frost went and the wet weather came, mud became omnipotent and destroyed all prettiness. And I found that the cold weather, let it be ever so cold, was not severe upon the men. It was wet which they feared and had cause to fear, both for themselves and for their horses. As to the horses, but few of them were protected by any shelter or covering whatsoever. Through both frost and wet they remained out, tied to the wheel of a waggon or to some temporary rack at which they were fed. In England we should imagine that any horse so treated must perish; but here the animals seemed to stand it. Many of them were miserable enough in appearance, but nevertheless they did the work required of them. I have observed that horses throughout the States are treated in a hardier manner than is usually the case with us.

At the period of which I am speaking, January, 1862, the health of the army of the Potomac was not as good as it had been, and was beginning to give way under the effects of the winter. Measles had become very prevalent, and also small-pox—though not of a virulent description; and men, in many instances, were sinking under fatigue. I was informed by various officers that the Irish regiments were on the whole the most satisfactory. Not that they made the best soldiers, for it was asserted that they were worse, as soldiers, than the Americans or Germans; not that they became more easily subject to rule, for it was asserted that they were unruly;—but because they were rarely ill. Diseases which seized the American troops on all sides seemed to spare them. The mortality was not excessive, but the men became sick and ailing, and fell under the doctor's hands.

Mr. Olmstead, whose name is well known in England as a writer on the southern States, was at this time secretary to a Sanitary Commission on the army, and published an abstract of the results of the inquiries made, on which I believe perfect reliance may be placed.[2] This inquiry was extended to two hundred regiments, which were presumed to be included in the army of the Potomac; but these regiments were not all located on the Virginian side of the river, and must not therefore be taken as belonging exclusively to the divisions of which I have been speaking. Mr. Olmstead says, "The health of our armies is evidently not above the average of armies in the field. The mortality of the army of the Potomac during the summer months averaged $3\frac{1}{2}$ per cent., and for the whole army it is stated at 5 per cent." "Of the camps inspected, 5 per cent.," he says, "were in admirable order; 44 per cent. fairly clean and well policed. The condition of 26 per cent. was negligent and slovenly, and of 24 per cent. decidedly bad, filthy, and dangerous." Thus 50 per cent. were either negligent and slovenly, or filthy and dangerous. I wonder what the report would have been had Camp Benton at St. Louis been surveyed! "In about 80 per cent. of the regiments the officers claimed to give systematic attention to the cleanliness of the men; but it is remarked that they rarely enforced the washing of the feet, and not always of the head and neck." I wish Mr. Olmstead had added that they never enforced the cutting of the hair. No single trait has been so decidedly disadvantageous to the appearance of the American army, as the long, uncombed, rough locks of hair which the men have appeared so loth to abandon. In reading the above one cannot but think of the condition of those other twenty regiments!

According to Mr. Olmstead two-thirds of the men were native-born, and one-third was composed of foreigners. These foreigners are either Irish or German. Had a similar report been made of the armies in the West, I think it would have been seen that the proportion of for-

2 Frederick Law Olmsted, or Olmstead (1822–1903), had secured a leave of absence as superintendent of New York City's Central Park to become general secretary of the United States Sanitary Commission, parent of the American Red Cross. He was a prolific writer; his books on the South were A Journey in the Seaboard Slave States (1856); A Journey through Texas (1857); A Journey in the Back Country (1860); and Journeys and Explorations in the Cotton Kingdom (1861). The books and papers relating to the Sanitary Commission, in which publications Olmsted took no small part, run to 455 items filling 25 volumes.

eigners was still greater. The average age of the privates was something under twenty-five, and that of the officers thirty-four. I may here add, from my own observation, that an officer's rank could in no degree be predicated from his age. Generals, colonels, majors, captains, and lieutenants, had been all appointed at the same time and without reference to age or qualification. Political influence or the power of raising recruits had been the standard by which military rank was distributed. The old West Point officers had generally been chosen for high commands, but beyond this everything was necessarily new. Young colonels and ancient captains abounded without any harsh feeling as to the matter on either side. Indeed in this respect the practice of the country generally was simply carried out. Fathers and mothers in America seem to obey their sons and daughters naturally, and as they grow old become the slaves of their grandchildren.

Mr. Olmstead says that food was found to be universally good and abundant. On this matter Mr. Olmstead might have spoken in stronger language without exaggeration. The food supplied to the American armies has been extravagantly good, and certainly has been wastefully abundant. Very much has been said of the cost of the American army, and it has been made a matter of boasting that no army so costly has ever been put into the field by any other nation. The assertion is, I believe, at any rate true. I have found it impossible to ascertain what has hitherto been expended on the army. I much doubt whether even Mr. Chase, the Secretary of the Treasury, or Mr. Stanton, the Secretary-at-War, know themselves, and I do not suppose that Mr. Stanton's predecessor much cared. Some approach, however, may be reached to the amount actually paid in wages and for clothes and diet, and I give below a statement which I have seen of the actual annual sum proposed to be expended on these heads, presuming the army to consist of 500,-000 men. The army is stated to contain 660,000 men, but the former numbers given would probably be found to be nearer the mark. To this must be added the cost of diet and clothing. The food of the men, I was informed, was supplied at an average cost of 17 cents a day, which, for an army of 500,000 men, would amount to 6,200,000*l*. per annum. The clothing of the men is shown by the printed statement of their war department to amount to 3 dollars a month for a period of five years. That, at least, is the amount allowed to a private of infantry or artillery. The cost of the cavalry uniforms and of the dress of the non-commissioned officers is something higher, but not sufficiently so to make it necessary to make special provision for the difference in a statement so rough as this. At 3 dollars a month the clothing of the

	Dollars.
Wages of privates, including sergeants and corporals	86,640,000
Salaries of regimental officers	23,784,000
Extra wages of privates; extra pay to mounted officers, and salary of officers above the rank of colonel	17,000,000
	127,424,000
	or
	£25,484,000 sterling.

army would amount to 3,600,000*l*. The actual annual cost would therefore be as follows:—

Salaries and wages	£25,484,400
Diet of the soldiers	6,200,000
Clothing for the soldiers. . . .	3,600,000
	£35,284,400

I believe that these figures may be trusted, unless it be with reference to that sum of $17,000,000 or 3,400,000*l*., which is presumed to include the salaries of all general-officers with their staffs, and also the extra wages paid to soldiers in certain cases. This is given as an estimate, and may be over or under the mark. The sum named as the cost of clothing would be correct, or nearly so, if the army remained in its present force for five years. If it so remained for only one year the cost would be one-fifth higher. It must of course be remembered that the sum above named includes simply the wages, clothes, and food of the men. It does not comprise the purchase of arms, horses, ammunition, or waggons; the forage of horses; the transport of troops, or any of those incidental expenses of warfare which are always, I presume, heavier than the absolute cost of the men, and which in this war have been probably heavier than in any war ever waged on the face of God's earth. Nor does it include that terrible item of peculation as to which I will say a word or two before I finish this chapter.

The yearly total payment of the officers and soldiers of the armies is as follows. As regards the officers it must be understood that this includes all the allowances made to them, except as regards those on the staff. The sums named apply only to the infantry and artillery. The pay of the cavalry is about ten per cent. higher.

> Lieutenant-General. General Scott alone
> holds that rank in the States' army . £1,850
> Major-General   1,150
> Brigadier-General   800
> *Colonel   530
> *Lieutenant-Colonel   475
> Major   430
> Captain   300
> First Lieutenant   265
> Second Lieutenant   245
> First Sergeant   48
> Sergeant   40
> Corporal   34
> Private   31

In every grade named the pay is, I believe, higher than that given by us, or, as I imagine, by any other nation. It is, however, probable that the extra allowances paid to some of our higher officers when on duty may give to their positions for a time a higher pecuniary remuneration. It will of course be understood that there is nothing in the American army answering to our colonel of a regiment. With us the officer so designated holds a nominal command of high dignity and emolument as a reward for past services.

I have already spoken of my visits to the camps of the other armies in the field, that of General Halleck, who held his head-quarters at St. Louis, in Missouri, and that of General Buell, who was at Louisville, in Kentucky. There was also a fourth army under General Hunter in Kansas, but I did not make my way as far west as that. I do not pretend to any military knowledge, and should be foolish to attempt military criticism; but as far as I could judge by appearance, I should say that the men in Buell's army were, of the three, in the best order. They seemed to me to be cleaner than the others, and, as far as I could learn, were in better health. Want of discipline and dirt have, no doubt, been the great faults of the regiments generally, and the latter drawback may probably be included in the former. These men have not been accustomed to act under the orders of superiors, and when they entered

* A Colonel and Lieutenant-Colonel are attached to each regiment.

on the service hardly recognized the fact that they would have to do so in ought else than in their actual drill and fighting. It is impossible to conceive any class of men to whom the necessary discipline of a soldier would come with more difficulty than to an American citizen. The whole training of his life has been against it. He has never known respect for a master, or reverence for men of a higher rank than himself. He has probably been made to work hard for his wages,—harder than an Englishman works,—but he has been his employer's equal. The language between them has been the language of equals, and their arrangement as to labour and wages has been a contract between equals. If he did not work he would not get his money,—and perhaps not if he did. Under these circumstances he has made his fight with the world; but those circumstances have never taught him that special deference to a superior, which is the first essential of a soldier's duty. But probably in no respect would that difficulty be so severely felt as in all matters appertaining to personal habits. Here at any rate the man would expect to be still his own master, acting for himself and independent of all outer control. Our English Hodge, when taken from the plough to the camp, would, probably, submit without a murmur to soap and water and a barber's shears; he would have received none of that education which would prompt him to rebel against such ordinances; but the American citizen, who for a while expects to shake hands with his captain whenever he sees him, and is astonished when he learns that he must not offer him drinks, cannot at once be brought to understand that he is to be treated like a child in the nursery;— that he must change his shirt so often, wash himself at such and such intervals, and go through a certain process of cleansing his outward garments daily. I met while travelling a sergeant of an old regular American regiment, and he spoke of the want of discipline among the volunteers as hopeless. But even he instanced it chiefly by their want of cleanliness. "They wear their shirts till they drop off their backs," said he; "and what can you expect from such men as that?" I liked that sergeant for his zeal and intelligence, and also for his courtesy when he found that I was an Englishman; for previous to his so finding he had begun to abuse the English roundly,—but I did not quite agree with him about the volunteers. It is very bad that soldiers should be dirty, bad also that they should treat their captains with familiarity and desire to exchange drinks with the majors. But even discipline is not everything; and discipline will come at last even to the American soldiers, distasteful as it may be, when the necessity for it is made apparent. But these volunteers have great military virtues. They are intelligent, zealous in their cause, handy with arms, willing enough to work at all military duties, and personally brave. On the other hand they are sickly, and there has been a considerable amount of drunkenness among them. No man who has looked to the subject can, I think, doubt that a native American has a lower physical development than an Irishman, a German, or an Englishman. They become old sooner, and die at an earlier age. As to that matter of drink, I do not think that much need be said against them. English soldiers get drunk when they have the means of doing so, and American soldiers would not get drunk if the means were taken away from them. A little drunkenness goes a long way in a camp, and ten drunkards will give a bad name to a company of a hundred. Let any man travel with twenty men of whom four are tipsy, and on leaving them he will tell you that every man of them was a drunkard.

I have said that these men are brave, and I have no doubt that they are so. How should it be otherwise with men of such a race? But it must be remembered that there are two kinds of courage, one of which is very common and the other very uncommon. Of the latter description of courage it cannot be expected that much should be found among the privates of any army, and perhaps not very many examples among the officers. It is a courage self-sustained, based on a knowledge of the right and on a life-long calculation that any results coming from adherence to the right will be preferable to any that can be produced by a departure from it. This is the courage which will enable a man to stand his ground in battle or elsewhere, though broken worlds should fall around him. The other courage, which is mainly an affair of the heart or blood and not of the brain, always requires some outward support. The man who finds himself prominent in danger bears himself gallantly, because the eyes of many will see him; whether as an old man he leads an army, or as a young man goes on a forlorn hope, or as a private carries his officer on his back out of the fire, he is sustained by the love of praise. And the men who are not individually prominent in danger, who stand their ground shoulder to shoulder, bear themselves gallantly also, each trusting in the combined strength of his comrades. When such combined strength has been acquired, that useful courage is engendered which we may rather call confidence, and which of all courage is the most serviceable in the army. At the battle of Bull's Run the army of the North became panic-stricken and fled. From this fact many have been led to believe that the American soldiers would not fight well, and that they could not be brought to stand their ground under fire. This I think has been an unfair conclusion. In the first place the history of the battle of Bull's Run has yet to be written; as yet the history of the flight only has been given to us. As far as I can learn, the northern soldiers did at first fight well;—so well, that the army of the South believed itself to be beaten. But a panic was created—at first, as it seems, among the teamsters and waggons. A cry was roused, and a rush was made by hundreds of drivers with their carts and horses; and then men who had never seen war before, who had not yet had three months' drilling as soldiers, to whom the turmoil of that day must have seemed as though hell were opening upon them, joined themselves to the general clamour, and fled to Washington, believing that all was lost. But at the same time the regiments of the enemy were going through the same farce in the other direction! It was a battle between troops who knew nothing of battles; of soldiers who were not yet soldiers. That individual high-minded courage, which would have given to each individual recruit the self-sustained power against a panic, which is to be looked for in a general, was not to be looked for in them. Of the other courage of which I have spoken, there was as much as the circumstances of the battle would allow.

On subsequent occasions the men have fought well. We should, I think, admit that they have fought very well when we consider how short has been their practice at such work. At Somerset, at Fort Henry, at Fort Donnelson, at Corinth, the men behaved with courage, standing well to their arms, though at each place the slaughter among them was great. They have always gone well into fire, and have generally borne themselves well under fire. I am convinced that we in England can make no greater mistake than to suppose that the Americans as soldiers are deficient in courage.

But now I must come to a matter in which a terrible deficiency has been shown, not by the soldiers, but by those whose duty it has been to provide for the soldiers. It is impossible to speak of the army of the North and to leave untouched that hideous subject of army contracts. And I think myself the more specially bound to allude to it because I feel that the iniquities which have prevailed, prove with terrible earnestness the demoralizing power of that dishonesty among men in high places, which is the one great evil of the American States. It is there that the deficiency exists, which must be supplied before the public men of the nation can take a high rank among other public men. There is the gangrene, which must be cut out before the government, as a government, can be great. To make money is the one thing needful, and men have been anxious to meddle with the affairs of government, because there might money be made with the greatest ease. "Make money," the Roman satirist said; "make it honestly if you can, but at any rate make money." That first counsel would be considered futile and altogether vain by those who have lately dealt with the public wants of the American States.

This is bad in a most fatal degree, not mainly because men in high places have been dishonest, or because the government has been badly served by its own paid officers. That men in high places should be dishonest, and that the people should be cheated by their rulers is very bad. But there is worse than this. The thing becomes so common, and so notorious, that the American world at large is taught to believe that dishonesty is in itself good. "It behoves a man to be smart, sir!" Till the opposite doctrine to that be learned; till men in America,—ay, and in Europe, Asia, and Africa,—can learn that it specially behoves a man not to be smart, they will have learned little of their duty towards God, and nothing of their duty towards their neighbour.

In the instances of fraud against the States' government to which I am about to allude, I shall take all my facts from the report made to the House of Representatives at Washington by a Committee of that House in December, 1861. "Mr. Washbourne, from the Select Committee to inquire into the Contracts of the Government, made the following Report." That is the heading of the pamphlet.[3] The Committee was known as the Van Wyck Committee, a gentleman of that name having acted as chairman.

The Committee first went to New York, and began their inquiries with reference to the purchase of a steam-boat called the "Catiline." In this case a certain Captain Comstock had been designated from Washington as the agent to be trusted in the charter or purchase of the vessel. He agreed on behalf of the Government to hire that special boat for 2000*l.* a month for three months, having given information to friends of his on the matter, which enabled them to purchase it out-and-out for less than 4000*l.* These friends were not connected with shipping matters, but were lawyers and hotel proprietors. The Committee conclude "that the vessel was chartered to the Government at an unconscionable price; and that Captain Comstock by whom this was effected, while enjoying *the peculiar confidence of the Government,* was acting for and in concert with the parties who chartered the vessel, and was in fact their agent." But the report does not explain why Captain Comstock was selected for this work by authority from Washing-

---

[3] *House Report No. 2, 37th Congress, 2nd Session.* Since Trollope speaks of this work as a "pamphlet," he must have seen a reprint of the report proper, which occupies only 84 pages. The supporting testimony runs to an additional 1,615 pages!

ton, nor does it recommend that he be punished. It does not appear that Captain Comstock had ever been in the regular service of the Government; but that he had been master of a steamer.

In the next place one Starbuck is employed to buy ships. As a government agent he buys two for 1300*l.*, and sells them to the government for 2900*l.* The vessels themselves, when delivered at the Navy Yard, were found to be totally unfit for the service for which they had been purchased. But why was Starbuck employed, when, as appears over and over again in the report, New York was full of paid government servants ready and fit to do the work? Starbuck was merely an agent, and who will believe that he was allowed to pocket the whole difference of 1600*l.*? The greater part of the plunder was, however, in this case refunded.

Then we come to the case of Mr. George D. Morgan, brother-in-law of Mr. Welles, the Secretary of the Navy. I have spoken of this gentleman before, and of his singular prosperity. He amassed a large fortune in five months, as a government agent for the purchase of vessels, he having been a wholesale grocer by trade. This gentleman had had no experience whatsoever with reference to ships. It is shown by the evidence that he had none of the requisite knowledge, and that there were special servants of the government in New York at that time, sent there specially for such services as these, who were in every way trustworthy, and who had the requisite knowledge. Yet Mr. Morgan was placed in this position by his brother-in-law the Secretary of the Navy, and in that capacity made about 20,000*l.* in five months, all of which was paid by the government, as is well shown to have been the fact in the report before me. One result of such a mode of agency is given;—one other result, I mean, besides the 20,000*l.* put into the pocket of the brother of the Secretary of the Navy. A ship called the "Stars and Stripes" was bought by Mr. Morgan for 11,000*l.*, which had been built some months before for 7000*l.* This vessel was bought from a company which was blessed with a President. The President made the bargain with the government agent, but insisted on keeping back from his own company 2000*l.* out of the 11,000*l.* for expenses incident to the purchase. The company did not like being mulcted of its prey, and growled heavily; but their President declared that such bargains were not got at Washington for nothing. Members of Congress had to be paid to assist in such things. At least he could not reduce his little private bill for such assistance below 1600*l.* He had, he said, positively paid out so much to those venal Members of Congress, and had made nothing for himself to compensate him for his own exertions. When this President came to be examined, he admitted that he had really made no payments to Members of Congress. His own capacity had been so great that no such assistance had been found necessary. But he justified his charge on the ground that the sum taken by him was no more than the company might have expected him to lay out on Members of Congress, or on ex-Members who are specially mentioned, had he not himself carried on the business with such consummate discretion! It seems to me that the Members or ex-Members of Congress were shamefully robbed in this matter.

The report deals manfully with Mr. Morgan, showing that for five months' work,—which work he did not do and did not know how to do, he received as large a sum as the President's salary for the whole Presidential term of four years. So much better is it to be an agent of government than simply an officer! And the Committee adds, that they "do not find in this transaction the less to censure in the fact that this arrangement between the Secretary of the Navy and Mr. Morgan was one between brothers-in-law." After that who will believe that Mr. Morgan had the whole of that 20,000*l.* for himself? And yet Mr. Welles still remains Secretary of the Navy, and has justified the whole transaction in an explanation admitting everything, and which is considered by his friends to be an able State paper. "It behoves a man to be smart, sir." Mr. Morgan and Secretary Welles will no doubt be considered by their own party to have done their duty well as high trading public functionaries. The faults of Mr. Morgan and of Secretary Welles are nothing to us in England; but the light in which such faults may be regarded by the American people is much to us.

I will now go on to the case of a Mr. Cummings. Mr. Cummings, it appears, had been for many years the editor of a newspaper in Philadelphia, and had been an intimate political friend and ally of Mr. Cameron. Now at the time of which I am writing, April, 1861, Mr. Cameron was Secretary-at-War, and could be very useful to an old political ally living in his own State. The upshot of the present case will teach us to think well of Mr. Cameron's gratitude.

In April, 1861, stores were wanted for the army at Washington, and Mr. Cameron gave an order to his old friend Cummings to expend 2,000,000 dollars, pretty much according to his fancy, in buying stores. Governor Morgan, the Governor of New York State and a relative of our other friend Morgan, was joined with Mr. Cummings in this commission, Mr. Cameron no doubt having felt himself bound to give the friends of his colleague at the Navy a chance. Governor Morgan at once made over his right to his relative; but better things soon came in Mr.

Morgan's way, and he relinquished his share in this partnership at an early date. In this transaction he did not himself handle above 25,000 dollars. Then the whole job fell into the hands of Mr. Cameron's old political friend.

The 2,000,000 of dollars, or 400,000*l*., were paid into the hands of certain government treasurers at New York, but they had orders to honour the draft of the political friend of the Secretary-at-War, and consequently 50,000*l*. was immediately withdrawn by Mr. Cummings, and with this he went to work. It is shown that he knew nothing of the business; that he employed a clerk from Albany whom he did not know, and confided to this clerk the duty of buying such stores as were bought; that this clerk was recommended to him by Mr. Weed, the editor of a newspaper at Albany, who is known in the States as the special political friend of Mr. Seward, the Secretary of State; and that in this way he spent 32,000*l*. He bought linen pantaloons and straw hats to the amount of 4200*l*., because he thought the soldiers looked hot in the warm weather; but he afterwards learned that they were of no use. He bought groceries of a hardware dealer at Albany, named Davidson, that town whence came Mr. Weed's clerk. He did not know what was Davidson's trade, nor did he know exactly what he was going to buy; but Davidson proposed to sell him something which Mr. Cummings believed to be some kind of provisions, and he bought it. He did not know for how much,—whether over 2000*l*. or not. He never saw the articles and had no knowledge of their quality. It was out of the question that he should have such knowledge, as he naïvely remarks. His clerk Humphreys saw the articles. He presumed they were brought from Albany, but did not know. He afterwards bought a ship,—or two or three ships. He inspected one ship "by a mere casual visit": that is to say, he did not examine her boilers; he did not know her tonnage, but he took the word of the seller for everything. He could not state the terms of the charter, or give the substance of it. He had had no former experience in buying or chartering ships. He also bought 75,000 pair of shoes at only 25 cents, or one shilling a pair, more than their proper price. He bought them of a Mr. Hall, who declares that he paid Mr. Cummings nothing for the job, but regarded it as a return for certain previous favours conferred by him on Mr. Cummings in the occasional loans of 100*l*. or 200*l*.

At the end of the examination it appears that Mr. Cummings still held in his hand a slight balance of 28,000*l*., of which he had forgotten to make mention in the body of his own evidence. "This item seems to have been overlooked by him in his testimony," says the report. And when the report was made nothing had yet been learned of the destiny of this small balance.

Then the report gives a list of the army supplies miscellaneously purchased by Mr. Cummings:—280 dozen pints of ale at 9s. 6d. a dozen; a lot of codfish and herrings; 200 boxes of cheeses and a large assortment of butter; some tongues; straw hats and linen "pants"; 23 barrels of pickles; 25 casks of Scotch ale, price not stated; a lot of London porter, price not stated; and some Hall carbines of which I must say a word more further on. It should be remembered that no requisition had come from the army for any of the articles named; that the purchase of herrings and straw hats was dictated solely by the discretion of Cummings and his man Humphreys,— or, as is more probable, by the fact that some other person had such articles by him for sale; and that the government had its own established officers for the supply of things properly ordered by military requisition. These very same articles also were apparently procured, in the first place, as a private speculation, and were made over to the government on the failure of that speculation. "Some of the above articles," says the report, "were shipped by the 'Catiline,' which were probably loaded on private account, and not being able to obtain a clearance was in some way, through Mr. Cummings, transferred over to the government,—*Scotch ale, London porter, selected herrings,* and all." The italics as well as the words are taken from the report.

This was the confidential political friend of the Secretary-at-War, by whom he was intrusted with 400,000l. of public money! 28,000l. had not been accounted for when the report was made, and the army supplies were bought after the fashion above named. That Secretary-at-War, Mr. Cameron, has since left the Cabinet; but he has not been turned out in disgrace; [4] he has been nominated as minister to Russia,

[4] Simon Cameron (1799–1899) was a political phenomenon of the first order. His long-undisputed control of the state of Pennsylvania represents one of the most striking records of "boss rule" in American history. Though Lincoln was reluctant to make him Secretary of War, Cameron's power was sufficient to force the appointment. Cameron's career subsequent to his removal from the Cabinet is an impressive instance of those recuperative powers in Americans that Trollope found so remarkable. On April 30, 1862 (while *North America* was in the press) the House passed a resolution declaring that Cameron as Secretary of War had "adopted a policy highly injurious to the public service," and voted its censure upon his head. Despite this ignominy, Cameron returned from Russia the following November to set about campaigning for election to the Senate. He failed in the race of 1863; four years later, after a "struggle of unexampled desperation," he came out triumphant.

For the next ten years Cameron remained in the Senate, serving after 1872 as chairman of the Committee on Foreign Relations. In 1876, during the closing months of Grant's administration, he had the pleasure of seeing his son installed in the post he himself had once been forced to vacate under such unsatisfactory condi-

XV   Interior of the New York Post Office
Frank Leslie's Illustrated Newspaper, II (*June* 11, 1856), 72

XVI Ladies' Drawing-Room in the Fifth Avenue Hotel: "But in the States of America the first sign of an incipient settlement is an hotel five stories high, with an office, a bar, a cloak-room, three gentlemen's parlours, two ladies' parlours, a ladies' entrance, and two hundred bedrooms."

Harper's Weekly, III (*October* 1, 1859), 633

and the world has been told that there was some difference of opinion between him and his colleagues respecting slavery! Mr. Cameron in some speech or paper declared on his leaving the Cabinet that he had not intended to remain long as Secretary-at-War. This assertion, I should think, must have been true.

And now about the Hall carbines, as to which the gentlemen on this Committee tell their tale with an evident delight in the richness of its incidents which at once puts all their readers in accord with them. There were altogether some five thousand of these, all of which the government sold to a Mr. Eastman in June, 1861, for 14*s.* each, as perfectly useless, and afterwards bought in August for 4*l.* 8*s.* each, about 4*s.* a carbine having been expended in their repair in the mean time. But as regards 790 of these now famous weapons, it must be explained they had been sold by the government as perfectly useless, and at a nominal price, previously to this second sale made by the government to Mr. Eastman. They had been so sold, and then, in April, 1861, they had been bought again for the government by the indefatigable Cummings for 3*l.* each. Then they were again sold as useless for 14*s.* each to Eastman, and instantly re-bought on behalf of the government for 4*l.* 8*s.* each! Useless for war purposes they may have been, but as articles of commerce it must be confessed that they were very serviceable.

This last purchase was made by a man named Stevens on behalf of General Fremont, who at that time commanded the army of the United States in Missouri. Stevens had been employed by General Fremont as an agent on the behalf of government, as is shown with clearness in the report, and on hearing of these muskets telegraphed to the General at once. "I have 5000 Hall's rifled cast-steel muskets, breech-loading, new, at 22 dollars." General Fremont telegraphed back instantly, "I will take the whole 5000 carbines . . . I will pay all extra charges. . . ." And so the purchase was made. The muskets, it seems, were not absolutely useless even as weapons of war. "Considering the emergency of the times," a competent witness considered them to be worth "10 or 12 dollars." The government had been as much cheated in selling them as it had in buying them. But the nature of the latter transaction is shown by the facts that Stevens was employed, though irresponsibly employed, as a government agent by General Fremont; that he bought the muskets

tions. When President Hayes refused next year to continue the younger Cameron as Secretary of War, the father made a place for him by resigning from the Senate, having first obtained assurances from the pliant legislature of Pennsylvania that it would elect his son to the seat. In the campaign of 1880 Cameron was chairman of the Republican National Committee. He lived to see his son three times elected to the Senate.

in that character himself, making on the transaction 1*l*. 18*s*. on each musket; and that the same man afterwards appeared as an aide-de-camp on General Fremont's staff. General Fremont had no authority himself to make such a purchase, and when the money was paid for the first instalment of the arms, it was so paid by the special order of General Fremont himself out of moneys intended to be applied to other purposes. The money was actually paid to a gentleman known at Fremont's head-quarters as his special friend, and was then paid in that irregular way because this friend desired that that special bill should receive immediate payment. After that who can believe that Stevens was himself allowed to pocket the whole amount of the plunder?

There is a nice little story of a clergyman in New York who sold for 40*l*. and certain further contingencies, the right to furnish 200 cavalry horses; but I should make this too long if I told all the nice little stories. As the frauds at St. Louis were, if not in fact the most monstrous, at any rate the most monstrous which have as yet been brought to the light, I cannot finish this account without explaining something of what was going on at that western Paradise in those halcyon days of General Fremont.

General Fremont, soon after reaching St. Louis, undertook to build ten forts for the protection of that city. These forts have since been pronounced as useless, and the whole measure has been treated with derision by officers of his own army. But the judgment displayed in the matter is a military question with which I do not presume to meddle. Even if a general be wrong in such a matter, his character as a man is not disgraced by such error. But the manner of building them was the affair with which Mr. Van Wyck's committee had to deal. It seems that five of the forts, the five largest, were made under the orders of a certain Major Kappner at a cost of 12,000*l*., and that the other five could have been built at least for the same sum. Major Kappner seems to have been a good and honest public servant, and therefore quite unfit for the superintendence of such work at St. Louis. The other five smaller forts were also in progress. The works on them having been continued from 1st September to 25th September, 1861; but on the 25th September General Fremont himself gave special orders that a contract should be made with a man named Beard, a Californian, who had followed him from California to St. Louis. This contract is dated the 25th of September. But nevertheless the work specified in that contract was done previous to that date, and most of the money paid was paid previous to that date. The contract did not specify any lump sum, but agreed that the work should be paid for by the yard and by the square foot. No less a sum was paid to Beard for this work—the cormorant Beard, as the report calls him—than 24,200*l.*, the last payment only, amounting to 400*l.*, having been made subsequent to the date of the contract. 20,200*l.* was paid to Beard before the date of the contract! The amounts were paid at five times, and the last four payments were made on the personal order of General Fremont. This Beard was under no bond, and none of the officers of the government knew anything of the terms under which he was working. On the 14th of October General Fremont was ordered to discontinue these works, and to abstain from making any further payments on their account. But, disobeying this order, he directed his Quartermaster to pay a further sum of 4000*l.* to Beard out of the first sums he should receive from Washington, he then being out of money. This however was not paid. "It must be understood," says the report, "that every dollar ordered to be paid by General Fremont on account of these works was diverted from a fund specially appropriated for another purpose." And then again, "The money appropriated by Congress to subsist and clothe and transport our armies was then, in utter contempt of all law and of the army regulations, as well as in defiance of superior authority, ordered to be diverted from its lawful purpose and turned over to the cormorant Beard. While he had received 170,000 dollars (24,200*l.*) from the Government, it will be seen from the testimony of Major Kappner that there had only been paid to the honest German labourers, who did the work on the first five forts built under his directions, the sum of 15,500 dollars (3100*l.*), leaving from 40,000 to 50,000 dollars (8000*l.* to 10,000*l.*) still due; and while these labourers, whose families were clamoring for bread, were besieging the Quartermaster's department for their pay, this infamous contractor Beard is found following up the army and in the confidence of the Major-General, who gives him orders for large purchases, which could only have been legally made through the Quartermaster's department." After that who will believe that all the money went into Beard's pocket? Why should General Fremont have committed every conceivable breach of order against his government, merely with the view of favouring such a man as Beard?

The collusion of the Quartermaster M'Instry with fraudulent knaves in the purchase of horses is then proved. M'Instry was at this time Fremont's Quartermaster at St. Louis. I cannot go through all these. A man of the name of Jim Neil comes out in beautiful pre-eminence. No dealer in horses could get to the Quartermaster except through Jim Neil, or some such go-between. The Quartermaster contracted with Neil and Neil with the owners of horses; Neil at the time being also military inspector of horses for the Quartermaster. He bought horses as cavalry horses for 24*l.* or less, and passed them himself as artillery horses for 30*l.* In other cases the military inspectors were paid by the sellers to pass horses. All this was done under Quartermaster M'Instry, who would himself deal with none but such as Neil. In one instance, one Elleard got a contract from M'Instry, the profit of which was 8000*l.* But there was a man named Brady. Now Brady was a friend of M'Instry's, who scenting the carrion afar off, had come from Detroit, in Michigan, to St. Louis. M'Instry himself had also come from Detroit. In this case Elleard was simply directed by M'Instry to share his profits with Brady, and consequently paid to Brady 4000*l.*, although Brady gave to the business neither capital nor labour. He simply took the 4000*l.* as the Quartermaster's friend. This Elleard, it seems, also gave a carriage and horses to Mrs. Fremont. Indeed Elleard seems to have been a civil and generous fellow. Then there is a man named Thompson, whose case is very amusing. Of him the Committee thus speaks:—"It must be said that Thompson was not forgetful of the obligations of gratitude, for, after he got through with the contract, he presented the son of Major M'Instry with a riding pony. That was the only mark of respect," to use his own words, "that he showed to the family of Major M'Instry."

General Fremont himself desired that a contract should be made with one Augustus Sacchi for a thousand Canadian horses. It turned out that Sacchi was "nobody: a man of straw living in a garret in New York whom nobody knew, a man who was brought out there"—to St. Louis—"as a good person through whom to work." "It will hardly be believed," says the report, "that the name of this same man Sacchi appears in the newspapers as being on the staff of General Fremont, at Springfield, with the rank of captain."

I do not know that any good would result from my pursuing further the details of this wonderful report. The remaining portion of it refers solely to the command held by General Fremont in Missouri, and adds proof upon proof of the gross robberies inflicted upon the government of the States by the very persons set in high authority to protect the government. We learn how all utensils for the camp, kettles, blankets, shoes, mess-pans, &c., were supplied by one firm, without a contract, at an enormous price, and of a quality so bad as to be almost useless, because the Quartermaster was under obligations to the partners. We learn that one partner in that firm gave 40*l.* towards a service of plate for the Quartermaster, and 60*l.* towards a carriage for Mrs. Fremont. We learn how futile were the efforts of any honest tradesman to supply good shoes to soldiers who were shoeless, and the history of one special pair of shoes which was thrust under the nose of the Quartermaster is very amusing. We learn that a certain paymaster properly refused to settle an account for matters with which he had no concern, and that General Fremont at once sent down soldiers to arrest him unless he made the illegal payment. In October 1000*l.* was expended in ice, all which ice was wasted. Regiments were sent hither and thither with no military purpose, merely because certain officers, calling themselves generals, desired to make up brigades for themselves. Indeed every description of fraud was perpetrated, and this was done not through the negligence of those in high command, but by their connivance and often with their express authority.

It will be said that the conduct of General Fremont [5] during the days of his command in Missouri is not a matter of much moment to us in England; that it has been properly handled by the Committee of Representatives appointed by the American Congress to inquire into the matter; and that after the publication of such a report by them, it is ungenerous in a writer from another nation to speak upon the subject. This would be so if the inquiries made by that Committee and their report had resulted in any general condemnation of the men whose misdeeds and peculations have been exposed. This, however, is by no means the case. Those who were heretofore opposed to General Fremont on political principles are opposed to him still; but those who heretofore supported him are ready to support him again.* He has not been placed beyond the pale of public favour by the record which has been made of his public misdeeds. He is decried by the Democrats because he is a Republican, and by the anti-abolitionists because he is an abolitionist; but he is not decried because he has shown himself to be dishonest in the service of his government. He was dismissed from his command in the West, but men on his side of the question declare that

[5] Allan Nevins (*Frémont, Pathmaker of the West* [1939]) would apparently absolve Frémont from a conscious part in the corrupt dealings that went on at St. Louis. The general was wanting in high executive ability, he says, and deficient in the power to judge men; but "much of the irregularity in letting contracts, the general confusion . . . arose from the fact that he was crushed under a mountain of labor."

* Since this was written General Fremont has been restored to high military command, and now holds equal rank and equal authority with Maclellan and Halleck. In fact, the charges made against him by the Committee of the House of Representatives have not been allowed to stand in his way. He is politically popular with a large section of the nation, and therefore it has been thought well to promote him to high place. Whether he be fit for such place, either as regards capability or integrity, seems to be considered of no moment.

he was so dismissed because his political opponents had prevailed. Now, at the moment that I am writing this, men are saying that the President must give him another command. He is still a major-general in the army of the State, and is as probable a candidate as any other that I could name for the next Presidency.

The same argument must be used with reference to the other gentlemen named. Mr. Welles is still a Cabinet Minister and Secretary for the Navy. It has been found impossible to keep Mr. Cameron in the Cabinet, but he was named as the Minister of the States government to Russia after the publication of the Van Wyck report, when the result of his old political friendship with Mr. Alexander Cummings was well known to the President who appointed him and to the Senate who sanctioned his appointment. The individual corruption of any one man—of any ten men—is not much. It should not be insisted on loudly by any foreigner in making up a balance-sheet of the virtues and vices of the good and bad qualities of any nation. But the light in which such corruption is viewed by the people whom it most nearly concerns is very much. I am far from saying that democracy has failed in America. Democracy there has done great things for a numerous people, and will yet, as I think, be successful. But that doctrine as to the necessity of smartness must be eschewed before a verdict in favour of American democracy can be pronounced. "It behoves a man to be smart, sir." In those words are contained the curse under which the States' government has been suffering for the last thirty years. Let us hope that the people will find a mode of ridding themselves of that curse. I, for one, believe that they will do so.

CHAPTER XXVII

From Louisville we returned to Cincinnati, in making which journey
we were taken to a place called Seymour in Indiana, at which spot we
were to "make connection" with the train running on the Mississippi
and Ohio line from St. Louis to Cincinnati. We did make the connection, but were called upon to remain four hours at Seymour in consequence of some accident on the line. In the same way, when going
eastwards from Cincinnati to Baltimore a few days later, I was detained
another four hours at a place called Crossline, in Ohio. On both occasions I spent my time in realizing, as far as that might be possible, the
sort of life which men lead who settle themselves at such localities. Both
these towns,—for they call themselves towns,—had been created by the
railways. Indeed this has been the case with almost every place at which
a few hundred inhabitants have been drawn together in the western
States. With the exception of such cities as Chicago, St. Louis, and Cincinnati, settlers can hardly be said to have chosen their own localities.
These have been chosen for them by the originators of the different
lines of railway. And there is nothing in Europe in any way like to
these western railway settlements. In the first place the line of the rails
runs through the main street of the town, and forms not unfrequently
the only road. At Seymour I could find no way of getting away from the
rails unless I went into the fields. At Crossline, which is a larger place,
I did find a street in which there was no railroad, but it was deserted,
and manifestly out of favour with the inhabitants. As there were railway junctions at both these posts, there were of course cross-streets, and
the houses extended themselves from the centre thus made along the
lines, houses being added to houses at short intervals as new comers
settled themselves down. The panting and groaning, and whistling of
engines is continual; for at such places freight trains are always kept
waiting for passenger trains, and the slower freight trains for those
which are called fast. This is the life of the town; and indeed as the
whole place is dependent on the railway, so is the railway held in favour and beloved. The noise of the engine is not disliked, nor are its
puffings and groanings held to be unmusical. With us a locomotive
steam-engine is still, as it were, a beast of prey, against which one has
to be on one's guard,—in respect to which one specially warns the chil-

dren. But there, in the western States, it has been taken to the bosoms of them all as a domestic animal; no one fears it, and the little children run about almost among its wheels. It is petted and made much of on all sides,—and, as far as I know, it seldom bites or tears. I have not heard of children being destroyed wholesale in the streets, or of drunken men becoming frequent sacrifices. But had I been consulted beforehand as to the natural effects of such an arrangement, I should have said that no child could have been reared in such a town, and that any continuance of population under such circumstances must have been impracticable.

Such places, however, do thrive and prosper with a prosperity especially their own, and the boys and girls increase and multiply in spite of all dangers. With us in England, it is difficult to realize the importance which is attached to a railway in the States, and the results which a railway creates. We have roads everywhere, and our country had been cultivated throughout, with more or less care, before our system of railways had been commenced; but in America, especially in the North, the railways have been the precursors of cultivation. They have been carried hither and thither, through primeval forests and over prairies, with small hope of other traffic than that which they themselves would make by their own influences. The people settling on their edges have had the very best of all roads at their service; but they have had no other roads. The face of the country between one settlement and another is still in many cases utterly unknown; but there is the connecting road by which produce is carried away, and new comers are brought in. The town that is distant a hundred miles by the rail is so near that its inhabitants are neighbours; but a settlement twenty miles distant across the uncleared country is unknown, unvisited, and probably unheard of by the women and children. Under such circumstances the railway is everything. It is the first necessity of life, and gives the only hope of wealth. It is the backbone of existence from whence spring, and by which are protected, all the vital organs and functions of the community. It is the right arm of civilization for the people, and the discoverer of the fertility of the land. It is all in all to those people, and to those regions. It has supplied the wants of frontier life with all the substantial comfort of the cities, and carried education, progress, and social habits into the wilderness. To the eye of the stranger such places as Seymour and Crossline are desolate and dreary. There is nothing of beauty in them, given either by nature or by art. The railway itself is ugly, and its numerous sidings and branches form a mass of iron road which is bewildering and, according to my ideas, in itself disagreeable. The wooden houses open down upon the line, and have no gardens to relieve them. A foreigner, when first surveying such a spot, will certainly record within himself a verdict against it; but in doing so he probably commits the error of judging it by a wrong standard. He should compare it with the new settlements which men have opened up in spots where no railway has assisted them, and not with old towns in which wealth has long been congregated. The traveller may see what is the place with the railway; then let him consider how it might have thriven without the railway.

I confess that I became tired of my sojourn at both the places I have named. At each I think that I saw every house in the place, although my visit to Seymour was made in the night; and at both I was lamentably at a loss for something to do. At Crossline I was all alone, and began to feel that the hours which I knew must pass before the missing train could come, would never make away with themselves. There were many others stationed there as I was, but to them had been given a capability for loafing which niggardly Nature has denied to me. An American has the power of seating himself in the close vicinity of a hot stove and feeding in silence on his own thoughts by the hour together. It may be that he will smoke; but after a while his cigar will come to an end. He sits on, however, certainly patient, and apparently contented. It may be that he chews, but if so, he does it with motionless jaws, and so slow a mastication of the pabulum on which he feeds, that his employment in this respect only disturbs the absolute quiet of the circle when, at certain long, distant intervals, he deposits the secretion of his tobacco in an ornamental utensil which may probably be placed in the furthest corner of the hall. But during all this time he is happy. It does not fret him to sit there and think and do nothing. He is by no means an idle man,—probably one much given to commercial enterprise. Idle men out there in the West we may say there are none. How should any idle man live in such a country? All who were sitting hour after hour in that circle round the stove of the Crossline Hotel hall,—sitting there hour after hour in silence, as I could not sit,—were men who earned their bread by labour. They were farmers, mechanics, storekeepers; there was a lawyer or two, and one clergyman. Sufficient conversation took place at first to indicate the professions of many of them. One may conclude that there could not be place there for an idle man. But they all of them had a capacity for a prolonged state of doing nothing, which is to me unintelligible, and which is very much to be envied. They are patient as cows, which from hour to hour lie on the grass chewing their cud. An Englishman, if he be kept waiting by a train in some forlorn station in which he can find no employment, curses his fate and all that has led to his present misfortune with an energy which tells the story of his deep and thorough misery. Such, I confess, is my state of existence under such circumstances. But a western American gives himself up to "loafing," and is quite happy. He balances himself on the back legs of an arm-chair, and remains so, without speaking, drinking, or smoking for an hour at a stretch; and while he is doing so he looks as though he had all that he desired. I believe that he is happy, and that he has all that he wants for such an occasion; —an arm-chair in which to sit, and a stove on which he can put his feet, and by which he can make himself warm.

Such was not the phase of character which I had expected to find among the people of the West. Of all virtues, patience would have been the last which I should have thought of attributing to them. I should have expected to see them angry when robbed of their time, and irritable under the stress of such grievances as railway delays; but they are never irritable under such circumstances as I have attempted to describe, nor, indeed, are they a people prone to irritation under any grievances. Even in political matters they are long-enduring, and do not form themselves into mobs for the expression of hot opinion. We in England thought that masses of the people would rise in anger if Mr. Lincoln's government should consent to give up Slidell and Mason; but the people bore it without any rising. The habeas corpus has been suspended, the liberty of the press has been destroyed for a time, the telegraph wires have been taken up by the government into their own hands; but nevertheless the people have said nothing. There has been no rising of a mob, and not even an expression of an adverse opinion. The people require to be allowed to vote periodically, and having acquired that privilege permit other matters to go by the board. In this respect we have, I think, in some degree misunderstood their character. They have all been taught to reverence the nature of that form of government under which they live, but they are not specially addicted to hot political fermentation. They have learned to understand that democratic institutions have given them liberty, and on that subject they entertain a strong conviction which is universal. But they have not habitually interested themselves deeply in the doings of their legislators or of their government. On the subject of slavery there have been and are different opinions, held with great tenacity, and maintained occasionally with violence; but on other subjects of daily policy the American people have not, I think, been eager politicians. Leading men in public life have been much less trammelled by popular will than among us. Indeed with us the most conspicuous of our statesmen and legislators do not lead, but are led. In the States the noted politicians of the day have been the leaders, and not unfrequently the coercers of opinion. Seeing this, I claim for England a broader freedom in political matters than the States have as yet achieved. In speaking of the American form of government, I will endeavour to explain more clearly the ideas which I have come to hold on this matter.

I survived my delay at Seymour, after which I passed again through Cincinnati, and then survived my subsequent delay at Crossline. As to Cincinnati, I must put on record the result of a country walk which I took there,—or rather on which I was taken by my friend. He professed to know the beauties of the neighbourhood, and to be well acquainted with all that was attractive in its vicinity. Cincinnati is built on the Ohio, and is closely surrounded by picturesque hills which overhang the suburbs of the city. Over these I was taken, ploughing my way through a depth of mud which cannot be understood by any ordinary Englishman. But the depth of mud was not the only impediment, nor the worst which we encountered. As we began to ascend from the level of the outskirts of the town we were greeted by a rising flavour in the air, which soon grew into a strong odour, and at last developed itself into a stench that surpassed in offensiveness anything that my nose had ever hitherto suffered.[1] When we were at the worst we hardly knew whether to descend or to proceed. It had so increased in virulence, that at one time I felt sure that it rose from some matter buried in the ground beneath my feet. But my friend, who declared himself to be quite at home in Cincinnati matters, and to understand the details of the great Cincinnati trade, declared against this opinion of mine. Hogs, he said, were at the bottom of it. It was the odour of hogs going up to the Ohio heavens;—of hogs in a state of transit from hoggish nature to clothes-brushes, saddles, sausages, and lard. He spoke with an authority that constrained belief; but I can never forgive him in that he took me over those hills, knowing all that he professed to know. Let the visitors to Cincinnati keep themselves within the city, and not wander forth among the mountains. It is well that the odour of hogs should ascend to heaven and not hang heavy over the streets; but it is not well to intercept that odour in its ascent. My friend became ill with fever, and had to betake himself to the care of nursing friends; so that I parted company with him at Cincinnati. I did not tell him that his

[1] For Frances Trollope's excursion perhaps along the same pathway, certainly in the same atmosphere, see the quotation from *Domestic Manners* given in the note to page 374.

illness was deserved as well as natural, but such was my feeling on the matter. I myself happily escaped the evil consequences which his imprudence might have entailed on me.

I passed again through Pittsburg, and over the Alleghany mountains by Altoona, and down to Baltimore,—back into civilization, secession, conversation, and gastronomy. I never had secessionist sympathies and never expressed them. I always believed in the North as a people,—discrediting, however, to the utmost the existing northern Government, or, as I should more properly say, the existing northern Cabinet; but nevertheless, with such feelings and such belief, I found myself very happy at Baltimore. Putting aside Boston, which must, I think, be generally preferred by Englishmen to any other city in the States. I should choose Baltimore as my residence if I were called upon to live in America. I am not led to this opinion, if I know myself, solely by the canvasback ducks; and as to the terrapins, I throw them to the winds. The madeira, which is still kept there with a reverence which I should call superstitious were it not that its free circulation among outside worshippers prohibits the just use of such a word, may have something to do with it; as may also the beauty of the women,—to some small extent. Trifles do bear upon our happiness in a manner that we do not ourselves understand, and of which we are unconscious. But there was an English look about the streets and houses which I think had as much to do with it as either the wine, the women, or the ducks; and it seemed to me as though the manners of the people of Maryland were more English than those of other Americans. I do not say that they were on this account better. My English hat is, I am well aware, less graceful, and I believe less comfortable, than a Turkish fez and turban; nevertheless I prefer my English hat. New York I regard as the most thoroughly American of all American cities. It is by no means the one in which I should find myself the happiest, but I do not on that account condemn it.

I have said that in returning to Baltimore I found myself among secessionists. In so saying, I intend to speak of a certain set whose influence depends perhaps more on their wealth, position, and education than on their numbers. I do not think that the population of the city was then in favour of secession, even if it had ever been so. I believe that the mob of Baltimore is probably the roughtest mob in the States, —is more akin to a Paris mob, and I may, perhaps, also say to a Manchester mob, than that of any other American city. There are more roughs in Baltimore than elsewhere, and the roughs there are rougher. In those early days of secession, when the troops were being first hurried down from New England for the protection of Washington, this mob was vehemently opposed to its progress. Men had been taught to think that the rights of the State of Maryland were being invaded by the passage of the soldiers; and they also were undoubtedly imbued with a strong prepossession for the southern cause. The two ideas had then gone together. But the mob of Baltimore had ceased to be secessionists within twelve months of the first exploit. In April, 1861, they had refused to allow Massachusetts soldiers to pass through the town on their way to Washington; and in February, 1862, they were nailing Union flags on the door-posts of those who refused to display such banners as signs of triumph at the northern victories!

That Maryland can ever go with the South, even in the event of the South succeeding in secession, no Marylander can believe. It is not pretended that there is any struggle now going on with such an object. No such result has been expected, certainly since the possession of Washington was secured to the North by the army of the Potomac. By few, I believe, was such a result expected even when Washington was insecure. And yet the feeling for secession among a certain class in Baltimore is as strong now as ever it was. And it is equally strong in certain districts of the State,—in those districts which are most akin to Virginia in their habits, modes of thought, and ties of friendship. These men, and these women also, pray for the South if they be pious, give their money to the South if they be generous, work for the South if they be industrious, fight for the South if they be young, and talk for the South morning, noon, and night in spite of General Dix and his columbiads on Federal Hill. It is in vain to say that such men and women have no strong feeling on the matter, and that they are praying, working, fighting, and talking under dictation. Their hearts are in it. And judging from them, even though there were no other evidence from which to judge, I have no doubt that a similar feeling is strong through all the seceding States. On this subject the North, I think, deceives itself in supposing that the southern rebellion has been carried on without any strong feeling on the part of the southern people. Whether the mob of Charleston be like the mob of Baltimore I cannot tell; but I have no doubt as to the gentry of Charleston and the gentry of Baltimore being in accord on the subject.

In what way, then, when the question has been settled by the force of arms, will these classes find themselves obliged to act? In Virginia and Maryland they comprise, as a rule, the highest and best educated of the people. As to parts of Kentucky the same thing may be said, and probably as to the whole of Tennessee. It must be remembered that this is not as though certain aristocratic families in a few English counties should find themselves divided off from the politics and national aspirations of their countrymen,—as was the case long since with reference to the Roman Catholic adherents of the Stuarts, and as has been the case since then in a lesser degree with the firmest of the old Tories who had allowed themselves to be deceived by Sir Robert Peel.[2] In each of these cases the minority of dissentients was so small that the nation suffered nothing, though individuals were all but robbed of their nationality. But as regards America it must be remembered that each State has in itself a governing power, and is in fact a separate people. Each has its own legislature, and must have its own line of politics.

The secessionists of Maryland and of Virginia may consent to live in obscurity; but if this be so, who is to rule in those States? From whence are to come the senators and the members of Congress; the governors and attorney-generals? From whence is to come the national spirit of the two States, and the salt that shall preserve their political life? I have never believed that these States would succeed in secession. I have always felt that they would be held within the Union, whatever might be their own wishes. But I think that they will be so held in a manner and after a fashion that will render any political vitality almost impossible till a new generation shall have sprung up. In the meantime life goes on pleasantly enough in Baltimore, and ladies meet together, knitting stockings and sewing shirts for the southern soldiers, while the gentlemen talk southern politics and drink the health of the (southern) President in ambiguous terms, as our Cavaliers used to drink the health of the king.

During my second visit to Baltimore I went over to Washington for a day or two, and found the capital still under the empire of King Mud. How the élite of a nation—for the inhabitants of Washington consider themselves to be the élite—can consent to live in such a state of thraldom, a foreigner cannot understand. Were I to say that it was intended to be typical of the condition of the government, I might be considered cynical; but undoubtedly the sloughs of despond which were deepest in their despondency were to be found in localities which gave an appearance of truth to such a surmise. The Secretary of State's office in which Mr. Seward was still reigning, though with diminished glory, was divided from the Head-Quarters of the Commander-in-Chief, which are immediately opposite to it, by an opaque river which admitted of no transit. These buildings stand at the corner of President

[2] For Sir Robert Peel's deception of the old Tories (in securing abolition of the corn laws), see the note to page 159.

Square, and it had been long understood that any close intercourse between them had not been considered desirable by the occupants of the
military side of the causeway. But the Secretary of State's office was altogether unapproachable without a long circuit and begrimed legs.
The Secretary-at-War's department was, if possible, in a worse condition. This is situated on the other side of the President's house, and
the mud lay, if possible, thicker in this quarter than it did round Mr.
Seward's chambers. The passage over Pennsylvania Avenue, immediately in front of the War Office, was a thing not to be attempted in
those days. Mr. Cameron, it is true, had gone, and Mr. Stanton was installed; but the labour of cleansing the interior of that establishment
had hitherto allowed no time for a glance at the exterior dirt, and Mr.
Stanton should, perhaps, be held as excused. That the Navy Office
should be buried in mud, and quite debarred from approach, was to
be expected. The space immediately in front of Mr. Lincoln's own
residence was still kept fairly clean, and I am happy to be able to give
testimony to this effect. Long may it remain so. I could not, however,
but think that an energetic and careful President would have seen to
the removal of the dirt from his own immediate neighbourhood. It was
something that his own shoes should remain unpolluted; but the foul
mud always clinging to the boots and leggings of those by whom he was
daily surrounded must, I should think, have been offensive to him.
The entrance to the Treasury was difficult to achieve by those who had
not learned by practice the ways of the place; but I must confess that
a tolerably clear passage was maintained on that side which led immediately down to the halls of Congress. Up at the Capitol the mud
was again triumphant in the front of the building; this however was
not of great importance, as the legislative chambers of the States are
always reached by the back-door. I, on this occasion, attempted to leave
the building by the grand entrance, but I soon became entangled
among rivers of mud and mazes of shifting sand. With difficulty I recovered my steps, and finding my way back to the building was forced
to content myself by an exit among the crowd of senators and representatives who were thronging down the back-stairs.

Of dirt of all kinds it behoves Washington and those concerned in
Washington to make themselves free. It is the Augean stables through
which some American Hercules must turn a purifying river before the
American people can justly boast either of their capital or of their government. As to the material mud, enough has been said. The presence
of the army perhaps caused it, and the excessive quantity of rain which
had fallen may also be taken as a fair plea. But what excuse shall we

find for that other dirt? It also had been caused by the presence of the army, and by that long-continued down-pouring of contracts which had fallen like Danaë's golden shower into the laps of those who understood how to avail themselves of such heavenly waters. The leaders of the rebellion are hated in the North. The names of Jefferson Davis, of Cobb, Tombes, and Floyd are mentioned with execration by the very children. This has sprung from a true and noble feeling; from a patriotic love of national greatness and a hatred of those who, for small party purposes, have been willing to lessen the name of the United States. I have reverenced the feeling even when I have not shared it. But, in addition to this, the names of those also should be execrated who have robbed their country when pretending to serve it; who have taken its wages in the days of its great struggle, and at the same time have filched from its coffers; who have undertaken the task of steering the ship through the storm in order that their hands might be deep in the meal-tub and the bread-basket, and that they might stuff their own sacks with the ship's provisions. These are the men who must be loathed by the nation,—whose fate must be held up as a warning to others before good can come! Northern men and women talk of hanging Davis and his accomplices. I myself trust that there will be no hanging when the war is over. I believe there will be none, for the Americans are not a blood-thirsty people. But if punishment of any kind be meted out, the men of the North should understand that they have worse offenders among them than Davis and Floyd.

At the period of which I am now speaking, there had come a change over the spirit of Mr. Lincoln's cabinet. Mr. Seward was still his Secretary of State, but he was, as far as outside observers could judge, no longer his Prime Minister. In the early days of the war, and up to the departure of Mr. Cameron from out of the cabinet, Mr. Seward had been the Minister of the nation. In his despatches he talks ever of We or of I. In every word of his official writings, of which a large volume has been published, he shows plainly that he intends to be considered as the man of the day,—as the hero who is to bring the States through their difficulties. Mr. Lincoln may be King, but Mr. Seward is Mayor of the Palace and carries the King in his pocket. From the depth of his own wisdom he undertakes to teach his ministers in all parts of the world, not only their duties, but their proper aspiration. He is equally kind to foreign statesmen, and sends to them messages as though from an altitude which no European politician had ever reached. At home he has affected the Prime Minister in everything, dropping the We and using the I in a manner that has hardly made up by its audacity for its deficiency in discretion. It is of course known everywhere that he had run Mr. Lincoln very hard for the position of Republican candidate for the Presidency. Mr. Lincoln beat him, and Mr. Seward is well aware that in the States a man has never a second chance for the Presidential chair. Hence has arisen his ambition to make for himself a new place in the annals of American politics. Hitherto there has been no Prime Minister known in the Government of the United States. Mr. Seward has attempted a revolution in that matter, and has essayed to fill the situation. For awhile it almost seemed that he was successful. He interfered with the army, and his interferences were endured. He took upon himself the business of the police, and arrested men at his own will and pleasure. The habeas corpus was in his hand, and his name was current through the States as a covering authority for every outrage on the old laws. Sufficient craft, or perhaps cleverness, he possessed to organize a position which should give him a power greater than the power of the President; but he had not the genius which would enable him to hold it. He made foolish prophecies about the war, and talked of the triumphs which he would win. He wrote state papers on matters which he did not understand, and gave himself the airs of diplomatic learning while he showed himself to be sadly ignorant of the very rudiments of diplomacy. He tried to joke as Lord Palmerston jokes, and nobody liked his joking. He was greedy after the little appanages of power, taking from others who loved them as well as he did, privileges with which he might have dispensed. And then, lastly, he was successful in nothing. He had given himself out as the commander of the Commander-in-Chief; but then under his command nothing got itself done. For a month or two some men had really believed in Mr. Seward. The policemen of the country had come to have an absolute trust in him, and the underlings of the public offices were beginning to think that he might be a great man. But then, as is ever the case with such men, there came suddenly a downfall. Mr. Cameron went from the cabinet, and everybody knew that Mr. Seward would be no longer commander of the Commander-in-Chief. His prime ministership was gone from him, and he sank down into the comparatively humble position of Minister for Foreign Affairs. His lettres de cachet no longer ran. His passport system was repealed. His prisoners were released. And though it is too much to say that writs of habeas corpus were no longer suspended, the effect and very meaning of the suspension was at once altered. When I first left Washington Mr. Seward was the only minister of the cabinet whose name was ever mentioned with reference to any great political measure. When I returned to Washington Mr. Stanton was Mr. Lincoln's leading minister, and, as Secretary-at-War, had practically the management of the army and of the internal police.

I have spoken here of Mr. Seward by name, and in my preceding paragraphs I have alluded with some asperity to the dishonesty of certain men who had obtained political power under Mr. Lincoln and used it for their own dishonest purposes. I trust that I may not be understood as bringing any such charges against Mr. Seward. That such dishonesty has been frightfully prevalent all men know who knew anything of Washington during the year 1861. In a former chapter I have alluded to this more at length, stating circumstances and in some cases giving the names of the persons charged with offences. Whenever I have done so, I have based my statements on the Van Wyck Report, and the evidence therein given. This is the published report of a Committee appointed by the House of Representatives; and as it has been before the world for some months without refutation, I think that I have a right to presume it to be true.* On no less authority than this would I consider myself justified in bringing any such charge. Of Mr. Seward's incompetency I have heard very much among American politicians; much also of his ambition. With worse offences than these I have not heard him charged.

At the period of which I am writing, February, 1862, the long list of military successes which attended the northern army through the late winter and early spring had commenced. Fort Henry, on the Tennessee river, had first been taken, and after that, Fort Donnelson on the Cumberland river, also in the State of Tennessee. Price had been driven out of Missouri into Arkansas by General Curtis, acting under General Halleck's orders. The chief body of the Confederate army in the West had abandoned the fortified position which they had long held at Bowling Green, in the south-western district of Kentucky. Roanoke Island on the coast of North Carolina, had been taken by General Burnside's expedition, and a belief had begun to manifest itself in Washington that the army of the Potomac was really about to advance. It is impossible to explain in what way the renewed confidence of the northern party showed itself, or how one learned that the hopes of the secessionists were waxing dim; but it was so; and even a stranger became aware of the general feeling as clearly as though it were a defined and established fact. In the early

* I ought perhaps to state that General Fremont has published an answer to the charges preferred against him. That answer refers chiefly to matters of military capacity or incapacity, as to which I have expressed no opinion. General Fremont does allude to the accusations made against him regarding the building of the forts; —but in doing so he seems to me rather to admit than to deny the facts as stated by the Committee.

part of the winter, when I reached Washington, the feeling ran all the other way. Northern men did not say that they were despondent; they did not with spoken words express diffidence as to their success; but their looks betrayed diffidence, and the moderation of their self-assurance almost amounted to despondency. In the capital the parties were very much divided. The old inhabitants were either secessionists or influenced by "secession proclivities," as the word went; but the men of the government and of the two houses of Congress were, with a few exceptions, of course northern. It should be understood that these parties were at variance with each other on almost every point as to which men can disagree. In our civil war it may be presumed that all Englishmen were at any rate anxious for England. They desired and fought for different modes of government; but each party was equally English in its ambition. In the States there is the hatred of a different nationality added to the rancour of different politics. The Southerners desire to be a people of themselves,—to divide themselves every possible mark of division from New England; to be as little akin to New York as they are to London,—or if possible less so. Their habits, they say, are different; their education, their beliefs, their propensities, their very virtues and vices are not the education, or the beliefs, or the propensities, or the virtues and vices of the North. The bond that ties them to the North is to them a Mezentian marriage,[3] and they hate their northern spouses with a Mezentian hatred. They would be anything sooner than citizens of the United States. They see to what Mexico has come, and the republics of Central America; but the prospect of even that degradation is less bitter to them than a share in the glory of the Stars and Stripes. Better, with them, to reign in hell than serve in heaven! It is not only in politics that they will be beaten, if they be beaten,—as one party with us may be beaten by another; but they will be beaten as we should be beaten if France annexed us, and directed that we should live under French rule. Let an Englishman digest and realize that idea, and he will comprehend the feelings of a southern gentleman as he contemplates the probability that his State will be brought back into the Union. And the northern feeling is as strong. The northern man has founded his national ambition on the territorial greatness of his nation. He has panted for new lands, and for still extended boundaries. The western world has opened her arms to him, and has seemed to welcome him as her only lord. British America has tempted him towards the north, and Mexico has been as a prey to him

[3] Mezentius, a sadistic Etruscan King who fought Æneas, tied living people face to face with corpses and left them to starve.

on the south. He has made maps of his empire, including all the continent, and has preached the Monroe doctrine as though it had been decreed by the gods. He has told the world of his increasing millions, and has never yet known his store to diminish. He has pawed in the valley, and rejoiced in his strength. He has said among the trumpets, Ha, ha! [4] He has boasted aloud in his pride, and called on all men to look at his glory. And now shall he be divided and shorn? Shall he be hemmed in from his ocean and shut off from his rivers? Shall he have a hook run into his nostrils, and a thorn driven into his jaw? Shall men say that his day is over, when he has hardly yet tasted the full cup of his success? Has his young life been a dream, and not a truth? Shall he never reach that giant manhood which the growth of his boyish years has promised him? If the South goes from him, he will be divided, shorn, and hemmed in. The hook will have pierced his nose, and the thorn will fester in his jaw. Men will taunt him with his former boastings, and he will awake to find himself but a mortal among mortals.

Such is the light in which the struggle is regarded by the two parties, and such the hopes and feelings which have been engendered. It may therefore be surmised with what amount of neighbourly love secessionist and northern neighbours regarded each other in such towns as Baltimore and Washington. Of course there was hatred of the deepest dye; of course there were muttered curses, or curses which sometimes were not simply muttered. Of course there were wretchedness, heartburnings, and fearful divisions in families. That, perhaps, was the worst of all. The daughter's husband would be in the northern ranks, while the son was fighting in the South; or two sons would hold equal rank in the two armies, sometimes sending to each other frightful threats of personal vengeance. Old friends would meet each other in the street, passing without speaking; or, worse still, would utter words of insult for which payment is to be demanded when a southern gentleman may again be allowed to quarrel in his own defence.

And yet society went on. Women still smiled, and men were happy to whom such smiles were given. Cakes and ale were going and ginger was still hot in the mouth. When many were together no words of unhappiness were heard. It was at those small meetings of two or three that women would weep instead of smiling, and that men would run their hands through their hair and sit in silence, thinking of their ruined hopes and divided children.

[4] Trollope's Biblical paraphrases in this and the following sentences come principally from the Book of Job, Chapters xxxix and xli.

I have spoken of southern hopes and northern fears, and have endeavoured to explain the feelings of each party. For myself I think that the Southerners have been wrong in their hopes, and that those of the North have been wrong in their fears. It is not better to rule in hell than serve in heaven. Of course a southern gentleman will not admit the premises which are here by me taken for granted. The hell to which I allude is, the sad position of a low and debased nation. Such, I think, will be the fate of the Gulf States, if they succeed in obtaining secession, —of a low and debased nation, or, worse still, of many low and debased nations. They will have lost their cotton monopoly by the competition created during the period of the war, and will have no material of greatness on which either to found themselves or to flourish. That they had much to bear when linked with the North, much to endure on account of that slavery from which it was all but impossible that they should disentangle themselves, may probably be true. But so have all political parties among all free nations much to bear from political opponents, and yet other free nations do not go to pieces. Had it been possible that the slave-owners and slave properties should have been scattered in parts through all the States and not congregated in the South, the slave party would have maintained itself as other parties do; but in such case, as a matter of course, it would not have thought of secession. It has been the close vicinity of slave-owners to each other, the fact that their lands have been coterminous, that theirs was especially a cotton district, which has tempted them to secession. They have been tempted to secession, and will, as I think, still achieve it in those Gulf States,—much to their misfortune.

And the fears of the North are, I think, equally wrong. That they will be deceived as to that Monroe doctrine is no doubt more than probable. That ambition for an entire continent under one rule will not, I should say, be gratified. But not on that account need the nation be less great, or its civilization less extensive. That hook in its nose and that thorn in its jaw will, after all, be but a hook of the imagination and an ideal thorn. Do not all great men suffer such ere their greatness be established and acknowledged? There is scope enough for all that manhood can do between the Atlantic and the Pacific, even though those hot, swampy cotton-fields be taken away; even though the snows of the British provinces be denied to them. And as for those rivers and that sea-board, the Americans of the North will have lost much of their old energy and usual force of will, if any southern Confederacy be allowed to deny their right of way or to stop their commercial enterprises. I believe that the South will be badly off without the North; but I feel certain that the North will never miss the South when once the wounds to her pride have been closed.

From Washington I journeyed back to Boston through the cities which I had visited in coming thither, and stayed again on my route for a few days at Baltimore, at Philadelphia, and at New York. At each town there were those whom I now regarded almost as old friends, and as the time of my departure drew near I felt a sorrow that I was not to be allowed to stay longer. As the general result of my sojourn in the country, I must declare that I was always happy and comfortable in the eastern cities, and generally unhappy and uncomfortable in the West. I had previously been inclined to think that I should like the roughness of the West, and that in the East I should encounter an arrogance which would have kept me always on the verge of hot water; but in both these surmises I found myself to have been wrong. And I think that most English travellers would come to the same conclusion. The western people do not mean to be harsh or uncivil, but they do not make themselves pleasant. In all the eastern cities,—I speak of the eastern cities north of Washington,—a society may be found which must be esteemed as agreeable by Englishmen who like clever genial men, and who love clever pretty women.

I was forced to pass twice again over the road between New York and Boston, as the packet by which I intended to leave America was fixed to sail from the former port. I had promised myself, and had promised others, that I would spend in Boston the last week of my sojourn in the States, and this was a promise which I was by no means inclined to break. If there be a gratification in this world which has no alloy, it is that of going to an assured welcome. The belief that men's arms and hearts are open to receive one,—and the arms and hearts of women, too, as far as they allow themselves to open them,—is the salt of the earth, the sole remedy against sea-sickness, the only cure for the tedium of railways, the one preservative amidst all the miseries and fatigue of travel. These matters are private, and should hardly be told of in a book; but in writing of the States, I should not do justice to my own convictions of the country if I did not say how pleasantly social intercourse there will ripen into friendship, and how full of love that friendship may become. I became enamoured of Boston at last. Beacon Street was very pleasant to me, and the view over Boston Common was dear to my eyes. Even the State House, with its great yellow-painted dome, became sightly; and the sunset over the western waters that encompass the city beats all other sunsets that I have seen.

During my last week there the world of Boston was moving itself on sleighs. There was not a wheel to be seen in the town. The omnibuses and public carriages had been dismounted from their axles and put themselves upon snow runners, and the private world had taken out its winter carriages, and wrapped itself up in buffalo robes. Men now spoke of the coming thaw as of a misfortune which must come, but which a kind Providence might perhaps postpone,—as we all, in short, speak of death. In the morning the snow would have been hardened by the night's frost, and men would look happy and contented. By an hour after noon the streets would be all wet, and the ground would be slushy and men would look gloomy and speak of speedy dissolution. There were those who would always prophesy that the next day would see the snow converted into one dull, dingy river. Such I regarded as seers of tribulation, and endeavoured with all my mind to disbelieve their interpretations of the signs. That sleighing was excellent fun. For myself I must own that I hardly saw the best of it at Boston, for the coming of the end was already at hand when I arrived there, and the fresh beauty of the hard snow was gone. Moreover when I essayed to show my prowess with a pair of horses on the established course for such equipages, the beasts ran away, knowing that I was not practised in the use of snow chariots, and brought me to grief and shame. There was a lady with me on the sleigh whom, for a while, I felt that I was doomed to consign to a snowy grave,—whom I would willingly have overturned into a drift of snow, so as to avoid worse consequences, had I only known how to do so. But Providence, even though without curbs and assisted only by simple snaffles, did at last prevail; and I brought the sleigh, horses, and lady alive back to Boston, whether with or without permanent injury I have never yet ascertained.

At last the day of tribulation came, and the snow was picked up and carted out of Boston. Gangs of men, standing shoulder to shoulder, were at work along the chief streets, picking, shovelling, and disposing of the dirty blocks. Even then the snow seemed to be nearly a foot thick; but it was dirty, rough, half-melted in some places, though hard as stone in others. The labour and cost of cleansing the city in this way must be very great. The people were at it as I left, and I felt that the day of tribulation had in truth come.

Farewell to thee, thou western Athens! When I have forgotten thee my right hand shall have forgotten its cunning, and my heart forgotten its pulses. Let us look at the list of names with which Boston has honoured itself in our days, and then ask what other town of the same size has done more. Prescott, Bancroft, Motley, Longfellow, Lowell, Emerson, Dana, Agassiz, Holmes, Hawthorne! Who is there among us in England who has not been the better for these men? Who does not owe to some of them a debt of gratitude? In whose ears is [5] not their names familiar? It is a bright galaxy and far extended, for so small a city. What city has done better than this? All these men, save one, are now alive and in the full possession of their powers. What other town of the same size has done as well in the same short space of time? It may be that this is the Augustan æra of Boston,—its Elizabethan time. If so, I am thankful that my steps have wandered thither at such a period.

While I was at Boston I had the sad privilege of attending the funeral of President Felton, the head of Harvard College. A few months before I had seen him a strong man, apparently in perfect health and in the pride of life. When I reached Boston, I heard of his death. He also was an accomplished scholar, and as a Grecian has left few behind him who were his equals. At his installation as President, four ex-Presidents of Harvard College assisted. Whether they were all present at his funeral I do not know, but I do know that they were all still living. These are Mr. Quincy, who is now over ninety; Mr. Sparks; Mr. Everett, the well-known orator; and Mr. Walker. They all reside in Boston or its neighbourhood, and will probably all assist at the installation of another President.

[5] Thus in the manuscript of *North America*. Trollope apparently thinks of *names* in its use here as a collective noun.

CHAPTER XXVIII

THE POST-OFFICE

A NY Englishman or Frenchman residing in the American States cannot fail to be struck with the inferiority of the Post-office arrangements in that country to those by which they are accommodated in their own country. I have not been a resident in the States, and as a traveller might probably have passed the subject without special remark, were it not that the service of the Post-office has been my own profession for many years. I could therefore hardly fail to observe things which to another man would have been of no material moment. At first I was inclined to lean heavily in my judgment upon the deficiencies of a department which must be of primary importance to a commercial nation. It seemed that among a people so intelligent, and so quick in all enterprises of trade, a well arranged Post-office would have been held to be absolutely necessary, and that all difficulties would have been made to succumb in their efforts to put that establishment, if no other, upon a proper footing. But as I looked into the matter, and in becoming acquainted with the circumstances of the Post-office learned the extent of the difficulties absolutely existing, I began to think that a very great deal had been done, and that the fault, as to that which had been left undone, rested, not with the Post-office officials, but was attributable partly to political causes altogether outside the Post-office, and partly, —perhaps chiefly,—to the nature of the country itself.

It is, I think, undoubtedly true that the amount of accommodation given by the Post-office of the States is small,—as compared with that afforded in some other countries, and that that accommodation is lessened by delays and uncertainty. The point which first struck me was the inconvenient hours at which mails were brought in and despatched. Here, in England, it is the object of our Post-office to carry the bulk of our letters at night; to deliver them as early as possible in the morning, and to collect them and take them away for despatch as late as may be in the day;—so that the merchant may receive his letters

---

1 Trollope was well qualified to deal with the subject of this chapter. Ever since 1834 he had been in the service of the British Post Office. By the time of his American tour he was an official of rank and importance, with a broad knowledge of postal matters both in and outside England. He had spent several years in the postal service in Ireland, and in 1858 and 1859 he had been entrusted with three separate missions for the Post Office to Egypt, Scotland, and the West Indies.

before the beginning of his day's business, and despatch them after its close. The bulk of our letters is handled in this manner, and the advantage of such an arrangement is manifest. But it seemed that in the States no such practice prevailed. Letters arrived at any hour in the day miscellaneously, and were despatched at any hour, and I found that the postmaster at one town could never tell me with certainty when letters would arrive at another. If the towns were distant, I would be told that the conveyance might take about two or three days; if they were near, that my letter would get to hand, "some time to-morrow." I ascertained, moreover, by painful experience that the whole of a mail would not always go forward by the first despatch. As regarded myself this had reference chiefly to English letters and newspapers.—"Only a part of the mail has come," the clerk would tell me. With us the owners of that part which did not "come," would consider themselves greatly aggrieved and make loud complaint. But, in the States, complaints made against official departments are held to be of little moment.

Letters also in the States are subject to great delays by irregularities on railways. One train does not hit the town of its destination before another train, to which it is nominally fitted, has been started on its journey. The mail trains are not bound to wait; and thus, in the large cities, far distant from New York, great irregularity prevails. It is, I think, owing to this,—at any rate partly to this,—that the system of telegraphing has become so prevalent. It is natural that this should be so between towns which are in the due course of post perhaps forty-eight hours asunder; but the uncertainty of the post increases the habit, to the profit, of course, of the companies which own the wires,—but to the manifest loss of the Post-office.

But the deficiency which struck me most forcibly in the American Post-office, was the absence of any recognized official delivery of letters. The United States Post-office does not assume to itself the duty of taking letters to the houses of those for whom they are intended, but holds itself as having completed the work for which the original postage has been paid, when it has brought them to the window of the Post-office of the town to which they are addressed. It is true that in most large towns,—though by no means in all,—a separate arrangement is made by which a delivery is afforded to those who are willing to pay a further sum for that further service; but the recognized official mode of delivery is from the office window. The merchants and persons in trade have boxes at the windows, for which they pay. Other old-established inhabitants in towns, and persons in receipt of a considerable correspondence, receive their letters by the subsidiary carriers and pay for them separately. But the poorer classes of the community, those persons among which it is of such paramount importance to increase the blessing of letter writing, obtain their letters from the Post-office windows.

In each of these cases the practice acts to the prejudice of the department. In order to escape the tax on delivery, which varies from two cents to one cent a letter, all men in trade, and many who are not in trade, hold office boxes; consequently immense space is required. The space given at Chicago, both to the public without and to the officials within, for such delivery, is more than four times that required at Liverpool for the same purpose. But Liverpool is three times the size of Chicago. The corps of clerks required for the window delivery is very great, and the whole affair is cumbrous in the extreme. The letters at most offices are given out through little windows, to which the inquirer is obliged to stoop. There he finds himself opposite to a pane of glass with a little hole; and when the clerk within shakes his head at him, he rarely believes but what his letters are there if he could only reach them. But in the second case, the tax on the delivery, which is intended simply to pay the wages of the men who take them out, is paid with a bad grace; it robs the letter of its charm, and forces it to present itself in the guise of a burden. It makes that disagreeable which for its own sake the Post-office should strive in every way to make agreeable. This practice, moreover, operates as a direct prevention to a class of correspondence, which furnishes in England a large proportion of the revenue of the Post-office. Mercantile houses in our large cities send out thousands of trade circulars, paying postage on them; but such circulars would not be received, either in England or elsewhere, if a demand for postage were made on their delivery. Who does not receive these circulars in our country by the dozen, consigning them generally to the waste-paper basket, after a most cursory inspection? As regards the sender, the transaction seems to us often to be very vain; but the Post-office gets its penny. So also would the American Post-office get its three cents.

But the main objection in my eyes to the American Post-office system, is this,—that it is not brought nearer to the poorer classes. Everybody writes or can write in America, and therefore the correspondence of their millions, should be, million for million, at any rate equal to ours. But it is not so: and this, I think, comes from the fact that communication by Post-office is not made easy to the people generally. Such communication is not found to be easy by a man who has to attend at a Post-office window on the chance of receiving a letter. When no arrangement more comfortable than that is provided, the Post-office will be used for the necessities of letter-writing, but will not be esteemed as a luxury. And thus not only do the people lose a comfort which they might enjoy, but the Post-office also loses that revenue which it might make.

I have said that the correspondence circulating in the United States is less than that of the United Kingdom. In making any comparison between them I am obliged to arrive at facts, or rather at the probabilities of facts, in a somewhat circuitous mode, as the Americans have kept no account of the number of letters which pass through their post-offices in a year. We can, however, make an estimate which, if incorrect, shall not at any rate be incorrect against them. The gross postal revenue of the United States, for the year ended 30th June, 1861, was in round figures 1,700,000*l*. This was the amount actually earned, exclusive of a sum of 140,000*l*. paid to the Post-office by the government for the carriage of what is called in that country free mail matter; otherwise, books, letters, and parcels franked by members of Congress. The gross postal revenue of the United Kindom was in the last year, in round figures, 3,358,000*l*., exclusive of a sum of 179,000*l*. claimed as earned for carrying official postage, and also exclusive of 127,866*l*., that being the amount of money order commission which in this country is considered a part of the Post-office revenue. In the United States there is at present no money order office. In the United Kingdom the sum of 3,358,000*l*. was earned by the conveyance and delivery of

> 593 millions of letters,
> 73 millions of newspapers,
> 12 millions of books.

What number of each was conveyed through the post in the United States we have no means of knowing; but presuming the average rate of postage on each letter in the States to be the same as it is in England, and presuming also that letters, newspapers, and books, circulated in the same proportion there as they do with us, the sum above named of 1,700,000*l*. will have been earned by carrying about 300 millions of letters. But the average rate of postage in the States is, in fact, higher than it is in England. The ordinary single rate of postage there is three cents or three half-pence, whereas with us it is a penny; and if three half-pence might be taken as the average rate in the United States, the number of letters would be reduced from 300 to 200 millions a year. There is however a class of letters which in the States are passed through the Post-office at the rate of one half-penny a letter, whereas there is no rate of postage with us less than a penny. Taking these halfpenny letters into consideration, I am disposed to regard the average rate of American postage at about five farthings, which would give the number of letters at 250 millions. We shall at any rate be safe in saying that the number is considerably less than 300 millions, and that it does not amount to half the number circulated with us. But the difference between our population and their population is not great. The population of the States during the year in question was about 27 millions, exclusive of slaves, and that of the British isles was about 29 millions. No doubt, in the year named, the correspondence of the States had been somewhat disturbed by the rebellion; but that disturbance, up to the end of June, 1861, had been very trifling. The division of the southern from the northern States, as far as the Post-office was concerned, did not take place till the end of May, 1861; and therefore but one month in the year was affected by the actual secession of the South. The gross postal revenue of the States which have seceded, was, for the year prior to secession, twelve hundred thousand five hundred dollars, and for that one month of June it would therefore have been a little over one hundred thousand dollars, or 20,000l. That sum may therefore be presumed to have been abstracted by secession from the gross annual revenue of the Post-office. Trade, also, was no doubt injured by the disturbance in the country, and the circulation of letters was, as a matter of course, to some degree affected by this injury; but it seems that the gross revenue of 1861 was less than that of 1860 by only one thirty-sixth. I think, therefore, that we may say, making all allowance that can be fairly made, that the number of letters circulating in the United Kingdom is more than double that which circulates, or ever has circulated, in the United States.

That this is so, I attribute not to any difference in the people of the two countries,—not to an aptitude for letter writing among us which is wanting with the Americans,—but to the greater convenience and wider accommodation of our own Post-office. As I have before stated, and will presently endeavour to show, this wider accommodation is not altogether the result of better management on our part. Our circumstances as regards the Post-office have had in them less of difficulties than theirs. But it has arisen in great part from better management; and in nothing is their deficiency so conspicuous as in the absence of a free delivery for their letters.

In order that the advantages of the Post-office should reach all persons, the delivery of letters should extend not only to towns, but to the country also. In France all letters are delivered free. However remote may be the position of a house or cottage, it is not too remote for the postman. With us all letters are not delivered; but the exceptions refer to distant solitary houses and to localities which are almost without correspondence. But in the United States there is no free delivery, and there is no delivery at all except in the large cities. In small towns, in villages, even in the suburbs of the largest cities, no such accommodation is given. Whatever may be the distance, people expecting letters must send for them to the Post-office;—and they who do not expect them, leave their letters uncalled for. Brother Jonathan goes out to fish in these especial waters with a very large net. The little fish, which are profitable, slip through; but the big fish, which are by no means profitable, are caught,—often at an expense greater than their value.

There are other smaller sins upon which I could put my finger,—and would do so were I writing an official report upon the subject of the American Post-office. In lieu of doing so, I will endeavour to explain how much the States' office has done in this matter of affording Post-office accommodation,—and how great have been the difficulties in the way of Post-office reformers in that country.

In the first place, when we compare ourselves to them, we must remember that we live in a tea-cup, and they in a washing-tub. As compared with them we inhabit towns which are close to each other. Our distances, as compared with theirs, are nothing. From London to Liverpool the line of railway traverses about two hundred miles, but the mail train which conveys the bags for Liverpool, carries the correspondence of probably four or five millions of persons. The mail train from New York to Buffalo passes over about four hundred miles, and on its route serves not one million. A comparison of this kind might be made with the same effect between any of our great internal mail routes, and any of theirs. Consequently, the expense of conveyance to them is, per letter, very much greater than with us, and the American Post-office is as a matter of necessity driven to an economy in the use of railways for the Post-office service, which we are not called on to practise. From New York to Chicago is nearly 1000 miles. From New York to St. Louis is over 1600.[2] I need not say that in England we know nothing of such distances, and that therefore our task has been comparatively easy. Nevertheless the States have followed in our track, and have taken advantage of Sir Rowland Hill's wise audacity in the reduction of postage with greater quickness than any other nation but our own. Through all the States letters pass for three cents over a distance less

---

[2] Trollope must not have calculated by the shortest routes, even among those available in 1861–2.

than 3000 miles. For distances above 3000 miles the rate is ten cents or five-pence. This increased rate has special reference to the mails for California, which are carried daily across the whole continent at a cost to the States Government of two hundred thousand pounds a year.

With us the chief mail trains are legally under the management of the Postmaster-General. He fixes the hours at which they shall start and arrive, being of course bound by certain stipulations as to pace. He can demand trains to run over any line at any hour, and can in this way secure the punctuality of mail transportation. Of course such interference on the part of a government official in the working of a railway is attended with a very heavy expense to the Government. Though the British Post-office can demand the use of trains at any hour, and as regards those trains can make the despatch of mails paramount to all other matters, the British Post-office cannot fix the price to be paid for such work. This is generally done by arbitration, and of course for such services the payment is very high. No such practice prevails in the States. The Government has no power of using the mail lines as they are used by our Post-office, nor could the expense of such a practice be borne or nearly borne by the proceeds of letters in the States. Consequently the Post-office is put on a par with ordinary customers, and such trains are used for mail matter as the directors of each line may see fit to use for other matter. Hence it occurs that no offence against the Post-office is committed when the connection between different mail trains is broken. The Post-office takes the best it can get, paying as other customers pay, and grumbling as other customers grumble when the service rendered falls short of that which has been promised.

It may, I think, easily be seen that any system such as ours, carried across so large a country, would go on increasing in cost at an enormous ratio. The greater the distance, the greater is the difficulty in securing the proper fitting of fast-running trains. And moreover, it must be remembered that the American lines have been got up on a very different footing from ours, at an expense per mile of probably less than a fifth of that laid out on our railways. Single lines of rail are common, even between great towns with large traffic. At the present moment—May, 1862—the only railway running into Washington, that namely from Baltimore, is a single line over the greater distance. The whole thing is necessarily worked at a cheaper rate than with us; not because the people are poorer, but because the distances are greater. As this is the case throughout the whole railway system of the country, it cannot be expected that such despatch and punctuality should be achieved in

America as are achieved here, in England, or in France. As population and wealth increase, it will come. In the mean time that which has been already done over the extent of the vast North American continent is very wonderful. I think, therefore, that complaint should not be made against the Washington Post-office, either on account of the inconvenience of the hours, or on the head of occasional irregularity. So much has been done in reducing the rate to three cents, and in giving a daily mail throughout the States, that the department should be praised for energy, and not blamed for apathy.

In the year ended 30th June, 1861, the gross revenue of the Post-office of the States was, as I have stated, 1,700,000*l.* In the same year its expenditure was in round figures 2,720,000*l.* Consequently there was an actual loss, to be made up out of general taxation, amounting to 1,020,000*l.* In the accounts of the American officers this is lessened by 140,000*l.*, that sum having been arbitrarily fixed by the Government as the amount earned by the Post-office in carrying free mail matter. We have a similar system in computing the value of the service rendered by our Post-office to the Government in carrying government despatches; but with us the amount named as the compensation depends on the actual weight carried. If the matter so carried be carried solely on the Government service, as is I believe the case with us, any such claim on behalf of the Post-office is apparently unnecessary. The Crown works for the Crown, as the right hand works for the left. The Post-office pays no rates or taxes, contributes nothing to the poor, runs its mails on turnpike roads free of toll, and gives receipts on unstamped paper. With us no payment is in truth made, though the Post-office in its accounts presumes itself to have received the money. But in the States the sum named is handed over by the State Treasury to the Post-office Treasury. Any such statement of credit does not in effect alter the real fact, that over a million sterling is required as a subsidy by the American Post-office, in order that it may be enabled to pay its way. In estimating the expenditure of the office the department at Washington debits itself with the sums paid for the ocean transit of its mails, amounting to something over 150,000*l.* We also now do the same, with the much greater sum paid by us for such service, which now amounts to 949,228*l.*, or nearly a million sterling. Till lately this was not paid out of the Post-office moneys, and the Post-office revenue was not debited with the amount.

Our gross Post-office revenue is, as I have said, 3,358,250*l.* As before explained, this is exclusive of the amount earned by the money order department, which, though managed by the authorities of the Post-office cannot be called a part of the Post-office; and exclusive also of the official postage, which is, in fact, never received. The expenditure of our British Post-office, inclusive of the sum paid for the ocean mail service, is 3,064,527*l*. We therefore make a net profit of 293,723*l*. out of the Post-office, as compared with a loss of 1,020,000*l*., on the part of the United States.

But perhaps the greatest difficulty with which the American Post-office is burdened, is that "free mail matter" to which I have alluded, for carrying which, the Post-office claims to earn 140,000*l*., and for the carriage of which, it might as fairly claim to earn 1,350,000*l*., or half the amount of its total expenditure, for I was informed by a gentleman whose knowledge on the subject could not be doubted, that the free mail matter so carried, equalled in bulk and weight all that other matter which was not carried free. To such an extent has the privilege of franking been carried in the States! All members of both Houses frank what they please,—for in effect the privilege is stretched to that extent. All Presidents of the Union, past and present, can frank, as, also, all Vice-Presidents, past and present; and there is a special act, enabling the widow of President Polk to frank. Why it is that widows of other Presidents do not agitate on the matter, I cannot understand. And all the Secretaries of State can frank; and ever so many other public officers. There is no limit in number to the letters so franked, and the nuisance has extended itself to so huge a size, that members of Congress in giving franks, cannot write the franks themselves. It is illegal for them to depute to others the privilege of signing their names for this purpose, but it is known at the Post-office that it is done. But even this is not the worst of it. Members of the House of Representatives have the power of sending through the post all those huge books which, with them as with us, grow out of Parliamentary debates and workings of Committees. This, under certain stipulations, is the case also in England; but in England, luckily no one values them. In America, however, it is not so. A voter considers himself to be noticed if he gets a book. He likes to have the book bound, and the bigger the book may be, the more the compliment is relished. Hence it comes to pass that an enormous quantity of useless matter is printed and bound, only that it may be sent down to constituents and make a show on the parlour shelves of constituents' wives. The Post-office groans and becomes insolvent, and the country pays for the paper, the printing, and the binding. While the public expenses of the nation were very small, there was, perhaps, no reason why voters should not thus be indulged; but now the matter is different, and it would be well that the conveyance by post of these Congressional libraries should be brought to an end. I was also assured that members very frequently obtain permission for the printing of a speech which has never been delivered,—and which never will be delivered,—in order that copies may be circulated among their constituents. There is in such an arrangement an ingenuity which is peculiarly American in its nature. Everybody concerned is no doubt cheated by the system. The constituents are cheated; the public, which pays, is cheated; and the Post-office is cheated. But the House is spared the hearing of the speech, and the result on the whole is perhaps beneficial.

We also, within the memory of many of us, had a franking privilege, which was peculiarly objectionable inasmuch as it operated towards giving a free transmission of their letters by post to the rich, while no such privilege was within reach of the poor. But with us it never stretched itself to such an extent as it has now achieved in the States. The number of letters for members was limited. The whole address was written by the franking member himself, and not much was sent in this way that was bulky. I am disposed to think that all government and Congressional jobs in the States bear the same proportion to government and Parliamentary jobs which have been in vogue among us. There has been an unblushing audacity in the public dishonesty,—what I may perhaps call the State dishonesty,—at Washington, which I think was hardly ever equalled in London. Bribery, I know, was disgracefully current in the days of Walpole, of Newcastle, and even of Castlereagh; —so current, that no Englishman has a right to hold up his own past government as a model of purity. But the corruption with us did blush and endeavour to hide itself. It was disgraceful to be bribed, if not so to offer bribes. But at Washington corruption has been so common that I can hardly understand how any honest man can have held up his head in the vicinity of the Capitol, or of the State office.

But the country has, I think, become tired of this. Hitherto it has been too busy about its more important concerns, in extending commerce, in making railways, in providing education for its youth, to think very much of what was being done at Washington. While the taxes were light and property was secure, while increasing population gave daily increasing strength to the nation, the people as a body were content with that theory of being governed by their little men. They gave a bad name to politicians, and allowed politics, as they say, "to slide." But all this will be altered now. The tremendous expenditure of the last twelve months has allowed dishonesty of so vast a grasp to make its ravages in the public pockets, that the evil will work its own cure.

Taxes will be very high, and the people will recognize the necessity of having honest men to look after them. The nation can no longer afford to be indifferent about its Government, and will require to know where its money goes, and why it goes. This franking privilege is already doomed, if not already dead. When I was in Washington a Bill was passed through the Lower House by which it would be abolished altogether. When I left America its fate in the Senate was still doubtful, and I was told by many that that Bill would not be allowed to become law without sundry alterations. But, nevertheless, I regard the franking privilege as doomed, and offer to the Washington Post-office officials my best congratulations on their coming deliverance.

The Post-office in the States is also burdened by another terrible political evil, which in itself is so heavy, that one would at first sight declare it to be enough to prevent anything like efficiency. The whole of its staff is removable every fourth year,—that is to say, on the election of every new President. And a very large proportion of its staff is thus removed periodically to make way for those for whom a new President is bound to provide, by reason of their services in sending him to the White House. They have served him and he thus repays them by this use of his patronage in their favour. At four hundred and thirty-four Post-offices in the States,—those being the offices to which the highest salaries are attached,—the President has this power, and exercises it as a matter of course. He has the same power with reference, I believe, to all the appointments held in the Post-office at Washington. This practice applies by no means to the Post-office only. All the government clerks,—clerks employed by the central government at Washington,—are subject to the same rule. And the rule has also been adopted in the various States with reference to State offices.

To a stranger this practice seems so manifestly absurd, that he can hardly conceive it possible that government service should be conducted on such terms. He cannot, in the first place, believe that men of sufficient standing before the world could be found to accept office under such circumstances; and is led to surmise that men of insufficient standing must be employed, and that there are other allurements to the office beyond the very moderate salaries which are allowed. He cannot, moreover, understand how the duties can be conducted, seeing that men must be called on to resign their places as soon as they have learned to make themselves useful. And, finally, he is lost in amazements as he contemplates this barefaced prostitution of the public employ to the vilest purposes of political manœuvring. With us also patronage has been used for political purposes, and to some small extent is still so used. We have not yet sufficiently recognized the fact, that in selecting a public servant nothing should be regarded but the advantage of the service in which he is to be employed. But we never, in the lowest times of our political corruption, ventured to throw over the question of service altogether, and to declare publicly, that the one and only result to be obtained by Government employment was political support. In the States political corruption has become so much a matter of course, that no American seems to be struck with the fact that the whole system is a system of robbery.

From sheer necessity some of the old hands are kept on when these changes are made. Were this not done the work would come absolutely to a dead lock. But it may be imagined how difficult it must be for men to carry through any improvements in a great department, when they have entered an office under such a system, and are liable to be expelled under the same. It is greatly to the praise of those who have been allowed to grow old in the service that so much has been done. No men, however, are more apt at such work than Americans, or more able to exert themselves at their posts. They are not idle. Independently of any question of remuneration, they are not indifferent to the well-being of the work they have in hand. They are good public servants, unless corruption come in their way.

While speaking on the subject of patronage, I cannot but allude to two appointments which had been made by political interest, and with the circumstances of which I became acquainted. In both instances a good place had been given to a gentleman by the incoming President, —not in return for political support, but from motives of private friendship,—either his own friendship or that of some mutual friend. In both instances I heard the selection spoken of with the warmest praise, as though a noble act had been done in the nomination of a private friend instead of a political partisan. And yet in each case a man was appointed who knew nothing of his work; who, from age and circumstances, was not likely to become acquainted with his work; who, by his appointment, kept out of the place those who did understand the work, and had earned a right to promotion by so understanding it. Two worthy gentlemen,—for they were both worthy,—were pensioned on the government for a term of years under a false pretence. That this should have been done is not perhaps remarkable; but it did seem remarkable to me that everybody regarded such appointments as a good deed—as a deed so exceptionably good as to be worthy of great praise. I do not allude to these selections on account of the political vice shown by the Presidents in making them, but on account of the political virtue;—

in order that the nature of political virtue in the States may be understood. It had never occurred to any one to whom I spoke on the subject, that a President in bestowing such places was bound to look for efficient work in return for the public money which was to be paid.

Before I end this chapter I must insert a few details respecting the Post-office of the States, which, though they may not be specially interesting to the general reader, will give some idea of the extent of the department. The total number of post-offices in the States on 30th June, 1861, was 28,586. With us the number in England, Scotland, and Ireland, at the same period was about 11,400. The population served may be regarded as nearly the same. Our lowest salary is 3*l.* per annum. In the States the remuneration is often much lower. It consists of a commission on the letters, and is sometimes less than ten shillings a year. The difficulty of obtaining persons to hold these offices, and the amount of work which must thereby be thrown on what is called the "appointment branch," may be judged by the fact that 9235 of these offices were filled up by new nominations during the last year. When the patronage is of such a nature it is difficult to say which give most trouble, the places which nobody wishes to have, or those which everybody wishes to have.

The total amount of postage on European letters, *i.e.,* letters passing between the States and Europe, in the last year as to which accounts were kept between Washington and the European post-offices, was 275,-000*l.* Of this over 150,000*l.* was on letters for the United Kingdom; and 130,000*l.* was on letters carried by the Cunard packets.

According to the accounts kept by the Washington office, the letters passing from the States to Europe and from Europe to the States are very nearly equal in number, about 101 going to Europe for every 100 received from Europe. But the number of newspapers sent from the States is more than double the number received in the States from Europe.

On 30th June, 1861, mails were carried through the then loyal States of the Union over 140,400 miles daily. Up to 31st May preceding, at which time the Government mails were running all through the United States, 96,000 miles were covered in those States which had then virtually seceded, and which in the following month were taken out from the Post-office accounts,—making a total of 236,400 miles daily. Of this mileage something less than one third is effected by railways, at an average cost of about six-pence a mile. Our total mileage per day is 151,000 miles, of which 43,823 are done by railway, at a cost of about sevenpence-halfpenny per mile.

As far as I could learn the servants of the Post-office are less liberally paid in the States than with us,—excepting as regards two classes. The first of these is that class which is paid by weekly wages,—such as letter-carriers and porters. Their remuneration is of course ruled by the rate of ordinary wages in the country; and as ordinary wages are higher in the States than with us, such men are paid accordingly. The other class is that of postmasters at second-rate towns. They receive the same compensation as those at the largest towns;—unless indeed there be other compensation than those written in the books at Washington. A post-master is paid a certain commission on letters, till it amounts to 400*l.* per annum: all above that going back to the Government. So also out of the fees paid for boxes at the window he receives any amount forthcoming, not exceeding 400*l.* a year; making in all a maximum of 800*l.* The postmaster of New York can get no more. But any moderately large town will give as much, and in this way an amount of patronage is provided which in a political view is really valuable.

But with all this the people have made their way, because they have been intelligent, industrious, and in earnest. And as the people have made their way, so has the Post-office. The number of its offices, the mileage it covers, its extraordinary cheapness, the rapidity with which it has been developed, are all proofs of great things done; and it is by no means standing still even in these evil days of war. Improvements are even now on foot, copied in a great measure from ourselves. Hitherto the American office has not taken upon itself the task of returning to their writers undelivered and undeliverable letters. This it is now going to do. It is, as I have said, shaking off from itself that terrible incubus, the franking privilege. And the expediency of introducing a money-order office into the States, connected with the Post-office as it is with us, is even now under consideration. Such an accommodation is much needed in the country; but I doubt whether the present moment, looking at the fiscal state of the country, is well adapted for establishing it.

I was much struck by the great extravagance in small things manifested by the Post-office through the States, and have reason to believe that the same remark would be equally true with regard to other public establishments. They use needless forms without end,—making millions of entries which no one is ever expected to regard. Their expenditure in stationery might, I think, be reduced by one half, and the labour might be saved which is now wasted in the abuse of that useless stationery. Their mail-bags are made in a costly manner, and are often large beyond all proportion or necessity. I could greatly lengthen this list if I were addressing myself solely to Post-office people; but as I am not doing so I will close these semi-official remarks, with an assurance to my colleagues in Post-office work on the other side of the water that I greatly respect what they have done, and trust that before long they may have renewed opportunities for the prosecution of their good work.

CHAPTER XXIX

AMERICAN HOTELS

I FIND it impossible to resist the subject of inns. As I have gone on with my journey, I have gone on with my book, and have spoken here and there of American hotels as I have encountered them. But in the States the hotels are so large an institution, having so much closer and wider a bearing on social life than they do in any other country, that I feel myself bound to treat them in a separate chapter as a great national feature in themselves. They are quite as much thought of in the nation as the legislature, or judicature, or literature of the country; and any falling off in them, or any improvement in the accommodation given, would strike the community as forcibly as a change in the constitution, or an alteration in the franchise.

Moreover I consider myself as qualified to write a chapter on hotels; —not only on the hotels of America but on hotels generally. I have myself been much too frequently a sojourner at hotels. I think I know what an hotel should be, and what it should not be; and am almost inclined to believe, in my pride, that I could myself fill the position of a landlord with some chance of social success, though probably with none of satisfactory pecuniary results.

Of all hotels known to me, I am inclined to think that the Swiss are the best. The things wanted at an hotel are, I fancy, mainly as follows: —a clean bedroom with a good and clean bed, and with it also plenty of ̗water. Good food, well dressed and served at convenient hours, which hours should on occasions be allowed to stretch themselves. Wines that shall be drinkable. Quick attendance. Bills that shall not be absolutely extortionate, smiling faces, and an absence of foul smells. There are many who desire more than this;—who expect exquisite cookery, choice wines, subservient domestics, distinguished consideration, and the strictest economy. But they are uneducated travellers who are going through the apprenticeship of their hotel lives;—who may probably never become free of the travellers' guild, or learn to distinguish that which they may fairly hope to attain from that which they can never accomplish.

Taking them as a whole I think that the Swiss hotels are the best.

They are perhaps a little close in the matter of cold water, but even as to this, they generally give way to pressure. The pressure, however, must not be violent, but gentle rather, and well continued. Their bedrooms are excellent. Their cookery is good, and to the outward senses is cleanly. The people are civil. The whole work of the house is carried on upon fixed rules which tend to the comfort of the establishment. They are not cheap, and not always quite honest. But the exorbitance or dishonesty of their charges rarely exceeds a certain reasonable scale, and hardly ever demands the bitter misery of a remonstrance.

The inns of the Tyrol are, I think, the cheapest I have known, affording the traveller what he requires for half the price, or less than half, that demanded in Switzerland. But the other half is taken out in stench and nastiness. As tourists scatter themselves more profusely, the prices of the Tyrol will no doubt rise. Let us hope that increased prices will bring with them besoms, scrubbing-brushes, and other much needed articles of cleanliness.

The inns of the north of Italy are very good, and indeed, the Italian inns throughout, as far as I know them, are much better than the name they bear. The Italians are a civil, kindly people, and do for you, at any rate, the best they can. Perhaps the unwary traveller may be cheated. Ignorant of the language, he may be called on to pay more than the man who speaks it, and who can bargain in the Italian fashion as to price. It has often been my lot, I doubt not, to be so cheated. But then I have been cheated with a grace that has been worth all the money. The ordinary prices of Italian inns are by no means high.

I have seldom thoroughly liked the inns of Germany which I have known. They are not clean, and water is very scarce. Smiles too are generally wanting, and I have usually fancied myself to be regarded as a piece of goods out of which so much profit was to be made.

The dearest hotels I know are the French;—and certainly not the best. In the provinces they are by no means so cleanly as those of Italy. Their wines are generally abominable, and their cookery often disgusting. In Paris grand dinners may no doubt be had, and luxuries of every description,—except the luxury of comfort. Cotton-velvet sofas and ormolu clocks stand in the place of convenient furniture, and logs of wood at a franc a log fail to impart to you the heat which the freezing cold of a Paris winter demands. They used to make good coffee in Paris, but even that is a thing of the past. I fancy that they import their brandy from England, and manufacture their own cigars. French wines you may get good at a Paris hotel; but you would drink them as good and much cheaper if you bought them in London and took them with you.

The worst hotels I know are in the Havana. Of course I do not speak here of chance mountain huts, or small far-off roadside hostels in which the traveller may find himself from time to time. All such are to be counted apart, and must be judged on their merits, by the circumstances which surround them. But with reference to places of wide resort, nothing can beat the hotels of the Havana in filth, discomfort, habits of abomination, and absence of everything which the traveller desires. All the world does not go to the Havana, and the subject is not, therefore, one of general interest. But in speaking of hotels at large, so much I find myself bound to say.

In all the countries to which I have alluded the guests of the house are expected to sit down together at one table. Conversation is at any rate possible, and there is the show if not the reality of society.

And now one word as to English inns. I do not think that we Englishmen have any great right to be proud of them. The worst about them is that they deteriorate from year to year instead of becoming better. We used to hear much of the comfort of the old English wayside inn, but the old English wayside inn has gone. The railway hotel has taken its place, and the railway hotel is too frequently gloomy, desolate, comfortless, and almost suicidal. In England too, since the old days are gone, there are wanting the landlord's bow, and the kindly smile of his stout wife. Who now knows the landlord of an inn, or cares to inquire whether or no there be a landlady? The old welcome is wanting, and the cheery warm air which used to atone for the bad port and tough beef has passed away;—while the port is still bad and the beef too often tough.

In England, and only in England, as I believe, is maintained in hotel life the theory of solitary existence. The sojourner at an English inn,—unless he be a commercial traveller, and, as such, a member of a universal, peripatetic, tradesman's club,—lives alone. He has his breakfast alone, his dinner alone, his pint of wine alone, and his cup of tea alone. It is not considered practicable that two strangers should sit at the same table, or cut from the same dish. Consequently his dinner is cooked for him separately, and the hotel keeper can hardly afford to give him a good dinner. He has two modes of life from which to choose. He either lives in a public room,—called a coffee-room, and there occupies during his comfortless meal a separate small table too frequently removed from fire and light, though generally exposed to draughts; or else he indulges in the luxury of a private sitting-room, and endeavours to find solace on an old horse-hair sofa, at the cost of seven shillings a day. His bedroom is not so arranged that he can use it as a sitting-room. Under either phase of life he can rarely find himself comfortable, and therefore he lives as little at an hotel as the circumstances of his business or of his pleasure will allow. I do not think that any of the requisites of a good inn are habitually to be found in perfection at our Kings' Heads and White Horses, though the falling off is not so lamentably distressing as it sometimes is in other countries. The bedrooms are dingy rather than dirty. Extra payment to servants will generally produce a tub of cold water. The food is never good, but it is usually eatable, and you may have it when you please. The wines are almost always bad, but the traveller can fall back upon beer. The attendance is good, provided always that the payment for it is liberal. The cost is generally too high, and unfortunately grows larger and larger from year to year. Smiling faces are out of the question unless specially paid for; and as to that matter of foul smells there is often room for improvement. An English inn to a solitary traveller without employment is an embodiment of dreary desolation. The excuse to be made for this is that English men and women do not live much at inns in their own country.

The American inn differs from all those of which I have made mention, and is altogether an institution apart, and a thing of itself. Hotels in America are very much larger and more numerous than in other countries. They are to be found in all towns, and I may almost say in all villages. In England and on the Continent we find them on the recognized routes of travel and in towns of commercial or social importance. On unfrequented roads and in villages there is usually some small house of public entertainment in which the unexpected traveller may obtain food and shelter, and in which the expected boon companions of the neighbourhood smoke their nightly pipes, and drink their nightly tipple. But in the States of America the first sign of an incipient settlement is an hotel five stories high, with an office, a bar, a cloak-room, three gentlemen's parlours, two ladies' parlours, a ladies' entrance, and two hundred bedrooms.

These, of course, are all built with a view to profit, and it may be presumed that in each case the originators of the speculation enter into some calculation as to their expected guests. Whence are to come the sleepers in those two hundred bedrooms, and who is to pay for the gaudy sofas and numerous lounging chairs of the ladies' parlours? In all other countries the expectation would extend itself simply to travellers;—to travellers or to strangers sojourning in the land. But this is by no means the case as to these speculations in America. When the new hotel rises up in the wilderness, it is presumed that people will come there with the express object of inhabiting it. The hotel itself will create a population,—as the railways do. With us railways run to the towns; but in the States the towns run to the railways. It is the same thing with the hotels.

Housekeeping is not popular with young married people in America, and there are various reasons why this should be so. Men there are not fixed in their employment as they are with us. If a young Benedict cannot get along as a lawyer at Salem, perhaps he may thrive as a shoemaker at Thermopylæ. Jefferson B. Johnson fails in the lumber line at Eleutheria, but hearing of an opening for a Baptist preacher at Big Mud Creek moves himself off with his wife and three children at a week's notice. Aminadab Wiggs takes an engagement as a clerk at a steam-boat office on the Pongowonga river, but he goes to his employment with an inward conviction that six months will see him earning his bread elsewhere. Under such circumstances even a large wardrobe is a nuisance, and a collection of furniture would be as appropriate as a drove of elephants. Then, again, young men and women marry without any means already collected on which to commence their life. They are content to look forward and to hope that such means will come. In so doing they are guilty of no imprudence. It is the way of the country; and, if the man be useful for anything, employment will certainly come to him. But he must live on the fruits of that employment, and can only pay his way from week to week and from day to day. And as a third reason I think I may allege that the mode of life found in these hotels is liked by the people who frequent them. It is to their taste. They are happy, or at any rate contented at these hotels, and do not wish for household cares. As to the two first reasons which I have given I can agree as to the necessity of the case, and quite concur as to the expediency of marriage under such circumstances. But as to that matter of taste, I cannot concur at all. Anything more forlorn than a young married woman at an American hotel, it is impossible to conceive.

Such are the guests expected for those two hundred bedrooms. The chance travellers are but chance additions to these, and are not generally the main stay of the house. As a matter of course the accommodation for travellers which these hotels afford increases and creates travelling. Men come because they know they will be fed and bedded at a moderate cost, and in an easy way, suited to their tastes. With us, and throughout Europe, inquiry is made before an unaccustomed journey is commenced, on that serious question of wayside food and shelter. But in the States no such question is needed. A big hotel is a matter of course, and therefore men travel. Everybody travels in the States. The railways and the hotels have between them so churned up the people that an untravelled man or woman is a rare animal. We are apt to suppose that travellers make roads, and that guests create hotels; but the cause and effect run exactly in the other way. I am almost disposed to think that we should become cannibals if gentlemen's legs and ladies' arms were hung up for sale in purveyors' shops.

After this fashion and with these intentions hotels are built. Size and an imposing exterior are the first requisitions. Everything about them must be on a large scale. A commanding exterior, and a certain interior dignity of demeanour is more essential than comfort or civility. Whatever an hotel may be it must not be "mean." In the American vernacular the word "mean" is very significant. A mean white in the South is a man who owns no slaves. Men are often mean, but actions are seldom so called. A man feels mean when the bluster is taken out of him. A mean hotel, conducted in a quiet unostentatious manner, in which the only endeavour made had reference to the comfort of a few guests, would find no favour in the States. These hotels are not called by the name of any sign, as with us in our provinces. There are no "Presidents' Heads" or "General Scotts." Nor by the name of the land-lord, or of some former landlord, as with us in London, and in many cities of the Continent. Nor are they called from some country or city which may have been presumed at some time to have had special pa-tronage for the establishment. In the nomenclature of American hotels the speciality of American hero-worship is shown, as in the nomencla-ture of their children. Every inn is a house, and these houses are gen-erally named after some hero, little known probably in the world at large, but highly estimated in that locality at the moment of the christening.

They are always built on a plan which to a European seems to be most unnecessarily extravagant in space. It is not unfrequently the case that the greater portion of the ground-floor is occupied by rooms and halls which make no return to the house whatever. The visitor enters a great hall by the front door, and almost invariably finds it full of men who are idling about, sitting round on stationary seats, talking in a listless manner, and getting through their time as though the place were a public lounging room. And so it is. The chances are that not half the crowd are guests at the hotel. I will now follow the visitor as he makes his way up to the office. Every hotel has an office.

To call this place the bar, as I have done too frequently, is a lamentable error. The bar is held in a separate room appropriated solely to
drinking. To the office, which is in fact a long open counter, the guest
walks up, and there inscribes his name in a book. This inscription was
to me a moment of misery which I could never go through with equanimity. As the name is written, and as the request for accommodation
is made, half a dozen loungers look over your name and listen to what
you say. They listen attentively, and spell your name carefully, but the
great man behind the bar does not seem to listen or to heed you. Your
destiny is never imparted to you on the instant. If your wife or any
other woman be with you, (the word "lady" is made so absolutely distasteful in American hotels that I cannot bring myself to use it in
writing of them,) she has been carried off to a lady's waiting room,
and there remains in august wretchedness till the great man at the bar
shall have decided on her fate. I have never been quite able to fathom
the mystery of these delays. I think they must have originated in the
necessity of waiting to see what might be the influx of travellers at the
moment, and then have become exaggerated and brought to their
present normal state by the gratified feeling of almost divine power
with which for the time it invests that despotic arbiter. I have found
it always the same, though arriving with no crowd, by a conveyance
of my own, when no other expectant guests were following me. The
great man has listened to my request in silence, with an imperturbable
face, and has usually continued his conversation with some loafing
friend, who at the time is probably scrutinizing my name in the book.
I have often suffered in patience; but patience is not specially the badge
of my tribe, and I have sometimes spoken out rather freely. If I may
presume to give advice to my travelling countrymen how to act under
such circumstances I should recommend to them freedom of speech
rather than patience. The great man when freely addressed generally
opens his eyes, and selects the key of your room without further delay.
I am inclined to think that the selection will not be made in any way
to your detriment by reason of that freedom of speech. The lady in the
ballad who spoke out her own mind to Lord Bateman was sent to her
home honourably in a coach and three. Had she held her tongue we
are justified in presuming that she would have been returned on a
pillion behind a servant.[1]

[1] Trollope refers to *The Loving Ballad of Lord Bateman*, a popular ballad that
he probably knew in the cockney-dialect version issued with spirited illustrations
by George Cruikshank in 1839 and again in 1851. It is not the "lady in the ballad"
who speaks out her mind, however, but the lady's mother. The marriage ceremony

I have been greatly annoyed by that silence on the part of the hotel clerk. I have repeatedly asked for room, and received no syllable in return. I have persisted in my request, and the clerk has nodded his head at me. Until a traveller is known, these gentlemen are singularly sparing of speech,—especially in the West. The same economy of words runs down from the great man at the office all through the servants of the establishment. It arises, I believe, entirely from that want of courtesy which democratic institutions create. The man whom you address, has to make a battle against the state of subservience, presumed to be indicated by his position, and he does so by declaring his indifference to the person on whose wants he is paid to attend. I have been honoured on one or two occasions by the subsequent intimacy of these great men at the hotel offices, and have then found them ready enough at conversation.

That necessity of making your request for rooms before a public audience, is not in itself agreeable, and sometimes entails a conversation which might be more comfortably made in private. "What do you mean by a dressing-room, and why do you want one?" Now that is a question which an Englishman feels awkward at answering before five-and-twenty Americans, with open mouths and eager eyes; but it has to be answered. When I left England, I was assured that I should not find any need for a separate sitting-room, seeing that drawing-rooms more or less sumptuous were prepared for the accommodation of "ladies." At first we attempted to follow the advice given to us, but we broke down. A man and his wife travelling from town to town, and making no sojourn on his way, may eat and sleep at an hotel without a private parlour. But an Englishwoman cannot live in comfort for a week, or even, in comfort, for a day, at any of these houses, without a sitting-room for herself. The ladies' drawing-room is a desolate wilder-

---

is scarcely over when Sophia, a Turkish maiden who once freed Lord Bateman from her father's prison, appears to claim her reward.

> Then up and spoke this young bride's mother,
> Who never vos heerd to speak so free:
> Sayin, "You'll not forget my ounly darter,
> If so be as Sophia has crossed the sea."

> "O it's true I made a bride of your darter,
> But she's neither the better nor the vorse for me;
> She came to me with a horse and saddle,
> But she may go home in a coach and three."

For the authorship of this Victorian version, frequently attributed to Thackeray, see Anne Lyon Haight: "Charles Dickens Tries to Remain Anonymous: Notes on the Loving Ballad of Lord Bateman" (*Colophon*, New Graphic Series, No. 1 [1939], pp. 39–66).

ness. The American women themselves do not use it. It is generally empty, or occupied by some forlorn spinster, eliciting harsh sounds from the wretched piano which it contains.

The price at these hotels throughout the Union is nearly always the same, viz., two and a half dollars a day, for which a bedroom is given, and as many meals as the guest can contrive to eat. This is the price for chance guests. The cost to monthly boarders is, I believe, not more than the half of this. Ten shillings a day, therefore, covers everything that is absolutely necessary, servants included. And this must be said in praise to these inns: that the traveller can compute his expenses accurately, and can absolutely bring them within that daily sum of ten shillings. This includes a great deal of eating, a great deal of attendance, the use of reading-rooms and smoking-rooms—which, however, always seem to be open to the public as well as to the guests,—and a bedroom with accommodation which is at any rate as good as the average accommodation of hotels in Europe. In the large Eastern towns baths are attached to many of the rooms. I always carry my own, and have never failed in getting water. It must be acknowledged that the price is very low. It is so low that I believe it affords, as a rule, no profit whatsoever. The profit is made upon extra charges, and they are higher than in any other country that I have visited. They are so high that I consider travelling in America, for an Englishman with his wife or family, to be more expensive than travelling in any part of Europe. First in the list of extras comes that matter of the sitting-room, and by that for a man and his wife the whole first expense is at once doubled. The ordinary charge is five dollars, or one pound a day! A guest intending to stay for two or three weeks at an hotel, or perhaps for one week, may, by agreement, have this charge reduced. At one inn I stayed a fortnight, and having made no such agreement was charged the full sum. I felt myself stirred up to complain, and did in that case remonstrate. I was asked how much I wished to have returned,—for the bill had been paid,—and the sum I suggested was at once handed to me. But even with such reduction the price is very high, and at once makes the American hotel expensive. Wine also at these houses is very costly, and very bad. The usual price is two dollars, or eight shillings, a bottle. The people of the country rarely drink wine at dinner in the hotels. When they do so, they drink champagne; but their normal drinking is done separately, at the bar, chiefly before dinner, and at a cheap rate. "A drink," let it be what it may, invariably costs a dime, or fivepence. But if you must have a glass of sherry with your dinner, it costs two dollars; for sherry does not grow into pint bottles in the States. But the guest who remains for two days can have his wine kept for him. Washing also is an expensive luxury. The price of this is invariable, being always fourpence for everything washed. A cambric handkerchief or muslin dress all come out at the same price. For those who are cunning in the matter this may do very well; but for men and women whose cuffs and collars are numerous it becomes expensive. The craft of those who are cunning is shown, I think, in little internal washings, by which the cambric handkerchiefs are kept out of the list, while the muslin dresses are placed upon it. I am led to this surmise by the energetic measures taken by the hotel keepers to prevent such domestic washings, and by the denunciations which in every hotel are pasted up in every room against the practice. I could not at first understand why I was always warned against washing my own clothes in my own bedroom, and told that no foreign laundress could on any account be admitted into the house. The injunctions given on this head are almost frantic in their energy, and therefore I conceive that hotel keepers find themselves exposed to much suffering in the matter. At these hotels they wash with great rapidity, sending you back your clothes in four or five hours if you desire it.

Another very stringent order is placed before the face of all visitors at American hotels, desiring them on no account to leave valuable property in their rooms. I presume that there must have been some difficulty in this matter in bygone years, for in every State a law has been passed declaring that hotel keepers shall not be held responsible for money or jewels stolen out of rooms in their houses, provided that they are furnished with safes for keeping such money, and give due caution to their guests on the subject. The due caution is always given, but I have seldom myself taken any notice of it. I have always left my portmanteau open, and have kept my money usually in a travelling desk in my room. But I never to my knowledge lost anything. The world, I think, gives itself credit for more thieves than it possesses. As to the female servants at American inns, they are generally all that is disagreeable. They are uncivil, impudent, dirty, slow,—provoking to a degree. But I believe that they keep their hands from picking and stealing.

I never yet made a single comfortable meal at an American hotel, or rose from my breakfast or dinner with that feeling of satisfaction which should, I think, be felt at such moments in a civilized land in which cookery prevails as an art. I have had enough, and have been healthy and am thankful. But that thankfulness is altogether a matter apart, and does not bear upon the question. If need be I can eat food that is disagreeable to my palate, and make no complaint. But I hold it to be compatible with the principles of an advanced Christianity to prefer food that is palatable. I never could get any of that kind at an American hotel. All meal-times at such houses were to me periods of disagreeable duty; and at this moment, as I write these lines at the hotel in which I am still staying, I pine for an English leg of mutton. But I do not wish it to be supposed that the fault of which I complain,—for it is a grievous fault,—is incidental to America as a nation. I have stayed in private houses, and have daily sat down to dinners quite as good as any my own kitchen could afford me. Their dinner parties are generally well done, and as a people they are by no means indifferent to the nature of their comestibles. It is of the hotels that I speak, and of them I again say that eating in them is a disagreeable task,—a painful labour. It is as a schoolboy's lesson, or the six hours' confinement of a clerk at his desk.

The mode of eating is as follows. Certain feeding hours are named, which generally include nearly all the day. Breakfast from six till ten. Dinner from one till five. Tea from six till nine. Supper from nine till twelve. When the guest presents himself at any of these hours he is marshalled to a seat, and a bill is put into his hand containing the names of all the eatables then offered for his choice. The list is incredibly and most unnecessarily long. Then it is that you will see care written on the face of the American hotel liver, as he studies the programme of the coming performance. With men this passes off unnoticed, but with young girls the appearance of the thing is not attractive. The anxious study, the elaborate reading of the daily book, and then the choice proclaimed with clear articulation. "Boiled mutton and caper sauce, roast duck, hashed venison, mashed potatoes, poached eggs and spinach, stewed tomatoes. Yes; and waiter,—some squash." There is no false delicacy in the voice by which this order is given, no desire for a gentle whisper. The dinner is ordered with the firm determination of an American heroine, and in some five minutes' time all the little dishes appear at once, and the lady is surrounded by her banquet.

How I did learn to hate those little dishes and their greasy contents! At a London eating-house things are often not very nice, but your meat is put on a plate and comes before you in an edible shape. At these hotels it is brought to you in horrid little oval dishes, and swims in grease. Gravy is not an institution at American hotels, but grease has taken its place. It is palpable, undisguised grease, floating in rivers,—not grease caused by accidental bad cookery, but grease on purpose. A beef-steak is not a beef-steak unless a quarter of a pound of butter be added to it. Those horrid little dishes! If one thinks of it how could they have been made to contain Christian food? Every article in that long list is liable to the call of any number of guests for four hours. Under such circumstances how can food be made eatable? Your roast mutton is brought to you raw;—if you object to that you are supplied with meat that has been four times brought before the public. At hotels on the continent of Europe different dinners are cooked at different hours, but here the same dinner is kept always going. The house breakfast is maintained on a similar footing. Huge boilers of tea and coffee are stewed down and kept hot. To me those meals were odious. It is of course open to any one to have separate dinners and separate breakfasts in his own room; but by this little is gained and much is lost. He or she who is so exclusive pays twice over for such meals,—as they are charged as extras on the bill; and, after all, receives the advantage of no exclusive cooking. Particles from the public dinners are brought to the private room, and the same odious little dishes make their appearance.

But the most striking peculiarity of the American hotels is in their public rooms. Of the ladies' drawing-room I have spoken. There are two and sometimes three in one hotel, and they are generally furnished, at any rate expensively. It seems to me that the space and the furniture are almost thrown away. At watering places, and sea-side summer hotels they are, I presume, used; but at ordinary hotels they are empty deserts. The intention is good, for they are established with the view of giving to ladies at hotels the comforts of ordinary domestic life; but they fail in their effect. Ladies will not make themselves happy in any room, or with ever so much gilded furniture, unless some means of happiness be provided for them. Into these rooms no book is ever brought, no needle-work is introduced; from them no clatter of many tongues is ever heard. On a marble table in the middle of the room always stands a large pitcher of iced water, and from this a cold, damp, uninviting air is spread through the atmosphere of the ladies' drawing-room.

Below, on the ground floor, there is, in the first place, the huge entrance hall, at the back of which, behind a bar, the great man of the place keeps the keys and holds his court. There are generally seats around it, in which smokers sit,—or men not smoking but ruminating. Opening off from this are reading rooms, smoking rooms, shaving rooms, drinking rooms, parlours for gentlemen in which smoking is prohibited, and which are generally as desolate as the ladies' sitting-rooms above. In those other more congenial chambers is always gathered together a crowd, apparently belonging in no way to the hotel. It would seem that a great portion of an American inn is as open to the public as an Exchange, or as the wayside of the street. In the West, during the months of this war, the traveller would always see many soldiers among the crowd,—not only officers, but privates. They sit in public seats, silent but apparently contented, sometimes for an hour together. All Americans are given to gatherings such as these. It is the much-loved institution to which the name of "loafing" has been given.

I do not like the mode of life which prevails in the American hotels. I have come across exceptions, and know one or two that are comfortable,—always excepting that matter of eating and drinking. But taking them as a whole I do not like their mode of life. I feel, however, bound to add that the hotels of Canada, which are kept, I think, always after the same fashion, are infinitely worse than those of the United States. I do not like the American hotels; but I must say in their favour that they afford an immense amount of accommodation. The traveller is rarely told that an hotel is full, so that travelling in America is without one of those great perils to which it is subject in Europe. It must also be acknowledged that for the ordinary purposes of a traveller they are very cheap.

CHAPTER XXX

LITERATURE

IN speaking of the literature of any country we are, I think, too much inclined to regard the question as one appertaining exclusively to the writers of books,—not acknowledging, as we should do, that the literary character of a people will depend much more upon what it reads than what it writes. If we can suppose any people to have an intimate acquaintance with the best literary efforts of other countries, we should hardly be correct in saying that such a people had no literary history of their own because it had itself produced nothing in literature. And, with reference to those countries which have been most fertile in the production of good books, I doubt whether their literary histories would not have more to tell of those ages in which much has been read than of those in which much has been written.

The United States have been by no means barren in the production of literature. The truth is so far from this that their literary triumphs are perhaps those which of all their triumphs are the most honourable to them, and which, considering their position as a young nation, are the most permanently satisfactory. But though they have done much in writing, they have done much more in reading. As producers they are more than respectable, but as consumers they are the most conspicuous people on the earth. It is impossible to speak of the subject of literature in America without thinking of the readers rather than of the writers. In this matter their position is different from that of any other great people, seeing that they share the advantages of our language. An American will perhaps consider himself to be as little like an Englishman as he is like a Frenchman. But he reads Shakespeare through the medium of his own vernacular, and has to undergo the penance of a foreign tongue before he can understand Molière. He separates himself from England in politics and perhaps in affection; but he cannot separate himself from England in mental culture. It may be suggested that an Englishman has the same advantages as regards America; and it is true that he is obtaining much of such advantage. Irving, Prescott, and Longfellow are the same to England as though she herself had produced them. But the balance of advantage must be greatly in favour of America. We have given her the work of four hundred years, and have received back in return the work of fifty.

And of this advantage the Americans have not been slow to avail themselves. As consumers of literature they are certainly the most conspicuous people on the earth. Where an English publisher contents himself with thousands of copies an American publisher deals with ten thousands. The sale of a new book, which in numbers would amount to a considerable success with us, would with them be a lamentable failure. This of course is accounted for, as regards the author and the publisher, by the difference of price at which the book is produced. One thousand in England will give perhaps as good a return as the ten thousand in America. But as regards the readers there can be no such equalization. The thousand copies cannot spread themselves as do the ten thousand. The one book at a guinea cannot multiply itself, let Mr. Mudie do what he will, as do the ten books at a dollar. Ultimately there remain the ten books against the one; and if there be not the ten readers against the one, there are five, or four, or three. Everybody in the States has books about his house. "And so has everybody in England," will say my English reader, mindful of the libraries, or book-rooms, or book-crowded drawing-rooms of his friends and acquaintances. But has my English reader who so replies examined the libraries of many English cabmen, of ticket porters, of warehousemen, and of agricultural labourers? I cannot take upon myself to say that I have done so with any close search in the States. But when it has been in my power I have done so, and I have always found books in such houses as I have entered. The amount of printed matter which is poured forth in streams from the printing-presses of the great American publishers is, however, a better proof of the truth of what I say than anything that I can have seen myself.

But of what class are the books that are so read? There are many who think that reading in itself is not good unless the matter read be excellent. I do not myself quite agree with this, thinking that almost any reading is better than none; but I will of course admit that good matter is better than bad matter. The bulk of the literature consumed in the States is no doubt composed of novels,—as it is also, now-a-days, in this country. Whether or no an unlimited supply of novels for young people is or is not advantageous, I will not here pretend to say. The general opinion with ourselves I take it is, that novels are bad reading if they be bad of their kind. Novels that are not bad are now-a-days accepted generally as indispensable to our households. Whatever may be the weakness of the American literary taste in this respect, it is, I think, a weakness which we share. There are more novel readers among them than with us, but only, I think, in the proportion that there are more readers.

I have no hesitation in saying, that works by English authors are more popular in the States, than those written by themselves; and, among English authors of the present day, they by no means confine themselves to the novelists. The English names of whom I heard most during my sojourn in the States, were perhaps those of Dickens, Tennyson, Buckle, Tom Hughes, Martin Tupper, and Thackeray. As the owners of all these names are still living, I am not going to take upon myself the delicate task of criticising the American taste. I may not perhaps coincide with them in every respect. But if I be right as to the names which I have given, such a selection shows that they do get beyond novels. I have little doubt but that many more copies of Dickens's novels have been sold during the last three years, than of the works either of Tennyson or of Buckle; but such also has been the case in England. It will probably be admitted that one copy of the "Civilization" should be held as being equal to five-and-twenty of "Nicholas Nickleby," and that a single "In Memoriam" may fairly weigh down half-a-dozen "Pickwicks." Men and women after their day's work are not always up to the "Civilization." As a rule they are generally up to "Proverbial Philosophy," and this, perhaps, may have had something to do with the great popularity of that very popular work.

I would not have it supposed that American readers despise their own authors. The Americans are very proud of having a literature of their own. Among the literary names which they honour, there are none, I think, more honourable than those of Cooper and Irving. They like to know that their modern historians are acknowledged as great authors, and as regards their own poets will sometimes demand your admiration for strains with which you hardly find yourself to be familiar. But English books are, I think, the better loved;—even the English books of the present day. And even beyond this,—with those who choose to indulge in the costly luxuries of literature,—books printed in England are more popular than those which are printed in their own country; and yet the manner in which the American publishers put out their work is very good. The book sold there at a dollar, or a dollar and a quarter, quite equals our ordinary five shilling volume. Nevertheless English books are preferred,—almost as strongly as are French bonnets. Of books absolutely printed and produced in England the supply in the States is of course small. They must necessarily be costly, and as regards new books, are always subjected to the rivalry of a cheaper American copy. But of the reprinted works of English authors the supply is unlimited, and the sale very great. Almost everything is reprinted; certainly everything which can be said to attain any home popularity. I do not know how far English authors may be aware of the fact; but it is undoubtedly a fact that their influence as authors, is greater on the other side of the Atlantic than on this. It is there that they have their most numerous school of pupils. It is there that they are recognized as teachers by hundreds of thousands. It is of those thirty millions that they should think, at any rate in part, when they discuss within their own hearts that question which all authors do discuss, whether that which they write shall in itself be good or bad,—be true or false. A writer in England may not, perhaps, think very much of this with reference to some trifle of which his English publisher proposes to sell some seven or eight hundred copies. But he begins to feel that he should have thought of it when he learns that twenty or thirty thousand copies of the same have been scattered through the length and breadth of the United States. The English author should feel that he writes for the widest circle of readers ever yet obtained by the literature of any country. He provides not only for his own country and for the States, but for the readers who are rising by millions in the British colonies. Canada is supplied chiefly from the presses of Boston, New York, and Philadelphia, but she is supplied with the works of the mother country. India, as I take it, gets all her books direct from London, as do the West Indies. Whether or no the Australian colonies have as yet learned to reprint our books I do not know, but I presume that they cannot do so as cheaply as they can import them. London with us, and the three cities which I have named on the other side of the Atlantic, are the places at which this literature is manufactured; but the demand in the western hemisphere is becoming more brisk than that which the old world creates. There is, I have no doubt, more literary matter printed in London than in all America put together. A greater extent of letter-press is put up in London than in the three publishing cities of the States. But the number of copies issued by the American publishers is so much greater than those which ours put forth, that the greater bulk of literature is with them. If this be so, the demand with them is of course greater than it is with us.

I have spoken here of the privilege which an English author enjoys by reason of the ever widening circle of readers to whom he writes. I speak of the privilege of an English author as distinguished from that of an American author. I profess my belief that in the United States an English author has an advantage over one of that country merely in the fact of his being English, as a French milliner has undoubtedly an advantage in her nationality let her merits or demerits as a milliner be what they may. I think that English books are better liked because they are English. But I do not know that there is any feeling with us either for or against an author because he is American. I believe that Longfellow stands in our judgment exactly where he would have stood had he been a tutor at a college in Oxford instead of a Professor at Cambridge in Massachusetts. Prescott is read among us as an historian without any reference as to his nationality, and by many, as I take it, in absolute ignorance of his nationality. Hawthorne, the novelist, is quite as well known in England as he is in his own country. But I do not know that to either of these three is awarded any favour or is denied any justice because he is an American. Washington Irving published many of his works in this country, receiving very large sums for them from Mr. Murray, and I fancy that in dealing with his publisher he found neither advantage nor disadvantage in his nationality;—that is, of course, advantage or disadvantage in reference to the light in which his works would be regarded. It must be admitted that there is no jealousy in the States against English authors. I think that there is a feeling in their favour, but no one can at any rate allege that there is a feeling against them. I think I may also assert on the part of my own country that there is no jealousy here against American authors. As regards the tastes of the people, the works of each country flow freely through the other. That is as it should be. But when we come to the mode of supply, things are not exactly as they should be; and I do not believe that any one will contradict me when I say that the fault is with the Americans.

I presume that all my readers know the meaning of the word copyright. A man's copyright, or right in his copy, is that amount of legal possession in the production of his brains which has been secured to him by the laws of his own country and by the laws of others.[1] Unless an author were secured by such laws, his writings would be of but little pecuniary value to him, as the right of printing and selling them would be open to all the world. In England and in America, and as I conceive in all countries possessing a literature, there is such a law securing to authors and to their heirs for a term of years the exclusive right over their own productions. That this should be so in England as regards English authors is so much a matter of course, that the copyright of an author would seem to be as naturally his own as a gentleman's deposit at his bank or his little investment in the three per cents.

[1] For Trollope's battle with Harper & Brothers over their right to publish *North America* without the author's sanction, see our Introduction, section VIII.

The right of an author to the value of his own productions in other countries than his own is not so much a matter of course; but nevertheless, if such productions have any value in other countries, that value should belong to him. This has been felt to be the case between England and France, and treaties have been made securing his own property to the author in each country. The fact that the languages of England and France are different makes the matter one of comparatively small moment. But it has been found to be for the honour and profit of the two countries, that there should be such a law, and an international copyright does exist. But if such an arrangement be needed between two such countries as France and England,—between two countries which do not speak the same language or share the same literature,—how much more necessary must it be between England and the United States? The literature of the one country is the literature of the other. The poem that is popular in London will certainly be popular in New York. The novel that is effective among American ladies will be equally so with those of England. There can be no doubt as to the importance of having a law of copyright between the two countries. The only question can be as to the expediency and the justice. At present there is no international copyright between England and the United States, and there is none because the States have declined to sanction any such law. It is known by all who are concerned in the matter on either side of the water that as far as Great Britain is concerned such a law would meet with no impediment.

Therefore it is to be presumed that the legislators of the States think it expedient and just to dispense with any such law. I have said that there can be no doubt as to the importance of the question, seeing that the price of English literature in the States must be most materially affected by it. Without such a law the Americans are enabled to import English literature without paying for it. It is open to any American publisher to reprint any work from an English copy, and to sell his reprints without any permission obtained from the English author or from the English publisher. The absolute material which the American publisher sells, he takes, or can take for nothing. The paper, ink, and composition he supplies in the ordinary way of business; but of the very matter which he professes to sell,—of the book which is the object of his trade, he is enabled to possess himself for nothing. If you, my reader, be a popular author, an American publisher will take the choicest work of your brain and make dollars out of it, selling thousands of copies of it in his country, whereas you can, perhaps, only sell hundreds of it in your own; and will either give you nothing for that he takes,—or else will explain to you that he need give you nothing, and that in paying you anything he subjects himself to the danger of seeing the property which he has bought taken again from him by other persons. If this be so that question whether or no there shall be a law of international copyright between the two countries cannot be unimportant.

But it may be inexpedient that there shall be such a law. It may be considered well, that as the influx of English books into America is much greater than the out-flux of American books back to England, the right of obtaining such books for nothing should be reserved, although the country in doing so robs its own authors of the advantage which should accrue to them from the English market. It might perhaps be thought anything but smart to surrender such an advantage by the passing of an international copyright bill. There are not many trades in which the tradesman can get the chief of his goods for nothing; and it may be thought, that the advantage arising to the States from such an arrangement of circumstances should not be abandoned. But how then about the justice? It would seem that the less said upon that subject the better. I have heard no one say that an author's property in his own works should not, in accordance with justice, be insured to him in the one country as well as in the other. I have seen no defence of the present position of affairs, on the score of justice. The price of books would be enhanced by an international copyright law, and it is well that books should be cheap. That is the only argument used. So would mutton be cheap, if it could be taken out of a butcher's shop for nothing!

But I absolutely deny the expediency of the present position of the matter, looking simply to the material advantage of the American people in the matter, and throwing aside altogether that question of justice. I must here, however, explain that I bring no charge whatsoever against the American publishers. The English author is a victim in their hands, but it is by no means their fault that he is so. As a rule, they are willing to pay for the works of popular English writers, but in arranging as to what payments they can make, they must of course bear in mind the fact that they have no exclusive right whatsoever in the things which they purchase. It is natural, also, that they should bear in mind when making their purchases, and arranging their prices, that they can have the very thing they are buying without any payment at all, if the price asked do not suit them. It is not of the publishers that I complain, or of any advantage which they take; but of the legislators of the country, and of the advantage which accrues, or is thought by them to accrue to the American people from the absence of an international copyright law. It is mean on their part to take such advantage if it existed; and it is foolish in them to suppose that any such advantage can accrue. The absence of any law of copyright no doubt gives to the American publisher the power of reprinting the works of English authors without paying for them,—seeing that the English author is undefended. But the American publisher who brings out such a reprint is equally undefended in his property. When he shall have produced his book, his rival in the next street may immediately reprint it from him, and destroy the value of his property by underselling him. It is probable that the first American publisher will have made some payment to the English author for the privilege of publishing the book honestly,—of publishing it without recurrence to piracy,—and in arranging his price with his customers he will be, of course, obliged to debit the book with the amount so paid. If the author receive ten cents a copy on every copy sold, the publisher must add that ten cents to the price he charges for it. But he cannot do this with security, because the book can be immediately reprinted, and sold without any such addition to the price. The only security which the American publisher has against the injury which may be so done to him, is the power of doing other injury in return. The men who stand high in the trade, and who are powerful because of the largeness of their dealings, can in a certain measure secure themselves in this way. Such a firm would have the power of crushing a small tradesman who should interfere with him. But if the large firm commits any such act of injustice, the little men in the trade have no power of setting themselves right by counter injustice. I need hardly point out what must be the effect of such a state of things upon the whole publishing trade; nor need I say more to prove that some law which shall regulate property in foreign copyrights would be as expedient with reference to America, as it would be just towards England. But the wrong done by America to herself does not rest here. It is true that more English books are read in the States than American books in England, but it is equally true that the literature of America is daily gaining readers among us. That injury to which English authors are subjected from the want of protection in the States, American authors suffer from the want of protection here. One can hardly believe that the legislators of the States would willingly place the brightest of their own fellow countrymen in this position, because in the event of a copyright bill being passed, the balance of advantage would seem to accrue to England!

Of the literature of the United States, speaking of literature in its ordinary sense, I do not know that I need say much more. I regard the literature of a country as its highest produce, believing it to be more powerful in its general effect, and more beneficial in its results, than either statesmanship, professional ability, religious teaching, or commerce. And in no part of its national career have the United States been so successful as in this. I need hardly explain that I should commit a monstrous injustice were I to make a comparison in this matter between England and America. Literature is the child of leisure and wealth. It is the produce of minds which by a happy combination of circumstances have been enabled to dispense with the ordinary cares of the world. It can hardly be expected to come from a young country, or from a new and still struggling people. Looking around at our own magnificent colonies I hardly remember a considerable name which they have produced, except that of my excellent old friend, Sam Slick.[2] Nothing, therefore, I think, shows the settled greatness of the people of the States more significantly than their firm establishment of a national literature. This literature runs over all subjects. American authors have excelled in poetry, in science, in history, in metaphysics, in law, in theology, and in fiction. They have attempted all, and failed in none. What Englishman has devoted a room to books, and devoted no portion of that room to the productions of America?

But I must say a word of literature in which I shall not speak of it in its ordinary sense, and shall yet speak of it in that sense which of all perhaps, in the present day, should be considered the most ordinary. I mean the every-day periodical literature of the press. Most of those who can read, it is to be hoped, read books; but all who can read do read newspapers. Newspapers in this country are so general that men cannot well live without them; but to men, and to women also, in the United States they may be said to be the one chief necessary of life. And yet in the whole length and breadth of the United States there is not published a single newspaper which seems to me to be worthy of praise.

A really good newspaper,—one excellent at all points,—would indeed be a triumph of honesty and of art! Not only is such a publication much to be desired in America, but it is still to be desired in Great Britain also. I used, in my younger days, to think of such a newspaper as a possible publication, and in a certain degree I then looked for it. Now I expect it only in my dreams. It should be powerful without

[2] The Canadian humorist Thomas Chandler Haliburton was famous for the creation of his character Sam Slick, a shrewd but boastful itinerant Yankee clockmaker and peddler. *The Clockmaker* (1837–40), first of the Sam Slick series, tells of this hero's adventures selling clocks to the farmers of Nova Scotia.

tyranny, popular without triumph, political without party passion, critical without personal feeling, right in its statements and just in its judgments, but right and just without pride. It should be all but omniscient, but not conscious of its omniscience; it should be moral, but not strait-laced; it should be well-assured, but yet modest; though never humble, it should be free from boasting. Above all these things it should be readable; and above that again it should be true. I used to think that such a newspaper might be produced, but I now sadly acknowledge to myself the fact that humanity is not capable of any work so divine.

The newspapers of the States generally may not only be said to have reached none of the virtues here named, but to have fallen into all the opposite vices. In the first place they are never true. In requiring truth from a newspaper the public should not be anxious to strain at gnats. A statement setting forth that a certain gooseberry was five inches in circumference, whereas in truth its girth was only two and a half, would give me no offence. Nor would I be offended at being told that Lord Derby was appointed to the premiership, while in truth the Queen had only sent for his lordship, having as yet come to no definite arrangement. The demand for truth which may reasonably be made upon a newspaper amounts to this,—that nothing should be stated not believed to be true, and that nothing should be stated as to which the truth is important, without adequate ground for such belief. If a newspaper accuse me of swindling, it is not sufficient that the writer believe me to be a swindler. He should have ample and sufficient ground for such belief;—otherwise in making such a statement he will write falsely. In our private life we all recognize the fact that this is so. It is understood that a man is not a whit the less a slanderer because he believes the slander which he promulgates. But it seems to me that this is not sufficiently recognized by many who write for the public press. Evil things are said, and are probably believed by the writers; they are said with that special skill for which newspaper writers have in our days become so conspicuous, defying alike redress by law or redress by argument; but they are too often said falsely. The words are not measured when they are written, and they are allowed to go forth without any sufficient inquiry into their truth. But if there be any ground for such complaint here in England, that ground is multiplied ten times—twenty times—in the States. This is not only shown in the abuse of individuals, in abuse which is as violent as it is perpetual, but in the treatment of every subject which is handled. All idea of truth has been thrown overboard. It seems to be admitted that the only object is to produce a sensation, and that it is admitted by both writer and reader that sensation and veracity are incompatible. Falsehood has become so much a matter of course with American newspapers that it has almost ceased to be falsehood. Nobody thinks me a liar because I deny that I am at home when I am in my study. The nature of the arrangement is generally understood. So also is it with the American newspapers.

But American newspapers are also unreadable. It is very bad that they should be false, but it is very surprising that they should be dull. Looking at the general intelligence of the people, one would have thought that a readable newspaper, put out with all pleasant appurtenances of clear type, good paper, and good internal arrangement, would have been a thing specially within their reach. But they have failed in every detail. Though their papers are always loaded with sensation headings, there are seldom sensation paragraphs to follow. The paragraphs do not fit the headings. Either they cannot be found, or if found they seem to have escaped from their proper column to some distant and remote portion of the sheet. One is led to presume that no American editor has any plan in the composition of his newspaper. I never know whether I have as yet got to the very heart's core of the daily journal, or whether I am still to go on searching for that heart's core. Alas, it too often happens that there is no heart's core! The whole thing seems to have been put out at hap-hazard. And then the very writing is in itself below mediocrity;—as though a power of expression in properly arranged language was not required by a newspaper editor, either as regards himself or as regards his subordinates. One is driven to suppose that the writers for the daily press are not chosen with any view to such capability. A man ambitious of being on the staff of an American newspaper should be capable of much work, should be satisfied with small pay, should be indifferent to the world's good usage, should be rough, ready, and of long sufferance; but, above all, he should be smart. The type of almost all American newspapers is wretched—I think I may say of all;—so wretched that that alone forbids one to hope for pleasure in reading them. They are ill-written, ill-printed, ill-arranged, and in fact are not readable. They are bought, glanced at, and thrown away.

They are full of boastings,—not boastings simply as to their country, their town, or their party,—but of boastings as to themselves. And yet they possess no self-assurance. It is always evident that they neither trust themselves, or expect to be trusted. They have made no approach to that omniscience which constitutes the great marvel of our own daily press; but finding it necessary to write as though they possessed it, they fall into blunders which are almost as marvellous. Justice and right judgment are out of the question with them. A political party end is always in view, and political party warfare in America admits of any weapons. No newspaper in America is really powerful or popular; and yet they are tyrannical and overbearing. The "New York Herald" has, I believe, the largest sale of any daily newspaper; but it is absolutely without political power, and in these times of war has truckled to the Government more basely than any other paper. It has an enormous sale, but so far is it from having achieved popularity, that no man on any side ever speaks a good word for it. All American newspapers deal in politics as a matter of course; but their politics have ever regard to men and never to measures. Vituperation is their natural political weapon; but since the President's ministers have assumed the power of stopping newspapers which are offensive to them, they have shown that they can descend to a course of eulogy which is even below vituperation.

I shall be accused of using very strong language against the newspaper press of America. I can only say that I do not know how to make that language too strong. Of course there are newspapers as to which the editors and writers may justly feel that my remarks, if applied to them, are unmerited. In writing on such a subject, I can only deal with the whole as a whole. During my stay in the country, I did my best to make myself acquainted with the nature of its newspapers, knowing in how great a degree its population depends on them for its daily store of information. Newspapers in the States of America have a much wider, or rather closer circulation, than they do with us. Every man and almost every woman sees a newspaper daily. They are very cheap, and are brought to every man's hand without trouble to himself, at every turn that he takes in his day's work. It would be much for the advantage of the country, that they should be good of their kind; but, if I am able to form a correct judgment on the matter, they are not good.

CHAPTER XXXI

CONCLUSION

In one of the earlier chapters of this volume,—now some seven or eight chapters past,—I brought myself on my travels back to Boston. It was not that my way homewards lay by that route, seeing that my fate required me to sail from New York; but I could not leave the country without revisiting my friends in Massachusetts. I have told how I was there in the sleighing time, and how pleasant were the mingled slush and frost of the snowy winter. In the morning the streets would be hard and crisp, and the stranger would surely fall if he were not prepared to walk on glaciers. In the afternoon he would be wading through rivers,—and if properly armed at all points with india-rubber, would enjoy the rivers as he waded. But the air would be always kindly, and the east wind there, if it was east as I was told, had none of that power of dominion which makes us all so submissive to its behests in London. For myself, I believe that the real east wind blows only in London.

And when the snow went in Boston I went with it. The evening before I left I watched them as they carted away the dirty uncouth blocks which had been broken up with pickaxes in Washington Street, and was melancholy as I reflected that I too should no longer be known in the streets. My weeks in Boston had not been very many, but nevertheless there were haunts there which I knew as though my feet had trodden them for years. There were houses to which I could have gone with my eyes blindfold; doors of which the latches were familiar to my hands; faces which I knew so well that they had ceased to put on for me the fictitious smiles of courtesy. Faces, houses, doors, and haunts, where are they now? For me they are as though they had never been. They are among the things which one would fain remember as one remembers a dream. Look back on it as a vision and it is all pleasant. But if you realize your vision and believe your dream to be a fact, all your pleasure is obliterated by regret.

I know that I shall never again be at Boston, and that I have said that about the Americans which would make me unwelcome as a guest if I were there. It is in this that my regret consists;—for this reason that I would wish to remember so many social hours as though they had been passed in sleep. They who will expect blessings from me, will say among themselves that I have cursed them. As I read the pages which I have written I feel that words which I intended for blessings when I prepared to utter them have gone nigh to turn themselves into curses.

I have ever admired the United States as a nation. I have loved their liberty, their prowess, their intelligence, and their progress. I have sympathized with a people who themselves have had no sympathy with passive security and inaction. I have felt confidence in them, and have known, as it were, that their industry must enable them to succeed as a people, while their freedom would insure to them success as a nation. With these convictions I went among them wishing to write of them good words,—words which might be pleasant for them to read, while they might assist perhaps in producing a true impression of them here at home. But among my good words there are so many which are bitter, that I fear I shall have failed in my object as regards them. And it seems to me, as I read once more my own pages, that in saying evil things of my friends, I have used language stronger than I intended; whereas I have omitted to express myself with emphasis when I have attempted to say good things. Why need I have told of the mud of Washington, or have exposed the nakedness of Cairo? Why did I speak with such eager enmity of those poor women in the New York cars, who never injured me, now that I think of it? Ladies of New York, as I write this, the words which were written among you, are printed and cannot be expunged; [1] but I tender to you my apologies from my home in England. And as to that Van Wyck committee! Might I not have left those contractors to be dealt with by their own Congress, seeing that that Congress committee was by no means inclined to spare them? I might have kept my pages free from gall, and have sent my sheets to the press unhurt by the conviction that I was hurting those who had dealt kindly by me! But what then? Was any people ever truly served by eulogy; or an honest cause furthered by undue praise?

O my friends with thin skins,—and here I protest that a thick skin is a fault not to be forgiven in a man or a nation, whereas a thin skin is in itself a merit, if only the wearer of it will be the master and not the slave of his skin,—O, my friends with thin skins, ye whom I call my cousins and love as brethren, will ye not forgive me these harsh words

---

[1] In a letter to Frederic Chapman, his publisher, written February 13, 1862, Trollope proposed that he send on the manuscript of the first volume of *North America* ready for the printers while he finished the second volume by installments. His impression was that he had already completed two thirds of the entire work.

that I have spoken? They have been spoken in love,—with a true love, a brotherly love, a love that has never been absent from the heart while the brain was coining them. I had my task to do, and I could not take the pleasant and ignore the painful. It may perhaps be that as a friend I had better not have written either good or bad. But no! To say that would indeed be to speak calumny of your country. A man may write of you truly, and yet write that which you would read with pleasure;—only that your skins are so thin! The streets of Washington are muddy and her ways are desolate. The nakedness of Cairo is very naked. And those ladies of New York: is it not to be confessed that they are somewhat imperious in their demands? As for the Van Wyck committee, have I not repeated the tale which you have told yourselves? And is it not well that such tales should be told?

And yet ye will not forgive me; because your skins are thin, and because the praise of others is the breath of your nostrils.

I do not know that an American as an individual is more thin-skinned than an Englishman; but as the representative of a nation it may almost be said of him that he has no skin at all. Any touch comes at once upon the net-work of his nerves and puts in operation all his organs of feeling with the violence of a blow. And for this peculiarity he has been made the mark of much ridicule. It shows itself in two ways; either by extreme displeasure when anything is said disrespectful of his country; or by the strong eulogy with which he is accustomed to speak of his own institutions and of those of his countrymen whom at the moment he may chance to hold in high esteem. The manner in which this is done is often ridiculous. "Sir, what do you think of our Mr. Jefferson Brick? Mr. Jefferson Brick, sir, is one of our most remarkable men." And again. "Do you like our institutions, sir? Do you find that philanthropy, religion, philosophy, and the social virtues are cultivated on a scale commensurate with the unequalled liberty and political advancement of the nation?" There is something absurd in such a mode of address when it is repeated often. But hero-worship and love of country are not absurd; and do not these addresses show capacity for hero-worship and an aptitude for the love of country? Jefferson Brick may not be a hero; but a capacity for such worship is something. Indeed the capacity is everything, for the need of a hero will at last produce the hero needed. And it is the same with that love of country. A people that are proud of their country will see that there is something in their country to justify their pride. Do we not all of us feel assured by the intense nationality of an American that he will not desert his nation in the hour of her need? I feel that assurance respecting them; and at those moments in which I am moved to laughter by the absurdities of their addresses, I feel it the strongest.

I left Boston with the snow, and returning to New York found that the streets there were dry and that the winter was nearly over. As I had passed through New York to Boston the streets had been by no means dry. The snow had lain in small mountains over which the omnibuses made their way down Broadway, till at the bottom of that thoroughfare, between Trinity Church and Bowling Green, alp became piled upon alp, and all traffic was full of danger. The accursed love of gain still took men to Wall Street, but they had to fight their way thither through physical difficulties which must have made even the state of the money market a matter almost of indifference to them. They do not seem to me to manage the winter in New York so well as they do in Boston. But now, on my last return thither, the alps were gone, the roads were clear, and one could travel through the city with no other impediment than those of treading on women's dresses if one walked, or having to look after women's band-boxes and pay their fares and take their change, if one used the omnibuses.

And now had come the end of my adventures, and as I set my foot once more upon the deck of the Cunard steamer I felt that my work was done. Whether it were done ill or well, or whether indeed any approach to the doing of it had been attained, all had been done that I could accomplish. No further opportunity remained to me of seeing, hearing, or of speaking. I had come out thither, having resolved to learn a little that I might if possible teach that little to others; and now the lesson was learned, or must remain unlearned. But in carrying out my resolution I had gradually risen in my ambition, and had mounted from one stage of inquiry to another, till at last I had found myself burdened with the task of ascertaining whether or no the Americans were doing their work as a nation well or ill; and now if ever, I must be prepared to put forth the result of my inquiry. As I walked up and down the deck of the steamboat I confess I felt that I had been somewhat arrogant.

I had been a few days over six months in the States, and I was engaged in writing a book of such a nature that a man might well engage himself for six years, or perhaps for sixty, in obtaining the materials for it. There was nothing in the form of government, or legislature, or manners of the people, as to which I had not taken upon myself to say something. I was professing to understand their strength and their weakness; and was daring to censure their faults and to eulogize their virtues. "Who is he," an American would say, "that he comes and judges us? His judgment is nothing." "Who is he," an Englishman would say, "that he comes and teaches us? His teaching is of no value."

In answer to this I have but a small plea to make. I have done my best. I have nothing "extenuated, and have set down nought in malice." I do feel that my volumes have blown themselves out into proportions greater than I had intended;—greater not in mass of pages, but in the matter handled. I am frequently addressing my own muse, who I am well aware is not Clio,² and asking her whither she is wending. "Cease, thou wrong-headed one, to meddle with these mysteries." I appeal to her frequently, but ever in vain. One cannot drive one's muse, nor yet always lead her. Of the various women with which a man is blessed, his muse is by no means the least difficult to manage.

But again I put in my slight plea. In doing as I have done, I have at least done my best. I have endeavoured to judge without prejudice, and to hear with honest ears, and to see with honest eyes. The subject, moreover, on which I have written, is one which, though great, is so universal in its bearings, that it may be said to admit of being handled without impropriety by the unlearned as well as the learned;—by those who have grown gray in the study of constitutional lore, and by those who have simply looked on at the government of men as we all look on at those matters which daily surround us. There are matters as to which a man should never take a pen in hand unless he has given to them much labour. The botanist must have learned to trace the herbs and flowers before he can presume to tell us how God has formed them. But the death of Hector is a fit subject for a boy's verses though Homer also sang of it. I feel that there is scope for a book on the United States' form of government as it was founded, and as it has since framed itself, which might do honour to the lifelong studies of some one of those great constitutional pundits whom we have among us; but, nevertheless, the plain words of a man who is no pundit need not disgrace the subject, if they be honestly written, and if he who writes them has in his heart an honest love of liberty. Such were my thoughts as I walked the deck of the Cunard steamer. Then I descended to my cabin, settled my luggage, and prepared for the continuance of my work. It was fourteen days from that time before I reached London, but the fourteen days to me were not unpleasant. The demon of seasickness usually spares me, and if I can find on board one or two who are equally fortunate—who can eat with me, drink with me, and talk with me—I do not know that a passage across the Atlantic is by any means a terrible evil.

² The Muse of history.

In finishing these volumes after the fashion in which they have been written throughout, I feel that I am bound to express a final opinion on two or three points, and that if I have not enabled myself to do so, I have travelled through the country in vain. I am bound by the very nature of my undertaking to say whether, according to such view as I have enabled myself to take of them, the Americans have succeeded as a nation politically and socially; and in doing this I ought to be able to explain how far slavery has interfered with such success. I am bound also, writing at the present moment, to express some opinion as to the result of this war, and to declare whether the North or the South may be expected to be victorious,—explaining in some rough way what may be the results of such victory, and how such results will affect the question of slavery. And I shall leave my task unfinished if I do not say what may be the possible chances of future quarrel between England and the States. That there has been and is much hot blood and angry feeling no man doubts; but such angry feeling has existed among many nations without any probability of war. In this case, with reference to this ill-will that has certainly established itself between us and that other people, is there any need that it should be satisfied by war and allayed by blood?

No one, I think, can doubt that the founders of the great American Commonwealth made an error in omitting to provide some means for the gradual extinction of slavery throughout the States. That error did not consist in any liking for slavery. There was no feeling in favour of slavery on the part of those who made themselves prominent at the political birth of the nation. I think I shall be justified in saying that at that time the opinion that slavery is itself a good thing, that it is an institution of divine origin and fit to be perpetuated among men as in itself excellent, had not found that favour in the southern States in which it is now held. Jefferson, who has been regarded as the leader of the southern or Democratic party, has left ample testimony that he regarded slavery as an evil. It is, I think, true that he gave such testimony much more freely when he was speaking or writing as a private individual than he ever allowed himself to do when his words were armed with the weight of public authority. But it is clear that, on the whole, he was opposed to slavery, and I think there can be little doubt that he and his party looked forward to a natural death for that evil. Calculation was made that slavery when not recruited afresh from Africa could not maintain its numbers, and that gradually the negro population would become extinct. This was the error made. It was easier to look forward to such a result and hope for such an end of the difficulty, than to extinguish slavery by a great political movement, which must doubtless have been difficult and costly. The northern States got rid of slavery by the operation of their separate legislatures, some at one date and some at others. The slaves were less numerous in the North than in the South, and the feeling adverse to slaves, was stronger in the North than in the South. Mason and Dixon's line which now separates slave soil from free soil, merely indicates the position in the country at which the balance turned. Maryland and Virginia were not inclined to make great immediate sacrifices for the manumission of their slaves; but the gentlemen of those States did not think that slavery was a divine institution, destined to flourish for ever as a blessing in their land.

The maintenance of slavery was, I think, a political mistake;—a political mistake, not because slavery is politically wrong, but because the politicians of the day made erroneous calculations as to the probability of its termination. So the income tax may be a political blunder with us;—not because it is in itself a bad tax, but because those who imposed it conceived that they were imposing it for a year or two, whereas, now, men do not expect to see the end of it. The maintenance of slavery was a political mistake; and I cannot think that the Americans in any way lessen the weight of their own error, by protesting, as they occasionally do, that slavery was a legacy made over to them from England. They might as well say, that travelling in carts without springs, at the rate of three miles an hour, was a legacy made over to them by England. On that matter of travelling they have not been contented with the old habits left to them, but have gone ahead and made railroads. In creating those railways the merit is due to them; and so also is the demerit of maintaining those slaves.

That demerit and that mistake have doubtless brought upon the Americans the grievances of their present position; and will, as I think, so far be accompanied by ultimate punishment that they will be the immediate means of causing the first disintegration of their nation. I will leave it to the Americans themselves to say, whether such disintegration must necessarily imply that they have failed in their political undertaking. The most loyal citizens of the northern States would have declared a month or two since,—and for aught I know would declare now,—that any disintegration of the States implied absolute failure. One stripe erased from the banner, one star lost from the firmament, would entail upon them all the disgrace of national defeat! It had been their boast that they would always advance, never retreat. They had looked forward to add ever State upon State, and territory to territory, till the whole continent should be bound together in the same union. To go back from that now, to fall into pieces and be divided, to become smaller in the eyes of the nations,—to be absolutely halfed, as some would say of such division, would be national disgrace, and would amount to political failure. "Let us fight for the whole," such men said, and probably do say. "To lose anything is to lose all!"

But the citizens of the States who speak and think thus, though they may be the most loyal, are perhaps not politically the most wise. And I am inclined to think that that defiant claim of every star, that resolve to possess every stripe upon the banner, had become somewhat less general when I was leaving the country than I had found it to be at the time of my arrival there. While things were going badly with the North,—while there was no tale of any battle to be told except of those at Bull's Run and Springfield, no northern man would admit a hint that secession might ultimately prevail in Georgia or Alabama. But the rebels had been driven out of Missouri when I was leaving the States, they had retreated altogether from Kentucky, having been beaten in one engagement there, and from a great portion of Tennessee, having been twice beaten in that State. The coast of North Carolina, and many points of the southern coast, were in the hands of the northern army, while the army of the South was retreating from all points into the centre of their country. Whatever may have been the strategical merits or demerits of the northern generals, it is at any rate certain that their apparent successes were greedily welcomed by the people, and created an idea that things were going well with the cause. And, as all this took place, it seemed to me that I heard less about the necessary integrity of the old flag. While as yet they were altogether unsuccessful, they were minded to make no surrender. But with their successes came the feeling, that in taking much they might perhaps allow themselves to yield something. This was clearly indicated by the message sent to Congress by the President in February (1862), in which he suggested that Congress should make arrangements for the purchase of the slaves in the border States; so that in the event of secession—accomplished secession—in the gulf States, the course of those border States might be made clear for them.[3] They might hesitate as to going willingly with the North, while possessing slaves,—as to setting themselves peaceably down as a small slave adjunct to a vast free soil nation, seeing that their property would always be in peril. Under such circumstances a slave adjunct to the free soil nation would not long be possible. But if it could be shown to them that in the event of their adhering to the North, com-

---

[3] For the action of Congress upon this proposal, see the note on page 360.

pensation would be forthcoming; then, indeed, the difficulty in arranging an advantageous line between the two future nations might be considerably modified. This message of the President's was intended to signify, that secession on favourable terms might be regarded by the North as not undesirable. Moderate men were beginning to whisper that, after all, the gulf States were no source either of national wealth or of national honour. Had there not been enough at Washington of cotton lords and cotton laws? When I have suggested that no senator from Georgia would ever again sit in the United States senate, American gentlemen have received my remark with a slight demur, and have then proceeded to argue the case. Six months before they would have declaimed against me and not have argued.

I will leave it to Americans themselves to say whether that disintegration of the States, should it ever be realized, will imply that they have failed in their political undertaking. If they do not protest that it argues failure, their feelings will not be hurt by any such protestations on the part of others. I have said that the blunder made by the founders of the nation with regard to slavery has brought with it this secession as its punishment. But such punishments come generally upon nations as great mercies. Ireland's famine was the punishment of her imprudence and idleness, but it has given to her prosperity and progress. And indeed, to speak with more logical correctness, the famine was no punishment to Ireland, nor will secession be a punishment to the northern States. In the long result step will have gone on after step, and effect will have followed cause, till the American people will at last acknowledge, that all these matters have been arranged for their advantage and promotion. It may be that a nation now and then goes to the wall, and that things go from bad to worse with a large people. It has been so with various nations and with many people since history was first written. But when it has been so, the people thus punished have been idle and bad. They have not only done evil in their generation, but have done more evil than good, and have contributed their power to the injury rather than to the improvement of mankind. It may be that this or that national fault may produce or seem to produce some consequent calamity. But the balance of good or evil things which fall to a people's share will indicate with certainty their average conduct as a nation. The one will be the certain consequence of the other. If it be that the Americans of the northern States have done well in their time, that they have assisted in the progress of the world, and made things better for mankind rather than worse, then they will come out of this trouble without eventual injury. That which came in the guise of punishment for a special fault, will be a part of the reward resulting from good conduct in the general. And as to this matter of slavery, in which I think that they have blundered both politically and morally,—has it not been found impossible hitherto for them to cleanse their hands of that taint? But that which they could not do for themselves the course of events is doing for them. If secession establish herself, though it be only secession of the gulf States, the people of the United States will soon be free from slavery.

In judging of the success or want of success of any political institutions or of any form of government, we should be guided, I think, by the general results, and not by any abstract rules as to the right or wrong of those institutions or of that form. It might be easy for a German lawyer to show that our system of trial by jury is open to the gravest objections, and that it sins against common sense. But if that system gives us substantial justice, and protects us from the tyranny of men in office, the German lawyer will not succeed in making us believe that it is a bad system. When looking into the matter of the schools at Boston, I observed to one of the committee of management that the statements with which I was supplied, though they told me how many of the children went to school, did not tell me how long they remained at school. The gentleman replied that that information was to be obtained from the result of the schooling of the population generally. Every boy and girl around us could read and write, and could enjoy reading and writing. There was therefore evidence to show that they remained at school sufficiently long for the required purposes. It was fair that I should judge of the system from the results. Here in England, we generally object to much that the Americans have adopted into their form of government, and think that many of their political theories are wrong. We do not like universal suffrage. We do not like a periodical change in the first magistrate; and we like quite as little a periodical permanence in the political officers immediately under the chief magistrate. We are, in short, wedded to our own forms and therefore opposed by judgment to forms differing from our own. But I think we all acknowledge that the United States, burdened as they are with these political evils,—as we think them, have grown in strength and material prosperity with a celerity of growth hitherto unknown among nations. We may dislike Americans personally, we may find ourselves uncomfortable when there, and unable to sympathize with them when away; we may believe them to be ambitious, unjust, self-idolatrous, or irreligious. But, unless we throw our judgment altogether overboard, we cannot believe them to be a weak people, a poor people, a people with low spirits or a people with idle hands. To what is it that the government of a country should chiefly look? What special advantages do we expect from our own government? Is it not that we should be safe at home and respected abroad;—that laws should be maintained, but that they should be so maintained that they should not be oppressive? There are, doubtless, countries in which the government professes to do much more than this for its people,—countries in which the government is paternal; in which it regulates the religion of the people, and professes to enforce on all the national children respect for the governors, teachers, spiritual pastors, and masters. But that is not our idea of a government. That is not what we desire to see established among ourselves or established among others. Safety from foreign foes, respect from foreign foes and friends, security under the law and security from the law,—this is what we expect from our government; and if I add to this that we expect to have these good things provided at a fairly moderate cost, I think I have exhausted the list of our requirements.

And if the Americans with their form of government have done for themselves all that we expect our government to do for us; if they have with some fair approach to general excellence obtained respect abroad, and security at home from foreign foes; if they have made life, liberty, and property safe under their laws, and have also so written and executed their laws as to secure their people from legal oppression,—I maintain that they are entitled to a verdict in their favour, let us object as we may to universal suffrage, to four years' Presidents, and four years' presidential cabinets. What, after all, matters the theory or the system, whether it be King or President, universal suffrage or ten-pound voter, so long as the people be free and prosperous? King and President, suffrage by poll and suffrage by property, are but the means. If the end be there, if the thing has been done, King and President, open suffrage and closed suffrage may alike be declared to have been successful. The Americans have been in existence as a nation for seventy-five years, and have achieved an amount of foreign respect during that period greater than any other nation ever obtained in double the time. And this has been given to them, not in deference to the statesman-like craft of their diplomatic and other officers, but on grounds the very opposite of those. It has been given to them because they form a numerous, wealthy, brave, and self-asserting nation. It is, I think, unnecessary to prove that such foreign respect has been given to them: but were it necessary, nothing would prove it more strongly than the regard which has been universally paid by European governments to the blockade placed during this war on the southern ports, by the government of the United States. Had the United States been placed by general consent in any class of nations below the first, England, France, and perhaps Russia, would have taken the matter into their own hands, and have settled for the States, either united or disunited, at any rate that question of the blockade. And the Americans have been safe at home from foreign foes; so safe, that no other strong people but ourselves have enjoyed anything approaching to their security since their foundation. Nor has our security been equal to theirs if we are to count our nationality as extending beyond the British Isles. Then as to security under their laws and from their laws! Those laws and the system of their management have been taken almost entirely from us, and have so been administered that life and property have been safe, and the subject also has been free from oppression. I think that this may be taken for granted, seeing that they who have been most opposed to American forms of government, have never asserted the reverse. I may be told of a man being lynched in one State, or tarred and feathered in another, or of a duel in a third being "fought at sight." So I may be told also of men garotted in London, and of tithe proctors buried in a bog without their ears in Ireland. Neither will seventy years of continuance nor will seven hundred secure such an observance of laws as will prevent temporary ebullition of popular feeling, or save a people from the chance disgrace of occasional outrage. Taking the general, life and limb and property have been as safe in the States as in other civilized countries with which we are acquainted.

As to their personal liberty under their laws, I know it will be said that they have surrendered all claim to any such precious possession by the facility with which they have now surrendered the privilege of the writ of habeas corpus. It has been taken from them, as I have endeavoured to show,[4] illegally, and they have submitted to the loss and to the illegality without a murmur! But in such a matter I do not think it fair to judge them by their conduct in such a moment as the present. That this is the very moment in which to judge of the efficiency of their institutions generally, of the aptitude of those institutions for the security of the nation, I readily acknowledge. But when a ship is at sea in a storm, riding out all that the winds and waves can do to her, one does not condemn her because a yard-arm gives way, nor even though the mainmast should go by the board. If she can make her

---

[4] Trollope devotes several pages to the suspension of the writ of habeas corpus in a chapter entitled "The Constitution of the United States," omitted in the present edition. See Appendix A.

port, saving life and cargo, she is a good ship, let her losses in spars and rigging be what they may. In this affair of the habeas corpus we will wait a while before we come to any final judgment. If it be that the people, when the war is over, shall consent to live under a military or other dictatorship,—that they shall quietly continue their course as a nation without recovery of their rights of freedom, then we shall have to say that their institutions were not founded in a soil of sufficient depth, and that they gave way before the first high wind that blew on them. I myself do not expect such a result.

I think we must admit that the Americans have received from their government, or rather from their system of policy, that aid and further-ance which they required from it; and, moreover, such aid and further-ance as we expect from our system of government. We must admit that they have been great, and free, and prosperous, as we also have become. And we must admit, also, that in some matters they have gone forward in advance of us. They have educated their people, as we have not edu-cated ours. They have given to their millions a personal respect, and a standing above the abjectness of poverty, which with us are much less general than with them. These things, I grant, have not come of their government, and have not been produced by their written constitution. They are the happy results of their happy circumstances. But so, also, those evil attributes which we sometimes assign to them are not the creatures of their government, or of their constitution. We acknowl-edge them to be well educated, intelligent, philanthropic, and indus-trious; but we say that they are ambitious, unjust, self-idolatrous, and irreligious. If so, let us at any rate balance the virtues against the vices. As to their ambition, it is a vice that leans so to virtue's side, that it hardly needs an apology. As to their injustice, or rather dishonesty, I have said what I have to say on that matter. I am not going to flinch from the accusation I have brought, though I am aware that in bring-ing it I have thrown away any hope that I might have had, of carrying with me the good will of the Americans for my book. The love of money,—or rather of making money,—carried to an extreme, has less-ened that instinctive respect for the rights of meum and tuum which all men feel more or less, and which, when encouraged within the hu-man breast, finds its result in perfect honesty. Other nations, of which I will not now stop to name even one, have had their periods of natural dishonesty. It may be that others are even now to be placed in the same category. But it is a fault which industry and intelligence com-bined will after a while serve to lessen and to banish. The industrious man desires to keep the fruit of his own industry, and the intelligent man will ultimately be able to do so. That the Americans are self-idolaters is perhaps true,—with a difference. An American desires you to worship his country, or his brother; but he does not often, by any of the usual signs of conceit, call upon you to worship himself. As an American, treating of America, he is self-idolatrous; but that is a self-idolatry which I can endure. Then, as to his want of religion—and it is a very sad want—I can only say of him, that I, as an Englishman, do not feel myself justified in flinging the first stone at him. In that matter of religion, as in the matter of education, the American, I think, stands on a level higher than ours. There is not in the States so absolute an ignorance of religion as is to be found in some of our manufacturing and mining districts, and also, alas! in some of our agricultural districts; but also, I think, there is less of respect and veneration for God's word among their educated classes, than there is with us; and, perhaps, also less knowledge as to God's word. The general religious level is, I think, higher with them; but there is with us, if I am right in my supposition, a higher eminence in religion, as there is also a deeper depth of ungodliness.

I think then that we are bound to acknowledge that the Americans have succeeded as a nation, politically and socially. When I speak of social success, I do not mean to say that their manners are correct according to this or that standard. I will not say that they are correct, or are not correct. In that matter of manners I have found that those, with whom it seemed to me natural that I should associate, were very pleasant according to my standard. I do not know that I am a good critic on such a subject, or that I have ever thought much of it with the view of criticising. I have been happy and comfortable with them, and for me that has been sufficient. In speaking of social success I allude to their success in private life as distinguished from that which they have achieved in public life;—to their successes in commerce, in mechanics, in the comforts and luxuries of life, in medicine and all that leads to the solace of affliction, in literature, and I may add also, considering the youth of the nation, in the arts. We are, I think, bound to acknowledge that they have succeeded. And if they have succeeded, it is vain for us to say that a system is wrong which has, at any rate, admitted of such success. That which was wanted from some form of government, has been obtained with much more than average excellence; and therefore the form adopted has approved itself as good. You may explain to a farmer's wife with indisputable logic, that her churn is a bad churn; but as long as she turns out butter in greater quantity, in better quality, and with more profit than her neighbours, you will hardly induce her to change it. It may be that with some other churn she might have done even better; but, under such circumstances, she will have a right to think well of the churn she uses.

The American constitution is now, I think, at the crisis of its severest trial. I conceive it to be by no means perfect, even for the wants of the people who use it; and I have already endeavoured to explain what changes it seems to need. And it has had this defect,—that it has permitted a falling away from its intended modes of action, while its letter has been kept sacred. As I have endeavoured to show, universal suffrage and democratic action in the Senate were not intended by the framers of the constitution. In this respect, the constitution has, as it were, fallen through, and it is needed that its very beams should be re-strengthened. There are also other matters as to which it seems that some change is indispensable. So much I have admitted. But, not the less, judging of it by the entirety of the work that it has done, I think that we are bound to own that it has been successful.

And now, with regard to this tedious war, of which from day to day we are still, in this month of May, 1862, hearing details which teach us to think that it can hardly as yet be near its end;—to what may we rationally look as its result? Of one thing I myself feel tolerably certain, —that its result will not be nothing, as some among us have seemed to suppose may be probable. I cannot believe that all this energy on the part of the North will be of no avail, more than I suppose that southern perseverance will be of no avail. There are those among us who say that as secession will at last be accomplished, the North should have yielded to the South at once, and that nothing will be gained by their great expenditure of life and treasure. I can by no means bring myself to agree with these. I also look to the establishment of secession. Seeing how essential and thorough are the points of variance between the North and the South, how unlike the one people is to the other, and how necessary it is that their policies should be different; seeing how deep are their antipathies, and how fixed is each side in the belief of its own rectitude and in the belief also of the other's political baseness, I cannot believe that the really southern States will ever again be joined in amicable union with those of the North. They, the States of the Gulf, may be utterly subjugated, and the North may hold over them military power. Georgia and her sisters may for a while belong to the Union, as one conquered country belongs to another. But I do not think that they will ever act with the Union;—and, as I imagine, the Union before long will agree to a separation. I do not mean to prophesy that the result will be thus accomplished. It may be that the

South will effect their own independence before they lay down their arms. I think, however, that we may look forward to such independence, whether it be achieved in that way, or in this, or in some other.

But not on that account will the war have been of no avail to the North. I think it must be already evident to all those who have looked into the matter that had the North yielded to the first call made by the South for secession all the slave States must have gone. Maryland would have gone, carrying Delaware in its arms; and if Maryland, all south of Maryland. If Maryland had gone, the capital would have gone. If the Government had resolved to yield, Virginia to the east would assuredly have gone, and I think there can be no doubt that Missouri, to the west, would have gone also. The feeling for the Union in Kentucky was very strong, but I do not think that even Kentucky could have saved itself. To have yielded to the southern demands would have been to have yielded everything. But no man now believes, let the contest go as it will, that Maryland and Delaware will go with the South. The secessionists of Baltimore do not think so, nor the gentlemen and ladies of Washington, whose whole hearts are in the southern cause. No man thinks that Maryland will go; and few, I believe, imagine that either Missouri or Kentucky will be divided from the North. I will not pretend what may be the exact line, but I myself feel confident that it will run south both of Virginia and of Kentucky.

If the North do conquer the South, and so arrange their matters that the southern States shall again become members of the Union, it will be admitted that they have done all that they sought to do. If they do not do this;—if instead of doing this, which would be all that they desire, they were in truth to do nothing;—to win finally not one foot of ground from the South,—a supposition which I regard as impossible;—I think that we should still admit after a while that they had done their duty in endeavouring to maintain the integrity of the empire. But if, as a third and more probable alternative, they succeed in rescuing from the South and from slavery four or five of the finest States of the old Union,—a vast portion of the continent, to be beaten by none other in salubrity, fertility, beauty, and political importance, —will it not then be admitted that the war has done some good, and that the life and treasure have not been spent in vain?

That is the termination of the contest to which I look forward. I think that there will be secession, but that the terms of secession will be dictated by the North, not by the South; and among these terms I expect to see an escape from slavery for those border States to which I have alluded. In that proposition which, in February last (1862), was made by the President, and which has since been sanctioned by the Senate, I think we may see the first step towards this measure. It may probably be the case that many of the slaves will be driven south; that as the owners of those slaves are driven from their holdings in Virginia they will take their slaves with them, or send them before them. The manumission, when it reaches Virginia, will not probably enfranchise the half million of slaves who, in 1860, were counted among its population. But as to that I confess myself to be comparatively careless. It is not the concern which I have now at heart. For myself, I shall feel satisfied if that manumission shall reach the million of whites by whom Virginia is populated; or if not that million in its entirety then that other million by which its rich soil would soon be tenanted. There are now about four millions of white men and women inhabiting the slave States which I have described, and I think it will be acknowledged that the northern States will have done something with their armies if they succeed in rescuing those four millions from the stain and evil of slavery.

There is a third question which I have asked myself, and to which I have undertaken to give some answer. When this war be over between the northern and southern States will there come upon us Englishmen a necessity of fighting with the Americans? If there do come such necessity, arising out of our conduct to the States during the period of their civil war, it will indeed be hard upon us, as a nation, seeing the struggle that we have made to be just in our dealings towards the States generally, whether they be North or South. To be just in such a period, and under such circumstances, is very difficult. In that contest between Sardinia and Austria it was all but impossible to be just to the Italians without being unjust to the Emperor of Austria. To have been strictly just at the moment one should have begun by confessing the injustice of so much that had gone before! But in this American contest such justice, though difficult, was easier. Affairs of trade rather than of treaties chiefly interfered; and these affairs, by a total disregard of our own pecuniary interests, could be so managed that justice might be done. This I think was effected. It may be, of course, that I am prejudiced on the side of my own nation; but striving to judge of the matter as best I may without prejudice, I cannot see that we, as a nation, have in aught offended against the strictest justice in our dealings with America during this contest. But justice has not sufficed. I do not know that our bitterest foes in the northern States have accused us of acting unjustly. It is not justice which they have looked for at our hands, and looked for in vain;—not justice, but gen-

erosity! We have not, as they say, sympathized with them in their
trouble! It seems to me that such a complaint is unworthy of them as
a nation, as a people, or as individuals. In such a matter generosity is
another name for injustice,—as it too often is in all matters. A generous
sympathy with the North would have been an ostensible and crushing
enmity to the South. We could not have sympathized with the North
without condemning the South, and telling to the world that the South
were our enemies. In ordering his own household a man should not
want generosity or sympathy from the outside; and if not a man, then
certainly not a nation. Generosity between nations must in its very
nature be wrong. One nation may be just to another, courteous to another, even considerate to another with propriety. But no nation can
be generous to another without injustice either to some third nation,
or to itself.

But though no accusation of unfairness has, as far as I am aware,
ever been made by the government of Washington against the government of London, there can be no doubt that a very strong feeling
of antipathy to England has sprung up in America during this war,
and that it is even yet so intense in its bitterness, that were the North
to become speedily victorious in their present contest very many Americans would be anxious to turn their arms at once against Canada. And
I fear that that fight between the Monitor and the Merrimac has
strengthened this wish by giving to the Americans an unwarranted confidence in their capability of defending themselves against any injury
from British shipping. It may be said by them, and probably would be
said by many of them, that this feeling of enmity had not been engendered by any idea of national injustice on our side;—that it might
reasonably exist, though no suspicion of such injustice had arisen in the
minds of any. They would argue that the hatred on their part had been
engendered by scorn on ours,—by scorn and ill words heaped upon
them in their distress.

They would say that slander, scorn, and uncharitable judgments
create deeper feuds than do robbery and violence, and produce deeper
enmity and worse rancour. "It is because we have been scorned by
England, that we hate England. We have been told from week to week,
and from day to day, that we were fools, cowards, knaves, and madmen.
We have been treated with disrespect, and that disrespect we will
avenge." It is thus that they speak of England, and there can be no
doubt that the opinion so expressed is very general. It is not my purpose here to say whether in this respect England has given cause of
offence to the States, or whether either country has given cause of of-

fence to the other. On both sides have many hard words been spoken, and on both sides also have good words been spoken. It is unfortunately the case that hard words are pregnant, and as such they are read, digested, and remembered; while good words are generally so dull that nobody reads them willingly, and when read they are forgotten. For many years there have been hard words bandied backwards and forwards between England and the United States, showing mutual jealousies and a disposition on the part of each nation to spare no fault committed by the other. This has grown of rivalry between the two, and in fact proves the respect which each has for the other's power and wealth. I will not now pretend to say with which side has been the chiefest blame, if there has been chiefest blame on either side. But I do say that it is monstrous in any people or in any person to suppose that such bickerings can afford a proper ground for war. I am not about to dilate on the horrors of war. Horrid as war may be, and full of evil, it is not so horrid to a nation, nor so full of evil, as national insult unavenged, or as national injury unredressed. A blow taken by a nation and taken without atonement is an acknowledgment of national inferiority than which any war is preferable. Neither England nor the States are inclined to take such blows. But such a blow, before it can be regarded as a national insult, as a wrong done by one nation on another, must be inflicted by the political entity of the one on the political entity of the other. No angry clamours of the press, no declamations of orators, no voices from the people, no studied criticisms from the learned few or unstudied censures from society at large, can have any fair weight on such a question or do aught towards justifying a national quarrel. They cannot form a casus belli.[5] Those two Latin words, which we all understand, explain this with the utmost accuracy. Were it not so, the peace of the world would indeed rest upon sand. Causes of national difference will arise,—for governments will be unjust as are individuals. And causes of difference will arise because governments are too blind to distinguish the just from the unjust. But in such cases the government acts on some ground which it declares. It either shows or pretends to show some casus belli. But in this matter of threatened war between the States and England it is declared openly that such war is to take place because the English have abused the Americans, and because, consequently, the Americans hate the English. There seems to exist an impression that no other ostensible ground for fighting need be shown, although such an event as that of war between the two nations would,

---

[5] "casus belli": an event or group of events that leads to war or may be used as a justification for going to war.

as all men acknowledge, be terrible in its results. "Your newspapers insulted us when we were in our difficulties. Your writers said evil things of us. Your legislators spoke of us with scorn. You exacted from us a disagreeable duty of retribution just when the performance of such a duty was most odious to us. You have shown symptoms of joy at our sorrow. And, therefore, as soon as our hands are at liberty, we will fight you." I have known schoolboys to argue in that way, and the arguments have been intelligible. But I cannot understand that any government should admit such an argument.

Nor will the American government willingly admit it. According to existing theories of government the armies of nations are but the tools of the governing powers. If at the close of the present civil war the American government,—the old civil government consisting of the President with such checks as Congress constitutionally has over him, —shall really hold the power to which it pretends, I do not fear that there will be any war. No President, and I think no Congress, will desire such a war. Nor will the people clamour for it, even should the idea of such a war be popular. The people of America are not clamorous against their government. If there be such a war it will be because the army shall have then become more powerful than the Government. If the President can hold his own the people will support him in his desire for peace. But if the President do not hold his own,—if some General with two or three hundred thousand men at his back shall then have the upper hand in the nation,—it is too probable that the people may back him. The old game will be played again that has so often been played in the history of nations, and some wretched military aspirant will go forth to flood Canada with blood, in order that the feathers of his cap may flaunt in men's eyes and that he may be talked of for some years to come as one of the great curses let loose by the Almighty on mankind.

I must confess that there is danger of this. To us the danger is very great. It cannot be good for us to send ships laden outside with iron shields instead of inside with soft goods and hardware to those thickly thronged American ports. It cannot be good for us to have to throw millions into those harbours instead of taking millions out from them. It cannot be good for us to export thousands upon thousands of soldiers to Canada of whom only hundreds would return. The whole turmoil, cost, and paraphernalia of such a course would be injurious to us in the extreme, and the loss of our commerce would be nearly ruinous. But the injury of such a war to us would be as nothing to the injury which it would inflict upon the States. To them for many years it would be absolutely ruinous. It would entail not only all those losses which such a war must bring with it; but that greater loss which would arise to the nation from the fact of its having been powerless to prevent it. Such a war would prove that it had lost the freedom from which it had struggled, and which for so many years it has enjoyed. For the sake of that people as well as for our own,—and for their sakes rather than for our own,—let us, as far as may be, abstain from words which are needlessly injurious. They have done much that is great and noble, even since this war has begun, and we have been slow to acknowledge it. They have made sacrifices for the sake of their country which we have ridiculed. They have struggled to maintain a good cause, and we have disbelieved in their earnestness. They have been anxious to abide by their constitution, which to them has been as it were a second gospel, and we have spoken of that constitution as though it had been a thing of mere words in which life had never existed. This has been done while their hands were very full and their back heavily laden. Such words coming from us, or from parties among us, cannot justify those threats of war which we hear spoken; but that they should make the hearts of men sore and their thoughts bitter against us can hardly be matter of surprise.

As to the result of any such war between us and them, it would depend mainly, I think, on the feelings of the Canadians. Neither could they annex Canada without the good-will of the Canadians, nor could we keep Canada without that good-will. At present the feeling in Canada against the northern States is so strong and so universal that England has little to fear on that head.

I have now done my task, and may take leave of my readers on either side of the water with a hearty hope that the existing war between the North and South may soon be over, and that none other may follow on its heels to exercise that new-fledged military skill which the existing quarrel will have produced on the other side of the Atlantic. I have written my book in obscure language if I have not shown that to me social successes and commercial prosperity are much dearer than any greatness that can be won by arms. The Americans had fondly thought that they were to be exempt from the curse of war,—at any rate from the bitterness of the curse. But the days for such exemption have not come as yet. While we are hurrying on to make twelve-inch shield-plates for our men-of-war, we can hardly dare to think of the days when the sword shall be turned into the ploughshare. May it not be thought well for us if, with such work on our hands, any scraps of iron shall be left to us with which to pursue the purposes of peace? But at least let us not have war with these children of our own. If we must fight, let us fight the French, "for King George upon the throne." The doing so will be disagreeable, but it will not be antipathetic to the nature of an Englishman. For my part, when an American tells me that he wants to fight with me, I regard his offence as compared with that of a Frenchman under the same circumstances, as I would compare the offence of a parricide or a fratricide with that of a mere common-place murderer. Such a war would be plus quam civile bellum.[6] Which of us two could take a thrashing from the other and afterwards go about our business with contentment?

On our return to Liverpool, we stayed for a few hours at Queenstown, taking in coal, and the passengers landed that they might stretch their legs and look about them. I also went ashore at the dear old place which I had known well in other days, when the people were not too grand to call it Cove, and were contented to run down from Cork in river steamers, before the Passage railway was built. I spent a pleasant summer there once in those times;—God be with the good old days! And now I went ashore at Queenstown, happy to feel that I should be again in a British isle, and happy also to know that I was once more in Ireland. And when the people came around me as they did, I seemed to know every face and to be familiar with every voice. It has been my fate to have so close an intimacy with Ireland, that when I meet an Irishman abroad, I always recognize in him more of a kinsman than I do in an Englishman. I never ask an Englishman from what county he comes, or what was his town. To Irishmen I usually put such questions, and I am generally familiar with the old haunts which they name. I was happy therefore to feel myself again in Ireland, and to walk round from Queenstown to the river at Passage by the old way that had once been familiar to my feet.

Or rather I should have been happy if I had not found myself instantly disgraced by the importunities of my friends! A legion of women surrounded me, imploring alms, begging my honour to bestow my charity on them for the love of the Virgin, using the most holy names in their adjurations for halfpence, clinging to me with that half joking, half lachrymose air of importunity which an Irish beggar has assumed as peculiarly her own. There were men too, who begged as well as women. And the women were sturdy and fat, and, not knowing me as well as I knew them, seemed resolved that their importunities should be successful. After all, I had an old world liking for them in their rags. They were endeared to me by certain memories and associations which

6 "a worse [war] even than a civil war."

I cannot define. But then what would those Americans think of them; —of them and of the country which produced them? That was the reflection which troubled me. A legion of women in rags clamorous for bread, protesting to heaven that they are starving, importunate with voices and with hands, surrounding the stranger when he puts his foot on the soil so that he cannot escape, does not afford to the cynical American who then first visits us,—and they all are cynical when they visit us,—a bad opportunity for his sarcasm. He can at any rate boast that he sees nothing of that at home. I myself am fond of Irish beggars. It is an acquired taste,—which comes upon one as does that for smoked whisky, or Limerick tobacco. But I certainly did wish that there were not so many of them at Queenstown.

I tell all this here not to the disgrace of Ireland;—not for the triumph of America. The Irishman or American who thinks rightly on the subject will know that the state of each country has arisen from its opportunities. Beggary does not prevail in new countries, and but few old countries have managed to exist without it. As to Ireland we may rejoice to say that there is less of it now than there was twenty years since. Things are mending there. But though such excuses may be truly made,—although an Englishman when he sees this squalor and poverty on the quays at Queenstown, consoles himself with reflecting that the evil has been unavoidable, but will perhaps soon be avoided,—nevertheless he cannot but remember that there is no such squalor and no such poverty in the land from which he has returned. I claim no credit for the new country. I impute no blame to the old country. But there is the fact. The Irishman when he expatriates himself to one of those American States loses much of that affectionate, confiding, masterworshipping nature which makes him so good a fellow when at home. But he becomes more of a man. He assumes a dignity which he never has known before. He learns to regard his labour as his own property. That which he earns he takes without thanks, but he desires to take no more than he earns. To me personally he has perhaps become less pleasant than he was. But to himself—! It seems to me that such a man must feel himself half a god, if he has the power of comparing what he is with what he was.

It is right that all this should be acknowledged by us. When we speak of America and of her institutions we should remember that she has given to our increasing population rights and privileges which we could not give;—which as an old country we probably can never give. That self-asserting, obtrusive independence which so often wounds us, is, if viewed aright, but an outward sign of those good things which a new country has produced for its people. Men and women do not beg in the States;—they do not offend you with tattered rags; they do not complain to heaven of starvation; they do not crouch to the ground for halfpence. If poor, they are not abject in their poverty. They read and write. They walk like human beings made in God's form. They know that they are men and women, owing it to themselves and to the world that they should earn their bread by their labour, but feeling that when earned it is their own. If this be so,—if it be acknowledged that it is so, —should not such knowledge in itself be sufficient testimony of the success of the country and of her institutions?

APPENDIX A

Textual Note

This edition of *North America* reproduces the text of the first English edition without change except for alterations that fall under one of the following three categories:

1. Correction of a few errors clearly due to oversight on the part of Trollope or his printer (for example, *brought* for *bought, commnad* for *command, beween* for *between*). As a general policy, on the other hand, Trollope's inconsistencies in the use of italics, capitals, and punctuation have been allowed to stand. They appear in his manuscript as well as in the printed text and seem part of his manner of expression. His idiosyncrasies in spelling (*Caffre, Dacotah, Bull's Run, dead lock, going a head, storeage, Texians*) have been permitted to remain for the same reason.

2. A few slight alterations to make the text conform to the manuscript of *North America* where the reading in the first English edition seems awkward or confusing though not positively incorrect (for example, *music!* for *music?, hold* for *held,* insertion of an omitted indefinite article in a series). The text of the first English edition is, on the whole, a remarkably good one, and few alterations have been required.

3. The omission of five chapters and three appendixes. The chapters omitted are: Volume I, Chapter xv, pages 326–37, "The Constitution of the State of New York"; Volume II, Chapter ix, pages 247–301, "The Constitution of the United States"; Chapter x, pages 302–23, "The Government"; Chapter xi, pages 324–39, "The Law Courts and Lawyers of the United States"; Chapter xii, pages 340–66, "The Financial Position." The three appendixes omitted reproduce the Declaration of Independence, the Articles of Confederation, and the Constitution of the United States. The publishers feel, and the editors are inclined to agree, that this material would add little to the value of the edition but would add formidably and unnecessarily to the cost of publication. The omitted chapters represent Trollope's attempt to explain the workings of state and Federal government in the United States to an English audience presumed to know little or nothing of the subject.

These are surely the chapters Allan Nevins had in mind when he remarked that Trollope thrust into *North America* "much material that
can be found, in more accurate form, in any good manual of civics." [1]

The second and third English editions of *North America* follow the
first verbatim except for correction of a few typographical errors, the
commission of a few new ones, and the slight alteration of a few
phrases. Later editions consulted offer no really significant variations
from the first nor any evidence that Trollope gave much thought to
the text of *North America* after 1862.

THE MANUSCRIPT OF *North America*

The manuscript of *North America*, now in the Trollope collection
of Garrett L. Reilly, of Rosemont, Pennsylvania, is bound in two heavy
red-morocco volumes containing 492 and 574 pages. The sheets, measur-
ing approximately $8\frac{1}{2}$ by 10 inches, are written in Anthony Trollope's
rather difficult script. The cancelings reveal no dramatic *volte-face,* no
suppressed indiscretions; they are, in the main, words or brief phrases
that Trollope rejected for the words or phrases written above them.
At infrequent intervals canceled passages of up to fifty words occur
where Trollope denied himself needless particulars or generalizations.
For some of these he substituted a succinct phrase or sentence above the
canceled lines. There are few places in the manuscript where a person
would conceivably be moved to question Trollope's wisdom in preferring his second thoughts to his first.

On two occasions in the second volume Trollope seems to have
made deletions of considerable length. For some distance following
page 178 in Chapter vi of the second volume, the chapter devoted to
Cairo and Camp Wood, Trollope renumbered to allow for the omission of twenty-three pages. One would like to know what he left out
at this point, but the chances are that he was merely eliminating a
digression from the subject matter he had allotted for this chapter and
that the material appears later on in a more appropriate place. On
page 476, Chapter xiii of the second volume, the chapter devoted to the
American Post Office, Trollope canceled the beginning of a digression
on universal suffrage, a subject he had discussed at length in an earlier
chapter. He apparently omitted five pages; page 482, the next included
in the manuscript, resumes the main topic of the chapter. All in all, the
manuscript of *North America,* like other Trollope manuscripts, bears
witness to Trollope's clarity of purpose and his workmanlike habits.

---

[1] *American Social History as Recorded by British Travellers,* compiled and
edited by Allan Nevins (New York, 1923).

[531]

APPENDIX B

Trollope's Itinerary of His 1861–2 American Tour

The following itinerary is taken from the pages of Trollope's account book. These jottings were set down very hastily and at times illegibly for the author's own reference. The editors have normalized a few inconsistencies of style and have regretfully omitted one or two proper names that defy deciphering. Such omissions, however, are properly indicated. For permission to publish the itinerary the editors wish to thank Miss Muriel Rose Trollope, in whose possession the account book rests.

AUGUST 1861		
Friday 23	To Liverpool	
Saturday 24		
Sunday 25		
Monday 26		
Tuesday 27		To Boston
Wednesday 28		
Thursday 29		
Friday 30		
Saturday 31		

SEPTEMBER 1861		
Sunday 1	En route
Monday 2	
Tuesday 3	Reached Halifax
Wednesday 4	En route
Thursday 5	Reached Boston— 7 am. Quincy. Mr Lee's lawn.
Friday 6	Cambridge. Dined at Dr Lothrop's. Sumner. Palfrey. Homans &c
Saturday 7	Dined at Quincey

with Adams and
. . .

Sunday 8	Unitarian church. Rose went to Mr Otis
Monday 9	Went to Newport
Tuesday 10	Drove to Lawton Valley
Wednesday 11	Rain all day
Thursday 12	Rose on horseback
Friday 13	Saw Miss Knawer [?]. Went to the Kalins [?]
Saturday 14	Returned to Boston
Sunday 15	Boston
Monday 16	Boston
Tuesday 17	To Portland
Wednesday 18	To Gorham after House
Thursday 19	Mount Washington & Gorham

Friday 20 To Crawford House & Mount Willard

Saturday 21 To Gorham & Island Pond

Sunday 22 At Island Pond

Monday 23 To Quebec

Tuesday 24 To Mountmorency [*sic*] Falls

Wednesday 25 Dined with the Governor

Thursday 26 To Sherbrook[e]

Friday 27 To Magog. Memphramagog & Mountain House

Saturday 28 Up the mountain, & Georgeville

Sunday 29 By Massawippi to Sherbrook[e]

Monday 30 To Montreal

OCTOBER 1861

Tuesday 1 Round the mountain at Montreal

Wednesday 2 Over tubular bridge & back

Thursday 3 To Ottawa

Friday 4 At Ottawa. Rideau & Chaudiere Fall

Saturday 5 To Prescott & Toronto

Sunday 6 At Toronto

Monday 7 At Toronto

Tuesday 8 To Niagara Falls

Wednesday 9 At Niaraga

Thursday 10 To Buffalo, & Detroit. Elevators

Friday 11 At Detroit. (Big black) trees

Saturday 12 To Grand Haven. Kept there by wind (sand)

Sunday 13 To Milwaukie [*sic*]. Tents of recruits

Monday 14 To La Crosse. Regiment from Minnesota. 1000 men

Tuesday 15 To St Paul

Wednesday 16 To St Anthony & back

Thursday 17 At St Paul

Friday 18 Down river

Saturday 19 To Dubuque. Broken wheel

Sunday 20 At Dubuque

Monday 21 To leadmine with Mr Langworthy. To Dixon

Tuesday 22 To Prairie. To Chicago

Wednesday 23 At Chicago

Thursday 24 To Cleveland

Friday 25 To Buffalo

Saturday 26 To Utica

Sunday 27 To Trenton Falls & back

Monday 28 To West Port

Tuesday 29 At West Port. College

Wednesday 30 To New York

Thursday 31 At New York

NOVEMBER 1861

Friday 1 At New York. Schools. 23 street

Saturday 2 At New York

Sunday 3 New York. Park

Monday	4	New York
Tuesday	5	New York
Wednesday	6	New York. Manhattan asylum, Deaf & Dumb. Historic Society
Thursday	7	New York
Friday	8	New York. Staten Island
Saturday	9	New York. Mr Bancroft
Sunday	10	New York
Monday	11	To Hartford
Tuesday	12	To Boston
Wednesday	13	Boston
Thursday	14	Boston
Friday	15	Boston
Saturday	16	Boston
Sunday	17	Boston
Monday	18	Boston
Tuesday	19	Boston
Wednesday	20	Boston
Thursday	21	Boston
Friday	22	Boston. Everett at Roxbury
Saturday	23	Boston. Pinebank
Sunday	24	Boston
Monday	25	Boston
Tuesday	26	Boston. Dinner at Tremont
Wednesday	27	Boston. Wendell Phillips
Thursday	28	Concord. Emerson & Hawthorne
Friday	29	Cambridge. Longfellow
Saturday	30	Boston. Dinner

DECEMBER 1861

Sunday	1	Boston
Monday	2	Lowell & back

Tuesday	3	To New York. (oh that morning) E. L. H.
Wednesday	4	New York
Thursday	5	New York
Friday	6	To Philadelphia
Saturday	7	Philadelphia. Mr Reed
Sunday	8	Philadelphia
Monday	9	Philadelphia. Mr Biddle
Tuesday	10	To Baltimore
Wednesday	11	Baltimore. Camps
Thursday	12	Baltimore. Mr Kennedy
Friday	13	Baltimore
Saturday	14	To Washington
Sunday	15	Washington
Monday	16	Washington
Tuesday	17	Washington
Wednesday	18	Washington
Thursday	19	Washington. At the army
Friday	20	Washington. Review
Saturday	21	Washington. Miss Auchmintz's [?]
Sunday	22	Washington. Down the river
Monday	23	Washington
Tuesday	24	Washington. Russell's
Wednesday	25	Washington. Breakfast. . . . Dinner Pyne's [?]
Thursday	26	Washington
Friday	27	Washington. Mr Seward
Saturday	28	Washington. Mr Hooper
Sunday	29	Washington. M^r

Taylor. Mr Eames
[?]

Monday 30 Washington.
Pyne's [?]

Tuesday 31 Washington. Russell's

1862

Wednesday
Jany 1 Washington. At
the camp. Ash-
mound [?]

Thursday 2 Washington. At
the camp

Friday 3 Washington. At
the camp. Gun-
nery

Saturday 4 Washington. Lord
Lyons

Sunday 5 Washington.
Anderson

Monday 6 Washington. Senate & House of
Representatives

Tuesday 7 Washington.
Navy yard

Wednesday 8 Washington. Lord
Lyons

Thursday 9 Washington. Dinner party. Sum-
ner's speech

Friday 10 Washington

Saturday 11 Washington

Sunday 12 Washington.
Judge Loring's

Monday 13 Washington. Taylor's

Tuesday 14 Mr Taylor's. To
Baltimore

Wednesday 15 To Harrisburgh

Thursday 16 To Altoona

Friday 17 To Pittsburgh

Saturday 18 By this post letters will be sent to
N. Y.

Sunday 19 To Cincinnati

Monday 20 At Cincinnati

Tuesday 21 To Lexington

Wednesday 22 To Frankford
[*sic*] & Woodford
Stud Farm

Thursday 23 To Louisville. To
be . . . at S^t
Louis

Friday 24 At Louisville

Saturday 25 To St Louis

Sunday 26 At St Louis

Monday 27 At St Louis

Tuesday 28 At St Louis

Wednesday 29 To Rolla

Thursday 30 At Rolla

Friday 31 To St Louis

1862

Saturday
Feb. 1 At St Louis

Sunday 2 At St Louis

Monday 3 To Cairo

Tuesday 4 At Cairo

Wednesday 5 At Cairo

Thursday 6 To Louisville

Friday 7 At Louisville

Saturday 8 At Louisville

Sunday 9 To Camp Wood—
Green River &
Mumfordsville

Monday 10 Back to Louisville

Tuesday 11 To Cincinnati

Wednesday 12 At Cincinnati

Thursday 13 To Pittsburgh

Friday 14 and Baltimore

Saturday	15	Baltimore. M*r* Kennedy
Sunday	16	Baltimore. Bernals [?]
Monday	17	Baltimore. Glenn's
Tuesday	18	Baltimore
Wednesday	19	To Washington
Thursday	20	Washington
Friday	21	Washington. Taylor's
Saturday	22	To Baltimore. Bernals [?]
Sunday	23	Baltimore & To Philadelphia
Monday	24	Philadelphia
Tuesday	25	At Philadelphia. Reed
Wednesday	26	At Philadelphia. Field
Thursday	27	To New York
Friday	28	At New York
Saturday *March*	1	At New York. To Boston
Sunday	2	At Boston. Lothrop's

Monday	3	Boston. Private theatricals
Tuesday	4	Boston. Longfellow. Felton's funeral
Wednesday	5	Boston. Homans. Agazziz's [*sic*] lecture
Thursday	6	Boston. Fields. M*rs* Mears
Friday	7	Boston. Peabody's M*rs* Homans
Saturday	8	Boston. Runaway sleigh. Sturgis. M*rs* Ames
Sunday	9	Fields. To New York. (Ah, me, West S*t*)
Monday	10	New York. M*rs* Knawer [?]
Tuesday	11	New York. Bancroft's
Wednesday	12	Went to sea
Thursday	13	At sea
to Monday	24	
Tuesday	25	Liverpool
Wednesday	26	Home

APPENDIX C

TROLLOPE'S FIRST VISIT TO AMERICA [1]

From Bermuda I took a sailing vessel to New York, in company with a rather large assortment of potatoes and onions. I had declared during my unlucky voyage from Kingston to Cuba that no consideration should again tempt me to try a sailing vessel, but such declarations always go for nothing. A man in his misery thinks much of his misery; but as soon as he is out of it it is forgotten, or becomes matter for mirth. Of even a voyage in a sailing vessel one may say that at some future time it will perhaps be pleasant to remember that also. And so I embarked myself along with the potatoes and onions on board the good ship "Henrietta."

Indeed, there is no other way of getting from Bermuda to New York; or of going anywhere from Bermuda—except to Halifax and St. Thomas, to which places a steamer runs once a month. In going to Cuba I had been becalmed, starved, shipwrecked, and very nearly quaranteened. In going to New York I encountered only the last misery. The doctor who boarded us stated that a vessel had come from Bermuda with a sick man, and that we must remain where we were till he had learnt what was the sick man's ailment. Our skipper, who knew the vessel in question, said that one of their crew had been drunk in Bermuda for two or three days, and had not yet worked it off. But the doctor called again in the course of the day, and informed us that it was intermittent fever. So we were allowed to pass. It does seem strange that sailing vessels should be subjected to such annoyances. I hardly think that one of the mail steamers going to New York would be delayed because there was a case of intermittent fever on board another vessel from Liverpool.

It is not my purpose to give an Englishman's ideas of the United States, or even of New York, at the fag end of a volume treating about the West Indies. On the United States I should like to write a volume, seeing that the government and social life of the people there—of that

[1] Chapter xxiii of Trollope's *The West Indies and the Spanish Main* (London, 1859). Trollope had sailed from Southampton in the fall of 1858 on a mission for the postal service. He touched at New York in the spring of 1859 on his return voyage.

people who are our children—afford the most interesting phenomena which we find as to the new world;—the best means of prophesying, if I may say so, what the world will next be, and what men will next do. There, at any rate, a new republic has become politically great and commercially active; whereas all other new republics have failed in those points, as in all others. But this cannot be attempted now.

From New York I went by the Hudson river to Albany, and on by the New York Central Railway to Niagara; and though I do not mean to make any endeavor to describe that latter place as such descriptions should be—and doubtless are and have been—written, I will say one or two words which may be of use to any one going thither.

The route which I took from New York would be, I should think, the most probable route for Englishmen. And as travelers will naturally go up the Hudson river by day, and then on from Albany by night train,* seeing that there is nothing to be seen at Albany, and that these trains have excellent sleeping accommodation—a lady, or indeed a gentleman, should always take a double sleeping-berth, a single one costs half a dollar, and a double one a dollar. This outlay has nothing to do with the traveling ticket;—it will follow that he, she, or they will reach Niagara at about 4 a.m.

In that case let them not go on to what is called the Niagara Falls Station, but pass over at a station called the Suspension Bridge—very well known on the road—to the other or Canada side of the water, and thence go to the Clifton Hotel. There can be no doubt as to this being the site at which tourists should stop. It is one of those cases in which to see is to be sure. But if the traveler be carried on to Niagara Falls station, he has a long and expensive journey to make back; and the United States side of the water will be antagonistic to him in doing so. The ticket from Albany to Niagara cost me six dollars; the carriage from Niagara to the Clifton Hotel cost me five. It was better to pay the five than to remain where I was; but it would have been better still to have saved them. I mention this as passengers to the Falls have no sort of intimation that they should get out at the Suspension Bridge; though they are all duly shaken out of their berths, and inquired of whether or not they be going west.

Nothing ever disappointed me less than the Falls of Niagara—but my raptures did not truly commence for the first half-day. Their charms grow upon one like the conversation of a brilliant man. Their depth and breadth and altitude, their music, color, and brilliancy, are not

---

* It would be well, however, to visit Trenton Falls by the way, which I did not do. They are but a short distance from Utica, a town on this line of railway.

fully acknowledged at the first moment. It may be that my eye is slow; but I can never take in to its full enjoyment any view or any picture at the first glance. I found this to be especially the case at Niagara. It was only by long gazing and long listening that I was able to appreciate the magnitude of that waste of waters.

My book is now complete, and I am not going to "do the Falls," but I must bid such of my readers as may go there to place themselves between the rocks and the waters of the Horseshoe Fall after sunset—well after sunset; and there remain—say for half an hour. And let every man do this alone; or if fortune have kindly given him such a companion, with one who may leave him as good as alone. But such companions are rare.

The spot to which I allude will easily make itself known to him, nor will he have any need of a guide. He will find it, of course, before the sun shall set. And, indeed, as to guides, let him eschew them, giving a twenty-five cent piece here and there, so that these men be not ruined for want of custom. Into this spot I made my way, and stood there for an hour, dry enough. The spray did reach my coat, and the drops settled on my hair; but nevertheless, as a man not over delicate, I was dry enough. Then I went up, and when there was enticed to put myself into a filthy oil-skin dress, hat, coat, and trousers, in order that I might be conducted under the Falls. Under the Falls! Well; I had been under the Falls; but still, wishing to see everything, I allowed myself to be caparisoned.

A sable conductor took me exactly to the spot where I had been before. But he took me also ten yards further, during which little extra journey I became soaking wet through, in spite of the dirty oil-cloth. The ducking cost me sixty cents, or half a crown.

But I must be allowed one word as to that visit after sunset; one word as to that which an obedient tourist will then see. In the spot to which I allude the visitor stands on a broad safe path, made of shingles, between the rock over which the water rushes and the rushing water. He will go in so far that the spray rising back from the bed of the torrent does not incommode him. With this exception, the further he can go the better; but here also circumstances will clearly show him the spot. Unless the water be driven in by a very strong wind, five yards make the difference between a comparatively dry coat and an absolutely wet one.

And then let him stand with his back to the entrance, thus hiding the last glimmer of the expiring day. So standing he will look up among the falling waters, or down into the deep misty pit, from which they reascend in almost as palpable a bulk. The rock will be at his left hand, high and hard, and dark and straight, like the wall of some huge cavern, such as children enter in their dreams. For the first five minutes he will be looking but at the waters of a cataract,—at the waters, indeed, of such a cataract as we know no other, and at their interior curves, which elsewhere we cannot see. But by-and-by all this will change. He will no longer be on a shingly path beneath a waterfall; but that feeling of a cavern wall will grow upon him, of a cavern deep, deep below roaring seas, in which the waves are there, though they do not enter in upon him; or rather not the waves, but the very bowels of the deep ocean. He will feel as though the floods surrounded him, coming and going with their wild sounds, and he will hardly recognize that though among them he is not in them. And they, as they fall with a continual roar, not hurting the ear, but musical withal, will seem to move as the vast ocean waters may perhaps move in their internal currents. He will lose the sense of one continued descent, and think that they are passing round him in their appointed courses. The broken spray that rises from the depth below, rises so strongly, so palpably, so rapidly, that the motion in every direction will seem equal. And then, as he looks on, strange colors will show themselves through the mist; the shades of gray will become green and blue, with ever and anon a flash of white; and then, when some gust of wind blows in with greater violence, the sea-girt cavern will become all dark and black. Oh, my friend, let there be no one there to speak to thee then; no, not even a heart's brother. As you stand there speak only to the waters.

So much for Niagara. From thence, I went along Lake Ontario, and by the St. Lawrence to Montreal, being desirous of seeing the new tubular railway bridge which is being erected there over the St. Lawrence close to that town. Lake Ontario is uninteresting, being altogether too large for scenery, and too foggy for sight-seeing if there were anything to see. The travelling accommodation however is excellent. The points of interest in the St. Lawrence are the thousand islands, among which the steamer glides as soon as it enters the river; and the rapids, of which the most singularly rapid is the one the vessel descends as it nears Montreal. Both of these are very well, but they do not require to be raved about. The Canadian towns at which one touches are interesting as being clean and large, and apparently prosperous;—also as being English, for we hardly reach the French part of Canada till we get down to Montreal.

This tubular bridge over the St. Lawrence, which will complete the whole trunk line of railway from Portland on the coast of Maine, through the two Canadas, to the States of Michigan and Wisconsin, will certainly be one of the most wonderful works of scientific art in the world. It is to consist of different tubes, resting on piers placed in the river bed at intervals sufficient to provide for the free navigation of the water. Some of these, including the centre and largest one, are already erected. This bridge will be over a mile and a half in length, and will cost the enormous sum of one million four hundred thousand pounds, being but two hundred thousand pounds short of the whole cost of the Panamá railway. I only wish that the shareholders may have as good a dividend.

From Montreal I went down Lake Champlain to Saratoga Springs, the great resort of New Yorkers when the weather in the city becomes too hot for endurance. I was there late in June, but was very glad at that time to sit with my toes over a fire. The country about Saratoga is by no means pretty. The waters I do not doubt are very healthy, and the hotels very good. It must, I should think, be a very dull place for persons who are not invalids.

From Saratoga I returned to New York, and from New York sailed for Liverpool in the exceedingly good ship "Africa," Captain Shannon. I have sailed in many vessels, but never in one that was more comfortable or better found.

And on board this most comfortable of vessels I have now finished my book, as I began it on board that one, of all the most uncomfortable, which carried me from Kingston in Jamaica to Cien Fuegos in the island of Cuba.

APPENDIX D

TROLLOPE'S VISIT TO CALIFORNIA [1]

New York

My way home from the Sandwich Islands to London took me to San Francisco, across the American continent and [to] New York, whence I am now writing to you my last letter of this series. I had made this journey before, but had on that occasion reached California too late to visit the now world-famous valley of the Yo Semite, and the big pine trees which we call Wellingtonias. On this occasion I made the excursion, and will presently tell the story of the trip; but I must first say a few words as to the town of San Francisco.

I do not know that in all my travels I ever visited a city less interesting to the normal tourist, who, as a rule, does not care to investigate the ways of trade, or to employ himself in ascertaining how the people around him earn their bread. There is almost nothing to see in San Francisco that is worth seeing. There is a new park in which you may drive for six or seven miles on a well-made road, and which, as a park for the use of the city, will, when completed, have many excellences. There is also there the biggest hotel in the world—so the people of San Francisco say—which has cost a million sterling—five millions of dollars—and is intended to swallow up all the other hotels. It was just finished, but not opened, when I was there. There is an inferior menagerie of wild beasts, and a place called the Cliff House, to which strangers are taken to hear seals bark. Everything, except hotel prices, is dearer here than at any other large town I know, and the ordinary traveller has no peace left him, either in public or private, by touters who wish to persuade him to take this or the other railway route into the Eastern States. There is always a perfectly cloudless sky overhead, unless when rain is falling in torrents, and perhaps nowhere in the world is there a more sudden change from heat to cold on the same day. I think I may say that strangers will generally desire to get out of San Francisco as quickly as they can, unless, indeed, circumstances may

---

1 Letter XX of *The Tireless Traveler: Twenty Letters to the Liverpool Mercury by Anthony Trollope, 1875,* edited, with an Introduction, by Bradford Allen Booth (University of California Press, 1941). Trollope landed at San Francisco on September 26, 1875, on his return to England from his second visit to Australia.

have enabled them to enjoy the hospitality of the place. There is little or nothing to see, and life at the hotels is not comfortable. But the trade of the place, and the way in which money is won and lost, are alike marvellous. I found 10s. a-day to be about the lowest rate of wages paid to a man for any kind of work in the city; and the average wages of a housemaid—who is, of course, found in everything but her clothes—to be over £70 per annum. All payments in California are made in coin, whereas in the other States of the Union except California, Oregon, and Nevada, moneys are paid in depreciated notes, so that the two dollars and a-half per day which the labourer earns in San Francisco are as good as three and a quarter in New York. No doubt this high rate of pay is met by an equivalent in the high cost of many articles, such as clothing and rent; but it does not affect the price of food, which to the labouring man is the one important item of expenditure. Consequently, the labouring man in California has a position which I have not known him to achieve elsewhere.

In trade there is a speculative rashness which ought to ensure ruin, according to our old-world ideas, but seems to be rewarded by very general success. The stranger may of course remember, if he pleases, that the millionaire who builds a mighty palace is seen and heard of and encountered at all corners, while the bankrupt will probably sink unseen into obscurity. But in San Francisco there is not much of bankruptcy, and, when it does occur, no one seems to be so little injured as the bankrupt. There is a good nature, a forbearance, and an easy giving of trust, which to an old-fashioned Englishman like myself seems to be most dangerous, but which I was assured there forms the readiest mode of building up a great commercial community. The great commercial community is there, and I am not prepared to deny that it has been built after that fashion. If a young man there can make friends, and can establish a character for honesty to his friends and for smartness to the outside world, he can borrow almost any amount of money without security, for the purpose of establishing himself in business. The lender, if he feel sure that he will not be robbed by his protégé, is willing to run the risk of unsuccessful speculation.

As we steamed into the Golden Horn [2] the news reached us that about a month previously the leading bank in San Francisco, the Bank of California, had "burst up" for some enormous amount of dollars, and that the manager, who was well known as one of the richest men and as perhaps the boldest speculator in the state, had been drowned

2 A slip of the traveler's pen for Golden Gate.

the day following.[3] But we also heard that payments would be resumed in a few days—and payments were resumed before I left the city; that no one but the shareholders would lose a dollar, and that the shareholders were ready to go on with any amount of new capital; and that not a single bankruptcy in the whole community had been caused by the stoppage of the bank, which had been extended for a period over a month! How came it to pass, I asked, of course, that the collapse of so great a monetary enterprise as the Bank of California should pass on without a general panic, at any rate in the city? Then I was assured that all those concerned were good-natured, that everybody gave time, that bills were renewed all round, and that in an hour or two it was understood that no one in San Francisco was to be asked for money just at that crisis. To me all this seemed to be wrong. I have always imagined that severity to bankrupt debtors—that amount of severity which requires that a bankrupt shall really be a bankrupt—is the best and indeed the only way of ensuring regularity in commerce, and of preventing men from tossing up with other people's money in the confidence that they may win and cannot lose. But such doctrines are altogether out of date in California. The money of depositors was scattered broadcast through the mining speculations of the district, and no one was a bit the worse for it except the unfortunate gentleman who had been, perhaps happily, removed from a community which had trusted him long with implicit confidence, and which still believed him to be an honest man, but which would hardly have known how to treat him had he survived. To add to the romance of the story it should be said that, though this gentleman was drowned while bathing, it seems to be certain that his death was accidental. It is stated that he was struck with apoplexy while in the water.

I was taken to visit the Stockbrokers' Board in San Francisco—that is, the room in which mining shares are bought and sold. The reader should understand that in California, and, still more, in the neighbouring State of Nevada, gold mining and silver mining are now very lively. The stock-jobbing created by these mines is carried on in San Francisco, and is a business as universally popular as was the buying and selling of railway shares during our railway mania. Everybody is at it. The housemaid of whom I have spoken as earning £70 per annum buys Consolidated Virginia or Ophir stock with that money; or perhaps she prefers Chollar Potosi, or Best and Belcher, or Yellow Jacket,

<hr>

[3] The failure of the Bank of California, to which Trollope refers, occurred August 25. See John P. Young: *San Francisco* (San Francisco, 1912), II, 504–8.

or Buckeye. She probably consults some gentleman of her acquaintance, and no doubt in 19 cases out of 20 loses her money. But it is the thing to do, and she enjoys that charm which is the delectation of all gamblers. Of course, in such a condition of things there are men who know how the wind is going to blow, who make the wind blow this way or that, who can raise the price of shares by fictitious purchases and then sell, or depreciate them by fictitious sales and then buy. The housemaids and others go to the wall, while the knowing men build palaces, and seem to be troubled by no seared consciences. In the meantime the brokers drive a roaring trade—whether they purchase legitimately for others, or speculate on their own account. The Stock Exchange in London is, I believe, closed to strangers. The Bourse in Paris is open to the world, and at a certain hour affords a scene to those who choose to go and look at it of wild noise, unintelligible action, and sometimes apparently of demoniac fury. The uninitiated are unable to comprehend that the roaring herd in the pen beneath them are doing business. The Stock Exchange Board in San Francisco is not open to strangers as it is in Paris, but may be visited with an order, and by the kindness of a friend I was admitted. Paris is more than six times as large as San Francisco; but the fury at San Francisco is even more demoniac than in Paris. I thought that the gentlemen employed were going to hit each other between the eyes, and that the apparent quarrels which I saw already demanded the interference of the police. But the uproarious throng were always obedient, after slight delays, to the ringing hammer of the chairman, and as each five minutes' period of internecine combat was brought to an end I found that a vast number of mining shares had been bought and sold. Perhaps a visit to this chamber when the stockbrokers are at work, between the hours of eleven and twelve, is, of all sights in San Francisco, the one best worth seeing.

A visit to the Yo Semite Valley from San Francisco requires a long and very tedious journey. The tourist first travels by railway from the city to Merced, about 140 miles, the first 100 of which are on the line which runs across the continent. At Merced he sleeps, finding there a very comfortable American hotel, at which, however, they will refuse to clean his boots. On the following morning he will start at six by a four-horse stage-coach, which, travelling at the rate of five miles an hour, will bring him to the end of his first day's journey at six in the evening. Here he will be accommodated at a ranche or farm-house, which has gradually grown to be an inn, and will be treated with smiling, good-natured courtesy. The next day's coaching will take him into the valley, and on his way he will have passed through a grove of the immense pine trees which first gave celebrity to these regions.

The latter portion of this journey is made through a picturesque country, with fine hills and handsome timber, but it is not comparable in beauty to very many roads of a similar nature in Europe. The first part of the road—from Merced, through Snelling, and as far as Coulterville—is altogether interesting. I travelled over it in September, when the dust was almost unbearable. The beds of the river were almost dry; the greenswards had become yellow, and the mid-day heat was extreme. I can easily believe that in May and June it bears a very different aspect. But in May and June the visitors who unfortunately belong to the unprivileged sex can seldom be accommodated with beds. The dormitories in the hotels are devoted to ladies, while the gentlemen repose either under or upon the dinner tables. The crowd is apt to be so great that, when the meals are spread, enormous energy is required, or at least is often used, by those who are anxious to secure their meals. We had no grass and no water in the streams, but we had every attention shown to us at Mr. Black's hotel, at which we were the only guests.

Sightseeing in the valley has to be done on horse-back, and the horses provided for our use were very good. You would not give me space were I to attempt to convert your columns into a guide book for the Yo Semite. I may perhaps best use the few words which are at my command by saying that the chief glory of the place depends on the almost perpendicular steepness and on the enormous altitude of the rocks which hem it in. The Clouds Nest [4] rises to a height of 6450 feet above the valley, and the rock called Le Capitaine,[5] which to the naked eye seems to hang over if it be not perpendicular, is 3000 feet high. The highest summits of the valley are about 12,000 feet above the sea. The highest mountains of Europe are of course higher than any that there are here; but I know of no rocks in Europe or elsewhere which are to be compared to them. Early in the morning, just as the sun is rising, and again for perhaps an hour before it has set, the colours are beautiful and the effects magnificent. But during the close of the day everything is painfully white. It is not the whiteness of snow or of marble, but rather that of plaster of Paris. The substance which produces this effect is in fact granite. The shapes of the summits are graceful and

4 I.e., Clouds' Rest.
5 I.e., El Capitan.

bold, but the mountains do not run into sharp peaks and serrated edges. Two of the most conspicuous are called the North and South Domes. The grandeur of the scene—and it is very grand—arises chiefly from the manner in which the precipitous sides of the mountains have been cut sheer down into the valley. In the spring and early summer the waterfalls must be very beautiful. They were beautiful when I was there, though from the scantiness of the mountain streams they were shorn of their great glory.

The return from the valley was exactly the same as the journey to it—hot, tedious, long, and dusty. Both going and coming I measured some of the big trees, finding the girth of the largest which I saw to be 78 feet. From the irregularity of the ground and the knobby excrescences which add to the size of the trees, accurate measurement is impossible, but I feel sure that I have rather understated than overstated the amount. The height of the highest trees yet discovered in California is by no means equal to that of some that have been found in Australia. I do not think that any tree exceeding 400 feet in height has been found in America, but a tree has been measured in Victoria which, when standing, exceeded 500 feet.

The traveller about to proceed from San Francisco to the East may accomplish a part of the journey to Yo Semite on his way. On returning he will stop at Latrop [6] and pick up the railway cars for New York, or whatever place may be his destination, thus saving the run of 100 miles back to San Francisco. As to myself, business required me to return to the city, and I thus had the opportunity of making the unbroken journey from the Pacific to the Atlantic.

So many accounts have already been given of this journey that I need hardly detain your readers by describing it at length. It occupies seven days and seven nights, the start from San Francisco being made at eight a.m. During this time the traveller is continually travelling, except for the three spaces of twenty minutes each per diem which are allowed for eating. The undertaking seems to be, if not dangerous on account of fatigue, at any rate liable to great tedium and very much discomfort. I can only say that I never made a journey with less fatigue, less tedium, or less discomfort. I was peculiarly happy in my fellow-travellers; but as I have crossed twice and was thus lucky on both occasions, meeting people in the carriages whom I had never seen before and from whom I parted as old friends, I may presume that such is the usual condition of things. The traveller should, I think, trouble himself with the carriage of no eatables, as those supplied on the road

[6] I.e., Lathrop.

are in every way sufficient. If he wishes the solace of wine or spirits he should take them with him. He will find himself provided with an excellent bed and with ample accommodation for washing his hands and face. The need of a bath at the end of the journey is certainly much felt.

APPENDIX E
Bibliography

1. NEWSPAPERS [1]

Boston Daily Evening Transcript, 1861–2.
Chicago Daily Tribune, 1861–2.
Chicago Evening Journal, 1861.
Cincinnati Daily Commercial, 1861–2.
Liberator (Boston), 1861.
National Intelligencer (Washington), 1861–2.
New York Daily Times, 1861–2.
New York Herald, 1861–2.
New York Tribune, 1861–2.
Saint Louis Democrat, 1861–2.
Sun (Baltimore), 1861–2.

2. BOOKS AND PERIODICALS

ADAMS, CHARLES FRANCIS: *Richard Henry Dana: A Biography* (Boston, 1929).

"American Sleeping Cars," *All the Year Round,* IV (1860–1), 328–32.

ANDERSON, GALUSHA: *A Border City during the Civil War* (Boston, 1908).

[APPLETON'S] *The American Annual Cyclopædia,* issues for 1861 and 1862 (New York, 1862, 1863).

BANCROFT, FREDERIC: *The Life of William A. Seward* (New York, 1900).

BERGER, MAX: *The British Traveller in America, 1836–60* (New York, 1943).

Bohn's Hand-Book of Washington (Washington, D. C., 1856).

BOOTH, BRADFORD A.: "Trollope and the *Pall Mall Gazette,*" *Nineteenth-Century Fiction,* IV (1949), 51–61, 137–58.

BROOKS, JOHN GRAHAM: *As Others See Us, a Study of Progress in the United States* (New York, 1910).

---

[1] Years significant for this edition, not complete runs, are indicated. Also of great value in following the weekly course of events during the early 1860's are the pictorial journals *Frank Leslie's Illustrated Newspaper, Harper's Weekly,* and *The Illustrated London News.*

BROOKS, NOAH: *Washington in Lincoln's Time* (New York, 1895).

BRYCE, JAMES, "Anthony Trollope," *Studies in Contemporary Biography* (New York, 1903), 116–30.

Cairo Guide, compiled and written by [the] Federal Writers' Project (Cairo, Illinois, 1938).

Chicago: a Stranger's and Tourist's Guide (Chicago, 1866).

"Clark Mill's Equestrian Statue of Washington," *Frank Leslie's Illustrated Magazine,* IX (1859–60), 218.

COLE, ARTHUR CHARLES: *The Irrepressible Conflict* (*A History of American Life,* Vol. VII) (New York, 1934).

COWLEY, CHARLES: *Illustrated History of Lowell* (Boston, 1868).

COWPER, WILLIAM: *The Poetical Works of William Cowper* (London, 1910).

CROSS, ARTHUR LYON: *A History of England and Greater Britain* (New York, 1923).

CRUSE, AMY: *The Victorians and Their Books* (London, 1935).

CURTIS, GEORGE WILLIAM: *The Potiphar Papers* (New York, 1856).

DAWSON, S. E.: *Hand-Book for the Dominion of Canada* (Montreal, 1884).

"Descent of a Timber-Slide by His Royal Highness," *Illustrated London News,* XXXVII (1860), 376.

DICEY, EDWARD: *Six Months in the Federal States* (London, 1863).

DICKENS, CHARLES: *Martin Chuzzlewit* (New York: National Library Edition, n.d.).

Dictionary of American Biography, Dumas Malone, editor (New York, 1928–36).

Dictionary of American History, James Truslow Adams and R. V. Coleman, editors (New York, 1940).

Dictionary of National Biography, Sidney Lee, editor (London, 1894).

DUNBAR, SEYMOUR: *A History of Travel in America* (New York, 1937).

EMERSON, RALPH WALDO: "The Fortune of the Republic," *The Complete Works of Ralph Waldo Emerson* (Boston, 1904), Vol. XI.

ESCOTT, T. H. S.: *Anthony Trollope: His Public Services, Private Friends, and Literary Originals* (London, 1913).

EVERETT, EDWARD: *The Great Issues before Our Country: an Oration . . . Delivered at the New York Academy of Music, July 4, 1861* (New York, 1861).

FAIRMAN, CHARLES EDWIN: *Art and Artists of the Capitol of the United States of America* (Washington, 1927), 69th Congress, 1st Session, Senate Document No. 95.

FAITHFULL, EMILY: *Three Visits to America* (New York, 1884).

FAITHFULL, EMILY, editor: *A Welcome: Original Contributions in Poetry and Prose* (London, 1863).

FERGUSON, WILLIAM: *America by River and Rail* (London, 1856).

FROTHINGHAM, P. R.: *Edward Everett, Orator and Statesman* (New York, 1925).

GEROULD, WINIFRED GREGORY, and JAMES THAYER GEROULD: *A Guide to Trollope* (Princeton University Press, 1948).

GILMAN, ARTHUR: "The Gold-Fields of Nova Scotia," *Atlantic Monthly,* XIII (1864), 576–86.

Guide to the City of Chicago, A (Chicago, 1868).

HARRINGTON, BERNARD J.: *The Life of Sir William Edmond* (Montreal, 1883).

HOLLEY, GEORGE W.: *The Falls of Niagara* (New York, 1883).

HOWELLS, WILLIAM DEAN, and others: *The Niagara Book* (New York, 1901).

IRWIN, MARY LESLIE: *Anthony Trollope: A Bibliography* (New York, 1926).

JOHNSON, RICHARD W.: *Reminiscences in Peace and War* (Philadelphia, 1886).

JORDAN, DONALDSON, and EDWIN J. PRATT: *Europe and the American Civil War* (Boston, 1931).

JOSEPHSON, HANNAH: *The Golden Threads: New England's Mill Girls and Magnates* (New York, 1949).

KENNGOTT, GEORGE F.: *The Record of a City: a Social Survey of Lowell, Massachusetts* (New York, 1912).

LANSDEN, JOHN M.: *A History of the City of Cairo, Illinois* (Chicago, 1910).

"Lindell Hotel Fire, The," *Harper's Weekly,* XI (1867), 264.

LOWELL, JAMES RUSSELL: *The Biglow Papers, The Writings of James Russell Lowell* (Boston, 1899), Vol. IX.

MACKAY, CHARLES: *Life and Liberty in America* (New York, 1859).

MAGUIRE, JOHN FRANCIS: *Father Mathew: a Biography* (London, 1863).

McINNIS, EDGAR: *Canada: a Political and Social History* (New York, 1947).

McMASTER, JOHN BACH: *A History of the People of the United States during Lincoln's Administration* (New York, 1927).

MENEELY, A. HOWARD: *The War Department, 1861: a Study in Mobilization and Administration* (New York, 1928).

MESICK, JANE LOUISE: *The English Traveller in America, 1785–1835* (New York, 1922).

MOORE, THOMAS: *The Poetical Works of Thomas Moore,* John Francis Walker, editor (New York, 1880).

MOTLEY, JOHN LOTHROP: *The Causes of the Civil War, a Letter to the London Times* (New York, 1861).

NEVINS, ALLAN: *The Emergence of Lincoln* (New York, 1950).

——: *Frémont, Pathmaker of the West* (New York, 1939).

——: *Ordeal of the Union* (New York, 1947).

"Palace Homes for the Traveller," *Godey's Lady's Book,* LX (1860), 465–6.

PHILLIPS, WENDELL: *Speeches, Lectures, and Letters* (Boston, 1894).

Population of the United States in 1860; Compiled from the . . . Eighth Census (Washington, 1864).

PRATT, EDWIN J.: see JORDAN, DONALDSON.

RANDALL, J. G.: *The Civil War and Reconstruction* (Boston, 1937).

RHODES, JAMES FORD: *History of the Civil War 1861–65* (New York, 1917).

ROBINSON, HARRIET H.: *Early Factory Labor in New England* (Boston, 1889).

ROWSOME, FRANCIS: "The Strange Story of the 'Great Eastern,'" *Harper's Monthly Magazine,* CLXXVIII (1939), 507–14.

RUSSELL, WILLIAM HOWARD: *My Diary North and South* (Boston, 1863).

SADLEIR, MICHAEL: *Trollope: A Bibliography* (London, 1928).

——: *Trollope: A Commentary* (New York, 1947).

SCUDDER, HORACE ELISHA: *James Russell Lowell: A Biography* (Boston, 1901).

STEBBINS, LUCY POATE, and RICHARD POATE STEBBINS: *The Trollopes: the Chronicle of a Writing Family* (Columbia University Press, 1945).

STRYKER, PHILIP DAVID: "Anthony Trollope in the United States" (unpublished doctoral dissertation, Northwestern University, 1947).

——: "The Significance of Trollope's *The American Senator,*" *Nineteenth-Century Fiction,* V (1950), 141–9.

TAYLOR, ROBERT H.: "The Manuscript of Trollope's *American Senator,*" *Papers of the Bibliographical Society of America,* XLI (1947), 123–9.

THACKERAY, WILLIAM MAKEPEACE: *The Newcomes* (London, 1899).

TOCQUEVILLE, ALEXIS DE: *Democracy in America,* Phillips Bradley, editor (New York, 1945).

"Trollope in Boston," *More Books: the Bulletin of the Boston Public Library,* Sixth Series, XXI (1946), 30–1.

TROLLOPE, ANTHONY: "American Literary Piracy [letter to James Russell Lowell]," *Athenæum*, No. 1819 (September 6, 1862), pp. 306–7.

——: "American Literary Piracy [letter to the editor]," *Athenæum*, No. 1826 (October 25, 1862), pp. 529–30.

——: "American Reconstruction," *Saint Paul's Magazine*, II (1868), 662–75.

——: *The American Senator* (London, 1877).

——: *Australia and New Zealand* (London, 1873).

——: *An Autobiography*, with an Introduction by Bradford Allen Booth (University of California Press, 1947).

——: "*The Civil War in America* . . . by Goldwin Smith" [a review], *Fortnightly Review*, V (1866), 251–4.

——: "The Courtship of Susan Bell," *Harper's New Monthly Magazine*, XXI (1860), 366–78.

——: *The Duke's Children* (London, 1880).

——: "The Genius of Nathaniel Hawthorne," *North American Review*, CXXIX (1879), 203–22.

——: *He Knew He Was Right* (London, 1869).

——: "Henry Wadsworth Longfellow," *North American Review*, CXXXII (1881), 383–406.

——: *The Landleaguers* (London, 1883).

——: "Miss Ophelia Gledd," in *A Welcome*, Emily Faithfull, editor (London, 1863). Reprinted in *Lotta Schmidt and Other Stories* (London, 1867).

——: *North America:* for editions of this work, see Part 3 of the Bibliography.

Principal Reviews of *North America*
(listed in order of appearance)

Athenæum, No. 1804 (May 24, 1862), 685–6.

Saturday Review, XIII (May 31, 1862), 625–6.

Spectator, XXXV (June 7, 1862), 635–6.

Times (London), June 11, 1862, p. 6.

Chambers' Journal, XVII (June 28, 1862), 408–9.

London Review and Weekly Journal, IV (June 28, 1862), 597–8.

Presbyterian Quarterly Review, No. XLI (July 1862), p. 173.

American Theological Review, IV (July 1862), 581–2.

Dublin University Magazine, LX (July 1862), 78–82.

Harper's New Monthly Magazine, XXV (July 1862), 262–4.

Home and Foreign Review, I (July 1862), 111–28.

Fraser's Magazine, LXVI (August 1862), 256–64.

Ladies' Repository, XXII (August 1862), 509.

Blackwood's Magazine, XCII (September 1862), 372–90.

London Quarterly Review, XIX (October 1862), 234–58.

North American Review, XCV (October 1862), 416–36.

Quarterly Review, CXII (October 1862), 535–70.

Westminster Review (American edition), LXXVIII (October 1862), 288.

——: "The Present Condition of the Northern States of the American Union," in *Four Lectures*, Morris L. Parrish, editor (London, 1938).

——: "*Resources and Prosperity of America*, by Sir M. Peto" [a review], *Fortnightly Review*, V (1866), 126–8.

——: *The Tireless Traveler*, edited, with an Introduction, by Bradford Allen Booth (University of California Press, 1941).

——: *The Way We Live Now* (London, 1875).

——: *The West Indies and the Spanish Main* (London, 1859).

TROLLOPE, FRANCES: *Domestic Manners of the Americans*, edited, with a History of Mrs. Trollope's Adventures in America, by Donald Smalley (New York, 1949).

TROLLOPE, THOMAS ADOLPHUS: *What I Remember* (New York, 1888).

TUCKERMAN, HENRY T.: *America and Her Commentators* (New York, 1864).

["Van Wyck Report"], *House Report* No. 2, 37th Congress, 2nd Session.

Washington, D. C.: a Guide to the Nation's Capital, American Guide Series (New York, 1942).

WILDMAN, JOHN HAZARD: "Trollope Illustrates the Distinction," *Nineteenth-Century Fiction*, IV (1949), 101–10.

WILLIAMS, KENNETH P.: *Lincoln Finds a General: a Military Study of the Civil War* (New York, 1949).

WILLIAMSON, JEFFERSON: *The American Hotel: an Anecdotal History* (New York, 1930).

WITTKE, CARL: *A History of Canada* (New York, 1942).

3. EDITIONS OF "NORTH AMERICA"

North America (London: Chapman & Hall, 1862), two volumes. Three editions within 1862.

North America (Philadelphia: J. B. Lippincott & Co., 1862), authorized edition.[2] Printings continued into 1863.

[2] For Trollope's quarrel with Harper's over the right to publish *North America*, see section VIII of our Introduction to the present edition. All editions of *North*

North America (New York: Harper & Brothers, 1862). Printings continued into 1863.

Nord-Amerika, translated into German by A. Diezman (1862), three volumes.[3]

North America (Leipzig: Bernhard Tauchnitz, 1862), Volumes 606–8 of the Tauchnitz Collection of British Authors.

North America (London: Chapman & Hall, 1864), two volumes, "Fourth and Cheaper Edition." [4]

North America (London: Chapman & Hall, 1866), Fifth Edition.

North America (London: Chapman & Hall, 1869), "New Edition."

America listed in this bibliography are in one volume unless otherwise indicated.

[3] Listed in Mary Leslie Irwin: *Anthony Trollope: A Bibliography* (New York, 1862).

[4] Listed in Michael Sadleir: *Trollope: A Bibliography* (London, 1928).

Acknowledgments

The editors take pleasure in acknowledging their indebtedness to Mr. Garrett L. Reilly for permission to consult and quote from the manuscript of *North America*; to Miss Muriel Rose Trollope, granddaughter of Anthony Trollope, for permission to reproduce the itinerary of Trollope's tour from his account book; to Houghton Mifflin Company for permission to quote from Horace Elisha Scudder's *James Russell Lowell: a Biography* (1901). Friends who have given advice and encouragement during the making of this edition are too numerous to mention in the limits of this note, but their aid is gratefully remembered. The editors are indebted for various kindnesses to the librarians and officers of Indiana University Library, the Library of the University of California at Los Angeles, the Newberry Library, the New York Public Library, the Library of Congress, and the University of Chicago Library.

INDEX